Medi

Media Law

SECOND EDITION

RALPH L. HOLSINGER

Professor Emeritus, Journalism
Indiana University, Bloomington

McGRAW-HILL, INC.

New York St. Louis San Francisco Auckland Bogotá Caracas
Hamburg Lisbon London Madrid Mexico Milan Montreal New Delhi
Paris San Juan São Paulo Singapore Sydney Tokyo Toronto

Media Law

1 2 3 4 5 6 7 8 9 0 DOC DOC 9 0 9 8 7 6 5 4 3 2 1

ISBN 0-07-029647-2

This book was set in Times Roman by the College Composition Unit
in cooperation with Monotype Composition Company.
The editors were Hilary Jackson and James R. Belser;
the production supervisor was Kathryn Porzio.
The cover was designed by Joseph Gillians.
The photo editor was Elyse Rieder.
R. R. Donnelley & Sons Company was printer and binder.

Library of Congress Cataloging-in-Publication Data

Holsinger, Ralph L.
    Media law / Ralph L. Holsinger.—2nd ed.
       p.   cm.
    Includes index.
    ISBN 0-07-029647-2
    1. Mass media—Law and legislation—United States.   2. Press law
—United States.   I. Title.
KF2750.H65   1991
343.7309′9—dc20
[347.30399]   90-25088

CONTENTS

PART 2. NEWS MEDIA AND THE LAW

Chapter 3   The Law of Defamation: An Overview   90

Chapter 4   The Anatomy of a Libel Case   128

Chapter 5   Invasion of Privacy   194

Chapter 6   A Fair and Public Trial

PART 3. LEGAL REGULATION OF THE MEDIA

PREFACE

Media Law is written for today's journalism students—in the broad meaning that term assumed in the 1980s. Thus, while major chapters are designed to help future reporters and editors recognize and avoid the many legal pitfalls that await the unwary, there is essential information here, too, for students planning careers in broadcasting, advertising, public relations, and corporate communications.

I began this book because my students made it clear to me that they wanted a text written in the language of journalists, and they wanted it to be interesting. Because I had worked as a newspaper reporter and editor for eighteen years before I became a teacher, I thought I could meet their demands. During my newspaper career, I had covered state and federal courts, the Ohio Legislature, Congress, and federal administrative agencies, which gave me a good grounding in how laws are made and applied. As a reporter, I had to meet the daily challenge of gathering news, frequently from reluctant sources, and writing for a mass audience. This gave me experience in translating the complexities of government and law into language readers could understand.

Later, as managing editor of a metropolitan daily newspaper, my horizons were broadened. I learned to consult lawyers to avoid legal problems that had not seemed very important to me as a reporter. I also became much more aware of those gray boundaries of the law where ethical considerations come into play, which not only made me appreciate the many points at which journalists risk collision with the legal system, but aroused my interest in learning more about what we mean when we talk about the First Amendment guarantee of freedom of speech and press.

Thus, when I joined the journalism faculty at Indiana University, Bloomington, more than twenty-five years ago, I began a systematic reading of First Amendment and media law cases. I am forever indebted to the late Austin Clifford, professor of torts at the Indiana University School of Law, who taught me at an early stage that the meaning of the law is found in the cases and cannot be understood without them. Thus, *Media Law* is based firmly on the cases. Some of these have defined the constitutional limits of the freedom of the press clause of the First Amendment. Others have interpreted the many statutes applying to journalists and the mass media. The major Supreme Court cases—most notably *New York Times* v. *Sullivan, Gertz* v. *Robert Welch, Inc.,* and *Branzburg* v. *Hayes*—are given extensive treatment. Students need to become familiar with these cases, above all others, because courts look to them for guidance in the important areas of libel and the right of journalists to protect their confidential sources.

While I place great reliance on the cases, I recognize that decisions usually are written by judges for lawyers. This means that students, and even journalism professors, can find them hard to understand. Thus, I have used verbatim excerpts only where I thought the judges wrote more clearly than I could. Where they did not, I have tried to translate their legal language into words students can understand. In this I have been guided by my students who have been kind enough to evaluate my lectures as usually clear and interesting. As a teacher, I have always acted in the belief that to be boring is to commit a cardinal sin. I have tried to apply that belief to my writing.

Media Law is written on three levels. At its heart, it is a practical guide to the legal problems likely to confront professional journalists. At this level, I have given a great deal of emphasis to libel, invasion of privacy, and the clash between lawyers and journalists over the right of accused persons to a fair trial and the right of journalists to protect their confidential sources and information. But there is also practical guidance for students who plan careers in broadcast news, corporate communications, advertising, and public relations. The chapter on copyright law should be of interest to students thinking of a career in the creative arts.

At a second level, *Media Law* is a guide to the meaning of the speech and press clauses of the First Amendment. I have written these parts of the book in the belief that the right to speak and write without hindrance from government is absolutely essential to a free society. The First Amendment says flatly, "Congress shall make no law . . . abridging the freedom of speech, or of the press." And yet the Congress has passed laws restricting both freedoms, and the Supreme Court has upheld them. I think it is important that students get some idea of why we have a First Amendment and of why limits have been imposed on it. Freedom can not be taken for granted—in today's world, the freedoms of speech and press are endangered species. Each generation must care enough about freedom of expression to protect it, or it will be lost here, too. Therefore, I have written about the development of the idea of freedom, the philosophy underlying the First Amendment, the various theories as to its meaning, and the major cases interpreting the speech and press clauses.

At the third level, I have gone beyond the law into the realm of ethics. I think this dimension makes *Media Law* unique among communications law texts. Each chapter ends with a section, "In the Professional World," that discusses the ethical aspects of its subject matter. These sections are not exhaustive, but they are written to suggest that the question, "Is it right?" is sometimes as important as the question, "Is it legal?"

Shortly after I became a teacher, the late Richard G. Gray became chairman of Indiana University's then Department of Journalism. He entrusted me with organizing our first senior seminar on the philosophy and ethics of the media. That has developed into a course all seniors are required to take. In the early 1970s, I was cochairman, along with George Gill of the *Louisville Courier-Journal* and Paul Poorman of the *Detroit News*, of the first Professional Standards Committee of the Associated Press Managing Editors Association. In effect, it was a committee on ethics and later under other leadership drafted the association's code of ethics. Over the years, its studies have contributed significantly to raising the level of ethical performance among newspaper professionals and to the growing body of literature on journalism ethics. I hope that "In the Professional World" will stimulate students to think about the ethical dimension of whatever branch of journalism they enter.

New to the Second Edition

I have retained both the organization and treatment of cases many users say they liked in the first edition. In addition, I also have listened to users who suggested broadening my scope to include more content of particular interest to students who are planning careers in corporate communications, advertising, and public relations.

Part 1, as in the first edition, deals with the origins and development of freedom of expression as an idea that serves the public interest; however, the three chapters of the first edition have been condensed into two. The first chapter begins with the historical development of the idea that the people should have a voice in how they are governed and leads up to the adoption of the First Amendment to the U.S. Constitution. New to this chapter are the following:

— A section on symbolic speech, which includes summaries of the two cases in which the Supreme Court held that flag-burning is a form of political expression protected by the First Amendment

Chapter 2 has been rewritten to include both the punishment of speech considered harmful to government and the attempts to prevent such speech, commonly called prior restraint. It also includes new sections on:

— The recent use of espionage law to punish a civilian employee of the U.S. Navy who gave a British magazine copies of secret satellite photos of a Soviet nuclear-powered aircraft carrier

— The Supreme Court's *Hazelwood* decision, which upheld the authority of public school teachers and administrators to censor high school newspapers published as part of course work in journalism

Part 2 covers libel, invasion of privacy, fair trial, the right of journalists to protect their confidential sources, and access to government information. These are the major areas of conflict between the news media on one side and government officials and the judicial system on the other. These topics are the ones most frequently misunderstood by users of the news media.

Libel has become such a complex topic that I have divided its discussion over two chapters. Chapter 3 offers an overview of libel, starting with a survey of the common law of defamation. The second part of the chapter summarizes the Supreme Court's decisions in *New York Times* v. *Sullivan* and *Gertz* v. *Robert Welch*, which federalized the treatment of libel by bringing it into the realm of constitutional law and the First Amendment's guarantee of freedom of speech and press. The first edition reflected the view, found in court decisions of the mid-1980s, that the common law of defamation was all but dead. That view has proved to be wrong. The Supreme Court's 1985 decision in *Dun & Bradstreet* established that states may apply their common law to nonmedia cases. This chapter closes with the following:

— A new section on common law and the business communicator beginning with a discussion of *Dun & Bradstreet* and proceeding to a summary of several cases in which courts have applied common law to corporate communications

Chapter 4 builds on the overview by leading the student step-by-step through the trial of a media libel case. The treatment draws in part on the author's experience as an expert witness in three such cases, including one that went to the Minnesota Supreme Court, which upheld the trial judge's reversal of a jury verdict in favor of the plaintiff. New material includes

— The constitutional status of opinion as derived from the Supreme Court's decisions in *Hustler Magazine* v. *Falwell* and *Milkovich* v. *Lorain Journal Co.*

— The District of Columbia Circuit's conclusion, in *Tavoulareas* v. *Piro*, that aggressive investigative reporting does not in itself prove actual malice

Chapter 5 deals with invasion of privacy. Although polls show that many persons perceive the media, particularly television, as invaders of privacy, the cases show that courts have been reluctant to return judgments against the media, primarily because newsworthiness is a strong defense. Further, the Supreme Court has held that facts found in the public records of a court are not actionable. The new material includes

— The Supreme Court's decision in *The Florida Star* v. *B.J.F.*, holding that there was no invasion of privacy in a newspaper's publishing the name of a rape victim, despite a state law forbidding release of the name by police

Chapter 6, on fair and public trials, begins with a survey of criminal justice procedures and moves to an examination of the meaning of a fair trial. At the heart of this chapter is a conflict between two guarantees found in the Bill of Rights—the freedom of press clause of the First Amendment and the right to a fair trial as defined by the Sixth Amendment. New material includes

— The right to photograph trial proceedings, formerly treated in the chapter on access to information

— A discussion of the circumstances under which names of jurors may be withheld from the news media

Chapter 7 deals with another major source of conflict between the courts and the media, the right of journalists to protect their confidential sources. The chapter reflects the willingness of courts in most jurisdictions to grant journalists a limited First Amendment testimonial privilege based on the Supreme Court's decision in *Branzburg* v. *Hayes*. There are notable exceptions, including a U.S. Seventh Circuit Court of Appeals decision denying the existence of a privilege in criminal cases. The chapter also includes a survey of reporters' rights under state shield laws.

Chapter 8, on The Right to Know, is devoted in large part to the Freedom of Information Act, which has greatly increased the right of access to documents held by federal administrative agencies. The chapter also includes an expanded survey of state laws providing for access to records and meetings. The new material includes summaries of three recent cases in which the Supreme Court held that

— The Justice Department does not have to release to the media the criminal histories it compiles on certain individuals for distribution to law enforcement agencies

— The American Bar Association committee that regularly advises the Justice Department on the qualifications of candidates for federal judgeships is not subject to the open meetings law

— A Florida law making it a crime for grand jury witnesses to disclose their testimony violates the First Amendment

Part 3 covers speech and media that are regulated by government because courts have held that the First Amendment interests involved are subordinate to more compelling public interests. The subject matter includes obscenity, which the Supreme Court has held is so lacking in ideas that it can be banned altogether; broadcasting, the only news medium licensed by the federal government; cable systems, which are subject to both local and federal controls; advertising, which only recently has come under limited First Amendment protection; copyright, which permits creators of original works in any medium to protect them from unauthorized copying, and the business aspects of the media, which are subject to the same kinds of regulation as other businesses.

Chapter 9, on Obscenity, focuses on the Supreme Court's decision in *Miller* v. *California*, which gives local juries wide discretion in determining how far the media can go in depicting or describing sexual activity. New to this edition are

— A section on licensing as a means of preventing or controlling dissemination of allegedly obscene materials

— The Supreme Court's decision in *Fort Wayne Books* defining the circumstances under which racketeering laws may be used against sellers of allegedly obscene materials

Chapter 10 focuses on those aspects of broadcasting law that have survived a movement toward deregulation that began with President Carter. The chapter has undergone major revision to reflect

— Abolition of the fairness doctrine, which for years required broadcasters to identify controversial public issues and present a balanced discussion of them

— The Supreme Court's decision upholding regulations designed to favor minority applicants for broadcasting licenses

Cable systems have grown so rapidly since the first edition was written that they have become the subject of a new Chapter 11. The treatment is based on The Cable Communications Policy Act of 1984 and court cases interpreting it. The second part of the chapter summarizes the First Amendment status of cable systems with respect to antitrust law, attempts by local franchising authorities to specify channels cable systems must carry, public access channels, and sexually oriented programming.

Chapter 12, on Advertising, has been expanded to make it of greater use to students considering careers in that field. It begins with a survey of the cases through which the Supreme Court extended First Amendment protection to commercial speech and then defined the limits of that protection. This part of the chapter pays considerable attention to

— Advertising by professionals, mainly lawyers

— The regulation of signs and billboards

— Advertising for products, such as alcoholic beverages, and for services, such as gambling, that are subject to regulation

The middle part of the chapter deals with government regulation of advertising. In the first edition, the focus was on the Federal Trade Commission. It became relatively inactive during the Reagan administration, leading to increased efforts by state attorneys general to police allegedly deceptive advertising and by business firms bringing civil actions against competitors to halt extravagant advertising claims. The latter part of the chapter deals with the right to refuse advertising and with corporate cause advertising.

Chapter 13, on Copyright Law, is concerned with the distinction between fair use and infringement. It has been expanded to include

— Recent Supreme Court decisions defining ownership of the copyright on works commissioned by others and on movies made prior to 1978, when the current copyright law took effect

— A section concerning trademarks that will be of particular interest to business communicators, public relations practitioners, and advertisers

Chapter 14, on The News Media as Businesses, is little changed except to deal more extensively with recent decisions defining the terms under which municipalities may regulate the placement of newspaper vending machines in public places.

This edition, like the first, will be updated at least once a year. Newsletters will be written at the end of each Supreme Court term in July summarizing the Court's media-related decisions and other developments affecting subjects treated in the text. Our intent is to distribute the newsletters to users of *Media Law* before the start of the fall semester.

Acknowledgments

While it was student reaction to the textbooks I chose that spurred me to think about a book of my own, nothing would have happened had it not been for two persons, Dr. Gray and Roth Wilkofsky. Dick not only was my chairman, director, and dean for fifteen years, he was my friend. He believed that I had a book in me and he let me know during our annual review chats that I ought to write it. When I decided to give it a try, Roth, as a senior editor at Random House, was willing to consider a proposal. From the beginning, he gave me strong support, and showed the utmost patience when time proved that writing a book is not as easy as I once naively thought it was. He went many extra miles with me to bring the work to fruition. For that, I wish there were stronger words than "thank you." I deeply regret that Dick Gray died before I finished this book.

At a critical moment in the project, Dr. Peter Sandman, professor of journalism at Rutgers University, agreed with Roth's request to read the manuscript. His helpful advice resulted in major restructuring designed to make the book a better teaching instrument, and I am grateful for his help.

I also wish to thank the following reviewers of various drafts of the first edition manuscript for their helpful suggestions: Douglas Anderson, Arizona State University; Edmund Blinn, Iowa State University; John J. Breen, University of Connecticut; James K. Buckalew, San Diego State University; T. Barton Carter, Boston University; Bill Chamberlin, University of North Carolina, Chapel Hill; Carolyn Stewart Dyer, University of Iowa; Marian Huttenstine, University of Alabama; Paul Jess, University of Kansas; Kelly Leiter, University of Tennessee; Kent R. Middleton, University of Georgia; John Murray, Michigan State University; James M. Neal, University of Nebraska, Lincoln; Mack Palmer, University of Oklahoma; P. E. Paulin, Oklahoma State University; David Protess, Northwestern University; J. D. Rayburn, University of Kentucky; Jack Schnedler, Northwestern University; Todd Simon, Michigan State University; Don Smith, Pennsylvania State University; William Steng, Oklahoma State University; and John D. Stevens, University of Michigan.

I also want to acknowledge support from two lawyers, my long-time friend Francis T. Martin of Cincinnati and Ralph Fuchs, emeritus professor of law at the Indiana University School of Law. Both were formidable advocates who were willing to tolerate a journalist's attempts to talk law and offer constructive advice. I regret that neither lived to judge a pupil's work.

I have been helped, too, by my students who were willing, semester after semester for twenty years, to enroll in my communications law class despite my reputation as a tough grader. They taught me what sells and what does not when your audience is comprised of 20-year-olds trying to learn enough law to pass a required course on the way to a degree. A goodly number of my students thought enough of the course to desert journalism and go on to law school.

In the preparation of the second edition, I owe special thanks to Hilary Jackson, who became my editor at McGraw-Hill and pushed me when I needed pushing to get this book done. I also thank the following reviewers whose comments offered both help and encouragement in shaping this new version of *Media Law*: Lamar Bridges, East Texas State University; Judith Buddenbaum, Colorado State University; Thomas Dickson, South West Missouri State; Robert Humphrey, California State University at Sacramento; Paul Jess, University of Kansas; Jerry Morgan Medley, Auburn University at Montgomery; and William Roach, University of North Florida.

Finally, I acknowledge the support of Elizabeth, my wife. It has not been easy for her to share me with a project that has demanded a good part of my time on more days than I care to count. I thank, too, John and Cynthia Chirtea, our daughter and son-in-law, whose gift of a personal computer at first complicated and then greatly expedited the preparation of the second edition.

Despite their involvement in the work, none of the persons mentioned above should be held responsible for any errors or omissions that may mar this work. The buck stopped at the point where my fingers met the keyboard of my word processor.

Ralph L. Holsinger

PART 1

FREEDOM OF SPEECH AND FREEDOM OF THE PRESS

CHAPTER 1

For more than 2000 years, people have struggled to win the right to speak freely and critically about political, economic, religious, and social issues. For most of that time, in most places, people did so at the risk of severe punishment, including death. Even today despite the cleansing winds of democracy that have swept away many long-established one-party regimes, many governments consider critics of official policies enemies of the state, to be tortured, imprisoned, or exiled.

Those who believe in freedom of speech and press argue that such freedom ensures government that is responsive to the needs of the people. Only if men and women are free to talk about their problems can they arrive at mutually acceptable solutions. The Supreme Court of the United States has endorsed that view, holding in many cases that debate on public issues should be robust, uninhibited, and wide open.

FREEDOM OF SPEECH AND PRESS: HISTORY AND PHILOSOPHY

There are also those who believe that the news media should serve government by helping it win public approval for policies designed by government officials to meet the people's needs. In this view, uninformed criticism merely creates dissatisfaction and interferes with the ability of government to perform.

The debate between those who advocate freedom of expression and those who argue for restraint continues today. Every recent American president has complained that a "negative press" has made it difficult to carry out his policies. Nor are critics of freedom of speech and press confined to government. When American Nazis have demonstrated in Jewish neighborhoods, or when Ku Klux Klansmen have burned crosses in cities with a large black population, riots have resulted. At another level, people have sought to censor or ban MTV, the lyrics of popular rock songs, and movies featuring sex and violence because they believe such things contribute to the decay of our culture. So the question of how far freedom of speech and press should be permitted to go remains important as we approach the end of the twentieth century.

This chapter presents a brief history of the development of the idea that people ought to be free to criticize their rulers. The first part is designed to highlight the forces that led to the American Declaration of Independence and the Constitution, particularly the First Amendment guarantees of freedom of speech and press. The second part examines the philosophy supporting and limiting freedom of speech and press.

Major Cases

- *American Communications Association* v. *Douds,* 339 U.S. 382, 70 S.Ct. 674, 94 L.Ed.2d 925 (1950).

- *Schenck* v. *United States,* 249 U.S. 47, 39 S.Ct. 247, 63 L.Ed. 470 (1919).

- *Texas* v. *Johnson,* 491 U.S. _ _ _, 109 S.Ct. 2533, 105 L.Ed.2d 342 (1989).

THE HISTORY OF FREEDOM OF SPEECH AND PRESS

The Idea of Freedom

In the fifth century B.C., the city-state of Athens adopted a form of democracy. The experiment proved short-lived, but the idea that people should be able to govern themselves survived. So did the companion idea that people should be free to talk about the policies of government and decide for themselves which are good and which are bad. Socrates and, later, Plato based their philosophy on the belief that truth is best reached through a process called *dialectic*—rigorous discussion from which no fact or argument is withheld. Plato believed that such discussion is essential if a government is to serve its people well. He wrote a book, the *Republic,* describing an ideal form of government in which the good, the beautiful, and the true would prevail.

However, Plato was realistic enough to recognize that those who achieve power in government are not always willing to submit their policies to rigorous discussion. A notable passage from the *Republic* illustrates the dilemma faced not only by Plato but by other advocates of freewheeling discussion of government policies:

> Till philosophers become kings, or those now named kings and rulers give themselves to philosophy truly and rightly, and these two things—political power and philosophic thought—come together, and the commoner minds, which at present seek only the one or the other, are kept out by force, states will have no rest from their troubles...and, if I am right, man will have none.[1]

Plato put those words in the mouth of Socrates, who had been executed by order of the Athenian rulers before the *Republic* was written. Socrates had fought bravely for Athens against its enemies, but when he was not serving as a soldier he wandered the streets questioning authority, particularly that based on religious belief. He acquired followers, Plato among them, and at the age of thirty-one was deemed such a threat to Athens that he was charged with corrupting the morals of the young and sentenced to death by drinking hemlock.

The Athenian flirtation with government by the people, and with the freedom of speech that accompanied it, did not last long. But the writings of Plato gave birth to an idea that has lived ever since—Truth can best be reached through free discussion.

Divine Right versus the Rights of the People

Ancient Rome also experimented with a form of popular rule. During the Roman Republic, 509–265 B.C., the people elected two chief executives, and nobles and plebeians elected members of a senate, which enacted laws. But as Rome

---

1. Benjamin Jowett, trans., *Republic of Plato* (Oxford: Clarendon Press, 1908), V: 473.

gobbled up more and more of what is now Italy, the fruits of conquest enriched relatively few of its citizens. In time, the Republic foundered on internal dissension between wealthy aristocrats and the masses of the poor. Some of the forms remained, but rule henceforth was by the rich and the powerful.

For more than fifteen centuries thereafter, most of the peoples of the Western world lived under various forms of autocracy, a system in which a few persons at the top impose their will on the masses at the bottom. Such rulers drew their power from three sources: (1) The rulers were in active command of the nation's armed forces. (2) The rulers either controlled the nation's economic wealth or were closely allied with those who did. (3) And in most states, especially from the fourth century on, the rulers invoked the spiritual power of the church to preach the doctrine of obedience, reinforced by the promise of a better life in the world hereafter. In time, this alliance between church and state became formalized in the political system known as divine right: Kings ruled because they were ordained by God to do so. Therefore, to question their authority was not only a crime, known as sedition, but blasphemy as well. Critics of a king's decisions might lose their livelihoods or their property, or they might be tortured or killed by the king's soldiers. Finally, as blasphemers, critics might be condemned to eternal damnation.

In the fifteenth century, the triple ramparts of autocratic power came under siege. The development of printing, the Protestant Reformation, and the Renaissance set in motion forces that even the cruelest tyrants could not put down. Printing, generally attributed to Johann Gutenberg in Germany, took from the clergy its power to control the dissemination of knowledge. For centuries, books had been copied by hand, generally in the monasteries, which meant that the ability to read, and to transfer written information, was in large part the domain of the clergy. When printing made books more readily available, many more people had an incentive to learn to read. From the mid-sixteenth century on, what they read, among other things, were tracts written by various religious dissenters, starting with Martin Luther. Luther, also a German, was a member of the Roman Catholic clergy who became appalled by what he saw as that body's corruption. He and his followers, who came to be known as Protestants, took the position that anyone who could read the Bible could figure out what it meant without having to rely on the official doctrine imposed by the pope and his bishops.

Authority was being questioned in other areas, too. Throughout Western Europe, writers, painters, sculptors, artisans, musicians, natural scientists, and others demonstrated that one did not have to look backward to ancient authority to find truth or beauty. Explorers demonstrated that the earth was not flat, as the Church had said it was. In Italy, Galileo peered at the planets through a crude telescope and concluded that, despite passages in Scripture, the earth was not the center of the universe. Such heresy did not go unchallenged by the Inquisition, the Church's tribunal, and in his old age, Galileo was forced to recant.

The forces of knowledge, once set in motion, could not be stayed. By the seventeenth century, dissenters in England were questioning not only the authority of the Church, but that of the Crown. One king, Charles I, was beheaded in 1649, leading the English monarchy to agree to share its power with an elected Parliament. Today, in royal ritual, Queen Elizabeth II is referred to as the Protector of

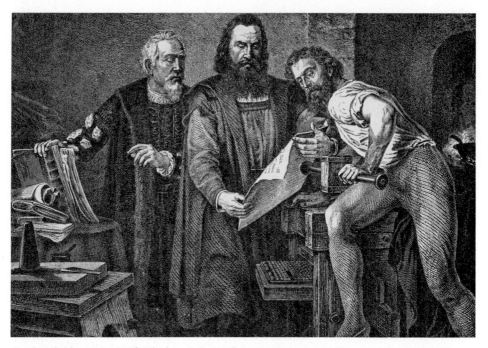

By developing the art of printing, Johann Gutenberg (center) offered an incentive for people in all walks of life to learn to read. This fifteenth-century development was one of the forces that created that remarkable explosion of knowledge known as the Renaissance. With knowledge came the questioning of authority that ultimately made possible both religious and political freedom. (Culver Pictures)

the Faith, meaning the Church of England, but that is about all that remains of the divine right of kings.

The transfer of power from monarchs to people required drastic changes in political theory. When kings ruled because they were ordained by God to do so, the people were their subjects. Kings gave orders; underlings were expected to obey those orders without question. Those rash enough to question the wisdom of a king's policies might find themselves charged with seditious libel, a crime punishable with death. But when most of a king's power had been transferred to an elected parliament, the old rules came under question. Members of Parliament represented the people, in whom the authority of the state ultimately resided. Did this not mean that the people had a right to inform themselves about government policies? And did it not mean that they could criticize those policies without being charged with seditious libel?

One who raised these questions was John Milton, who is remembered today mainly for such enduring classics as *Paradise Lost*. However, during the Civil War that followed Charles's beheading, Milton served as an official of, and apologist for, the parliamentary government of Oliver Cromwell. During that period, Milton came under attack from some of the Puritan members of Parliament because he had written a tract arguing that partners to an unhappy marriage should have the right to get a divorce. Puritans disapproved of divorce. To compound Milton's crime, he had managed to get his tract published without first obtaining approval from a government censor. According to the law in effect at that time, nothing could be published until it had received a license from the government. The purpose was to nip any seditious libel in the bud.

As Milton's experience suggests, the licensing system had begun to break down in the seventeenth century as printing presses became more common. Milton responded to the attack on his works by proposing that the system be abolished. In 1644, he composed "A Speech for the Liberty of Unlicenc'd Print-ing," which, published in essay form, bears the title *Areopagitica*. It is a passionate yet well-reasoned argument against government censorship of written works dealing with political policy.

It is illogical to assume, Milton wrote, that any government can satisfy all its people. It is equally illogical to assume that everything a government does will be done justly. But if the people are free to talk and write about government policies, and if those who govern are willing to pay attention, the result should be an improvement in the quality of government and the well-being of the people.

Milton, like Plato, had reservations about how far freedom of expression ought to go and who could be trusted with it. Note the conflicting currents running through this passage from *Areopagitica:*

> I deny not, but that it is of greatest concernment in the Church and Common-wealth, to have a vigilant eye how Bookes demeane themselves, as well as men; and thereafter to confine, imprison, and do sharpest justice on them as malefactors; for Bookes are not absolutely dead things, but do contain a potencie of life in them to be as active as that soule was whose progeny they are; nay they do preserve as in a violl the purest efficacie and extraction of that living intellect that bred them.[2]

Milton's contribution to the advancement of freedom of expression lies in his recognition that such freedom is in the public interest. He summarized his message in a notable passage:

> And though all the windes of doctrine were let loose to play upon the earth, so Truth be in the field, we do injuriously by licencing and prohibiting to misdoubt her strength. Let her and Falshood grapple; who ever knew Truth put to the wors, in a free and open encounter.[3]

Two hundred years later, Milton's idea was put in stronger terms by another English philosopher, John Stuart Mill. In his essay *On Liberty,* he argued that even when the power of government is backed by near-unanimous public opinion, that power should not be used to suppress dissent. Mill wrote:

> If all mankind minus one were of one opinion, and only one person were of the contrary opinion, mankind would be no more justified in silencing that one person, than he, if he had the power, would be justified in silencing mankind....[T]he pe-

2. *Complete Poetry and Works of John Milton* (New York: Modern Library, 1950), pp. 681–82.
3. Ibid., p. 719.

culiar evil of silencing the expression of an opinion is, that it is robbing the human race: posterity as well as the existing generation; those who dissent from the opinion, still more than those who hold it. If the opinion is right, they are deprived of the opportunity of exchanging error for truth; if wrong, they lose, what is almost as great a benefit, the clearer perception and livelier impression of truth, produced by its collision with error.

Mill recognized what Milton did not, that truth cannot always prevail, at least in the short run, against the cruel refinements of repression and propaganda used by some determined dictators. Nor could either Mill or Milton have anticipated the impasse created when both sides of a dispute take unyielding positions based on opposing principle, as in the debate over a woman's right to have an abortion. Milton himself did not always practice what he preached. Secure in the belief that his own Protestant views were correct, he had no objections to censoring the works of Catholic writers.

Nor did Milton's arguments sound the death knell of political oppression in England. After 1660, when the English Parliament restored Charles II to the throne, but with less power than his father had had, Englishmen continued to suffer cruel deaths for the crime of seditious libel. One of the more interesting of the many cases reported in *Howell's State Trials*[4] involved a printer, John Twyn, whose shop was raided by constables in the early hours of the morning. They found smudged page proofs of a book arguing that a king whose decrees violated the "law of God" should be called to account by the people. Twyn and his helpers were thrown into jail and denied contact with even their wives until they were brought out months later to stand trial. Accused of "imagining and intending the death" of the king, they were tried without counsel. After thirty minutes of testimony, dominated by the judge, a jury found them guilty and condemned Twyn to a horrible death.

The trial had overtones that are at issue today. The author of the book was not known, and much of the judge's questioning was directed at persuading Twyn to name the author. Such questions followed Twyn to the scaffold, where he was told that his soul might rest more easily in the hereafter if he were to identify the source of the offending work. It is not clear from Twyn's answers whether he remained silent because he did not know who had written the draft, or because he was protecting the author. But the terms of the sentence were carried out. He was forced to straddle a triangular wooden beam on which he was carried at shoulder height to the place of execution. There he was hanged, but not in such a way as to kill him. He was cut down, revived, and then forced to watch while his "privy-members" were cut off and burned. Finally, he was beheaded, and his body was hacked into four pieces. Each part was nailed above a different gate to the city to stand as a warning to others who might dare urge the overthrow of the king.

Twyn was a victim of a final Royalist backlash surrounding the king's return to England and the throne after exile in France. Milton, too, was a victim of it, but

---

4.   15 Charles II 1663, p. 513.

only to the extent of being driven out of public life. He died in 1674, twenty-one years before Parliament let the Printing Act expire; thus, he did not live to see licensed printing abolished in England.

There is a striking similarity between the ideas for which Twyn was executed and those that survive in John Locke's *Treatises on Government,* published in 1690. Locke designed these *Treatises* to rationalize the transfer of power from a king, who ruled by divine right, to a parliament that represented the people. This was a serious matter, as is evidenced by the fact that the shift of power was marked by nearly a century of turmoil, including a bloody civil war. In writing his *Treatises,* Locke borrowed the social-compact theory of the origins of government from Thomas Hobbes, an earlier political philosopher. This theory rests on the assumption that at some time in the past people recognized that they would be better off working together than they were in a "state of nature," where every family had to provide for all its needs. In that state, the only law was the "law of the jungle," which meant, in effect, that only the strongest or the most clever survived. Hobbes theorized that at some point people had become tired of fending for themselves and had agreed to surrender some of their independence in return for security. These agreements, or compacts, signaled the beginning of organized society and of rudimentary governments.

Locke expanded on Hobbes's social-compact theory and sought to formalize it. He wrote as one who had escaped Twyn's fate, although he, too, believed that those who govern should be held accountable to the people. Locke recognized that tyranny is not the sole province of absolute monarchs; majorities can also oppress minorities. To counter that possibility in newly created democracies, Locke advocated two safeguards:

1. People creating new governments should reduce the compact to writing in the form of a constitution. That document should clearly establish the limits of the government's power.

2. The people should make clear that they are not giving up all of the personal rights that were theirs in the state of nature. Life in the jungle may have been hard, but, Locke argued, some aspects of the freedom that went with it ought not be surrendered to any government.

As a further barrier against oppression by majority vote, Locke argued that the powers of government ought to be divided three ways: An elected legislature should have the power to adopt laws; an independent executive branch should have the power to carry the laws into effect; and a court system should have the power to "dispense justice and decide the rights of the subject." Finally, all three branches of government should be constrained by a duty to the law of nature, which, in Locke's view, guaranteed the personal, or natural, rights retained by the people.

Under Locke's system, then, there would be a check on the will of the majority. People who believed a law violated their natural rights could appeal to the courts for justice. If the judges decided that the law did indeed infringe those rights, they had the duty to hold that the law was void. Further, Locke argued, the people have a right to resist officials who exceed the powers given them by the compact.

Locke's views gradually prevailed in England and, later, in the American colonies. In the eighteenth century, the rights of the people came to the fore in Anglo-Saxon countries and, at the end of the century, in France. Political thought literally was turned upside down. No longer was the power to govern seen as flowing from the top down. No longer were the common people required to obey without question whatever order a monarch might give them. Authority had shifted, in some parts of the world, to the people. With that authority came the right to choose their rulers, and to oust them if they abused their powers. This implied, at the least, the people's right to criticize those they had elevated to public office. Divine right had given way in some places to the rights of the people.

Speech in Colonial America ====================================

When Locke wrote his *Treatises on Government,* the English colonies in America had been in existence for nearly a century. Already, some colonists were beginning to object to the idea of being ruled from London. Although each colony had a legislative body of some kind, the governors were appointed in London, and colonial laws were subject to veto by the British Parliament. In addition, laws enacted by Parliament were to be obeyed by the colonists as they were in the homeland. One of these was the law of seditious libel.

In 1734, that law was challenged in an action in the New York courts. John Peter Zenger, publisher of the *New York Weekly Journal,* had published articles accusing Governor William Cosby of dishonesty and oppression.[5] Cosby reacted by charging Zenger with seditious libel. Zenger spent nine months in jail awaiting trial, while his wife continued to publish the paper. When Zenger came to trial, he faced a rule of law that made it almost impossible for him to win. Under that rule, any words, whether they were true or false, that tended to undermine the people's faith in their government were punishable. During the trial, the judge instructed the jury that the truth of Zenger's articles was not at issue. Zenger's lawyer, Andrew Hamilton, invoked English precedent to argue that the jury could disregard the judge's instruction without fear of punishment. He also argued so eloquently that truth ought never to be libelous that the jury found Zenger not guilty. The verdict did not change the law of seditious libel—truth was still not officially recognized as a defense for harmful criticism of government. However, because the decision was widely publicized and became a rallying point for foes of press censorship, the decision sent a message to British prosecutors in the American colonies. There is no record of seditious libel trials in the colonial

---

5. Frederic Breakspear Farrar, "A Printer, a Lawyer, and the Free Press," *Editor & Publisher,* 3 August 1985. The article includes a facsimile of the *New York Weekly Journal* for 2 December 1734 reporting the order to burn several issues of the *Journal* because they had been declared seditious.

courts after Zenger's acquittal. Thus, the case generally is regarded as the beginning of press freedom in what was to become, half a century later, the United States of America.

During those fifty years, the belief in freedom of speech and press was by no means universal. If the government would not act against unpopular speakers and writers, the people on occasion did. Some editors who favored English rule in the years leading up to the Revolution were victims of mob violence. However, persons who believed that the colonists were victims of oppressive laws enacted by a Parliament in which they had no representation found a ready outlet for their protests in newspapers, in pamphlets, and in the pulpits of many churches. Historian Lawrence Henry Gipson, in his definitive thirteen-volume study *The British Empire Before the American Revolution*,[6] lists freedom of discussion as one of the factors responsible for the break with Great Britain.

In his concluding volume, he says many Americans were familiar with the writings used to justify England's earlier rebellion against its monarchs:

> Thus armed, the colonial leaders seized their pens. The ideas they expressed were widely disseminated from the pulpit and other public rostrums and especially by the American press in innumerable letters to the editors of the forty-three colonial newspapers (published for brief or extended periods between 1763 and 1775), as well as in broadsides, pamphlets, and books. Some of the writings were mere emotional outpourings, but others of a much higher order were addressed to the intellect and sought to rationalize the rights that all mankind should demand of any government. Taken together these expressions of intense opposition to the policies of the mother country by their very volume could have had only one effect—the implanting in the minds of Americans of a sense of urgency for the establishment of a new political order.[7]

That urgency took tangible form in 1776 in the Declaration of Independence, which touched off more than five years of war, leading to the creation of the United States of America. Both the Declaration and the Constitution, which established our present form of government in 1789, draw heavily from Locke's *Treatises on Government*. The first paragraph of the Declaration invokes the authority of "the Laws of Nature and of Nature's God" to justify separation from English authority. The Constitution, enacted in the name of "[w]e, the people of the United States," is a social compact of the kind Locke recommended.

The Constitution and the Bill of Rights

. It is impossible at this distance to imagine what it must have been like to establish a new government stretching from Maine to Georgia along the Atlantic coast two hundred years ago. Having experienced what they regarded as tyranny under English rule, the founders seemed to have been clear about several things.

6. New York: Knopf, 1958–1967.
7. Gipson, vol. 13, *The Triumphant Empire*, 1967, pp. 193–94.

They did not want a monarch, or an executive who could assume the powers of one. They believed that the people were the source of the government's power. They thought the primary responsibility for day-to-day governing should rest with the states. But they needed a central government to conduct relations with foreign countries, to protect them from foreign enemies, to create a monetary system, and to ensure the flow of commerce among the states and with other countries. However, they did not want that government to become strong enough to take away the powers of the states or certain basic liberties of the people.

After the colonists had won their freedom at Yorktown, with help from the French army and navy, they tried to get along with an almost powerless central government operating under the Articles of Confederation. When it became evident that such a government was not going to work, the states elected delegates who met in secret in Philadelphia for four months in 1787 and produced a brief document of seven articles. Including the names of its forty signers, the Constitution takes up about four pages of the *World Almanac.* Amendments added since it went into effect in 1789 take up another three and a half pages.

In simplest terms, the Constitution is a plan of government. It established the institutions of government—Congress, the Executive, headed by the president, and the Judiciary, headed by the Supreme Court of the United States. Numbered sections and subsections define the powers of each. Other articles define the relationship between the federal and state governments. Another prescribes the slow, deliberate procedure by which the Constitution can be amended.

As presented to the states for adoption, the Constitution said nothing about the rights of the people, including the right to speak and write freely about the actions of the central government. The drafters had acted on the theory that they were creating a central government of carefully defined, limited powers. In their view, they had given that government no authority to meddle with the rights of its citizens. The Constitution's silence on the people's rights raised suspicions in some states. They made a point of conditioning their approval of the new union on the promise that the Constitution would be amended to protect the rights of individuals.

Within two years after the federal government began functioning in 1789, Congress proposed twelve amendments making up a Bill of Rights designed to prevent the new central government from trampling on the people's natural or personal rights. Interestingly, in light of the importance the guarantee of the freedom of speech, press, and religion has assumed in our time, those freedoms were not the subject of the original First Amendment. That dealt with the apportionment of representatives to Congress, and the second with their compensation. When both failed to win ratification, the original Third became the First.

In large part, the subject matter of the ten adopted amendments reflects grievances against specific injustices experienced by Americans during the latter days of British colonial rule. First among these injustices is a concern with religion. Congress is neither to tax the people to support a state church nor to interfere with the right to worship as one pleases. Next in the same amendment is what appears to be a flat prohibition against any attempt by Congress to limit freedom of speech or of the press. Then there is a guarantee of the right of the people to assemble peacefully and to ask government "for a redress of grievances." Three of the amendments are designed to protect the privacy of the home and to prevent seizure of property. Five, with some overlapping, detail the rights of persons accused of crime.

Our focus is on the First Amendment, which reads:

> Congress shall make no law respecting an establishment of religion, or prohibiting the free exercise thereof; or abridging the freedom of speech, or of the press; or the right of the people peaceably to assemble, and to petition the Government for a redress of grievances.

Strangely, there is little in the debates of the time to show what the drafters meant when they wrote and adopted that amendment. Read literally, it seems to say that Congress has no authority to limit freedom of speech or of the press. The realities of the time suggest otherwise.

According to one view, the founders were influenced by Sir William Blackstone, whose *Commentaries on the Laws of England* was considered the definitive discussion of the meaning of the common law here as well as in England. He wrote that punishment of "blasphemous, immoral, treasonable, schismatical, seditious, or scandalous libels" did not infringe on freedom of the press:

> The liberty of the press is indeed essential to the nature of a free state; but this consists in laying no previous restraints upon publications, and not in freedom from censure for criminal matter when published. Every freeman has an undoubted right to lay what sentiments he pleases before the public: to forbid this is to destroy the freedom of the press: but if he publishes what is improper, mischievous, or illegal, he must take the consequences of his own temerity.[8]

In this view, England had enjoyed liberty of the press since the Printing Act had expired in 1695, and the American colonies since 1725 when the licensing act was permitted to expire on this side of the Atlantic. But if writers knew they might suffer Twyn's fate or languish in jail like Zenger, how likely were they to share their views with the public?

Clearly, Blackstone's view of liberty of the press was a limited one. People could say or write what they pleased as long as they were prepared to take the consequences. If words violated a law, or were even considered "improper [or] mischievous," the writer might well end up in prison, if not on the scaffold.

Only scanty written evidence remains as to what the founders meant when they sought to protect freedom of speech and of the press. Thomas Jefferson, who wrote the Declaration of Independence, and James Madison, who wrote the First Amendment, seem to have rejected the English common law of seditious libel.[9] Benjamin Franklin, a member of the committee that drafted the Declaration and a delegate to the convention that drafted the Constitution, said in 1789 during a discussion of the freedom of speech clause in the Pennsylvania constitution: "[I]f by the liberty of the press were to be understood merely the liberty

---

8. William Blackstone, *Commentaries on the Laws of England,* facsimile ed. (Chicago: University of Chicago Press, 1979), vol. 4, pp. 151–52.
9. Zechariah Chafee, Jr., *Free Speech in the United States* (Cambridge: Harvard University Press, 1941), and Leonard W. Levy, *Legacy of Suppression* (Cambridge: Belknap Press of Harvard University Press, 1960).

of discussing the propriety of public measures and political opinions, let us have as much of it as you please. On the other hand, if it means liberty to calumniate another, there ought to be some limit."[10] That he would put some limits on liberty of speech is notable in light of the fact that he made his living as a successful printer and publisher until he became caught up in public life in 1748.

The first ten amendments to the Constitution—the Bill of Rights—took effect in 1791. At that point, the United States not only had a form of government based squarely on John Locke's *Treatises on Government,* it also had taken steps to guarantee the rights of the people, an idea borrowed from Thomas Hobbes. In a sense, the Bill of Rights created a law above the law to which people could appeal, through the courts, when they believed their freedom was being violated. The Supreme Court has held on numerous occasions that laws, or acts of public officials, which violate rights guaranteed by the first ten amendments are void.

The Sedition Act of 1798

Within a decade after the adoption of the First Amendment, freedom of speech was put to the test and lost. Reacting to the possibility that inflamed passions might draw the United States into a renewed war between England and France, Congress adopted the Sedition Act of 1798, which was plainly a seditious libel law. The Act made it a crime, punishable by fine and imprisonment, to engage in harmful criticism of President John Adams and his policies.

The Sedition Act had its origins in the highly charged partisan politics of the time. President Adams headed the Federalist party, which was sympathetic to England while it wanted to keep the United States out of the war. The Federalists also believed in a strongly centralized government in which the president played a dominant role. Ranged in opposition were the Republicans, headed by Vice-President Thomas Jefferson. Theirs was a party of small farmers and artisans who mistrusted a strong central government. Party members leaned toward the French, remembering their help in the Revolution. It soon became apparent that the Sedition Act was aimed primarily at the editors of Republican newspapers.

Viewed from the vantage point of today, there is no doubt that the Sedition Act was a serious abridgment of freedom of speech and of the press. And yet, judging from the records of the time, there were few who believed in 1798 that it violated the First Amendment guarantees. The debate in Congress preceding passage of the Act indicates that the amendment was seen only as a protection against direct censorship. One speaker said that the First Amendment could not prevent punishment of an editor who published material that "offends against the law."[11] Alexander Hamilton, who had been President Washington's secretary of state and remained one of the leaders of the Federalist party, defended the Sedition Act, partly because it contained at his insistence a clause making truth a de-

---

10.   Chafee, *Free Speech in the United States,* Atheneum ed. (New York, 1969), p. 17.
11.   Robert Harper, a representative from South Carolina, 8 *Annals of Congress,* 5th Cong. 1797–1799, p. 2101.

fense. In a 1799 letter, Hamilton argued that officers of government could serve effectively only if law protected "their reputations from malicious and unfounded slanders."[12]

This view was shared by Justice Samuel Chase of the Supreme Court of the United States. As was the practice in those days, he also sat as a trial judge assigned to a "circuit" comprised of one or more states. In his decision finding Dr. Thomas Cooper, editor of the *Sunbury and Northumberland Gazette*, guilty of sedition, Justice Chase noted that "all governments which I ever heard of" have laws to protect themselves and their officials from harmful criticism. In a passage that might have been written by some present-day politicians, he said:

> A Republican government can only be destroyed in two ways; the introduction of luxury or the licentiousness of the Press. The latter is the more slow, but more sure and certain, means of bringing about the destruction of the government. The legislature of this country, knowing this maxim, has thought proper to check the licentiousness of the press.[13]

Cooper's crime was the writing of an editorial taking issue with President Adams's trade policies. He wrote that when Adams had taken office, "he was hardly in the infancy of political mistake." That was enough to put him among the approximately twenty-five persons arrested on charges of sedition in 1798 and 1799. Fifteen were indicted, eleven tried, and ten were found guilty.[14] The crime was a misdemeanor punishable by a fine or a jail term, or both. Almost all of those who were tried were editors of Republican newspapers.

The Act aroused opposition. Two states, Kentucky and Virginia, passed resolutions condemning it; the former written by Thomas Jefferson, the latter by James Madison. The resolutions took the position that in passing the Sedition Act, Congress had usurped powers expressly denied it by the Constitution. This left the inference that a similar act might be legal if it was drafted and adopted by the various state legislatures.

The Act expired, by its own terms, in March 1801 with the expiration of Adams's term. Historians differ as to the role public resentment over its enforcement played in the election of Thomas Jefferson as president in 1800. One of the first things he did was to pardon all who had been convicted under the Act. Because all of the victims were members of his Republican party, it is impossible to know whether he acted on a firm belief in freedom of speech or out of political motives. During his first term he took no action to prevent the trial of one of his critics, Harry Croswell, who was charged with violating New York's seditious libel law.[15]

Justice Chase was impeached by the House and tried by the Senate in 1805, largely for his role in the trials of Dr. Cooper and of James Callender, author of a

---

12. *The Papers of Alexander Hamilton,* vol. 23, April-October 1799 (New York: Columbia University Press, 1976), p. 604.
13. United States v. Cooper, 25 Fed. Cas. 631, 635 (1800).
14. Clifton O. Lawhorne, *Defamation and Public Officials: The Evolving Law of Libel* (Carbondale: Southern Illinois University Press, 1971), p. 51.
15. People v. Croswell, 3 Johns. Cas. 337 (1804).

book written with Jefferson's encouragement attacking the Adams administration. Evidence indicates that Chase read the book, instigated the prosecution, presided during the trial, and charged the jury in terms that left no doubt he believed Callender guilty. More than half the Senate voted to remove Chase from the Supreme Court, but the total did not reach the required two-thirds majority.[16] In 1840, Congress voted to refund the fines imposed on the victims of the Act. In the process, the House Committee on the Judiciary declared the law "unconstitutional, null and void, passed under a mistaken notion of delegated power." This was simply an opinion, with no force as legal precedent.

The episode lies embedded deep within American history, but its lessons remain valid. Even in a nation with a Constitution that guarantees freedom of speech and press, the urge to suppress unpopular speakers and writers lies just beneath the surface. When foreign enemies threaten, or economic hardship creates unrest, that urge may well be translated into action, official or unofficial. Experience with the Sedition Act did nothing to demonstrate how much protection the First Amendment offers to critics of government because none of the cases reached the Supreme Court.

THE PHILOSOPHY OF FREEDOM OF SPEECH AND PRESS

For more than a century after the Sedition Act expired in 1801, the First Amendment lay dormant. Censorship of news dispatches from the war zones was accepted without legal challenge during the Civil War. Without a sedition law in the statutes, criticism of government and of government officials was accepted as part of the game of party politics. When individuals in and out of government felt that they had been defamed by an overly abusive editor, they might sue for libel in the state courts. But not until well into this century was the Supreme Court ever asked to decide how far the First Amendment goes in protecting freedom of speech and of the press.

The limits of the guarantees were tested first in World War I when Congress enacted the Espionage Act of 1917, followed quickly by the Sedition Act of 1918. Since then, and especially since 1945, courts at all levels have decided thousands of First Amendment cases. These cases have dealt not only with the right to criticize government and government officials, but with the right to picket in labor disputes, the right to demonstrate against racial and other forms of discrimination, the right to protect one's privacy, the right to protect one's reputation, the right to see sexually explicit movies, the right to insist that broadcasters present a wide spectrum of opinion, and the right to advertise. Few aspects of our lives have not been touched by the expanding definition of First Amendment freedoms.

---

16. Samuel Eliot Morison and Henry Steele Commager, *The Growth of the American Republic* (New York: Oxford University Press, 1937), vol 1, p. 293.

Court decisions, especially those of the Supreme Court of the United States, tell us what is legal with respect to speech and the media at any given time. Much of the subject matter of this book is devoted to the major cases defining the rights of the media. But there is also the question of how far freedom of speech and of the press ought to go. This is the realm of philosophy and ethics. Several respected scholars have attempted to develop a rational theory of the meaning of the First Amendment. In doing so, they have sought to offer guidance to those who would use speech for the maximum benefit of society. At a personal level, we know from experience that we sometimes feel better when we have "let off steam" or given someone "a piece of our mind." The First Amendment theorists have sought to demonstrate, in the tradition of John Milton, that unfettered debate is the best means of arriving at the truth about important public issues. In the process, most have discerned limits beyond which words can become harmful. Ethics is concerned with the moral aspects of freedom of speech and of the press. In some areas both law and theory permit speech that some might believe to be harmful. In some instances, media professionals must draw on their own sense of ethics in deciding what to do.

The rest of this chapter presents a sampling of the theories about freedom of speech and of the press. It also outlines the Supreme Court's application of various theories to speech and press cases. A knowledge of First Amendment theory can help us understand why the Supreme Court decided a case as it did. Within limits, it might permit us to anticipate the outcome of a case. However, the Court is made up of nine justices, each of whom looks at any given case in his or her own way. Prediction is therefore best treated as a game of chance rather than a certainty.

The most important reason for studying First Amendment theory is to build a foundation on which to decide for ourselves how important it is to insist that others be permitted to speak their minds. In a society such as ours, no person's right to speak and write freely is any more secure than that of the least rational and most repulsive member of society. If any person is to be punished for his or her views, or forced to be silent, we need a clear understanding of why it is done. Because public opinion does prevail in a rough way in American society, each of us ought to have a theory of the meaning of the First Amendment.

The Meaning of Freedom of Speech and Press

The belief that free discussion offers society the best hope for peaceful resolution of its differences has advanced haltingly and still is held by only a minority of the world's peoples. Such belief assumes that the participants in the debate are rational and willing to compromise on something short of each side's view of absolute truth. The alternative is suppression of one side or the other.

This section summarizes the work of three First Amendment scholars: Zechariah Chafee, Jr., for many years a professor of law at Harvard; Alexander Meiklejohn, a professor of philosophy at Brown, Amherst, and the University of

Wisconsin; and Thomas I. Emerson, professor of law at Yale. It also includes the views of Walter Lippmann, for many years a respected newspaper columnist and author of books on public affairs. Each came to firm conclusions about the meaning of the First Amendment.

Zechariah Chafee, Jr.

Chafee's masterwork is *Free Speech in the United States,* published in 1941 just prior to this country's entry into World War II. It was completed at a time when freedom was the exception, not the rule, for a majority of the world's people. Chafee was by no means an absolutist in his view of the First Amendment. He saw freedom of speech as only one interest, but a very important one, which government must protect for its own good and that of society. When debate focuses on government policies, it must be "absolutely unlimited," because only through the free play of ideas is truth likely to be found. If the government uses its power to suppress a point of view, "it becomes a matter of chance whether it is thrown on the false side or the true, and truth loses all the natural advantages of the contest."[17]

But government, Chafee noted, also has other interests to protect, "such as order, the training of the young, protection against external aggression." If speech threatens to interfere with these other interests, courts must balance one against the other. In such instances, Chafee said, speech "ought to weigh very heavily in the scale." It should be punished "only when the interest in public safety is really impaired." The line between acceptable speech and unacceptable speech should be drawn, he argued, "close to the point where words will give rise to unlawful acts."[18]

Chafee's theory of the First Amendment is important because it embodies the approach—the balancing test—that the Supreme Court has commended to lower courts in freedom of speech cases. Each attempt at suppression is treated as a balancing of interests: the speaker's right to participate in the search for truth, for example, versus the government's right to raise an army in time of war. The same test also is applied to cases in which it is alleged that the news media have harmed a person's reputation, or have interfered with the right to a fair trial.

Walter Lippmann

At about the time Chafee was writing his book, Lippmann was writing in a different style but to the same end in his newspaper columns and in an article, "The Indispensable Opposition," published in the *Atlantic Monthly* in 1939.[19]

---

17. Chafee, Atheneum ed., pp. 31–32.
18. Ibid., p. 35.
19. Reprinted in Henry Steele Commager, ed., *Living Ideas in America* (New York: Harper & Row, 1951), pp. 400–03.

Lippmann focused on people rather than government. He argued, as did Alexander Hamilton in *The Federalist*,[20] that any guarantee of freedom of speech or press means nothing unless the people are strongly committed to supporting it. Lippmann noted that if you ask them about it, most people will say they are willing to tolerate speakers with whom they disagree. But in his view, toleration is not enough. Freedom of speech cannot survive in any society, he wrote, echoing Mill, unless people realize that "because freedom of discussion improves our own opinion, the liberties of other[s]...are our own vital necessity." He said we must listen to those whose opinions seem obnoxious to us because they are the most likely to point out our errors. To listen only to those who agree with us, Lippmann argued, is to court disaster.

Thus Lippmann's view that freedom of speech is indispensable is not to be shrugged off as simply good advice for people in authority. The urge to censor, intimidate, or join a noisy mob lies just beneath the surface in most of us. It is one thing to take part in a noisy debate or even to heckle a speaker. That is part of the political process. So are sign-waving demonstrators. But it is a much more serious matter to use physical coercion to prevent someone from speaking at all, to set fire to an abortion clinic, or to insist that a news organization suspend a commentator whose views on gender, race, or religion are considered repugnant.[21]

Alexander Meiklejohn

After World War II, Alexander Meiklejohn addressed the same streak of oppression Lippmann had observed. In a series of lectures later expanded into a book, this long-time commentator on the meaning of freedom in the university focused on the meaning of freedom of expression guaranteed by the First Amendment. He argued that there are two layers of freedom: at the higher level, speech devoted to public affairs; at a lower level, actions that distort debate on public matters, speech that directly provokes illegal acts, and speech that brings harm to other individuals.

Speech devoted to public affairs, Meiklejohn continued, should receive a very high degree of protection from the First Amendment. Such speech is in the public interest and should therefore be encouraged. Starting from the belief that the Constitution not only makes the public at large, which he called "the electorate," a branch of the government, but the most important one, he wrote:

> The First Amendment seems to me to be a very uncompromising statement. It admits of no exceptions. It tells us that the Congress and, by implication, all other agencies of government are denied any authority whatever to limit the political freedom of the citizens of the United States. It declares that with respect to political

---

20. *The Federalist: A Commentary on the Constitution of the United States,* The Modern Library edition (New York: Random House, 1937), p. 560.
21. As CBS News did Andy Rooney from *60 Minutes* for one month in 1990 in response to complaints from homosexuals. Michael Gartner, "Silencing Rooney, or Anyone, Hurts Us All," *Wall Street Journal,* 22 February 1990.

belief, political discussion, political advocacy, political planning, our citizens are sovereign, and the Congress is their subordinate agent.[22]

Meiklejohn's repeated use of the word "political" to describe the kind of speech worthy of absolute protection under the First Amendment should not be misconstrued. He was not limiting himself to the kind of oratory that takes place during political campaigns. Taken in connection with his references to public policy, it is clear that his theory would extend full First Amendment protection to economic and social issues—to arguments over factory closings, air pollution, abortion, and racial or sexual discrimination—because all involve government intervention at some point.

Building on his belief that the First Amendment should give absolute protection to the debate over public policy, Meiklejohn argued that the government should do more than merely tolerate all shades of opinion. Nor is it enough to extend the protection of the courts to the participants in this debate. Government should open public buildings and other public places to those who want to debate public policy. Such places should be as open to those who attack the government's policies as they are to those who support them.

However, Meiklejohn relegated speech-related action and some forms of pure speech to a lower level where they were protected, not by the First Amendment, but by the due process clause of the Fifth Amendment. While he expressly rejected the application of Chafee's balancing test to speech having to do with public policy,[23] he was willing to apply it to lower-level speech. Some such speech grows out of personal relationships: one person, for instance, does not have an absolute right to speak ill of another. Other such speech is a product of commercial relationships: A merchant does not have a right to make false advertising claims for his wares, or to misrepresent the terms of a contract. Meiklejohn also put on his lower level some speech directed at government. Once the debate on policy has ended and has been formalized into statute law, the people are required to obey the law until it has been changed. Speech or speech-related action, in defiance of law, may be punished if the punishment is carried out in accord with the due process guarantees of the Fifth Amendment.

"The First Amendment...is not the guardian of unregulated talkativeness," Meiklejohn wrote.[24] Thus, to ensure orderly debate of the issues, noisy obstructionists can be removed from the forum. Or if twenty persons are of the same mind, it is time-wasting to insist that each should have time to say the same thing. "What is essential is not that everyone shall speak, but that everything worth saying shall be said." Nor does the First Amendment mean that an individual should be permitted to use a sound truck in a residential neighborhood in the middle of the night to argue a point of view. Nor does it mean that demonstrators should be permitted to stop traffic in rush hour to make a point. In short, Meiklejohn was saying, as the Supreme Court has said consistently, that the state

22. Alexander Meiklejohn, *Political Freedom* (New York: Harper & Row, 1960), pp. 107–08.
23. Ibid., pp. 58–59.
24. Ibid., p. 26.

may regulate the *process* of debate—the time, place, and manner of speaking. But, in doing so, it must be neutral as to the *content* of the speech.

Meiklejohn differs from Chafee and Lippmann in two respects: He would give absolute protection to debate over public policy and he injected a positive element into First Amendment theory. As he saw it, the amendment imposes a mandate on government to encourage debate. The Supreme Court has not yet gone all the way with Meiklejohn on either premise, but it has come close to doing so. However, Meiklejohn, like Chafee and Lippmann, was not willing to interpret "Congress shall make no law" as an absolute protection for all kinds of speech.

Thomas I. Emerson

Emerson wrote *The System of Freedom of Expression* in the late 1960s.[25] Turmoil boiled around him as he wrote. A law professor at Yale, he was able to observe firsthand the demonstrations fueled in the 1960s by opposition to the war in Vietnam and the struggle of blacks for a greater degree of equity in society. What he saw obviously disquieted him. In an epilogue he expresses doubt that freedom of expression could survive an assault on one side from a New Left that equated freedom of speech with lack of conviction, and on the other from a Right determined to preserve the status quo.

Emerson went beyond the others in arguing that all "expression" which bears on government policy ought to have the full protection of the First Amendment. Further, he went beyond Meiklejohn and included some kinds of speech-related action in his definition of "expression." He would protect peaceful picketing, demonstrations, the carrying of signs, and symbolic speech, such as burning an American flag. He also sought to answer a question Chafee and Meiklejohn left unanswered, except in general terms: At what point does speech-related action become a criminal act that can be punished?

Emerson found no room in a system of free expression for application of the balancing test advocated by Chafee. In his view, courts considering First Amendment cases would be limited to defining the "key elements" of that Amendment, which he listed as "expression," "abridge," and "law." Any form of speech or action that met his definition of "expression" would be protected absolutely against any act of government that sought to limit it.

Like Lippmann, Emerson recognized that private individuals and institutions, as well as organized groups, can discourage freedom of speech. Under current interpretations of First Amendment law, the courts can do little to prevent such abridgments unless a criminal act, such as vandalism, is involved. Emerson argued that the courts ought to be able to deal directly with nongovernmental acts intended to silence unpopular speakers.

Like Meiklejohn, he found a positive element in the First Amendment. Not only should government offer its facilities to those who would debate public policy, but it should attempt, through education, to expand the understanding of

---

25. New York: Random House, 1970.

such policy. Further, he argued that the First Amendment imposes a mandate on government to release information essential to proper appraisal of its actions. Finally, he saw an expanded role for radio and television in the discussion of public affairs. As the only media licensed by government, they should be required to seek out and present all sides of controversial public issues.

A major portion of Emerson's work is devoted to exploring the boundary between speech and action that Chafee saw as the test of how free any society is. Emerson would push that line far into territory usually perceived as the domain of action. In his view, a peaceful strike is expression, not action. So are street gatherings and marching. Where, then, is the line between the permissible and the impermissible?

Emerson saw no problems with the discussion of violence as a means of solving a political impasse. Speakers could point out that certain kinds of oppression had led to violence in the past. They could warn that if oppressive policies were not changed, they might lead to violence. But there is a limit:

> ...[T]he urging of immediate, specific acts of violence would, under circumstances where violence was possible and likely, fall within the category of "action." Such communication would be so interlocked with violent conduct as to constitute for all practical purposes part of the action; it would be in effect the beginning of the action itself. In short the basic effort would be to formulate the definition of "expression" in terms of the difference between the ideational preparation for subsequent conduct and actual participation in it.[26]

By way of illustration, there would be nothing wrong, in Emerson's view, with a speaker's urging an audience in Peoria "to evict that rotten president from his Oval Office." But if the same speaker were to say the same thing to an angry crowd in Lafayette Square in Washington, D.C., and that crowd seemed on the point of crossing Pennsylvania Avenue to assault the White House, he could be punished for his words. "Expression" would have become a strong likelihood of harmful "action."

Chafee, Lippmann, Meiklejohn, and Emerson's differing views of the First Amendment can be made clearer by applying them to the announcement that the Ku Klux Klan plans a rally in a city park in a community where racial tensions are near the flash point. In Chafee's view, persons opposed to the rally could go to court and argue that it was likely to cause violence. If a reasonable case could be made, the court would be required to balance it against the probable message of the Klan speakers. If the court concluded that the possibility of violence outweighed the speakers' likely contribution to the debate on racial policy, it could issue an injunction forbidding the rally.

The Lippmann who wrote "The Indispensable Opposition" might take the position that while the Klan's message was likely to be distasteful to some, the speakers should be permitted to deliver it because they might make some contri-

---

26. Emerson, pp. 17–18.

bution to the debate over race relations. He would argue that some worthwhile speech, like some medicine, leaves a bitter taste.

Meiklejohn would have looked at the rally in two ways. He would regard the speechmaking in one way, but the surrounding elements—the robes, the hoods, the possibility of a march through the streets, the number of participants, and the likelihood of a cross being burned—in another. Whatever the speakers might have to say about race relations ought to be given the utmost protection, in Meiklejohn's view, because it would be a contribution to the debate on the public policy. If police were required to protect the speakers from violence originating among opponents of the Klan, then police protection ought to be provided. Further, Meiklejohn would see the park as an appropriate forum for the speakers. Its use would be in conformity with the government's obligation to encourage debate on public policy. But if the Klan members were to wear hoods, or march through a black neighborhood, or burn a cross, that would be another matter. Such actions might well be intimidating rather than persuasive. They might provoke violence. In Meiklejohn's view, they could be challenged in the courts. If, after a hearing with both sides represented, the court concluded that any speech-related action was likely to cause violence, such action could be forbidden.

Emerson's theory of the First Amendment would protect not only the speeches, but any peaceful action Klan members might take to draw attention to their cause. They could march, as long as they did not block traffic, they could wear robes and hoods, and they could burn a cross if they wanted to. What they could not do is create a situation in which it appeared likely that they might resort to violence against others. But the likelihood that the speeches would spur members to action would have to be clear. By the same token, Emerson would expect the police to intervene if others should attempt violence against the Klan. But their actions would be directed at those who were threatening violence, not at the participants in the rally.

Thus, all the theories start with the assumption that members of the Ku Klux Klan are entitled to participate in the debate over public policy. So are those who hold other points of view. All the theories further assume that those who do not participate in the debate, and even the debaters themselves, will weigh the various arguments and decide for themselves what the policy ought to be. Finally, First Amendment theorists assume that most people are rational. Therefore, they will reject extreme positions and reach an accommodation that will be acceptable to a majority. This is the process through which public opinion is formed and shapes public policy.

The Supreme Court's Interpretation of Freedom of Speech and Press

The Supreme Court of the United States is made up of lawyers, many of whom have had experience as judges of lower courts. A few have been professors of law. Most come to think of themselves as legal philosophers. Nevertheless, critics, including some members of the present Court, have complained that the Court has not been able to settle on any consistent theory of First Amendment law. Whether any one theory can be applied to the great variety of cases that reach the Court is an open question. In any case, in the seventy years in which it has dealt with First Amendment cases, the Court has applied several theories, or tests.

One theory can be rejected at the start: the Court has never agreed with Meiklejohn or Emerson that some kinds of speech should be given absolute protection. Between 1939 and 1971, two members of the Court, Hugo L. Black and William O. Douglas, argued on occasion that the First Amendment means precisely what it says—Congress shall make no law abridging freedom of speech, press, religion, and assembly. But Black drew back from that position in the late 1960s and told an interviewer he could not support the right of demonstrators to gather outside the homes of public officials.

A majority has come close on occasion to granting absolute protection to speech, but has always left an exception which could be applied as a check in an extreme case. The Court's actions have rested on the following grounds: the bad tendency theory, the clear and present danger test, the theory of the balancing of interests, the preferred position theory, and a positive theory of the First Amendment. The Court also has recognized some kinds of action as symbolic speech, protected by the First Amendment, and has expanded the concept of a public forum.

The Bad Tendency Theory

This theory came out of the kind of English common law that was used against poor Twyn and that justified the convictions of the Republican editors caught up in the Sedition Act of 1798. If words had a tendency to undermine the authority of government or to corrupt the morals of some members of society, the writer or speaker could be punished. Under this theory, there was no need to show that any harm had been done. The mere likelihood of harm was enough to support a conviction.

The Clear and Present Danger Test

This test was formulated by Justice Oliver Wendell Holmes in *Schenck* v. *United States* in 1919. Charles Schenck was general secretary of the Socialist party. During World War I, he and an associate printed and distributed fifteen thousand leaflets urging resistance to the draft. The two were charged with violating the Espionage Act, found guilty, and sentenced to prison. They appealed to the Supreme Court, arguing that their right to free speech had been violated. The case was not decided until four months after the war had ended in victory for the United States and its allies. Nevertheless, the Court found, with Holmes writ-

Schenck v. *United States,*
249 U.S. 47, 39 S. Ct.
247, 63 L. Ed. 470 (1919).

ing a unanimous decision, that the leaflets presented a "clear and present danger" to the draft system, and thus to the nation's efforts to win the war. In time, the decision was seen as giving speech greater protection than that offered by the bad tendency test, but in its early applications, in the 1920s, the distinction was hard to see.

In the *Schenck* decision, Holmes made the following points:

1. Government must, under mandate from the Constitution, protect certain vital interests—the lives and properties of its citizens, peace and good order, and the security of the nation against threats from foreign enemies. Anything that would prevent government from carrying out its required functions is a "substantive evil that Congress has a right to prevent."

2. In protecting vital interests, there are times when government must override First Amendment interests and punish persons whose words might bring harm to the state. This is especially true in time of war. Another such time might be a period of turmoil brought on by economic depression. At such times, government is particularly vulnerable to agitators seeking to capitalize on heightened emotion.

3. Speech may also lose its protection because of the place in which it is uttered or the audience to which it is addressed. A disgruntled speaker who chooses to shout his discontent into the wind blowing across an empty beach is no threat to anyone. But those same words spoken to a mob outside the White House would be another matter.

4. The circumstances surrounding the speech must also be taken into account. Holmes illustrated with a sentence which has been more frequently quoted than fully understood, even by some judges: "The most stringent protection of free speech would not protect a man in falsely shouting fire in a theater and causing a panic." If this sentence is examined closely, its meaning is found to be much closer to Meiklejohn and Emerson than the decision in *Schenck* put it. First, Holmes was saying that the content of the speech must be a lie. Not a mistaken opinion; not an illegal appeal based on emotion: only a deliberate misstatement of fact can be punished. Clearly, his choice of words means that there could be no punishment for the person who found a fire in a theater and whose warning saved the lives of the audience. Nor could the law punish an actor whose lines required him to shout "Fire!" The speaker must have resorted to falsehood in order to cause trouble. Second, Holmes was saying that there must be a direct connection between the false speech and a harmful act—in this instance, panic, the kind of action that leads to people getting trampled or piled up against the doors, causing injury or death.

In later cases, Holmes and Justice Brandeis were to say that the meaning of the clear and present danger test was wrapped up in that one sentence about "shouting fire." Speech creates a clear and present danger only when it is obvious that it will immediately produce actions harmful to a vital interest Congress has the authority to protect. If the test is properly applied, it puts the line between speech and action very close to the latter, as Chafee, Meiklejohn, and Emerson advocated.

The Theory of the Balancing of Interests

Under this theory, the First Amendment interest in free discussion is seen merely as one of many interests safeguarded by the Constitution. When one comes into conflict with another, it is the duty of the courts to weigh the competing interests against each other and decide which has the greater value to society under the circumstances. Obviously, the outcome of the contest is as subject to the personal leanings of the individual judges involved as under any other theory.

Balancing in speech cases had its formal origins in *American Communications Association* v. *Douds*. The case involved the refusal of an officer of a labor union to sign an affidavit stating that he was not a member of the Communist party or of any other organization advocating violent overthrow of the government, and that he did not believe in violent overthrow. A union could not take advantage of the National Labor Relations Act unless all its officers signed such affidavits. Lower courts upheld the requirement. A majority of the Supreme Court agreed that labor union officers should be required to forswear affiliation with subversive organizations, but the justices split evenly on whether they should be required to take an oath as to what they believed, thus upholding the right to require union officers to sign the affidavits.

American Communications Association v. *Douds,* 339 U.S. 382, 70 S.Ct. 674, 94 L.Ed. 925 (1950).

Chief Justice Fred M. Vinson, who wrote the prevailing opinion, explained the balancing concept applied by the Court. He reasoned that the oath did not prevent anyone from believing what he or she pleased. All it did was deny certain federal benefits to persons who believed in overthrowing the source of those benefits. Vinson saw this as a limited restriction on freedom of expression, both in terms of the numbers of persons affected and in the degree of restriction on speech.

On the other hand, there is considerable societal interest in preventing those who believe in violent overthrow from achieving positions of power. Communist leaders of labor unions might well call for strikes for political purposes rather than to achieve economic goals. Further, if the Court held the oath invalid for labor union leaders, for whom else might a similar oath be invalid? Could the government be denied the right to ask a prospective member of the Secret Service if he believed in assassinating presidents? Vinson wrote, "An affirmative answer hardly commends itself to reason," and he concluded that the oath "does not unduly infringe freedoms protected by the First Amendment."

The balancing theory is still the most common method used by the courts in determining when expression can be punished. However, in recent years, the Supreme Court usually has given First Amendment rights a greater weight in the scale of justice than did the Vinson court in *Douds*.

The Preferred Position Theory

A series of recent Court decisions has held that First Amendment rights, and some others guaranteed by the Bill of Rights, occupy a "preferred position." The Court also has held that these guarantees stand, through the Fourteenth Amendment, in a preferred position as a barrier against state interference. Preferred position theory is used in all instances in which government is seen as trying to prevent allegedly harmful speech. Thus it is a weapon against censorship, also called prior, or previous, restraint. The theory begins with the assumption that the people enjoyed freedom of speech before they entered into the compact that resulted in the Constitution. Therefore, while the Constitution specifically protects that right, it did not grant it. Because freedom of speech lies at the heart of a free society, it must be guarded diligently. Any encroachment by government is a serious matter, so serious that the courts assume that any restriction on freedom of speech is unconstitutional until proved otherwise. In such cases, the burden of proof is on the government. It must show (1) that the restriction has been imposed to protect an interest it is entitled to protect under the Constitution, (2) that the law has been drafted in such specific terms that it will do what it is supposed to do with a minimum of harm to freedom of speech, and (3) that the government's vital interest cannot be protected without some restriction on speech. If there is more than one way to protect the government's basic interest, it must use the method that does the least harm to speech.

The government must show in such cases that its need to act is "compelling." The courts assume that government has acted improperly until it proves otherwise. If speech is the subject of an attempted restraint, the Court has said there is both a "heavy presumption" that the restraint is unconstitutional[27] and a "heavy burden of showing justification for such a restraint."[28]

The effect of the preferred position theory has been to grant pure speech—that is, speech untainted by action—a high degree of freedom. At times the Supreme Court has come very close to the positions advocated by Meiklejohn and Emerson, especially when speech concerns the actions of government and government officials.

Symbolic Speech

Both Meiklejohn and Emerson believed that the First Amendment should protect conduct designed to express a position on public issues. The Supreme Court has embraced that belief and for more than fifty years has given almost as much

---

27. Bantam Books, Inc., v. Sullivan, 372 U.S. 58, 83 S.Ct. 631, 9 L.Ed.2d 584 (1963).
28. Organization for a Better Austin v. Keefe, 402 U.S. 415, 91 S.Ct. 1575, 29 L.Ed.2d 1 (1971).

protection to peaceful political action as it has to political argument. Such action is called symbolic speech.

In 1989, the Court demonstrated how far it is willing to go to protect such speech when it upheld the right to burn a U.S. flag to make a political point. The decision split the Court five-to-four and was made possible only because two Reagan appointees considered conservatives, Anthony Kennedy and Antonin Scalia, signed the opinion written by William J. Brennan, Jr. Kennedy wrote separately to note his "distaste for the result," but he said settled principles of First Amendment law gave the Court no right to rule otherwise, "however painful this judgment is to announce."

Texas v. *Johnson,* **491 U.S. _ _ _, 109 S.Ct. 2533, 105 L.Ed.2d 342 (1989).**

Police arrest Scott "Dred Scott" Tyler of Chicago for burning a United States flag on the Capitol steps in Washington, D.C. His act challenged a federal law enacted to counter the Supreme Court's holding that a Texas flag desecration law violated the First Amendment. This arrest and others led to the Court's again holding that flag burning as an expression of political protest is symbolic speech protected by the Constitution. (AP/Wide World Photos)

Brennan built the majority's decision on speech cases dating to World War I and more specifically on precedents established in symbolic speech and flag desecration cases decided by the Court during the Vietnam war. In those cases, the Court held that the First Amendment protects the right to speak disrespectfully of the flag and urge others not to honor it,[29] to tape a peace symbol to a U.S. flag and display it in a public place,[30] or to sew a flag to the seat of one's pants.[31] In those cases, the Court held that when otherwise illegal acts are committed to express a point of view on an important public issue, they may be protected as symbolic speech. The test is whether the actor's purpose is to convey a particular message and that his audience understands that message. Further, the conduct must be such that its First Amendment value overrides the state's interest in punishing it. The symbolic speech doctrine obviously does not encompass murder, assault, or armed robbery committed with the intent to convey a political message, nor did it protect a man who burned his draft card to protest the Vietnam war. The Court held that the government's interest in identifying men eligible for the draft overcame any First Amendment point made by the card's destruction.[32]

In *Johnson,* Texas authorities said the state's flag desecration law was designed to prevent breaches of the peace and to preserve the flag "as a symbol of nationhood and national unity." Brennan noted that no one had reacted violently when Gregory Lee Johnson poured kerosene on a U.S. flag and lighted it in front of Dallas City Hall to protest the renomination of President Reagan. Had anyone used violence, Brennan said, the state could have acted under another statute punishing breaches of the peace.

Nor was the state's interest in protecting the flag sufficient to overcome Johnson's First Amendment interest in burning it to make his point. Brennan said the Court has held on numerous occasions that the right to express dissatisfaction with national policy is "situated at the core of our First Amendment values." He added: "If there is a bedrock principle underlying the First Amendment, it is that the Government may not prohibit the expression of an idea simply because society finds the idea itself offensive or disagreeable." To forbid the use of the flag or other symbols as a means of expression "would be to enter territory having no discernible or defensible boundaries...."

Where Brennan found an expression of ideas worthy of the Court's protection, Chief Justice William H. Rehnquist found only "an inarticulate grunt or roar that, it seems fair to say, is most likely to be indulged in not to express any particular idea, but to antagonize others." He said Johnson's burning of the flag "conveyed nothing that could not have been conveyed...just as forcefully in a dozen different ways." The chief justice said Johnson could not have been punished for saying whatever he pleased about the flag or the government, but, in his view, he should have been punished for burning the flag.

---

29. Street v. New York, 394 U.S. 576, 89 S.Ct. 1354, 22 L.Ed.2d 572 (1969).
30. Spence v. Washington, 418 U.S. 405, 94 S.Ct. 2727, 41 L.Ed.2d 842 (1974).
31. Smith v. Goguen, 415 U.S. 566, 94 S.Ct. 1242, 39 L.Ed.2d 605 (1974).
32. United States v. O'Brien, 391 U.S. 367, 88 S.Ct. 1673, 20 L.Ed.2d 672 (1968).

Congress reacted by enacting a law making it a crime to mutilate the flag. Immediately after it became effective, demonstrators tested it by again burning a flag and getting arrested. A U.S. district court judge in Seattle found the law in violation of the First Amendment. The Supreme Court affirmed, citing *Johnson* as its precedent.[33]

A Positive Theory of the First Amendment

Until 1980, the Court had flirted with, but generally rejected, the idea advanced by Meiklejohn and made more specific by Emerson that the First Amendment requires positive steps by government to ensure free and informed debate on its policies. Fifty years ago, the Court noted in *Hague* v. *CIO*[34] that "time out of mind public streets and sidewalks have been used for purposes of assembly, communicating thoughts between citizens, and discussing public questions." In such places, the government's right to restrict the content of speech "is very limited," the Court said. Thus it long has been established that government has, at the least, a passive role in providing a forum for the communication of ideas.

In cases since, the Court has refined the limits it mentioned in *Hague*. In 1988, it held in *Boos* v. *Berry*[35] that the District of Columbia could not prevent sign-waving pickets from getting within 500 feet of the embassies of foreign governments. The problem with the District's ordinance was that it applied only to signs tending to bring the targeted nation into "public odium" or "public disrepute." That made the law a content-based restriction on political speech in a public forum, thus violating the First Amendment. The Court noted a well-established legal principle that speech can be restricted in a public forum only if the restriction is content-neutral.

This is not to say that people can take over public places and use them for political purposes as they see fit. Government can control the time, place, and manner of the use. Restrictions must be reasonable and cannot be used to prohibit speech altogether. The Court has upheld restrictions imposed to preserve order, although it has required strong evidence that a riot was likely. The Court has been more likely to uphold restrictions designed to keep traffic moving or to protect those outside the forum from undue disturbance, as from excessively loud amplifying systems. For instance, in 1989 the Court held that the city of New York could impose decibel limits on the sound systems used by rock bands during concerts at the Band Shell in Central Park.[36] Years earlier, the Court had held that cities can regulate the loudness of sound trucks used on public streets during political campaigns.[37]

---

33.   United States v. Eichman and United States v. Haggerty, _ _ _ U.S. _ _ _, 110 S.Ct. 2404, 110 L.Ed. 2d 287 (1990)
34.   307 U.S. 496, 59 S.Ct. 954, 83 L.Ed. 1423 (1939).
35.   485 U.S. 312, 108 S.Ct. 1157, 99 L.Ed.2d 333 (1988).
36.   Ward v. Rock against Racism, _ _ _ U.S. _ _ _, 109 S.Ct. 2746, 105 L.Ed.2d 661 (1989).
37.   Kovacs v. Cooper, 336 U.S. 77, 69 S.Ct. 448, 93 L.Ed. 513 (1949).

Chinese students gather near their nation's embassy in Washington, D.C., in May 1989 to show their opposition to China's Communist regime. Their right to do so was established less than a year earlier when the Supreme Court struck down a law forbidding political protest within 500 feet of a foreign embassy. Days after this picture was taken, Chinese authorities used tanks and troops to sweep supporters of democracy from Tiananmen Square in Beijing, killing many. (AP/Wide World Photos)

Public forums are not limited to parks, street, sidewalks, and other outdoor areas. Public forums include public auditoriums,[38] public schools,[39] and airport terminals.[40] The Court has held that if an agency of government permits one speaker to discuss public issues in one of its facilities, that agency must open that facility to others for the same purpose.

At one time, the Supreme Court embraced Meiklejohn's belief that radio and television, as media licensed by the government, are required by the First Amendment to seek out and present both sides of public issues; for example, in 1969 the Court upheld the fairness doctrine imposed on broadcasters by the Federal Communications Commission.[41] However, that doctrine was abandoned by

---

38. Southeastern Promotions v. Conrad, 420 U.S. 546, 95 S.Ct. 1239, 43 L.Ed.2d 448 (1975).
39. Tinker v. Des Moines School Dist. 393 U.S. 503, 89 S.Ct. 733, 21 L.Ed.2d 731 (1969).
40. Heffron v. International Society for Krishna Consciousness, 452 U.S. 640, 101 S.Ct. 2559, 69 L.Ed.2d 298 (1981).
41. Red Lion Broadcasting Co. v. Federal Communications Commission, 395 U.S. 367, 89 S.Ct. 1794, 23 L.Ed.2d 371 (1969).

the commission in 1987 except as it applies to public referenda. An appellate court in the District of Columbia affirmed its right to do so.[42]

The Supreme Court has held flatly that any attempt by government to enforce "fairness" on newspapers violates the First Amendment. Nor has the Court found in the First Amendment any levers that can be used to pry information out of the government. It has held that the amendment protects a reporter's right to share information with the public but offers no help in getting information. Congress moved into that breach by adopting the Freedom of Information Act, establishing by law a right of access to much of, but not all, the information generated by government agencies. The Supreme Court has upheld that Act in numerous decisions but has construed it rather narrowly.

In 1980, the Court handed down its first First Amendment access decision in *Richmond Newspapers* v. *Virginia*.[43] The case grew out of an order by a judge who ejected journalists and other spectators from his courtroom while he conducted a murder trial. On appeal, a majority of the Court held that the First Amendment protects the right to be present in a courtroom during a trial. Chief Justice Burger reasoned that courtrooms historically have been public assemblies and therefore come within the First Amendment's guarantee of the right to assemble. That right, he said, is not absolute but can be restricted only for the most compelling reasons. Justice John Paul Stevens noted the potentially far-reaching aspects of that ruling. The Court, he said, had for the first time found in the First Amendment a right of access to the news. The case stands as at least a first step toward the positive role for the First Amendment postulated by Meiklejohn and Emerson. However, in the decade since, the Court has done little to expand the meaning of *Richmond Newspapers* to establish a right of access to other newsworthy government activities.

A LOOK AHEAD

In the chapters that follow, we will examine the Supreme Court's application of First Amendment theory to the many forms of communication. We will find that the Court has:

1. Come very close to giving absolute protection to speech directed at influencing government policy. This includes peaceful action, such as picketing, demonstrating, and even burning the U.S. flag. Theoretically, sedition is still a crime, but the government has not been able to win a conviction in the past thirty years.

2. Held that public officials and public figures cannot win a libel suit against the media unless they can offer clear and convincing proof they were vic-

---

42. Syracuse Peace Council v. Federal Communications Commission, 867 F.2d 654 (D.C.Cir. 1989).
43. 448 U.S. 555, 100 S.Ct. 2814, 65 L.Ed.2d 973 (1980).

tims of a false and defamatory assertion of fact. Further, public figures must prove that the publisher either knew the assertion was false or acted with a reckless disregard for the truth. States have the option under the First Amendment of permitting private individuals to win libel suits by proving negligence, a lesser degree of fault. Pure opinion characterizing the actions of individuals, public or private, enjoys absolute protection under the First Amendment.

3. Extended First Amendment protection to truthful advertising for legal products or services. The government can regulate such advertising only if it can prove that regulation is necessary to further an overriding public interest and does not encroach on otherwise protected speech.

4. Greatly narrowed the ability of government to censor moving pictures. It can act only if it can prove that such pictures are obscene, meaning that they serve no serious purpose and portray sexual or excretory activity in a manner that appeals to a prurient interest to a degree unacceptable to the community in which the movie is exhibited.

5. Held that, because broadcasters must be licensed by the government in order to obtain access to the people's airwaves, they have a lesser degree of First Amendment freedom than do owners of print media. This means primarily that broadcasters can be required to carry some political campaign messages and must offer contending candidates equal opportunities to reach the public.

6. Begun to carve out a First Amendment niche for cable television that is somewhere between the near-absolute freedom enjoyed by the print media and the lesser degree of freedom afforded broadcasters.

7. Held, in a recent case, that public high school newspapers published as part of a classroom exercise enjoy no more First Amendment freedom than school authorities are willing to grant them. However, in other respects, the Court has held that the First Amendment does not stop at the schoolhouse gate, giving students and faculty the right to express support for various causes as long as they do not disrupt the learning process.

8. Held that there is no First Amendment protection for obscene materials, so-called fighting words, false or misleading advertising, advertising for illegal products or services, and language that directly incites illegal acts. However, the Court acts on the assumption that communications directed at the general public are protected by the First Amendment. If the government attempts to punish or suppress such communications, it carries the burden of proving that it has the authority to do so, that its interest in doing so is greater that the public's right to know, and that its proposed action will sweep no more broadly than necessary to protect its asserted interest.

In the Professional World

If history teaches any lessons, one of them surely must be that we cannot take for granted the right to say or publish what we please. Another must be that, as Milton put it, words "are not absolutely dead things, but do contain a potencie of life in them." He went on to compare them to the dragon's teeth of mythology which, "being sown up and down, may chance to spring up armed men." Through history, that "potencie" has created tensions which have fueled the urge to censor, lest unbridled speech tear apart the fabric that holds society together. The opposing view is that a society can become strong only by listening to its critics and shoring up the weaknesses they expose.

The authors of the First Amendment, guided by Milton, Locke, and others, adopted the latter view, embracing the idea that freedom of expression is one of the natural rights retained by the people when they entered the social compact. One purpose of the amendment was to place political speech beyond the reach of a majority's power to suppress ideas it does not like.

That goal has been endorsed by the Supreme Court. Halfway through World War II, when it was by no means certain that the United States and its allies would prevail over the Axis powers, the Court wrote one of its most eloquent decisions upholding the right of dissent. At issue was a law adopted by the state of West Virginia requiring all public school pupils to start the day by pledging their allegiance to the flag. The purpose was to promote loyalty to the government in a time of peril. To a handful of Jehovah's Witnesses, the flag salute was idolatry, forbidden by the tenets of their faith. When their children refused to mouth the pledge, the children were expelled from school and the parents were prosecuted for contributing to their delinquency.

The Supreme Court told the state its law violated the freedom of speech clause of the First Amendment.[44] Justice Robert H. Jackson, writing for the Court, noted that when rulers attempt to coerce an end to dissent, they "soon find themselves exterminating dissenters." Nor is the punishment of dissenters made any more palatable when it is done by a majority for the purpose of promoting national unity. Jackson wrote:

> The very purpose of a Bill of Rights was to withdraw certain subjects from the vicissitudes of political controversy, to place them beyond the reach of majorities and officials and to establish them as legal principles to be applied by the courts. One's right to life, liberty, and property, to free speech, a free press, freedom of worship and assembly, and other fundamental rights may not be submitted to vote; they depend on the outcome of no elections.

---

44. West Virginia State Board of Education v. Barnette, 319 U.S. 624, 63 S.Ct. 1178, 87 L.Ed. 1628 (1943).

> If there is any fixed star in our constitutional constellation, it is that no official, high or petty, can prescribe what shall be orthodox in politics, nationalism, religion, or other matters of opinion, or to force citizens to confess by word or act their faith therein. If there are any circumstances which permit an exception, they do not now occur to us.

Jackson's words erased a law enacted by the West Virginia legislature, but implicit in them is a recognition of the same repressive force decried by Walter Lippman in his "Indispensable Opposition." As Walt Kelly once said through his cartoon character Pogo, "We have met the enemy, and they is us." Whether we succeed in getting a legislature to enact our views into law, many of us will use such force as we can muster to silence those whose views we abhor. That some such views are indeed abhorrent—racial slurs directed at blacks, Hispanics, and others; sexual harassment; and callousness toward the physically handicapped are some examples—makes repression easier, even makes it seem the nobler course. Some see words such as "nigger," "kike," "honky," "slut," and "faggot" as Rehnquist saw flag burning, as a "grunt or roar" designed to provoke anger rather than express an idea. In keeping with that view, administrators at such prestigious universities as Dartmouth, Stanford, Smith, Wisconsin, and Michigan either have acted to punish students for discriminatory remarks or have considered rules to provide for such punishment.[45] They were moved to action by evidence of an increase in racist slurs, antigay taunts, and anti-Semitic remarks on theirs and other campuses. Their rationale is that college students and faculty should serve as examples in accepting diversity and rejecting stereotypes of all kinds.

Michigan acted after a university radio station aired anti-Semitic comments and racist jokes. The faculty adopted a code providing for punishment of any conduct that "stigmatizes or victimizes" people on the basis of race, ethnicity, religion, sexual orientation, national origin, marital status, handicap, and "Vietnam-era veteran status."

However, that is not the end of it. At Dartmouth, four editors of a conservative weekly newspaper, *The Dartmouth Review,* were suspended from school after President James O. Freedman accused the publication of "dangerously affecting—in fact, poisoning—the intellectual environment of our campus."[46] The *Review's* crowning offense was publication of a transcript of a rambling lecture given by a black professor of music, which was followed by a confrontation when the students sought comment from the professor.

---

45. Richard Bernstein, "On Campus, How Free Should Free Speech Be?" *New York Times,* 10 September 1989.
46. Allan R. Gold, "Dartmouth President Faults Right-Wing Student Journal," *New York Times,* 29 March 1988.

Officially, the students were suspended, not for what they wrote, but for harassing a professor. However, in his speech to the faculty justifying the filing of disciplinary charges, President Freedman focused on the content of the weekly. He said, "What it has done has been irresponsible, mean-spirited, cruel and ugly." He said he felt morally obligated to respond to the publication's "bullying tactics," which, he said, "seems virtually designed to have the effect of discouraging women and members of minority groups from joining our faculty or enrolling as students." Freedman called *Review* staffers "ideological provocateurs posing as journalists." He said his own "profound commitment to protecting freedom of expression is entirely consistent with the personal and moral obligation of exercising one's own First Amendment rights in criticizing the press upon appropriate circumstances." Thus, he said, we "must not stand by silently when a newspaper recklessly sets out to create a climate of intolerance and intimidation that destroys our mutual sense of community and inhibits the reasoned examination of the widest possible range of ideas." The speech brought a standing ovation from the faculty.

Freedman was responding to a problem provoked by the *Review's* tactics. Black students, charging that articles questioning the academic value of the music professor's classes were racially motivated, conducted rallies, forums, and marches in protest. Freedman met with black students several times in an attempt to ease tensions on the campus. From his point of view, he was seeking to remove an irritant that disturbed the harmony of an integrated campus.

While his speech was applauded on campus, it was deplored by critics elsewhere, including Laurence Silberman, a Dartmouth graduate and a judge of the U.S. Court of Appeals for the District of Columbia Circuit. He made public the letter he wrote declining the Daniel Webster Award offered by the Dartmouth Club of Washington.[47] He said his purpose in declining the award was to indicate his "strong disapproval of the present Dartmouth atmosphere of intolerance to unfashionable opinion." Contributing to that atmosphere, he continued, is the "official position of the college that there is a morally right and wrong answer" to controversial social and political questions. "The Dartmouth Administration and many of the faculty use 'racism' and 'sexism' and other 'isms' loosely...to label their critics as morally inferior." Silberman said he found that approach offensive.

A Yale student was put on probation for displaying posters satirizing the university's annual GLAD Week—Gay and Lesbian Awareness Days. His posters promoted BAD Week—Bestiality Awareness Days. The Yale College Executive Committee, made up of deans, faculty, and students, found the student guilty of "harassment and intimidation against the gay and lesbian community."[48]

---

47. Excerpts from it were published in the *Wall Street Journal*, 28 December 1988.
48. "Yale's Beastly Behavior," editorial in *Wall Street Journal*, 23 September 1986.

There was a somewhat different result at Northwestern University when an English professor led a demonstration that prevented a Nicaraguan *Contra* leader from speaking. She took over the stage, announced that she was a member of the International Committee against Racism, and said she and sympathizers in the audience were not going to let the *Contra* leader speak. They made such a clamor that the meeting was canceled. A faculty disciplinary committee concluded that the professor had "committed a grave violation of academic freedom and the right of a speaker to speak and be heard in a university." Nevertheless, the English faculty and the university's tenure committees later recommended that she be given tenure. Provost W. Raymond Mack rejected the tenure recommendation, holding that the professor had "violated widely accepted principles of academic freedom and responsibility." President Arnold W. Weber upheld Mack's decision.[49]

These instances and others raise the question asked in a *New York Times* headline: "On Campus, How Free Should Free Speech Be?" Traditionally, the core of the university has been its college of the liberal arts. That term dates to the middle of the eighteenth century, when *artes liberales* was translated from the Latin, meaning "works befitting a free man." The word "liberal" comes from the same Latin root as "liberty": "*liber*," which meant "free." To be free, of course, has many meanings. In this text, "free" generally will mean the freedom to express ideas—good, bad, significant, silly, profound, trivial, and, yes, even abhorrent. But free also means the right to be free from harassment, from discrimination, from intimidation, and worse. And because words "are not absolutely dead things," on some occasions one person's freedom of speech becomes harassment of another. Philosophers seek a moral balance among these sometimes conflicting freedoms. Judges sometimes are compelled to strike a legal balance. Because ours is a society that rests ultimately on public opinion, each of us must also decide which freedoms we value most.

The measure of freedom, as Justice Jackson and Walter Lippmann suggested during World War II, is our willingness as individuals to permit speech that outrages us. It is easy, if one has no deep commitment to church or country, to tolerate antireligious or antigovernment diatribe. Religious and governmental authorities are remote figures, able to take care of themselves. In any event, they have been subject to criticism as far back as anyone can remember and seem none the worse for it.

But the new kinds of criticism, especially on college campuses, attack more vulnerable targets. Equality for women, affirmative action for minorities, and respect for homosexual preferences are values that have come to the fore relatively recently. They have not yet struck deep roots into our culture and hence seem more vulnerable to attack than the older values of

---

49. "Freedom 101 (Ltd. Enrollment)," editorial in *Wall Street Journal*, 25 February 1987.

church and state. When racist, sexist, and homophobic slurs appear on campus buildings overnight, are broadcast on a campus radio station, or uttered in a classroom, real people suffer immediate real pain. Black students at Indiana University said they found it difficult to concentrate on lectures in a classroom dominated by a Thomas Hart Benton mural portraying part of the state's history. They wanted the mural scraped off the wall. Their objection was to one figure, a hooded Klansman bearing a torch, which they found intimidating. The fact that when Benton painted the mural the Ku Klux Klan had been a major force in Indiana politics, which any accurate portrayal of the period could not ignore, made the mural no less bothersome.

People who feel vulnerable, for whatever reason, do not want to be reminded of that vulnerability. At such times, these people may believe that language seen as an outrageous insult will sway public opinion and sweep away such gains as have been made. But such outbursts are equally likely to be the last shots of a dwindling rear guard reacting to what it sees as the crumbling of its values. If the new values are indeed another step in the direction of truth, the better course would be not to suppress racist, sexist, homophobic, or anti-Semitic speech but to counter it with fact and reasoned argument. We do not need a First Amendment to protect speech that makes no one mad. Freedom is measured by how far we are willing to go to protect speech that does make us mad because we consider it irresponsible and even harmful. Most of us hail and mourn the Chinese students and workers who were martyred in Tiananmen Square in Beijing in 1989. As we do so, we should keep in mind that they were shot down because their government believed that what they said there was irresponsible and even harmful.

FOR REVIEW

1. Beginning with Plato, philosophers have recognized, and sometimes been victims of, tension between political authority and the right to question that authority. List and examine arguments used to justify the exercise of authority by government. Do the same for arguments supporting the right to question authority. Is there any common ground between the two lists?

2. Milton saw words as potent forces, capable, if sown in the right soil, of "springing up armed men." Does this possibility support the argument that some speech is so outrageous that it ought to be suppressed? Like what? Who should have the authority to determine which speech should be suppressed? How should it be exercised?

3. A sometimes humorous television commentator on human foibles writes a letter in which he says he finds certain homosexual practices abhorrent to him. He also is alleged to have made disparaging remarks about blacks.

This leads to his being characterized as a bigot. Should he be removed from his program? What principles should guide your decision?

4. At this distance, what is the significance of the Zenger case? Of the Alien and Sedition Acts and the enforcement of them? What factors are common to both?

5. Does the First Amendment mean what it says? Should it? Why or why not?

6. If you could be appointed to the Supreme Court, what theory or philosophy would you adopt in interpreting the meaning of the speech and press clause of the First Amendment? To which of the philosophers discussed in this chapter would you look for guidance?

7. How valid is the clear and present danger test as applied to speech or writing? How precise? Was it applied in *Schenck?* What would happen if you were to use it as your guide in answering question 2 above?

8. Emerson believed that there was no room in First Amendment theory for a balancing test. Is this a realistic position? Was there a role for it, for instance, in the flag-burning case? For a clear and present danger test?

9. A considerable number of people in your town believe so strongly that abortion is wrong that they are determined to force the closing of the town's only abortion clinic. How far can they go under the doctrine of symbolic speech to do so?

10. Meiklejohn and, to a greater degree, Emerson believed that the First Amendment should not just protect speech but encourage speech. Others have argued that this positive view of the amendment should go so far as to provide a right of access not only to public forums but to the media. List and examine arguments supporting a positive role for the First Amendment.

CHAPTER 2

A government trying to win a war, keep vital secrets, or ensure what the Preamble to the Constitution calls "domestic tranquility" can take one of three courses with those whose words might cause trouble:

1. It can adopt the First Amendment theories of Emerson and Meiklejohn and take its chances that the people will reject advocates of harmful action and do what is best for the nation.

2. It can adopt laws providing for punishment of those whose words might help the enemy, or who would disclose vital secrets, or try to stir up trouble.

SEDITION AND CENSORSHIP

3. It can impose censorship, thus cutting off at the source any words that might help the enemy, disclose vital secrets, or provoke harmful action. Obviously, if censorship can be made effective, it offers the most certain way of preventing speech the government considers harmful. On the other hand, it is also the most stringent possible abridgment of the freedom of speech and press guaranteed by the First Amendment.

As this book will demonstrate, the first course has been the one usually taken in the United States. On numerous occasions, the Supreme Court has held that free debate is the preferred method of resolving differences in our society. The Court has so held even when the debaters have played fast and loose with the truth, or have used language that others have found offensive. However, the Court also has upheld laws designed to punish persons whose speech is considered harmful to national security, to an orderly society, or to the rights of others. If such laws are carefully drafted to protect governmental interests, and if they do not restrict speech unduly, they can be enforced. People have been sent to prison for long terms because it was believed that their speech might help an enemy in time of war or might have led to overthrow of the government in time of peace. The third course, censorship, has rarely been imposed. In modern times, the Supreme Court has held in several notable instances that censorship violated the First Amendment guarantees of freedom of speech and press, but the Court also has refused to hold that it can never be imposed. The Court has always left open the possibility that at some time, under certain extreme circumstances, government could use its power to suppress speech that posed a direct threat to a vital interest.

At this point, it might be well to reflect on the difference between punishing someone for speech considered harmful and suppressing that speech altogether. People who know they might go to prison or be fined heavily if they criticize government officials too severely will think twice before they do so. But as we saw in Chapter 1, in the discussion of the Sedition Act of 1798, there are people who will go ahead and criticize anyway. They do so for several reasons. They know that their comments will reach the public and may even have an influence on policy in the long run. They may also reason that a possible arrest will lead more people to pay attention to their comments. And it is possible, as is Zenger's case, also described in Chapter 1, that a jury may find the critics not guilty. Thus, laws designed to punish some participants in the debate on public policy may have a deterrent effect, but they do not prevent determined speakers from being heard at all. That is what censorship attempts to do. Thus, the difference can be quite significant. The Supreme Court once expressed the difference this way: it said laws punishing speakers can be said to chill speech; censorship freezes it.

Direct censorship of the media has been rare in the United States. The federal government used its control of the telegraph system during the Civil War to censor dispatches from battlefield reporters to their newspapers. A censorship law was in effect during World War I and was used mainly against socialist publications. During World War II, mail from servicemen and women abroad was censored. In this country, the news media generally complied with an informal system of censorship under which editors were expected to check with the Office of War Information before disseminating sensitive information. More common, starting with World War I and continuing through the Great Depression into the Cold War following World War II, has been the use of sedition law to punish those whose speech or writings were believed to pose a threat to national security.

For governments, as for individuals, the instinct for self-preservation is a powerful force. Thus, all nations have laws providing for punishment of those who would attempt to destroy them. People who plot the overthrow of their own government had better be prepared to win. To lose is to face imprisonment, exile, or death. In many nations, laws designed to prevent violent overthrow make advocating such overthrow a crime. Despite the First Amendment, the United States is no exception. Since 1940, the Smith Act[1] has made it a crime to advocate violence to effect a change in the form of government. The problem with such laws lies in drawing the line between words advocating a change in government policies or the form of government and words designed to provoke rebellion. Advocacy of peaceful change is politics. Advocacy of violent change can be punished as sedition.

This chapter examines the use of sedition law and censorship in the United States. After the Sedition Act of 1798 was permitted to lapse in 1801, no federal sedition law existed until the United States entered World War I in 1917. However, various military commanders used martial law to punish dissenters during the Civil War. During World War I, nearly 2000 Socialists, pacifists, and German immigrants were punished for sedition. In the immediate aftermath of the war, in response to fears raised by the Bolshevik Revolution in Russia, sedition law was used against U.S. Communists and others who advocated an end to what they saw as capitalist oppression. Appeals from some of the convictions reached the U.S. Supreme Court, which, for the first time, had to decide how far the First Amendment goes in protecting unpopular speech. Some of the cases from that era remain as landmarks defining the right of individuals and groups to defy government policy or advocate changes in the form of government.

Our current sedition law, the Smith Act, was a product of the contending ideologies, Communist and Fascist, seeking to draw the United States into, or keep

---

1.   18 U.S.C.A. § 2385.

it out of, World War II. The act's purpose was to punish those who might be tempted to impose either form of government on the United States. The Japanese attack on Pearl Harbor in December 1941 so united the American people that few were accused of sedition during World War II, although President Roosevelt used his war powers to confine most U.S. citizens of Japanese descent to internment camps for the duration. After the war ended in 1945, prosecution of Communists was renewed during the period of mutual suspicion between the United States and the Soviet Union known as the Cold War. During that time, the entire leadership of the U.S. Communist Party was found guilty of sedition and sent to prison. In the late 1950s, when relations between the two powers entered into the period known as détente, prosecutions dwindled and ended. The Supreme Court held that people could not be punished for advocating violent overthrow of the government unless they clearly intended to incite immediate harmful action. Sedition law has been little used since.

Thus, Americans remain free to say pretty much what they please about the president, Congress, and government at all levels, as every political campaign illustrates anew. Those who talk about a violent change in the system may find themselves watched by the FBI, but unless they plant bombs in public buildings, as a few have, they are not likely to be arrested. The line is drawn at death threats, particularly those directed at the president. Persons who talk openly about killing the president are likely to be arrested, and, if a court concludes the talk was serious enough to present a threat, punished.

The latter part of this chapter examines several instances in which the government sought to freeze speech by imposing a prior restraint, which is the legal term for government censorship. We will start where the Court started, in 1931, when the state of Minnesota ordered a weekly newspaper to stop publishing. In that case, and in two more recent cases, the Court erected high barriers that government must overcome before a prior restraint can be imposed. However, these barriers are not so high as to rule out prior restraint in all instances. On one occasion, the government was able to hold up for two weeks newspaper publication of a top secret report on the Vietnam war. On another, for seven months the government prevented a magazine from publishing an article the government believed might help other nations build a hydrogen bomb. On others, the government was able to enforce contracts that prevent former CIA agents from publishing secrets learned while they were with the agency. And, most recently, the Supreme Court held that public school officials can censor newspapers published as part of the course work in journalism. Later in the book, we will see that prior restraint can be imposed to protect privacy, suppress obscenity, and prevent infringement of copyright. Thus, although the Supreme Court has made censorship difficult, it has refused to hold that the First Amendment makes it impossible.

Major Cases

- *Abrams* v. *United States,* 250 U.S. 616, 40 S.Ct. 17, 63 L.Ed. 1173 (1919).
- *Bantam Books* v. *Sullivan,* 372 U.S. 58, 83 S.Ct. 631, 9 L.Ed.2d 584 (1963).

- *Carroll* v. *President and Commissioners of Princess Anne,* 393 U.S. 175, 89 S.Ct. 347, 21 L.Ed.2d 325 (1968).

- *Dennis* v. *United States,* 341 U.S. 494, 71 S.Ct. 857, 95 L.Ed. 1137 (1951).

- *Gitlow* v. *People of the State of New York,* 268 U.S. 652, 45 S.Ct. 625, 69 L.Ed. 1138 (1925).

- *Hazelwood School District* v. *Kuhlmeier,* 484 U.S. 260, 108 S.Ct. 562, 98 L.Ed.2d 592 (1988).

- *Near* v. *Minnesota,* 283 U.S. 697, 51 S.Ct. 625, 75 L.Ed. 1357 (1931).

- *New York Times Co.* v. *United States,* 403 U.S. 713, 91 S.Ct. 2140, 29 L.Ed.2d 822 (1971).

- *Organization for a Better Austin* v. *Keefe,* 402 U.S. 415, 91 S.Ct. 1575, 29 L.Ed.2d 1 (1971).

- *Snepp* v. *United States,* 444 U.S. 507, 100 S.Ct. 763, 62 L.Ed.2d 704 (1980).

- *United States* v. *Morison,* 844 F.2d 1057 (4th Cir. 1988).

- *Yates* v. *United States,* 354 U.S. 298, 77 S.Ct. 1064, 1 L.Ed.2d 1356 (1957).

SEDITION

The Prosecution of Sedition

When Congress declared war on Germany and its allies in April 1917, many Americans doubted that it acted wisely. To them Europe was far away, its wars no concern of ours. Consequently, some in Congress believed that the people's doubts would undermine the will to fight. Two groups were viewed with particular suspicion: the large numbers of Germans who had come to this country in the 1890s, and Socialists, who were numerous enough to have elected mayors in several cities and who believed the war was part of an evil design to shore up declining capitalist systems.

To cope with anticipated antiwar talk from such as these, Congress quickly followed up its declaration of war by adopting the Espionage Act of 1917, which made it a crime to speak or write in a way that could be seen as helping the enemy.[2] When that law turned out not to be broad enough to catch all who spoke their doubts about the war, Congress passed the much more stringent Sedition Act of 1918. That law made it a crime to talk against the draft, or the sale of war bonds, or to interfere with production of war goods, as by advocating a strike. Even to question the constitutionality of the draft or the official version of why we entered the war became a crime. Consequently, nearly 2000 espionage and sedition arrests were made in fewer than eighteen months. The attorney general

---

2. Zechariah Chafee, Jr., *Free Speech in the United States,* Atheneum ed. (New York: Atheneum, 1969), pp. 37–39.

reported that 877 resulted in convictions. Other cases were dismissed after the war ended in 1918.[3] No other period in history has seen so many arrests for the crime of talking against the government.

The cases were decided on the theory that the right of the government to preserve itself from conquest by foreign enemies and from violent overthrow by domestic enemies is foremost among all rights. Under this theory, words that have a tendency to help either kind of enemy may be punished. Convictions were based on the belief that forces which might be set in motion by seditious words must be checked at the start before they can cause harm. In this view, liberty of speech protects reasoned discourse in which truth is used for good purposes. But when speech becomes ''license'' in the old sense of ''licentiousness,'' it becomes destructive of orderly discourse and therefore punishable. Obviously, reasonable persons can disagree widely as to when liberty becomes license. Under the pressures of fear generated by the war, the field of license expanded. It was seen by judges and juries to cover words that in ordinary times would have been dismissed as the spoutings of harmless hotheads or pondered as valid debate on public policy.

Two Supreme Court cases from the World War I era remain of interest in helping us understand the extent to which the First Amendment protects those who protest government policies. They are *Schenck* v. *United States*[4] and *Abrams* v. *United States*.[5] A third, from the mid-1920s, *Gitlow* v. *People of the State of New York*,[6] is of enduring importance because it led the Supreme Court to stretch the First Amendment, through the Fourteenth, to apply to state attempts to restrict freedom of speech and press.

In *Schenck,* which was summarized in Chapter 1, the Supreme Court for the first time interpreted the meaning of the First Amendment and found it to be far from an absolute guarantee of the right to speak freely, particularly in time of war. Justice Oliver Wendell Holmes, writing for the Court, took note of the bad tendency theory, summarized above, and said it permitted the government to move too easily to repress unpopular speakers. It should be replaced, he said, by a test that would permit punishment only of those speakers whose words ''create a clear and present danger'' of harm to an interest the government is entitled to protect. In this instance, the Court found that interest in Article I, Section 8, of the Constitution, which gives Congress the power to ''raise and support armies.'' In the Court's view, Schenck's pamphlets urging resistance to the draft directly threatened the government's ability to do that. Had the campaign succeeded, the Court reasoned, the United States could have lost the war with Germany. Actually, there was no evidence that anyone who read Schenck's pamphlets had refused to serve. In addition, the justices knew when they decided the case, four months after the war ended, that the United States had won. This has led some legal scholars to conclude that despite Holmes's rhetoric, the Court decided the case on a bad tendency theory.

---

3.   Ibid., p. 52.
4.   249 U.S. 47, 39 S.Ct. 247, 63 L.Ed. 470 (1919).
5.   250 U.S. 616, 40 S.Ct. 17, 63 L.Ed. 1173 (1919).
6.   268 U.S. 652, 45 S.Ct. 625, 69 L.Ed. 1138 (1925).

That conclusion is reinforced by the fact that within a few months Holmes found himself joining the Court's most liberal justice, Louis D. Brandeis, in dissent as other appellants also were found to have been a clear and present danger to the war effort. Holmes wrote the most eloquent of those dissents in *Abrams,* a case involving five self-described "revolutionaries, anarchists, and socialists." Their crime had been to write and distribute pamphlets attacking President Wilson because he had sent troops to Russia to fight against the Bolsheviks during the Revolution. The majority had no doubt that the five intended "to excite, at the supreme crisis of the war, disaffection, sedition, riots, and, as they hoped, revolution in this country." Nor did the majority doubt that the threat was real. It confirmed the twenty-year prison sentences imposed on Abrams and his associates by the court below.

Abrams v. *United States,*
250 U.S. 616, 40 S.Ct. 17,
63 L.Ed. 1173 (1919).

In Holmes's view the defendants' leaflets were to be given no more credence than a claim that they had found a formula to square the circle. He found the urge to persecute unpopular speakers understandable. Once you conclude that your views are correct, "you naturally express your wishes in law and sweep away all opposition." Any other course might be a confession "that you doubt either your power or your premises." Holmes continued:

> But when men have realized that time has upset many fighting faiths, they may come to believe even more than they believe the very foundation of their own conduct that the ultimate good desired is better reached by free trade in ideas—that the best test of truth is the power of the thought to get itself accepted in the competition of the market; and that truth is the only ground upon which their wishes safely can be carried out. That, at any rate, is the theory of our Constitution. It is an experiment, as all life is an experiment. Every year, if not every day, we have to wager our salvation upon some prophecy based upon imperfect knowledge. While that experiment is part of our system I think that we should be eternally vigilant against attempts to check the expression of opinions that we loathe and believe to be fraught with death, unless they so imminently threaten immediate interference with the lawful and pressing purposes of the law that an immediate check is required to save the country.

That passage comes closer to defining the clear and present danger test than does Holmes's majority opinion in *Schenck.* The passage also elaborates on the argument advanced by Milton, that the test of truth is the ability of an idea to win acceptance in free and open encounter with other ideas. But neither Holmes's eloquence nor the clear and present danger test prevented the Court from upholding prison sentences imposed on Abrams, Schenck, and others, including Eugene Debs, a one-time member of the Indiana Legislature who became the leader of the Socialist Party and was sentenced to ten years in prison for his opposition to World War I. Holmes wrote the Court's decision sustaining the conviction.[7] Debs ran as his party's candidate for president while he was in prison and received almost a million votes. His sentence was commuted in 1921.

---

7. Debs v. United States, 249 U.S. 211, 39 S.Ct. 252, 63 L.Ed. 566 (1919).

The First Amendment and the States ═══════════════════

In the 1920s, the fears and tensions that led to sedition prosecutions subsided somewhat at the federal level. However, states continued prosecution of Communists, anarchists, and members of a left-wing labor union, the Industrial Workers of the World. One of these cases led to a Supreme Court decision that upset a century-old constitutional principle limiting application of the Bill of Rights to actions by the federal government. In 1833, in *Barron* v. *Baltimore*,[8] Chief Justice John Marshall had held that the Constitution had been adopted by the people of the United States "for themselves, for their own government, and not for the government of the individual states." Each state, he noted, had its own constitution when the federal Constitution was adopted. Those constitutions remained in effect, establishing the limits within which state authorities could act. Marshall went on to hold that in this instance the due process clause of the Fifth Amendment could not be invoked by a Baltimore wharf owner to collect damages against the city. From that time on, courts acted on the theory that rights guarantees contained in other amendments, including the First, could be used to bar federal action but not infringements by state authorities.

Thus, when New York authorities prosecuted Benjamin Gitlow under a state law making it a crime to advocate violence against the government they did so in the belief that they need only satisfy the state constitution's free speech clause. Gitlow was a member of the left-wing section of the Socialist Party. His crime was the publication of a ponderous *Manifesto* calling for a general strike as a first step toward the toppling of the capitalist system. A New York court found him guilty of criminal anarchy and sentenced him to prison.

Gitlow v. *People of the State of New York,* **268 U.S. 652, 45 S.Ct. 625, 69 L.Ed. 1138 (1925).**

The Supreme Court agreed to review the conviction and affirmed it, despite a strong protest by Justice Holmes. In doing so, the Court also held that a state's attempts to restrict freedoms of speech and press are subject to review under the standards established by the First Amendment. Speaking for a majority, Justice Edward T. Sanford wrote:

> For present purposes we may and do assume that freedom of speech and of the press—which are protected by the First Amendment from abridgment by Congress—are among the fundamental personal rights and "liberties" protected by the Fourteenth Amendment from impairment by the States. We do not regard the incidental statement in Prudential Ins. Co. v. Cheek, 259 U.S. 530, 543, that the Fourteenth Amendment imposes no restrictions on the States concerning freedom of speech, as determinative of this question.

Two points in that paragraph require explanation. In deciding *Prudential* only a few years earlier, the Court had said, in language not essential to the decision, that states were not bound by the First Amendment's guarantees of freedom of

---

8. 7 Pet. 243, 8 L.Ed. 672 (1833).

speech and press. Now, in language that clearly was essential, the Court said just the opposite. Had it held otherwise, it would have had no jurisdiction over *Gitlow* because the case dealt with a prosecution in a state court under a state law. It could be reviewed by a federal court only if a federal question—in this instance, Gitlow's right to freedom of speech—was involved. The second point requiring explanation is Sanford's reference to the "liberties" protected by the Fourteenth Amendment. That amendment, adopted in the aftermath of the Civil War, was drafted to prevent states from adopting laws designed to deny freed slaves the rights enjoyed by white people. The language alluded to by Sanford says:

> ...No state shall make or enforce any law which shall abridge the privileges or immunities of citizens of the United States; nor shall any State deprive any person of life, liberty, or property without due process of law; nor deny to any person within its jurisdiction the equal protection of the laws.

With the passage of time, the *Gitlow* decision has assumed an importance far greater than it had in 1925. Then its only result was to assure that Gitlow went to prison. But in more recent times the Supreme Court has used the rationale of *Gitlow* not only to ensure freedom of speech and press but to prevent the states from restricting most of the rights, or "liberties," guaranteed by the Bill of Rights. Sanford's seemingly casual invocation of the Fourteenth Amendment in *Gitlow* permeates much of the remainder of this book. That decision made possible the broad application of the First Amendment that protects freedom of speech and press in our time.

The Smith Act

The World War I Sedition Act was permitted to expire in the 1920s. The nation was at peace and was enjoying prosperity. By 1940, the Great Depression and the outbreak of war in Europe had brought on a new period of stress in the United States. With as many as a quarter of the nation's adults out of work, ideologues offering various economic panaceas sought changes in business and government. Communist sympathizers with Stalinist Russia and brown-shirted followers of Hitler's Nazi Germany contended for support. When the war in Europe began in 1939, strife arose between those who believed we should join forces with England and those who wanted peace at any price.

The atmosphere was made to order for a revival of the belief that a law could protect the nation from harmful talk. With little fanfare, Congress enacted the first peacetime sedition law since the Alien and Sedition Act had been permitted to expire in 1801. It was known as the Smith Act because its language was offered as an amendment to an alien deportation bill by Howard W. Smith, a representative to Congress from Virginia. The Act made it a crime to

> knowingly or willfully advocate, abet, advise, or teach the duty, necessity, desirability, or propriety of overthrowing or destroying the government of the United

States, or the government of any State...or...any political subdivision therein, by force or violence, or by the assassination of any officer of any such government.

Oddly, Representative Smith's law received little use either in the short time remaining before the United States entered the war at the end of 1941 or during the four years of the war. For one thing, Japan's surprise attack on Pearl Harbor united the nation as have few events in its history. For another, Germany's invasion of the Soviet Union in 1940 made the United States an ally of Communist Russia, thus converting U.S. Communists into ardent patriots. This left only a few U.S. Nazis and a more numerous population of Japanese-Americans as potential targets of sedition law. Although history has taught that there was little to fear from the Americans of Japanese descent, the government reacted by rounding them up and putting them in detention camps until the war ended. Not until 1988 did the government partially atone for that act by agreeing to pay the surviving internees a few thousand dollars each.

The Prosecution of American Communists

With the end of World War II in 1945, the United States' longstanding fear of communism quickly revived. The United States and the Soviet Union had been uneasy and mistrusting allies at best. With the defeat of Germany and Japan, old suspicions were revived, creating an era of distrust that became known as the Cold War. Because at that time U.S. Communists were seen as taking orders from Moscow, they, too, became subjects of suspicion and distrust. Very quickly, covert investigations of party members by the FBI resulted in prosecutions under the Smith Act. Before the Cold War gave way to a period of détente at the end of the 1950s, nearly 200 alleged Communists, including the entire leadership of the Communist Party U.S.A., had been prosecuted under federal law. Others suspected of harboring subversive ideas were targets of state sedition laws or subjects of congressional committee investigations designed to hound them out of public life.

The prosecutions of the Communists, and at a later period of an Ohio Ku Klux Klan leader, led to three significant Supreme Court decisions that drew the line between speech that may be punished as sedition and speech that is an acceptable part of political debate. The cases remain of interest in the light of the Reagan administration's use of sedition law against Puerto Rican nationalists and U.S. white supremacists. The cases are *Dennis* v. *United States,*[9] *Yates* v. *United States,*[10] and *Brandenberg* v. *Ohio.*[11]

During and after World War II, Eugene Dennis was the general secretary of the Communist Party U.S.A. On the strength of reports from FBI informants who had infiltrated the party organization, Dennis and his fellow members of the

---

9. 341 U.S. 494, 71 S.Ct. 857, 95 L.Ed. 1137 (1951).
10. 354 U.S. 298, 77 S.Ct. 1064, 1 L.Ed.2d 1356 (1957).
11. 395 U.S. 444, 89 S.Ct. 1827, 23 L.Ed.2d 430 (1969).

Central Committee were indicted in 1948 on charges of plotting the overthrow of the government. At the time, the Communist party had a known membership of about 74,000 in the United States, but such was the political climate that it was widely believed to have hundreds of thousands of secret sympathizers.

After a trial that lasted nine months, a jury in a U.S. district court in New York City found Dennis and twelve members of the party's governing board guilty of advocating violent overthrow of the government. Prosecution witnesses had testified that the leaders were preparing their followers to use force to topple the government if another depression should cause unrest. All of the defendants were sentenced to prison. They appealed, arguing that they were doing no more than talk about violent overthrow as one of several means of achieving power. As they saw it, such talk is protected by the First Amendment. The circuit court of appeals disagreed. The Communists took their case to the Supreme Court. It held six to two that the trial court jury's verdict was correct.

Four of the six justices concluded that the party represented a clear and present danger to the nation's security. They started with the premise that Con-

Dennis **v.** *United States,* **341 U.S. 494, 71 S. Ct. 857, 95 L.Ed. 1137 (1951).**

gress has power under the Constitution to draft laws designed to protect the nation from armed rebellion. Theoretically, as recognized by the Declaration of Independence, there is a right to rebel against a dictatorial government. But that right has no meaning, the plurality wrote, when "the existing structure of government provides for peaceful and orderly change." This was a reminder that, in the United States, the route to power runs through the ballot box.

Lawyers for Dennis argued that the language of the Smith Act swept more broadly than was needed to protect the government from those who would destroy it. They argued that if the Act were strictly enforced as written it could be used to punish classroom discussion of Communist party doctrine.

The plurality disagreed. It said the law was directed at advocacy, not discussion. Indeed, the trial judge had told the jury it could not convict the party leaders if it concluded they were engaged only in peaceful discussion of ideas. He also had told the jury the Smith Act did not make it a crime to study the principles of communism in colleges and universities. The plurality concluded that when Congress wrote the law, lawmakers were concerned with speech and writing used to plan and set in motion illegal acts against the government.

The outcome of the case hinged on the distinction between advocacy and discussion. The plurality said that speech urging illegal action against the government is advocacy of a kind not protected by the First Amendment. People are free to discuss violent overthrow as long as they don't prepare themselves to strike when the time seems ripe for successful action. But, as the Court saw it, the Communist party was preparing to strike. Chief Justice Fred M. Vinson, who wrote for the plurality, used some of his strongest language in condemning the party's purpose. He said the clear and present danger test

cannot mean that before the Government may act, it must wait until the *putsch* is about to be executed, the plans have been laid and the signal is awaited. If Govern-

During the Vietnam war, the courts protected opponents of government policy even when they conducted demonstrations in the shadow of the Capitol in Washington, D.C. Such demonstrations were held to be a form of symbolic speech fully protected by the First Amendment even when they bordered on violence. (J. Berndt/Stock, Boston)

ment is aware that a group aiming at its overthrow is attempting to indoctrinate its members and to commit them to a course whereby they will strike when the leaders feel the circumstances permit, action by the Government is required.

Justice Felix Frankfurter, usually a liberal on First Amendment rights, concurred in the Court's holding that the defendants were guilty, but not in the plurality's reasoning. He clearly was bothered by Vinson's attempt to distinguish between "advocacy" and "discussion." The plurality said that the party leaders' crime was advocacy—in this instance, of violent overthrow of the government. Frankfurter was not willing to concede that all advocacy is illegal, nor was he certain that a clear line always can be drawn between advocacy and discussion. As he saw it, a certain degree of advocacy of change is at the heart of the political process. Therefore, courts ought to be cautious about restricting advocacy, even when its purpose is to change the form of government. However, Frankfurter concluded that Congress was within its constitutional powers in making advocacy of violent overthrow a crime. Despite his misgivings, he held that the Communist party leaders had urged such overthrow.

Justice Robert H. Jackson, the sixth member of the majority, did not share Frankfurter's doubts. Nor did he see any First Amendment issue in the case. In his view, Dennis and his associates were involved in a conspiracy to commit illegal acts against the government. Under criminal law, such conspiracies always have been punishable. He chided the other justices for making more out of the case than that.

That decision, reached at the depth of the Cold War in 1951, cleared the way for vigorous prosecution of lower-level Communist party leaders, including Oleta O'Connor Yates and other officers of the party

Yates v. *United States,* in California. At their trial in a federal court in
354 U.S. 298, 77 S.Ct. Los Angeles, the judge read the Supreme
1064, 1 L.Ed.2d 1356 (1957) Court's decision in *Dennis* and told the jurors
they could find the defendants guilty if they concluded the Communists had advocated violent overthrow of the government "unrelated to [the] tendency [of their words] to produce forcible actions." The jury found the officers guilty. The judge sentenced each to spend five years in prison and pay a $10,000 fine. When the case reached the Supreme Court in 1957, it reversed. The Court said the judge had gone too far in telling the jury that the Smith Act punishes all advocacy of violent overthrow. People can talk all they want about the desirability of using violence against government. They can even express the hope that a revolution will succeed. As Justice John Marshall Harlan put it, "The essential distinction [between legal and illegal advocacy] is that those to whom the advocacy is addressed must be urged to *do* something, now or in the future, rather than merely believe in something." The Court said there was no evidence that Yates and the other officers of the California branch of the Communist party had urged anyone to commit illegal acts.

The government made no attempt to retry them so as to offer such evidence. Indeed, with the decision in *Yates,* Smith Act prosecutions dwindled and died. By 1961, the government's attempt to suppress its Communist critics ended.

The decisions in *Dennis* and *Yates,* only six years apart, illustrate that even the justices of the Supreme Court, the branch of government most remote from the pressures of politics, are not altogether insulated from public opinion. In 1951, when *Dennis* was decided, Joseph Stalin was in control of the Soviet Union and the Communist party, including its branches in other countries. Investigations conducted by committees of both houses of Congress were exposing persons in labor unions, civil rights organizations, and the moving picture industry who were alleged to be either Communists or "fellow travelers" who were doing Stalin's bidding. At the same time that the Supreme Court was pondering its decision in *Dennis,* a court in New York City was finding Julius and Ethel Rosenberg and Morton Sobell guilty of giving the secrets of the atom bomb to the Soviet Union. The Rosenbergs were executed in 1953. In that same year, Stalin died and was succeeded as Soviet leader in 1955 by Nikita Khrushchev. In a secret speech to the Twentieth Congress of the Soviet Communist party Khrushchev denounced Stalin and announced a policy of peaceful coexistence with the West. The speech created a worldwide sensation when it was leaked to Western correspondents. By 1957, when the Court decided *Yates,* the Soviet Union and the United States were enjoying an improvement in relations known as "détente." The danger that had impressed five justices of the Supreme Court as being clear and present in 1951 was not mentioned by a single justice in *Yates.* In 1959, Khrushchev became the first Soviet premier to visit the United States, where he was greeted by large and generally friendly crowds. The Cold War was not over, but relations between the two powers were noticeably warmer.

The Civil Rights Movement and Sedition Law ════════════

Constitutional amendments adopted during and after the Civil War abolished slavery and sought to protect the rights of freed persons,[12] but these amendments by no means brought about equality for blacks with whites. Indeed, the Supreme Court in the 1890s had endorsed a doctrine of "separate but equal" treatment of blacks with respect to such things as segregated railroad cars, schools, restrooms, and even drinking fountains. Under this doctrine, local governments could enforce rigid patterns of racial segregation justified by the fiction that facilities provided for blacks were the same as those provided for whites. Such patterns were enforced officially by states in the Deep South and unofficially virtually every place else.

In the 1950s, blacks mounted a challenge to the separate-but-equal doctrine. The Supreme Court held in 1954, in *Brown* v. *Board of Education,*[13] that public schools should be integrated. In 1955, in Montgomery, Alabama, Rosa Parks began another challenge to the system when she refused to give up her bus seat to a white man, as the local law required. Her act started a movement toward integration that grew into a major confrontation between militant blacks and white officialdom through boycotts, lunch counter sit-ins, demonstrations, and reaction to court-ordered integration of public schools. State sedition laws were among the legal devices invoked in a vain attempt to preserve segregation. In Mississippi, for instance, the state charged that William Ware was promoting anarchy and arrested him. The charge was based on his attempt to get blacks registered so they could vote. A federal trial court said the law defining anarchy as a crime was written so broadly that it could be used to punish mere advocacy or teaching of violent overthrow as an abstract theory.[14] Therefore, the Supreme Court's decision in *Yates* made it unconstitutional.

Ironically, the arrest of a Ku Klux Klansman in southwestern Ohio gave the Supreme Court an opportunity to hold that all similar state laws were unconstitutional. Clarence Brandenberg, owner of a television repair shop in a Cincinnati

---

12. The Thirteenth, ratified in 1865, abolished slavery. The Fourteenth, ratified in 1868, sought to prevent states from depriving blacks of rights enjoyed by other citizens. The Fifteenth, ratified in 1870, sought to protect the voting rights of blacks.
13. 347 U.S. 483, 74 S.Ct. 686, 98 L.Ed. 873 (1954).
14. Ware v. Nichols, 266 F.Supp. 564 (S.D.Miss. 1967).

suburb, was an officer in the Klan. In the mid-1960s, he invited a reporter for a Cincinnati television station to cover a Klan rally and cross burning. Police who saw part of Brandenberg's speech on television heard him talk about taking revenge against officials who were trying to bring about racial integration. Brandenberg was charged with violating Ohio's Criminal Syndicalism Act. A county court found him guilty. A judge sentenced him to ten years in prison and fined him $1000. Brandenberg's appeal reached the Supreme Court, which held the Ohio law and all others like it unconstitutional. The court said the law was written so broadly that it could be used to punish people for doing no more than talk about resorting to violence. The Court said that laws seeking to protect government against violent overthrow can survive only if they are aimed narrowly at speech directly linked to ''imminent lawless action'' or likely to ''incite or produce such action.''

With that decision, the Court brought to an end the line of sedition cases starting with *Schenck* in 1919. In those decisions the Court has said that governments, federal and state, have a right to protect themselves against those who would resort to violence to change the system. Governments also can protect themselves against those who advocate such violence. As defined in *Dennis,* ''advocacy'' was broad enough to include the leaders of the Communist party whose crime was said to be creating a disciplined group primed to act when its leaders gave the signal. However, in *Yates* and *Brandenberg,* the Court said that ''advocacy'' cannot be punished unless its purpose is to incite direct and immediate violence. Any law that fails to make clear the distinction between urging people to take up arms against their government and merely talking about doing so violates the First Amendment.

The Vietnam War: Advocacy and Action

The Vietnam war divided the American people as have few events since the Civil War. And yet, despite violent demonstrations against our involvement in Vietnam, sedition law was not used against those who opposed the war. Events that once might have been considered seditious led to three significant lawsuits, all of which the government lost. The courts held that government could not violate the basic rights of individuals to put down demonstrations against its policies.

Two of the lawsuits, *Sullivan* v. *Murphy*[15] and *Apton* v. *Wilson,*[16] grew out of the attempt of antiwar demonstrators to shut down the operations of the government in May 1971. Tens of thousands gathered in Washington, D.C., and sought to block streets leading into the city and the entrances to government buildings. So many demonstrators were arrested that police failed to follow their usual identification and reporting procedures and, as a result, were unable to prove their charges in court. Some of those who had been detained sued the police, arguing that they had been arrested without cause.

---

15.   478 F.2d 938 (D.C.Cir. 1973).
16.   506 F.2d 83 (D.C.Cir. 1974).

In *Sullivan,* the U.S. Court of Appeals for the District of Columbia Circuit held that all persons against whom a valid case could not be made were entitled to refund of bail, which ranged up to $250, and to have the arrest expunged from their records. In *Apton,* the same court held that if demonstrators could prove they had been arrested although they had done nothing wrong, they could sue police officials for damages.

The third lawsuit, *Dellums* v. *Powell,*[17] grew out of a demonstration on the Capitol Plaza, where demonstrations were forbidden. When Ronald V. Dellums, a representative to Congress from California, sought to address the crowd, police moved in and began arresting members of the audience. Some of those arrested sued James M. Powell, chief of the Capitol Police, on grounds that he had interfered with their First Amendment rights. A federal district court jury agreed with that view and awarded damages, which were upheld, but reduced in amount, on appeal.

The case is of additional interest because in his decision Circuit Judge J. Skelly Wright wrote that demonstrations "for better or worse [have become] a major vehicle by which those who wish to express dissent can create a forum in which their views may be brought to the attention of a mass audience and, in turn, to the attention of a national legislature." He said that demonstrations can be more effective than writing a letter to a member of Congress because "the staging and theatrics...of the demonstration [can express] the passion and emotion with which a point of view is held." Thus the decision can be seen as putting the circuit court's stamp of approval on demonstrations as a legitimate means of influencing the resolution of public issues.

Sedition Law's Revival

After a lapse of more than thirty years, the Sedition Act was used with mixed results during the Reagan administration to prosecute several disparate groups of dissidents. The targets included Puerto Rican nationalists, white supremacists preaching hatred of Jews and blacks, and Marxist-Leninists accused of bombing firms that do business with South Africa.

In 1985, a federal court in Chicago convicted on sedition charges four persons the government said were members of the Armed Forces of National Liberation, a Puerto Rican group. Three members of the group had been filmed by hidden cameras in the act of making bombs. The group claimed responsibility for 120 bombings in New York City and elsewhere between 1974 and 1983 in which 5 persons were killed and about 100 injured. According to a government attorney involved in the prosecution, the case did not involve a First Amendment issue. She was quoted as saying, "There is no protected right to oppose the Government by force and violence and to say so is to debase the First Amendment."[18]

In 1988, a federal district court jury in Fort Smith, Arkansas, acquitted thirteen white supremacists who were accused of conspiring to overthrow the gov-

---

17. 566 F.2d 167 (D.C.Cir. 1977).
18. Katherine Bishop, "U.S. Dusts Off an Old Law," *New York Times,* 27 March 1988.

ernment of the United States and to kill a federal judge and a federal agent. Prosecutors said the group was planning to start an all-white government in the Pacific Northwest.[19]

In 1989, a federal court jury in Springfield, Massachusetts, cleared three avowed revolutionaries of charges alleging that they robbed banks and bombed buildings along the East Coast as part of a plot to overthrow the government. The jurors were unable to reach a verdict on racketeering charges based on the same incidents.[20]

These instances serve as a reminder that the Smith Act, as interpreted by the Supreme Court in *Yates,* remains in force and can be invoked when prosecutors conclude that opponents of the government are plotting action aimed at the government's overthrow. It matters not how long the odds are against success. As the Court said in *Dennis,* officials who are aware that action is being planned need not "wait until the *putsch* is about to be executed" before taking action. But, as two of the cases above illustrate, whether they can convince a jury that there is a real threat to the government is another matter.

OTHER RESTRICTIONS ON SPEECH ABOUT GOVERNMENT

Espionage Law and the News Media

As noted at the beginning of this chapter, the first thing Congress did when the United States entered World War I was enact the Espionage Act of 1917. This law, unlike the sedition act of that era, was not permitted to lapse. It still is the law used to prosecute as spies people who pass military secrets to other countries. However, in 1985 the Espionage Act was used for the first time to prosecute and convict a government employee for disclosing information to the news media rather than to agents of a foreign government.[21] Many journalists found the conviction disquieting. In the higher echelons of Washington correspondence, leaks of classified materials are almost routine. Officials, high and low, give such materials to reporters, on a selective basis, to advance their own policies or disparage those of their rivals. The conviction, which was upheld on appeal, can be seen as a warning to those who may be tempted to leak classified information to reporters, no matter what their motives for doing so. And it raises a question as to whether reporters might be punished for failure to disclose on request the identity of the source of a leak of classified information.

---

19. "Jury Acquits 9 of Conspiracy against the U.S.," *New York Times,* 7 April 1988.
20. "Jury Clears 3 on Sedition Charges But Is Undecided on Racketeering," *New York Times,* 28 November 1989; "Judge Declares Mistrial for 3 after Jury Deadlocks in Sedition Case," *New York Times,* 30 November 1989.
21. George Garneau, "Conviction of Classified Photo Leaker Upheld," *Editor & Publisher,* 9 April 1988, p. 20 + ; Stuart Taylor, Jr., "Court Ruling on Leaks Could Make It a Crime to Talk to the Press," *New York Times,* 10 April 1988.

Samuel Loring Morison (left) leaves the federal courthouse in Baltimore with his lawyer during the trial at which he was found guilty of peacetime espionage. As a naval intelligence analyst for the U.S. government, he had access to classified photos of Soviet ships, which he leaked to a British magazine. An appeals court ruled that the government's interest in security was sufficient to overcome any First Amendment interest served by Morison's "thievery." (AP/Wide World Photos)

The case began in 1984 when Samuel Loring Morison, a naval intelligence analyst and a part-time correspondent for a British naval publication, was looking for a way to convince the editor of that publication that he should be given a full-time job. Morison worked in the Naval Intelligence Support Section in a room known as a "vaulted area," because all of the employees were cleared to handle "top secret" materials. One day, he glanced at a colleague's desk and saw photographs taken by a spy satellite of the Soviet Union's first nuclear aircraft carrier, then under construction in a Black Sea shipyard. The borders of the photographs were stamped "Top Secret" and carried a warning that intelligence sources or methods could be disclosed were the wrong persons to see them. Morison surreptitiously took the photographs, clipped off the borders, and made copies, which he sent to the editor of *Jane's Defence Weekly,* with whom he had been talking about a job. Morison also sent the editor a summary of what the U.S. Navy knew about an explosion that recently had occurred at a Soviet naval base.

United States v. *Morison,* **844 F.2d 1057 (4th Cir. 1988).**

When the photos were published in *Jane's* they were considered so newsworthy that other magazines and newspapers, including the *Washington Post,* republished them. When the Navy began an investigation, Morison denied ever seeing the photos and gave officers the names of two fellow employees who he said should be questioned. He continued his denials after his fingerprint was found on one of the photos. Investigators also analyzed his typewriter ribbon, finding several letters to *Jane's* and the report on the explosion. A federal district court jury found Morison guilty of espionage, and a judge sentenced him to two years in prison.

On appeal, Morison argued, with support from the *Post,* CBS, and other news organizations, that he was not acting as a spy but was serving a First Amendment interest in providing information of public importance to the news media. His primary motive, he said, was to alert the public to a significant advance in Soviet naval power, thus making people more willing to support increased expenditures for our own Navy. He also argued that Congress never intended that the Espionage Act be used to stifle dissemination of legitimate news. Its intent, he said, was that the law be used only against those who pass vital information to foreign powers for the purpose of harming the United States. In briefs filed with the court, the news organizations argued that upholding Morison's conviction would have a chilling effect on the First Amendment by deterring others in the government who might otherwise leak newsworthy information to the media.

The appellate court rejected all the arguments, although all three judges felt compelled to write about the First Amendment issues raised by the case. The court said the language of the Espionage Act is clear. Under its terms, it is a crime for persons with access to government secrets to disclose them to persons not entitled to receive them. Those persons need not be agents of a foreign government. Nor does the First Amendment give people a right to break the law to obtain news or disseminate it. The court's opinion said:

> ...[I]t seems beyond controversy that a recreant intelligence department employee who had abstracted from the government files secret intelligence information and had willfully transmitted or given it to one "not entitled to receive it" as did the defendant in this case, is not entitled to invoke the First Amendment as a shield to immunize his act of thievery. To permit the thief thus to misuse the Amendment would be to prostitute the salutary purposes of the First Amendment.

The court's opinion was written by Judge Donald Russell. The other members of the panel, Judges J. Harvey Wilkinson, III, and James Dickson Phillips, wrote separately to stress that the case raised significant First Amendment questions. Wilkinson said that "[t]he First Amendment interest in informed popular debate does not simply vanish at the invocation of the words 'national security.'" He noted that leaks sometimes serve a useful public purpose in countering the tendency "for government to withhold reports of disquieting developments and to manage news in a fashion most favorable to itself." That tendency, he said, threatens harm to the public interest because it diminishes access to "unfiltered facts." However, Morison's actions also were potentially harmful to the public interest. On his own, he gave away secrets that may have compromised "the security of sensitive government operations." Wilkinson noted that in a less than perfect world, it is essential that even democratic governments keep some things secret from their own people lest potential enemies be given an advantage. Thus, despite misgivings, in which he was joined by Phillips, Wilkinson concluded that Morison's conviction should be affirmed.

Death Threats Directed at Public Officials

Although the courts will tolerate speech, and even some kinds of action, aimed at demonstrating opposition to government policies, one kind of speech can lead to a prison term. Law enforcement officers and the courts have taken a serious view of threats to the lives of public officials, particularly the president. That this is so reflects a disturbing fact of political life in the latter part of the twentieth century: Some people make targets of presidents and other prominent persons. The victims of assassins include President John F. Kennedy; his brother, Robert, a candidate for president; and the Rev. Martin Luther King, Jr., a giant among civil rights advocates. Others have survived attempts on their lives, among them former Presidents Gerald Ford and Ronald Reagan; former presidential candidate and Alabama Governor George Wallace, paralyzed for life from the waist down; and Vernon Jordan, another civil rights leader.

It should be no surprise, then, that courts have not been disposed to interfere with punishment of those who threaten to kill the president, if the threat has even a remote credence. Presidents can be and have been portrayed in words and cartoons as inept, as liars, and as robbers of the poor, all part of the political game. But individuals have been sent to prison for threatening to kill the president, even when the threat was made by a person who was many miles distant from his target. The statute defining the crime is 18 U.S.C. §871, adopted in 1948. Two recent court decisions illustrate the circumstances under which a threat directed at the president can be punished.

To be actionable, a threat on the president's life must be made in such circumstances that it is taken seriously by those who are charged with protecting her or him from harm. In *United States* v. *Hoffman*,[22] the Seventh Circuit Court of Appeals affirmed the conviction of David L. Hoffman of Milwaukee, who sent a letter to the White House saying, "Ronnie, Listen Chump! Resign or You'll Get Your Brains Blown Out." Below those words, Hoffman had made a crude drawing of a pistol with a bullet emerging from its barrel. Despite the distance between Milwaukee and Washington, D.C., a trial court jury concluded that the threat violated the law. At the trial, Hoffman's mother testified that he was angry with the president because Reagan would not pardon Sun Myung Moon, the leader of the Unification Church, with which her son was then affiliated. Hoffman also had been arrested for carrying a concealed weapon and had a history of psychiatric disorders. The court held that under the circumstances reasonable people could

---

22.   806 F.2d 703 (7th Cir. 1986).

conclude that the letter was intended as a threat and was therefore not political speech protected by the First Amendment. Quoting from *Watts* v. *United States,*[23] the court said, "Because the statute 'makes criminal a form of pure speech, [it] must be interpreted with the commands of the First Amendment clearly in mind.'...To protect these First Amendment values, the Court held that 'the statute initially requires the government to prove a true "threat."' The Court concluded that 'political hyperbole' does not constitute a 'true threat.'"

In 1988, the Supreme Court concluded there was no "true threat" in the comment made by a deputy constable in Houston, Texas, when she heard that President Reagan survived the attempt on his life in 1981. She was working at a computer terminal in an inner room of the constable's office when she heard the news. She said to her boyfriend, who was working nearby, "If they go after him again, I hope they get him." When another deputy reported the remark to the constable, he fired the woman. She sued to get her job back, and the case reached the Supreme Court. In *Rankin* v. *McPherson,*[24] the Court held that under the circumstances, the comment could not be construed as a serious threat on the life of the president. The Court's majority concluded that the woman's comment, tasteless as it may have been, was an expression of political opinion protected by the First Amendment. Therefore, the constable violated the deputy's free speech rights by firing her.

These cases round out our look at the punishment of speech that threatens harm to the government or its officials. If that speech is merely critical of the government's policies, or of how officials carry out those policies, it is protected by the First Amendment. Demonstrations designed to influence government policy likewise are protected, as the Vietnam war era cases tell us. But if a speaker's words are designed to provoke harmful action, and are likely to do so, the government can punish the speaker. Such punishment is most likely when the words take the form of a death threat directed at the president under circumstances that lead authorities to take the threat seriously.

PRIOR RESTRAINT

The Supreme Court and Prior Restraint

Censorship has rarely been imposed in the United States, even in time of war. During the Civil War, the army sometimes used its control of the telegraph system to prevent newspapers from receiving dispatches describing Union defeats. However, such steps served only to delay publication of the bad news.[25] As mentioned, during World War I, censorship was imposed through the postal system

---

23. 394 U.S. 705, 89 S.Ct. 1399, 22 L.Ed.2d 664 (1969).
24. 483 U.S. 378, 107 S.Ct. 2891, 97 L.Ed.2d 315 (1987).
25. An interesting account of how northern newspapers covered the Civil War and bypassed army censors is found in J. Cutler Andrews, *The North Reports the Civil War* (Pittsburgh: University of Pittsburgh Press, 1955).

and was directed mainly at Socialist party newspapers.[26] In neither war was the Supreme Court asked to rule whether censorship violated the First Amendment guarantees of freedom of speech and press.

Indeed, it was not until 1931, when the nation was at peace, that the Court had its first opportunity to decide whether the First Amendment forbids censorship. When the test did come, it had nothing to do with national security. The question was: could a newspaper be shut down because it was considered scandalous?

Authorities in Minnesota, acting under powers given them by a state law, had obtained a court order forbidding J. M. Near and Howard Guilford to publish further issues of the weekly *Saturday Press* until they promised to print only the truth, and that "with good motives and for justifiable ends."[27] The Supreme Court ruled, five to four, that Near and Guilford could resume publication without making such a promise. The decision in *Near* v. *Minnesota,* written by Chief Justice Charles Evans Hughes, has become a landmark case quoted frequently by lower courts. While the majority held that prior restraint usually violates the First Amendment guarantee of freedom of speech and press, it also suggested several specific instances in which restraint might be justified. Thus, *Near* has proved to be both a victory and a defeat for those who believe that whatever else it does, the First Amendment ought to stand as a barrier against censorship.

Near v. *Minnesota,* **283 U.S. 697, 51 S.Ct. 625, 75 L.Ed. 1357 (1931).**

The *Saturday Press* was one of many unexpected by-products of a constitutional amendment, adopted in 1919, that prohibited the manufacture and sale of alcoholic beverages. It soon became evident that while the amendment cut off the legal sale of beer, wine, and spirits, it did not end the people's thirst for such beverages. To satisfy that thirst, an illegal network of distillers, brewers, distributors, and sellers came into existence. This illegal network was able to exist in part because police chose to ignore it, or because they were bribed to do so. Because laws in some states made mere possession of alcoholic beverages a crime, one of the effects of the prohibition amendment was to make lawbreakers out of everyone who wanted to drink something stronger than soda pop. Near and Guilford sought to capitalize on the situation by publishing a weekly newspaper devoted to exposing wrongdoers, of whom there obviously were many.

At one level, the *Saturday Press* served a public purpose by pointing to public officials who were taking bribes to ignore the illegal traffic in liquor. But their critics alleged that at another level Near and Guilford used their paper for a form of blackmail. The critics charged that some people were given a chance to keep their names out of the paper if they agreed to buy advertising or make a direct payment to the publishers. Additionally, the *Saturday Press* published derogatory comments about Jews and others. Its content and the tactics of its publishers made many people angry. As a result, Guilford was shot and wounded by un-

---

26. For a discussion of the actions taken by the Post Office to bar allegedly subversive publications from the mails, see Zechariah Chafee, Jr., *Free Speech in the United States* (New York: Atheneum, 1969).

27. "Scandal and Defamation! The Right of Newspapers to Defame," American Civil Liberties Union, 1931. See also Fred W. Friendly, *Minnesota Rag* (New York: Random House, 1981).

known assailants shortly after publication began, and there were threats of further violence. After the ninth issue of the paper appeared, a county attorney went to court and, without notice to either Near or Guilford, obtained an order shutting the paper down. In this court order, the *Saturday Press* was condemned as a nuisance devoted to fomenting violence. The publishers, with help from the *Chicago Tribune,* the American Civil Liberties Union, and the American Newspaper Publishers Association, were able to take their case to the Supreme Court of the United States.

That Court overturned the state court's order. Chief Justice Hughes, writing for the majority, saw the case as a conflict between two important interests. On one side was the First Amendment interest in freedom of speech and press, which lies at the heart of a free society. On the other side was another vitally important interest—the preservation of an orderly society. Hughes noted that states inherently have the authority to protect the health, safety, morals, and general welfare of their residents. This authority, called the "police power," is exercised in many ways. Some courts have held that it is of equal importance with freedom of speech and press, reasoning that if society cannot maintain itself in an orderly manner, freedom of speech and press will have little meaning. Hughes noted that the Minnesota law used to shut down the *Saturday Press* was designed to promote public safety, and therefore was an exercise of the police power. Under it, a judge could suppress any publication which, in his opinion, might provoke violence. However, and this was critical to the judgment in *Near,* the law made no distinction between truthful and untruthful articles. Nor did it establish any clear guidelines for determining when a publication might provoke violence. In short, the law's language was so broad that the decision was entirely up to the judge's discretion. That, Hughes concluded, was "the very essence of censorship."

The chief justice then examined what Blackstone and other legal commentators have said about previous restraint. His conclusion was that where libel is concerned, the generally approved remedy is a suit for damages, not suppression of the libelous publication. However, Hughes continued, some commentators have argued that the First Amendment, despite its seemingly absolute terms, does not prohibit all previous restraints. He agreed that it does not:

> No one would question but that a government might prevent actual obstruction to its recruiting service or the publication of the sailing dates of transports or the number and location of troops. On similar grounds, the primary requirements of decency may be enforced against obscene publications. The security of community life may be protected against incitements to acts of violence and the overthrow of orderly government. The constitutional guaranty of free speech does not "protect a man from an injunction against uttering words that may have all the effect of force."

The majority of the Court concluded that the *Saturday Press* did not come under any of these categories and therefore had been shut down in violation of the First Amendment. The Court also held that the Minnesota law was unconstitutional because it did not define with precision when a paper might be suppressed, and because it permitted suppression of truth as well as falsehood.

It should be emphasized that decisions written by five justices are as strong in establishing precedent as decisions written by all nine. But it is also worth noting that the first time the Court was confronted by a prior restraint of a newspaper, four of the nine justices acted on the belief that abuse of First Amendment freedoms could justify prior restraint. In the opinion of the minority, Near and Guilford were engaged in the publishing business for purposes of blackmail and extortion. Such businesses, the minority reasoned, could be shut down by court order.

The decision illustrates the dilemma that lies at the heart of many First Amendment cases. Beyond question, by the standards of most publishers of the era, the *Saturday Press* was a product of bad journalism. Some of its contents were highly offensive; other parts of it were false. In short, in the eyes of many people, it was garbage, and the Minnesota court treated it as such. So did the minority in the Supreme Court. It took the position that a rag like the *Saturday Press* was not entitled to First Amendment protection. But the majority took the position that the First Amendment was designed to protect speech that some people condemn as garbage. In fact, that is the point of having constitutional protection for freedom of speech and press. No one makes an issue of speech everyone agrees with. Nor is there likely to be a problem with publications reflecting the opinions of a majority. It is only when speakers begin making someone uncomfortable that they run into problems. In *Near,* the majority held that the state could not use its power to put shabby journalists out of business, even when much of what they published was considered trash.

The *Near* decision is of continuing importance for two reasons:

1. A majority of the Court condemned prior restraint of a newspaper on First Amendment grounds. Its reasons for doing so were not particularly strong, but the precedent was established and would be followed by other courts.

2. However, a majority of the Court also suggested that under certain specified circumstances, listed in the passage quoted above, prior restraint might be proper. Thus, in striking down a restraint imposed to prevent libelous assertions deemed likely to provoke violence, the Court opened the way for attempts to impose censorship for other purposes. Indeed, this is what has happened, as the remainder of this chapter will illustrate. *Near,* then, must be seen in perspective as a paradox. It extended the meaning of the First Amendment in a specific case, but also seemed to approve some limits to its scope.

Barriers against Prior Restraint

For thirty years, *Near* was the Supreme Court's only authority to which lower courts could refer in prior restraint cases. Not until 1963 did it have any more to say about the matter. Then in 1971 came a second decision further defining procedures that must be followed if a prior restraint is to be upheld. These two cases, taken with *Near,* have erected high barriers that must be surmounted if censorship is to survive appeal to the courts.

The first of these cases, *Bantam Books* v. *Sullivan,* grew out of an attempt by the state of Rhode Island to prevent allegedly obscene publications from reaching young people. Members of a state commission were given the authority to determine which books and magazines were suitable for children and which were not. The commission's periodical listing of works unfit for children was distributed to bookstores and other places selling books and magazines. Police officers visited the stores to check on whether the proscribed publications were being displayed where minors could get at them. To avoid being hassled, some stores stopped selling books and magazines listed by the commission, including such widely read novels as *Peyton Place* and such magazines as *Playboy.*

Bantam Books v. *Sullivan,*
372 U.S. 58, 83 S.Ct. 631,
9 L.Ed.2d 584 (1963).

Bantam Books took the lead in challenging the state's action. It argued that even though the state had pursued no prosecutions, the listing system's intimidation provided a form of prior restraint. Rhode Island courts disagreed, but the U.S. Supreme Court reversed. Writing for the majority, Justice William J. Brennan, Jr., drafted a standard that went beyond the Court's holding in *Near* and since has been applied in prior restraint cases. The key passage in the Court's decision is: "Any system of prior restraints of expression comes to this Court bearing a heavy presumption against its constitutional validity.... We have tolerated such a system only where it has operated under judicial superintendence and assured an almost immediate judicial determination of the validity of the restraint." At a minimum, Brennan suggested, a proper system for imposing a prior restraint to prevent distribution of materials considered harmful to minors would include notice to the subject that a restraint was contemplated. Such notice should lead quickly to an appearance before a judge who would hear both sides of the argument. At that time, the agency seeking the restraint would be required to offer a precise statement of the standard that had been applied in determining that the materials were unfit for minors. Finally, the agency would have to explain why it had found the works objectionable. A restraint could be imposed only if the judge could be convinced that it was justified. Brennan concluded that the Rhode Island law was unconstitutional because it provided none of the suggested safeguards.

Eight years later, the Supreme Court reinforced those procedures in a case involving an attempt to prevent distribution of handbills in a Chicago suburb. *Organization for a Better Austin* v. *Keefe* originated with Jerome M. Keefe, owner of a real estate agency. The Organization for a Better Austin, a group of homeowners formed to protect the racially mixed nature of their community, accused Keefe of trying to upset that mixture by promoting "block-busting" and "panic peddling" designed to induce white owners to sell and move out. The organization prepared leaflets denouncing Keefe's sales tactics and distributed them widely in the community where Keefe lived. Contending that his privacy was being invaded, Keefe went to court and was able to get an order forbidding further distribution of the leaflets. State

Organization for a Better Austin v. *Keefe,* 402 U.S. 415, 91 S.Ct. 1575, 29 L.Ed.2d 1 (1971).

courts affirmed, but the Supreme Court reversed, holding that the organization was a victim of an impermissible prior restraint. The Court held that anyone seeking a prior restraint through the procedures outlined in *Bantam Books* "carries a heavy burden of showing justification" for its request.

The key points of *Near, Bantam Books,* and *Organization for a Better Austin* may be summarized thus: Despite its seemingly absolute wording, the speech and press clause of the First Amendment does not stand as a barrier against all forms of censorship. If words have "all the effect of force," or if they obstruct the recruiting service in time of war or give away vital military secrets, if they are obscene, or incite violent overthrow of the government, they may be restrained. But such restraint cannot be done casually or arbitrarily. There is a "heavy presumption" that any restraint of speech or press is unconstitutional. The government can prevail only if it "carries [the] heavy burden of showing justification" for restraint. The government must show that it is trying to protect a vital interest, such as national security, that the Constitution gives it a right to protect. Or the government must show that the offending speech is of a type, such as obscenity, not protected by the First Amendment. The government must show that the restraint will accomplish its intended purpose without also restraining speech that offers no threat to a vital interest. The victim of the intended restraint must be given an opportunity to counter the government's evidence. In short, prior restraint can be imposed only after an adversary hearing before a judge.

Because of the principles explained above, judicially approved prior restraint is uncommon. This does not keep private individuals, business organizations, and government officials from trying to impose such restraints. Nor do all these entities fail. In the remainder of this chapter, we will examine some of those attempts. (We will encounter others in later chapters.)

The Protection of Unpopular Opinions

Starting in the 1930s, when a small religious movement, Jehovah's Witnesses, was the victim of widespread persecution in the United States,[28] the Supreme Court wrote a remarkable series of decisions banning the use of prior restraint to prevent the spread of unpopular doctrines. The precedents established by the Court have protected labor unions and civil rights advocates, along with white racists and anti-Semites. Summaries of some of the more significant cases follow.

It was not easy to be a Jehovah's Witness in the 1930s. The religious movement's literature portrayed the Roman Catholic Church as the creation of the devil, with the pope as his vicar. The salute to the flag was condemned as a form of idolatry. Further, Witnesses made themselves highly visible by going door-to-door or accosting people on the streets to sell or give away religious pamphlets.

---

28. For a sampling of the more than a thousand recorded instances of persecution of Jehovah's Witnesses, see Leonard A. Stevens, *Salute! The Case of the Bible vs. the Flag* (New York: Coward, 1973).

In reaction, city governments everywhere adopted ordinances designed to discourage distribution of handbills or other printed matter.

An ordinance adopted in Griffin, Georgia, was typical. Under its terms anyone who wanted to distribute pamphlets or leaflets had to get a permit from the city manager, who had the sole authority to deny, grant, or revoke a permit. Alma Lovell, a Jehovah's Witness, ignored the ordinance. When she was arrested for trying to sell tracts at two for a nickel, she was found guilty of soliciting without a license and was fined $50. The case, *Lovell* v. *Griffin*,[29] reached the Supreme Court, which held unanimously that the Griffin ordinance was an unconstitutional form of prior restraint. The Court focused on the city manager's arbitrary authority to grant or revoke a license at will. Invoking echoes of John Milton's *Areopagitica,* the Court said, "The ordinance would restore...licensing and censorship in its baldest form." Although on its face the ordinance did not interfere with the right of the Witnesses to publish whatever they pleased, the Court said it was a form of restraint nevertheless because its purpose was to prevent distribution of the movement's views. The Court noted that "without circulation, the publication would be of little value."

With its decision in *Lovell* in 1938, the Court extended the protection of the First Amendment to newspaper carriers, to pamphleteers, to corner soapbox speakers, itinerant evangelists, and all others who seek to spread the word, on paper or orally, in public places.

Two years later, in *Thornhill* v. *Alabama,*[30] the Court extended the First Amendment's protection of the dissemination of unpopular ideas to cover peaceful picketing by labor unions. The target this time was an Alabama law that forbade loitering or picketing "without just cause or legal excuse." "Just cause" was not defined, nor was "legal excuse." Nevertheless, police concluded that several men who were picketing a wood-preserving plant had no justifiable reason for doing so even though a strike was in progress. Police arrested the pickets and a court found them guilty. The Supreme Court reversed, holding that the law permitted the same kind of arbitrary interference with speech that it had condemned in *Lovell.* Under the law's terms, officials could jail pickets simply because they didn't approve the pickets' cause. Thus the law served as "a continuous and pervasive restraint on all freedom of discussion that might reasonably be regarded as within" its reach.

In a real sense, the victories won by Jehovah's Witnesses in *Lovell* and by organized labor in *Thornhill* made possible the victories of the black civil rights movement in the 1950s and 1960s. Courts cited those and related cases in striking down attempts to prevent or suppress the protest marches and demonstrations that brought the movement to public attention. Some of these cases reached the Supreme Court.[31] In its decisions, the Court reiterated principles in the Witnesses' and labor cases: Government cannot prevent the use of streets and other

---

29. 303 U.S. 444, 58 S.Ct. 666, 82 L.Ed. 949 (1938).
30. 310 U.S. 88, 60 S.Ct. 736, 84 L.Ed. 1093 (1940).
31. See, for instance, Shuttlesworth v. City of Birmingham, 394 U.S. 147, 89 S.Ct. 935, 22 L.Ed.2d 162 (1969).

public places for the dissemination of ideas, no matter how unpopular. Government can require that demonstrations be peaceful and can limit the time, place, and manner of dissemination, but such regulation must be reasonable.

Further, the Supreme Court has held that governments cannot prevent speakers from presenting unpopular, or even repugnant, views in order to head off possible violence. A restraint to prevent bloodshed can be imposed only if the threat of violence is so imminent, and so beyond the control of the authorities, that no other remedy will work.

The leading case, *Carroll* v. *President and Commissioners of Princess Anne,* grew out of an ugly series of events on Maryland's eastern shore when members of the National States' Rights Party conducted a rally in Princess Anne, a community of fewer than a thousand. About a quarter of the 150 persons present were black. The audience was subjected to a series of antiblack and anti-Semitic tirades. Feelings were running high, and state police were on hand to prevent a riot. There was no trouble that night, but one of the speakers promised that even stronger speeches would be made at a similar rally the next night.

Carroll v. *President and Commissioners of Princess Anne,* **393 U.S. 175, 89 S.Ct. 347, 21 L.Ed.2d 325 (1968).**

That rally was not held. Early in the day, local officials went to Somerset County Circuit Court and, without notice to any members of the States' Rights Party or even a hearing, obtained a restraining order forbidding any further rallies in the county during the next ten days. After a trial at the end of that time, the court extended its order to cover the next ten months.

The Maryland Court of Appeals endorsed the ten-day order but reversed the ten-month order on the ground that a restraint of that length was unreasonable. On further appeal, the Supreme Court of the United States held that even a ten-day order was unconstitutional. However, the Court focused its decision narrowly on the arbitrary nature of the proceeding in the Maryland trial court. The Court reiterated its holding in *Bantam Books* that a restraint can be imposed only after an adversary hearing. But in doing so, the Court also reiterated its holding in *Near*—a prior restraint can be imposed to prevent violence. Quoting from an earlier decision,[32] the Court said, "No one would have the hardihood to suggest that the principle of freedom of speech sanctions incitement to riot." The Court said there was no clear evidence of such incitement in Princess Anne.

What can a community do when advocates of highly offensive racial or religious views insist on their right to express those views under circumstances that seem designed to provoke violence? That question has no clear answer, as is illustrated by the experience of Skokie, Illinois, when self-proclaimed U.S. Nazis sought permission to conduct a rally there in the 1970s. Skokie has a predominantly Jewish population and at the time some of its residents were survivors of

---

32. Cantwell v. Connecticut, 310 U.S. 396, 60 S.Ct. 900, 84 L.Ed. 1213 (1940), a Jehovah's Witnesses case in which the Court found that the threat of violence was not so imminent as to justify the arrest of a Witness who played an anti-Catholic recording on a public street in a Catholic neighborhood, provoking listeners to threaten to punch him in the nose.

American Nazis use shields to ward off debris thrown at them during a demonstration in Federal Building Plaza in Chicago in 1978. At the time, the group was awaiting the outcome of legal actions in which state and federal courts reluctantly upheld their right to march in Skokie, Illinois, the home of many survivors of Hitler's World War II death camps. (AP/Wide World Photos)

Hitler's World War II death camps. Members of the Nazi group wore uniforms patterned on those worn by Hitler's infamous SS squads, who enforced his attempt to exterminate Jews. When they asked to conduct a rally on the steps of the Skokie Village Hall, residents reacted with fear and indignation. Militant Jewish groups threatened violence. Caught in the middle, the Skokie Village Council adopted three ordinances designed to make it difficult if not impossible for the meeting to be held. This set off a series of lawsuits in both state and federal courts, resulting in decisions holding that the ordinances were unconstitutional attempts at prior restraint. The Supreme Court refused pleas that the decisions should be overturned because they would lead to violence.[33]

The Nazi group's right to freedom of speech and assembly was upheld. But as Justice Harry A. Blackmun noted, every court that considered the case felt a need to apologize for its verdict. Blackmun argued that the Supreme Court should have taken the case to determine how far a community must go to protect inflammatory and provocative speakers. It is interesting to compare his view with

---

33. Smith v. Collin, 439 U.S. 916, 99 S.Ct. 291, 58 L.Ed.2d 264 (1978). See also 447 F.Supp. 676 (N.D.Ill. 1978), 578 F.2d 1197 (7th Cir. 1978), and Village of Skokie v. National Socialist Party, 373 N.E.2d 21 (Ill. 1978).

that of Thomas I. Emerson, the First Amendment scholar whose views are summarized in Chapter 1. Emerson argued that the First Amendment imposes a duty on government to provide a forum for all shades of opinion. Blackmun, confronted with an extreme application of that argument, wrote:

> I...feel that the present case affords the Court an opportunity to consider whether...there is no limit whatsoever to the exercise of free speech. There indeed may be no such limit, but when citizens assert, not casually but with deep conviction, that the proposed demonstration is scheduled at a place and in a manner that is taunting and overwhelmingly offensive to the citizens of that place, that assertion, uncomfortable though it may be for the judges, deserves to be examined. It just might fall into the same category as one's "right" to cry "fire" in a crowded theater, for "the character of every act depends upon the circumstances in which it is done." [Quoting Holmes in *Schenck*.]

Blackmun's concern raises serious questions. How far must society go to provide a forum for those whose only purpose seems to be to stir up racial, religious, or political hatred? How much exposure should the news media give to persons whose arguments are based on deliberate misstatement of fact or are devoid of both reason and logic? In short, is all speech equally free? Is there an obligation under the First Amendment to provide a forum for any kind of expression uttered in the name of a cause? It is a question that vexes not only judges in these times, but journalists, university administrators, and all who believe that issues should be resolved without resort to force.

The Protection of National Security

Twice in recent times the federal government has asked the courts to prevent publication of information believed harmful to national security. In the first instance the *New York Times,* the *Washington Post,* and other newspapers were prevented for about two weeks from publishing secret documents dealing with the Vietnam war. The Supreme Court ruled that the government had not met the heavy burden of proving that the restraint was essential to the nation's security. In the second instance, a U.S. district court prevented a magazine from publishing an article purporting to describe how a hydrogen bomb is made. That episode ended indecisively when the information was disclosed in other media. At the time, both cases caused considerable controversy, but neither established enduring principles of media law. However, because each did involve imposition of a temporary prior restraint believed necessary to protect national security, the cases are still worth study.

The Pentagon Papers

The first case, known as the "Pentagon Papers" case, began in June 1971 when readers of the *New York Times* were offered the first installment of a top-secret government study of how the United States became involved in the Vietnam war. The newspaper said it would publish those parts of the 7000-page document its editors believed to be of public interest. Henry Kissinger, President Nixon's national security adviser, said in his memoirs that the disclosure "came as a profound shock to the Administration."[34] That shock quickly was converted into action of an unprecedented nature. Within three days, the attorney general of the United States obtained court orders that stopped first the *Times* and then the *Washington Post* from publishing further installments of the documents. Only one court, the U.S. Court of Appeals for the Second Circuit, ruled that the facts justified a prior restraint. Other courts in New York City and Washington, D.C., granted government motions for temporary restraint pending the outcome of an appeal to the Supreme Court. That Court, acting with unusual speed, granted certiorari, heard arguments, and issued its decision in one week. That fact alone speaks volumes about how seriously courts view an attempt to prevent publication of government information. Normally two to four months elapse between argument and the Court's decision, and commonly a year will pass between the Court's agreeing to take a case and its decision.

In this instance, the justices voted six to three to lift the restraint immediately. The unsigned *per curiam* decision disposed in two short paragraphs of the government's argument that the president had a

New York Times Co. v. United States, **403 U.S. 713, 91 S.Ct. 2140, 29 L.Ed.2d 822 (1971).**

right to restrain publication of information he believed to be harmful to national security. Quoting directly from *Near, Bantam Books,* and *Organization for a Better Austin,* the Court said it agreed with a New York federal district court and the District of Columbia Circuit Court, which had held that the government had not carried the "heavy burden" required to justify its request for a restraint. Thus, it had not overcome "the heavy presumption against" the restraint's constitutional validity. Even the three dissenters took pains to say that they opposed prior restraints in general but thought this case had moved through the courts too quickly to develop a factual basis on which to judge whether national security was indeed in danger. They wanted the case returned to the lower courts for trial so that a record might be developed.

Although the decision broke no new legal ground, the case was of great importance to the news media because for the first time the Department of Justice had asked the courts to restrain publication of government information. One of the lower-court judges involved in the case noted that it was the first time in 200 years that "the executive department has succeeded in stopping the presses."[35]

The individual opinions written by each of the nine justices of the Supreme Court reflect a similar concern for the gravity of the action. Only two of the justices, William O. Douglas and Hugo L. Black, took the position that the press never can be prevented from publishing what it knows. Justice Brennan relied on

---

34. Henry Kissinger, *White House Years* (Boston: Little, Brown, 1979), p. 729. The book contains background information on the context in which the Pentagon Papers case arose. See also Floyd Abrams, "The Pentagon Papers a Decade Later," *New York Times Magazine,* 7 June 1981, p. 22, for one view of the consequences of the publication.
35. Judge J. Skelly Wright of the U.S. Court of Appeals for the District of Columbia Circuit in United States v. Washington Post Co., 446 F.2d 1322 (D.C.Cir. 1971).

Near and concluded that publication of the Pentagon Papers did not raise the same kind of danger as publication of the sailing date of transports or of troop dispositions in time of war. The three other members of the majority avoided the First Amendment issue by concluding that no law authorized the government to prevent newspapers from publishing top-secret documents.

Only one of the opinions, that of Chief Justice Warren E. Burger writing in dissent, raised questions that continue to plague relations between the news media and the government. Lawyers for the *Times* had asserted in argument to the Court that the paper was serving the public's "right to know" when it began publication of the documents. Burger said he could not find that right in the First Amendment. Even if it were there, as the *Times* lawyer seemed to argue, it would not be absolute, Burger wrote, but might have to yield in some instances to other important interests. If the Court were to recognize such a right, and ground it in the Constitution, Burger asked, who would be responsible for fulfilling it? The news media? Or the government, which is the main repository of information on its own activities? Burger could not resist pointing out that the editors of the *Times* had held up publication of the papers for three months while they decided what parts of them would be published. Why, in the fulfillment of a "right to know," should the courts be required to act in a few days?

Burger's questions are good ones. They will arise in different contexts later in this book. "The right to know" is a phrase that slips easily off the tongue, especially when a journalist is denied access to information that seems important. Usually it is asserted in a context that suggests the journalist is acting on behalf of the people, who are the ultimate possessors of "right to know." That people who govern themselves have a right to know everything their various governments are doing is an appealing concept in a free society. If that indeed is the ultimate nature of the right, it has awesome implications, as Burger suggests. If such a right were to be found in the First Amendment, would it not compel journalists to transmit in unedited form every last word they found in public government documents and in the utterances of government officials? Would not any abridgment of that flow by an editor become a violation of the public's "right to know"? This may sound far-fetched, but a constitutional right, once defined, holds a preeminent position in the legal hierarchy.

Burger also taunted the *Times* for its willingness to accept and publish documents he saw as stolen property. *Times* editors, he wrote, should have known something was wrong when they were handed such a vast quantity of documents, clearly marked "top secret" and clearly the property of the United States government. It should have occurred to them to notify the proper government departments of their windfall and to seek declassification of the materials through proper channels. "With such an approach—one that great newspapers have in the past practiced and stated editorially to be the duty of an honorable press—the newspapers and Government might well have narrowed the area of disagreement" and settled it through litigation.

Burger let fly a final arrow:

> To me it is hardly believable that a newspaper long regarded as a great institution in American life would fail to perform one of the basic and simple duties of every

citizen with respect to the discovery or possession of stolen property or secret Government documents. That duty, I had thought—perhaps naively—was to report forthwith to responsible public officers. This duty rests on taxi drivers, justices and the *New York Times*.

Chief Justice Burger's belief that documents, or even copies of them, are property and therefore subject to criminal law defining theft was to surface in each succeeding session of Congress through 1977. Proposals were made to make unauthorized possession of such documents a crime. But each time, representatives of the news media and civil libertarians raised enough objections to defeat the attempt.[36] However, in 1987 in another context, the Supreme Court itself held that information is property and can be protected from theft like any other kind of property. The Court's decision, in *Carpenter* v. *United States*,[37] upheld the conviction for securities fraud of two *Wall Street Journal* employees and a stockbroker who used information taken from the paper in advance of publication to profit from changes in securities prices. A unanimous Court held that *Journal* editors could protect information gathered by reporters for the paper's use until it is published. The decision is summarized in the chapter on copyright law.

With the benefit of hindsight, the publication of the Pentagon Papers seems to have had little effect on the nation's security. Still, questions persist. Should information considered so vital to security that government officials stamp it "top secret" be subject to disclosure by any reporter who can lay hands on it? Or should disclosure be permitted only by "responsible" reporters, such as those employed by the *New York Times* and the *Washington Post?* If reporters may tell the world about matters the government deems secret, who else may do so?

Or does the problem lie, as Justice Potter Stewart suggested, in the government's trying to keep too many secrets? When the secrecy stamp is applied, as it has been, to clippings from newspapers and magazines, doesn't this make a mockery of the classification system? And isn't the system further mocked when government officials, including presidents, selectively disclose classified information that will help them score a political point? In its brief in this case the *New York Times* pointed to many instances of such disclosure in memoirs, in press conferences, and in "don't quote me" leaks to favored reporters.

If Congress should try to enact a law, as some members of the Court suggested, providing for punishment of the publisher of classified information, what is to be done in those instances in which a knowledgeable reporter, working with readily available information, reaches conclusions that have also been reached in a classified document? Would shrewd analysis of a broad range of sensitive information thus become a crime?

Despite the troubling questions raised by publication of the Pentagon Papers, the fact remains that a majority of the Supreme Court again struck down a prior restraint. In doing so, the Court did not write any new law, placing its reliance on

---

36. *Congressional Quarterly Almanac* (Washington, D.C.: Congressional Quarterly), ed. from 1971 through 1980.
37. 484 U.S. 19, 108 S.Ct. 316, 98 L.Ed.2d 275 (1987).

Near, Bantam Books, and *Organization for a Better Austin,* but it reinforced the principle that censorship is a weapon of last resort, to be used only when the danger is so serious that nothing less stringent will work.

The H-Bomb Secret

In 1979, a federal district court judge in Wisconsin thought he was confronted with just such a danger. Justice Department lawyers told him that *The Progressive* magazine was going to publish an article that would tell how to make a hydrogen bomb—the most powerful force under the control of human beings. In this instance the Justice Department lawyers pointed to a law which authorizes restraint to prevent disclosure of nuclear secrets.[38] The government argued that under terms of the law, all information dealing with nuclear weapons technology is "classified at birth"; that is, it must be treated as a secret as soon as it takes tangible form.

Howard Morland, the author of the article, argued that the article disclosed no secrets. He said he had obtained all of his information from previously published material found in libraries. His point, he said, was that no longer are any secrets involved in making hydrogen bombs. Because that is true, he said he and the magazine's editors hoped that publication of the article would lead to more diligent efforts to abolish nuclear weapons.

Judge Robert W. Warren listened to both sides and then ruled for the government. He issued an order forbidding publication of the article. He conceded that his decision was a serious blow to First Amendment freedoms. But he said those freedoms wouldn't matter if publication of the article were to make it possible for someone to build and use a hydrogen bomb.[39]

The Progressive appealed the ruling, but the case was dropped six months later when a newspaper in Madison, Wisconsin, and several other newspapers elsewhere ran a letter from a computer programmer containing essentially the same information about the working of a hydrogen bomb. The programmer had even prepared a diagram purportedly of the bomb's mechanism. The programmer, like Morland, said he had found all his information in the public domain, although he conceded that some of it had been made public by three scientists who allegedly had violated their security clearances. However, no one was punished.[40] *The Progressive* published Morland's article in the November 1979 issue under the title "The H-Bomb Secret: To Know How Is to Ask Why."

At the time of the district court's decision, the *Progressive* case seemed to put the First Amendment issue squarely—a serious risk to the nation's security was countered by imposition of a prior restraint, the most serious infringement of freedom of the press. Had it gone up through the appeals process, the case might well have resulted in a decision defining the point at which harmful disclosures

---

38. Atomic Energy Act, 42 U.S. Code §§ 2274, 2280.
39. United States v. The Progressive, 467 F.Supp. 990 (W.D.Wis. 1979).
40. John Consoli, "The Progressive Triumphs in H-Bomb Case," *Editor & Publisher,* 22 September 1979, pp. 9, 36.

can be prevented. However, the multiple publications that brought the case to an end suggest that the editors of *The Progressive* may have been right when they argued that as of 1979 there no longer was any secret to protect.

Prior Restraint by Contract

The Supreme Court has held that under some circumstances the government can censor books and articles even without a breach of national security. The Court upheld the contractual relationship between the federal government and those of its employees who have regular access to classified information.

As one might expect, people who go to work for the Central Intelligence Agency must agree not to disclose any information learned during their employment that would expose "intelligence sources or methods." Some of the agency's employees occupy such sensitive positions that they cannot even tell outsiders for whom they work. This insistence on secrecy continues when employees leave the CIA for whatever reason. The employment agreement has been construed to require former employees to submit to the agency for security clearance any article, book, or speech based on their previous work. The purpose is to prevent disclosure of information learned during the course of their employment that still might be classified. The same restrictions apply to former employees of the Defense and State Departments or of the White House who had regular access to classified intelligence data.

Three court decisions, one of them by the Supreme Court, have upheld the government's right to require review of works prepared for publication by parties who have signed such contracts. The leading case involved a book, *Decent Interval*,[41] written by Frank Snepp, a former CIA agent. The book described the United States's pell-mell withdrawal from Vietnam in 1975. The author did not submit the manuscript for review, although he had signed the usual employment contract when he went to work for the agency. Although the government conceded that there was no still-classified material in the book, it filed suit in a federal district court to compel Snepp to surrender his profits from the work. Lower courts disagreed as to whether he should do so, but the Supreme Court had no doubts. In a brusque *per curiam* decision, the Court held that a former agent's judgment as to what may be disclosed safely is not to be substituted for that of the CIA. The Court wrote:

Snepp v. *United States,* 444 U.S. 507, 100 S.Ct. 763, 62 L.Ed.2d 704 (1980).

> Undisputed evidence in this case shows that a CIA agent's violation of his obligation to submit writings about the agency for prepublication review impairs the CIA's ability to perform its statutory duties. Admiral Turner, director of the CIA, testified without contradiction that Snepp's book and others like it have seriously impaired the effectiveness of American intelligence operations.

41. Frank W. Snepp, *Decent Interval* (New York: Random House, 1977).

As a consequence, the Court required that all Snepp's earnings from the book, estimated at $125,000 or more,[42] be placed in trust for the benefit of the government. The Court said its order "simply requires him to disgorge the benefits of his faithlessness."

Two earlier decisions by the U.S. Court of Appeals for the Fourth Circuit resulted in publication of a book containing blank spaces to reflect material deleted by order of government censors. The book, *The CIA and the Cult of Intelligence*,[43] was written by Victor L. Marchetti, a former official of the CIA, and John Marks, a former employee of the State Department. Its purpose was to expose what the authors believed to be improper interference by the CIA in the internal affairs of other countries, most notably Chile, Cuba, and China. When the CIA learned that the manuscript was being offered to publishers, it asked Marchetti to submit the work for review. He resisted, arguing that he had a right under the First Amendment to question government policy. The circuit court held, in *United States* v. *Marchetti*,[44] that Marchetti had such a right. But it also held that he had no right to use classified material in doing so. His contract with the government was valid. He would have to submit his manuscript for review.

When he did so, the CIA ordered deletion of 339 passages, or nearly 20 percent of the book. Again Marchetti appealed to the courts for relief. This led to negotiation during which about half the deleted material was restored. Litigation over the remainder resulted in a second appellate court decision, *Alfred A. Knopf* v. *Colby*,[45] establishing the rules to be applied by the CIA in ordering deletions from works submitted for review. It put the burden of proof on the author to show (1) that a questioned item was not classified properly, or (2) that it was not classified when the author came into possession of it, or (3) that it had been declassified. The court said Marchetti could not publish still-classified information because the gist of it had been published by someone else. The court reasoned that a foreign agent who read a story written by a reporter might have doubts about its truth. But if he were to read the same information in an article written by a former CIA agent, his doubts would be resolved. Knopf published the book before the case was decided, perhaps to capitalize on the publicity surrounding the case. Some passages are printed in boldface to show that the CIA first ordered their deletion and then relented. But the book also contains 168 blank spaces up to 2 pages in length to show how much was taken out by order of the government.

The book stands as a reminder that people who decide to work for the government in sensitive positions can be required to give up some of their freedom of speech, not only while they are employed but for the rest of their lives. If such employees have access to classified information, they cannot write for publication unless they first submit their work for review. The courts have held that the

---

42. "Top Court Rules CIA Has Power to Screen Writings by Past and Current Employees," *Wall Street Journal*, 20 February 1980.
43. New York: Knopf, 1974.
44. 466 F.2d 1309 (4th Cir. 1972).
45. 509 F.2d 1362 (4th Cir. 1975).

government can prevent them from using classified information learned in the course of their employment. And the Supreme Court has held that if they evade review they can be forced to give up their profits from the work in question, even though it disclosed no classified information.

Prior Restraint and Student Publications

Students who work on school publications long have been torn between two forces. One force is whatever impels them to go into journalism in the first place, ranging from a narrowly personal interest in showing off one's writing ability or in having a little fun to an altruistic interest in helping change the world. Students who choose journalism also usually are aware that the First Amendment to the Constitution protects freedom of the press, which presumably includes school newspapers. The second force is school authorities—the publication's faculty adviser backed up by the principal, the superintendent, and the board of education. At the best, such authorities tolerate or may even encourage a student press free to explore any issue of interest to its staff. But anyone who has ever worked on a student newspaper is aware that freedom has its limits. Go too far, stir up too many people, and school authorities not only will talk about the responsibilities that go along with freedom but may enforce their view of those responsibilities on the student staff. Until recently, despite a scattering of lower-level court cases, no one involved in this tense equation could say with certainty whether the First Amendment supported the students' freedom to publish what they pleased or the school officials' right to enforce responsibility. In January 1988, the Supreme Court resolved those doubts. It held five to three that when a public school newspaper is published as part of a journalism class, school officials, not the student editors, have the ultimate authority to decide what is printed and what is not as long as the decision is not made for political reasons. Put in its bluntest terms, the Court's decision affirmed the right of public school officials—agents of the state—to impose an arbitrary prior restraint on articles, photographs, or drawings a student editor has decided to publish.

The case had its origins in just such an act. In May 1983, the student editors of *Spectrum,* a newspaper serving students at Hazelwood East High School in the suburbs of St. Louis, put together the final edition for the school year. It included an article on teenage pregnancy, featuring interviews with several Hazelwood students who had had babies. The students were not named, and the editors believed they had changed the stories enough to keep the girls from being identified. The issue also contained an article in which the writer described his reactions to being torn between divorced parents. He was particularly hard on his father. When students received their copies of *Spectrum* neither article appeared. The two pages on which they had been dummied by the editors had been removed from the newspaper. Hazelwood East Principal Robert E. Reynolds said later, "The students and families in the articles

Hazelwood School District v. *Kuhlmeier,* **484 U.S. 260, 108 S.Ct. 562, 98 L.Ed.2d 592 (1988).**

A student editor holds up a copy of the Hazelwood East High School *Spectrum* reporting a Supreme Court decision growing out of the school principal's censorship of an earlier edition of the paper. The Court held that public school authorities have a right to control the content of school newspapers that are published as part of classroom work in journalism. (AP/Wide World Photos)

[on pregnancy and divorce] were described in such an accurate way that the readers could tell who they were. When it became clear that the articles were going to tread on the right of privacy of students and their parents, I stepped in to stop the process."[46]

Reynolds stopped one process but started another. Cathy Kuhlmeier and two other *Spectrum* staffers asked a federal district court in St. Louis to overrule the principal. It refused to do so. The Eighth Circuit Court of Appeals reversed. School officials took the case to the Supreme Court, which agreed to consider it. Five justices, over vigorous protests from three others, ruled that the principal had acted reasonably. Further, the majority held that "no violation of First Amendment rights occurred." Justice Byron R. White, writing for the majority, said the principal was merely playing the role of a good teacher by correcting a substandard classroom exercise. That view was not shared by Justice Brennan, who wrote for the minority, and by others who commented on the decision. Brennan called the principal's action "brutal censorship." A headline in *Editor &*

---

46. "From Hazelwood to the High Court," *New York Times Magazine,* 13 September 1987, p. 102.

Publisher, the newspaper trade magazine, called the decision a "First Amendment disaster."[47]

How could there be such widely diverse views of the same action and the same decision? Within the Court, the split occurred over which of the Court's previous decisions was seen as the applicable precedent. The majority, made up of White, Chief Justice William H. Rehnquist, and Justices John Paul Stevens, Sandra Day O'Connor, and Antonin Scalia, found its guidance in *Bethel School District No. 403* v. *Fraser.*[48] In that case, the Court approved actions by school officials who disciplined a student speaker for using vulgar language in a speech to a high school assembly. The majority said such language was offensive to some students and inappropriate for the younger members of the student body. In the *Hazelwood* decision, White noted that in *Bethel* the Court had held that "[a] school need not tolerate student speech that is inconsistent with its 'basic educational mission,' even though the government could not censor similar speech outside the school.... We thus recognized that '[t]he determination of what manner of speech in the classroom or in school assembly is inappropriate properly rests with the school board' rather than with the federal courts. It is in this context that [the student editors'] First Amendment claims must be considered."

The minority, as had the appeals court below, found its guidance in *Tinker* v. *Des Moines Independent Community School Dist.*[49] In that case the Court had told school officials they acted improperly in disciplining students for wearing black arm bands to class to protest the Vietnam war. It reminded school officials, in language that has become classic, that First Amendment freedoms do not stop at the schoolhouse gate. School officials can restrict student expression only if the officials can prove that the expression seems likely to disrupt the educational process. In a considerable number of cases, as in this one, lower courts had quoted *Tinker* in upholding the right of students to publish alternative newspapers or to resist censorship of the student press.

The lower court's reliance on *Tinker* in this instance was mistaken, White said. The action approved in *Tinker*—the wearing of black arm bands to protest the nation's involvement in the Vietnam war—had nothing to do with the school's educational mission. The Tinker children were expressing their objections to events outside the school. Their actions were not a part of any lesson being taught in a classroom.

White noted that *Hazelwood* brought an altogether different set of facts to the Court. *Spectrum* was published as part of the work in a class for which the student reporters and editors received grades and academic credit. Whatever else the newspaper was, it was a laboratory production to which the students applied their lessons in journalism. Because *Spectrum* was intimately involved in the educational process, White and his colleagues concluded that they must look to *Bethel,* not *Tinker,* for guidance, because *Bethel,* too, had its origins in a school function—an assembly that was a part of the process of electing student body officers. As the Court saw it, the assembly was part of the educational process,

---

47. *Editor & Publisher,* 16 January 1988, p. 12.
48. 478 U.S. 675, 106 S.Ct. 3159, 92 L.Ed.2d 540 (1986).
49. 393 U.S. 503, 89 S.Ct. 733, 21 L.Ed.2d 731 (1969).

because students were required to attend it. Therefore, school officials could exercise control over what was said in the assembly to make certain that the speech served an educational purpose and was not inappropriate for some members of the audience. Once that line of reasoning was applied to the facts of *Hazelwood,* the next step was inevitable. *Spectrum,* too, was a part of the educational process. As such, it could be controlled by school authorities, like any other part of the educational process, without raising First Amendment questions, as long as the control served a reasonable educational purpose.

White next sought to define how far officials could go before their regulation of content might be considered unreasonable. In doing so, he expanded the scope of the decision to include not only school-sponsored publications, but also "theatrical productions, and other expressive activities that students, parents, and members of the faculty might reasonably perceive to bear the imprimatur of the school." Such activities, White said, are supervised by faculty members "and designed to impart particular knowledge or skills to student participants and audiences." At that point, in the eyes of a majority of the Court, *Spectrum* no longer was a newspaper entitled to full First Amendment protection but was a part of the school's classroom-oriented extracurricular activities over which "[e]ducators are entitled to exercise greater control." The purpose of that control, White said, is "to assure that participants learn whatever lessons the activity is designed to teach, that readers or listeners are not exposed to material that may be inappropriate for their level of maturity, and that the views of the individual speakers are not erroneously attributed to the school."

With respect to a school-sponsored newspaper, White wrote, a school may "disassociate itself," quoting from *Fraser,* "from speech that is, for example, ungrammatical, poorly written, inadequately researched, biased or prejudiced, vulgar or profane, or unsuitable for immature audiences. A school must be able to set high standards for the student speech that is disseminated under its auspices—standards that may be higher than those demanded by some newspaper publishers or theatrical producers in the 'real' world—and may refuse to disseminate student speech that does not meet those standards." Lest there be any doubt about the limits to reasonable control of course-related activities, White added: "A school must also retain the authority to refuse to sponsor student speech that might reasonably be perceived to advocate drug or alcohol use, irresponsible sex, or conduct otherwise inconsistent with 'the shared values of a civilized social order,'" again quoting from *Fraser,* "or to associate the school with any position other than neutrality on matters of political controversy."

One other question had to be answered before the Court could complete its decision. Was the newspaper a public forum? The court of appeals had said it was. If so, school officials could control the time, place, and manner of its publication, but that control would have to be content neutral. The Supreme Court had said so on many occasions. In this instance, there was no doubt that Principal Reynolds had removed the two pages because he objected to their content. He had said so.

That made no difference, White wrote, because the evidence clearly proved that *Spectrum* was not a public forum. Schools are not like public streets or parks, "that 'time out of mind, have been used for purposes of assembly, communicating thoughts between citizens, and discussing public questions.'" Schools can become public forums only if officials open classrooms or auditoriums "for indiscriminate use by the general public." That had not been done with *Spectrum.* Quite to the contrary, the Hazelwood School Board had adopted a policy statement providing that "[s]chool sponsored publications are developed within the adopted curriculum and its educational implications in regular classroom activities." The policy statement paid lip service to the principle of free expression "within the rules of responsible journalism," but also stated that "school officials retained ultimate control over what constitutes 'responsible journalism.'"

The school's Curriculum Guide described the Journalism II course, which produced *Spectrum,* as a "laboratory situation in which the students publish the school newspaper applying skills they have learned in Journalism I." White noted further that Journalism II was taught by a faculty member "who selected the editors of *Spectrum,* scheduled publication dates, decided the number of pages for each issue, assigned story ideas to class members, advised students on the development of their stories, reviewed the use of quotations, edited stories, selected and edited the letters to the editor, and dealt with the printing company." The instructor had final authority over content, but as a matter of routine submitted all copy to Principal Reynolds for review prior to publication.

Nevertheless, a statement of policy published at the beginning of each school year said, "*Spectrum,* as a student-press publication, accepts all rights implied by the First Amendment." Contrary to the position taken by the court of appeals, White concluded that the statement did not reflect an intent to have the newspaper serve as a public forum. All it suggested, he wrote, was "that the administration will not interfere with the students' exercise of those First Amendment rights that attend the publication of a school-sponsored newspaper." White did not attempt to define those rights except to say that because they were exercised within the framework of "a supervised learning experience for journalism students, . . . school officials were entitled to regulate the contents of *Spectrum* in any reasonable manner."

The Court concluded that Principal Reynolds had acted reasonably, out of concern for privacy and for the immature students in the paper's audience, when he removed 2 pages from *Spectrum.* He was simply acting as a teacher to correct students who had not learned their lessons. As White put it, "Reynolds could reasonably have concluded that the students who had written and edited these articles had not sufficiently mastered those portions of the Journalism II curriculum that pertained to the treatment of controversial issues and personal attacks, the need to protect the privacy of individuals whose most intimate concerns are to be revealed in the newspaper, and 'the legal, moral, and ethical restrictions imposed upon journalists within [a] school community' that includes adolescent subjects and readers."

By thus reducing the student newspaper to a classroom exercise, putting it on the same footing with U.S. history tests and English grammar essays, White and his colleagues were able to sum up their decision by asserting, "Accordingly, no violation of First Amendment rights occurred."

Justice Brennan wrote a strong dissent, but stopped short of endorsing absolute freedom for student editors. Standing squarely on the Court's rationale in *Tinker,* he indicated he would uphold a "narrowly tailored" right to censor student expression that "disrupts class work [or] invades the rights of others." He did not find that kind of narrow tailoring in the actions of the school principal. Brennan conceded that some kinds of speech can be "illegitimate." But when such speech is found, those who would eliminate it must use "sensitive tools" to separate it from speech protected by the First Amendment. In Brennan's view that is not what Reynolds did. In an area where precision was called for, "the principal used a paper shredder." Brennan was joined in dissent by Justices Thurgood Marshall and Blackmun. At the time of the decision, the Court had only eight members because Congress and President Reagan were deadlocked over a replacement for Justice Lewis Powell.

The dissenters did not agree that there had been "no violation of First Amendment rights." In their view, *Spectrum* was first a newspaper and only secondarily a classroom exercise. Seeing it as an outlet for student news and opinion, they would have given it First Amendment protection up to the limits established by the Court in *Tinker*. In their view, the majority's reliance on *Fraser* was nothing more than an excuse to justify "brutal censorship." As they saw it, the principal's action "served no legitimate pedagogical purpose." If he had been trying to teach a lesson, Brennan suggested, Reynolds might have chosen "obvious alternatives, such as precise deletions or additions..., rearranging the layout, or delaying publication. Such unthinking contempt for individual rights is intolerable from any state official. It is particularly insidious from one to whom the public entrusts the task of inculcating in its youth an appreciation for the cherished democratic liberties that our Constitution guarantees."

Brennan began his dissent by observing that "[w]hen the young men and women of Hazelwood East High School registered in Journalism II, they expected a civics lesson." The school's statement of policy and the course description promised them an opportunity to express their views and gain "an appreciation of their rights and responsibilities under the First Amendment to the United States Constitution." He rounded out that theme with the last sentence in his dissent: "The young men and women of Hazelwood East expected a civics lesson, but not the one the Court teaches them today."

Despite Brennan's protests, the majority's lesson, reduced to a few words, can be summed up as follows: A public school newspaper published in connection with a class, as about half of them are,[50] is primarily an educational tool and only secondarily a limited exercise in First Amendment freedoms. Therefore, teachers and administrators can change or even delete articles that fall short of the standards of good journalism as long as those changes or deletions serve a reasonable educational purpose. In the Court's view, student victims of administrative censorship can seek relief under the First Amendment only if they can prove that changes in their stories were made for other than educational reasons.

The decision apparently does not affect the considerable number of public school newspapers that are not published as part of the required work in a jour-

---

50. Mark Goodman, director of the Student Press Law Center, Washington, D.C., as quoted in Stephen Wermiel, "High Court to Review School Officials' Authority to Censor Student Newspapers," *Wall Street Journal*, 21 January 1987.

nalism or English course. Nor does it have any effect on student newspapers published by private or parochial schools. Because teachers and officials of such schools are not agents of the state, and because students are under no compulsion to attend such schools, authorities may control private school student publications without raising First Amendment questions.

Immediate reaction to the decision, as reflected in newspaper and magazine articles and in editorial comment, was more favorable than unfavorable. Much of the comment could be summed up in the sentence used by one editorial writer: "Welcome to the real world."[51] The strongest unfavorable reaction came from organizations representing the student press. Jane Kirtley, director of the Reporters Committee for Freedom of the Press, told *Editor & Publisher:* "It's a terrible decision, it's really a disaster. It sends a very clear message to students that they are second-class citizens when it comes to First Amendment rights. It sends a message that First Amendment rights can be taken away at the whim of a court. For the high school press this is a very dark day."[52]

The president of the National School Boards Association, Jonathan T. Howe, took a different position. He said the decision gives school districts responsibility as publishers "no different from the publisher of any other newspaper." In his view, the decision does not limit the rights of student journalists beyond those of others.

Two years later, the Freedom of Information Committee of the American Society of Newspaper Editors (ASNE) concluded that the *Hazelwood* decision "has turned too many high school newspaper staff members and their advisers into journalistic wimps."[53] A survey conducted by the committee found only a small increase in the number of reported instances of direct censorship. But it noted considerable change in the content of public school newspapers as a result of self-censorship. Persons associated with high school publications told the committee that "student staff members and their advisers are carefully steering away from tackling controversies."

There are exceptions. In California, section 48907 of the State Education Code guarantees essentially the degree of freedom for which Brennan argued in his dissent.[54] The section says school officials cannot censor a story unless it is "obscene, libelous, slanderous," or advocates "substantial disruption" of the school.

Soon after the *Hazelwood* decision was handed down, the school board in Clear Creek County, Colorado, unanimously adopted a policy statement recognizing the high school newspaper as a "forum for public expression."[55] The policy gives strong support to freedom of expression and ends as follows:

---

51. Mark Fitzgerald, "Editorials Support Censorship Decision," *Editor & Publisher,* 23 January 1988, p. 11 + .

52. George Garneau, "A 'First Amendment Disaster,'" *Editor & Publisher,* 16 January 1988, p. 12.

53. David Zweifel, "Self-censorship Is Flourishing at High School Newspapers," *The Bulletin,* March 1990, p. 19 + . Zweifel is editor of the *Capital Times* in Madison, Wisconsin, and a member of ASNE's Freedom of Information Committee.

54. Allan Wolper, "California Students Protected from Censorship," *Editor & Publisher,* 6 February 1988, p. 17 + .

55. Mark Fitzgerald, "Colorado School Board Bans High School Newspaper Censorship," *Editor & Publisher,* 1 April 1988, p. 17.

Each year, the student newspaper staff assisted by the sponsors and administrators shall devise an editorial policy to guide its operations. Such policy shall address procedures for handling sensitive and controversial issues, including, but not limited to, obscenity, libel, advocacy of school or community disruption and individuals' right of privacy.

Nevertheless, the Supreme Court's decision in *Hazelwood* stands as an important watershed in First Amendment law. Before it was handed down, it was possible to argue that a public school official's censorship of a student newspaper was in most instances an unacceptable prior restraint. A few courts had ruled that way. It no longer is possible to take that position with respect to public school newspapers published as part of the school's course work. School officials can exercise reasonable control over the content of such newspapers to further an educational purpose. That control can take the form, as it did in *Hazelwood,* of an arbitrary prior restraint.

In the Professional World

For most journalists, advertising copywriters, and public relations practitioners, "sedition" and "censorship" are words found in history books or in the news from countries with governments that permit no political opposition. Professionals in the conventional media, like the overwhelming majority of the American people, take the U.S. political and economic systems as givens.

However, there are a few Americans who take a different view of society. They see the conventional political process as a sham. Politicians seeking to hold or win office make a big fuss every two years, but they offer voters a choice between Tweedledum and Tweedledee. Whether the Democrats or Republicans win, they believe the government will continue to shore up an economic system that oppresses the poor, pollutes the environment, rapes the world's natural resources, and keeps the Third World in bondage. Such believers are few in number in this country, but they argue there can be no change for the better until the people rise up and take control of the land, the factories, the transportation system, and all other private businesses. Only then can the nation's resources be used to give everyone a comfortable living, rather than to enrich the few.

There are enough such opponents of the establishment to organize political parties and qualify for a place on the ballot in most states. In presidential elections in recent times, candidates have represented the Communist, Socialist Workers, Workers World, Libertarian, and Socialist parties. Along with candidates of other unconventional political parties, they have campaigned with little or no attention from television, the wire services, newspapers, and magazines. Most people aren't even aware of the existence of minor party candidates until they enter the voting booth and see the names on the ballots. Thus, candidates who argue that the existing political and economic structure should be scrapped so that a better one can replace it must resort to their own party publications. In one sense, they are talking to themselves, because the usual readers of such publications have already been converted to the cause. Few outsiders are aware of the existence of the *Revolutionary Worker* or other organs published more or less regularly by antiestablishment parties.

This situation raises questions not of law, but of ethics: If the mass media lean so far on the side of safety that they give time and space only to those who work within and support the system, is there a true marketplace of ideas? Milton complained that truth and falsehood could not truly grapple if government used its power to keep some ideas out of the arena. Is the contest any less rigged when media indifference keeps them out? When Eugene McCarthy, a former United States senator and by no stretch of the imagination a radical opponent of the system, ran for president as an independent in 1976, he complained with elegance and wit that he was ignored by the major media. Editors responded that they were merely reflecting the perceived interests of their audience. Everyone knew McCarthy's cause was doomed from the start, so why give it any attention? The circular logic of such a position is evident.

There are those who believe that mainstream journalism has become subversive. This is not a new idea. In Chapter 1, we saw that advocates of the Sedition Act of 1798 believed it necessary to curb a "licentious" press in order to preserve the government. Today, questions are being raised about the adversary stance adopted by most journalists in their reporting of government.

Even more questions were raised during the 1988 presidential campaign, when reporters seemed to spend more time delving into the private lives of the candidates than they did into the issues. One candidate, Gary Hart, was driven out early by allegations that he had an affair with a Florida model. Another, Delaware Senator Joseph Biden, dropped out after newspapers reported that he had borrowed his most effective campaign speech from an English candidate for Parliament and may have cheated to get through law school. Stories about Dan Quayle's Vietnam war-era National Guard service, his grades as a college student, and how he became admitted to law school far overshadowed discussion of his eight years in the Senate. The campaign was further trivialized by the nature of the television advertisements used by the two major parties. Vice President George Bush, the Republican candidate for president, made major issues of the Pledge of Allegiance and of a prisoner furlough system in Massachusetts which had been abused by one prisoner who used his temporary release to commit other crimes. Governor Michael Dukakis repeatedly portrayed his opponent as a friend of the rich and, in the last weeks of the campaign, as an "outright liar." Reporters covering the campaign found themselves being taunted by the crowds who came to hear the candidates. Polls showed that nearly three-fourths of the voters disapproved the tactics used by both sides, and many of them blamed the media for the low level of the campaign.

None of this qualifies as seditious, of course. But it does raise questions about the relationship between the media's coverage of government and the government's ability to function. If the big stories are those that play up the failings of public officials, the flaws in policy, or the shortcomings of the government, what happens to the public trust that is essential to the working of a democratic system? The truth is, no one knows. Nor can one argue that it is not news when a president lies to the people, as Nixon did during the Watergate episode or as Johnson did about events in the Gulf of Tonkin. Nor is there any question that policy should be debated. Few proposals for dealing with problems as persistent and complex as poverty, racial relations, drug abuse, farm debt, and the reduction of armaments are likely to offer perfect solutions. Precisely because such problems, and others, are persistent and complex, their every aspect needs to be studied critically and attacked logically. The question is, what happens to any administration's ability to deal with such problems when its proposals are overwhelmed by instant reaction, much of it originating with those who have vested interests in seeing that the status quo is maintained? One effect may be a form of paralysis that rules out any significant change. Another effect may be a loss of faith in the ability of the system to meet the people's needs. This is indicated by the steady decline over the last two decades of the percentage of eligible voters who go to the polls, especially in nonpresidential years. In recent off-year elections, fewer than half the eligible voters have cast ballots for members of Congress, which may be one reason why the reelection rate in the House is close to 98 percent.

In the legal sense, there is nothing seditious in proclaiming that our emperors aren't wearing clothes. The First Amendment does not require that journalists be cheerleaders for government. One of the most important purposes of that amendment is to prevent government from punishing journalists and others who expose its mistakes and hoot at its follies. For more than twenty-five years, the courts have protected this purpose with zeal. The freedom to criticize government is near or at the absolute level advocated by Meiklejohn and Emerson.

Should that freedom go so far, as some media lawyers argued in the *Morison* case, as to condone the publication of secret photographs stolen from the government? There is no question, of course, that the Soviets knew all there is to know about the nuclear-powered aircraft carrier photographed from a U.S. spy satellite. And it may well be, as Morison hoped, that some members of Congress would be more inclined to vote money for the Navy if they knew such a carrier was being built. The government's immediate fear was that by publishing the photos, *Jane's* might help the Soviets learn more about our surveillance systems, and how to counter them, than they already knew. But beyond that is the larger ethical question: Are journalists, who usually are not fully informed on intelligence questions, qualified to determine when sensitive defense and foreign policy information can be published without harm to the government? Or should they care whether publication will cause harm or not? As U.S. airborne troops were on their way to Panama in December 1989, at least two news organizations were disseminating stories about their departure and their probable destination. Is the story all that matters?

Obviously, such questions have no easy answers. Equally obvious is that some journalists will publish government secrets, as is evidenced by the Pentagon Papers and the *Progressive* cases. Those cases, and others, also tell us that journalists will oppose vigorously any attempt by government to keep them from publishing what they know, government secrets or not. And yet on some occasions journalists have chosen not to publish what they know. Editors of the *New York Times* knew that President Kennedy was planning an invasion of Cuba to attempt the overthrow of Fidel Castro. At the president's request, they chose not to publish it. After the invasion had failed, both the *Times* editors and the president said they wished the newspaper had published the story. Also in the Kennedy era, many reporters knew that the president was a philanderer, and yet the story was not published until many years after his death.

As these episodes suggest, information can be withheld from the people without resort to court orders. At all levels of government, reporters deal with sources who offer them information "off the record" or for background. Sometimes such information is offered in the expectation that the reporter will publish it without identifying the source. But at other times, the reporter and the source agree that the information will not be disclosed to the public. On such occasions, if the information has any value to the public, has not the reporter self-imposed a form of prior restraint?

The "right to know" is a phrase that comes easily to reporters in pursuit of stories that sources are reluctant to disclose. But, as the discussion above suggests, that right, if it exists, is not easy to define. The questions raised by former Chief Justice Burger in his dissent in the Pentagon Papers case will not go away. If there is such a right, who decides what the people are entitled to know? Can we govern ourselves wisely if some information about the functioning of government is withheld? Does it make any difference whether information is withheld because government officials refuse to disclose it or because journalists conclude it does not fit the conventional definitions of news?

FOR REVIEW

1. What is the rationale for a sedition law in time of peace? Is the rationale valid in a democracy?

2. On its face, the First Amendment seems to stand as a barrier only against acts of Congress designed to limit freedom of speech or press. How, then, can courts use that amendment to overrule attempts by state governments to limit expression?

3. With reference to the Supreme Court's decisions in *Dennis, Yates,* and *Brandenberg,* are there circumstances in which advocacy of violent overthrow of the government might be punished? Should there be?

4. In the *Morison* case, Judge J. Harvey Wilkinson, III, wrote that "[t]he First Amendment interest in informed popular debate does not simply vanish at the invocation of the words 'national security.'" But he also noted that in a less than perfect world even democratic governments must keep some things secret from their own people. How can these statements be reconciled?

5. What is the crucial fact question in determining whether someone who threatens to kill the president is likely to be prosecuted and found guilty?

6. Define a prior restraint. How can such action be justified in light of that part of the First Amendment which says, "Congress shall make no law...abridging the freedom of speech, or of the press..."?

7. The Supreme Court's decision in *Near* v. *Minnesota* has been called both a victory and a defeat for the First Amendment. Explain.

8. What elements distinguish the Wisconsin district court's decision in the *Progressive* case from the Supreme Court's decision in the Pentagon Papers case? What questions do the cases raise?

9. Under what circumstances can information be treated as private property? Can such treatment be justified in light of the First Amendment? Why or why not?

10. Analyze the Supreme Court's decision in *Hazelwood School District* v. *Kuhlmeier* with specific reference to First Amendment values. Now, suppose that Justice Brennan's dissent had been the majority opinion of the Court. What difference might it have made in the operation of public high school student newspapers?

PART 2

NEWS MEDIA AND THE LAW

CHAPTER 3

For more than six centuries, courts in England and the United States have recognized the value of reputation—what others think of us. They also have recognized that reputation can be harmed by words—particularly by accusations of
crime, of immorality, or of dishonesty. Therefore, as a matter of common law,
courts permitted victims of harmful words to sue their detractors and recover
sums of money calculated to compensate for the loss of reputation. The great
body of law that grew out of such actions is called the "law of defamation," commonly known as the law of libel and slander. In libel, the harmful words are written, printed, or otherwise put into a form that will endure and be disseminated to
the public. In slander, they are spoken.

In the last half of this century, libel law became of greater concern to journalists and other communicators than any other kind of law. During a twenty-five-

THE LAW OF DEFAMATION: AN OVERVIEW

year period reaching a peak in the mid-1980s, libel actions were brought against the media in record numbers. Ironically, this surge came when the Supreme Court, in a notable series of decisions, was making libel actions more difficult for plaintiffs to win. The Court did so by removing libel involving the media from the realm of common law and making it subject to federal constitutional law. In the first and most important of its libel decisions, *New York Times* v. *Sullivan*[1] in 1964, the Court held that the First Amendment protects the media against libel actions brought by public officials, even when the official has been the victim of a lie. In such instances, the Court said, officials cannot recover damages unless they can prove that the publisher knowingly published a lie or showed reckless disregard for the truth. With that holding, the Court embarked on a course that revolutionized libel law. In later cases, the Court expanded the *New York Times* principle to cover public figures—people who hold no public office but have an influence on events—and, in a modified form, even private individuals.

Although most libel cases involve the mass media, no one involved in communications is exempt from the reach of libel law. In recent years, corporate communicators, advertisers, and book publishers, as well as journalists, have been targets of libel actions. An employer's in-plant bulletin defining sexual harassment and noting that one supervisor had been fired for that offense led to a libel action. A book based on the life of a noted Texas sheriff led to another. Journalists are vulnerable because they are constantly involved in reporting crime and other wrongdoing. They are particularly vulnerable when they attempt to expose those in and out of government who abuse the public trust. An Indiana newspaper was sued for libel because it asked in a news item whether an automobile salvage yard should continue to hold a towing contract with the city after one of its owners was charged with receiving stolen property. The *Washington Post* spent more than five years in litigation when it looked into allegations that an oil company executive had set up his son in a tanker chartering firm that hauled the company's oil and published its findings. In the instances mentioned here, the defendants won, as nine out of ten usually do,[2] but they spent thousands of dollars doing so. Floyd Abrams, a lawyer with extensive experi-

---

1. 376 U.S. 254, 84 S.Ct. 710, 11 L.Ed.2d 686 (1964).
2. Randall P. Bezanson, Gilbert Cranberg, and John Soloski, "Libel and the Press, Setting the Record Straight," *Iowa L.Rev.*, October 1985, pp. 215–33.

ence in defending libel cases, estimated in 1985 that media defendants' legal costs averaged $150,000 in those lawsuits that went to trial.[3] Some media defendants have spent as much as $600,000.[4] Professional communicators can and do buy libel insurance to guard against such costs, but that, too, is expensive.

It is even more expensive, of course, to lose a libel action, and that does happen despite the First Amendment barriers erected by the Supreme Court. Judgments in six figures have been common, and a few of the jury awards have run into the millions of dollars. Many of these were reduced or wiped out on appeal, but the defendants and their insurers still had to pay the legal costs involved. The expenses associated with libel actions are not without consequences. During the 1987 national conference of Investigative Reporters & Editors, several journalists and media lawyers said that publishers' fears of incurring heavy legal costs had a chilling effect on investigative journalism.[5]

There are encouraging signs as this is being written that the chill may be lifting. In 1988, several prominent media lawyers told a Practicing Law Institute seminar that the number of libel actions aimed at the media had significantly declined. Further, of the cases being filed, many more than in previous years were being dismissed in response to defense motions for summary judgment. Such motions are made at an early stage in the proceedings and, when granted, can greatly reduce the defendant's costs. Seminar participants attributed these trends to recent Supreme Court decisions encouraging summary judgment and to indications that after more than two decades of turmoil and uncertainty, the law of libel has at last become settled.[6] This means that courts have come to agreement on the meaning and application of principles announced by the Supreme Court in its twenty or more libel decisions since 1964.

To understand why there was such a long period of uncertainty, we will look in this chapter at a little of the history of defamation law, which began to take form in the common law of England as early as the thirteenth century. That law was transported to the colonies by the English settlers and became a part of the common law of each of the states after the Revolution. Thus, by the middle of this century, the common law of defamation was based on nearly 700 years of court decisions and had been written into the statutes of many states. In practice, the law favored those who believed they had been defamed. When a libel suit was filed, courts assumed that the defamatory assertions were false and that the plaintiff had been harmed by them. The defendant bore the entire burden of proof and could avoid paying damages only by proving one of three defenses: truth, fair

---

3. Floyd Abrams, "Why We Should Change Libel Law," *New York Times Magazine,* 29 September 1985, p. 34 + .

4. "The Cost of Libel: Economic and Policy Implications," a report on a Cost of Libel Conference conducted by the Gannett Center for Media Studies and Columbia University's Center for Telecommunications and Information Studies in June 1986. The report was published by the Gannett Center, 2950 Broadway, New York, N.Y., 10027.

5. M.L. Stein, "The Chilling Effect," *Editor & Publisher,* 4 July 1987, p. 10 + .

6. Mary A. Anderson, "Media Lawyers Are Sanguine about Libel Trends, Less Optimistic about Other Legal Challenges," *Presstime,* December 1988, p. 40.

comment, or privilege. In some instances, even the truth could be libelous if the plaintiff could prove that its publication was motivated by ill will. To be fair, comment had to be based on known facts. Privilege required proof that the alleged libel was a fair and accurate report of a government or judicial proceeding. Frequently, a jury's only task was to determine the size of the award of damages because the publisher could prove none of the defenses.

Long-established principles of law are not easily changed. Thus lower courts were left without landmarks when, with its decision in *New York Times,* the Supreme Court began to turn the assumptions around. In that decision, the Court said public officials who sue the news media for libel have to prove that they were the victims of a false assertion of fact. Further, they have to prove with "clear and convincing" evidence that the assertion was published with "actual malice," which the Court defined as publishing with knowledge of falsity or with reckless disregard for the truth. Within a decade, the Court had extended that burden of proof to public figures. These it defined as people who do not hold public office but who have thrust themselves "into the vortex" of the discussion of a public controversy in an attempt to influence its outcome and who can reasonably be expected to do so. In later decisions, the Court held that even private individuals who sue the mass media for libel must prove falsity and some degree of fault. They also must prove that they were harmed by the alleged libel.

The Supreme Court's decisions have literally stood the old law of libel on its head, if the mass media are the targets of the lawsuit. It has held that truth can never be libelous, no matter what the reason for publishing it. Further, assertions of fact are assumed to be true until the plaintiff proves their falsity. The old defense of fair comment has been pushed aside by the Court's holding that opinion—assertions not subject to being proved true or false—is given absolute protection by the First Amendment. Further, the Court has held that hyperbole—assertions that seem to be factual but are so outlandish no reasonable person would believe them to be such—also are protected. Privilege remains as a defense but has been extended to embrace what is known as a "constitutional privilege." This flows out of *New York Times* v. *Sullivan* and protects the right to report and comment on public issues. Indeed, the constitutional privilege has become the defense of choice in libel actions against the media because it is difficult to overcome.

In *New York Times,* the Court said it brought libel under the protection of the First Amendment to ensure that debate on the performance of public officials is "uninhibited, robust, and wide-open." By reducing the fear of expensive libel actions, the Court reasoned that it would encourage publishers and broadcasters to dig into controversial issues and report their findings.

Many in the news media have done just that. However, because the Court's decision in *New York Times* raised more questions than it answered, such digging also has led to numerous libel actions. Through these actions, courts have forged the answers to such questions as: Who is a public official? How do you prove that someone deliberately published a falsehood? What is reckless disregard for the truth? What makes a person a public figure? What is a public controversy?

How is the line drawn between an opinion protected by the First Amendment and an opinion that implies a false and defamatory assertion of fact? When public officials or public figures are the targets, does "uninhibited, robust" debate mean that anything goes? What about an inference that a prominent clergyman's "first time" was with his mother in an outhouse? How much fault must private individuals prove in order to win a libel action? What standards are applied in determining whether journalists are at fault in reporting derogatory information that later is found to be false?

This chapter, and the next, which should be treated as a unit, summarize the court decisions, many at the Supreme Court level, answering the questions above. We will find that in the process it seemed for awhile that the Court had swept away the old common law, making all libel cases exercises in First Amendment law. But in the mid-1980s, a more conservative Court, led by Chief Justice William H. Rehnquist, signaled a change. The Court held that states may apply most common-law principles to nonmedia cases. This means that public relations practitioners, corporate communicators, and advertising agencies may find themselves caught up in libel cases to which widely divergent principles of law are applied. If an alleged libel arises out of internal corporate communications, or in a narrowly circulated business medium, the communicators involved may find themselves carrying the burdens of proof prescribed by common law. They may have to carry a similar burden if a news release is based on an event deemed not to involve the public interest. But if the communication involves such an interest, First Amendment principles will shift the burden of proof to the plaintiff, as it does for the news media.

We will begin by examining the common law of defamation. We do this in part because it was the only defamation law for many centuries. The early modern decisions, starting with *New York Times,* were written with reference to the common law. Therefore, some grasp of common law is essential to an understanding of them. We start with common law also because the considerable number of journalism students bent on careers in public relations, corporate communications, or advertising may find themselves coping with it. Then we will move to an overview of the great landmark cases through which the Supreme Court used the First Amendment to erect a bulwark between the mass media and libel plaintiffs. The chapter will close with a section summarizing several common-law cases growing out of business communications.

Chapter 4 will take us step by step through the procedures and principles involved in the resolution of a libel action against the media. The chapter expands on the overview in Chapter 3 to show the student how courts apply the precedents established by the Supreme Court.

Despite the decline in the number of libel actions, students should not assume that the study of libel law no longer is important. On the contrary, a knowledge of such law is more important than ever for those who become involved in any kind of public communication. Now that the law seems settled, a media practitioner who blunders into a libel suit through ignorance of the established principles will be an almost certain loser. That conclusion is reinforced by two recent Supreme Court decisions upholding sizable libel judgments against newspapers.

Major Cases

- *Calder* v. *Jones*, 465 U.S. 783, 104 S.Ct. 1482, 79 L.Ed.2d 804 (1984).

- *Dun & Bradstreet* v. *Greenmoss Builders*, 472 U.S. 479, 105 S.Ct. 2939, 86 L.Ed.2d 593 (1985).

- *Garziano* v. *E.I. Du Pont de Nemours & Co.*, 818 F.2d 380 (5th Cir. 1987).

- *Gertz* v. *Robert Welch, Inc.*, 418 U.S. 323, 94 S.Ct. 2997, 41 L.Ed.2d 789 (1974).

- *Keeton* v. *Hustler Magazine*, 465 U.S. 770, 104 S.Ct. 1473, 79 L.Ed.2d 790 (1984).

- *Moncrief* v. *Lexington Herald-Leader*, 807 F.2d 217 (D.C.Cir. 1986).

- *New York Times* v. *Sullivan*, 376 U.S. 254, 84 S.Ct. 710, 11 L.Ed.2d 686 (1964).

- *Rosenbloom* v. *Metromedia, Inc.*, 403 U.S. 29, 91 S.Ct. 1811, 29 L.Ed.2d 296 (1971).

- *Ryder* v. *Time, Inc.*, 557 F.2d 824 (4th Cir. 1976); 3 Med.L.Rptr. 1170 (1977).

THE COMMON LAW OF DEFAMATION

An Overview

In general terms, the law of defamation is concerned with protection of reputation. One dictionary defines the root word, "defame," thus: "to attack the good name of an individual by slander or libel." A usage note goes on to explain that defamation implies the open circulation of an evil report calculated to harm the reputation of an identifiable person. Legal reference works, reflecting decisions of the courts, attempt to be more precise. *Restatement of Torts,* which is prepared by lawyers specializing in tort law and published by the American Law Institute,[7] says: "A communication is defamatory if it tends to so harm the reputation of another as to lower him in the estimation of the community or to deter third persons from associating or dealing with him."

The problem with any definition is that it cannot anticipate the variety of ways in which allegedly defamatory words will confront the unsuspecting communicator. The *Restatement's* definition is followed by five paragraphs of elaboration that can be boiled down to another principle: Any communicator who feels com-

---

7. *Restatement of the Law, Second, Torts,* as adopted and promulgated by the American Law Institute, Washington, D.C., 19 May 1976 (St. Paul, Minn.: American Law Institute Publishers, 1977), vol. 3, § 559, p. 156.

pelled to report in tangible form or in a broadcast that an identifiable person or business firm may be involved in illegal, unethical, immoral, or dishonest activity risks being sued for defamation. This does not mean that such reports should not be made. The public needs to know when individuals, particularly those in government or other influential positions, seem to be doing wrong. An employer considering an applicant for a position has a right to know if a previous employer found that candidate untrustworthy. Potential customers are entitled to know if a business firm is selling shoddy or dangerous products or providing inferior service.

Long ago, courts recognized those needs and established defenses that could be used against defamation suits. However, when a libel suit was filed, courts assumed that the offending language was false and that if it made certain particularly serious charges, such as accusation of a crime, the victim had been harmed. Defendants carried the burden of justifying the defamation and could do so only by convincing juries that one or more of three options protected them:

1. The assertions at issue were true. This option was sometimes difficult because what seems true to one person may not seem so to another.

2. The assertions were part of a fair and accurate account of a trial, of legislative debate, or of some other government action or report. This was the defense of qualified privilege. Courts also have recognized a qualified privilege protecting the right of business firms to exchange essential, if sometimes defamatory, information with each other and with their employees.

3. The assertions were fair comment on the actions of someone such as a performer or author who had invited public attention. Comment was considered fair only if it was based on facts either stated in the article or commonly known.

Defendants who could not prove one of those defenses to a jury's satisfaction were required to pay whatever damages the jurors considered appropriate, even if there was no evidence that the plaintiff had been harmed. None of this had anything to do with the First Amendment, because the most important assumption of all was that libel, like obscenity, lay outside the realm of protected speech.

Common law recognized two kinds of defamation, *libel* and *slander*. Libel is defamation stated in a tangible medium—in print, in a photograph, or in some other form with a capacity to endure. Slander rises out of spoken words. Because libel usually exists in a medium capable of being widely circulated, courts applying common-law principles treated it seriously. In contrast, slander was taken much more lightly by the courts. Slanderous words usually were heard by relatively few persons, and the defamatory sting of the statement might soon be dissipated. Therefore, slander victims were required to prove that they had suffered some harm before they could collect damages.

With the advent of radio in the 1920s, and its capacity to carry harmful words to a large audience, the legal distinctions between libel and slander began to blur, although a few slander cases continue to arise in the business world. Today, courts treat an action in defamation directed at a radio or television station as they would a libel suit directed at a newspaper, magazine, or book publisher. Such differences as there are concern the question of fault. A broadcaster is more likely to be found at fault for a libel written into a script or found in a previously taped segment of a newscast than for defamatory remarks that come out of the blue from a caller to a radio talk show.

Common law divided libel into two kinds, libel per se and libel *per quod*. Once there was a significant difference in the way courts treated them. Certain classes of words are considered harmful on their face—that is, per se. These include accusations of crime. To say that someone is a thief, a rapist, a drug pusher, or a murderer means that person will be shunned by most of society. Courts in England established seven centuries ago that it is libelous on its face to accuse women and men of immoral behavior. Despite the relaxation of moral standards, it still is. It also is libelous per se to label a person as mentally ill or as the victim of a "loathsome disease." The nature of such diseases has changed with the times, but there is little doubt that a person wrongfully identified as a victim of AIDS would have a cause of action. Other words considered harmful on their face include assertions that a physician is a "quack," a lawyer is a "shyster," that a priest repeats secrets heard in the confessional, or that a business firm cheats its customers or can't pay its bills. There are circumstances under which all the allegations listed above, and others equally serious, can safely be published. Because jurors are likely to see such allegations as particularly harmful, their appearance in copy being prepared for publication or broadcast should be treated like a flashing red light calling for the utmost caution before proceeding.

A libel *per quod* is not evident on its face. Indeed, the language may seem harmless, and to many persons it will be. But to those who know what the unstated facts are, the language is defamatory. Under the common-law rules of libel *per quod,* the victim had to prove that others knew the circumstances that made the apparently harmful assertion defamatory and that he had suffered a loss of reputation as a consequence. In one classic case, a court found libel *per quod* in a false newspaper report that a woman had given birth. Some knew she had only recently been married. West Virginia's Supreme Court found libel in headlines reporting that a candidate for governor was "enriched" by the sale of land near a new national park.[8] The candidate had done nothing wrong, and the stories made that clear, but the court said the headlines would evoke harmful comparisons with a former governor who had been found guilty of corruption because he had used his office to enrich himself.

Courts still use the terms libel per se and libel *per quod* in their decisions. Judges are not likely to dismiss cases based on assertions that are libelous on their face. The distinction also may have some influence on jurors assessing damages against a losing defendant. Journalists who have no problem identifying a potential libel per se need to keep up with the news to avoid being tripped up by a libel *per quod*. A business-page story reporting a savings and loan executive's

---

8. Sprouse v. Clay Communications, 211 S.E.2d 674 (W. Va. 1975).

investments in race horses and an Arizona resort takes on another cast if her institution previously has appeared on a list of troubled thrifts.

Courts consider libel a *tort*—that is, an injury or wrong, other than violation of a contract, committed with or without force, against the person or property of another. The usual remedy is a lawsuit for damages. Thus, libel generally is a private matter, to be resolved by the parties involved. However, several states still have criminal libel statutes in their codes. Such statutes make it a crime to libel individuals, including public officials in some instances. The rationale is that the state has an interest in preventing the dissemination of false statements that may provoke violence. Such laws are rarely invoked and in some instances have been held to violate the Constitution; as a result, some states recently have repealed their criminal libel statutes.

In the normal course of events, people who believe they have been defamed have three options. They can do nothing, hoping that whatever damage has been done to their reputations will disappear in time. They can ask the offending medium to run a correction or let them tell their side of the story. Or they can hire a lawyer and commence what is called a "civil action." Only if they do the latter—and win in court or reach a settlement—can they be compensated for the harm to their reputation.

Beginning a Libel Case

Six elements basic to the filing of a libel action under common and statute law remain valid. Persons who feel they have been wronged by the publication of a libel must prove (1) publication, (2) identification, and (3) defamation if they file suit. (4) Libel plaintiffs must file suit within a fixed time or find their action barred by what is called a "statute of limitations." (5) The action must be brought in a court that has jurisdiction over the defendant. (6) Finally, in a majority of the states, libel defendants can seek to mitigate damages by publishing a retraction or correction of the defamatory language. Statute law in a few states requires libel plaintiffs to seek a retraction from the offending publisher as a condition to filing suit.

Publication

In virtually all libel actions, *publication* is proved by a copy of the offending item. This can be a certified copy of a newspaper article or editorial, the transcript of a broadcast, or a photograph, if the alleged libel was pictorial in nature. It is assumed from the fact of publication that someone read, heard, or saw the offending words or image. The case reports contain a few instances in which publishers tried to argue that, owing to the paper's poor circulation, no one probably saw the story. Such arguments are rejected. At law, publication is proved if the circumstances suggest that anyone other than the author of the libel and its target saw the offending words. Cases have been based on letters typed by a secretary and seen otherwise only by the person who dictated the letter and its recipient, who was the subject of the libel. At the minimum, it takes only three people to lay the groundwork for a libel case: the libeler, the target of the libel, and a third person who read the libel or heard it broadcast by a radio or television station. Therefore, the fact of publication is not likely to be at issue in a case involving the news media.

Identification

Sometimes the element of *identification* may be at issue. Occasionally, a reporter will write a story in the belief that there can be no libel if no names are mentioned. And, on occasion, reporters have found the hard way that they were wrong. A Hearst newspaper columnist lost a suit based on an item reporting gossip in Palm Beach of an affair between the wife of a wealthy pillar of society and a former FBI agent who had become a lawyer. No names were mentioned, but there was only one lawyer in Palm Beach who had been an FBI agent and who mixed with the upper levels of society. He won a judgment for $60,000.[9]

Libel cases sometimes can result from too little identification. For instance, at the time of Watergate, when several lawyers on the White House staff were found guilty of misconduct, *Time* magazine published an article on unprofessional conduct by lawyers in general. One lawyer whose conduct was described by the article was Richard R. Ryder, who practiced in Virginia. He had been accused of hiding evidence for a client suspected of dealing in narcotics. Following its usual editorial style, *Time* omitted the middle initial and did not name the town in which Richard R. Ryder practiced.

Ryder v. *Time, Inc.,* 557 F.2d 824 (4th Cir. 1976); 3 Med.L. Rptr. 1170 (1977).

Richard J. Ryder, who also practiced law in Virginia, sued *Time* for libel, asserting that he had suffered embarrassment because some persons thought he was the subject of the article. Eventually, *Time* won the case, but the magazine was put to the expense of defending itself in more than three years of litigation that reached the federal appeals level. The action ended when a federal magistrate held that *Time* could not reasonably be expected to check the roster of lawyers in Virginia to make certain there was only one Richard Ryder.

Thus, win or lose, mistakes in identification in connection with libelous assertions can be costly. To avoid them, reporters should obtain precise identification of anyone mentioned in a story involving wrongdoing. This should include exact spelling of first and last names—some Smiths spell it Smythe—middle initials, age, address, and occupation. This is especially important if the last name is common in the community. The telephone directory in even a medium-sized city may show two or three Ralph Johnsons, Raymond Johnsons, or Robert Johnsons. Under such circumstances, to report simply that Ralph Johnson was arrested for as-

---

9. Hope v. Hearst Consolidated Publications, 294 F.2d 681 (2d Cir. 1961).

sault is to invite, at the least, an outraged telephone call from the Ralph Johnsons who weren't arrested and their families.

Defamation

In many libel cases, the decisive question is whether the language at issue is defamatory; that is, whether it is of such a nature as to lower the plaintiff in the estimation of others. At an early stage of the proceedings, a judge must look at the evidence and decide as a matter of law whether defamation is present.

As we have seen, at common law, certain kinds of allegations were considered libelous per se—so damaging that they were held to be defamatory on their face. Therefore, if the item in question accused the plaintiff of committing a serious crime, the judge's decision was easy to make. Defamation was present. The case could proceed, and its outcome would depend on the proofs the defendant could muster.

The judge's decision is also easy if the item in question clearly is not defamatory. There are occasions in which people feel highly insulted by accusations that strike others as reasonable. For instance, the case reports include instances in which persons sued because they were identified as police informants. Courts have held that such accusations are not defamatory because it is the duty of every person who has knowledge of crime to report it to the police.

The problems come with statements that do not make clearly defamatory assertions but are not clearly harmless. Suppose, for instance, that an officeholder has been accused of neglecting his duties. How is "neglect" defined? At what point does an observer's "neglect" become the officeholder's wise discretion? Do the facts point to a failure to perform duties required by law or simply to a difference of opinion as to what the officeholder should have done? In such instances, the judge may decline to rule on whether defamation is present. That question would be reserved for trial where it would be decided by the "trier of fact," usually a jury, in the light of the evidence presented and argued by both sides. If the trial were by jury, the judge would instruct the jurors to consider the words at issue in their ordinary meanings and determine for themselves whether they would lower the plaintiff in the esteem of the community.

Two states, Illinois[10] and Ohio,[11] follow what is called the "innocent construction" rule. If a statement is capable of two meanings, one defamatory and the other not, the rule requires that the innocent meaning prevail. In making a decision, the judge must consider a statement as a whole, give the words their natural and obvious meanings, and reach a conclusion that an appellate court would find reasonable.

In private libel actions, of the kind in which business firms can be involved, the assumption is that defamatory assertions are false. But if the news media, or matters of public interest, are involved, the plaintiff must prove that the assertions at issue are false. Discussion of that proof will be found in the next chapter.

---

10.   Chapski v. Copley Press, 442 N.E.2d 195 (Ill. 1982).
11.   Yeager v. Local Union 20, 6 Ohio St.3d 369, 453 N.E.2d 666 (1983).

Statutes of Limitations and the Single Publication Rule

All states have statutes of limitations, which establish time periods within which tort actions must be brought. These limits are coupled in twenty-eight states, the District of Columbia, and Puerto Rico[12] with what is known as the "single publication rule" to establish strict time frames within which libel actions must be brought.

The single publication rule, in effect, permits only one libel action to be based on a defamatory article or broadcast. This is particularly important if the defamation has occurred in a publication that circulates in two or more states or in a radio or television network program. The rule assumes that all damages, no matter where suffered, can be recovered in a single action. Further, a judgment in any one jurisdiction bars any other actions between the same plaintiff and defendant in all other jurisdictions.[13]

Under statutes of limitations, a libel action must be filed within a specified period, which varies from one to three years, depending on the state.[14]

Time limits established by statute are enforced strictly. Usually, the limit is based on the date on which the matter at issue was made public, rather than when it became known to the plaintiff. That distinction was decisive in *Morgan* v. *Hustler Magazine,* decided by a federal district court in Ohio in 1987.[15] In December 1975, the magazine published photographs of Donda R. Morgan which were made in 1973 when she was a fashion model. Although one of the photographs appeared on the front cover, Morgan did not learn about the publication until January 1984. She filed suit against the magazine a year later. *Hustler's* lawyer filed a motion to dismiss, citing Ohio's one-year statute of limitations for libel actions. Morgan's lawyer argued that the limit should be tolled from the date of the discovery of the alleged libel rather than from the date of publication. He cited rulings in medical malpractice cases in which courts have held that the right to file suit is measured from the patient's discovery of the alleged harm. A few states

---

12. Compiled from *50-State Survey 1987,* Henry R. Kaufman, editor (New York: Libel Defense Resource Center, 1987). The states are Alabama, Arizona, Arkansas, California, Colorado, Connecticut, Florida, Georgia, Idaho, Illinois, Kansas, Louisiana, Minnesota, Mississippi, Missouri, Nebraska, New Hampshire, New Jersey, New Mexico, New York, North Dakota, Ohio, Oklahoma, Oregon, Pennsylvania, Tennessee, Texas, and Virginia. In California, Illinois, and New York, courts have held that a paperback version of a book originally published in hard covers is a separate publication. Only Hawaii and Montana have rejected the single publication rule. In other states, neither statute nor case law has had occasion to address the question.
13. Restatement § 577A, Comment a (1971).
14. States with a one-year limit are in the majority. They are Arizona, California, Colorado, Georgia, Illinois, Kansas, Kentucky, Louisiana, Maryland, Michigan, Mississippi, Nebraska, New Jersey, New York, North Carolina, Ohio, Oklahoma, Oregon, Pennsylvania, Rhode Island, Tennessee, Texas, Utah, Virginia, West Virginia, and Wyoming. The District of Columbia and Puerto Rico also have a one-year limit.

    A two-year limit is in effect in Alabama, Alaska, Connecticut, Delaware, Florida, Hawaii, Idaho, Indiana, Iowa, Maine, Minnesota, Missouri, Montana, Nevada, North Dakota, South Carolina, South Dakota, Washington, and Wisconsin.

    A three-year limit is in effect in Arkansas, Massachusetts, New Hampshire, New Mexico, and Vermont.
15. 653 F.Supp. 711 (N.D. Ohio 1987).

also permit the statute of limitations in libel actions to be tolled from the date of discovery. The district court held there was nothing to show that Ohio courts had applied the discovery rule to libel actions. Rather, Ohio courts had adopted the single publication rule, meaning that the cause of action began with the date the magazine first reached the public. Because that had happened more than nine years before Morgan filed her lawsuit, the court ruled that the statute of limitations barred her action. The court dismissed the case.

Where Libel Actions May be Filed

In the overwhelming majority of libel actions, the lawsuit is filed in a state court having jurisdiction over the community in which the defendant is located. But, as a result of two Supreme Court cases, publishers of magazines and national newspapers, or owners of broadcasting networks, may find themselves being sued in state or federal courts far from their headquarters. This can add considerably to the cost of defending against a libel action.

When the plaintiff and defendant in a libel action are domiciled in different states, the plaintiff can file suit in either state or federal courts. Libel plaintiffs suing media defendants have access to federal courts because such actions raise First Amendment questions. However, federal courts are required to apply pertinent state law to such cases as long as the law does not conflict with constitutional principles established by the Supreme Court.

As a result of the Court's decisions, the plaintiff's lawyer also may have a choice as to the state in which to bring suit. That choice is controlled by state "long-arm" statutes and by U.S. Supreme Court decisions interpreting the due process clause of the Fourteenth Amendment. Long-arm statutes define the rules governing court jurisdiction over civil actions involving parties who live or have their headquarters in different states. In figurative terms, the statutes define how far a state court can reach out to gather in a distant defendant.

The controlling Supreme Court cases are *Calder* v. *Jones* and *Keeton* v. *Hustler Magazine*. A third case, *Moncrief* v. *Lexington Herald-Leader,* decided by the U.S. Court of Appeals for the District of Columbia Circuit, defines procedures protecting news agencies with Washington bureaus.

Calder v. *Jones,* **465 U.S. 783, 104 S.Ct. 1482, 79 L.Ed.2d 804 (1984).**

In *Calder,* Shirley Jones, an actress living in southern California, was the target of a story in the *National Enquirer*. The weekly tabloid is published from offices in Florida and has a circulation of more than 4 million. In 1979, when the article appeared, almost 600,000 copies were sold in California each week, more than in any other state. When Jones decided to sue the weekly for libel, her attorney filed the action in a California Superior Court, a trial court in the county in which she lived. The *Enquirer*'s lawyer asked that the suit be dismissed on the ground that the court had no jurisdiction over the weekly's employees because she lived and worked in Florida. The trial court granted the motion, but the California Court of Appeal reversed. The Supreme Court accepted the case for review and affirmed the reversal, thus holding that the lawsuit could proceed in California.

The Supreme Court based its decision on two cases interpreting the Fourteenth Amendment's due process clause.[16] In those cases the Court held that the clause "permits personal jurisdiction over a defendant in any State with which the defendant has 'certain minimum contacts...such that the maintenance of the suit does not offend "traditional notions of fair play and substantial justice."'"

In this instance, the Court found sufficient "contacts" in the *Enquirer*'s circulation in California and in the actions of a reporter and his editor, neither of whom had visited the state in preparing the story. But the Court said both should have known that the story would have a "potentially devastating effect" on Jones.

In *Keeton,* the Court stretched the idea of "minimum contacts" still further, holding that a libel plaintiff who lived in New York could file suit in New Hampshire against a magazine published by an Ohio

Keeton v. _Hustler_ _Magazine,_ 465 U.S. 770, 104 S.Ct. 1473, 79 L.Ed.2d 790 (1984).

corporation with its principal place of business in California. The plaintiff, Kathy Keeton, first filed suit against *Hustler* magazine and its publisher, Larry Flynt, in Ohio. The case was dismissed because that state's one-year statute of limitations had expired. By the time that happened, it was too late to file in California or New York or, indeed, in any other state except New Hampshire, which then had a six-year limit for filing libel actions. It since has been reduced to three. When Keeton filed suit in a U.S. district court in that state, the court ruled the due process clause forbade use of New Hampshire's long-arm statute to reach across the country and acquire personal jurisdiction over Flynt and his magazine. The judge concluded that the New Hampshire contacts of both parties were less than minimal. Keeton's only association with New Hampshire was that her name appeared as an editor on the masthead of a magazine with a limited circulation in the state. *Hustler*'s contacts were limited to the circulation of 10,000 to 15,000 copies each month. The U.S. Court of Appeals for the First Circuit affirmed, holding that "the New Hampshire tail is too small to wag so large an out-of-state dog."[17]

A unanimous Supreme Court disagreed. Pointing to the effect of the single publication rule, the Court said that New Hampshire's then extra-long statute of limitations afforded Keeton an opportunity to redress whatever harm the *Hustler* story had done to her reputation in her home state of New York or anywhere else that she might be known. Further, it held that *Hustler*'s sales in the state, however few, were the product of an effort on the magazine's part to reach and have an effect on New Hampshire readers. That was enough to satisfy the "minimum contacts" requirement.

Keeton and *Calder* serve notice that magazines, national newspapers, and network broadcasters can be sued for libel in any state in which they do some part of their business or have enough of an audience to meet the "minimum contacts" requirement of the due process clause of the Fourteenth Amendment.

---

16. Milliken v. Meyer, 311 U.S. 457, 61 S.Ct. 339, 85 L.Ed. 278 (1940), and International Shoe Co. v. Washington, 326 U.S. 310, 66 S.Ct. 154, 90 L.Ed. 95 (1945).
17. 682 F.2d 33 (1st Cir. 1982).

Kathy Keeton leaves the U.S. district court in Concord, New Hampshire, with her lawyer after winning a $2 million libel judgment against Larry Flynt, publisher of *Hustler* magazine. Keeton, publisher of *Omni* magazine, was able to file the suit because the Supreme Court ruled that *Hustler* did enough business in New Hampshire to give that state, with its then six-year statute of limitations, jurisdiction over the lawsuit. Shorter limits for filing suit had expired in all other states. (UPI/Bettmann Newsphotos)

One significant exception applying to news organizations with Washington correspondents needs to be noted. The District of Columbia's long-arm statute contains language that in most instances protects correspondents and their employers from being sued for libel in District courts.[18] That language was upheld by the U.S. Court of Appeals for the District of Columbia Circuit in a libel action brought in the District against the *Lexington Herald-Leader,* a Kentucky newspaper. The paper's Washington correspondent had written a highly critical story about an attorney employed by the Department of Labor.

Moncrief v. *Lexington Herald-Leader,* 807 F.2d 217 (D.C.Cir. (1986).

When the attorney sued for libel, the *Herald-Leader* moved to dismiss, arguing that the U.S. District Court for the District of Columbia had no jurisdiction over the newspaper. The attorney argued that the court did have jurisdiction because

18. D.C. Code Ann. § 13–423 (1981).

the newspaper met the minimum contacts standard defined in *Keeton* and *Calder;* the newspaper had a full-time Washington correspondent and sold twenty-two mail subscriptions to residents of the District. The district court dismissed the suit, and the appellate court affirmed, relying on the news-gathering exception in the District's long-arm statute. The appellate court noted with approval an earlier decision holding that "the mere collection of news" in Washington for publication elsewhere is not "a doing of business" in the city.[19]

Retraction

In a majority of the states, a news medium's honest confession of a defamatory error may lower an award of damages, but it can't ward off a libel suit if the plaintiff is determined to go forward. Such a confession is called a "retraction." In fourteen states,[20] courts have held as a matter of common law that a full and prompt retraction, given prominent display in the offending medium, can be introduced at trial and considered by the jury in fixing the award of damages. In twenty-five states,[21] legislatures have enacted statutes defining the nature and effect of a retraction. Tennessee appears on both lists because its courts have recognized a common-law right to introduce a retraction in mitigation of damages and it has a statute that prohibits an award of punitive damages if a proper retraction is made.

Retraction statutes vary. At one end of the scale, they provide only, as in common law, that a proper retraction can be used in an attempt to lower the award of damages. At the other end of the scale, Indiana, Mississippi, North Carolina, South Dakota, and Wisconsin require plaintiffs to seek a retraction before filing a libel suit. North Dakota has a similar requirement unless the publication involves "the libel of a female." Commonly, the statutes limit plaintiffs to recovery of actual or general damages if a timely and complete retraction is made. Actual damages are defined in some statutes as provable financial loss. General damages include compensation for such intangibles as humiliation and embarrassment, or being shunned in the community.

Editors, and lawyers who advise them, differ on publication of retractions. If the alleged libel involves a simple mistake in fact resulting from a misunderstanding, or reliance on an uninformed or malicious source, most editors and lawyers would agree that a retraction be made. However, the stories most likely to lead to a libel suit are the result of complex investigations into the conduct of public officials or public figures. Or they grow out of the coverage of highly charged disagreements over public policy. In such instances, a retraction could lead only to further trouble. The *Moncrief* case, discussed in the preceding section, illustrates the problem. The *Herald-Leader*'s story covered many facets of the lawyer's work. Some close observers of that work clearly didn't believe that Moncrief was a very good lawyer. Others had a better opinion of him. Readers would have to consider the story as a

---

19. Neely v. Philadelphia Inquirer Co., 62 F.2d 873 (D.C.Cir. 1932).
20. Arizona, Arkansas, Colorado, Illinois, Kansas, Louisiana, Maryland, Massachusetts, New York, Ohio, Pennsylvania, South Carolina, Tennessee, and Washington.
21. Alabama, California, Connecticut, Idaho, Indiana, Iowa, Kentucky, Maine, Michigan, Minnesota, Mississippi, Montana, Nebraska, Nevada, North Carolina, North Dakota, Oklahoma, Oregon, South Dakota, Tennessee, Texas, Utah, Virginia, West Virginia, and Wisconsin.

whole and come to their own conclusions. Moncrief naturally objected to those passages quoting his critics. If he had asked for a retraction, what could the newspaper retract? Clearly, it would not be in the paper's interest to say that the sources used by the reporter did not say what they were quoted as saying. Nor would it be in the paper's interest to say that the sources were quoted accurately, but the reporter and editor didn't believe the harsh things said about Moncrief. In such instances, lawyers will advise against a retraction.

At this point, we have established the grounds on which a libel suit can be based. An action begins with publication of a false and defamatory assertion of fact about an identifiable living person, corporation, association, or other kind of business firm. Small groups of people also can be libeled by statements that seem to defame each member of the group. Publication takes place when the defamatory assertion is seen by someone other than the publisher or the target of the assertion. In most states, the date of publication marks the beginning of a period, running from one year in a majority of the states to three years, within which a suit must be filed. The action must be brought in a court with jurisdiction over the defendant. That does not mean that the suit must be filed in the community in which the defendant lives, or, in the case of a business firm, has its headquarters. The Supreme Court has held that an action can be filed in a jurisdiction in which the defendant does enough business to establish the "minimum contact" required by the due process clause of the Fourteenth Amendment. An exception has been made for news organizations with correspondents in the District of Columbia. In a few states, a libel suit cannot be filed until the subject of the alleged defamation has asked the publisher for a retraction. In most states, publication of a retraction can reduce an award of damages.

At common law, a plaintiff whose lawsuit survived the procedures above was well on the way to a judgment. This is still true of libel actions involving forms of business communications that are deemed not in the public interest. These could include statements damaging to a firm's credit rating, negative recommendations for former employees, statements of the reasons for firing an employee, or disparagement of a competitor. In such instances, the common law imposes the burden of proof on the defendant to justify the allegedly defamatory assertions. This can be done by proving truth, privilege, or fair comment, which will be discussed later.

THE FIRST AMENDMENT AND THE LAW OF LIBEL

The Constitutional Defense: *New York Times* v. *Sullivan*

In 1908, Kansas was the first state to apply the *public principle* to libel actions.[22] Under this principle, which was adopted by a few other states, public

---

22. Coleman v. MacLennan, 98 P. 281 (Kans. 1908).

officeholders were required to carry a heavier burden of proof than that carried by other libel plaintiffs. The public principle was grounded in the belief that persons who seek and hold public office ought to expect searching examination of their public actions. Such people enjoy advantages that private citizens do not, including access to the media, where they can respond to criticism. Courts in the public principle states reasoned, therefore, that it ought to be more difficult for public persons to win libel actions.

In 1964, the Supreme Court of the United States accepted an appeal by the *New York Times* and ruled that the First Amendment requires all state and federal courts to apply the public principle to libel suits brought by public officials. With its decision in *New York Times* v. *Sullivan,* it federalized important elements of libel law, moving them out of the realm of common law and state statute and into the realm of constitutional law.

New York Times v. *Sullivan,* 376 U.S. 254, 84 S.Ct. 710, 11 L.Ed.2d 686 (1964).

At the same time, the Supreme Court literally revolutionized libel law, shifting most of the burden of proof from the defendant onto the plaintiff, at least in actions involving the news media. The importance of the case cannot be overstated. An understanding of the present status of libel law must begin with mastery of *New York Times* v. *Sullivan.*

The case was one of the byproducts of the civil rights movement that swept the South in the late 1950s. Racial segregation was the rule in all parts of the United States at that time, but it reached its extremes in the former slave states stretching from Virginia to Louisiana. In those states, law as well as custom forced blacks to live separated from whites.

About 1955, this segregated system came under challenge from blacks seeking the right to do such things as sit where they pleased in city buses, or eat at lunch counters in downtown department stores. In 1960, whites used violence against demonstrations by black students at Alabama State College in Montgomery who were seeking to integrate such public facilities. In March of that year, an advertisement appeared in the *New York Times* appealing for financial support for the embattled students of Alabama State. The ad was signed by sixty-four persons, white and black, many of them prominent in public affairs, religion, trade unions, and the performing arts. Headed "Heed Their Rising Voices," the ad said in part:

> In Montgomery, Ala., after students sang "My Country, 'tis of Thee" on the State Capitol steps, their leaders were expelled from school, and truckloads of police armed with shotguns and tear gas ringed the Alabama State College campus. When the entire student body protested to state authorities by refusing to register, their dining hall was padlocked in an attempt to starve them into submission....
>
> Again and again, the Southern violators have answered Dr. [Martin Luther] King's peaceful protests with intimidation and violence. They have bombed his home almost killing his wife and child. They have assaulted his person. They have arrested him seven times—for "speeding," "loitering," and similar "offenses." And now they have charged him with "perjury"—a felony under which they could imprison him for *10 years.*

Attorneys representing Police Commissioner L. B. Sullivan, one of three elected commissioners of the city of Montgomery, wrote the *Times* asserting that those two paragraphs libeled their client. In accordance with Alabama law, they asked for a retraction, a published admission from the *Times* that it had published untruths. The *Times* responded by asking the attorneys to point to specific libelous passages in the advertisement. Sullivan's response was to file a lawsuit in a Montgomery court.

At trial, Sullivan argued that the ad's general references to "police" pointed a finger at him because he supervised the police force. Therefore, he reasoned, the ad accused him of being responsible for padlocking the dining hall in order to starve the students into submission. And, since arrests ordinarily are made by police, it accused him of arresting Dr. King seven times, perhaps illegally, thus making Sullivan one of the "Southern violators." Further, he said, the ad made it look as though he encouraged the violence directed at Dr. King and his family. Six witnesses testified that they had read the ad and concluded it was referring to Sullivan in a derogatory way.

Other witnesses testified that much of the detail in the offending paragraphs was false. The students had not sung "America"; they had sung "The Star-Spangled Banner." Only nine students were expelled, but not for leading the demonstration at the Capitol. Only part of the student body had protested the expulsions, not by refusing to register, but by boycotting classes for a single day. The campus dining hall was not padlocked at any time. The only students who may have been refused service were those who did not have meal tickets, and there were few of them. Police were deployed near the campus in large numbers, but at no time did they ring the campus.

Nor were those the only errors. Dr. King had been arrested four times, not seven. Although he claimed he had been assaulted when he was arrested for loitering outside a courtroom, one of the officers involved denied at the libel trial that there had been an assault. Dr. King's house had indeed been bombed, but that had happened before Sullivan became police commissioner. No evidence ever implicated police in the bombing. Three of Dr. King's four arrests also took place before Sullivan's election. Dr. King was indicted on two counts of perjury, for which the maximum term was five years, not ten, but he had been acquitted on both. Sullivan testified that he had had nothing to do with either charge.

Clippings in the *Times's* own files showed that some of the allegations made in the ad were false. The manager of the newspaper's Advertising Acceptability department testified that he had not checked the files because the ad had been prepared by a reputable agency. It was accompanied by a letter from A. Philip Randolph, president of the Brotherhood of Sleeping Car Porters and a New York City resident, certifying that all the persons whose names appeared in the ad had given their permission. The manager said he knew and respected Randolph. He said he had approved the ad for publication because he knew nothing to cause him to believe it was false, and because it bore the endorsement of "a number of people who are well known and whose reputations [he] had no reason to question."

The jury found that Sullivan had been libeled and awarded him a judgment for $500,000. The Alabama Supreme Court affirmed. In light of the facts as presented in court it had no other course. The decision was in accord with the law of libel as it was at that time. Sullivan and his witnesses had proved the only issue in doubt—identification. Once that was established, he stood accused of condoning, if not participating in, a series of felonies. Such accusations were libelous on their face. Nor, according to the law of the time, did the *Times* have any workable defenses. The proven errors in fact undercut any attempt to establish truth, privilege, that is, that the ad was a fair and accurate report of materials found in official records, or fair comment. The only question left for the jury was to establish the degree of harm to Sullivan's reputation and, hence, the size of the award.

The outcome of the suit in the state courts struck not only at the *Times,* but at other news media. The *Times* faced eleven other libel suits in Alabama courts in which plaintiffs were seeking more than $5 million. The Columbia Broadcasting System was defending five libel suits in Southern states in which plaintiffs were asking for nearly $2 million. Most of these suits were based on news coverage of the racial integration movement. Against that background the Supreme Court agreed to review the case and reversed unanimously.

Justice William J. Brennan, Jr., wrote the Court's opinion. He was joined by four others. From the outset, he took the position that comment on the public conduct of public officials is protected by the First Amendment. His clear intent was to take the case out of the realm of Alabama's common and statute law, where the *Times* could not win, onto the higher ground of constitutional law, where, the decision would prove, it could. In the process, the Court made four fundamental changes in legal principles.

The Protection of Editorial Advertising

The first change in traditional law was made to counter Sullivan's contention that "Heed Their Rising Voices" was not protected by the First Amendment because it was a paid advertisement. In making this point, Sullivan's lawyers relied on the Supreme Court's decision in *Valentine* v. *Chrestensen* in 1942.[23] In that case, in which the Court held that the owner of a submarine had no right to distribute commercial advertising handbills on the streets of New York City, the majority had seemed to say that advertising was not protected by the Constitution. In response to Sullivan's argument, Brennan wrote:

> The publication here...communicated information, expressed opinion, recited grievances, protested claimed abuses, and sought financial support on behalf of a movement whose existence and objectives are matters of the highest public concern. That the *Times* was paid for publishing the advertisement is as immaterial in this connection as the fact that newspapers and books are sold. Any other conclusion would discourage newspapers from carrying "editorial advertisements" of this type, and so might shut off an important outlet for the promulgation of information and ideas by persons who do not themselves have access to publishing facilities—who wish to exercise their freedom of speech even though they are not members of the

---

23.   316 U.S. 52, 62 S.Ct. 920, 86 L.Ed. 1262 (1942).

press. The effect would be to shackle the First Amendment in its attempt to secure "the widest possible dissemination of information from diverse and antagonistic sources."[24] To avoid placing such a handicap upon the freedom of expression, we hold that if the allegedly libelous statements would otherwise be constitutionally protected from the present judgment, they do not forfeit that protection because they were published in the form of a paid advertisement.

With those words, the Court established its first new principle. Editorial advertising stands on higher constitutional ground than does ordinary commercial advertising. Editorial advertising gives people an opportunity to plead their cause in the news media. It is concerned with ideas. In contrast, commercial advertising simply offers a product or a service at a price. By bringing editorial advertising under the protection of the First Amendment, the Court was raising a barrier against successful libel suits, thus encouraging publishers to accept such appeals. Ten years later, the Court would extend limited First Amendment protection to commercial advertising, too (See chapter 12).

The First Amendment and Libel Per Se

Sullivan's next argument went to the heart of the common law of libel, the concept of libel per se. Under Alabama law, a statement was libelous on its face if it imputed misconduct to a public official. If a jury found that the complained-of words applied to the official, it was assumed that he had suffered harm to reputation. The defendant could escape an award of damages only by proving that the allegedly defamatory allegations were true in all respects or that they were fair comment based on a solid bed of fact. If either defense was tried and failed, the law further assumed that publication of a libel per se was a product of malice, in the sense of ill will. This meant that a jury could require the defendant to pay not only compensatory damages, a sum designed to make good the plaintiff's harm, but punitive damages, an additional sum levied as punishment.

The question thus became, could the First Amendment be invoked to interrupt this march to a costly conclusion once a publication had been found to be libelous on its face? Sullivan's lawyers quoted from numerous decisions in which Supreme Court majorities had seemed to say that libel per se, like obscenity and other language devoid of idea content, was outside the scope of First Amendment protection. But, responded Brennan, none of those cases involved criticism of the public conduct of public officials:

> [W]e are compelled neither by precedent nor policy to give any more weight to the epithet "libel" than we have to other "mere labels" of state law. Like insurrection, contempt, advocacy of unlawful acts, breach of the peace, obscenity, solicitation of illegal business, and the other various formulae for the repression of expression that have been challenged in this court, libel can claim no talismanic immunity

---

24. Quoting the Court's 1945 decision in Associated Press v. United States, an antitrust case, 326 U.S. 1, 65 S.Ct. 1416, 89 L.Ed. 2013 (1945).

from constitutional limitations. It must be measured by standards that satisfy the First Amendment.

The general proposition that freedom of expression upon public questions is secured by the First Amendment has long been settled by our decisions.

Brennan thus forged the second link in the progression required to reverse the Alabama courts. Even statements libelous on their face must be examined in the light of First Amendment guarantees if they arise out of the discussion of public issues. With this platform built, the Court proceeded to the heart of its decision:

Thus we consider this case against the background of a profound national commitment to the principle that debate on public issues should be uninhibited, robust, and wide-open, and that it may well include vehement, caustic, and sometimes unpleasantly sharp attacks on government and public officials. The present advertisement, as an expression of grievance and protest on one of the major public issues of our time, would seem clearly to qualify for the constitutional protection.

The Partial Protection of False Statements

Having established that "Heed Their Rising Voices" was protected by the First Amendment even though it had appeared as a paid advertisement and was libelous on its face, the Court had an even higher hurdle to jump. Beyond question, the ad contained false assertions of fact, and some of these were libelous. Does the First Amendment also condone falsehood?

Brennan examined the "public principle" cases and found that courts in a minority of the states had tolerated some error in the criticism of public officials. He concluded, quoting James Madison, who wrote much of the Constitution, that "some degree of abuse is inseparable from the proper use of everything; and in no instance is this more true than in that of the press." Brennan also noted that in some areas of law, the Supreme Court already had rejected the suggestion that the First Amendment protects only those statements that can be proved to be true. He added, again quoting Madison:

[E]rroneous statement is inevitable in free debate, and...it must be protected if the freedoms of expression are to have the "breathing space" that they "need...to survive."

With those words, Brennan, writing for a majority of the Court, established a third legal principle, and a most significant one: The First Amendment excuses some falsehoods uttered in the heat of debate over the public conduct of public officials.

Brennan expanded on the reasons for the Court's new approach. The *Times* had already been ordered to pay a $500,000 judgment, which Brennan likened to a fine, and faced other civil suits for comparable sums. Newspapers confronted with such prospects might well succumb to a "pall of fear and timidity" and mute their criticisms of public officials, Brennan said. In such an atmosphere, he noted, "First Amendment freedoms cannot survive." Nor can state libel laws be saved, Brennan added, by permitting publishers to win libel suits by proving the truth of their statements. He wrote:

> A rule compelling the critic of official conduct to guarantee the truth of all his factual assertions—and to do so on pain of libel judgments virtually unlimited in amount—leads to...''self-censorship.'' Allowance of the defense of truth, with the burden of proving it on the defendant, does not mean that only false speech will be deterred. Even courts accepting this defense as an adequate safeguard have recognized the difficulties in adducing legal proofs that the alleged libel was true in all its factual particulars....Under such a rule, would-be critics of official conduct may be deterred from voicing their criticism, even though it is believed to be true and even though it is in fact true, because of doubt whether it can be proved in court or fear of the expense of having to so do....The rule thus dampens the vigor and limits the variety of public debate. It is inconsistent with the First and Fourteenth Amendments.

The Plaintiff Must Prove Actual Malice

Brennan saved the Court's most explosive change for last:

> The constitutional guarantees require, we think, a federal rule that prohibits a public official from recovering damages for a defamatory falsehood relating to his official conduct unless he proves that the statement was made with ''actual malice''—that is, with knowledge that it was false or with reckless disregard of whether it was false or not.

The term ''actual malice'' was not new in court decisions, as is evidenced by the fact that Brennan put it in quotation marks. But it must be emphasized that his definition of the term was new. The dictionary defines ''malice'' in terms of ''evil intent or motive''—the desire to cause harm to another. But, as used in libel decisions, ''actual malice'' means precisely what the Supreme Court said it means in *New York Times,* no more and no less. It means that the publisher of the libel either acted in the knowledge that his assertion was false or in reckless disregard of whether it was true or not.

Seldom has a single paragraph in a Supreme Court decision brought about such a revolutionary change in the law. With that paragraph, the Court shifted most of the burden of proof in libel suits brought by public officials against the news media. Not only would public official plaintiffs have to prove publication, identification, and defamation, but they would have to prove that the defamatory passage was false, and that the publisher either knew it was false or acted in reckless disregard of the truth. Further, Brennan wrote, for a majority of the Court, public official plaintiffs would have to prove actual malice with ''convincing clarity.'' This, he made clear, would require a higher level of proof than the ''preponderance of the evidence'' test required in other civil actions. Lawyers say the difference is between the need to prove 90 percent of your case as against only 51 percent, which is a wide gap indeed.

To avoid the expense of returning the case to an Alabama court for possible retrial under the new rules, the Court proceeded to hold that Sullivan could not prove that the *Times* acted in actual malice. At the most, Brennan wrote, Sullivan might be able to prove that the *Times's* advertising department was negligent in not checking the assertions in the advertisement against clippings in the newspaper's own files. But, Brennan added, a mere failure to investigate is not reckless disregard. Such failure must be coupled with a showing that the publisher doubted the truth of the statement in question. In this instance, there was no doubt. The advertisement bore the signatures of respected persons of substance. There was no reason why anyone at the *Times* should doubt them.

The Supreme Court's decision in *New York Times* v. *Sullivan* sent lower courts everywhere a clear signal: Public officials should not be permitted to collect libel judgments from the news media except for a knowing or reckless lie. Further, the burden was on the public official plaintiff to prove knowledge of falsity or reckless disregard of truth on the part of the publisher.

It quickly became apparent that the Supreme Court's decision in *New York Times* raised significant questions:

— Sullivan was an elected public official with responsibility for overseeing a police department. The Court's decision was written with frequent reference to a "public official," and therefore seemed limited in its application. But who else on the public payroll might be classed as a public official?

— Some persons in public life have considerable influence even though they hold no public office. Others seek influence by becoming candidates for election to public offices. Shouldn't such persons be subject to robust and uninhibited debate?

— The Court defined "actual malice" in terms that looked deceptively easy. It is the knowing lie, or the assertion that is a product of a reckless disregard for the truth. But how might a public official prove either one with "convincing clarity"? Brennan had written that doubt on the part of the publisher is an element in reckless disregard, but how much doubt? And how can it be proved? Did the decision mean that libel plaintiffs could examine the editorial process? Could they pry into the state of mind of the reporter who gathered the facts and wrote the story, and of the editors who approved it?

There were also more subtle questions. Does the First Amendment protect discussion of persons or discussion of ideas? Could the same statement libel one person because he did not hold public office and not libel another because she did? If a public official plaintiff must prove actual malice, would he also have the burden of proving that the statement at issue was false? In view of the Court's robust commitment to freewheeling debate, even to the point of tolerating some degree of falsehood, were judges expected to dispose of more cases through summary judgment?

Cases seeking answers to some of these questions reached the Supreme Court during the decade after 1964. In its decision in three of the cases, the Court extended the scope of the *New York Times* rule, as the constitutional defense quickly came to be known. In 1966, in *Rosenblatt* v. *Baer*,[25] the Court defined

---

25. 383 U.S. 75, 86 S.Ct. 669, 15 L.Ed.2d 597 (1966).

"public official" to include "those among the hierarchy of government employees who have, or appear to the public to have, substantial responsibility for or control over the conduct of government affairs." A public official, then, is not just anyone on a government payroll, but only those employees who make policy or who have considerable discretion in how they carry out their duties.

In 1967, in *Curtis Publishing Co.* v. *Butts*,[26] the Court extended the application of the *New York Times* rule to "public figures." These it defined in part as persons who thrust themselves "into the 'vortex' of an important public controversy." That definition would prove to be too vague. Subsequent decisions refining and narrowing the definition of public figures will be treated later.

The Constitutional Defense Further Defined

The *New York Times* decision was a product of a Supreme Court led by Chief Justice Earl Warren. Warren had been appointed by President Dwight D. Eisenhower in 1953 and presided for sixteen years over one of the most liberal eras in the history of the Supreme Court. Particularly during the 1960s, the Court greatly expanded the protections afforded by the Bill of Rights, including freedom of speech and press. The *Rosenblatt* and *Butts* decisions were also products of the Warren Court.

In 1969, Warren retired as chief justice, giving Richard M. Nixon, a Republican who was elected president the previous year, an opportunity to make his first appointment to the Court. Nixon chose Warren E. Burger, then a judge of the United States Court of Appeals for the District of Columbia Circuit, to replace Warren. Burger was known to believe that the Warren Court had gone too far in applying federal constitutional law to cases that he thought best left to state courts for decision. A year later, Burger was joined on the Court by the second Nixon appointee, Harry A. Blackmun, who had been a judge of the Court of Appeals for the Eighth Circuit in Minnesota. He replaced Abe Fortas, who had been appointed to the Court by President Lyndon B. Johnson, a Democrat. With Nixon's first two appointments, the Court's membership began to move in a conservative direction.

Rosenbloom v. *Metromedia*

During its 1970–1971 term, the Court accepted for review a libel case growing out of the arrest of a book and magazine distributor in Philadelphia on obscenity charges. In reporting the arrest, a Philadelphia radio station owned by Metromedia had referred to the distributor as a "smut peddler." It did so even after the distributor had called the station and told its news staff the magazines in question had been held not to be obscene by courts else-

Rosenbloom v. *Metromedia, Inc.,* **403 U.S. 29, 91 S.Ct. 1811, 29 L.Ed.2d 296 (1971).**

---

26.   388 U.S. 130, 87 S.Ct. 1975, 18 L.Ed.2d 1094 (1967).

where. The epithet was also used to describe the distributor, Rosenbloom, after the charges against him had been dismissed. Rosenbloom sued the station for libel and won a six-figure judgment. The Supreme Court reversed, but was so badly divided that a majority could not agree on a rationale.

At issue was whether Rosenbloom should have to prove actual malice. He was not a public official, and the Court was in disagreement as to whether he was a public figure. Justice Brennan's view was decisive, although he could not get a majority of the Court to accept his position as he had in *New York Times*. Arguing that the purpose of the First Amendment is to protect the discussion of ideas and to protect the news media in the reporting of public affairs, he and three other justices concluded that Rosenbloom's status was immaterial. At the heart of the case was the bigger issue of obscenity and the attempt to control its distribution in the public interest. Rosenbloom was caught up in the attempt to resolve that issue. Therefore, he should be required to prove actual malice.

At that point, the Supreme Court had gone as far as it was going to go in extending First Amendment protection to libel defendants. Had Brennan been able to muster a majority behind his opinion, all libel plaintiffs suing the news media would have had to prove actual malice. The *Rosenbloom* decision continues to be of importance because courts in a few states have adopted its rationale. However, within three years, the Supreme Court was to accept another libel case and hold that states could permit private individuals to sue the news media for libel on a lesser showing of fault than actual malice.

Gertz v. *Robert Welch, Inc.*

In the same year that *Rosenbloom* was decided, Justices Hugo L. Black and John Marshall Harlan died. Black had taken the position that the First Amendment gives absolute protection to pure speech, including libel. Harlan, an Eisenhower appointee, was more conservative. After a long fight with the Senate, Nixon replaced them in 1972 with Lewis F. Powell, Jr., and William H. Rehnquist, both of whom took the position at the time that the Constitution should be construed in strict terms. Rehnquist, perhaps even more than Burger, has taken the position that many issues, including libel, should be resolved at the state level, without resort to federal constitutional law. Powell was to become more flexible on First Amendment issues.

Thus there were four Nixon appointees on the Court when it decided its next significant libel case in 1974. The plaintiff was a Chicago lawyer, Elmer Gertz, who had been criticized severely by an article in *American Opinion,* the magazine of the ultraconservative John Birch Society. Gertz drew the magazine's fire when he agreed to represent the parents of a youth who had been shot to death by a Chicago police officer. When police officials ruled that the shooting was unjustified, the parents sued their son's killer for damages. The magazine took the position that Gertz's role as the family's lawyer made him part of a plot to discredit the police. The writer referred to the lawyer as "Leninist Elmer Gertz" and "Communist-fronter Gertz." A photo caption re-

Gertz v. *Robert Welch, Inc.,* **418 U.S. 323, 94 S.Ct. 2997, 41 L.Ed.2d 789 (1974).**

ferred to Gertz as a member of the "Red Guild," a reference to the fact that some years earlier he had been active in the National Lawyers Guild. Its membership was made up largely of lawyers opposed to the dominant and somewhat conservative American Bar Association. Some Guild members had attracted attention in the McCarthy era by defending persons identified as Communists by congressional investigating committees. There was little doubt that the article made false statements about Gertz. For instance, it said the police file on the lawyer was so voluminous that only "a big Irish cop" could lift it. Gertz had no police record.

When Gertz sued the magazine's publisher, Robert Welch, Inc., for libel, the district court judge who heard the case was somewhat confused as to the meaning of the *New York Times* rule. He had decided at the start of the trial that it did not apply. After the jury had returned a $50,000 judgment in Gertz's favor, he held otherwise on grounds that the article in *American Opinion* discussed an issue of public importance. The United States Court of Appeals for the Seventh Circuit affirmed the judge's ruling. Gertz, who had seen his $50,000 award wiped out, asked the Supreme Court to accept the case for review, which it did.

Justice Powell, writing for a five-member majority that included Blackmun and Rehnquist, specifically repudiated the plurality ruling in *Rosenbloom*. The majority held that the nature of the plaintiff is the crucial element in deciding whether the *New York Times* rule protects a media libel defendant. Justice Powell's decision for the Court is not a model of judicial writing because he chose to discuss elements of libel law that were not properly a part of the case brought to the Court by Gertz. When judges write, as Powell did here, on issues that are not essential to a resolution of the case, such passages are called *dicta*. Strictly speaking, they are viewed as extraneous comment and are not considered as precedents that lower courts are expected to follow. However, Powell's dicta in *Gertz* have been looked to for guidance by most lower courts. Thus, the Court's decision has established important new guidelines for libel law, both supplementing and limiting *New York Times*.

LIBEL IS LIMITED TO FALSE AND DEFAMATORY ASSERTIONS OF FACT   Powell began by writing about the nature of defamation:

> We begin with the common ground. Under the First Amendment there is no such thing as a false idea. However pernicious an opinion may seem, we depend for its correction not on the conscience of judges and juries, but on the competition of other ideas. But there is no constitutional value in false statements of fact. Neither the intentional lie nor the careless error materially advances society's interest in "uninhibited, robust, and wide-open debate" on public issues.... They belong to that category of utterances which "are no essential part of any exposition of ideas, and are of such slight social value as a step to truth that any benefit that may be derived from them is clearly outweighed by the social interest in order and morality."[27]

---

27. Quoting Chaplinsky v. New Hampshire, 315 U.S. 568, 62 S.Ct. 766, 86 L.Ed. 1031 (1942), in which the Court held that "fighting words," in this instance insulting epithets, are devoid of idea content, hence not protected by the First Amendment.

With the second and third sentences of the above paragraph, the Court said that statements of opinion are not actionable as libel. Defamatory statements, the Court seemed to be saying, are actionable only if they make a false assertion of fact. Because Gertz's suit was based on demonstrably false assertions of fact, Powell's references to opinion were considered dicta. However, as we will see, courts today, with the Supreme Court's approval, take the position that the First Amendment gives absolute protection to expressions of pure opinion. Therefore, they cannot be the basis for a libel action.

THE STATES MAY MAKE IT EASIER FOR PRIVATE INDIVIDUALS TO WIN LIBEL ACTIONS AGAINST THE MEDIA   Powell next reviewed the Court's decision in *New York Times,* focusing on the protection it gave to falsehoods uttered in the heat of debate. To retreat from that holding, he said, would run the risk of restricting debate through "intolerable self-censorship." Some error must be protected, Powell added, "to protect speech that matters."

However, Powell noted for the majority, freedom of speech and press do not stand alone. Other interests must also be protected. For instance, the justice wrote, states have a legitimate interest in providing "compensation of individuals for harm inflicted on them by defamatory falsehoods." Therefore, the Supreme Court would not foreclose the right of any state to protect an individual's reputation. Here Powell was addressing an issue raised by the case and no longer was writing dicta.

However, without directly saying so, Powell was responding to the criticism that the Supreme Court, in writing the *New York Times* decision, had sought to bring all libel law within the scope of the First Amendment, thus federalizing it. The words above signaled the Court's intention to pull back somewhat from the extreme reading of *New York Times.* Powell made clear that the Court did not intend to weaken the actual malice rule as it applies to public persons. He wrote:

> Those who, by reason of the notoriety of their achievements or the vigor and success with which they seek the public's attention, are properly classed as public figures and those who hold governmental office may recover for injury to reputation only on clear and convincing proof that the defamatory falsehood was made with knowledge of its falsity or with reckless disregard of the truth.

The majority recognized that some deserving plaintiffs might not be able to surmount that barrier. But, on the other hand, its presence serves as "an extremely powerful antidote" for the tendency toward self-censorship induced by the old common law of libel. For that reason, Powell wrote, "the Court has concluded that the protection of the *New York Times* privilege should be available to publishers and broadcasters of defamatory falsehood concerning public officials and public figures." But, he added, the Court also had concluded that states should have the right to apply a less stringent rule to private individuals who might be defamed by the news media.

The majority offered a simple justification for its conclusion. Public officials and public figures are newsworthy. If they are subjected to criticism, they can fight back in print and on the air. Private individuals are less likely to reach the public with their views, even when they have been the subject of a defamatory story. Therefore, the Court concluded, they are "more vulnerable to injury, and the state interest in protecting them is correspondingly greater." On the other hand, persons who hold public office, or who try to influence public affairs, should do so in full knowledge of the likely consequences. They run "the risk of closer public scrutiny than might otherwise be the case."

At this point in its decision, the Court had delivered two clear signals to state and federal courts. It had no intention of backing away from its holding in *New York Times* so far as public officials and public figures were concerned. If they were to prevail in libel suits against the media, they would have to offer clear and convincing proof of falsehood and actual malice. But, if states so chose, they could permit private individuals to prevail against the media on some lesser degree of proof. A third signal was less clear. The Court seemed to be saying that any libel action against the media, no matter who the plaintiff, brings First Amendment guarantees into play, if the action is based on the discussion of a public issue.

PUBLIC FIGURES ARE DEFINED AND CATEGORIZED   If states were to be permitted to make it easier for some people to win libel suits, what criteria should be used to differentiate public figures from private individuals? Powell next turned to that question. He started by dividing public figures into three classes, involuntary, all-purpose, and limited:

> Hypothetically, it may be possible for someone to become a public figure through no purposeful action of his own, but the instances of truly involuntary public figures must be exceedingly rare. For the most part those who attain this status have assumed roles of especial prominence in the affairs of society. Some occupy positions of such persuasive power and influence that they are deemed public figures for all purposes. More commonly, those classed as public figures have thrust themselves to the forefront of particular public controversies in order to influence the resolution of the issues involved. In either event, they invite attention and comment.
>
> Even if the foregoing generalities do not obtain in every instance, the communications media are entitled to act on the assumption that public officials and public figures have voluntarily exposed themselves to increased risk of defamatory falsehoods concerning them. No such assumption is justified with respect to a private individual. He has not accepted a public office or assumed an "influential role in ordering society." He has relinquished no part of his interest in the protection of his own good name, and consequently he has a more compelling call on the courts for redress of injury inflicted by defamatory falsehood. Thus, private individuals are not only more vulnerable to injury than public officials and public figures; they are more deserving of recovery.
>
> For these reasons we conclude that the States should retain substantial latitude in their efforts to enforce a legal remedy for defamatory falsehood injurious to the reputation of a private individual.

PRIVATE INDIVIDUALS MUST PROVE SOME DEGREE OF FAULT ON THE PART OF THE MEDIA   The phrase "substantial latitude" was used for a purpose. The Supreme Court was willing to let the states apply their own rules to libel suits directed at the news media by private individuals, but it was not willing to let them restore the old rule of common law in its entirety. There were limits, which the Court sought to define as follows:

> We hold that, so long as they do not impose liability without fault, the States may define for themselves the appropriate standard of liability for a publisher or a broadcaster of defamatory falsehood injurious to a private individual. This approach provides a more equitable boundary between the competing concerns involved here. It recognizes the strength of the legitimate state interest in compensating private individuals for wrongful injury to reputation, yet shields the press and broadcast media from the rigors of strict liability for defamation. At least this conclusion obtains where, as here, the substance of the defamatory statement "makes substantial danger to reputation apparent."

While Powell did not define what he meant by "liability without fault," Chief Justice Burger, writing in dissent, did. He said the majority had established a "new negligence standard," as indeed it had. In most states that have chosen the option offered by *Gertz,* private individuals who sue the news media for libel need show only that reporters or editors have fallen short of a recognized standard of care. State courts have varied in defining that standard. Some have applied the well-established principles of ordinary negligence, in which persons are at fault if they have failed to do what a "prudent person" would have done under the circumstances. What such a person would do is a matter for a jury to determine after listening to witnesses for both sides. Other courts have held that the performance of journalists should be measured against the standard of care that would be followed by professional reporters and editors caught up in similar circumstances. Again, the determination is one to be made by the jury after listening to the testimony of witnesses deemed to have knowledge of professional practices.[28] In either event, *Gertz* has given courts responsibility for doing what journalists themselves have not done in a systematic fashion: that is, establish professional standards for performance.

In this section of its decision, the Court sought to protect the news media from libel judgments based on inadvertent mistakes, such things as typographical errors, confusion in addresses, or mistaken information accepted in good faith from usually reliable sources. The Court held that even private individuals should not be permitted to succeed in a libel suit against the media unless they could prove some kind of fault.

PRIVATE INDIVIDUALS MUST ALSO SHOW THAT THEY HAVE BEEN HARMED UNLESS THEY CAN PROVE ACTUAL MALICE   The Court moved next to the question of damages. If states were permitted to apply their old common-law standards in libel suits brought by private individuals, the sky might be the limit. Under those standards, juries could award damages to persons who had suffered no injury, such as loss of income or standing in the community. At common law, injury was

---

28. John B. McCrory, "Development of the Defense of Constitutional Privilege in Libel Law," *Communications Law 1983* (New York: Practicing Law Institute, 1983), vol. 1, pp. 167–71.

assumed from the fact of publication. Powell noted that common law gave juries "largely uncontrolled discretion" to "award substantial sums as compensation for supposed damages to reputation without any proof that such harm actually occurred." If states were to revert to common law in assessing damages, they would invite "juries to punish unpopular opinion rather than to compensate individuals for injury." The prospect of such awards might "inhibit the vigorous exercise of First Amendment freedoms by inviting self-censorship." To prevent that, Powell wrote for the Court, states could go no further in protecting the reputation of private individuals "than compensation for actual injury....[W]e hold that States may not permit recovery of presumed or punitive damages, at least when liability is not based on a showing of knowledge of falsity or reckless disregard of the truth."

After saying that it need not attempt to define "actual injury," the Court seemed to do just that. Powell wrote:

> Suffice it to say that actual injury is not limited to out-of-pocket loss. Indeed, the more customary types of actual harm inflicted by defamatory falsehood include impairment of reputation and standing in the community, personal humiliation, and mental anguish and suffering. Of course, juries must be limited by appropriate instructions, and all awards must be supported by competent evidence concerning the injury, although there need be no evidence which assigns an actual dollar value to the injury.

The Court turned next to a strong criticism of awards of punitive damages in libel suits, but it stopped short of outlawing them. Punitive damages are designed to punish a defendant for alleged wrongdoing, and to deter others who might be tempted to commit a similar offense. The Court said:

> We also find no justification for allowing awards of punitive damages against publishers and broadcasters held liable under state-defined standards of liability for defamation. In most jurisdictions jury discretion over the amounts awarded is limited only by the gentle rule that they not be excessive. Consequently, juries assess punitive damages in wholly unpredictable amounts bearing no necessary relation to the actual harm caused. And they remain free to use their discretion selectively to punish expressions of unpopular views. Like the doctrine of presumed damages, jury discretion to award punitive damages unnecessarily exacerbates the danger of media self-censorship, but unlike the former rule, punitive damages are wholly irrelevant to the state interest that justifies a negligence standard for private defamation actions. They are not compensation for injury. Instead, they are private fines levied by civil juries to punish reprehensible conduct and to deter future occurrence. In short, the private defamation plaintiff who establishes liability under a less demanding standard than that stated in *New York Times* may recover only such damages as are sufficient to compensate him for actual injury.

With that part of its decision, the majority seemed to be trying to bring awards of damages in libel cases under control. Recovery by private individuals would be limited to compensation for actual injury, unless they could prove actual malice. Public officials and public figures could not recover anything unless they could prove actual malice. However, the Court could not define harm in such a way as to reduce it to a tangible measurement. Juries were left with considerable discretion. What, for instance, is the dollar value of "impairment of reputation and standing in the community?" Or of "personal humiliation, and mental anguish and suffering?" How does one prove the latter? Subsequent cases have demonstrated that some juries are willing to put six- and seven-figure values on such intangibles despite Powell's condemnation of "private fines levied by civil juries."

The remainder of the decision was devoted to the Court's finding that Gertz was not a public figure, although he had had some minimal participation in public affairs in Chicago. In essence the Court concluded that he had attracted *American Opinion's* libelous lightning not because he was trying to influence public opinion against police in general, but because he had been hired to file suit against one police officer. He was simply a lawyer doing his job. That did not make him even a limited-purpose public figure. The case was sent back to the federal district court in Chicago.

There, seven years later in the spring of 1981, the case again reached trial. In the meantime, Gertz had achieved a sort of fame as the lawyer whose lawsuit had changed the law of libel. He was in demand as a lecturer. He had become a professor at the John Marshall Law School. Gertz commented in an interview with a reporter for the *Chicago Law Bulletin* that the case "may have made me a public figure."[29]

Nevertheless, the trial was conducted on the ground that he was a private individual, as the Supreme Court had held him to be at the time the libel was published in 1969. Gertz testified that when he saw the article he was shocked and that it "knocked me out emotionally for a long period of time." He also testified that he thought he had lost clients as a result of it.

This time, a six-member jury found that *American Opinion* not only was negligent in publishing the article, but had acted with actual malice. The jurors concluded that Gertz had suffered $100,000 in actual harm. They assessed an additional $300,000 in punitive damages against Robert Welch, Inc. Gertz was quoted as viewing the outcome as a "blow for responsible journalism."[30] More than a year later, an appeals court affirmed the award.[31] The Supreme Court refused to review the verdict.[32]

COMMON LAW AND THE BUSINESS COMMUNICATOR

In the decade following the Supreme Court's decision in *Gertz,* some courts acted on the assumption that the common law of libel had been supplanted by constitutional rules imposed by the Supreme Court. Other courts were not so sure. A few state courts read *Gertz* as condoning a limited application of common law to cases in which private individuals sued the mass media. The Pennsylvania Supreme Court, for instance, held that while *Gertz* required private plaintiffs to

---

29. "Landmark Libel Case Being Quietly Retried," *Chicago Law Bulletin,* 17 April 1981.
30. "Gertz Case Finally Settled," *Newsletter,* Inland Daily Press Association, 30 April 1981.
31. Gertz v. Robert Welch, Inc., 680 F.2d 527 (7th Cir. 1982).
32. Robert Welch, Inc., v. Gertz, 103 S.Ct. 1233 (1983).

prove fault, it did not require them to prove falsity.[33] Courts in Wisconsin[34] and Tennessee[35] had come to the same conclusion. The Supreme Court stopped that reversion to common law when it accepted the Pennsylvania case and reversed. It held in *Philadelphia Newspapers* v. *Hepps*[36] that private individuals who are defamed by the news media during the discussion of a matter of "public concern" must prove falsehood as well as fault and harm. But the Court was divided, five to four, and the dissenters all favored permitting the states to revive some parts of the common law to protect private plaintiffs from media abuse.

Only a few months earlier, the Supreme Court had also used the words "public concern" in taking a much kindlier approach to common law in a case involving a business reporting service, Dun & Bradstreet. Dun & Bradstreet relies on thousands of correspondents to gather from public agencies and other sources information that has a bearing on the creditworthiness of business firms. It disseminates that information on a confidential basis to thousands of clients. With respect to those clients it is as much a news organization as Associated Press or United Press International.

Yet when Dun & Bradstreet was sued for libel by a firm it had erroneously reported to be bankrupt, the Supreme Court held that Vermont courts had acted properly in trying the case under the state's common law without regard to *New York Times* and the First Amendment. Because the Court was divided five ways, with no more than four justices signing any of the opinions, the effect of the decision was not immediately apparent. But, taken with *Hepps,* scattered lower court cases since 1986 indicate that *Greenmoss* is of considerable importance to corporate communicators and conceivably could have application to the media. The two cases leave little doubt that state common and statute law can be applied when private individuals have been defamed in contexts with which the general public has no legitimate concern. As of this writing, the Arizona Supreme Court and the U.S. Courts of Appeals for the Fourth and Fifth circuits have held that states may apply their common law to such actions. The Supreme Court's holding has been applied in actions involving disclosure of false and damaging credit ratings, interoffice memoranda dealing with investigation of theft, and corporate communications reporting the firing of an employee found guilty of sexual harassment.

Private Individuals, Private Matters, and the Common Law of Libel

In 1976, the president of a Vermont construction firm, Greenmoss Builders, went to his bank to talk about the financing of several projects he had under consideration. He was shocked when the banker

Dun & Bradstreet v. *Greenmoss Builders,* 472 U.S. 479, 105 S.Ct. 2939, 86 L.Ed.2d 593 (1985).

told him he had received information from Dun & Bradstreet that Greenmoss had filed for protection under bankruptcy law. The firm had not done so. The seventeen-year-old high school

33.   Hepps v. Philadelphia Newspapers, 506 Pa. 304, 485 A.2d 374 (Pa. 1984).
34.   Denny v. Mertz, 106 Wis.2d 636, 318 N.W.2d 141 (Wis. 1982).
35.   Memphis Publishing Co. v. Nichols, 569 S.W.2d 412 (Tenn. 1978).
36.   475 U.S. 767, 106 S.Ct. 1558, 89 L.Ed.2d 783 (1986).

student who was paid by Dun & Bradstreet to check Vermont bankruptcy pleadings had mistakenly attributed to Greenmoss a bankruptcy petition filed by one of its former employees. Normally the credit-reporting firm would have checked the information with Greenmoss before disseminating it. In this instance, it had not done so. The false report was sent to five clients who, under terms of their contract, were not supposed to share the information with anyone else.

When Greenmoss's president called the credit reporting agency to ask for a correction, he also asked for the names of its clients who had received the false report. Dun & Bradstreet refused to give him the names, but it did issue a correction which it sent to the five clients who had received the misinformation.

Greenmoss sued for libel. At trial, the judge told the jury that because the credit agency's report was libelous on its face, Greenmoss did not have to prove it had been harmed because "damage and loss [are] conclusively presumed." In doing so, he was applying Vermont's common law. He also told the jury it could make an award of punitive damages if it concluded Dun & Bradstreet had acted with actual malice. However, the court gave the jury several definitions of the term, one of which was that given in *New York Times,* that is, that Dun & Bradstreet knew the report was false or had acted recklessly in disseminating it. But it also gave the traditional common-law definition of malice, which is a product of ill will, and included references to "bad faith" and "reckless disregard of the possible consequences." The jury awarded the builder $50,000 in compensatory or presumed damages and $300,000 in punitive damages.

Dun & Bradstreet asked for a new trial, arguing that the judge's instruction to the jury violated the constitutional requirements imposed by the Supreme Court in *Gertz.* The judge did so, the agency said, by permitting Greenmoss to recover compensatory damages without proving harm and punitive damages by proving something less than actual malice. The judge said he was in some doubt as to whether *Gertz* applied to nonmedia cases, and granted the motion. Greenmoss appealed to the Vermont Supreme Court, which reversed, thus reinstating the jury's verdict. The court concluded that credit-reporting firms, such as Dun & Bradstreet, are not "the type of media worthy of First Amendment protection as contemplated by *New York Times.*" Going further, it held "that as a matter of law, the media protections outlined in *Gertz* are inapplicable to nonmedia defamation actions." Therefore, the state's common law governed. This permitted the trial court to assume that Greenmoss had been harmed and award punitive damages on proof of something less than actual malice. The U.S. Supreme Court agreed to review the case and upheld the verdict, five to four.

However, the Supreme Court did not adopt the Vermont court's rationale. The prevailing justices did not attempt to distinguish between media and nonmedia defendants and say clearly that different standards apply to each in a libel case. Rather, they focused on the facts from which the case arose, reasoning that Greenmoss' credit rating was a private matter, of interest only to the contractor and the firms that did business with it. Justice Powell, writing for only two other members of the Court, reasoned that because the libel arose out of a private matter, the First Amendment did not come into play. Therefore, Vermont courts had acted properly in applying the state's common law to the case.

However, Powell muddied the waters by suggesting that statements which are not of public concern are "not totally unprotected by the First Amendment." In context, he seemed to be referring to the doctrine of commercial speech under which a lesser degree of First Amendment protection is afforded to purely commercial advertising than to speech dealing with public issues. In his discussion, Powell made much of the fact that Dun & Bradstreet "is solely motivated by the desire for profit" and that the speech in question was "solely in the individual interest of the speaker and its specific business audience." He saw the profit motive as an incentive to ensure the accuracy of the agency's service and a justification for penalizing its mistakes.

The four dissenting justices argued that Greenmoss's credit rating was not strictly a private matter. There was enough public interest in it, they said, to justify a holding that Greenmoss needed to prove both fault and harm. Powell accused the dissenters of trying "to constitutionalize the entire common law of libel."

At this writing, *Greenmoss,* coupled with *Hepps,* serves as a reminder that "the entire common law of libel" has not been "constitutionalize[d]." It is very much alive in the business world among nonmedia defendants and even quasi-media defendants such as credit-reporting services. All that is required is that the plaintiff be a private individual and the defamatory assertions not a matter of "public concern." Left open is the question of whether media defendants, too, may be subject to common law if a private plaintiff can convince a court that there was no legitimate public interest in the subject matter of a defamatory publication or broadcast.

Privilege and the Private Libel Action

In 1985, hard on the heels of *Greenmoss,* the U.S. Court of Appeals for the Fourth Circuit held that West Virginia's libel statutes and common law should apply to a case growing out of an interoffice memorandum on a theft of property in an insurance agency.[37] The next year, the Arizona Supreme Court wrote, in a case involving a newspaper, that "when a plaintiff is a private figure and the speech is of private concern, the states are free to retain common law principles."[38] However, the decision in the case did not depend on that observation. The plaintiff was deemed a limited-purpose public figure.

In reality, the *Greenmoss* decision has not changed the rules under which private libel defendants, most usually business firms or their officers, must defend themselves. It has simply made clear that the reach of *New York Times* and *Gertz* cannot be extended so far as to bring all libel law under the First Amendment. Private defendants under common law can use one of three defenses—truth, privilege, or fair comment. In this connection, "privilege" has a somewhat different meaning than it has where government and its officers and agencies are concerned. At common law, business firms have a qualified privilege to share infor-

---

37. Mutafis v. Erie Insurance Exchange, 775 F.2d 593 (4th Cir. 1985).
38. Dombey v. Phoenix Newspapers, 150 Ariz. 476, 724 P.2d 562 (Ariz. 1986).

mation essential to the conduct of their business. This includes such things as references for employment, credit reports, reasons for dismissals, accident investigatory reports, and other internal communications. In one instance, a federal court of appeals held that Du Pont was protected by privilege when it issued a press release announcing its decision to withdraw Teflon from the oil additive market because it concluded the product was ineffective in such usage.[39]

More recently, the U.S. Court of Appeals for the Fifth Circuit decided *Garziano* v. *E.I. Du Pont de Nemours & Co.,* in which Mississippi's common law of libel was applied. The plaintiff, Richard Garziano, was discharged after his supervisors concluded he had committed several acts of sexual harassment in the course of his work. When rumors about the discharge and the reasons for it circulated through the plant, the company issued a management information bulletin on sexual harassment. The bulletin referred to "the recent sexual harassment incident which resulted in an employee's termination." The remainder of the bulletin dealt with sexual harassment in general, describing the offense and prescribing procedures for reporting and investigating it. The bulletin was one of a series distributed to supervisors with instructions to share pertinent information with their subordinates. Subsequently, Garziano's termination and the reasons for it became the subject of talk not only in the plant but in the community outside.

Garziano v. *E.I. Du Pont de Nemours & Co.,* 818 F.2d 380 (5th Cir. 1987).

Garziano sued Du Pont for libel. Under the state's common law, the company argued that its bulletin was protected by privilege, that is, by its right to share accurate information about company actions and policies with its employees. After a jury had awarded Garziano $93,000 in compensatory damages, Du Pont asked the trial judge to overrule. The judge refused to do so. He conceded that Du Pont did indeed have a right to inform its employees as to its policies on sexual harassment, but he said the jury apparently concluded the company could have done so without associating Garziano with the offense. To the extent that Du Pont did the latter, it lost the right to be protected by the privilege.

On appeal, the circuit court reversed. It did not question the application of common law to the case. It agreed with the trial judge's holding that the management bulletin was protected by privilege and held that the privilege had not been abused by distribution of the bulletin to supervisors. However, it said there was a question, unresolved at trial, as to whether the privilege was abused by dissemination of information about Garziano to persons outside the plant who had no need to know it. The court remanded the case for resolution of that point.

This case is of further interest because it illustrates an instance in which even the truth can be libelous. Under common law, truth can be the subject of a libel action if there is no reasonable justification for publishing it. Thus, the courts found that Du Pont was justified in telling its own employees why Garziano was dismissed. To that point, the company was protected by privilege—by its right to

---

39. Flotech v. E.I. Du Pont de Nemours & Co., 627 F.Supp. 358 (D.Mass. 1985); 814 F.2d 775 (1st Cir. 1987).

share with its employees information to which they were entitled. But as the Fourth Circuit's decision clearly suggests, Du Pont had no reason to spread that information through the community. Students should not let themselves be confused by the court's holding in this case. It is confined only to the common law as it applies to libel actions brought by private individuals over matters that do not involve the public interest. If public officials or public figures are libel plaintiffs, or if private individuals are defamed because of their involvement in public issues, all must prove falsity. For such plaintiffs, the truth can't be libelous.

Greenmoss stands, then, as a reminder that libel law has not been completely brought under the realm of the First Amendment. For some professional communicators, the common law of libel, with its easy assumption of falsity and harm, is still there and can be used by private individuals whose private lives are needlessly defamed by their employers or by other nonmedia entities. Such plaintiffs need prove only identification, publication, and defamation. Harm is assumed. From then on, the burden of proof is on the defendant to justify his act. As *Garziano* illustrates, that can't always be done by proving truth. If the truth has been circulated to people who have no need to know it, plaintiffs can still win their cases. When business communications result in an action for libel—and no public issue is involved—the defense of choice is privilege, and the defendant must offer proof that sound business reasons supported circulation of the defamatory information. In the *Garziano* case, all courts agreed that the employees had a right to know that one of them had been terminated for violating the company's policy on sexual harassment. The trial judge believed the employees could have been notified without identifying the former employee, but the appellate court held that the use of his name within the company did not abuse the privilege. It was abused only if it could be proved that the employer was responsible for spreading word of Garziano and his offense to the public at large.

FOR REVIEW

1. With what is the law of defamation concerned? Distinguish between libel and slander; between libel per se and libel *per quod*.

2. Under common law, what elements had to be present to establish grounds for a lawsuit in defamation?

3. What factors control where such a lawsuit may be filed? Could the jurisdiction in which a libel action is filed make a difference in its outcome? Explain.

4. What is a retraction? Under what circumstances should one be made? When should one not be made?

5. Outline the Supreme Court's decision in *New York Times* v. *Sullivan*. What effect has it had on the common law of defamation?

6. Outline the Supreme Court's decision in *Gertz* v. *Robert Welch*. In what respect did it modify *New York Times?*

7. You are public relations director for a department store. Employee pilferage is a problem. The store manager decides to make an example of the principal suspect and fires him. No charges are filed. The manager also wants the remaining employees to know what happened and why, and she tells you it's your job to tell them. What do you do? Why?

8. Explain the significance of the Supreme Court's *Greenmoss* decision to business communicators. What meaning might it have for the news media?

CHAPTER 4

The constitutional ramparts erected around the media by *New York Times* and *Gertz* have made libel law one of the most complex fields of jurisprudence. Plaintiffs who sue a newspaper, magazine, book publisher, or broadcaster for libel under circumstances that raise any doubt whatsoever as to the validity of their case can anticipate years of litigation. One case in which the author served as an expert witness was in the courts for nine years, generating in the process a stack of documents nearly three feet high. Obviously, such extended litigation becomes very expensive for both sides.

Yet despite its complexity, any libel case has at the most four clearly defined points of contention, each subject to a judge's ruling that could bring the action to an end short of trial. At each of those points, the Supreme Court has said, the First Amendment compels the plaintiff to offer convincing proof that the case should go forward. If such proof is not offered, the judge is empowered to dismiss the case in response to a defendant's motion, if the facts are not in dispute. Such dismissal is called a "summary judgment." The crucial points of contention are:

THE ANATOMY
OF A LIBEL CASE

1. At the very start, the court must be convinced that the plaintiff was defamed. Only if it is reasonably clear that the plaintiff was the target of a false and defamatory assertion of fact will the case go forward.

2. Also to be established near the beginning of the case is the nature of the plaintiff. This is an important point of contention because public officials and public figures must prove a higher degree of fault in most states than is required of private individuals.

3. Once the nature of the plaintiff has been established, the next step is proving that the defendant was at fault. Public officials and public figures must offer clear and convincing proof of actual malice—that the defendant knew the defamatory assertion was false or acted in reckless disregard for the truth. In most states, private individuals must prove negligence—that the defendant acted carelessly.

4. In most states, private individual plaintiffs finally must prove that they have been harmed. This can include embarrassment and humiliation, being shunned by others, or actual loss of income.

Although the Supreme Court's decisions have put the entire burden of proof on the plaintiff, there still are proofs defendants can offer that will lead to dismissal of the lawsuit:

1. Although the plaintiff must prove falsity to get started, a defendant can win a judgment by offering convincing proof of the truth of the allegedly libelous assertions.

2. The defendant also can counter by proving that the alleged defamation was drawn from privileged sources, that is, from public officials acting in an official capacity, the proceedings of a public deliberative body, public records, highly placed participants in a public controversy, or other trusted sources. Journalists have a qualified First Amendment privilege to report public issues.

Overall in this chapter we will be exploring the defense of constitutional privilege established by *New York Times* and further defined by *Gertz* and other Supreme Court decisions. That defense is so pervasive that it is a part of every lawsuit in which someone sues the mass media for libel growing out of the reporting or discussion of a public issue. The Supreme Court has said that every such lawsuit requires the proofs listed above. In the pages that follow, we will examine the significant cases defining and applying to the four points of contention the principles found in *New York Times* and *Gertz*.

Major Cases

- *Anderson* v. *Liberty Lobby,* 477 U.S. 242, 106 S.Ct. 2505, 91 L.Ed.2d 282 (1986).

- *Bose Corporation* v. *Consumers Union,* 466 U.S. 485, 104 S.Ct. 1949, 80 L.Ed.2d 502 (1984).

- *Brown & Williamson Tobacco Co.* v. *Jacobson,* 713 F.2d 262 (7th Cir. 1983).

- *Edwards* v. *National Audubon Society,* 566 F.2d 113 (2d Cir. 1977).

- *Greenbelt Cooperative Publishing Co.* v. *Bresler,* 398 U.S. 6, 90 S.Ct. 1537, 26 L.Ed.2d 6 (1970).

- *Herbert* v. *Lando,* 441 U.S. 153, 99 S.Ct. 1635, 60 L.Ed.2d 115 (1979).

- *Hustler Magazine* v. *Falwell,* 485 U.S. 46, 108 S.Ct. 876, 99 L.Ed.2d 41 (1988).

- *Hutchinson* v. *Proxmire,* 443 U.S. 111, 99 S.Ct. 2675, 61 L.Ed.2d 411 (1979).

- *Liberty Lobby* v. *Dow Jones & Company,* 838 F.2d 1287 (D.C.Cir. 1988).

- *McCall* v. *Courier-Journal and Louisville Times,* 623 S.W.2d 882 (Ky. 1981).

- *Nelson* v. *Associated Press,* 667 F.Supp. 1468 (S.D.Fla. 1987).

- *Old Dominion Branch No. 496, National Association of Letter Carriers, AFL-CIO* v. *Austin,* 418 U.S. 264, 94 S.Ct. 2770, 41 L.Ed.2d 745 (1974).

- *Ollman* v. *Evans,* 750 F.2d 970 (D.C.Cir. 1984).

- *Rosenblatt* v. *Baer,* 383 U.S. 75, 86 S.Ct. 669, 15 L.Ed.2d 597 (1966).

- *St. Amant* v. *Thompson,* 390 U.S. 727, 88 S.Ct. 1323, 20 L.Ed.2d 262 (1968).

- *Stone* v. *Essex County Newspapers,* 330 N.E.2d 161 (Mass. 1975).

- *Tavoulareas* v. *Piro,* 817 F.2d 762 (D.C.Cir. 1987).

- *Time, Inc.* v. *Firestone,* 424 U.S. 448, 96 S.Ct. 958, 47 L.Ed.2d 154 (1976).

- *Wolston* v. *Reader's Digest Association,* 443 U.S. 157, 99 S.Ct. 2701, 61 L.Ed.2d 450 (1979).

THE BEGINNING: ESSENTIAL ELEMENTS ══════

Under the First Amendment, as under common law, three basic elements must be present before a plaintiff can begin a libel action. Two, publication and identification, have not been changed by the *New York Times* rule. They are summarized below only for review. The third, defamation, has undergone considerable change and will be treated in full.

Publication

Publication is proved by offering a copy of the offending article or photograph or a transcript of the broadcast. Courts require plaintiffs to specify the passages considered false and defamatory.

Identification

If the individual was named in the submitted material, no issue of identification exists, provided the allegedly defamatory portions were directed at the plaintiff. If the identification is not direct, evidence must be offered, as in *New York Times,* that others understood the defamatory language to be directed at the plaintiff.

Generally, libel is an individual matter, although some courts have held that members of small groups, usually defined as fewer than twenty-five members, can maintain an action if the defamatory language is inclusive. One court held that nine Neiman-Marcus models had grounds for suit against the author of a book describing the models as including the best call girls in Dallas.[1] But a California court held that three wives of members of the Hell's Angels motorcycle gang could not maintain an action against *Playboy* for an article describing the unusual sexual activities of the gang's "brides," because none was sufficiently identified.[2] There were more than a hundred wives of gang members. Libel actions cannot be begun in behalf of dead persons, but an action already in process can be pursued by a plaintiff's heirs.[3]

False and Defamatory Assertions of Fact

From the beginning, lower courts read *New York Times* as requiring public official libel plaintiffs to carry the burden of proving falsity. This conclusion was derived from the Supreme Court's holding that public officials must prove either knowledge of falsity or reckless disregard of probable falsity and must offer convincing evidence of one or the other. Lower court judges reasoned that public officials and, later, public figures could not prove knowledge of falsity without first proving falsity.

---

1. Neiman-Marcus v. Lait, 107 F.Supp. 96 (S.D.N.Y. 1952).
2. Barger v. Playboy Enterprises, 564 F.Supp. 1151 (N.D.Calif. 1983).
3. McBeth v. United Press International, 505 F.2d 959 (5th Cir. 1974).

With respect to private individuals, *Gertz* left doubt as to whether they, like public persons, must prove falsity. As we noted in the previous chapter, that doubt was not resolved until the Supreme Court decided *Philadelphia Newspapers* v. *Hepps*.[4] The case arose out of a series of articles in the *Philadelphia Inquirer* linking a beer distributor with organized crime. Holding that he was a private individual, the Pennsylvania Supreme Court said his libel suit against the newspaper should be controlled by the state's common law. That put the burden of proving one of the common-law defenses—truth, fair comment, or privilege—on the newspaper. The U.S. Supreme Court reversed, five to four. The majority said that if the decision were permitted to stand it would have "a chilling effect...antithetical to the First Amendment's protection of true speech on matters of public concern."

As a consequence, it is settled that anyone who sues the mass media for libel in connection with a public issue must offer specific evidence of falsity to have a case. Further, the language in question must defame the plaintiff, through an accusation either that is libelous on its face or that would otherwise harm the plaintiff's reputation. If the assertions in question are true, they are not actionable, no matter how defamatory they may be, nor how questionable the defendant's motives for using them. The Supreme Court held in *Garrison* v. *Louisiana*,[5] that truth "may not be the subject of either civil or criminal sanctions where the discussion of public affairs is concerned."

To be actionable, then, the assertions at issue in a libel case must be both false and defamatory. This is a question of law to be resolved by a judge. A case will go forward only if the judge is offered convincing evidence that a report is both false and defamatory or if the facts are in doubt. Questions of fact are to be resolved by the trier of fact, usually a jury, on the basis of evidence presented in court.

Thus, a report based on police records of an individual's arrest on a charge of dealing in cocaine provides no basis for a libel suit. To say that someone has been arrested for dealing in cocaine is defamatory among most elements of society, but an accurate report of the arrest would not be false. Nor would there be grounds for action if a magazine erroneously reported that a reporter had won a Pulitzer Prize. The reporter might be embarrassed, but there is nothing defamatory about winning the most prestigious prize in journalism.

Excerpts from two court decisions will illustrate the points made above. In the first, *Nelson* v. *Associated Press,* the court held that there was no cause of action because the assertions at issue either were true or were not defamatory. In the second, *Brown & Williamson Tobacco Co.* v. *Jacobson,* the court held that the assertions were both false and defamatory, eventually resulting in a multi-million-dollar judgment.

Nelson grew out of the news coverage given a lurid divorce trial in Palm Beach, Florida. Herbert ("Peter") Pulitzer sued his wife, Roxanne, for divorce,

Nelson v. *Associated Press,* 667 F.Supp. 1468 (S.D.Fla. 1987).

alleging, among other things, that she participated in séances while she was in bed surrounded by friends, some of whom engaged in sexual activity with her. During that period of

---

4.   475 U.S. 767, 106 S.Ct. 1558, 89 L.Ed.2d 783 (1986).
5.   379 U.S. 64, 85 S.Ct. 209, 12 L.Ed.2d 1042 (1964).

her life, Roxanne consulted frequently with Janis Nelson, a professional psychic, who also was her confidante. During the divorce trial, Peter summoned Nelson as a witness.

An Associated Press story on the trial was edited at the *Miami Herald* so that one sentence read as follows: "Nelson testified last month that she saw Mrs. Pulitzer share sex and cocaine with Brian Richards, an alleged cocaine dealer, at Richards' apartment."

Nelson sued for libel, alleging that the sentence defamed her by depicting her as a voyeur, which her complaint defined as "a prying observer who is usually seeking the sordid or scandalous." In ruling on a defense motion for dismissal, the trial judge focused on the word "usually." He said that to stretch the meaning of "saw" to imply that Nelson "is a prying observer *usually* seeking the sordid or scandalous...is a tortured reading of the words." The passage would be defamatory, he said, only if it "had said 'frequently saw,' 'usually saw,' 'regularly saw,' or 'enjoyed seeing.'" Further, the judge said, the language was essentially true. Nelson testified that she had seen Roxanne and Richards go into a bedroom and, when both of them emerged a "long time" later, Roxanne was zipping up her pants and adjusting her clothes. The court noted that literal truth is not always required in determining whether a statement is both false and defamatory. Although Nelson had not observed Roxanne and her lover engaging in sexual intercourse, "she unquestionably knew they did, so in the biblical sense of the word, she 'saw' it." Therefore, because the sentence as edited by the *Herald* was neither defamatory to Nelson nor false, it could not be the basis for a libel action.

The *Brown & Williamson* case grew out of the commentary segment of a WBBM television newscast in Chicago. Walter Jacobson, the anchor, said Brown & Williamson was conducting an advertising campaign designed to get young people to smoke Viceroy cigarettes. He said the company's strategy, based on a marketing study, related the brand to "pot, wine, beer and sex." Jacobson relied in part on a Federal Trade Commission staff report that concluded the tobacco company had hired a consultant to look into advertising approaches that would appeal to young people. But the report didn't say that the consultant's findings had been adopted.

Brown & Williamson Tobacco Co. v. *Jacobson,* 713 F.2d 262 (7th Cir. 1983).

Brown & Williamson sued Jacobson, WBBM, and the station's owner, CBS Inc., for libel. The defendants argued that the broadcast was neither false nor defamatory. A trial judge agreed, but, on appeal, the U.S. Court of Appeals, Seventh Circuit, held that Jacobson's assertions were libelous on their face. The court said the news item led viewers to believe that the company had adopted an advertising policy designed to persuade children to smoke cigarettes. The court also held that the newscast associated cigarette smoking "with slightly illicit activity." Thus, the tobacco company was portrayed as encouraging criminal activity, because most states have laws forbidding sale of cigarettes to minors. Brown & Williamson offered the FTC report as proof that it had not conducted the advertising campaign described by Jacobson. The case was remanded for trial. Eventually, a jury found for the tobacco company, awarding it $3,050,000 in damages.[6] The verdict survived appeal and was affirmed when the Supreme Court refused to review the case.[7]

Hyperbole

Dictionaries define "hyperbole" as an exaggerated statement used as a figure of speech to make a point, as in "this book weighs a ton." In reality, few books weigh more than 2 pounds, and everyone knows it. Twice the Supreme Court has recognized that some political speech also is exaggerated to make a point and therefore is not to be taken literally. In a third instance, it went further and applied the principle to crude social commentary.

In *Greenbelt Cooperative Publishing Co.* v. *Bresler,* a speaker, during a hearing on a zoning change, called a real estate developer's offer of compromise a form of blackmail. When a newspaper quoted the speaker, the developer sued for libel, arguing that he falsely had been accused of committing the crime of blackmail. Maryland courts agreed with him, awarding him a sizable judgment. The Supreme Court reversed, holding that the word "blackmail" could not reasonably be understood as an accusation of crime. It reasoned that taken in context, the ordinary reader would understand that the word simply summed up one opponent's strong objections to the developer's negotiating tactics. It was, in short, "rhetorical hyperbole" of a kind that could be expected of participants in a debate that could affect property values.

Greenbelt Cooperative Publishing Co. v. *Bresler,* 398 U.S. 6, 90 S.Ct. 1537, 26 L.Ed.2d 6 (1970).

Old Dominion Branch No. 496, National Association of Letter Carriers, AFL-CIO v. *Austin* grew out of a labor dispute. When several post office employees in Richmond, Virginia, refused to join the Letter Carriers union, the union published a leaflet denouncing them as "scabs." The epithet was reinforced by a quotation attributed to Jack London portraying scabs as traitors to their religion, their country, their families, and their class. The targets of the abuse sued for libel, arguing that they had falsely been accused of treason. The Supreme Court held that the leaflet's language, strong as it was, was protected political speech. The Court said that anyone who knew anything about labor disputes would know that "traitor" was used in a "loose, figurative sense" and not as an accusation of crime. Such persons also would know that "exaggerated rhetoric was commonplace in labor disputes."

Old Dominion Branch No. 496, National Association of Letter Carriers, AFL-CIO v. *Austin,* 418 U.S. 264, 94 S.Ct. 2770, 41 L.Ed.2d 745 (1974).

A more recent case added another dimension to the points made in those two decisions. In *Hustler Magazine* v. *Falwell,* the Court held that an "outrageous"

---

6.   644 F.Supp. 1240 (N.D.Ill. 1986).
7.   Stephen Wermiel, "Justices Let Stand Award of $3,050,000 against CBS, Anchorman in Libel Case," *Wall Street Journal,* 5 April 1988, quoting Henry Kaufman of the Libel Defense Resource Center in New York.

Hustler Magazine v. *Falwell*, 485 U.S. 46, 108 S.Ct. 876, 99 L.Ed.2d 41 (1988).

insult directed at a nationally known television evangelist was protected hyperbole even though it seemed to make an assertion of fact. At issue was a parody based on Campari liqueur's "first time" advertising campaign. In a cartoon drawn to resemble a Campari ad, *Hustler* said the Reverend Jerry Falwell's "first time" was during a drunken, incestuous rendezvous with his mother in an outhouse. The Supreme Court said the parody "suggested that [Falwell] is a hypocrite who preaches only when he is drunk." At the bottom of the page, a disclaimer in small type said, "Ad parody, not to be taken seriously."

Falwell did take it seriously. He sued for damages for libel, invasion of privacy, and intentional infliction of emotional distress. The court threw out the invasion of privacy claim, but the case went to trial on the other two counts. A federal court jury in Roanoke, Virginia, where Falwell has his headquarters, held

Larry Flynt, publisher of *Hustler* magazine, talks with reporters outside the Supreme Court building in Washington, D.C., after the Court heard arguments on his appeal of a $100,000 judgment in favor of the Rev. Jerry Falwell. The Court held that *Hustler*'s ad parody portraying Falwell's "first time" as with his mother in an outhouse was a protected expression of opinion. Flynt is in a wheelchair because a would-be assassin's bullet left him paralyzed below the waist. (AP/Wide World Photos)

that the evangelist had not been libeled because the ad parody could not reasonably be understood as making factual assertions about him. However, the jury found that there had been an intentional infliction of emotional distress and awarded Falwell $100,000 in compensatory damages and another $100,000 in punitive damages, with half of that levied against Flynt personally. The U.S. Court of Appeals for the Fourth Circuit affirmed.

The Supreme Court reversed unanimously. Chief Justice William H. Rehnquist, who wrote for the Court, said there was no doubt that the parody was "gross and repugnant" in the eyes of some people. The courts below had based their decisions on the conclusion that the cartoon was so outrageous as to be offensive and that it reflected an intent to insult Falwell. Rehnquist noted that in some branches of tort law bad motives may be taken into account, but, he added,

> we think the First Amendment prohibits such a result in the area of public debate about public figures.
>
> Were we to hold otherwise, there can be little doubt that political cartoonists and satirists would be subjected to damages awards without any showing that their work falsely defamed its subject.... The appeal of the political cartoon is often based on exploration of unfortunate physical traits or politically embarrassing events—an exploration often calculated to injure the feelings of the subject of the portrayal. The art of the cartoonist is often not reasoned or evenhanded, but slashing and one-sided.

Rehnquist rejected "outrageousness" as a standard for determining when political speech becomes so insulting that the speaker should be held accountable for it in court. To adopt such a standard, he said, "would allow a jury to impose liability on the basis of the jurors' tastes or views, or perhaps on their dislike of a particular expression." With that said, the Court returned to the standard established in *New York Times*. Whether public officials or public figures are suing for libel or for intentional infliction of emotional distress, they must prove that they have been victims of a false and defamatory statement of fact made with actual malice.

The decision is of great importance to cartoonists and satirists and to the media that disseminate their work. The decision upholds the right to deflate pompous or self-righteous public officials and public figures by "outrageous" treatment, even though the fault may be seen only through the eye of the beholder. *Falwell, Greenbelt,* and *Old Dominion* recognize a fact of political life in the late twentieth century: People who want to get the public's attention are more likely to do so with rhetoric than with logic. If that rhetoric goes beyond the bounds of belief, it is protected by the First Amendment.

Opinion

The constitutional protection of opinion in libel cases is based, as we have noted, on an almost offhand observation by Justice Lewis F. Powell, Jr., in *Gertz.* Writing for a majority of the Supreme Court, he said that "there is no such thing as a false idea." Opinion, he added, no matter how "pernicious" or mistaken it may seem, should be countered by debate, not by a judge or jury deciding a libel suit. At the time, most courts and legal scholars considered the passage as *dicta* because it was not essential to the Court's decision, and the passage therefore did not establish a precedent that lower courts were required to apply. However, within a few years some judges were citing Powell's language to support decisions to dismiss libel cases based on editorials, commentary, and other assertions of opinion. By 1984, the trend had assumed such force that the U.S. Court of Appeals for the Ninth Circuit asserted flatly that defamation actions cannot be based on statements of opinion.[8] In that same year, the U.S. Court of Appeals for the District of Columbia Circuit, sitting *en banc* (the entire panel of judges participated) went a step further and held that the distinction between fact and opinion is a question of law to be decided by a judge.[9]

The Supreme Court did not directly address the constitutional status of opinion until it decided the *Falwell* case discussed in the preceding section. Indeed, both Rehnquist and former Chief Justice Warren E. Burger had written in one instance that *Gertz* had not established a federal rule with respect to opinion.[10] In *Falwell,* Rehnquist reversed his field. He wrote, echoing Powell in *Gertz,* "The First Amendment recognizes no such thing as a 'false' idea." Expanding on that theme, he analyzed several of the Supreme Court's libel decisions, concluding that even when a critic of a public person is moved by "motives that are less than admirable," his opinion is protected by the Constitution. That also is true, Rehnquist added, when the unfavorable opinion is inspired by hatred or ill will. Because he was writing for a unanimous court, and because the *Hustler* cartoon did express an opinion of sorts, Rehnquist thus put the full weight of the Supreme Court behind the principle that the First Amendment gives absolute protection to expressions of opinion.

In the closing days of its 1989–90 term, the Court modified that position. It held in *Milkovich* v. *Lorain Journal Co.* that opinions implying, or based on, a false assertion of fact have no more protection than stories based on facts.[11] Chief Justice Rehnquist, who wrote for himself and six others, said:

> If a speaker says, "In my opinion John Jones is a liar," he implies a knowledge of facts which lead to the conclusion that Jones told an untruth. Even if the speaker states the facts upon which he bases his opinion, if those facts are either incorrect or incomplete, of if his assessment of them is erroneous, the statement may still imply a false assertion of fact. Simply couching such statements in terms of opinion does not dispel these implications; and the statement, "In my opinion Jones is a liar," can cause as much damage to reputation as the statement, "Jones is a liar."

The case at issue grew out of a sports column commenting on a court decision upholding a high school wrestling team's right to compete in a state tournament.

8. Church of Scientology of California v. Flynn, 744 F.2d 694 (9th Cir. 1984).
9. Ollman v. Evans, 750 F.2d 970 (D.C.Cir. 1984); cert. denied, 471 U.S. 1127 (1985).
10. Miskovsky v. Oklahoma Publishing Co., 459 U.S. 923, 103 S.Ct. 235, 74 L.Ed.2d 186 (1982).
11. Stephen Wermiel, "First Amendment Shield for Media Narrowed by Court," *Wall Street Journal,* 22 June 1990; Debra Gersh, "Opinion No Exception," *Editor & Publisher,* 30 June 1990, p. 12 + .

The decision overruled a state athletic association's finding that the team's coach provoked an altercation at a wrestling match. The columnist, relying on information obtained from the association's director, said the coach must have lied to the court. The case had been in litigation for fifteen years and twice previously the Supreme Court had refused to review it. Ohio courts found that the column was opinion protected by the First Amendment.

In doing so, Ohio joined thirty-five other states and virtually all of the twelve federal circuits in holding that as a matter of law expressions of opinion enjoy absolute First Amendment protection. Lacking firm guidance from the Supreme Court, lower courts have varied in establishing criteria for distinguishing fact from opinion, moving in four directions:

1. Some look at the context in which the alleged libel occurred. If it was in an editorial or in a column of political commentary, the defamatory assertions are considered opinion. Such courts reason that the average person knows that editorial writers and columnists deal in opinion.

2. Others look at the nature of the offending article. If devoted to commentary on government policy and aimed at government officials, the article is protected opinion.

3. Still other courts probe more deeply into the nature of the alleged libel and consider what they call "the totality of the circumstances." This involves a four-step analysis.

4. Finally, some courts go further and try to discern whether assertions of fact may be embedded in or implied from what appears to be opinion. If those underlying assertions are held to be false and defamatory, the libel action can go forward.

The most influential appellate court decision in this area was handed down by the U.S. Court of Appeals for the District of Columbia Circuit, sitting *en banc*.

Ollman v. *Evans,* 750 F.2d 970 (D.C.Cir. 1984); cert. denied, 471 U.S. 1127, 105 S.Ct. 2662, 86 L.Ed.2d 278 (1985).

The case, *Ollman* v. *Evans,* had been in the courts for seven years and presented such difficult issues that it divided the appellate panel six to five, with the judges writing seven different opinions. The Supreme Court declined an opportunity to review the decision, although Rehnquist and Burger wrote that they would have taken the case so as to try to draw a clear line between actionable fact and nonactionable opinion. They would have limited the latter to political ideas for which the test of truth "is indeed the market place and not the courtroom."

The opinion written by Judge Kenneth W. Starr for himself and five other members of the appellate court panel attempted to establish standards for separating fact from opinion. He noted that in many instances assertions of fact and opinion are so intertwined it is difficult to tell where one begins and the other ends. This was particularly true of *Ollman,* which grew out of a syndicated newspaper column written by Rowland Evans and Robert Novak. Their subject was a search committee's recommendation that Bertell Ollman be named chair of the Department of Government and Politics at the University of Maryland. In the columnists' opinion, the choice was bad because Ollman was an avowed Marxist who used his classroom "as an instrument for preparing what he calls 'the revolution.'" The columnists said Ollman was a political activist whose purpose in teaching was "to convert students to socialism." Near the end of the column, Evans and Novak quoted an unidentified political scientist as saying, "Ollman has no status within the profession, but is a pure and simple activist."

After the column appeared in the *Washington Post* and other newspapers, the university's board of trustees refused to appoint Ollman, who then sought a retraction from the authors. When the columnists refused his request, he filed suit for libel. A U.S. district court judge granted a motion for dismissal, holding that the article was opinion and thus protected absolutely by the First Amendment. On appeal, a three-judge panel of the District of Columbia Circuit Court went through the article paragraph by paragraph and concluded that false and defamatory assertions of fact were mixed with opinion. They sent the case back to the district court for trial. Again, the judge ruled for Evans and Novak. On further appeal, the circuit court's entire panel of judges wrestled with the overriding question: Was the column solely an expression of opinion? The majority concluded it was.

Judge Starr began by examining cases in which other courts sought to distinguish between fact and opinion. He found that some judges made "a judgment call" without attempting to justify it, others focused on whether the assertion in question could be proved true or false, while "still others adopted a multi-factor test, attempting to assess the allegedly defamatory proposition in the totality of the circumstances in which it appeared."

Starr chose the last approach and elaborated on it. Starting with the premise that assertions may be factual in some contexts but can be accepted as opinion in others, he concluded that in such instances "courts should analyze the totality of the circumstances in which the statements are made to decide whether they merit the absolute First Amendment protection enjoyed by opinion." He then conducted a four-step analysis that has come to be known as "the totality of circumstances test." Its components are:

1. *Common Usage*. What is "the common usage of meaning of the specific language of the challenged statement itself"? The purpose of this step is to determine "whether the statement has a precise core of meaning for which a consensus of understanding exists or, conversely, whether the statement is indefinite and ambiguous."

2. *Verifiability*. "...is the statement capable of being objectively characterized as true or false?" Facts may be proved true or false; opinions cannot be more than fair or unfair.

3. *Context*. If steps one and two do not lead to a conclusion, the disputed language must be looked at in the context of the entire article or column. Will the "unchallenged language surrounding the allegedly defamatory

statement...influence the average reader's readiness to infer that a particular statement has factual content?''

4. *Setting.* If there still is doubt, the inquiry must move to the larger setting in which the statement appears. ''Different types of writing have...widely varying social conventions which *signal* to the reader the likelihood of a statement's being either fact or opinion.'' Readers expect political cartoons or editorials to express opinion. Most also understand that the editorial page and, in some newspapers, the op-ed page are reserved for expressions of opinion.

The court of appeals concluded that because Evans and Novak make their living writing generally conservative columns that ordinarily appear on the editorial or op-ed pages of newspapers, readers would understand their comments on a Marxist professor to be opinion.

Judge Robert Bork concurred in that conclusion, but he and three other members of the panel would have adopted a much simpler, and broader, standard for distinguishing between fact and opinion. They would look at what the speaker or writer was trying to do. If the purpose was to influence public policy or comment on political matters, they would give such speech absolute protection. They noted that the primary purpose of the First Amendment is to protect political speech. Bork wrote that to preserve the ''vigorous and robust'' political arena required by that amendment, those who enter the arena must ''accept a degree of derogation that others need not.''

Although some courts have seemed to accept the Bork view by ruling that editorials stating political views enjoy absolute protection, far more have looked to

Liberty Lobby v. *Dow Jones & Company,* **838 F.2d 1287 (D.C.Cir. 1988).**

Judge Starr's ''totality of the circumstances'' test for guidance. Among them is Judge Bork himself, who, in one of his last decisions as a circuit court judge,[12] upheld dismissal of a libel suit brought by Liberty Lobby against Dow Jones & Company, publishers of the *Wall Street Journal.* The case is of interest because it illustrates how courts can view a characterization, in this instance ''anti-Semitic,'' as both an assertion of fact and as opinion. In 1984, a *Journal* reporter described Liberty Lobby, a citizens' action group, as anti-Semitic. The article was an investigative report linking the Lobby with a publisher of racist tracts. A year later, the characterization was repeated in an editorial page column commenting on a libel trial in which William F. Buckley, Jr., was defending himself and his magazine, *National Review,* against an action brought by Liberty Lobby. The magazine, like the *Journal,* had described the Lobby as anti-Semitic.

When Liberty Lobby sued Dow Jones for libel, the publisher moved that the action be dismissed. The trial court judge granted the motion, concluding that as-

---

12. President Reagan nominated Bork to fill a vacancy on the Supreme Court in the fall of 1987. After various groups had charged that Bork was insensitive to the rights of women and minorities, the Senate refused to confirm the nomination. Bork resigned from the court of appeals the next year.

sertions in the article and column were substantially true and that the description of the organization as anti-Semitic, while defamatory, was in all instances protected opinion. The court of appeals affirmed, but Bork, writing for the court, rejected the holding that the term "anti-Semitic" is an expression of opinion in all instances. He said the appellate court was "unwilling to say that the term has no core meaning so that it is an expression of opinion in any context and, as such, always constitutionally protected." He said that it "has both descriptive and normative content." Therefore, the use of the term had to be looked at in context to determine whether it was meant to describe the Liberty Lobby's factual position with respect to Jews or was invective not intended to be taken literally. In this instance, Bork concluded, the story contained sufficient factual evidence to support a reasonable conclusion that the characterization was true.

PURE OPINION VERSUS MIXED OPINION   The discussion above reflects the course taken by most courts with respect to expressions of opinion. However, two reservations must be noted. In 1977, only three years after the Supreme Court decided *Gertz,* the panel of lawyers who revised *Restatement of Torts* adopted a position on the First Amendment protection of opinion.[13] Their work necessarily was based on only a few cases, some of them decided by courts that considered Powell's comments *dicta.* Nevertheless, the panel concluded that opinion is protected by the First Amendment. However, the panel proceeded to muddy the waters by dividing opinion into two kinds, "pure" and "mixed"; the panel defined "pure" opinion as comment based on facts either expressed as a foundation for the comment or generally known. Such statements enjoy absolute protection. "Mixed" opinion either includes false and defamatory assertions of fact or implies their existence. The panel said that libel actions can be based on the false and defamatory assertions, either stated or implied, that are "mixed" with the opinion. One of the hazards of this position is the difficulty of knowing which false and defamatory "facts" a judge or jury will find as implied by an expression of opinion. Had that test been applied in *Ollman,* as a minority of the panel would have done, the result might well have been different. The minority argued, for instance, that the assertion, "Ollman has no status within the profession," was subject to being proved true or false. The *Restatement*'s view thus is narrower than that taken in Judge Starr's totality of the circumstances test, which excused that alleged false statement of fact because it was part of a column readers would consider to be an expression of opinion. The Supreme Court's decision in *Milkovich* seems to have endorsed the *Restatement*'s view.

A survey of the case reports shows that courts in the following states have either referred to the *Restatement*'s position with approval or have adopted its reasoning: Colorado, Florida, Maine, Massachusetts, Michigan, Nevada, New Mexico, New York, Pennsylvania, Rhode Island, and Washington. Although some of the decisions predate the 1984 decision in *Ollman,* others, particularly in New York, are of recent vintage.

---

13. Restatement (Second) of Torts § 566 (1977).

A Massachusetts case illustrates how courts apply the *Restatement*'s position. When a television reporter in Boston was fired after he had prepared a series of allegedly one-sided telecasts critical of the mayor, the station announced only that he had been guilty of "misconduct and insubordination." Reporters asked the station's spokeswoman for more details. She said the reporter had a history of "bad reporting techniques...[and of] sloppy and irresponsible reporting," and she was so quoted in the media. The reporter sued the station for libel. A trial judge dismissed the case, and the Supreme Judicial Court of Massachusetts affirmed.[14] It held that reasonable people can look at the facts and disagree on whether a reporter is sloppy and irresponsible without being able to offer conclusive proof either way. Thus the reporter was unable to offer convincing proof that he was the victim of a false and defamatory assertion of fact.

ACCUSATIONS OF CRIME DISGUISED AS OPINION   The second reservation involves accusations of crime couched as expressions of opinion. If the factual support for the accusation is ambiguous, or suggests that the accusation is to be taken seriously, courts are likely to consider it actionable. *Braig* v. *Field Communications,*[15] decided by the Superior Court of Pennsylvania, illustrates the point.

As a judge of the Court of Common Pleas of Philadelphia County, Joseph P. Braig had presided at the trial of a police officer accused of murdering a nineteen-year-old black man. Braig declared a mistrial on the ground of "intentional prosecutorial misconduct." His ruling was controversial and became the subject of discussion on a WKBS-TV public affairs program. An assistant district attorney said Braig was "no friend of the police brutality unit [of the prosecutor's office]. I don't care who we sent in to try that case, in my opinion, that case was going to get blown out." Braig took the position that the speaker accused him of being biased in favor of the police to the point of letting them get away with murder and a party to a "fix." He sued both the assistant district attorney and the station for libel. A trial court granted a defense motion for summary judgment, holding that the remark quoted above was a statement of opinion. On appeal, the superior court held otherwise. Despite the speaker's qualifying "in my opinion," the statement, taken in context, emerged as a possible assertion of fact. The court said a jury should be permitted to decide whether the ordinary listener would conclude that Braig has conspired with the police in a "fix."

Nevertheless, the First Amendment's protection for opinion has become a strong and frequently used defense in libel actions. If a judge can be persuaded to rule as a matter of law that an allegedly defamatory statement is an expression of opinion, the plaintiff has no cause of action. This means that unless the ruling is overturned on appeal the defendant will be spared the expense of going to trial. Opinion is loosely defined as comment that is not subject to being proved true or false.

---

14. Cole v. Westinghouse Broadcasting, 435 N.E.2d 1021 (1982).
15. 456 A.2d 1366 (Pa. 1983).

THE STATUS OF LIBEL PLAINTIFFS ========

Once libel plaintiffs have proved to a judge's satisfaction that they have been the victims of a false and defamatory assertion of fact, their cases can go forward. At that point, in all but a few states, the judge must resolve a second point of contention that will have a major bearing on how the case proceeds. The court must determine whether the plaintiff is a public official, a public figure, or a private individual. In all states, public persons can prevail only if they offer clear and convincing proof of actual malice. But in a majority of the states, under the option offered by the Supreme Court in *Gertz,* private individuals can prevail by proving that the defendant was negligent. In a few states, private individuals also must prove actual malice if they have been defamed by a news medium during the discussion of a public issue. Thus, in most libel suits, a judge's decision as to the status of the plaintiff can be a factor in who wins or loses. If the plaintiff is a mayor, a member of a legislative body, or a candidate for such offices, the question of status can be answered fairly easily, but if the plaintiff is a welfare department case worker, a teacher, a lawyer, or a party to a legal proceeding, status is more difficult to determine. This is especially so when the plaintiff also is newsworthy. The Supreme Court has offered lower courts guidance in making such determinations. This has been supplemented by appellate court decisions. The principles derived from these decisions are summarized below.

Public Officials

There is no doubt that L. B. Sullivan, whose libel suit resulted in the *New York Times* rule, was a public official. He held an elective office, and as supervisor of the police department in Montgomery, Alabama, made public policy and had considerable discretion in how he carried out his duties. Therefore, what he did and how he did it had an impact on a good many persons and were proper subjects for public debate.

However, only a minority of public officials is elected. Many are appointed to office, and still others are simply hired to do a job. Thus it is not surprising that *Rosenblatt* v. *Baer,* 383 U.S. 75, 86 S.Ct. 669, 15 L.Ed.2d 597 (1966). within two years after it decided *New York Times* v. *Sullivan,* the Supreme Court sought, in *Rosenblatt* v. *Baer,* to define public officials. Baer had been manager of a county-owned ski slope in Laconia, New Hampshire. He was caught in a political dispute and had to resign. During the following ski season, Rosenblatt wrote a column for the local newspaper commenting on how much more profitable the ski slope was under the new manager. Arguing that the column implied that he'd been skimming funds from the slope's till, Baer sued Rosenblatt for libel, winning a $31,500 judgment in the state courts. The Supreme Court took the case and reversed, holding that Baer was a public official who would have to prove actual malice, which he could not do. The Court's decision said:

We remarked in *New York Times* that we had no occasion "to determine how far down into the lower ranks of government employees the 'public official' designation would extend for purposes of this rule, or otherwise specify categories of persons who would or would not be included."...No precise lines need to be drawn for this case. The motivating force for the decision in *New York Times* was twofold....There is, first, a strong interest in debate on public issues, and, second, a strong interest in debate about those persons who are in a position significantly to influence resolution of those issues....It is clear, therefore, that the "public official" designation applies at the very least to those among the hierarchy of government employees who have, or appear to the public to have, substantial responsibility for or control over the conduct of government affairs.

In this instance, Baer's testimony at the trial helped the Court classify him as a public official. He had said that the public regarded him as the man responsible for the success or failure of the ski slope's operation. Thus he had both "responsibility for" and "control over" a function of government that was important in a snow state like New Hampshire.

As a consequence of the Supreme Court's decision in *Rosenblatt,* courts seek answers to two questions in deciding whether a libel plaintiff is a public official:

— Does he or she have policy-making authority?

— Does he or she ordinarily have access to the news media?

If the answer to both questions is yes, the person is a public official. Courts have held the following to be public officials:

— A physician who was under contract at $125,000 a year to provide medical services to prisoners in Alaska state correctional facilities.[16] The Alaska Supreme Court quoted *Rosenblatt* in holding that the public had an interest in how he performed his duties.

— The building inspector in Ocean Beach, New York.[17] Building permits were issued or denied on the basis of his recommendations.

— A territorial detective in the Virgin Islands.[18] Courts, with a few exceptions, have held that any law enforcement officer who has authority to make arrests is a public official. Police officers have broad discretion in deciding whether to take persons into custody. If they decide to make an arrest, the consequences are severe, resulting in at least temporary loss of freedom for the subject of the arrest.

— The executive director of the State Human Relations Commission in Georgia.[19] Although he was appointed, not elected, he exercised broad discretion in carrying out his duties.

---

16. Green v. Northern Publishing Co., 655 P.2d 736 (Alaska 1982).
17. Dattner v. Pokoik, 437 N.Y.S.2d 425 (N.Y.App. 1981).
18. Zurita v. Virgin Islands Daily News, 578 F.Supp. 306 (D.V.I. 1984).
19. Walker v. Southeastern Newspapers, 9 Med.L.Rptr. 1516 (1982).

— The director of financial aid at Weber State College in Utah.[20] As the official responsible for administering $2 million a year in student aid, he invited public scrutiny, especially because most of the money came from public funds.

Several recent decisions serve as a reminder that not everyone on the public payroll qualifies as a public official for purposes of a libel suit. Courts in California and New York held, for instance, that public school teachers do not become public officials by carrying out the duties assigned to them in the classroom.[21] The courts ruled that because teachers are expected to conform to policies set by school boards and administrators, they are employees.

The United States Court of Appeals, Fourth Circuit, ruled that an archeological firm hired as a consultant to a county government was not a public official.[22] The court said the firm was a "fact-finder...[with] no control over governmental affairs. It made no recommendations, participated in no policy determinations, and exercised no discretion."

At least four courts have taken the position that the passage of time does not alter an individual's status as a public official if the alleged defamation relates to his or her activity when in office. The U.S. Court of Appeals for the Fifth Circuit said in 1987 that it could see "no persuasive reason why [plaintiffs'] departure from their public positions should exempt them from meeting the *New York Times* standard when they sue for a news story on that departure."[23]

Public officials, then, may be elected or appointed, but they must be able to exercise discretion. They must be able to make public policy or make decisions that have an effect on others. They must be involved in duties in which some segment of the public has an interest and which they can influence through discussion. This means that those persons on a public payroll who do no more than perform a job under the direction of a superior are not public officials for purpose of a libel suit.

Public Figures

In its decision in *Gertz,* the Supreme Court recognized a class of persons known as public figures and held that they, like public officials, should be required to prove actual malice if they sue the news media for libel. Such persons, the Court said, invite public attention and, because they are newsworthy, have ready access to the news media to respond to their critics. The Court went on to define three kinds of public figures:

— All-purpose public figures. Such persons "have assumed roles of especial prominence in the affairs of society." They have "persuasive power and influence."

---

20. VanDyke v. KUTV, 663 P.2d 52 (Utah 1983).
21. Franklin v. Lodge 1108, 97 Cal.App.3d 915 (1979); DeLuca v. New York News, 109 Misc.2d 341 (N.Y.Sup. 1981).
22. Arctic v. Loudoun Times Mirror Co., 624 F.2d 518 (4th Cir. 1980).
23. Zerangue v. TSP Newspapers, 814 F.2d 1066 (5th Cir. 1987). See also Gray v. Udevitz, 656 F.2d 588 (10th Cir. 1981), Hart v. Playboy Enterprises, 5 Med.L.Rptr. 1811 (D.Kan. 1979), and Stripling v. Literary Guild of America, 5 Med.L.Rptr. 1958 (W.D.Tex. 1979).

— Limited or "vortex" public figures. These are persons who "have thrust themselves to the forefront of particular public controversies in order to influence the resolution of the issues involved."

— Involuntary public figures. These are persons who do nothing to attract attention or influence public policy, yet find themselves in the middle of a controversy over a public issue.

The Court was trying to define more precisely a category that had emerged casually seven years earlier in its decision in *Curtis Publishing Co.* v. *Butts*.[24] In that decision it had held that Edwin Walker, a retired army general who was active in trying to prevent blacks from entering southern universities, and Wally Butts, athletic director at the University of Georgia, were public figures. Therefore, they, like public officials, would have to prove actual malice if they were to prevail in a libel suit. The Court's decision offered few specific guidelines to judges seeking guidance in deciding whether a plaintiff was a public figure. That is what the Court tried to do in *Gertz*. However, the Court has had occasion three times since to refine the guidelines further. Those decisions, and the pertinent decisions in state and federal appeals courts, will be treated below.

ALL-PURPOSE   All-purpose public figures have continuing news value. Or they exercise "persuasive power and influence" in matters of public concern. They are celebrities whose names are recognized by the general public. The public follows their ideas and actions with great interest. Because they have so much influence, courts have held that the media have considerable leeway in commenting on their activities. Chief Judge Edward Allen Tamm of the United States Court of Appeals, District of Columbia Circuit, had this to say in *Waldbaum* v. *Fairchild Publications, Inc.*,[25] in 1980:

> The media serve as a check on the power of the famous and that check must be strongest when the subject's influence is strongest. Fame often brings power, money, respect, adulation, and self-gratification. It also may bring close scrutiny that can lead to adverse as well as favorable comment. When someone steps into the public spotlight, or when he remains there once cast into it, he must take the bad with the good.

Courts have held that Johnny Carson, for many years host of the "Tonight" show on NBC television, is an all-purpose public figure.[26] So is William F. Buckley, Jr., the nationally syndicated conservative columnist and novelist.[27] Institutions have been held to be all-purpose public figures, among them the Church of Scientology,[28] which has five million members, the Reliance Insurance Co.,[29] a billion-dollar corporation, and Ithaca College,[30] a private liberal arts col-

24.   388 U.S. 130, 87 S.Ct. 1975, 18 L.Ed.2d 1094 (1967).
25.   627 F.2d 1287 (D.C. Cir. 1980).
26.   Carson v. Allied News Co., 529 F.2d 206 (7th Cir. 1976).
27.   Buckley v. Littell, 539 F.2d 882 (2d Cir. 1976).
28.   Church of Scientology v. Siegelman, 475 F.Supp. 950 (S.D.N.Y. 1979).
29.   Reliance Insurance Co. v. Barron's, 442 F.Supp. 1341 (S.D.N.Y. 1977).
30.   Ithaca College v. Yale Daily News Publishing Co., 105 Misc.2d 793 (N.Y.Sup. 1980).

Johnny Carson, who for more than twenty years as host of NBC's *Tonight* show was the televised bedtime companion of millions of Americans, has been held to be an all-purpose public figure. This means, as one court put it, that his name is a household word. It also means that if he sues for libel he must prove actual malice; that is, that the publisher of a defamatory falsehood about him knew it was false, or acted in reckless disregard for the truth. (UPI/Bettmann Newsphotos)

lege that a New York court found to be pervasively involved in public affairs as an educational institution.

Several courts have held that individuals can be all-purpose public figures with respect to a limited geographic area. Kansas courts held that an attorney who had practiced in the same community for thirty-two years, during which time he had taken an active role in resolving many public issues, became an all-purpose public figure.[31] New York courts came to the same conclusion about an individual who for ten years had injected himself into the attempt to resolve public controversies in his community.[32] Montana courts held that a former state chairman of the Republican party, an author of books on stocks and commodities, and the subject of articles in several business magazines, was an all-purpose public figure within that state.[33]

Notoriety can also make an all-purpose public figure, as a federal court demonstrated by holding that James Earl Ray, the convicted assassin of Rev. Martin Luther King, Jr., has that status.[34]

---

31. Steere v. Cupp. 602 P.2d 1267 (Kans. 1979).
32. Clements v. Gannett Co., 5 Med.L.Rptr. 1657 (1979).
33. Williams v. Pasma, 656 P.2d 212 (Mont. 1982).
34. Ray v. Time, Inc., 452 F.Supp. 618 (W.D.Tenn. 1978).

A common theme runs through the cases. All-purpose public figures have achieved what the U.S. Circuit Court for the District of Columbia called "celebrity in society," adding that well-known athletes and entertainers are the archetypes.[35] But that is not the end of it. To become all-purpose public figures, individuals must seek and win widespread public attention. They must achieve such influence that when they talk, people listen. They have the power to shape events. They are dominant figures, whether on the national stage or the more limited platforms of their states or communities. Whatever the forum, they are quoted in the print media and appear on television. As the District of Columbia circuit court noted, not many achieve such status, but those who do must be prepared to accept criticism as well as adulation. In our society, that is the lot of those who "have knowingly relinquished their anonymity in return for fame, fortune, or influence."

LIMITED OR "VORTEX"   Limited public figures become so through their voluntary involvement in an attempt to resolve a specific public controversy. Courts, including the Supreme Court, have made the point that persons can be newsworthy without becoming public figures. Courts have said that the news media cannot create public figures simply by stirring up a controversy and drawing people into it by seeking them out and quoting them. The controversy must arise from events, and only those persons who enter it voluntarily for the purpose of resolving it are likely to be considered limited public figures if they become libel plaintiffs.

"Limited" must be understood two ways. Usually, a limited public figure is involved only in a particular controversy. Further, media comment on the individuals involved in the controversy must be limited to their role in that controversy if the actual malice rule is to be applied in a libel action. So, in most states, in any libel suit brought by people other than public officials or celebrities, a crucial question is, "Are the plaintiffs limited public figures?" In two cases out of three, the answer to that question is, "Yes," according to one survey.[36]

In determining whether a plaintiff is a limited public figure, courts look for guidance to four Supreme Court cases and, increasingly, to a decision of the U.S. Court of Appeals for the District of Columbia Circuit. The first of the Supreme Court cases is *Gertz*. The Court has further refined its definition of a public figure in *Time, Inc.* v. *Firestone,*[37] *Hutchinson* v. *Proxmire,*[38] and *Wolston* v. *Reader's Digest Association.*[39] The landmark circuit court case is *Waldbaum*, which was quoted and cited at the beginning of this section. The court found that Waldbaum, who had been discharged as president of the second largest consumer cooperative in the country, was a public figure because he was deeply involved in promoting cooperatives as competitors to privately owned supermarkets and was looked to as a leader in the field.

---

35. Tavoulareas v. Piro, 817 F.2d 762 (D.C.Cir. 1987).
36. Randall P. Bezanson, Gilbert Cranberg, John Soloski, "Libel Law and the Press: Setting the Record Straight," 71 Iowa L.Rev. 217, Oct. 1985. The authors analyzed 497 libel cases against media defendants.
37. 424 U.S. 448, 96 S.Ct. 958, 47 L.Ed.2d 154 (1976).
38. 443 U.S. 111, 99 S.Ct. 2675, 61 L.Ed.2d 411 (1979).
39. 443 U.S. 157, 99 S.Ct. 2701, 61 L.Ed.2d 450 (1979).

Three principles have emerged from these cases. When there is doubt as to whether a plaintiff is a limited public figure, courts start by (1) identifying the controversy at issue. They proceed to (2) an examination of the plaintiff's role in the controversy. The final step (3) is to determine if the alleged defamation grew out of the plaintiff's participation in the controversy.

We turn next to an examination of how these principles were applied to a specific case by Judge Starr, who wrote for the District of Columbia circuit court in

Tavoulareas v. Piro, 817 F.2d 762 (D.C.Cir. 1987).

Tavoulareas v. *Piro,* in which the *Washington Post* was the major defendant. The plaintiffs were William P. Tavoulareas, at the time president and chief operating officer of Mobil Corporation, and his son Peter, who, in his twenties, became a partner in a London-based shipping firm that leased oil tankers to Mobil. Acting on a tip from Philip Piro, the estranged husband of the elder Tavoulareas's daughter, the *Post* developed a story that said the father had set up his son in business and then steered Mobil's tanker leases to him. The story portrayed William Tavoulareas as a dominant figure who had deceived Mobil's board of directors as to his links with his son's business. Testimony offered at the trial indicated that he had not. A jury awarded William Tavoulareas $250,000 in compensatory damages and $1.8 million in punitive damages against the *Post* and the two reporters who prepared the article.

The trial judge overturned the verdict, setting off a round of appeals that led first to an order reinstating the jury's award and ultimately to a decision by the entire circuit court panel, which ruled, with one dissent, that the *Post* and its reporters did not have to pay the defendants anything. A crucial question for the panel was whether William Tavoulareas was a public figure.

The court quickly disposed of the contention that the plaintiff was an all-purpose public figure. It said the Supreme Court has established "stringent standards applicable to this class of public figure," and the oil executive did not come within them. His prominence was confined to business circles, and his celebrity in society at large did not "approach that of a well-known athlete or entertainer." The court also noted that in its *Waldbaum* decision it had held that "[b]eing an executive within a prominent and influential company does not by itself make one a public figure."

However, Judge Starr continued, individuals may become public figures because of their involvement in "certain issues or situations." Was Tavoulareas one of them? The court said he could be, but only if he had thrust himself into the resolution of a public controversy other than that created by the *Post*'s article. Beginning its analysis of the executive's status, the court said:

> First, we isolate the controversy at issue, because the scope of the controversy in which the plaintiff involves himself defines the scope of the public personality. The controversy must be public both in the sense that "persons actually were discussing" it, and that "persons beyond the immediate participants in the dispute [are likely] to feel the impact of its resolution."

In this instance, the court said, there was a public controversy of long standing. It had its origins in the oil shortages of the 1970s when Mideastern Moslem nations temporarily cut off shipments to the United States to show their opposition to this nation's ties to Israel. As a result of those shortages, the management and structure of the oil industry came under close scrutiny. "Many reform proposals were publicly advanced and considered, including measures to break up or divest the large oil companies, increase their taxes, install government representatives on their boards of directors, and subject them to more intense public regulation." The stakes were high. The public was directly involved. At the height of the embargo, motorists waited in long lines to buy gasoline from stations able to get it. In less than a decade, the price of petroleum products more than tripled, with effects that were felt throughout the economy. The resulting controversy had not been resolved when the *Post* wrote about Tavoulareas and Mobil in 1979.

Had Tavoulareas thrust himself into that controversy? Indeed he had. In November 1979, shortly before the *Post* ran its story, Tavoulareas made a speech in which he said:

> As you know, Mobil has gotten the reputation of being probably the most outspoken company on public issues, through our newspaper advocacy advertising and other public statements. It's not always comfortable being in the limelight, particularly when the President of the United States calls us perhaps the most irresponsible company in the country. But we think the effort has been worth making and we're going to go on with it. We see positive results in the press and in our meetings with elected officials.

Tavoulareas was referring to an unusual advertising campaign which Mobil conducted through much of the decade of the 1970s. At his direction, the company's public relations department prepared a series of quarter-page editorial advertisements which were published in the nation's leading newspapers. Through them, as the court noted, "Mobil and Tavoulareas played substantial roles in spearheading a public counterattack on the movement for reform in the oil industry." As evidence of Tavoulareas's involvement in the controversy, the *Post* compiled 500 pages of news clippings in which he was quoted. In the court's view, the collection left no doubt that

> Tavoulareas was outspoken in defending the oil industry's performance, in blaming the oil crisis on government regulation and interference with the free market, and in advocating rejection of efforts to further regulate or alter the oil industry. He made speeches, testified before Congress, published articles, and through Mobil's publicity apparatus enjoyed continuing access to the media. Even more than his counterparts in the industry, Tavoulareas sought and received public attention on the management and operations of the Nation's oil companies.

The conclusion was inevitable. He had thrust himself into the vortex of the debate over public policy toward the oil industry. That made him a limited public figure. Therefore, the court said, "[h]aving 'stepped into the public spotlight ...he must take the good with the bad,'" again quoting from *Waldbaum*.

There remained only one question, but it was crucial. Was the *Post*'s article, focusing as it did on a business relationship between father and son, and between the two companies they represented, germane to the public controversy? The court backed into its answer, saying, "The alleged nepotism by Tavoulareas was not 'wholly unrelated' to a public controversy where the credibility and integrity of representatives of the oil industry had become an issue." Further, the arrangement had become so much a subject of gossip within the oil industry during the crisis years that Mobil had released its version to an oil industry trade publication before the *Post*'s article appeared. The Securities and Exchange Commission had looked into the arrangement and had asked Tavoulareas to justify it. Mobil's board of directors was so concerned with the apparent conflict of interest that it had raised questions within the company. In the end, the court found "abundant evidence of the already 'public' nature" of the subject of the *Post*'s article and its bearing on Tavoulareas's stature as an influential figure in the debate over oil policy.

All this meant that Tavoulareas could not win his lawsuit against the *Post* unless he could prove actual malice. In a decision that examined in depth the role of investigative reporting in modern journalism, the court concluded that he had not done so. That part of the decision will be summarized later in the chapter in the section on actual malice.

A survey of the reported cases shows many other instances in which libel plaintiffs have been held to be limited public figures. One way to achieve that status is to run for political office.[40] Another is to attempt to influence the outcome of a referendum.[41] Journalists live in a glass house where libel is concerned. Courts have ruled that newspapers,[42] their editors,[43] columnists,[44] and reporters[45] are public figures. In other instances, people have become limited public figures because they made a diligent effort to publicize otherwise private causes or organizations with which they were associated. Among them are the director of a drug rehabilitation center who issued statements to the press and invited a reporter to be present when a state official inspected the center's records.[46] Another was the owner of an art school who sought press coverage when his operation of the school came under fire.[47] In one unusual case, a marine biologist who trained dolphins for the navy and the Central Intelligence Agency during the Vietnam war was held to be a public figure.[48] His work during the war was secret, but he entered the public arena later by writing articles, responding to requests for interviews, including an appearance on *60 Minutes,* and preparing brochures offering his services as a dolphin trainer.

TIME LAPSE AND PUBLIC FIGURE STATUS   The case brought by the marine biologist raised a question that has been a factor in several others. With the passage of time, can a limited public figure again become a private individual? The district court judge said the marine biologist might indeed do so, at least with respect to

40. Brown v. Herald Co., 698 F.2d 949 (8th Cir. 1983).
41. Cloyd v. Press, 629 S.W.2d 24 (Tenn.App. 1981).
42. Bee Publications v. Cheektowaga Times, 107 A.D.2d 382 (4th Dept. 1985).
43. Fried v. Daily Review, 11 Med.L.Rptr. 2145 (Cal.Ct.App., 1st Dist. 1985).
44. Warner v. Kansas City Star, 726 S.W.2d 384 (Mo.Ct.App., W.D. 1987).
45. Jensen v. Times Mirror, 634 F.Supp. 304; on reconsideration, 647 F.Supp. 1525 (D.Conn. 1986).
46. Major v. Drapeau, 507 A.2d 938 (R.I. 1986).
47. Cooper School of Art v. Plain Dealer, 12 Med.L.Rptr. 2283 (Ohio Ct.App., 8th Dist. 1986).
48. Fitzgerald v. Penthouse International, 525 F.Supp. 585 (D.Md. 1981).

some aspects of his career. However, two federal appellate courts and the Mississippi Supreme Court have held that once people become limited public figures they remain so for purposes of comment on the controversy in which they became involved. The Sixth Circuit court of appeals held that a major witness in a rape trial that led to the execution of several black youths in the 1930s remained a public figure for purposes of comment on that event more than 40 years later.[49] The Fifth Circuit court of appeals held that an entertainer who for several years had been Elvis Presley's girlfriend still was a public figure a dozen years later with respect to her association with the singer.[50] The Mississippi decision involved a man who had been a candidate for deputy sheriff in 1967 and thereafter retired from public life. The court said that for purposes of comment on that election, he remained a public figure in 1983.[51]

These examples, and the many others in the case reports, simply emphasize principles already listed. Individuals become limited public figures because they voluntarily involve themselves in the attempt to resolve a public controversy. Courts have said a controversy is public when it will affect people other than those directly involved in it. Further, the controversy must be of such a nature that its resolution depends to some extent on the power of public opinion. Limited public figures take their case to the media by issuing press releases and calling press conferences. They write letters to the editor. They appear on television. When they go public, they cannot expect that all that is printed or said about them will be favorable. If they should be defamed by the media in connection with their advocacy, they must prove actual malice if they are to prevail.

INVOLUNTARY   In *Gertz,* the Supreme Court used the word "hypothetically" to introduce the suggestion that some persons might become public figures "through no purposeful action" of their own. It added that "instances of truly involuntary public figures must be exceedingly rare." That prediction has proved accurate. In a half-dozen or so reported cases as of 1990, courts have recognized the possibility that some individuals might become public figures despite their efforts to stay out of the limelight. But in only one reported instance has a court ruled that a plaintiff was an involuntary public figure. The U.S. Court of Appeals for the District of Columbia Circuit held that an air traffic controller had become an "involuntary public figure for the very limited purpose" of the discussion of a crash that occurred while he was on duty.[52]

Public Personalities

Courts in a few jurisdictions have recognized a class of persons who do not precisely fit the public figure categories above but who nevertheless have ready access to the media. New York courts have taken the lead in calling such persons

---

49.   Street v. National Broadcasting Co., 645 F.2d 1227 (6th Cir.); cert. granted, 454 U.S. 815; cert. dismissed, 454 U.S. 1095 (1981).

50.   Brewer v. Memphis Publishing Co., 626 F.2d 1238 (5th Cir. 1980); cert. denied, 452 U.S. 962 (1981).

51.   Newson v. Henry, 443 So.2d 817 (Miss. 1983).

52.   Dameron v. Washington Magazine, 779 F.2d 736 (D.C.Cir. 1985).

"public personalities."[53] Courts in that state have applied the term to a famous National League baseball pitcher, to a belly dancer who was widely known in her community, to a writer for *Sports Illustrated,* and to the owner of radio stations in Buffalo. Courts in a few other jurisdictions have also applied the term to sports figures and to a former girlfriend of Elvis Presley. In these instances, the plaintiffs were not deemed to have reached the celebrity status that would have made them all-purpose public figures. Nor had they thrust themselves into a public controversy. However, they did have access to the media and, therefore, could respond to their detractors. For that reason, the courts held that they would have to prove actual malice to prevail in a libel action.

Private Individuals

Libel plaintiffs who do not meet the criteria required to make them public officials or public figures are regarded by the courts as private individuals. Thus in more than half the states they can prevail by proving a lesser degree of fault than actual malice, usually negligence.

Four times since the Supreme Court first identified public figures in the *Butts* case in 1967, the Court has agreed to review cases in which the status of the plaintiff was at issue. In all instances, the plaintiffs were, or had been, much in the news. In each instance, the Court held that the plaintiff nevertheless remained a private individual. Although the most recent of the cases was decided more than ten years ago, these cases remain important to journalists, serving as a reminder that newsworthiness alone does not make people public figures for libel actions.

The first of the decisions was *Gertz.* In it, the Court held that a lawyer hired to represent a client does not, by that act alone, become a public figure. Even though the lawyer may try a case that deals directly with a public controversy, as in *Gertz,* that involvement itself does not make the lawyer a public figure. Lawyers become public figures for purposes of comment on their handling of cases only when they go beyond the normal bounds of their professional duties. Lawyers must become advocates of causes, as well as agents of their clients, to become limited public figures.

Other professionals who work for fees or are hired to perform duties for, or give advice to, clients, including governments, also are private individuals as long as they simply do their jobs and do not enter the public forum as advocates. These professionals include engineers, accountants, physicians, consultants, marketing analysts, and the like. It is conceivable that public relations practitioners might become public figures as they carry out their missions for clients, but there are no reported cases defining their status.

The second decision defining a private individual is *Time, Inc.* v. *Firestone.* The case grew out of a brief item in *Time* magazine noting that Russell A. Firestone, Jr.,

Time, Inc. v. *Firestone,* **424 U.S. 448, 96 S.Ct. 958, 47 L.Ed.2d 154 (1976).**

heir to the tire fortune, had been granted a divorce from his wife, Mary Alice, on grounds of adultery. It also noted that she had been awarded $3000 a month in alimony. Under Florida law, a wife found

---

53. James v. Gannett Co., 40 N.Y.2d 415 (1976).

to have committed adultery cannot be awarded alimony. Although the judge who heard the divorce action said it had "produced enough evidence of extramarital adventures on both sides to make Dr. Freud's hair curl," he had ignored most of it, granting the divorce on other grounds. Mrs. Firestone sued the magazine for libel. A jury awarded her $100,000 in damages, and the Florida Supreme Court affirmed, holding that the magazine's reporter was negligent in not knowing enough law to realize that Mrs. Firestone could not have been awarded alimony if she had been found to be an adulteress. The U.S. Supreme Court took the case to review *Time*'s argument that Mrs. Firestone should have been regarded as a public figure because the divorce trial had been so highly publicized that she had arranged several news conferences to answer questions from reporters.

The Supreme Court said notoriety did not make her a public figure. Nor did her ready access to the media. And even though the most intimate details of her conflict with her husband were spread across the land, she was not involved in a public controversy of the kind contemplated in *New York Times* and *Gertz*. Only she, her husband, their families, and their friends had anything to gain or lose from the divorce action. The dispute was resolved by a judge, who applied the law to the evidence, not by public opinion. Moreover, Mrs. Firestone was involved in the dispute because she went to court to protect her interests, a right guaranteed by the Constitution.

From the point of view of the judicial bench, the decision made sense. Civil courts are for the use of persons who think they have been wronged. People who are thinking about filing a lawsuit, or responding to one, should not also have to think about whether those acts will open them to defamatory falsehood under a rule that makes recovery difficult. *Firestone* also can be seen as a logical extension of *Gertz*. Gertz did not become a public figure by representing a client in a lawsuit, even though that suit touched many nerves, reflected unfavorably on the performance of the police, and drew much public attention. Why, then, should participants in such a suit become fair game for libel solely because of their participation?

But from the point of view of the news media, the decision had an ominous note. It told journalists that they cannot be certain that highly visible newsmakers will be required to prove actual malice if they sue for libel. Some lawyers advise their clients in *Gertz* states never to assume that subjects of defamatory stories are public figures no matter how much they have been in the news.[54]

The Supreme Court reinforced the point it made in *Firestone* when it decided two cases brought by persons who had been dragged into the news through their association with highly publicized controversies. The Court held that neither person's newsworthiness had made him either an involuntary or a limited public figure.

The first of the cases, *Hutchinson* v. *Proxmire,* was unusual in two ways. The defendant, William Proxmire, was a U.S. senator, and the suit was based on a

Hutchinson v. *Proxmire,*
443 U.S. 111, 99 S.Ct. 2675,
61 L.Ed. 2d 411 (1979).

news release from his office. Dr. Ronald Hutchinson, who relied on federal grants to finance his research in psychology, was drawn out of the obscurity of the laboratory when Senator

---

54.   Alexander Greenfield, "Thirty Ways to Protect Yourself against Libel Lawsuits," *Editor & Publisher,* 3 June 1989, p. 56.

Proxmire awarded his "Golden Fleece" to the government agencies that paid for the research. In this, there was no honor. The senator gave the award periodically to individuals, government agencies, and projects he considered outrageously wasteful of public funds. In this instance, the primary targets were the Defense Department and NASA, which had given Hutchinson $500,000 to study stress. The researcher used monkeys as subjects and made thousands of feet of videotape of their facial expressions as they reacted to various kinds of stress. In Proxmire's opinion the whole project was monkey business of another kind, and he said so in a scathing press release. The story was used widely. Reporters sought out Hutchinson and published his reaction to the senator's charges.

Hutchinson sued Proxmire for libel. He said his work was made to appear worthless, and he was subjected to ridicule. A judge dismissed the lawsuit, ruling that Hutchinson was a public figure and that he could not prove actual malice. An appellate court affirmed. The Supreme Court took the case and reversed.

The lower courts looked to Hutchinson's federal grants and his access to the media in deeming him a public figure. The Supreme Court looked at the nature of the controversy and how Hutchinson became involved in it. The Court said the key issue was not Hutchinson's research. Only a few professionals in the same field knew about it. His work was not controversial until Proxmire made it so. The real public controversy was over the spending of public funds. Hutchinson did not enter that debate until Proxmire made an issue of his grants. Thus, the scientist was an unwilling player in Proxmire's game. He remained a private individual who need prove only negligence to prevail. Proxmire eventually settled with him for $10,000.

In the second case, *Wolston* v. *Reader's Digest Association,* the Supreme Court said that involvement in criminal conduct, without more, does not make one a public figure. Wolston had a brief brush with the law during the McCarthy era after World War II when he failed to appear before a federal grand jury and was held in criminal contempt.

Wolston v. Reader's Digest Association, 443 U.S. 157, 99 S.Ct. 2701, 61 L.Ed.2d 450 (1979).

Like many others who lived through those times, Wolston was more a victim of circumstances than a shaper of events. He was born in Russia, came to the United States after the Soviet Revolution, became a citizen, served in World War II, and remained in government service afterward. He was the nephew of a couple who pleaded guilty to espionage for the Soviet Union in 1958. It was for that reason that he was called by the grand jury. No charges were filed against him. However, years later a book published by Reader's Digest listed him, his aunt, and his uncle among those who had been identified as Soviet spies or who had been found guilty of perjury or contempt in connection with charges of spying during and after World War II. Wolston sued the book's publisher for libel. A federal district court judge dismissed the case, ruling that Wolston was a public figure and could not prove actual malice. The judge said Wolston became a public figure when he pleaded guilty to criminal contempt and became the subject of news stories in Washington, D.C., and New York City.

The Supreme Court said that he did not. The Court said he had done nothing on his own to thrust himself into the post–World War II controversy over Soviet spying. He had been brought into the controversy by the FBI and the grand jury. His failure to appear was not an act of defiance designed to call attention to a cause. He didn't show up because he was ill. When he appeared in court of his own volition the following day, he offered to testify, but the judge reacted by finding him in contempt. None of that made him a public figure. Nor did the news stories. They merely reported an event in which Wolston was an unwilling participant. To emphasize the point, Justice Rehnquist wrote for the Court's majority: "[W]e reject the further contention of respondents that any person who engages in criminal conduct automatically becomes a public figure for purposes of comment on a limited range of issues related to his conviction.... To hold otherwise would create an 'open season' for all who sought to defame persons convicted of crime."

In each instance, the Court said that libel plaintiffs who were not otherwise famous did not become public figures merely because they did something—or something was done to them—that made them newsworthy. In accord with the precedents established in the cases above, lower courts have held that the following were private individuals for purposes of a libel action: A file clerk in a county sheriff's office who married the sheriff,[55] the son of a town supervisor who was cited after a traffic accident,[56] and a Turkish national who was described as a specialist in drug smuggling.[57]

People who are engaged in private business, or who are employed by business firms, are private individuals unless they enjoy unusual prominence or, like Tavoulareas, seek to influence the outcome of a public controversy. Courts have held the following to be private individuals: A broker who sought investors in a proposed tax-exempt mutual fund,[58] a businessman who was "in the public eye in regard to certain of his business ventures" but who was accused of wrongdoing apart from those ventures,[59] a corporation's general counsel who was involved in a stockholder's dispute which was held to be a private controversy,[60] a seller of Olympic souvenirs,[61] and a milk producers association which did not initiate news coverage of a controversy over a request for a federal loan guarantee.[62]

It is also worth noting that courts have found the following to be private individuals: a former Miss Wyoming, who participated in the Miss America contest and who alleged that she was identified as the subject of a short story attributing amazing sexual powers to a "Miss Wyoming"[63]; the author of novels on human sexuality, when her name was used in connection with the nude photo of another person,[64] and a woman who was photographed on the street during filming of a televised documentary on prostitution.[65]

---

55. Sellars v. Stauffer Communications, 9 Kans.App.2d 573, 684 P.2d 450 (1984); affirmed, 236 Kans. 697, 695 P.2d 812 (1985).
56. Hogan v. Herald Co., 84 A.D.2d 470 (4th Dept.); affirmed, 58 N.Y.2d 630 (1983).
57. Karaduman v. Newsday, 51 N.Y.2d 531 (N.Y. 1980).
58. Jadwin v. Minneapolis Star, 367 N.W.2d 476 (Minn. 1985).
59. Mead Corporation v. Hicks, 448 So.2d 308 (Ala. 1983).
60. Denny v. Mertz, 106 Wis.2d 636, 318 N.W.2d 141; cert. denied, 459 U.S. 883 (1982).
61. Zates v. Richman, 86 A.D.2d 746 (N.Y.App. 1982).
62. Eastern Milk Producers Cooperative v. Milkweed, 8 Med.L.Rptr. 2100 (N.D.N.Y. 1982).
63. Pring v. Penthouse International, 695 F.2d 438 (10th Cir. 1982).
64. Lerman v. Chuckleberry Publishing, 521 F.Supp. 228 (S.D.N.Y. 1981).
65. Clark v. ABC, 684 F.2d 1208 (6th Cir. 1982).

This sampling of the reported decisions, and the four landmark Supreme Court cases discussed above, tell us that people do not become public figures for purposes of a libel suit simply because they are in the news. They serve as a reminder that the news media may be able to create all-purpose public figures or public personalities but are not likely to create limited public figures by dragging ordinary people into the news. All-purpose public figures are celebrities—in the language of one decision, their names are "household words." Such figures can be created by constant exposure on television screens, in newspapers, or in magazines. All-purpose public figures are recognized wherever they go, and people talk about them. If that talk is sometimes harshly critical, such is the price of fame.

Limited public figures are linked to events. They are people who take up causes and by doing so seek to change the course of human affairs. By their efforts, they may force the closing of a dump, limit the flight patterns at an airport, win approval of zoning for satellite television dishes, develop time-share condominiums, or force other changes that will affect their neighbors or society at large. Because limited public figures do have an effect on others, they, too, must expect criticism.

DEFINING THE STANDARDS OF FAULT

Let us assume that from the point of view of a communications medium the worst has happened. The matter at issue has been found to contain a false and defamatory assertion of fact. Thus, the judge has rejected a motion to dismiss. He also has ruled on the status of the plaintiff: public official, public figure, or private individual. That ruling will have a major influence on the next point of contention: To what degree was the communications medium at fault? How much, or how little, fault plaintiffs must prove depends not only on their status but also, in the case of private individuals, on the state in which the lawsuit is being tried. In any state, public officials or public figures must prove actual malice to win a judgment of any kind. This proof requires clear and convincing evidence that those responsible for putting the libel in circulation either knew it was false or acted with reckless disregard for the truth.

In four states, private individuals also must prove actual malice. But in those states that have elected the option offered by *Gertz,* a private individual needs prove only negligence—a failure to use ordinary care or to follow professional standards for reporting and editing—to win a judgment for compensatory or actual damages. If such plaintiffs can prove actual malice, they also may claim punitive damages.

We will look first at the standard of fault the various states require a private individual to prove and then examine the leading decisions defining actual malice and negligence.

State Standards and the *Gertz* Option

Courts in thirty states, the District of Columbia, Guam, Puerto Rico, and the Virgin Islands have accepted the option offered by the Supreme Court in *Gertz* and permit private individual plaintiffs to prevail against the news media by proving negligence.[66] These states are Alabama, Arizona, Arkansas, California, Connecticut, Delaware, Georgia, Hawaii, Iowa, Kansas, Kentucky, Louisiana, Maryland, Massachusetts, Michigan, Minnesota, New Hampshire, New Mexico, North Carolina, Ohio, Oklahoma, Oregon, Pennsylvania, South Carolina, Tennessee, Texas, Utah, Vermont, Washington, and West Virginia.

Four states require private individuals to prove actual malice if the defamation grows out of the reporting of, or comment on, a public issue. Colorado[67] and Indiana[68] do so because their courts have elected to follow the Supreme Court's plurality holding in *Rosenbloom,* taking the position that the First Amendment and the freedom of speech clause of their state constitutions protect the discussion of public issues, no matter what the status of the individuals involved. New Jersey bases its position on that state's common law. The fourth state, Illinois, has taken the position that its constitution protects the discussion of public issues.

New Jersey's adoption of the actual malice standard for private individuals is somewhat ambiguous. The state's supreme court wrote, in *Sisler* v. *Gannett Co., Inc.,*[69]

> We hold that when a *private person* with sufficient experience, understanding and knowledge enters into a personal transaction or conducts his *personal affairs* in a manner that one in his position would reasonably expect *implicates a legitimate public interest* with an attendant *risk of publicity,* defamatory speech that focuses upon that public interest will not be actionable unless it has been published with actual malice.

The wording leaves an inference that some private individuals could be deemed so lacking in knowledge of how the world works that they might be able to prevail on a lesser showing of fault.

The standard of proof required of private individuals in Illinois also requires qualification. Twice the Illinois Supreme Court has held that private individuals who are defamed as part of the reporting or discussion of "matters of public concern" must prove actual malice.[70] However, in a third decision, which did not involve a matter of public concern, the court said a private individual could recover by proving either knowledge of falsity or that the defendant, believing the defamatory assertion to be true, "lacked reasonable grounds for that belief."[71] Presumably, that language refers to a negligence standard.

---

66. The listings in this section are derived from case summaries included in the Libel Defense Resource Center's *50-State Survey 1989,* Henry Kaufman, editor, and the author's case files.
67. Walker v. Colorado Springs Sun, 188 Colo. 86, 538 P.2d 450; cert. denied, 423 U.S. 1025 (1975), and Diversified Management v. Denver Post, 653 P.2d 1103 (Colo. 1982).
68. Aafco Heating & Air Conditioning Co. v. Northwest Publications, 321 N.E.2d 580 (Ind.App. 1974).
69. 104 N.J. 506, 516 A.2d 1083 (N.J. 1986).
70. Farnsworth v. Tribune Co., 43 Ill.2d 286, 253 N.E.2d 408 (Ill. 1969), and Colson v. Stieg, 89 Ill.2d 205, 433 N.E.2d 246 (Ill. 1982).
71. Troman v. Wood, 62 Ill.2d 184, 340 N.E.2d 292 (1975).

Virginia courts also are ambivalent on the standard of proof of fault required of private individuals. In the only case in point,[72] the state supreme court said that if the language at issue "makes substantial danger to reputation apparent," presumably a reference to a libel per se, the plaintiff need prove only negligence. But if substantial danger is not apparent, which is a determination to be made by the trial court, the plaintiff must offer clear and convincing evidence of actual malice.

New York stands alone somewhere between the *Gertz* states and the four states that require private plaintiffs to prove actual malice. Private individual plaintiffs who are involved in a matter of legitimate public concern must prove by the preponderance of the evidence that the publication was made "in a grossly irresponsible manner" without regard for the standards ordinarily followed by responsible journalists.[73] This is something more than carelessness but does not require proof that the publisher had serious doubt.

The cases offer little in the way of precedent as to the distinction between "grossly irresponsible" journalistic conduct and either actual malice or negligence. However, New York's Court of Claims volunteered some guidance in an opinion that is *dicta*. The court said that editors of the student newspaper at a state university were grossly negligent in running a letter to the editor without checking to make certain it was written by the students whose names were signed to it.[74] The letter, which identified the signers as members of the gay community who were coming out of the closet, bore the names of two students who had not written it. When the two named students sued for libel, the claims court said the failure of the newspaper's editors to verify the identity of the writers, coupled with the lack of consistent procedures for verifying letters to the editor, was "grossly irresponsible." However, the suit was dismissed because the students had sued the state as owner of the paper through the university. The court held that state officials, including university faculty and administrators, had no authority to censor the newspaper. Therefore, the state could not be held responsible for publication of a libel. The court said the newspaper's editors were the proper target of a suit.

Missouri courts require private individuals to show that the media were at fault, but the cases do not define what that means.[75]

Florida and Wisconsin, as of 1990, must be listed as in doubt as to their standards for private individuals because of conflicting decisions by trial courts and lower-level appellate courts. However, some authorities list them as having adopted a negligence standard.[76] In Alaska, the state supreme court reserved a decision on the standard of proof required of private individuals.[77]

---

72. The Gazette v. Harris, 229 Va. 1, 325 S.E.2d 713 (Va. 1985).
73. Chapadeau v. Utica Observer-Dispatch, 38 N.Y.2d 196, 379 N.Y.S.2d 61, 341 N.E.2d 569 (N.Y. 1975).
74. Mazart v. State, 441 N.Y.S.2d 600 (N.Y.C.C. 1981).
75. McQuoid v. Springfield Newspapers, 502 F.Supp. 1050 (W.D.Mo. 1980); Joseph v. Elam, 709 S.W.2d 517 (Mo.App.W.D. 1986); Williams v. Pulitzer Publishing Co., 706 S.W.2d 508 (Mo.App.E.D. 1986).
76. *Communications Law 1987,* vol. 2, pp. 782–5.
77. Schneider v. Pay 'N Save Corp., 723 P.2d 619 (Alaska 1986).

Finally, as of this writing, in ten states courts have had no occasion to decide the standard of fault for private individuals: Idaho, Maine, Mississippi, Montana, Nebraska, Nevada, North Dakota, Rhode Island, South Dakota, and Wyoming.

Actual Malice

In *New York Times,* the Supreme Court defined actual malice as publishing with knowledge of falsity or with reckless disregard for the truth. Knowledge of falsity is clear cut and results in deliberate publishing of a lie. In a few instances plaintiffs have been able to prove such publication.[78]

Much more common have been cases in which plaintiffs have proved reckless disregard. In *New York Times,* the Supreme Court made only a general attempt to define the term. The Court noted that the advertisement was signed by a number of persons who were distinguished in various fields. The advertising staff of the *Times* would have no reason to doubt their version of the facts. It was true, the Court noted, that clippings in the *Times*'s own library contradicted statements in the ad. But in the absence of a "serious doubt," the advertising director's failure to check the files was not reckless disregard. At worst, the Court held, it was no more than negligence.

The key words in the paragraph above are "serious doubt." Subsequent decisions defining reckless disregard have focused on them. The critical questions in establishing reckless disregard are, "Did the defendant seriously doubt the truth of the libelous allegation?" "Were the sources or the nature of the evidence such that the defendant should have had serious doubt about the allegations?" Thus reckless disregard has its roots in the defendant's state of mind. Because one's state of mind is difficult to ascertain under the best of circumstances, the finding of reckless disregard is a subjective process, based on such evidence as the plaintiff can muster pointing to what the defendant knew or did not know when the libelous material was being prepared and when the decision was reached to publish it. Courts have the duty of assessing the facts and deciding whether they point to the presence or absence of a serious doubt.

Four years after its decision in *New York Times,* the Supreme Court felt compelled to further define what it meant by "actual malice" and particularly by "reckless disregard." The Court accepted for review a Louisiana case, *St. Amant* v. *Thompson,*[79] and made it the definitive guide to the meaning of the term. Three later decisions have offered further guidance. They are *Herbert* v. *Lando,*[80] *Bose Corp.* v. *Consumers Union,*[81] and *Anderson* v. *Liberty Lobby.*[82] In these decisions, the Court has emphasized several points, which may be stated briefly as follows:

---

78. Most notably, Goldwater v. Ginzburg, 414 F.2d 324 (2d Cir. 1969). The successful plaintiff, for many years a U.S. Senator from Arizona, was the Republican candidate for president in 1964.
79. 390 U.S. 727, 88 S.Ct. 1323, 20 L.Ed.2d 262 (1968).
80. 441 U.S. 153, 99 S.Ct. 1635, 60 L.Ed.2d 115 (1979).
81. 466 U.S. 485, 104 S.Ct. 1949, 80 L.Ed.2d 502 (1984).
82. 477 U.S. 242, 106 S.Ct. 2505, 91 L.Ed.2d 202 (1986).

— "Actual malice" means what the Supreme Court said it means. It is knowledge of falsity or reckless disregard of the truth. It does not embody the traditional meaning of "malice" as ill will or intent to harm.

— Public officials or public figures cannot prevail in a libel suit unless they prove actual malice with clear and convincing evidence. No plaintiff, public or private, can be awarded punitive damages in the absence of proof of actual malice.

— Actual malice is a subjective standard. This is particularly true of reckless disregard. Therefore, the Court held in *Herbert* that libel plaintiffs must be permitted to inquire into the state of mind of the journalist defendants. In practical terms, this means that journalists can be required to justify the editorial decisions that went into preparation of allegedly libelous material. Journalists can be asked why they believed one source and not another; why they used some facts harmful to the plaintiff while ignoring others that were favorable.

— Key elements in reckless disregard are "serious doubts" about the truth of the publication or "a high degree of awareness of their probable falsity."[83] The existence of such doubt, or awareness, need not be proved directly. It may be inferred from the circumstances, such as the nature of the defendant's sources, ready access to information contradicting the libelous assertion, and deadline pressures.

— The determination of actual malice is a mixed question of law and fact. If a plaintiff can offer no evidence pointing to knowledge of falsity or reckless disregard, the court may grant a defendant's motion for summary judgment. If the facts are in doubt, the question is submitted to a jury. However, in its *Bose* decision, the Supreme Court held that a jury's finding of actual malice can be reviewed by an appellate court, which is free to come to its own conclusions as to the meaning of the evidence.

— The Court took this rationale a step further in *Liberty Lobby*. It encouraged judges to grant motions for summary dismissal if they conclude the plaintiffs are unable to offer clear and convincing evidence of actual malice. Since then, one court has said that the effect of the decision was to extend to all jurisdictions the Second Circuit's liberal policy toward summary dismissal of public official/public figure libel suits.[84]

The *St. Amant* case had its origins in a political appeal broadcast over a Baton Rouge television station. Phil St. Amant, a candidate for public office, accused his opponent of accepting bribes. In doing so, he read a sworn statement from a Teamsters Union member which portrayed Herman Thompson, a deputy sheriff, as a middleman in the bribery. Thompson sued St. Amant for libel and won a

St. Amant v. Thompson, 390 U.S. 727, 88 S.Ct. 1323, 20 L.Ed.2d 262 (1968).

83. Garrison v. Louisiana, 379 U.S. 64, 85 S.Ct. 209, 13 L.Ed.2d 125 (1964).
84. Contemporary Mission v. New York Times Co., 665 F.Supp. 248 (S.D.N.Y. 1987).

$5000 judgment before Louisiana courts became hopelessly bogged down in try-ing to define actual malice. The Supreme Court agreed to take the case, holding that Thompson was not entitled to damages because there was no reckless disre-gard on St. Amant's part. Justice Byron R. White wrote the decision, in which he was joined by seven other members of the Court.

He started by emphasizing that reckless disregard is a product of the factual situation of each case. But it begins with evidence of doubt:

> There must be sufficient evidence to permit the conclusion that the defendant in fact entertained serious doubts as to the truth of his publication. Publishing with such doubts shows reckless disregard for truth or falsity and demonstrates actual malice.
>
> It may be said that such a test puts a premium on ignorance, encourages the ir-responsible publisher not to enquire, and permits the issue to be determined by the defendant's testimony that he published the statement in good faith and unaware of its probable falsity....
>
> The defendant in a defamation action brought by a public official cannot, how-ever, automatically insure a favorable verdict by testifying that he published with a belief that the statements were true. The finder of fact must determine whether the publication was indeed made in good faith. Professions of good faith will be unlikely to prove persuasive, for example, where a story is fabricated by the defendant, is the product of his imagination, or is based wholly on an unverified anonymous tele-phone call. Nor will they be likely to prevail when the publisher's allegations are so inherently improbable that only a reckless man would put them in circulation. Like-wise, recklessness may be found where there are reasons to doubt the veracity of the informant or the accuracy of his reports.
>
> ...Failure to investigate does not in itself establish bad faith.

With its decision in *St. Amant,* the Court did what it could to tell lower courts how to know actual malice when they see it. The standard does not require re-porters and editors to check every conceivable loose end as a story is being de-veloped, especially if it is "hot news" where time is of the essence.[85] Mere fail-ure to check will not, of itself, prove reckless disregard. But if such failure is coupled with the publisher's doubt, or with evidence suggesting he should have had doubts, then there can be reckless disregard. At that point, courts look at the events leading to publication. Who were the sources of information? What was known of their reputation for honesty? How many sources were there? Why did the publisher accept information from one source and reject contradictory infor-mation from another? Were the published allegations "so inherently improbable that only a reckless man would put them in circulation?"

The answers to some of those questions lie in the editorial process—in the de-cisions reporters and editors make in gathering and presenting news and com-ment. That process requires judgment, which is a factor of the state of mind of the participants. Obviously, individuals can and do disagree over news values and over the truth or falsehood of allegedly defamatory statements. What seems

---

85. Curtis Publishing Co. v. Butts, 388 U.S. 130, 87 S.Ct. 1975, 18 L.Ed.2d 1094 (1967).

obviously true to a person with one point of view may seem like an improbable falsehood to a person with another point of view.

Herbert v. *Lando* grew out of a libel plaintiff's efforts to obtain the answers to state-of-mind questions. Anthony Herbert, a retired army officer who had served in Vietnam, was the subject of a segment of "60 Minutes" produced by Barry Lando of CBS News and narrated by Mike Wallace. Herbert said the segment, which dealt with atrocities allegedly committed by American troops, made him appear to be a liar. He sued for libel and, because he conceded he was a public figure, sought to prove actual malice.

Herbert v. Lando, 441 U.S. 153, 99 S.Ct. 1635, 60 L.Ed.2d 115 (1979).

During the process of discovery, Herbert's lawyer questioned Lando at length about the news judgments that shaped the telecast. Discovery is a pretrial process that involves the questioning of potential witnesses under oath to narrow the issues that need to be resolved at trial. Lando was asked why he had believed some sources, but not others, and why he had used some information harmful to Herbert while rejecting information favorable to the officer. The lawyer also asked for details of the discussions between Lando and Wallace, and with others, that went into the shaping of the telecast. Lando refused to answer such questions, arguing that freedom of the press would be restricted if reporters and editors could be compelled to answer questions about their state of mind during the editorial process. A district court judge ordered Lando to answer the questions, but a federal appeals court reversed, holding that the First Amendment stood as a barrier against such questions. The Supreme Court agreed to review the decision. It held that the appeals court was wrong.

Justice White, joined by six others, wrote for the Court. He pointed out that *New York Times* had erected a strong safeguard for the media by requiring public official/public figure plaintiffs to prove actual malice. To do so, they must show that the defendant acted either with knowledge that the alleged libel was false, or with serious doubts about its truth. Both knowledge and doubt are states of mind. White concluded that if the Court were to shut off all inquiry into the editorial decision-making process, including the state of mind of defendants, proving actual malice would become virtually impossible. Despite the Supreme Court's decision in his favor, on remand Herbert was unable to prove actual malice, and thus was the loser.[86]

The *Herbert* decision has been a factor contributing to the expense of taking a libel suit to trial. Plaintiffs now commonly ask during discovery for the names of all persons who played any role in preparing allegedly defamatory material. These persons can be asked about what they said to each other, with focus on whether any of them raised doubts about any element of the story. Further, reporters can be asked to identify their sources of information and even to produce transcripts of their notes or copies of any audio tapes of interviews. If the offending story was based on an investigation of any consequence, discovery can result

---

86. Herbert v. Lando, 781 F.2d 298 (2d Cir. 1986).

in the preparation of thousands of pages of depositions, all of which is quite expensive. Questions are likely to focus on such matters as why reporters believed some sources, but not others; why they followed up some leads, but ignored others; what state of mind with respect to the plaintiff shaped the story, and what the intent was in deciding to publish at all.

The *Bose* decision also dealt with the process involved in proving actual malice. In it, the issue was how far appeals courts can go in reviewing the factual situation that led a trial court to conclude that a media defendant acted in actual malice. The case had its origins in a *Consumer Report* magazine article evaluating the quality of stereo speakers. Included was the Bose 901 speaker, which had only recently come into production. The magazine's engineers found that it had some virtues but that it was incapable of allowing the listener to pinpoint the location of individual instruments in an orchestra because the speakers made some of them seem "to wander about the room."

Bose Corporation v. Consumers Union, 466 U.S. 485, 104 S.Ct. 1949, 80 L.Ed.2d 502 (1984).

Bose sued Consumers Union, the magazine's publisher, for libel, alleging that the statement about the instruments' tending "to wander about the room" was false and defamatory. During discovery the engineer who wrote the review testified that in reality the sound of a solo instrument seemed to move back and forth along the wall between the two speakers of his stereo system. The judge examined excerpts from other articles written by the engineer and concluded that he was expert enough in the English language to know that his use of "about" would convey a different impression. The judge further concluded that the engineer had used that word deliberately and thus had knowingly falsified his report. A jury awarded the firm $115,296 in damages.

On appeal, a circuit court agreed that the article was both false and defamatory. It conceded that the engineer's language may have been imprecise but could find no evidence proving knowledge of falsity or reckless disregard for the truth. Bose took its case to the Supreme Court, arguing that the circuit court had violated the Federal Rules of Civil Procedure by overturning the district court's findings of fact with respect to actual malice. At issue was Rule 52(a), which provides: "Findings of fact shall not be set aside [by an appeals court] unless clearly erroneous, and due regard shall be given to the opportunity of the trial court to judge the credibility of the witnesses."

The Supreme Court affirmed the circuit court's decision, holding that in media libel cases the First Amendment requires appellate courts to "make an independent examination of the whole record." If the appellate court is not satisfied that the plaintiff offered clear and convincing proof of actual malice, the court has the power to reverse a contrary conclusion by the trier of fact, whether it be a judge or a jury.

However, not all courts agreed on the thrust of the decision. Some read it as encouraging greater use of summary judgment to dispose of libel actions short of trial unless the plaintiff could offer clear and convincing proof of actual malice. Others continued to permit cases to go to trial if there was even minimal proof of the defendant's fault. Two years later, in *Anderson* v. *Liberty Lobby,* the Supreme Court signalled that the former reading was correct.

The question at issue in *Liberty Lobby* was whether that organization, a self-described "citizens' lobby," had presented clear and convincing evidence of actual malice during the preliminary stages of its libel suit against columnist Jack Anderson. A magazine published by Anderson had carried three articles portraying Liberty Lobby and Willis Carto, its founder and treasurer, as neo-Nazi, anti-Semitic, racist and fascist. One of the articles called the author of a book published by Liberty Lobby "an American Hitler."

Anderson v. *Liberty Lobby,* 477 U.S. 242, 106 S.Ct. 2505, 91 L.Ed.2d 202 (1986).

After discovery, Anderson asked the U.S. District Court for the District of Columbia for summary judgment under Rule 56 of the Federal Rules of Civil Procedure. Under that rule, judges are to grant motions for summary judgment if the pleadings present no genuine disagreement over the meaning of material facts and the law supports the position taken by the moving party. In this instance, that Liberty Lobby and Carto were public figures were accepted as fact. Thus, they would have to prove actual malice. Liberty Lobby argued that some of the sources quoted in the articles were unreliable and that the author had not verified the information before publishing it. Liberty Lobby also offered evidence that the magazine's editor had said the articles were "terrible" and "ridiculous." Anderson's lawyers gave the court depositions detailing the research that had gone into preparation of the articles and the author's belief that the facts in the articles were truthful and accurate. An appendix listed the sources for each of the statements alleged to be libelous. The district court judge held that the author's thorough investigation and his reliance on numerous sources precluded a jury's finding of clear and convincing evidence of actual malice. Therefore, he dismissed the lawsuit.

On appeal, the circuit court held that the judge had acted properly with respect to most of the disputed passages. However, it said that with respect to nine of them, "a jury could reasonably conclude that the...allegations were defamatory, false, and made with actual malice." Further, it held that to defeat a motion for summary judgment the plaintiffs did not have to show that a jury could find actual malice with "convincing clarity." All that is required is enough evidence to support a reasonable likelihood that a jury might do so.

The Supreme Court disagreed and reversed. Justice White, writing for six members of the Court, held that in *Liberty Lobby,* the District of Columbia Circuit Court had taken a too liberal view of the proof required to support dismissal of the libel suit. Rule 56, he said, requires judges ruling on a motion for summary judgment to apply the same standard of proof that would be required at trial. In this instance, that meant that unless Liberty Lobby could show clear and convincing evidence of actual malice, the lawsuit should be dismissed. The Court thus supported the view that judges considering libel cases brought by public officials or public figures should hold them to a high level of proof of fault if they were to escape having their cases dismissed.

However, because the majority also said it did not intend to "denigrate the role of the jury," "authoriz[e] trial on affidavits," or "suggest that trial courts should act other than with caution in granting summary judgment," the effect of the decision may be more psychological than legal. Indeed, Brennan, usually the Court's most liberal justice on libel questions, said he was unable to discern how the majority's standard was to be applied by trial judges. The two most conservative members, Rehnquist and Burger, took the same position. They said the majority might have given some help to trial judges if it had demonstrated how its standard applied to the facts of *Liberty Lobby*.

Whatever the shortcomings of the Court's decision in *Liberty Lobby,* judges in the U.S. Second Circuit seem not to have any trouble with it. Judge Vincent L. Broderick of the U.S. District Court in New York City granted summary judgment to the *New York Times* in a libel suit brought by a religious group, Contemporary Mission. Citing *Liberty Lobby,* Judge Broderick said that in the absence of clear and convincing evidence of actual malice, he was required by that decision to dismiss the case. He noted, "The Second Circuit has construed *Liberty Lobby* to be a demonstration of the Supreme Court's 'willingness to dispose of libel claims brought by public figure plaintiffs on summary judgment.'"[87]

One of the most notable instances of a failure to prove actual malice occurred in 1985 and involved formidable opponents. Ariel Sharon, then the Israeli defense minister and the leader of that nation's invasion of Lebanon in 1982, was the plaintiff. *Time* magazine was the defendant. Israel's invasion was highly successful and led to the occupation of Beirut, Lebanon's capital. During that occupation, Christian Phalangist militia entered a Palestinian refugee camp in Beirut and killed hundreds of civilians in revenge for the assassination of President Bashir Gemayel. Rumors that Sharon had encouraged the massacre led to an investigation by a blue-ribbon commission appointed by the Israeli government. The commission found no evidence that Sharon had conspired with the Phalangists but said that he should have anticipated the killings and tried to prevent them.

Time's article on the investigation said a secret appendix to the commission's report showed that Sharon had talked with members of the Gemayel family and encouraged them to seek revenge. Sharon considered the article a "blood libel" and sued *Time* in a federal court in New York City for $50 million. Judge Abraham Sofaer made legal history by recognizing the complexities of the proofs required by the *New York Times* rule and attempting to simplify them.[88] He submitted the case to the jury one step at a time. The first question was, "Was the article capable of a defamatory meaning?" The jury said it was. Sharon was portrayed as a party to the murder of hundreds of innocent people. The second ques-

---

87. Contemporary Mission v. New York Times Co., 665 F.Supp. 248, 258 n. 1, (S.D.N.Y. 1987). The quotation is from Guccione v. Hustler Magazine, 800 F.2d 298 (2d Cir. 1986, cert. denied, 479 U.S. 1092, 107 S.Ct. 1303, 94 L.Ed.2d 158 (1987).

88. Andrew Radolf, "Hats off to the Judge," *Editor & Publisher,* 2 February 1985, pp. 9, 29; Paul Janensch, "Time's Costly 'Victory' in the Sharon Libel Case," *Louisville Courier-Journal,* 3 February 1985. For an extended analysis of the Sharon case and that brought by Gen. William Westmoreland against CBS and "60 Minutes," see Renata Adler, "Annals of Law: Two Trials," *New Yorker,* 16 June 1986, pp. 42 + , and 23 June 1986, pp. 34 + .

Ariel Sharon, former Israeli defense minister, was
both a winner and a loser when he sued *Time*
magazine for libel. In 1985, a jury held that the
magazine defamed Sharon by reporting falsely that
he had encouraged Lebanese Christians to massacre
Palestinians. But because Sharon was unable to
prove that the magazine's editors knew the story
was false, or had serious doubts about it, he lost his
suit for damages. (Tannenbaum/Sygma)

tion was, "Was *Time*'s allegation false?" Evidence given the court proved the
existence of a secret appendix to the commission's report. The Israeli government refused to declassify it. However, lawyers for both sides were permitted to
examine it. It did not say that Sharon had encouraged the Gemayels to seek revenge, as *Time* had reported. At that point, the magazine conceded its story was
false and apologized.

That left the final crucial question. "Did the reporter who wrote the story, and
the editors who put it in final form, have any reason to doubt what it said about
Sharon's role?" The original version of the story was written in Israel by a staff
correspondent, David Halevy, who had lived in Israel for forty-three years.

He did not see the appendix to the commission's report, but relied on "a
highly reliable source," who said Sharon had met with Phalangist leaders prior to
the massacre. Halevy also said he relied on hints from high-ranking Israeli army
officers and his own analysis to conclude that Sharon gave the Phalangists "the
feeling" that he understood their need for revenge. Editors in New York changed
Halevy's language to make the story say Sharon had discussed the need for revenge. Underlying the story was Sharon's reputation as an advocate of strong

measures against Palestinians suspected of acts of terrorism against Israelis. The defense minister was highly controversial, and there were many in his own country who believed him capable of doing what *Time*'s story said he did. Therefore, there was no reason for Halevy or his editors to doubt the story. The jury found that there was no actual malice, but the jurors felt compelled to issue a statement castigating *Time* for acting "negligently and carelessly." However, that was not enough to keep *Time* from winning the lawsuit.

Courts have also held that there is no actual malice in relying on the accuracy of news provided by a wire service, especially against a deadline.[89] Nor is there actual malice in relying on the work of a highly respected journalist,[90] or on articles previously published without question as to their accuracy.[91] Reporters who obtain information that later proves to be false from police reports, from reports of other government agencies, or in interviews with public officials will not be found in actual malice if the resulting article accurately reflects the source material.[92] Careful research, coupled with reliance on recognized authorities, has resulted in a finding that there was no actual malice.[93]

Journalists who have placed greater reliance on the word of criminals than on more reputable sources, including a former mayor of San Francisco, have been found in actual malice.[94] Reliance on gossip, rumor, and eavesdropping also can get journalists in trouble. Oklahoma courts found actual malice in an incredibly botched story written by a young photographer who had spent the night in a sheriff's office waiting to go along on a drug raid.[95] The photographer overheard parts of telephone conversations and police radio chatter that led him to believe a police officer had kidnapped a teenager at gun point. His belief was reinforced the next morning when he heard a deputy prosecutor talking on the telephone about the need to investigate the incident. Without asking questions of anyone, the photographer wrote a story that, even more incredibly, was accepted by an editor who doubted its truth but published it anyway. The editor's only check was to ask the writer if he had talked to the prosecutor. A jury concluded that the chain of error amounted to reckless disregard for the truth.

More recently, the Supreme Court upheld a libel judgment against a Hamilton, Ohio, newspaper that was ordered to pay a former candidate for municipal judge $5000 in compensatory damages and $195,000 in punitive damages.[96] Shortly before the election, the newspaper reported that the candidate had used "dirty tricks" to cause an investigation of bribery allegations involving employees of one of his opponents. When the candidate sued for libel, he was able to prove that he had done nothing of the kind. In preparing the story, the newspaper relied

---

89. "Suit v. 32 Papers Dropped," *Editor & Publisher,* 4 February 1984, p. 37.
90. Loeb v. Globe Newspaper Co., 489 F.Supp. 481 (D.Mass. 1980).
91. Dupler v. Mansfield Journal Co., 64 Ohio St.2d 116 (Ohio 1980).
92. Catalano v. Pechous, 83 Ill.2d 146 (Ill. 1980).
93. Yiamouyannis v. Consumers Union, 619 F.2d 932 (2d Cir. 1980).
94. Alioto v. Cowles Communications, 430 F.Supp. 1363 (N.D.Cal. 1977).
95. Akins v. Altus Newspapers, 609 P.2d 1263 (1977).
96. Harte-Hanks Communications v. Connaughton, 491 U.S. _ _ _, 109 S.Ct. 2678, 105 L.Ed.2d 562 (1989).

heavily on an interview with a woman who also had given her story to another newspaper. That newspaper found the story so lacking in credibility that it refused to publish it. Evidence showed that the Hamilton newspaper's reporter had not interviewed a key participant in the alleged bribery and had not listened to a tape recording of a meeting at which the episode had been discussed. On appeal, the Supreme Court reaffirmed the definition of actual malice found in its earlier decisions and held unanimously that in this instance the lower courts had applied those standards properly.

For centuries, "malice" in connection with libel meant ill will, spite, or an intent to cause harm. That history has been hard to overcome. Despite the Supreme Court's insistence that "actual malice" has nothing to do with how writers feel about their subjects, courts in two states, Indiana[97] and Texas,[98] have held that evidence of ill will can be introduced as part of the proof of actual malice. Courts in those states have adopted the theory that a reporter who has shown a dislike for persons involved in an unfavorable story is likely to have "a state of mind highly conducive to reckless disregard of falsity."

Actual Malice and Investigative Reporting

By definition and by reputation, investigative reporters are tough, aggressive pursuers of official skullduggery. If they do their jobs well, they are candidates for the most prestigious prizes in journalism, topped by the Pulitzer. If they cut corners in pursuit of their goals, and sometimes even if they don't, they may also be prime targets for a libel suit. In several recent cases, plaintiff's lawyers have argued that the tactics used by investigative reporters, and the pressures put on them by their editors, are in themselves proof of the state of mind that leads to actual malice. The most definitive rejection of that argument is found in the District of Columbia Circuit's decision in *Tavoulareas* v. *Piro,*[99] some aspects of which were summarized earlier in this chapter. One of the strongest disagreements among the judges was over the state of mind investigative reporters bring to their job and its role in proving actual malice.

Tavoulareas's lawyers argued that Patrick Tyler, the lead reporter on the story, was intent on "getting" the executive. To support that conclusion, they offered several pieces of evidence. At one point, the lawyers said Mobil had embarrassed Tyler by exposing to his editors "his false description of an interview" with Tavoulareas. Early in Tyler's investigation, he had talked to a colleague about "knock[ing] off one of the seven sisters," meaning Mobil, one of the seven largest oil companies. At another point, the reporter had characterized his article as part of a "case against Tavoulareas." After Tavoulareas had met with Tyler and some of his editors at the *Washington Post,* the reporter said the *Post* "blew [the executive] out of the water," and sent him home with his "tail between his legs."

---

97. Cochran v. Indianapolis Newspapers, 372 N.E.2d 1211 (Ind.App. 1978).
98. Frank B. Hall & Co. v. Buck, 678 S.W.2d 612 (Tex.Ct.App. 1984); cert. denied, 472 U.S. 1009 (1985).
99. 817 F.2d 762 (D.C.Cir. 1987).

This evidence was enough to convince a jury that Tyler and his editors had been so intent on getting Tavoulareas and his son that they had acted with actual malice. On appeal, the circuit court panel ruled otherwise. Judge Starr said that an intent to inflict harm is not a part of the Supreme Court's definition of actual malice. Conceding that on occasion evidence of ill will, coupled with substantial evidence of reckless conduct, might support a finding of actual malice, the court warned of the hazards involved:

> The danger of admitting ill-will or bad-motive evidence is that the jury will mistakenly hold the defendant liable for his attitude toward the plaintiff rather than his attitude toward the veracity of his statements concerning the plaintiff. If the trial judge nonetheless determines in his or her sound discretion that such evidence should be admitted..., the judge must seek to minimize the danger of unfair prejudice.[100]

In this instance, Judge Starr said he found nothing in the evidence against Tyler that proved actual malice. It did prove that he "had adopted an adversarial stance toward Tavoulareas." The judge found nothing wrong with that. He reminded his fellow judges that "as in other professions, an adversarial stance is fully consistent with professional investigative reporting." What other professions did he have in mind? Law, for one. Lawyers are expected to take an adversarial stance in favor of their clients. Judge Starr continued:

> It would be sadly ironic for judges in our adversarial system to conclude, as the dissent urges us to do, that the mere taking of an adversarial stance is antithetical to the truthful presentation of facts. We decline to take such a remarkable step in First Amendment jurisprudence. An adversarial stance is certainly not indicative of actual malice under the circumstances where, as here, the reporter conducted a detailed investigation and wrote a story that is substantially true.

Tavoulareas's lawyers argued that as a *Post* reporter, Tyler worked under editors who constantly applied pressure on him and others "to create sensationalistic stories." They found evidence of that pressure in the testimony of Bob Woodward, Tyler's supervising editor, who said he was looking for "holy shit" stories from his staff. Woodward said that term came from reaction he had heard to the stories he and Carl Bernstein had written about the Watergate episode that led to President Nixon's resignation in 1974. Starr said there was nothing in Woodward's testimony to indicate that he expected reporters to seek sensation at the expense of accuracy. The editor's Watergate stories had been checked rigorously for accuracy and won a Pulitzer Prize. The court rejected "the proposition that a jury question of actual malice is created whenever a libel plaintiff introduces evidence that the newspaper vigorously pursued high-impact stories of alleged wrongdoing."

Senior Judge George E. MacKinnon disagreed vigorously. He found an adversarial stance incompatible with the impartiality that should be expected of reporters. A reporter who sees himself as an opponent of the people he is writing

---

100. 817 F.2d 762, 795 n. 45.

about "is more likely to distort the fact than an impartial or objective reporter." MacKinnon noted that Tyler had further demonstrated his bias by encouraging commission of a felony to get material for his story. There was testimony that the reporter had asked Tavoulareas's estranged son-in-law if he knew a family member who would rifle the executive's safe and copy any incriminating documents found there. Starr accepted Tyler's assertion that he was joking, but MacKinnon took it seriously.

With respect to the pressure on *Post* reporters to produce sensational stories, MacKinnon poked at the newspaper's most vulnerable spot. The issue, he wrote, was not whether Woodward and the *Post* wanted its reporters to stretch the truth but whether the pressure led them to do so. That, MacKinnon said, was proved in 1981 when the *Post* had to return a Pulitzer Prize won by a reporter for a story describing "Jimmy's World," occupied by an eight-year-old heroin addict. It was a touching story, but events proved it was made up by the reporter. He pointed also to a paragraph from the *Post* ombudsman's postmortem on that episode: "[S]ome reporters said they felt strongly that the 'system' at the Post has editors making demands on reporters that cannot be met. That reporters are made to feel they are failures when they cannot meet those demands. In MacKinnon's view, those demands had led Tyler to slant all the evidence against Tavoulareas, producing a story that not only was inaccurate and defamatory, but one that showed a reckless disregard for the truth. The majority felt otherwise. Its view stands as the strongest defense in case law for the adversarial position taken by many investigative reporters. The court said that plaintiffs seeking to prove actual malice must do more than show that the defendants were trying to bring down the plaintiffs or were under pressure to produce a big story. The plaintiffs must offer proof that the defendants deliberately or recklessly distorted the facts in order to do so.

Negligence

In response to the Supreme Court's decision in *Gertz,* thirty states permit private individuals to prevail in libel suits if they can prove negligence on the part of the news media. As noted above, proving negligence is easier than actual malice, but plaintiffs still must offer convincing evidence that the defendant's reporting and editing practices fell short of accepted standards. Proof of doubt, serious or otherwise, is not required. Although the state of mind of the defendants is subject to examination, it is not decisive. The focus in determining whether reporters or editors are negligent is on their conduct. Private plaintiffs who sue the media in *Gertz* states must prove some departure from the standard of care ordinarily followed by journalists or any prudent person under the circumstances.

Restatement of Torts 2d, which reflects the conclusions of lawyers who practice libel law, offers the following definition of negligence:

> Negligence is conduct that creates an unreasonable risk of harm. The standard of conduct is that of a reasonable person under like circumstances....
> The defendant, if a professional disseminator of news, such as a newspaper, a magazine, or a broadcasting station, or an employee, such as a reporter, is held to the skill and experience normally possessed by members of that profession. Cus-

toms and practices within the profession are relevant in applying the negligence standard, which is, to a substantial degree, set by the profession itself, though a custom is not controlling.[101]

Restatement enlarges on these generalities by noting three factors that must be taken into consideration in determining whether a reporter or editor was negligent:

1. *Was time of the essence?* "Was the communication a matter of topical news requiring prompt publication to be useful, or was it one in which time and opportunity were freely available to investigate? In the latter situation, due care may require a more thorough investigation." This is a recognition of the "hot news" principle.

2. *What interest was being promoted by the publication?* Was the subject essential to an understanding of a public issue? Would it help people make up their minds about a candidate for public office? Or was it merely gossip? The latter has little public purpose, but great capacity for harm. Therefore, the publisher ought to go to great pains to ensure its accuracy. A lesser standard of care might prevail in the first two instances.

3. *How extensively would the private individual's reputation be damaged if the defamatory statement proved to be false?* This could involve considerations of whether the plaintiff had any reputation to lose, how widely the alleged libel was circulated, and its nature.

Obviously, negligence, like actual malice, must be determined in the light of the facts of each case. Courts trying libel cases brought by private individuals have shown willingness to seek guidance from expert witnesses. These include reporters and editors, journalism professors, consultants, and others who can demonstrate sufficient knowledge of reporting and editing practices to withstand challenge by counsel. Reflecting the lack of agreement on the standard of care expected by journalists, each side can usually produce experts who will support its position. In the end, then, the decision is one for the trier of fact, that is, a jury or a judge. Thus, the *Gertz* decision has put nonjournalists in the position of deciding the standard of care expected of reporters and editors.

Courts in Florida and Kansas expect reporters and editors to know enough law to cover legal proceedings accurately. In Florida, the supreme court said a *Time* magazine reporter was negligent in reporting the Firestone divorce, referred to earlier. He should have known, the court said, that Mrs. Firestone could not have been awarded alimony if she had been found guilty of adultery.[102] In Kansas, the supreme court held that a reporter and her editor were negligent in preparing a story on a farmer accused of starving his hogs.[103] The story said the

---

101. *Restatement*, §580B(g), pp. 227, 228.
102. Firestone v. Time, Inc., 405 So.2d 172 (Fla. 1974).
103. Gobin v. Globe Publishing Co., 531 P.2d 76 (Kans. 1975).

farmer had pleaded guilty to the charge when, in fact, it had only been filed. Both the Florida and Kansas courts used strong language in condemning the reporters' ignorance of the law. Noting the great harm to reputation that can come from mistakenly reporting that a person is guilty of a crime, the Kansas court said the least a journalist can do is "use due care in gathering and reporting court proceedings."

The highest court of Massachusetts also found negligence in a cub reporter's coverage of a court proceeding. The case is of special interest because it illustrates the distinction between negligence and ac-

Stone v. *Essex County Newspapers, Inc.* 330 N.E.2d 161 (1975).

tual malice, which, in this instance, were found in the same case. The reporter's problem came, not from a lack of knowledge of the law, but from timidity. Not knowing that a table was reserved for reporters at the front of the courtroom, the reporter sat at the back of the spectators' section during a narcotics trial. From there, he had difficulty hearing the witnesses. One of the defendants was the twenty-year-old son of the operator of the public schools' lunchrooms. When the prosecutor asked the town marshal who possessed the drugs in question, the reporter thought he heard the marshal respond, "Mr. Stone." The reporter assumed the reference was to the father—the only Mr. Stone he knew. Without checking further with the marshal or the prosecutor, the reporter used the father's first name in his story.

When the reporter submitted the story to his editor, the latter expressed surprise. He had known the elder Stone for twenty years and had never known him to do wrong. He asked the reporter if he was sure. The reporter said the marshal had said on the witness stand that Mr. Stone possessed the drugs. The editor had also known the marshal for a long time and knew he could be trusted. With a deadline approaching, the editor cleared the story for publication.

Stone sued for libel. Eventually, the Massachusetts Supreme Judicial Court ruled that if Stone were held to be a public figure there could be no recovery from the reporter. His failure to sit where he could hear clearly, coupled with his failure to ask someone for Stone's first name was "gross carelessness," but it did not rise to the level of reckless disregard. He was new to the town and to his job. He did not know many people and had no reason to doubt that the Stone mentioned in court was the only Stone he knew. But the editor's reaction to the reporter's story was enough in itself to prove actual malice. He did have doubts, and they could have been removed by a telephone call. His failure to react to his doubts was enough to establish reckless disregard.

An Illinois appeals court held that a reporter was negligent in placing too much reliance on a complaint filed in connection with a civil suit.[104] The reporter compounded his problem by omitting some of the detail in the complaint in order to make a better story. The resulting article was headlined: "SAVED PARROT, LET WOMAN DIE, SUIT SAYS." The defendant in the suit had indeed saved his parrot when he awakened to find his house on fire. But he had been unable to reach a

---

104.   Newell v. Field Enterprises, 415 N.E.2d 434 (Ill.App. 1980).

woman who was asleep in an upstairs room, and he had tried in vain to awaken her. These facts were stated more clearly in the petition to the court than they were in the news story. When the man who rescued the parrot filed a libel suit, the appeals court ruled that the discrepancy between the story and the facts in the petition, which was the reporter's sole source, permitted "an inference of negligent reporting." The court said the facts chosen for the story portrayed such callous conduct that the reporter should have made "a reasonable investigation" to make sure they were true.

The decision serves as a reminder that pleadings filed in connection with civil suits should be handled with care. Allegations made in pleadings present only one side of the case, and that usually in absolute terms. One purpose of a civil suit is to let a jury or judge determine where, between the extremes, the truth lies.

An Arizona court found a reporter negligent in relying on a disgruntled employee for information harmful to her boss.[105] The reporter checked the information with other sources, but had stopped short of confirming the employee's assertion that the Better Business Bureau had received more complaints about her boss's firm than about anyone else. In the end, the finding of negligence made no difference. At trial, a jury found that the story was substantially true.[106]

Courts have found that reporters are not negligent if they rely on the word of a police officer[107] or an officer of the immigration service,[108] even if the information proves to be incorrect.

State courts vary in the standard of proof required to show negligence. However, a survey of the cases indicates that the majority are holding it need be shown only by the preponderance of the evidence. At law, this is a lesser burden than the "clear and convincing evidence" required of public officials and public figures. Thus, in most of the states that have adopted a negligence standard, private plaintiffs not only may win libel suits against the media on a lesser showing of fault, but the rules of evidence make it easier for them to prove.

Obviously, people can and do differ over what is "reasonable care." However, reporters who have been trained well, or who have worked for careful editors, are not likely to be found negligent. Nor are public relations practitioners and advertising copy writers who adhere to the standards of their professions. Prudent professional communicators rely on documentary evidence when it is available. They know that even the best of memories can falter and that participants in a dispute usually make their side look good when they talk to outsiders. Thus potentially defamatory assertions are checked against other sources before they are passed along to the public. Courts have held on numerous occasions that negligence begins with a failure to check facts, especially the "little" facts like the correct spelling of names, street addresses, and the precise wording of court records.

---

105. Peagler v. Phoenix Newspapers, Inc., 560 P.2d 1216 (Ariz. 1977).
106. Peagler v. Phoenix Newspapers, Inc., 640 P.2d 1110 (Ariz. 1982).
107. Wilson v. Capital City Press, 315 So.2d 393 (La. App. 1975).
108. Karp v. Miami Herald Publishing Co., 359 So.2d 580 (Fla.App. 1978).

THE CALCULATION OF DAMAGES ═══════

Proving Harm

In *Gertz,* the Supreme Court held that if states elect to permit private individuals to win libel actions by proving something less than actual malice, they also must require such plaintiffs to prove that they have been harmed. This point of contention is perhaps the easiest for a plaintiff to prove. With proof of harm, private plaintiffs whose lawsuits have survived the three previous points of contention are entitled to recover such monetary damages as may be required to make good their loss. The terms used to describe such awards vary from state to state, but they are commonly referred to as "actual damages" or "compensatory damages."

As Powell noted in *Gertz,* plaintiffs can demonstrate injury by showing they have lost a job or have suffered loss of income as a consequence of the publication of defamatory assertions about them. In such instances, plaintiff's lawyers may call accountants and actuaries as witnesses to calculate the loss. The jury is then asked to require defendants to make it good. Plaintiffs who can prove that they were humiliated to a point that made them ill are permitted to seek recovery of out-of-pocket expenses for medical care, including psychiatric counselling. Jury awards to cover such calculable losses are called special damages.

However, Powell also wrote that "actual injury is not limited to out-of-pocket loss." It includes "impairment of reputation and standing in the community, personal humiliation, and mental anguish." These are intangibles that can be proved only through testimony from the victim or from sympathetic witnesses. Obviously, few, if any, standards will help a jury place a precise value on these elements. This lack gives plaintiffs' lawyers an opening to play on the sympathies of jurors who may have their own reasons for feeling antagonistic toward media defendants. As noted earlier in this chapter, more than half the libel suits that go to a jury result in verdicts for the plaintiff, and some of these have run into the millions of dollars.

A survey of the cases shows that only a few such awards survive modification if they are appealed. Appellate judges, who do not hear the rhetoric a plaintiff's lawyer used to sway the jury, insist on convincing proof of loss of reputation to support an award of damages. The Arkansas Supreme Court summed up the legal principle involved in its decision in *Little Rock Newspapers* v. *Dodrill*[109]: "It is settled law that damage to reputation is the *essence of libel* and protection of reputation is the fundamental concept of the law of defamation.... Such injury to the reputation is a *prerequisite* to making out a case of defamation."

Further, appellate courts have been reluctant to accept a plaintiff's unsupported testimony of loss of standing in the community. In rejecting a claim for damages against the Macmillan Publishing Company, a New York appellate court

---

109.   281 Ark. 25, 660 S.W.2d 933 (Ark. 1983).

said the plaintiff had been "unable to come forth with any proof of loss of reputation because he knows of no one who believes he was a child molester or thinks less of him due to the publication."[110] A federal trial court in New Jersey ruled that public figure plaintiffs do not have a cause of action unless they can prove "compensable injury to reputation."[111]

Courts are divided on the proof that must be offered to support a claim for damages for mental anguish, humiliation, or sorrow. In the cases cited in the paragraph above, the courts held that without proof of loss of reputation there could be no recovery for mental anguish. However, in at least three states, Louisiana, Maryland, and Florida, courts have held that mental distress alone is compensable if convincing proof is offered.[112]

The Vexing Question of Punitive Damages

In addition to special damages and actual or compensatory damages, courts may impose exemplary or punitive damages designed to punish defendants for their callousness and to serve as a deterrent to others who might be tempted to be careless with the truth. One media lawyer called punitive damage awards "the pot of gold" in libel cases.[113] In *Gertz,* the Supreme Court had harsh words for punitive damage awards, calling them "private fines levied by civil juries to punish reprehensible conduct and to deter future occurrence." The Court said if states permitted private libel plaintiffs to win suits against the media by showing some degree of fault short of actual malice, they could not also permit juries to award punitive damages on the same basis. Private plaintiffs can recover punitive damages, the Court said, only if they can prove actual malice. This is the rule in those states that have adopted the option offered in *Gertz,* particularly if a news medium is the defendant or if the libel occurs as part of the discussion of a public issue.

From the defendant's point of view, a major problem with punitive damages is that there are no clear guidelines for juries to follow in awarding them. Powell noted in *Gertz* that in some instances jurors may impose damages "to punish expressions of unpopular views." Such awards are subject to review by appellate courts. But even at that level, no firm rules determine when an award is excessive. Three cases will illustrate the point.

When a gossip item in the *National Enquirer* reported that Carol Burnett was drunk and annoying other diners in an exclusive Washington, D.C., restaurant, she sued for libel. A jury in California ordered the tabloid to pay her $300,000 in actual damages and $1.3 million in punitive damages. The trial judge considered both figures excessive, reducing the former to $50,000 and the latter to $750,000. A state appellate court found the first figure reasonable but further reduced the

---

110. Salamone v. Macmillan Publishing Co., 77 A.D.2d 501 (1st Dept. 1980).
111. Schiavone Construction Co. v. Time, 646 F.Supp. 1511 (D.N.J. 1986).
112. Freeman v. Cooper, 390 So.2d 1355 (La.App. 1980), aff'd, 414 So.2d 355 (La. 1982); Hearst Corp. v. Hughes, 297 Md. 112, 466 A.2d 486 (Md. 1983), and Miami Herald v. Ane, 458 So.2d 239 (Fla. 1984).
113. Richard Winfield, outside counsel to the Associated Press, quoted by Andrew Radolf in "Landmark Libel Case?" *Editor & Publisher,* 20 May 1989, p. 9.

punitive damages to $150,000. However, the court gave Burnett the option of accepting the latter figure or seeking a new trial limited to the question of punitive damages. She chose to settle with the *National Enquirer* for an undisclosed amount.[114]

When Bob Guccione, founder and publisher of *Penthouse* magazine, sued his rival in the soft porn business, Larry Flynt of *Hustler,* for libel, an Ohio jury awarded him $26 million in punitive damages. An appellate court concluded that the jury agreed on that figure for the sole purpose of putting *Hustler* out of business. It ruled that the award was excessive and ordered a new trial limited to the question of the amount of punitive damages.[115]

However, the *Pittsburgh Post-Gazette* was rebuffed at every level when it sought review of an award of $2 million in punitive damages. Neither the Pennsylvania nor the U.S. Supreme Court would consider the appeal.[116] The sum was ten times the jury's award of $200,000 in actual damages to a former Commonwealth Court judge. Further, Pennsylvania law, like statutes in some other states, forbids the newspaper's libel insurer to pay any part of the award of punitive damages. By the time the case ended in 1989, interest and fees had raised the award to $2.7 million, which is believed to be the largest ever imposed on a newspaper in a libel case.

During its 1988–1989 term, the Supreme Court decided two cases which it might have used either to establish standards for awards of punitive damages or to put some cap on them.[117] The Court did neither, although in one instance it seemed to invite litigants to take another approach to the issue.

The latter was a nonmedia case in which the size of an award of punitive damages was at issue. A Vermont jury had found that a waste disposal firm used unfair methods to drive a competitor out of business, assessing the firm $51,146 in compensatory damages and $6 million in punitive damages, which was upheld on appeal. In going to the Supreme Court, the loser argued that the award of punitive damages was an "excessive fine" of the kind prohibited by the Eighth Amendment.[118] The Supreme Court ruled, seven to two, that the amendment was intended to limit fines imposed by government to punish individuals for criminal acts and therefore does not apply to jury awards in civil actions. The Court left open the question as to whether excessive awards of punitive damages might violate the due process clause of the Fourteenth Amendment. Five justices have at one time or another raised questions as to whether awards of punitive damages that are far out of proportion to the actual damage that led to the lawsuit violate that clause.[119]

---

114. "Burnett Settles Libel Suit," *Editor & Publisher,* 26 January 1985, p. 33.
115. Guccione v. Hustler Magazine, 7 Med.L.Rptr. 2077 (1981).
116. Peter Pae, "Pittsburgh Paper Sues to Get Insurer to Cover Damages," *Wall Street Journal,* 13 July 1989.
117. Harte-Hanks Communications v. Connaughton, 491 U.S. _ _ _, 109 S.Ct. 2678, 105 L.Ed.2d 562 (1989), and Browning-Ferris Industries v. Kelco Disposal, 492 U.S. _ _ _, 109 S.Ct. 2909, 106 L.Ed.2d 219 (1989).
118. The amendment says, "Excessive bail shall not be required, nor excessive fines imposed, nor cruel and unusual punishments inflicted."
119. Stephen Wermiel, "Punitive Damage Amounts In Civil Lawsuits Aren't Restricted, Justices Rule," *Wall Street Journal,* 27 June 1989.

Five states prohibit awards of punitive damages in libel cases: Massachusetts,[120] Michigan,[121] New Hampshire,[122] Oregon,[123] and Washington.[124] In Oregon and Washington, the ban is found in the states' constitutions. In New Hampshire, recovery is prohibited by statute. In the other states, the prohibition is grounded in common law.

OTHER PRIVILEGES PROTECTING JOURNALISTS

As courts use the term, a privilege is a special right or immunity granted to individuals, either because the grant is necessary to serve the common good or because the grant will serve the purposes of justice in a legal proceeding. Most of this chapter has been devoted thus far to the First Amendment privilege established by the Supreme Court in *New York Times* v. *Sullivan* and further refined in subsequent decisions. *New York Times* gives the communications media powerful protection against libel suits to further the people's interest in robust debate on public issues.

Courts have recognized other privileges that also further that interest. One, the privilege of neutral reportage, is of recent vintage. It grew out of the long-established common-law privilege protecting fair and accurate accounts of government activities but carries a First Amendment gloss derived from *New York Times*. A second privilege protects public officials and government entities, such as legislatures, in the performance of their official duties. This privilege is absolute in that officials cannot be sued for libel successfully for allegations made in carrying out their duties. The privilege is derived from common law, and its purpose is to encourage the frank give and take that in the Miltonian view leads to truth. A third privilege, already noted, protects journalists in reporting what public officials say, what is found in government documents, and what is said and done in court or in debate in legislative or administrative bodies. That privilege is not absolute. It is qualified in that it protects only fair and accurate reports of those proceedings. This privilege has been strengthened by *New York Times,* which tolerates both unfairness and inaccuracy in the reporting of government activities unless the reporter's sloppiness is so reckless as to become actual malice.

Neutral Reportage

Since 1977, courts in a few jurisdictions have recognized a First Amendment privilege for news media confronted with highly charged and newsworthy public

---

120. Stone v. Essex County Newspapers, 367 Mass. 849, 330 N.E.2d 161 (Mass. 1975).
121. Peisner v. Detroit Free Press, 364 N.E.2d 600 (Mich. 1985).
122. RSA 508:16 (Supp. 1986).
123. Wheeler v. Green, 286 Ore. 99, 593 P.2d 777 (Ore. 1979).
124. Farrar v. Tribune Publishing Co., 57 Wash.2d 549, 358 P.2d 792 (1961).

controversies. In these jurisdictions, courts have held that when accusations are being flung back and forth, it is unreasonable to expect the media to investigate all of them and make reasonably certain that they are true. Therefore, as long as the media offer a neutral report of the accusations, and the reactions of the participants in the controversy, the media are protected. The protection will prevail even when reporters and editors may have had doubt as to the truth of the accusations. Such protection, called the privilege of neutral reportage, has not won general approval. Courts in a few jurisdictions have rejected it. The Supreme Court has refused to resolve the differences, rejecting opportunities to hear cases on both sides of the issue.[125]

The privilege was recognized first in 1977 by the United States Court of Appeals, Second Circuit, in *Edwards* v. *National Audubon Society*. The case began when a reporter for the *New York Times* read an editorial in a publication of the Audubon Society. The editorial said that some scientists who were defending the continued use of DDT as an insecticide were "paid liars." The reporter considered the allegation newsworthy, but so broad that it could hit a lot of innocent targets. He asked the society to be more specific. A vice-president of the society gave him five names, but insisted, as did the editor of the publication, that he did not know that the named scientists were in fact "paid liars." What he did know was that the five continued to cite the society's annual bird count as proof of their assertion that DDT was not harmful to bird life. In the society's view, the count was increasing year by year, not because there were more birds, but because more watchers were participating in the count. The vice-president said the five scientists he named had ignored the society's efforts to impress them with this point. This list included three professors at highly regarded state universities, a Nobel Prize winner who had developed high-yield varieties of food grains, and a lecturer for the National Agricultural Chemical Association. The *Times* reporter sought comment from the five and obtained it from three of them. The resulting news story used the expression "paid to lie," attributed to an Audubon Society spokesman, and the reaction of the scientists. The three university professors sued the society and the *Times* for libel. A jury awarded two of them $20,000 each and the third $21,000.

Edwards v. *National Audubon Society,* **566 F.2d 113 (2d Cir. 1977).**

On appeal, the circuit court reversed, holding that the *Times* was protected by an absolute constitutional privilege based on a right of neutral reportage. It defined that right:

> At stake in this case is a fundamental principle. Succinctly stated, when a responsible, prominent organization like the National Audubon Society makes serious charges against a public figure, the First Amendment protects the accurate and disinterested reporting of those charges, regardless of the reporter's private views regarding their validity.... What is newsworthy about such accusations is that they were made. We do not believe that the press may be required under the First

---

125. In Edwards and McCall, both discussed below.

Amendment to suppress newsworthy statements merely because it has serious doubts regarding their truth. Nor must the press take up cudgels against dubious charges in order to publish them without fear of liability for defamation. . . . The public interest in being fully informed about controversies that often rage around sensitive issues demands that the press be afforded the freedom to report such charges without assuming responsibility for them.

Edwards and subsequent decisions of other courts yield four elements that are essential to establish the privilege of neutral reportage:

1. A public controversy must exist, or it must be created by serious and newsworthy charges.

2. The allegations at issue must be made by a responsible person or organization, probably rising to the level of a public official or public figure.

3. The assertion at issue must be directed at a public official or a public figure.

4. It must be reported accurately and neutrally.

Decisions in the limited number of cases thus far indicate that the first two points are extremely important. The controversy must exist independently of the news media. The assertions at issue must be initiated by someone of stature who is seen by the media as both responsible and newsworthy. The media's role must be confined to that of a disinterested observer resisting the temptation to take sides or to add fuel to the controversy.

In *McManus* v. *Doubleday & Co.*,[126] a federal district court in New York City held that neutral reportage did not apply to charges resulting from investigative reporting. The court held that the charges were solicited by the reporter and that "no controversy raged around the libelous statement before the reporter entered the scene." The court emphasized that "journalist-induced charges" do not come under the protection of the *Edwards* privilege. Nor does a news story "particularly lacking in balanced reporting."[127]

The privilege of neutral reportage has been recognized in California,[128] Florida,[129] Georgia,[130] Indiana,[131] New Jersey,[132] Ohio,[133] Utah,[134] Vermont,[135] and Washington.[136] The federal district court with jurisdiction over Wyoming has

126. 513 F.Supp. 1383 (S.D.N.Y. 1981).
127. Cianci v. New Times Publishing Co., 639 F.2d 54 (2d Cir. 1980).
128. Barry v. Time, 584 F.Supp. 1110 (N.D.Cal. 1984).
129. Brake & Alignment Supply v. Post-Newsweek, 472 So.2d 517 (Fla.App. 3d Dist. 1985).
130. Minton v. Thomson Newspapers, 175 Ga.App. 525, 33 S.E.2d 913 (1985).
131. Woods v. Evansville Press Co., 11 Med.L.Rptr. 2201 (S.D.Ind. 1985); aff'd. on other grounds, 791 F.2d 480 (7th Cir. 1986).
132. Lavin v. New York News, 757 F.2d 1416 (3d Cir. 1985).
133. Horvath v. The Telegraph, 8 Med.L.Rptr. 1657 (Ohio App. 1982).
134. Ogden Bus Lines v. KSL, 551 P.2d 222 (Utah 1976).
135. Burns v. Times-Argus Association, 139 Vt. 381, 430 A.2d 773 (Vt. 1981).
136. Senear v. Daily Journal American, 8 Med.L.Rptr. 2489 (Wash.Super.Ct. 1982).

recognized the privilege, and state courts have twice referred favorably to it in *dicta*.[137] Alabama courts also have recognized the privilege in *dicta*.[138]

Illinois appellate courts have both accepted and rejected the neutral reportage privilege. A down-state court was one of the early endorsers of *Edwards*,[139] but Chicago area courts have twice rejected this privilege in *dicta*.[140]

Courts in four states and one federal circuit have rejected the doctrine of neutral reportage. In their view, the privilege gives the media an opening to publish dubious false and defamatory accusations simply because someone made them. That's what happened in *McCall* v. *Courier-Journal and Louisville Times*,[141] the case that led the Kentucky Supreme Court to reject the neutral reportage privilege.

From the beginning, the case did not fit the *Edwards* pattern. In this instance, the newsworthy accusation was made by woman charged with selling drugs, not by a public figure. Her target was a lawyer of some local renown who was neither so prominent as to qualify as an all-purpose public figure nor so deeply involved in a public issue as to qualify as a limited public figure. The woman told a *Louisville Times* reporter that when she asked lawyer John Tim McCall to defend her against a drug charge he told her he could clear her if she paid him a $10,000 fee. She said he had bragged about going fishing with a judge and had talked about a "fix." A friend who had accompanied the suspect corroborated her story.

McCall v. *Courier-Journal and Louisville Times*, 623 S.W.2d 882 (Ky. 1981).

Sensing an exposé, the reporter gave the suspect a tape recorder small enough to hide in her purse and coached her on questions she should ask on her next visit with the lawyer. The lawyer told her there would be no fix. He would simply work harder for $10,000 than he would for his usual fee of $1500. If his extra effort failed and she had to go to jail, he would charge her only $1500. All this was on tape. Nevertheless, the reporter wrote a story, played on page 1, that said McCall was "in possible violation of his professional ethics." The story gave the suspect's account of her first visit to the lawyer and included such words as "fix," "illegal," and "improper offers." The headline, spread across the top of the page, asked, "Lawyer's 'Guarantee' to Keep Woman Free for $10,000 Unethical?"

When McCall sued the newspaper for libel and invasion of privacy, the newspaper's lawyers argued that the story was protected by the neutral reportage privilege. The trial court dismissed the action, and a state appeals court affirmed. But the state supreme court reversed, holding that there were issues of fact that a jury

---

137. Whitaker v. Denver Post, 4 Med.L.Rptr. 1351 (D.Wyo. 1978); McMurray v. Howard Publications, 612 P.2d 14 (Wyo. 1980), and MacGuire v. Harriscope Broadcasting Corp., 612 P.2d 830 (Wyo. 1980).
138. Wilson v. Birmingham Post, 482 So.2d 1209 (Ala. 1986).
139. Krauss v. Champaign News Gazette, 59 Ill.App.3d 745, 375 N.E.2d 1362 (1978).
140. Newell v. Field Enterprises, 91 Ill.App.3d 735, 415 N.E.2d 434 (Ill.App. 1980), and Tunney v. American Broadcasting Co., 109 Ill.App.3d 769, 441 N.E.2d 86 (Ill.App. 1982).
141. 623 S.W.2d 882 (Ky. 1981).

should be permitted to resolve. In doing so, it denounced the *Times* reporter and editors for publishing the drug suspect's allegations even though, to quote the court, "the newspaper knew—and admitted it knew—that there was no evidence of any crime on the part of McCall." The court flatly rejected the neutral reportage defense. To embrace that doctrine, the court said, it would have to ignore all that the U.S. Supreme Court has said about actual malice. In its view, the news media have no right to circulate defamatory allegations that they know to be false, or about which they have serious doubt, no matter who makes them.

Courts in the other jurisdictions that have rejected a neutral reportage privilege have likewise chosen to place their reliance on the safeguards embodied in the proof of actual malice. They are Michigan,[142] New York,[143] South Dakota,[144] and the U.S. Court of Appeals for the Third Circuit applying what it understood to be Pennsylvania law.[145] It is worthy of note that although *Edwards* was decided by the U.S. Court of Appeals for the Second Circuit, which sits in New York City, New York's state courts have refused to be bound by that decision. And one U.S. district court judge within the circuit ruled that *Edwards* should be given a narrow interpretation.[146] He said that any claim for protection under the neutral reportage privilege should be given careful scrutiny to make certain that all four factors on which that decision was based are present. This means at a minimum that the squabble began without instigation from a news medium, that it was over an issue of genuine public importance, that the defamatory accusations were made by public officials/figures and directed at others of the same stature, and that the news media played the story straight down the middle. Anything short of that is not neutral reportage.

Qualified Privilege

Although the constitutional privilege created by *New York Times* v. *Sullivan* is the defense of choice for lawyers defending communications media against libel suits, the common-law defense of qualified privilege is still useful. The purpose of the privilege is to protect the news media when they act as the eyes and ears of the general public in covering the actions of government agencies and the statements of government officials. Under common law, such reports had to be fair and accurate or the privilege was lost. With the added protection afforded by the actual malice holding in *New York Times,* and the negligence option offered by *Gertz,* the qualified privilege defense has become much stronger. However, courts in several states have upheld libel actions based on the erroneous reporting of judicial proceedings.[147] In effect, the courts have told reporters that if they are going to cover the courts they had better know enough law to make sure their

---

142. Postill v. Booth Newspapers, 118 Mich.App. 608 (Mich.App. 1982).
143. Hogan v. Herald Co., 58 N.Y.2d 630, 458 N.Y.S.2d 538, 444 N.E.2d 1002 (N.Y. 1982).
144. Janklow v. Viking Press, 378 N.W.2d 875 (S.Dak. 1985).
145. Dickey v. CBS, 583 F.2d 1221 (3d Cir. 1978).
146. Lasky v. ABC, 631 F.Supp. 962 (S.D.N.Y. 1986).
147. See the *Firestone* and *Gobin* cases mentioned earlier in this chapter.

stories are accurate. However, if reporters use care in reporting official proceedings and in taking information from public records, they can rely on the defense of qualified privilege to protect them in libel actions. The following cases are illustrative.

Time magazine won dismissal of a libel suit brought against it by Schiavone Construction Co.[148] The article in question reported that the construction company had made improper payments to labor union officials to prevent strikes. This allegedly happened when Raymond J. Donovan, President Reagan's first secretary of labor, was an officer of the company. Whether or not such payments were made—and if so, Donovan's knowledge of them—became subjects of news reports and congressional hearings during the secretary's tenure in office. *Time*'s article was based on testimony offered at the hearings. A federal district court held that because the report was a reasonably accurate account of that testimony it was protected by a qualified privilege. A federal circuit court affirmed that holding.

In a broader application of the privilege, a federal district court in Colorado, interpreting that state's law, held that letters written to a state agency, to various county officials, and even to a newspaper in connection with a rezoning proceeding carried absolute protection. The court held that the letters were written in response to a request from the county board of commissioners for comment on, and public participation in, the rezoning. Since they were a part of the board's search for facts on which to base its decision, they became a function of government and thus privileged.[149]

Statements made by public officials, including law enforcement officers, are protected by absolute privilege when the officials are acting in an official capacity. A United States district court's decision in *Moorhead* v. *Millin*[150] indicates that some courts interpret the scope of official duties quite broadly. In this instance, the lieutenant governor of the Virgin Islands wrote a letter criticizing the performance of the director of the Division of Utilities and Sanitation. Some of the allegations in the letter were false. Parts of the letter, including the false allegations, were published by a newspaper. When the director sued the newspaper for libel, the district court ruled that the lieutenant governor's letter was written as part of his official duties and therefore was protected by absolute privilege. It ruled further that the libel suit against the newspaper should be dismissed because the director could not prove it had published the lieutenant governor's false assertions with actual malice.

A federal district court in Pennsylvania held in *Williams* v. *WCAU-TV* that the station was protected by privilege when it televised the arrest of a suspected bank robber, even though the suspect was released when police concluded he had no connection with the robbery. The court held that the arrest was an official action protected by the state's law defining privilege.[151]

---

148. Schiavone Construction Co. v. Time, Inc., 569 F.Supp. 614 (D.N.J. 1983); affirmed, 735 F.2d 94 (3d Cir. 1984).
149. Walters v. Linhof, 559 F.Supp. 1231 (D.Colo. 1983).
150. 542 F.Supp. 614 (D.V.I. 1982).
151. 555 F.Supp. 198 (E.D.Pa. 1983).

Courts also operate under absolute privilege. This protects witnesses, lawyers, and judges in their testimony or comment during any legal proceedings. The privilege extends to grand jury proceedings.[152] A federal court in Illinois held that a letter written to a judge by a psychologist in connection with a child custody proceeding was absolutely privileged because it was relevant to the proceeding.[153] In California, depositions taken in advance of a trial are protected by an absolute privilege. A state appellate court reasoned, in a libel case brought against the *Fresno Bee,* that depositions are as much a part of a trial as is testimony given in open court.[154] Therefore, the court held, the *Bee* was protected by a qualified privilege when it published a fair and accurate account of a deposition made by one of its own reporters. In the taking of a deposition, lawyers for one side in a legal action question prospective witnesses for the other side under oath in an attempt to narrow the issues that will be contested at the trial.

Although the privilege generally protects only fair and accurate accounts of legal proceedings, courts have held that a news story need not include every detail.

For instance, a federal court in Massachusetts held that a magazine was protected in reporting that the defendant in a criminal prosecution had threatened a witness in court. There was a difference of opinion over the nature of the threat, and the defendant's attorney asserted that no threat had been made. The magazine article omitted the lawyer's disclaimer. The court ruled that the account still was fair and accurate because inclusion of his disclaimer would not have erased the derogatory sting of the report that a threat had been made.[155] A federal court of appeals held that CBS News did not abuse the privilege by illustrating its account of a court proceeding with videotapes taken outside the courtroom. The court held that the combination of words and pictures did not go beyond the bounds of a fair and accurate report.[156]

The defense of qualified privilege can be abused, as is illustrated by the decision of a federal appeals court in *Bufalino* v. *Associated Press.*[157] The case began when an Associated Press (AP) reporter examined the list of contributors to Richard L. Thornburgh's successful campaign for governor of Pennsylvania. The reporter concluded, partly on the basis of information provided by an unidentified informant, that 4 of the 14,000 contributors had links to organized crime. This was news because Thornburgh had made a campaign issue of his opposition to organized crime. The governor-elect reacted by announcing that he was returning the contributions of three of the four persons named in the story. The fourth contributor, who did not get his money back, was Charles J. Bufalino, a lawyer who also served as the appointed attorney for a small town in northeastern Pennsylvania. He had given $140 to Thornburgh's campaign. Apparently, Thornburgh did not believe Bufalino had ties to organized crime.

152.   Reeves v. American Broadcasting Companies, Inc., 719 F.2d 602 (3d Cir. 1983).
153.   Bond v. Pecaut, 561 F.Supp. 1037 (D.Ill. 1983).
154.   "Calif. court rejects lawsuit against Bee," *Editor & Publisher,* 6 June 1987, p. 96.
155.   Ricci v. Venture Magazine, Inc., 574 F.Supp. 1563 (D.Mass. 1983).
156.   Lal v. CBS, Inc., 726 F.2d 97 (3d Cir. 1984).
157.   692 F.2d 266 (2d Cir. 1982).

When the lawyer sued AP for libel, the reporter said he had listed Bufalino because one or more members of the Pennsylvania Crime Commission had told him in confidence that the lawyer was related to an alleged Mafia leader. The sources also said Bufalino had testified for his relative in a deportation hearing and had represented organized crime figures as an attorney. At the time the story was written, the reporter had no other evidence linking Bufalino to organized crime. The appellate court held that because the reporter had not based his story on a public record or on the public statement of a government official acting in an official capacity, the Associated Press was not protected by a qualified privilege. Nor could the information be made privileged by the news agency's later discovery of records showing that Bufalino may have had financial and social ties with organized crime figures. The court ruled that the story was written without such documentary support and would have to be judged for libel purposes on what the AP reporter knew at the time. The court also held that because the reporter refused to identify his sources it could not tell whether they were public officials acting within the scope of their duties when they talked to the reporter.

In any discussion of privilege and the courts, the question arises: Does privilege protect the reporting of information found in a petition or pleading initiating a lawsuit? The answer depends upon each state's common law. In the majority of the states that have ruled on the question, courts have held that such petitions are not protected by privilege until a court has taken some legal notice of them. This can come about through a decision made on a motion, either by the defense or the plaintiff. In these majority states, reporters who act too soon in basing a story on defamatory material taken from a petition filed in court may not be able to rely on qualified privilege as a defense.

The *Pittsburgh Post-Gazette* case, mentioned in the section on punitive damages, grew out of stories based on documents filed in a dispute over a will. One story, published in 1979, suggested, on the basis of statements made in a deposition, that a former judge, then a lawyer in private practice, may have conspired with a beneficiary to alter a will. A jury concluded that the story was not a fair report of the entire proceeding. Earlier, another Pennsylvania jury ordered a newspaper to pay a physician $200,000 in damages for a story based in part on a petition filed in a malpractice suit. The reporter had added detail to the story by interviewing the woman who filed the suit but had not talked to the physician.[158]

Courts in a few states have held that pleadings in a lawsuit are privileged when they are filed with the clerk.[159] An Illinois appeals court listed four reasons for doing so:

1. The public has an interest in knowing what goes on in court, especially since many of society's problems are being attacked through litigation. Courts have been asked, for instance, to resolve issues affecting minority job rights, university admissions policies, wages paid to women, water and air pollution, and the safety of automobiles.

---

158. "Libel Award Is 'Message' to Newspaper," *Editor & Publisher,* 24 January 1987, p. 46.
159. For a discussion of this topic, see Newell v. Field Enterprises, 415 N.E.2d 434 (Ill. 1980).

2. The majority states have taken the position that by deferring privilege until some judicial action has been taken, they will discourage the filing of suits for the sole purpose of putting defamatory accusations in circulation. However, there is no guarantee that a suit pushed forward to litigation has any substance, or was brought in good faith.

3. Starting in 1927,[160] courts have recognized a growing public awareness of the reality of what happens in court. Most persons know that those who file suit base that filing on a one-sided version of the facts. Thus, most readers will apply more than a few grains of salt to allegations contained in a story of a suit's being filed.

4. In all states, the filing of most suits produces a public record. Petitions are filed in the office of the clerk of courts where they are open to inspection by anyone. Thus, all publication does is extend the range of knowledge of the filing. In some states, records of paternity proceedings, of charges of incest, and, in a few states, of some kinds of divorce proceedings are sealed by law; therefore, they are not public records. Most juvenile courts also operate under a cloak of secrecy that can be breached only by order of the court.

In general, however, professional communicators who are covering the actions of government and the activities of public officials enjoy double protection against libel suits. A story that accurately reflects a privileged situation is protected by qualified privilege. If the situation turns out not to have been privileged, or if some detail proves not to be accurate, the *New York Times* rule comes into play. At that point, the reporter's performance comes under examination. A public official or public figure plaintiff must offer clear and convincing evidence of actual malice. Private individuals in the states that have adopted the option offered by *Gertz* must prove negligence. In a few federal circuits, and in some states, reporters of public controversies enjoy an additional privilege—neutral reportage.

In the Professional World

New York Times v. *Sullivan* has accomplished one of the purposes of the justices who wrote it. By its twenty-fifth anniversary in 1989 it had effected a noticeable decrease in the number of libel suits brought against the news media. But critics in and out of the media were asking if that decrease had been bought at too high a price. *New York Times, Gertz,* and their many progeny have converted libel actions into elaborate and expensive rituals that only wealthy litigants can afford. This has led some publishers to discourage investigative reporting lest it lead to an expensive legal action. Looked at from the other side, however, the decisions have greatly length-

---

160. Campbell v. New York Evening Post, 157 N.E. 153 (N.Y. 1927).

ened the odds against a plaintiff's winning a substantial judgment. Consequently, some persons who have indeed been victims of false and defamatory falsehoods have hesitated to set in motion a process that may or may not result, many months or even years later, in clearing their names. That reluctance is based on a fact that troubles many, including some journalists and the lawyers who represent them: The law permits the news media to defame public officials, public figures, and even private individuals, and get away with it. Proving fault is difficult at best. The Supreme Court has made proving actual malice even more difficult by requiring appellate courts to review conclusions of fact reached by the trial jury. It is not surprising, then, that lawyers, academics, and others are advancing proposals designed to cut short, or by-pass, the legal process required to establish the truth or falsehood of an alleged defamation.

The Practising Law Institute's conclusions as to the decrease in the number of libel actions were noted in the introduction to the preceding chapter. Additional evidence comes from the two firms that write most of the libel insurance policies for the media. They estimated that the number of libel suits filed against all communications media dropped by a third between 1985 and 1988, with actions against newspapers declining by at least a fifth.[161]

The insurers attributed the decline in part to the failure of plaintiffs in three highly publicized cases—*Sharon* v. *Time Inc.*, *Westmoreland* v. *CBS*, and *Pring* v. *Penthouse*—to win judgments. These decisions and others have greatly raised the odds against a libel plaintiff's winning a large judgment. The *Journal* article quoted one libel lawyer as saying that the odds against collecting a judgment large enough to justify the expense of protracted litigation have become too long for most law firms. The lawyer noted that only 20 percent of the jury verdicts for plaintiffs are being upheld on appeal. The average judgment affirmed by appellate courts is $145,550. Plaintiff's attorneys usually take libel cases on a contingency fee basis. If the attorneys win, they may get up to 40 percent of the award. If they lose, they get nothing in most instances except reimbursement for direct expenses. A law firm that agrees to represent a libel plaintiff in an action against a determined defendant can anticipate five to seven years of preparation which may lead to little or no return.

The economics of a libel action cuts two ways. As we noted in the introduction, media defendants incur heavy legal fees even when they win. The prospect of such costs is leading more defendants to settle cases at an early stage, according to Chad Milton, vice president and assistant general counsel for one of the libel insurers. He was quoted by the *Journal* as saying: "A few years ago, libel cases weren't settled—period. Now it's being considered. It's often rejected, but it's considered. Settling can be the right thing to do in certain circumstances."

---

161. Betty Wong, "In Wake of Westmoreland, Sharon Cases, Libel Suits against the Media Decline," *Wall Street Journal,* 17 October 1988.

The high cost of defending a libel action is having other consequences. One session of the 1987 meeting of Investigative Reporters & Editors was devoted to a discussion of the chilling effect of libel actions. Sam Klein, a lawyer whose main client is the *Philadelphia Enquirer,* was quoted as saying there is a chill "in the sense that people have to take second, third and fourth looks at stories." He also said he knew of newspapers that no longer do any investigative reporting out of fear of being sued for libel. Bill Marimow, who twice has won Pulitzer Prizes as a reporter for the *Inquirer,* said he changed his interviewing methods to avoid libel cases. He said he has become more open with sources he is investigating and as a result may not always get as much of the story as he might have previously.

Floyd Abrams, a specialist in First Amendment law who has represented the *New York Times* and other major media clients, also says that fear of the costs of libel actions has deterred investigative reporting. He wrote that an article reporting "serious misconduct in the scientific community," including the publication of false and misleading statements by distinguished scientists, was withheld because it might have led to a lawsuit.[162] Abrams cited other instances in which articles and books by reputable journalists either had to be toned down before publication or were not published at all because of legal concerns.

In the view of Abrams and of speakers at the annual meetings of the investigative reporters' organization, fear of libel actions is depriving the public of helpful information. Others see few signs of such deprivation. Senior Judge George E. MacKinnon of the U.S. Court of Appeals for the District of Columbia Circuit, in his dissent in *Tavoulareas,* argued that management pressure on *Washington Post* reporters to produce sensational stories "could motivate reporters to stretch the truth." In his opinion, that's exactly what the *Post's* reporters did in their story about Mobil's chief executive officer. To build their "case against Tavoulareas," they "resolved practically all ambiguities against him, *consistently* accepting the most damaging statements from obviously biased...sources." Keep in mind that a majority of the court did not agree with MacKinnon, holding that the pressure on the staff, coupled with acknowledged distortions in the story, did not prove reckless disregard.

Others have argued that, far from stifling investigative journalism, *New York Times* has encouraged poorly prepared reporters to practice in a shoddy way. One who has advanced that view is Clark R. Mollenhoff, winner of three Sigma Delta Chi Distinguished Service Awards and a Pulitzer Prize before he became a journalism professor at Washington and Lee University. He spent many years as a Washington correspondent and investigative reporter for the *Des Moines Register* and other Cowles publications. On the twenty-fifth anniversary of *New York Times* he wrote an article as-

---

162. Floyd Abrams, "Why We Should Change the Libel Law," *New York Times Magazine,* 29 September 1985, p. 344.

serting that the decision has done more harm than good.[163] He said he cheered the Court's holding when it was made in 1964 but has come to the conclusion that the actual malice rule has encouraged sloppy journalism. In his view, the rule permits editors to justify their failure to fully corroborate damaging charges against public officials and public figures by saying their lack of doubt gave them no reason for digging deeper. With the bluntness for which he was known as a reporter, Mollenhoff wrote: "It has been said that patriotism is the last refuge of scoundrels. *New York Times* v. *Sullivan* similarly has provided a significant refuge for a few willful falsifying scoundrels, for larger numbers of scoop-minded incompetents, and for many reporters and editors who are just plain lazy." That commentary may be too extreme, but Mollenhoff's reservations about the effect of *New York Times* are shared by Justice White, who helped write it. Concurring in the Court's judgment in *Greenmoss,* he wrote: "I have become convinced that the Court struck an improvident balance in the *New York Times* case between the public's interest in being fully informed about public officials and public affairs and the competing interest of those who have been defamed in vindicating their reputation."

In White's view, as in Mollenhoff's, the culprit is the actual malice rule. It gives First Amendment protection "to false statements of fact about public officials." In White's view, such statements frustrate the core value of the amendment, which is protection of "that flow of intelligence" essential to our ability to govern ourselves through our elected representatives. That value, White wrote, is "even more disserved when the statements falsely impugn the honesty of those men and women and hence lessen the confidence in government." And yet officials who are the victims of false charges can't even get into court unless they can make out "a jury case of a knowing or reckless falsehood." That means, White concluded, that "[t]he lie will stand, and the public continue to be misinformed about public matters." The justice placed little stock in the remedy that is at the heart of *New York Times* and *Gertz:* the Supreme Court majority's assumption that public officials and public figures are powerful enough to reach the public in a convincing fashion with their version of the truth. Quoting from Brennan's opinion in *Rosenbloom,* he wrote, "It is a rare case where the denial overtakes the original charge. Denials, retractions, and corrections are not 'hot' news, and rarely receive the prominence of the original story."

Has *New York Times* outlived its usefulness? There are those who think so and who are making suggestions for other means of counteracting defamatory falsehoods. One set of suggestions grew out of a study of media credibility commissioned by the Associated Press Managing Editors Association in 1984 and a similar study conducted at about the same time for the *Los Angeles Times* by its media reporter, David Shaw. Both studies recom-

---

163. Clark R. Mollenhoff, "25 Years of *Times* v. *Sullivan, Quill,* March 1989, p. 27 + .

mended that reporters and editors set higher standards of professional performance, insist that they be met, and tell their readers what they do and
why.[164] Noting that the news media are perceived as powerful institutions,
Shaw argued that they should perform with the same degree of openness
they demand from the institutions they cover. In his view, journalists ought
to tell their audience how they developed controversial stories and why
those stories took the form they did. This is precisely what plaintiff's lawyers ask for when they pursue a libel action against a media defendant.

A study by three University of Iowa professors of libel plaintiffs, and of
all libel and privacy cases decided between 1974 and 1984, suggests that
such openness might help if it is coupled with a greater willingness to admit
the occasional serious mistake.[165] The study shows that most libel plaintiffs
said they went to court only after they had sought a correction and been
rebuffed, sometimes rudely. In a summary of their findings, the authors
said, "In a significant proportion of the cases, the *way* people were treated
when they contacted the media seems to account for, or be a factor in, their
anger and decision to sue."

David Lawrence, Jr., publisher of the *Detroit Free Press,* responded to
that finding in a talk to an Inland Daily Press Association meeting in
Chicago.[166] He said, "Journalists are people with great power that can be
used for good and bad and, in many cases, the public resents that power.
We're often seen as arrogant people who own the printing press and always
have the last word." That arrogance often shows up, Lawrence said, when
someone calls to complain about being mistreated or misrepresented in a
story. At such times, he said, "It is arrogant for a newspaper to be anything
but courteous. Journalists tend to think they are right most of the time, but
it is important to acknowledge errors of fact, tone or context." He recommended that reporters and editors make themselves accessible to critics of
their stories and that they treat critics with compassion.

One libel lawyer recommends anticipating complaints and attempting to
head them off while a potentially defamatory story is being prepared.
Alexander Greenfield, former corporate and libel counsel to the *New York
Times* and *U.S. News & World Report,* wrote: "The best protection always
is to get an interview or comment from a subject who is being pictured in a
bad light. You may learn you have errors, learn about other sources, and
deflect a lawsuit by giving the person his say and showing him a balanced
picture."[167]

---

164. "APME Credibility Research: What the Research Means," presentation by panel comprised
of Roberto Goizueta, chair of the board, Coca-Cola Co.; Norman Isaacs, former chair, National News Council; and David Shaw, media reporter, *Los Angeles Times,* at the APME
annual meeting in San Francisco, 29 October 1985.

165. Randall P. Bezanson, Gilbert Cranberg, John Soloski, "Libel Law and the Press: Setting the
Record Straight," *Iowa L.Rev.,* October 1985, p. 215 + .

166. Debra Gersh, "Arrogance in Journalism," *Editor & Publisher,* 13 December 1986, p. 24 + .

167. Alexander Greenfield, "Thirty Ways to Protect Yourself against Libel Lawsuits," *Editor &
Publisher,* 3 June 1989, p. 56.

Floyd Abrams, the First Amendment authority quoted earlier in this section, recommends a further step. He encourages media to make a prompt admission of error when they clearly have misstated facts. But Abrams would go further and make changes in the law that would both discourage libel suits and make it less expensive to resolve questions of truth when persons have been defamed. Abrams would start by denying plaintiffs the right to sue when the media make a prompt and complete retraction. He would continue by limiting damages for emotional injury and abolishing punitive damages. That would end the "pot of gold" potential that now encourages some lawyers to file suit hoping either to find a sympathetic jury or to force a generous settlement. To further discourage such suits, Abrams would give courts the power to require that the loser pay the winner's legal fees if the suit were brought or defended in disregard of settled principles of law. Finally, he suggests that states enact laws to permit public officials or public figures to sue for a declaratory judgment to determine the truth of what was published about them.

Those suggestions were made in 1985. They have not been put into effect. However, they were endorsed in part by a panel of eleven lawyers and others who were drawn together by the Annenberg Washington Program in 1988 to study libel law.[168] The panel's proposal, like Abrams's, would start with a request for a retraction or reply. If that were made to the complainant's satisfaction, the matter would end. If the request was refused, the complainant could sue, but either party could ask that the suit be limited to a finding of the truth or falsity of the item in question. In such event, the loser would be required to pay the winner's attorney fees.

The Iowa professors whose study of libel cases found that many plaintiffs would be content with a mechanism to clear their names proposed to bypass the legal system altogether. In 1987, the University of Iowa, in cooperation with the American Arbitration Association, received funding from the John and Mary R. Markle Foundation to give their proposal a try.[169] The resulting Libel Dispute Resolution Program was designed to determine within two months whether an alleged defamation was true or false. The original funding was for two years. At the end of that time, the program had resolved one dispute and another was pending. The funding was renewed.[170]

Meanwhile, *New York Times,* supplemented by *Gertz,* stands as a precedent that has brought under the protective shield of the First Amendment media coverage of public officials, public figures, and of private individuals caught up in matters of public importance. Behind that shield, the media can report on, or participate in, the debate on public policy. For media professionals willing to go to great lengths to ensure that their accounts are

---

168. George Garneau, "Libel Law Reform," *Editor & Publisher,* 22 October 1988, p. 36 + ; Stephen Wermiel, "Libel-Law Plan Could Eliminate Damage Awards," *Wall Street Journal,* 18 October 1988.
169. "Resolving Libel Disputes," *Editor & Publisher,* 2 May 1987, with a "Clarification," 20 June 1987.
170. Interview with John Soloski, 13 July 1989.

both accurate and fair, that shield offers nearly absolute protection from libel judgments but not from expensive libel suits. For the "willful falsifying scoundrels," "scoop-minded incompetents," and the "plain lazy," this shield offers less protection, depending on the ability of their victims to prove actual malice or negligence. At bottom then, libel becomes a question of ethics. The law permits the media to defame individuals and institutions and get away with it. Until the Supreme Court says otherwise, that is the reality faced by all who are caught in the media's spotlight. The critical question is: Should any professional communicator take comfort in avoiding liability only because the subject of a defamatory report could not prove fault?

FOR REVIEW

1. Define defamation. Who carries the burden of proving defamation? Assuming that defamation can be proved, what remains to be proved by libel plaintiffs if they are to win their lawsuits?

2. Is an accusation of crime always grounds for a libel action? Explain.

3. Although by the time it reached the Supreme Court, the central issue in *Falwell* was the intentional infliction of emotional distress, not libel, the decision nevertheless made important points with respect to libel law. What are they?

4. In those courts that look to *Ollman* for guidance, what criteria are used to distinguish between an assertion of opinion and a statement of fact?

5. Define a public official for purposes of a libel action. Illustrate.

6. Distinguish between an all-purpose and a limited public figure. Discuss the role of the news media in creating public figures. What criteria do courts use in determining whether a libel plaintiff is a limited public figure?

7. What standard of proof does your state require of private individuals who sue the news media for libel?

8. What is "actual malice"? How is it proved? What element is virtually essential to its proof? Illustrate by reference to a case.

9. A public official/public figure libel plaintiff offers proof that a publication's reporters and editors were out to get him or her, that their position was that of an adversary, not neutral fact-finders. The plaintiff also offers proof of some errors in the stories. Does this prove actual malice? Should it? Why or why not?

10. Distinguish between negligence, as it is defined in libel cases, and actual malice. Illustrate by reference to a case in which negligence was proved.

11. What is meant by the term "neutral reportage"? Is the concept compatible with the Supreme Court's definition of actual malice? Why or why not?

12. With respect to the news media, what is a qualified privilege? What is its value? Does the term have the same meaning for nonmedia libel defendants? Explain.

13. What is meant by an abuse of privilege in the context of a libel case? Explain.

14. The news media and other professional communicators have had more than twenty-five years of experience with *New York Times* and its progeny. On the whole, have the rules flowing from that decision strengthened or weakened the First Amendment's guarantee of freedom of the press? Have they served the public well or badly? If you could sit on the Supreme Court, would you change any element of libel law? If so, what? Why?

CHAPTER 5

When television cameras zoom in on people who have just learned that their friends or relatives were victims of an airplane crash, or when newspapers report, without apparent reason, that the man who deflected a shot aimed at the president is a homosexual, many people ask why. Are not such examples of journalistic enterprise an invasion of privacy?

It is not easy to answer that question when it is raised by critics of media performance. Twentieth-century law indeed recognizes that people have a right to be left alone. Persons who suffer humiliation or embarrassment because of the acts of others have a legal right of redress in most states. Problems arise, however, because the law varies widely from state to state and because the law recognizes that at some point an individual's asserted right to privacy limits the media's First Amendment right to inform the public. The problem is further compounded by a wide difference between the perception of the general public and that of media

INVASION OF PRIVACY

professionals as to what is an invasion of privacy. Polls show, for instance, that substantial majorities of the public think it is an invasion of privacy to publish photographs of accident victims, to report that a person committed suicide, or to give the addresses of burglary victims.[1] Obviously, the news media do all these things. It is equally obvious that none of them violate the law. Other studies show, however, that one factor in the media's low credibility with the public comes from the perception that journalists are invaders of privacy.[2]

This perception has resulted in lawsuits directed at the media, although by no means as frequently as libel actions. Nor have plaintiffs had the same degree of success. Major privacy judgments against media professionals are rare. However, the number of actions, and their nature, make privacy law a major area of concern not only for newspapers and television, but for photographers, advertisers, and public relations professionals as well.

Unlike the law of defamation, which has roots at least seven hundred years old, the law of privacy is of fairly recent origin. It was not recognized as a branch of tort law until early in this century, and still has not been recognized as an actionable tort in all states. It is a product of both common law and statutes. Also unlike the law of defamation, it has not been federalized, nor has it been brought into the realm of First Amendment law, except in one of its aspects. Therefore, the law of privacy, to a greater extent than the law of defamation, varies from state to state. However, a few reasonably clear principles have been established by court decisions, and these will be the subject of this chapter.

The law of privacy is concerned primarily with exploitation or harassment of the individual by the news media, employers, bill collectors, advertisers, and public relations practitioners. Lawsuits can be brought by persons who believe that others have poked too deeply into the former's private lives, exposing facts so outrageous and so lacking in news value that their publication is offensive. Reporters who use surreptitious methods—misrepresentation, hidden microphones,

---

1. Sam Cremin, "Public Tells When News Media Invade Privacy," *Editor & Publisher,* 19 May 1979, p. 13.
2. *Journalists and Readers: Bridging the Credibility Gap,* commissioned by the Associated Press Managing Editors Association and conducted by MORI Research, Inc., Minneapolis, October 1985.

or concealed cameras—to gather information may be open to a lawsuit for intrusion, even though their efforts produce a newsworthy story. Libel plaintiffs can recover damages only if they can prove they have been victims of false and defamatory assertions of fact. Privacy plaintiffs can recover if an overly favorable story portrays them in a false light that would be embarrassing to a person of ordinary sensibilities. Finally, privacy law recognizes that people have a property right in their names and portraits. Thus, advertisers who rely on endorsements or on likenesses of real people to sell their products open themselves to privacy actions. In recent times, this branch of the tort has been expanded to protect performers or other famous persons from being exploited without their consent.

Government, too, has become involved in protecting privacy. States have enacted laws permitting persons who have been arrested and even convicted of crime, but who have gone straight, to expunge or seal the records dealing with their offenses. This has made it difficult in some instances for journalists to investigate allegations or wrongdoing, or the performance of prosecutors and judges.

Because of the nature of privacy law, none of the cases have the stature of *New York Times* v. *Sullivan* or *Gertz* v. *Robert Welch, Inc.* Rather, this chapter will present a number of significant cases, each of which illustrates one or more of the general principles mentioned above.

Major Cases

- *Bahr* v. *Statesman Journal Co.*, 624 P.2d 664 (Ore. App. 1981).

- *Cantrell* v. *Forest City Publishing Co.*, 419 U.S. 245, 95 S. Ct. 465, 42 L. Ed. 2d 419 (1974).

- *Carson* v. *Here's Johnny Portable Toilets*, 698 F. 2d 831 (6th Cir. 1983).

- *Cher* v. *Forum International, Ltd.*, 692 F. 2d 634 (9th Cir. 1982).

- *Cox Broadcasting Co.* v. *Cohn*, 420 U.S. 469, 95 S. Ct. 1029, 43 L. Ed. 2d 328 (1975).

- *Diaz* v. *Oakland Tribune, Inc.*, 188 Cal. Rptr. 762 (Cal. Ct. App. 1st Dist. Div. 3 1983).

- *Dietemann* v. *Time, Inc.*, 284 F. Supp. 425 (C. D. Calif. 1968); 449 F. 2d 245 (9th Cir. 1971).

- *Jenkins* v. *Dell Publishing Co.*, 251 F. 2d 447 (3d Cir. 1958).

- *Kimbrough* v. *Coca-Cola/USA*, 521 S. W. 2d 719 (Tex. 1975).

- *Matter of Application to Adjudge Providence Journal Co. and Its Executive Editor, Charles M. Hauser, in Criminal Contempt*, 820 F. 2d 1342 (1st Cir. 1986).

- *Miller* v. *National Broadcasting Co.*, 187 Cal. App. 3d 1463, 232 Cal. Rptr. 668 (Cal. App. 2 Dist. 1986).

■ *National Bank of Commerce* v. *Shaklee Corp.,* 503 F.Supp. 719 (W. D. Tex. 1980).

■ *New Bedford Standard-Times Publishing Co.* v. *Clerk of Third Dist. Court,* 387 N. E. 2d 110 (Mass. 1979).

■ *Newspapers, Inc.* v. *Brier,* 279 N. W. 2d 179 (Wis. 1979).

■ *Oklahoma Publishing Co.* v. *District Court in and for Oklahoma County,* 430 U.S. 308, 97 S. Ct. 1045, 51 L. Ed. 2d 355 (1977).

■ *Shields* v. *Gross,* 7 Med. L. Rptr. 2349 (Sup. Ct. N. Y. Co. 1981); modified, 451 N.Y.S. 419 (N.Y. App. 1982); aff'd as modified, 448 N. E. 2d 108 (N.Y. 1983); 503 F. Supp. 533 (S.D.N.Y. 1983).

■ *Sidis* v. *F-R Publishing Corp.,* 113 F. 2d 806 (2d Cir. 1940).

■ *The Florida Star* v. *B.J.F.,* ___ U.S. ___, 109 S.Ct. 2603, 105 L. Ed. 2d 443 (1989).

■ *Time, Inc.* v. *Hill,* 385 U.S. 374, 87 S. Ct. 534, 17 L. Ed. 2d 456 (1967).

■ *Virgil* v. *Time, Inc.,* 527 F. 2d 1122 (9th Cir. 1975).

■ *Zacchini* v. *Scripps-Howard Broadcasting,* 433 U.S. 562, 97 S. Ct. 2849, 53 L. Ed. 2d 965 (1977).

THE LAW OF PRIVACY

Unlike libel law, which traces its lineage through at least six centuries of common law, the law of privacy is one of the few fields of law that can date its birth to a law journal article. The courts have drawn many of its principles from an article written by two Boston lawyers, Samuel D. Warren and Louis D. Brandeis, published in the *Harvard Law Review* in 1890.[3] Twenty-six years later, Brandeis was appointed to the Supreme Court of the United States, where his concern with privacy was reflected in some of his opinions.

When the article was written, Warren and Brandeis were young lawyers with entreé to Boston's top social circles. In their opinion, journalists were devoting too much attention to what happened in those circles. They wrote in protest:

> Instantaneous photographs and newspaper enterprise have invaded the sacred precincts of private and domestic life; and numerous mechanical devices threaten to make good the prediction that "what is whispered in the closet shall be proclaimed from the housetops." ...
>
> Of the desirability—indeed the necessity—of some ... protection there can be, it is believed, no doubt. The press is overstepping in every direction the obvious bounds of propriety and decency. Gossip is no longer the resource of the idle and

---

3. Samuel D. Warren and Louis D. Brandeis, "The Right to Privacy," 4 *Harvard Law Review* 193, 15 December 1890.

vicious, but has become a trade, which is pursued with industry as well as effrontery. To satisfy a prurient taste the details of sexual relations are spread broadcast in the columns of the daily papers. To occupy the indolent, column upon column is filled with idle gossip, which can only be procured by intrusion upon the domestic circle.

The article suggested that the same principles that give property owners the right to protect their houses and lands from trespassers should give all persons the right to protect themselves from intrusion into their private affairs. The authors argued for a right to be left alone, for a right to control the extent to which others can pry into an individual's private life.

Within a decade, courts began to recognize such a right. Some of the early cases were decided on the theory of trespass, as the authors had suggested. Others were decided on the theory that an individual's identity is a form of property that an individual can control.

Some courts rejected the Warren and Brandeis reasoning, most notably the New York Court of Appeals in *Roberson* v. *Rochester Folding Box Co.*[4] The action had been brought by a young woman whose portrait was used without her permission to advertise flour. She won an order from a trial court preventing further use of her likeness, but the appeals court reversed, holding it could find no precedents to support a right of privacy. The legislature reacted in 1903 by enacting a law designed to prevent such exploitation.[5]

Today, all but two states protect a right of privacy, either as defined by statute, as in New York, or by common law. In a few states, privacy is protected by a combination of the two. Courts in Minnesota have refused to recognize a legally defendable right of privacy. Those in North Dakota have had no occasion to do so. Several other states have had no media-related privacy cases but have recognized the tort in cases involving business firms and their treatment of customers or employees.

THE FOUR ELEMENTS OF INVASION OF PRIVACY

The phrase "invasion of privacy" seems simple, but under legal analysis in the courts it has proved to be highly complex. So much so that William L. Prosser, who for twenty years or so was a leading authority on torts law, finally concluded that invasion of privacy is not one tort but a bundle of four. His conclusions are embodied in *Restatement of Torts*[6]

> The law of privacy comprises four distinct kinds of invasion of four different interests of the plaintiff which are tied together by the common name, but otherwise have almost nothing in common except that each represents an interference with the right of the plaintiff "to be let alone."

---

4. 64 N.E. 442 (N.Y. 1903).
5. New York Civil Rights Law §§50–51.
6. 3rd ed., 1964, vol. 3, §652a, p. 832.

The four kinds of invasion comprising the law of privacy include:
(1) intrusion upon the plaintiff's physical and mental solitude or seclusion,
(2) public disclosure of private facts,
(3) publicity which places the plaintiff in a false light in the public eye,
(4) appropriation, for the defendant's benefit or advantage, of the plaintiff's name or likeness.

The summaries below point up the differences between the four elements that combine under the term "invasion of privacy."

Intrusion into Mental or Physical Solitude

Intrusion into a person's mental or physical solitude is closely related to the trespass mentioned by Warren and Brandeis. It involves entry without permission into another's private space. An Oklahoma court upheld trespass convictions against reporters and photographers who followed antinuclear demonstrators onto a utility company's property.[7] Journalists who use subterfuge to gain entrance to a private home are vulnerable to suit as intruders. A photographer who harasses a newsworthy subject may also be an intruder. So may an eavesdropper or wiretapper. Publication is not an essential element in an action for intrusion. Courts have held that the harm lies in the act of intrusion itself. Some courts have rejected the argument that a First Amendment right to gather news ought to justify an intrusion, while others have held that the reporter's First Amendment interest must be balanced against the victim's right of privacy.

Thirty-nine states, the District of Columbia, and Puerto Rico have recognized intrusion as a cause of an action for invasion of privacy. The states are Alabama, Alaska, Arizona, Arkansas, California, Colorado, Connecticut, Delaware, Florida, Georgia, Idaho, Illinois, Indiana, Iowa, Kansas, Kentucky, Louisiana, Maine, Maryland, Massachusetts, Michigan, Mississippi, Missouri, Nebraska, New Hampshire, New Jersey, New Mexico, New York, Ohio, Oklahoma, Oregon, Pennsylvania, Rhode Island, South Carolina, Texas, Utah, Washington, West Virginia, and Wisconsin.[8]

Disclosure of Private Fact

A disclosure of private fact occurs when some medium of communication disseminates personal information that the individual involved did not want made public. The information must be of a nature that would be offensive to a person of ordinary sensibilities. California courts held, for example, that a newspaper column commenting on a college student-body leader's sex-change operation was a

---

7. Stahl v. Oklahoma, 665 P.2d 839 (Okla.Ct.Crim.App. 1983).
8. This list and those in the following sections were compiled from Victor A. Kovner, "Recent Developments in Intrusion, Private Facts, False Light, and Commercialization Claims," *Communications Law 1987* (New York: Practising Law Institute, 1987), pp. 281–439; Henry R. Kaufman, ed., *LDRC 50-State Survey* (New York: Libel Defense Resource Center, 1989), and the author's files.

disclosure of embarrassing private fact.[9] Disclosure is the only media-related tort for which truth is not an absolute defense. However, if the facts at issue are held to be newsworthy, or are taken from the public record of a court or other governmental agency, publication is not an invasion of privacy. The principal problem with this branch of the tort lies in defining what is newsworthy. Some courts leave this determination to a jury. Generally, courts have taken a broad view of newsworthiness, as we will see later in this chapter. However, a federal judge, ruling in a case involving publication of a nude photo, said, "I am not persuaded that a woman taking a bath is newsworthy."[10]

Thirty-eight states, the District of Columbia, and the Virgin Islands have recognized disclosure of private fact as an actionable tort. The states are Alabama, Arizona, Arkansas, California, Colorado, Connecticut, Delaware, Florida, Georgia, Hawaii, Idaho, Indiana, Iowa, Kansas, Kentucky, Louisiana, Maine, Maryland, Massachusetts, Michigan, Mississippi, Missouri, New Hampshire, New Jersey, New Mexico, North Carolina, Ohio, Oklahoma, Oregon, Pennsylvania, Rhode Island, South Carolina, Tennessee, Texas, Vermont, Washington, West Virginia, and Wisconsin. However, in all but a few of the reported cases involving media defendants, courts held that publication was justified, either because the facts in question were not sufficiently outrageous, were newsworthy, or had been found in public records.

False Light

By definition, a person can be put in a false light only through publicity. He or she must be the subject of a publication, film, or broadcast that distorts his or her personality. Thus, this branch of the tort is related to defamation, and at some point merges into it. Short of that point, a false-light action can be based on neutral or even flattering statements. A baseball pitcher, a member of the sport's Hall of Fame, was able to stop publication of a book that falsely portrayed him as a war hero.[11] The essential element is that individuals must be portrayed as something other than they are to the point of embarrassment. To portray a Unitarian as a fundamentalist member of the Moral Majority, or vice versa, would defame neither, but probably would embarrass both. Such portrayal, then, could result in an action for false-light invasion of privacy.

In two cases brought by private individuals, the Supreme Court held that false-light plaintiffs must prove actual malice—knowledge of falsity or reckless disregard for the truth—if they were to prevail. Both preceded *Gertz,* and the Supreme Court has had no occasion since to rule on whether private individuals may prevail on a lesser showing of fault. However, in recent cases, courts in some states have held that private false-light plaintiffs need prove only negligence. The point is that courts treat false-light actions much like actions in libel, which means that the First Amendment stands as a strong barrier against a successful suit.

---

9.   Diaz v. Oakland Tribune, Inc., 188 Cal.Rptr. 762 (Calif.App. 1983).
10.   McCabe v. Village Voice, 550 F.Supp. 525 (E.D.Pa. 1982).
11.   Spahn v. Julian Messner, 18 N.Y.2d 324 (N.Y. 1966); 21 N.Y.2d 124 (N.Y. 1967).

Thirty-one states and the District of Columbia have recognized false-light invasion of privacy as an actionable tort. The states are Alabama, Arizona, Arkansas, California, Colorado, Connecticut, Florida, Georgia, Idaho, Illinois, Iowa, Kansas, Kentucky, Louisiana, Maine, Maryland, Michigan, Nebraska, New Jersey, New Mexico, New York, Oklahoma, Oregon, Pennsylvania, Rhode Island, South Carolina, South Dakota, Tennessee, Texas, Washington, and West Virginia.

The North Carolina Supreme Court rejected a false-light claim, holding that the plaintiff should not be compensated for mere embarrassment.[12] The Sixth Circuit Court of Appeals held that Ohio courts have not recognized false-light invasion of privacy as an actionable tort. The court did so in a case brought by a judge who was portrayed in a television reporter's commentary as a "macho trial judge who discriminated against women rape victims in favor of their assailants."[13] The Wisconsin Legislature enacted a privacy statute in 1977 and removed by amendment a section that would have permitted recovery for false light.[14]

Appropriation and the Right of Publicity

Appropriation involves the unauthorized use of one person's name or likeness to benefit another. Commonly, such use occurs in an advertisement or in other promotional material designed to help the user make a profit. Thus, it is of particular importance to advertising and public relations professionals. Courts act on the theory that a person whose identity has been used without consent to sell a product is entitled to a share of the user's profit. Advertisers can avoid a lawsuit for appropriation by getting written consent from any person whose name or likeness will appear in an advertisement or other promotional material. In effect, such consent is a contract, which can be drawn broadly to cover any use, or narrowly to cover a specific use. Usually, the contract includes a schedule of fees to be paid to the person whose name or likeness is used.

In recent years, courts have been broadening the scope of appropriation to cover what is called the right of publicity. In defining this right, courts have recognized that entertainers, athletes, actors, and others whose names become household words acquire an identity that is of value and can be protected against unauthorized exploitation by others. In a few instances, courts have held that such protection can prevail even against a use by the news media, thus raising serious First Amendment questions.

Thirty-eight states and the District of Columbia recognize the right to protect one's name or likeness against misappropriation by others. The states are Alabama, Alaska, Arizona, Arkansas, California, Connecticut, Florida, Georgia, Hawaii, Illinois, Indiana, Iowa, Kansas, Kentucky, Louisiana, Maine, Maryland, Massachusetts, Michigan, Mississippi, Missouri, Montana, Nebraska, New Jersey, New Mexico, New York, North Carolina, Ohio, Oklahoma, Oregon, Penn-

---

12. Renwick v. News and Observer, 310 N.C. 312, 312 S.E.2d 405 (N.C. 1984).
13. Angelotta v. American Broadcasting Corp., 820 F.2d 806 (6th Cir. 1987).
14. §895.50, Wis.Stats.

sylvania, Rhode Island, Tennessee, Texas, Utah, Virginia, West Virginia, and Wisconsin.

Invasions of privacy may thus occur in four quite different ways, but intrusion stands alone in that publication is not necessary. There can be no action for disclosure of private fact, false light, or appropriation unless there has been some sharing of information with the public.

The four branches also differ in the role truth plays as a defense. Truth is not a factor one way or the other in an intrusion case; the focus is on the alleged intruder's methods. Truth works against defendants in disclosure cases. The plaintiff has no cause of action unless the information at issue is true. Obviously, then, truth alone is not a defense. The defendant can prevail only if the facts were taken from a public record or are held to be newsworthy. However, truth is an absolute defense in a false-light action. Just as persons cannot be libeled by publication of the truth about them, neither can they be put in a false light by the truth. With appropriation, or violation of the right of publicity, as with intrusion, truth is not a factor, unless there is some question as to the identity of a likeness used in an advertisement. Once it has been established that an individual's name or likeness has been used of another's commercial gain, the only defense is proof of a valid consent for that use.

INTRUSION

From the earliest recorded days of Anglo-Saxon jurisprudence, courts have shown great respect for private property. This respect is recognized in two places in the Bill of Rights. The Third Amendment forbids the quartering of troops in private homes. The Fourth protects individuals and their property ''against unreasonable searches and seizures.'' The sanctity of property has long been recognized in the law of trespass. Property owners can take action against those who enter their premises without consent. Intrusion, as grounds for a civil action in invasion of privacy, is an extension of the law of trespass.

Professional communicators who keep in mind the origins of this branch of privacy law use caution whenever it seems necessary to enter private property to obtain information or make a photograph. In most instances, there are no problems. Most people are willing to consider a request for an interview, whether for print or for broadcast. If the request is granted, it is usually accompanied by an invitation to enter the source's home, office, or place of business. The vast majority of requests for information raise no privacy questions. But when the possessor of vital information, or a person suspected of violating the law, is unwilling to be interviewed or photographed, there can be problems.

Intrusion by Deception

The classic intrusion case, *Dietemann v. Time, Inc.*, involved a most reluctant source, a plumber who was believed to be practicing medicine without a license.

Dietemann v. *Time Inc.,*
284 F. Supp. 425 (C.D.
Calif. 1968), 449 F.2d 245
(9th Cir. 1971).

He worked in his home and was careful to admit only persons he knew or who were referred to him by someone he knew. When an editor in the Los Angeles bureau of *Life* magazine heard about the plumber, he assigned a female reporter and a male photographer to pose as husband and wife seeking treatment from him. The couple consulted the district attorney, who decided to use them to get information that could be used in a criminal prosecution. The reporter and photographer agreed to cooperate.

The reporter packed a radio transmitter in her handbag and the man wore a tie-clip camera. They gained admission to the plumber's home by posing as friends of previous clients. After an examination, the plumber told the reporter she had cancer as a result of eating rancid butter eleven years, nine months, and seven days earlier. He prescribed a cure of minerals, herbs, and other harmless substances. Every word was transmitted to a tape recorder in a police car parked nearby, while the photographer was getting pictures of the diagnostic process. The plumber was arrested and charged with practicing medicine without a license. He pleaded no contest.

Life's article appeared after the arrest but before the plea. The plumber sued for invasion of privacy, and a federal district court in Los Angeles awarded him $1,000 in damages. On appeal, the Court of Appeals, Ninth Circuit, affirmed.

Both courts recognized there was a public interest in stopping Dietemann's crude practice of medicine, but they held that that did not justify the intrusion. The court of appeals condemned the *Life* team's reporting methods in strong terms:

> Although the issue has not been squarely decided in California, we have little difficulty in concluding that clandestine photography of the plaintiff in his den and the recordation and transmission of his conversation without his consent resulting in his emotional distress warrants recovery for invasion of privacy....
>
> Plaintiff's den was a sphere from which he could reasonably expect to exclude eavesdropping newsmen. He invited two of defendant's employees to the den. One who invites another to his home or office takes a risk that the visitor may not be what he seems, and that visitor may repeat all he hears and observes when he leaves. But he does not and should not be required to take the risk that what is heard and seen will be transmitted by photograph or recording, or in our modern world, in full living color and hi-fi to the public at large or to any segment of it that the visitor may select.

Life's lawyers argued that the First Amendment protected the gathering of news as well as its dissemination. They argued that cameras and recording devices have become "indispensable tools" in investigative reporting. The court swept this argument aside:

> The First Amendment has never been construed to accord newsmen immunity from torts or crimes committed during the course of newsgathering. The First Amendment is not a license to trespass, to steal, or to intrude by electronic means

into the precincts of another's home or office. It does not become such a license simply because the person subjected to the intrusion is reasonably suspected of committing a crime.

The court thus condemned several methods that might be used by reporters who believe anything goes in pursuit of a good story. Foremost was the use of deception to gain entrance to Dietemann's house. There, if anywhere, he had the greatest expectation of privacy. While it was true that he also used his house as a medical office of sorts, it likewise was true that he normally accepted patients only if he knew them or knew someone who would vouch for them. Two other tools of the investigative reporter, the hidden microphone, connected by radio to a tape recorder, and the hidden camera, also were condemned by the court. We will see that there are times when reporters legally may use both. But in this instance, they were faulted because they were used in conjunction with an improper entry into private property.

The Camera and Intrusion

Photographers safely may use a camera to record anything they can see from a public place, provided they don't make nuisances of themselves. If people want to take off their clothes, or make fools of themselves in other ways, in places that can be seen from a public street or other public property, they are fair game. It needs to be emphasized that the subjects of such photographs must have done whatever it was they did of their own volition. But when photographers go onto private property to take their photographs, or harass their subjects, they may be open to an action in intrusion.

CBS News lost an action for criminal trespass because a camera crew entered an expensive French restaurant, Le Mistral, in New York City with camera running. Some of the videotape later used on WCBS-TV showed the restaurant's staff trying to eject the crew. Here, as in *Dietemann,* there was a reason for the intrusion. The restaurant was one of several cited by the New York City Health Service Administration for alleged health code violations. CBS was doing a news story on those violations.

The owners of Le Mistral did not like the way their restaurant was portrayed. They sued CBS for libel, false-light invasion of privacy, and trespass. A judge dismissed the first two counts, but, in *Le Mistral* v. *Columbia Broadcasting System,*[15] denied a motion to dismiss the trespass claim. Noting that the crew had entered the restaurant with no intention of eating and without permission to take photographs, he commented, "Patronizing a restaurant does not carry with it an obligation to appear on television." An appeals court sustained a $1500 judgment against CBS.

Although restaurants, like other businesses that cater to the public, normally are open to all, the New York courts held that those who patronize them retain some expectation of privacy. But when private property can be seen from public

---

15.   402 N.Y.S.2d 815 (1st Dept. 1978).

property, or a place normally open to the public, the camera may safely record what happens there. The Louisiana Supreme Court held that the *Crowley Post-Signal* did not intrude when it published a photograph of one of the city's older homes along with a caption referring to it as "a bit weather worn and unkempt."[16] The photo had been taken from the street. The Washington Supreme Court came to a similar conclusion in a privacy action against KING Broadcasting.[17] The action was brought by a pharmacist who was charged with fraud. When the pharmacist refused to be interviewed, a KING-TV camera operator stood in an alley alongside the store and photographed him through a window. Because the alley was open to the public, the court held there was no intrusion. The pharmacist could have been seen by anyone passing by.

A Florida court held that there are times when photographers safely may go onto private property in pursuit of a story, depending on who is in control of the property at the time. The case, *Florida Publishing Co.* v. *Fletcher*,[18] involved a newspaper photographer who had gone with firefighters into a house where a young girl had died from smoke inhalation. A fire marshal asked the photographer to record the scene for the department's investigatory file. One of the photos was published in the photographer's paper, the *Florida Times-Union*. The girl's mother, who was not at home at the time of the fire, sued the newspaper for intrusion. In holding that she had no cause of action, the state supreme court noted that photographers and reporters customarily accompany police and firefighters to newsworthy events. The court held that this implies the authorities' consent when an entry to private property occurs. In this instance, the fire marshal, not the dead girl's mother, was in control of the house during the fire. Thus, there was no illegal intrusion.

Miller v. *National Broadcasting Co.,* **187 Cal. App. 3d 1463, 232 Cal. Rptr. 668 (Cal. App. 2 Dist. 1986).**

However, a California appellate court held that there was an intrusion when an NBC camera crew followed paramedics into a home and recorded their futile attempt to save the life of a heart attack victim. An NBC producer had obtained permission from the Los Angeles Fire Department to accompany paramedics to obtain material for a minidocumentary on their work. On ten to fifteen occasions, the filming took the crew into private homes. In only a few instances did anyone question the members' right to be there.

No questions were asked when the crew followed paramedics into the home of Dave and Brownie Miller, although the crew passed Mrs. Miller in the hall outside the couple's bedroom where Dave Miller had suffered a heart attack. Weeks later, as Mrs. Miller tried to tune in a soap opera on television, she was shocked by a promotional spot for a documentary. It briefly showed paramedics trying to revive a man. A tattoo on his arm identified him as her late husband. She called the station to protest, then filed suit for trespass and intrusion.

---

16. Jaubert v. Crowley Post-Signal, 375 So.2d 1386 (La. 1979).
17. Mark v. KING Broadcasting, 635 P.2d 1081 (Wash. 1981).
18. 340 So.2d 914 (Fla. 1976).

A trial court dismissed the case, but the appellate court reversed. Noting that Miller was neither a statesman nor a public figure, the court wrote: "In our view, reasonable people could regard the NBC camera crew's intrusion into Dave Miller's bedroom at a time of vulnerability and confusion...as 'highly offensive' conduct." The court said that to require NBC to seek permission from residents before following paramedics into private homes ought not have "a chilling effect on the exercise of First Amendment rights. To hold otherwise might have extraordinarily chilling implications for all of us."

This decision, coupled with the decision of an Oklahoma appellate court in the *Stahl* case, mentioned earlier, suggests that journalists should not assume a right to enter private property in pursuit of news. As a general rule of trespass law, we are free to go onto another's property in the absence of fences or of signs telling us to stay out and can remain until we are told to get out. But if what journalists do on private property is later found to be offensive to persons of ordinary sensibilities, these journalists may find themselves on the losing end of an intrusion action, or even charged as criminal trespassers, as in *Stahl*.

In one case, a photographer's method of operation in public places was held to be an intrusion. For more than a decade, free-lance photographer Ron Galella followed Jacqueline Onassis and her children whenever they ventured out in public. He would bump into them on the streets and then record their reactions. He used telephoto lenses and ingenious vantage points to photograph their activities on private property. He would appear in the middle of the night to photograph Onassis emerging from friends' apartments or to catch her with male friends. Eventually, she became fed up with Galella's antics and asked a court to put a stop to them. The court did not go that far, but it did impose limits on how close the photographer could get to his subject. When Galella continued to harass Onassis, the court gave him a choice: He could keep his distance or go to jail.[19] He chose the former, promising not to take another picture of Onassis "as long as I live."[20]

Tape Recording and Wiretapping

As the Ninth Circuit Court pointed out in *Dietemann,* modern technology has made it possible for reporters and others to record and photograph interviews without the subject's knowledge. Until recently, such action may have been a violation of the Federal Wiretap Statute[21] as well as an intrusion subject to a civil suit for damages. However, Congress has amended the statute to permit journalists, or anyone else, to record interviews without informing the other participants.[22] Congress acted in response to a decision by the U.S. Court of Appeals for the Sixth Circuit in *Boddie*

---

19. Galella v. Onassis, 353 F.Supp. 196 (S.D.N.Y. 1972); 487 F.2d 986 (2d Cir. 1973); 8 Med.L.Rptr. 1321 (S.D.N.Y. 1982).
20. *Facts on File,* 18 June 1982, p. 447.
21. 18 U.S.C. §§2510–2520.
22. Stuart Pierson, "Congress Removes Restrictions on Journalists' Use of Recorders," *Editor & Publisher,* 14 February 1987, p. 72.

v. *ABC,*[23] holding that Geraldo Rivera and ABC News may have committed a crime when they videotaped an interview without the subject's consent. The court read the wiretap law as making it a crime to secretly record a conversation for an "injurious purpose." In reaction to that decision, Congress removed those two words from the law. Despite that change, ABC spent another three years in litigation before a federal judge ruled that Rivera had acted responsibly and had neither committed a crime nor invaded the subject's privacy.[24]

However, reporters who secretly record interviews, whether in person or over the telephone, may still be liable, either under common law or through state statutes. Eleven states prohibit by law the secret recording of telephone conversations: California, Florida, Georgia, Illinois, Maryland, Massachusetts, Montana, New Hampshire, Oregon, Pennsylvania, and Washington.[25] The California law has been upheld in a nonmedia case.[26] Obviously, such laws are difficult to enforce because the violation can be disclosed only by the person who did the recording.

It should go without saying that listening in on telephone conversations to which a journalist is not a party is a serious violation of both law and ethics. The Wiretap Statute imposes a maximum fine of $10,000 and up to five years in prison for illegal interception of "any wire or oral communication." Publishing information obtained through such interception also is a crime. However, the U.S. Court of Appeals for the First Circuit has held that if a newspaper obtains wiretap information legally, the paper may publish it without violating the law. Under extreme circumstances, the paper may even do so in defiance of a court order.

Matter of Application to Adjudge Providence Journal Co. and its Executive Editor, Charles M. Hauser, in Criminal Contempt, **820 F.2d 1342 (1st Cir. 1986).**

The *Providence Journal* used the Freedom of Information Act to obtain the transcripts of telephone conversations made in the 1960s by the late Raymond L.S. Patriarca and his son, Raymond J., both reputedly involved in ongoing criminal activity. The FBI had used illegal wiretaps to monitor their telephone calls. An attorney for Raymond J. Patriarca, arguing that publication of the transcripts would violate the privacy of his client and of others, obtained an order from a U.S. district court in Providence forbidding the *Journal* to use information from them. After consulting the newspaper's lawyer, *Journal* Executive Editor Charles M. Hauser concluded the order was unconstitutional and approved publication of a story based on the transcripts.

A week later, the district court judge came to the same conclusion and lifted the order. Nevertheless, at the instigation of Patriarca's attorney, the judge found

---

23. 731 F.2d 333 (6th Cir. 1984).
24. Christi Harlan, "Judge Dismisses Suit against ABC On Rivera Taping," *Wall Street Journal,* 6 September 1988. The dismissal was affirmed by the U.S. Court of Appeals for the Sixth Circuit. "Rivera Wins Hidden Microphone Case," *Editor & Publisher,* 26 August 1989.
25. Kovner, "Recent Developments," p. 295.
26. Air Transport Association of America v. Public Utilities Commission, State of California, 833 F.2d 200 (9th Cir. 1987).

the *Journal* and Hauser in contempt for disobeying his order. He fined the paper $100,000 and sentenced the editor to eighteen months in prison (suspended) and to 200 hours of public service.

A three-judge panel of the U.S. Court of Appeals for the First Circuit reversed, holding that a "party subject to an order that constitutes a transparently invalid prior restraint on pure speech may challenge the order by violating it."[27] The court said the only conceivable danger was to Patriarca's privacy and the remedy for that was an action for damages after publication, not a restraint.

On rehearing *en banc,* the full court adopted the panel's opinion, but suggested that in the future a publisher confronted with such an order ought to make a good-faith effort to seek emergency relief from an appellate court. "If timely access to the appellate court is not available or if timely decision is not forthcoming, the publisher may then proceed to publish and challenge the constitutionality of the order in contempt proceedings."[28] The Supreme Court agreed to review the decision but took no action after deciding that the special prosecutor representing the government lacked legal authority to make an appeal.[29]

New York Times reporter Hedrick Smith was the subject of an illegal wiretap ordered by President Nixon's national security adviser, Henry A. Kissinger. The White House was trying to find out who leaked information to the reporter on negotiations with Japan over the future of Okinawa. When Smith learned of the tap four years later, he sued for damages. Ultimately, a federal appellate court ruled that Smith could not recover damages because Kissinger acted on a reasonable belief that the nation's security could be harmed by the leak. On remand, a district court judge ordered the government to expunge all records made from the wiretaps.[30]

Copied or Stolen Documents

Letters, reports, memoranda, and other written materials prepared by an individual are that person's private property. Like any property, they can be protected from theft. Looked at from the journalist's point of view, the information contained in documents may be something other than private property—it may be news. Can that news be made public without committing an intrusion? The answer is yes—provided that the reporter did not intrude in order to obtain it. Two cases involving the legendary investigative reporter and Washington columnist Drew Pearson make the point.

The first, *Liberty Lobby* v. *Pearson,*[31] decided by the United States Court of Appeals for the District of Columbia Circuit in 1968, involved information con-

27. Matter of Application to Adjudge Providence Journal Co. and Its Executive Editor, Charles M. Hauser, in Criminal Contempt, 820 F.2d 1342 (1st Cir. 1986).

28. 820 F.2d 1354 (1st Cir. 1987).

29. United States v. Providence Journal Company, 485 U.S. 693, 108 S.Ct. 1502, 99 L.Ed.2d 785 (1988).

30. "Government Told to Expunge Records of Tap on Reporter's Phone," *Editor & Publisher,* 8 August 1987, p. 29.

31. 390 F.2d 489 (D.C.Cir. 1968).

tained in documents stolen from a private lobbying organization and given to Jack Anderson, then Pearson's assistant. When the organization asked a federal court to prevent further publication of information taken from its files, the court refused to do so. On appeal, the circuit court held that Liberty Lobby was not entitled to relief unless it could prove that it owned the documents in Pearson's possession and could also show that either Pearson or Anderson had taken them from the files. The court also held that there was a public interest in publication which, in a close case, would require a ruling in Pearson's favor.

The second case, *Pearson* v. *Dodd*,[32] involved information taken from the files of a United States senator. Thomas Dodd of Connecticut was suspected of dipping into campaign funds to pay for his living expenses. Disgruntled members of his office staff copied documents supporting these suspicions and gave them to Pearson and Anderson, who published information taken from them. Dodd sued the columnists for intrusion and for conversion, the crime of using stolen property. A federal district court held that there had been a conversion, but an appeals court reversed, dismissing both counts of the lawsuit. It wrote:

> If we were to hold [Pearson and Anderson] liable for invasion of privacy on these facts, we would establish the proposition that one who received information from an intruder, knowing it has been obtained by improper intrusion, is guilty of a tort. In an untried and developing area of tort law, we are not prepared to go so far. A person approached by an eavesdropper would perhaps play the nobler part should he spurn the offer and shut his ears. However, it seems to us that at this point it would place too great a strain on human weakness to hold one liable in damages who merely succumbs to temptation and listens.

There was no conversion, the court held, because the documents themselves had never left Dodd's office. Thus, there had been no theft of property. The senator had not been deprived of the use of the documents, even though he had been embarrassed when the information they contained left his office through the magic of a handy copying machine.

DISCLOSURE OF EMBARRASSING PRIVATE FACT

Courts have held that the news media can be required to pay damages to persons humiliated by the publication of private facts. If such publication would "outrage the community's notions of decency," as measured by a jury, the publication can be an invasion of privacy. But courts also have held that the media cannot be found liable if the allegedly private facts, no matter how outrageous, are newsworthy or are taken from a public record. For journalists, the problem lies in the further holding by some courts that juries should decide when allegedly private facts become newsworthy. Thus, this branch of the tort is marked by con-

---

32. 410 F.2d 701 (D.C.Cir. 1969).

siderable uncertainty. However, the news media have won more private-fact cases than they have lost. In the process, some guideposts have emerged to help journalists assess the hazards.

Constitutional Limits

On two occasions the Supreme Court has upheld the right of the media to publish the names of rape victims despite state laws forbidding such publication. On a third, it upheld the right of West Virginia newspapers to publish the name of a juvenile offender despite a law making such publication a crime. In each instance, however, the Court also said that it was not upholding the media's right to publish all facts, whatever their source or however outrageous they might be, about individuals. Thus, the Court has kept open the right to sue for disclosure of embarrassing private fact, but the Court has imposed First Amendment limits on that right.

Cox Broadcasting Co. v. Cohn, **420 U.S. 469, 95 S.Ct. 1029, 43 L.Ed.2d 328 (1975).**

The landmark decision is *Cox Broadcasting Co. v. Cohn*. The case grew out of the rape and murder of a seventeen-year-old girl in Atlanta. In compliance with a state law making it a crime to publish or broadcast the name of a rape victim, the news media did not identify her. Eight months later, the six men accused of the crime appeared in court. As part of a plea bargain, five of them pleaded guilty to attempted rape. The sixth pleaded not guilty. A reporter for WSB-TV, the Cox station in Atlanta, was present. He asked the court clerk to show him the indictments so that he could get the names and the details of the charge correctly. Each indictment carried the victim's name, which the reporter also copied into his notes. On the news that evening, WSB-TV disclosed her name to the public for the first time.

Normally, an action for disclosure of private fact can be brought only by the victim. But a provision in the Georgia statute forbidding publication of the name of a rape victim made it possible for close relatives to start a civil action in a deceased victim's behalf. Her father sued Cox Broadcasting for invasion of privacy, alleging disclosure of private fact. A trial court brushed aside First Amendment arguments and awarded summary judgment to the plaintiff, Cohn. The only question for the jury, the court ruled, was the amount of the judgment. Cox appealed, and the state supreme court upheld the verdict, ruling that the statute declared as state policy that a rape victim's name is not a matter of public concern. The statute, the state supreme court said, placed a limited, but legitimate, limitation on freedom of the press. Cox Broadcasting appealed to the United States Supreme Court, which took the case.

Justice Byron R. White, writing for himself and five other justices, focused the Court's decision on the question raised by the facts of the case: Could the news media be held liable for publishing facts found in the public records of a court? The majority held that a state neither can prevent such publication nor can it define such publication as an invasion of privacy. The Court gave two reasons for its holding:

1. The news media perform a valuable public service by covering news of government, including the courts. This is something few people have the time or the inclination to do for themselves. Therefore, the media, as surrogates for the general public, should not have needless limits placed on their coverage. In this instance, news of the crime of rape was of legitimate concern to the public.

2. Of particular importance is the right of the news media to report matters on the public record. Courts have recognized "a privilege in the press to report the events of judicial proceedings." The majority concluded that there can be no liability for the accurate reporting of matters taken from public records, especially those of the courts.

Repeatedly, the Court emphasized that its holding was a narrow one, limited solely to the facts of the case. The Court held that the young woman's name was both on the public record and an element of a legitimate news event—a particularly brutal gang rape. Further, the majority made a point of noting that in no way was the authority of states to seal court records containing embarrassing facts being limited. The majority noted that records of juvenile courts generally are considered private, subject to release only by a judge's order.

However, only four years later, in *Smith* v. *Daily Mail Publishing Co.,*[33] the Supreme Court struck down a West Virginia law making it a crime for newspapers to publish the names of juvenile offenders. In that instance, the name of a junior high school student who shot another student to death in a school parking lot was obtained not from a public record but from police, a prosecutor, and other students at the scene. The Court noted that the name was obtained lawfully and that the juvenile was involved in "a matter of public significance." The Court held that the state's interest in seeking rehabilitation of juvenile offenders by shielding them from public knowledge was not sufficient to override the First Amendment interest in publication of offenders' names.

More recently, the Supreme Court struck down a Florida law making it a misdemeanor to publish the names of rape victims. At the same time, it reversed a judgment awarding the victim $100,000 for invasion of privacy. It did so even though another Florida statute was designed expressly to keep the names of rape victims off the public record, as the Court had suggested in *Cox.*

The Florida Star v. *B.J.F.,* _ _ _ U.S. _ _ _, 109 S.Ct. 2603, 105 L.Ed.2d 443 (1989).

The case had its origins in a series of mistakes. A reporter-trainee employed by *The Florida Star,* a weekly serving Jacksonville's black community, was sent to the sheriff's office to gather material for the newspaper's "Police Reports." Among the items made available to her and other reporters was a complaint by a woman who was raped and robbed in a city park as she was on her way to a bus stop. Under Florida law, the victim's name should not have been in the report, but it was. In any event, signs in the press room reminded reporters that the names of the victims of sex crimes are not

---

33. 443 U.S. 97, 99 S.Ct. 2667, 61 L.Ed.2d 399 (1979).

matters of public record. The *Florida Star's* policy was not to use names of such victims. Nevertheless, the newspaper's one-paragraph item on the rape included the victim's name.

When the victim, identified only as B.J.F., sued for damages, the Sheriff's Department admitted it had done wrong and settled with her for $2500. The newspaper elected to go to trial. B.J.F. testified that she suffered emotional distress from seeing the assault described in print. The news item said the assailant had undressed her and had sexual intercourse with her before he fled "with her 60 cents, Timex watch and gold necklace." She also testified that a man had called her home and told her mother that he would rape her again. As a result, B.J.F. said she had to change her telephone number and her residence, seek police protection, and obtain mental health counseling. At the end of her testimony, the trial judge ruled that the newspaper's conduct was negligent on its face, leaving the jury to decide only the amount of the damages. It awarded B.J.F. $75,000 in compensatory damages and $25,000 in punitive damages. The newspaper appealed, arguing that it ought not be held liable for publishing truthful information freely made available to it by police. The Florida Supreme Court summarily affirmed the jury's award. The U.S. Supreme Court took the case on appeal and reversed, six to three.

As it had in *Cox,* the Court rejected the argument that the news media should never be held liable for publishing truthful information. It also rejected the suggestion that the rationale used in *Cox* should be applied to this case. Justice Thurgood Marshall, writing for the majority, noted that in *Cox* the rapists had been arrested and were involved in court proceedings, which usually are open to the public. In this instance, there had been no arrest. Further, by law the name of the victim was not part of the public record.

In Marshall's view, what the *Florida Star* did when it published B.J.F.'s name was on the same legal footing as the *Daily Mail*'s publication of the name of the juvenile offender in *Smith*. The paper had published truthful information which it had obtained lawfully, even if it was by mistake. Under such circumstances, the state can punish the media only to protect "a narrowly tailored...state interest of the highest order." Marshall said such an interest might be found in the need to protect a rape victim from retaliation or some other harm. The majority did not find that kind of interest in B.J.F.'s case.

Justice White, who wrote the *Cox* decision, led the dissent this time, flatly rejecting the majority's reasoning. He said he found no support for it in *Cox, Smith,* or anywhere else. Nor could he find any "public interest in publishing the names, addresses, and phone numbers of victims of crime" or in holding newspapers free from blame "where a state's efforts to protect a victim's privacy have failed."

A third Supreme Court decision involving possible identification of the victims of a sexual assault leaves doubt as to whether any professed state interest in protecting privacy can survive a First Amendment challenge. In *Globe Newspapers v. Superior Court,*[34] the Court struck down a Massachusetts law excluding the news media from the courtroom during the trial of sex crimes when minors were

---

34. 457 U.S. 596, 102 S.Ct. 2613, 73 L.Ed.2d 248 (1982).

the victims. The statute was grounded in a desire to protect the victims from additional trauma and in the belief that they might be more likely to testify as to details of the crime if they could do so in privacy. The Supreme Court said that a blanket exclusion swept too broadly. The Court did not rule out the possibility that some parts of such trials could be conducted behind closed doors but said that the judge would have to make such decisions on an individual basis. In this instance, the Court noted, the names of the victims were on the public record.

These decisions leave the media free to use the names of victims of sex crimes if they choose to do so. Most editors do not,[35] with notable exceptions. A Washington state newspaper publisher's policy of not only identifying rape victims but giving extensive coverage to rape trials was the subject of heated denunciation at the 1986 meeting of the Associated Press Managing Editors Association.[36] A Texas television station's use in a documentary of a rape victim's first name along with photographs of her residence led to a lawsuit that ultimately was resolved by the U.S. Court of Appeals for the Fifth Circuit.[37] The court said the details were of "unique importance" to the credibility of a story questioning the guilt of the man convicted of the rape. It held that the public interest in reversing a false conviction outweighed the victim's privacy interest. However, the court said its decision should not be construed as condoning routine identification of rape victims. In most instances, it said, the name is irrelevant.

Except in California, media run little risk of losing privacy actions based on disclosure of matter on the public record, no matter how old. Courts in Kansas and Iowa, among other states, have held that the lapse of time does not take away the right to publish embarrassing facts found in such records. The Kansas case involved a "Looking Backward" column's use of items reporting the discharge of a police officer ten years earlier.[38] The Iowa case grew out of a report that a young woman had been forced to undergo sterilization while she was a ward of a county home.[39] However, California courts still cite two early cases holding that the state's interest in rehabilitation of wrongdoers is sufficient to justify privacy actions against media that recall a subject's criminal past. The first, *Melvin* v. *Reid*,[40] was against the producer of a movie based on a crime committed by a prostitute many years earlier. The second involved a story in *Reader's Digest* about a truck driver who eleven years earlier had been arrested for hijacking.[41]

The Measure of an Embarrassing Private Fact

Cox and the related Supreme Court cases deal with two dimensions of the tort of disclosure of embarrassing private fact. In *Cox*, the Court said that matters

35. One survey indicates that fewer than 3 percent of newspaper editors identify victims of sexual assaults. "Survey Finds Trend away from Detailed Identification," *ASNE Bulletin*, July/August 1987, p. 5.
36. M. L. Stein, "Covering Sex Crimes," *Editor & Publisher*, 15 November 1986, p. 16+.
37. Ross v. Midwest Communications, 870 F.2d 271 (5th Cir. 1989).
38. Rawlins v. Hutchinson Publishing Co., 543 P.2d 988 (Kans. 1975).
39. Howard v. Des Moines Register & Tribune, 283 N.W.2d 289 (Iowa 1979).
40. 112 Cal.App. 285 (1931).
41. Briscoe v. Reader's Digest Association, 483 P.2d 34 (1971).

found in official public records, particularly those of the courts, can't be used as grounds for a disclosure action. Simply put, the decision says that public facts aren't private. *Smith* and *B.J.F.* carry the principle further. In those cases, the Court said that the state can't punish the media for disclosing some embarrassing facts not on the public record if those facts were obtained legally and if the state can't demonstrate some strong reason for restricting their use. What, then, is an embarrassing private fact that will support a privacy suit if it is made public?

The Iowa Supreme Court said in *Howard* that a publication is actionable if (1) it concerns "the private, as distinguished from the public, life of the individual" and (2) it "is not of legitimate concern to the public." The second element was quoted from *Restatement (Second) of Torts*,[42] which also says that the facts in question must "be highly offensive to a reasonable person." What would offend a reasonable person usually is for a jury to decide.

Sidis v. F-R Publishing Corp., 113 F.2d 806 (2d Cir. 1940)

Once they have determined that private fact is at issue, courts usually look to *Sidis* v. *F-R Publishing Corp.* for guidance as to whether it is actionable. At issue was a profile in the *New Yorker* magazine of William James Sidis, whose mathematical genius was such that he had attracted widespread attention as a child. He was graduated from Harvard at sixteen. He soon tired of life in the spotlight, however, and retreated from the academic world, became a recluse, and earned a bare existence as a clerk. More than twenty years later, a *New Yorker* writer caught up with Sidis. The resulting article was sympathetic in tone, but ruthless in detailing Sidis's rise and fall. He found it deeply offensive and sued the magazine for invasion of privacy. The courts were sympathetic, too, but not enough so to find in Sidis's favor. The appeals court noted that he was not an ordinary person, but a genius who, at one time, had attracted widespread public attention. That had made him a public figure. As such, he had lost most of his claim to a right of privacy. True, he had retreated into obscurity, but that, too, the court said, was "a matter of public concern." The article in the *New Yorker* "sketched the life of an unusual personality, and it possessed considerable popular news interest." The court added:

> We express no comment on whether or not the newsworthiness of the matter printed will always constitute a complete defense. Revelations may be so intimate and so unwarranted in the view of the victim's position as to outrage the community's notion of decency. But when focused upon public characters, truthful comments upon dress, speech, habits, and the ordinary aspects of personality will usually not transgress this line. Regrettably or not, the misfortunes and frailties of neighbors and "public figures" are subjects of considerable interest and discussion to the rest of the population. And when such are the mores of the community, it would be unwise for a court to bar their expression in the newspapers, books and magazines of the day.

---

42. §652D.

Diaz v. *Oakland Tribune, Inc.,* **188 Cal. Rptr. 762 (Cal. Ct. App. 1st Dist. Div. 3 1983)**

The publication of private facts is actionable, then, only if the disclosure would "outrage the community's notion of decency." The measure is not what would offend a sensitive person, like Sidis, but that composite known as the community, or the average person. A California jury found such outrage in a column that appeared in the *Oakland Tribune*. Columnist Sidney Jones thought there was news in his discovery that the female student-body president of the College of Alameda had had a sex-change operation. He wrote that the students would be surprised to learn that the president, Toni Ann Diaz, "is no lady, but in fact is a man whose real name is Antonio." The item added that students enrolled in a physical education class with her "may wish to make other showering arrangements." Diaz sued the newspaper and the columnist for invasion of privacy, alleging that the item disclosed private fact and was highly offensive. An Alameda county jury agreed, awarding her a $750,000 judgment against the *Tribune* and $25,000 against the columnist.

A California appeals court reversed, not because it disagreed with the result, but because it concluded that the judge had not properly instructed the jury on the burden of proof. The court noted that the gist of the column was true. Toni had been Antonio until undergoing surgery. Then she had gone to great lengths to change all the usual forms of identification to show her as a woman. Only her closest relatives knew what had happened. The columnist had acted on a tip from confidential sources. The information was confirmed by Oakland police, who had arrested Antonio Diaz some years before. The columnist did not talk to Toni Diaz.

The *Tribune,* seeking support from *Cox Broadcasting,* argued that because the arrest of Antonio had led to a trial at which he was acquitted, its item was based at least in part on the public record of a court. The sex change was confirmed not only by police, but by later records in the name of Toni Diaz. The California court held that all such records were beside the point. The fact at issue was the sex-change operation, and that was not on the public record of a court.

The court also held that the publication of a private fact is an invasion of privacy if the fact in question "would be offensive and objectionable to [a] reasonable person" and if it were "not of legitimate public concern." The latter was the court's way of saying that even an offensive fact would be protected if it were newsworthy. The trial judge had told the jury that the newspaper had the burden of proving that Diaz's sex change was newsworthy. That, the appeals court ruled, was error. The judge should have required Diaz to prove that her operation was not newsworthy. It said that burden was mandated by the same First Amendment interest found in the *New York Times* rule. Those who would restrict the flow of news must carry the burden of proving a need to do so.

In sending the case back for retrial, the court said that the jury, given proper instructions as to the burden of proof, would have to balance the competing interests and decide whether the item was newsworthy. That decision, the court said, "depends upon contemporary community mores and standards of decency," which is the kind of factual judgment best left to a jury. However, the appeals court volunteered the opinion that the item was not newsworthy. It also said that the jury was correct in its finding that the columnist had acted with malice when he added the sentence about showering arrangements. He knew, or should have known, that Diaz was not enrolled in a physical education class. The sentence could have had no other purpose than to make fun of her. That, the court said, was enough to support the jury's award of punitive damages.

The record does not show what happened on remand. Nor do the case records show many instances in which plaintiffs have been able to bring successful disclosure actions against news media. In the few instances resulting in awards of damages, disclosure was coupled with other factors.

The Georgia Supreme Court upheld a $4,166 judgment against the *Cullman Daily Times Democrat* based on a photograph taken at a county fair. It showed Mrs. Flora Bell Graham as she emerged from the fun house with her two young sons. An air jet had blown her skirt to her shoulders, and she was frantically trying to hold it down. The newspaper's editors thought the photo caught the spirit of the fair and used it on page 1. Mrs. Graham said she was mortified and sued the newspaper for disclosure of private fact. The newspaper argued that the photo was taken in a public place and was newsworthy. The supreme court held, in *Daily Times Democrat* v. *Graham*,[43] that it could find nothing newsworthy in a photo of Mrs. Graham's underpants. Further, it noted that they were exposed against her will. The court concluded that the jury properly concluded that such exposure outraged the public's sense of decency.

A New Mexico court awarded a prison guard $200,000 for a story that appeared in the *Dallas Times Herald* describing his experiences as a hostage during a riot.[44] Prisoners had beaten, stabbed, and sexually assaulted him. The reporter had obtained much of the information by entering the guard's hospital room and eavesdropping on his conversation with a friend. The guard said he was very upset by publication of details of the assault and by a part of the story saying that he and his wife were living in near poverty. In this instance, the disclosure of embarrassing private fact was coupled with an intrusion. The Ninth Circuit Court of appeals, citing *Briscoe* and *Diaz,* held that a jury should be permitted to decide whether a horse racing association violated a family's privacy when it issued a press release giving the true name of a police informant who had been given a new identity under a witness protection program.[45] The release said the witnesses' wife had been denied a racing license.

The cases discussed thus far tell us that an individual has no cause of action for disclosure if the facts in question were taken from a public record, particularly the public record of a court. If a plaintiff's case is to survive summary dismissal, the embarrassing facts must have come from nonpublic sources, and they must be of such a nature as to outrage the community's sense of decency. But, as the

---

43. 162 So.2d 474 (Ga. 1964).
44. "Dallas Times Herald Loses $200,000 Suit," *Editor & Publisher,* 16 October 1982, p. 57; Schmitt v. Dallas Times Herald, No. 5781-582 (New Mexico Dist.Ct., Santa Fe. Co.).
45. Capra v. Thoroughbred Racing Association, 787 F.2d 463 (9th Cir.); cert. denied, 479 U.S. 1017, 107 S.Ct. 669, 93 L.Ed.2d 721 (1986).

courts noted in *Sidis* and *Diaz,* even outrageous facts are protected if they possess "considerable popular news interest," if they are "of legitimate public concern," or if the subject of the article is a public figure. The record offers abundant proof that these elements offer the media powerful defenses against disclosure actions.

Newsworthiness and the Public Interest

From the beginning, courts have recognized a conflict between an individual's interest in privacy and the public's interest in being informed. When the Georgia Supreme Court recognized a common-law right of privacy more than eighty years ago, it grappled with that conflict. The court said, in *Pavesich* v. *New England Life Insurance Co.,*[46] that it believed the right of privacy to be one of the natural rights recognized by "the law of nature." But it also said that one of the stumbling blocks to its enforcement is that "it would inevitably tend to curtail the liberty of speech and of the press," which also is a natural right. The court added, "It will therefore be seen that the right of privacy must in some particulars yield to the right of speech and of the press." This has proved to be the case. In federal and state courts, newsworthiness—information deemed to serve a public interest—has become the strongest defense against an action for disclosure of embarrassing private fact.

Jenkins v. *Dell Publishing Co.,* **251 F.2d 447 (3d Cir. 1958).**

Courts have tended to define newsworthiness broadly. In a decision that is still cited as a precedent, the United States Court of Appeals for the Third Circuit offered one of the broadest definitions of newsworthiness in *Jenkins* v. *Dell Publishing Co.* The plaintiff was a widow who was noteworthy only because her husband had been beaten to death on the street by a pack of young hoodlums, leaving her with six young children. Immediately after the incident, Mrs. Jenkins agreed to pose with her children for a Pittsburgh newspaper photographer. The picture appeared the next day along with a story about the murder of her husband. Three months later, the widow was shocked to find the same photograph in *Front Page Detective* magazine along with a brief, factual account of the murder. She sued the publisher for invasion of privacy, alleging, among other things, that the facts of her tragic loss were offered as entertainment for the magazine's readers, causing her embarrassment. A federal district court dismissed the action, and the appeals court affirmed, holding that "information and entertainment are not mutually exclusive categories." The court then sought to define news:

> A large part of the matter that appears in newspapers and news magazines today is not published or read for the value or importance of the information it conveys. Some readers are attracted by shocking news. Others are titillated by sex in the news. Still others are entertained by news which has an incongruous or ironic aspect. Most news is in various ways amusing, and for that reason of special interest

---

46. 50 S.E. 68 (Ga. 1905).

to many people. Few newspapers or news magazines would long survive if they did not publish a substantial amount of news on the basis of entertainment value of one kind or another. This may be a disturbing commentary upon our civilization, but it is nonetheless a realistic picture of society which courts shaping new juristic concepts should take into account.

Virgil v. *Time Inc.,* 527 F.2d 1122 (9th Cir. 1975).   The United States Court of Appeals for the Ninth Circuit also has dealt with the line between news and entertainment. In a case, *Virgil* v. *Time Inc.,* brought by a noted body-surfer, that court was less generous with the news media than the *Jenkins* court, but its decision, too, has become a frequently cited precedent.

Mike Virgil was said to be the most reckless member of a group who surfed at the Wedge, reputed to be the world's most dangerous spot for body-surfing. *Sports Illustrated* assigned a writer to do a story on the sport, with Virgil as its focus. Virgil and his wife and others spoke freely with the writer. The completed article was rich in unusual facts about an unusual character. The article left no doubt that Virgil was as reckless on land as he was in the water. It said he had dived down a flight of stairs at a ski resort to "impress these chicks all around." He burned the back of his hand to win a bet that he could burn a hole with a cigarette in a dollar bill resting there. He ate spiders and insects. He injured himself deliberately on construction jobs so he could draw workers' compensation while he continued his surfing.

When one of the magazine's researchers telephoned Virgil to check on such details, he had second thoughts and asked that they not be published. Reasoning that whatever an adult says to a reporter is fair game, *Sports Illustrated* published the story. Virgil sued for invasion of privacy. A federal district court dismissed, but the appeals court reversed and remanded, holding that it thought a jury should decide whether details of Virgil's life out of the water were newsworthy. The court also held that one who speaks freely with a reporter does not necessarily consent to publication. If the subject of a story is given a chance to review it, as in this instance, and changes his or her mind about some of the revelations, the court said, "[T]he consequent publicity is without consent." Nevertheless, the court said Virgil could not recover damages if a jury decided that the public had a legitimate interest in the facts, that the facts had previously become public knowledge, or that they would not be offensive to a reasonable person of ordinary sensibilities.

Despite the circuit court's decision, Virgil never got a chance to present his case to a jury. On remand, the United States District Court for the Southern District of California granted summary judgment to *Sports Illustrated*.[47] Applying the circuit court's prescribed test of newsworthiness, the district judge concluded that no reasonable juror could find the story highly offensive. He conceded that the facts would embarrass Virgil, but he said they were neither morbid nor sensational. Nor were they published "for their own sake." The writer had a pur-

---

47.   Virgil v. Sports Illustrated and Time Inc., 424 F.Supp. 1286 (S.D. Calif. 1976).

pose, which was to give his readers an insight into Virgil's daring style of body-surfing. Thus the story fulfilled a legitimate public interest.

The *Diaz* court also offered jurors guidelines for determining when private facts become newsworthy, borrowing from the earlier decision in *Briscoe*.[48] It said the jury should "consider (1) the social value of the facts published, (2) the depth of the article's intrusion into ostensibly private affairs, and (3) the extent to which the party voluntarily acceded to a position of public notoriety...."

Strict application of such guidelines has made it difficult for plaintiffs to win suits for disclosure of embarrassing private fact. Even when they have been able to convince a jury that the disclosure was not newsworthy, appeals courts have shown a disposition to hold otherwise. One case, *Cape Publications, Inc.,* v. *Bridges,*[49] illustrates the point. A woman was held hostage by her estranged husband. She managed to escape and ran into the street clutching a hand towel that just managed to conceal the fact that she was nude. A photographer for *Cocoa Today* took her picture as she fled, and the newspaper used it. She convinced a jury that the photo was not newsworthy and that the newspaper exceeded the limits of decency in causing her extreme embarrassment. The jury awarded her $10,000. The appellate court reversed, holding:

> Just because the story and photograph may be embarrassing or distressful to the plaintiff does not mean the newspaper cannot publish what is otherwise newsworthy. At some point, the public interest in obtaining information becomes dominant over the individual's right of privacy.

This examination of newsworthiness and the public interest ends where it began: When an individual's asserted right of privacy collides with the public's right to be informed about matters of public interest, the latter almost always prevails. Courts have recognized that the public has a legitimate interest not only in the fate of nations but in human frailties, foibles, and misfortunes. Thus, there is little doubt that Gary Hart had no basis for legal action when the *Miami Herald* reported that he had a weekend rendezvous with a young model. The newspaper obtained the information by assigning reporters to watch Hart's home in the Georgetown section of Washington, D.C. At the time, Hart was considered a leading candidate for the Democratic Party's presidential nomination. Some journalists condemned the reporters' methods as an egregious invasion of privacy,[50] but the story was newsworthy and in fact dominated the news in all media and led within weeks to Hart's withdrawal from the presidential race.

Defenses against a disclosure action are not absolute, but they are nearly so. The successful plaintiff must prove that the facts in question were not found in the public record, that he did not make them public himself, that they would outrage the community's sense of decency, and that their revelation serves no legitimate public interest. These are formidable barriers, but they reserve for the media what is perhaps the most important question of all: How far should the media

---

48. Briscoe v. Reader's Digest Association, 483 P.2d 34, at 43 (Calif. 1971).
49. 423 So.2d 426 (Fla.App.Ct. 5th Dist. 1982).
50. Ron Dorfman, "Peeping Watchdogs," *Quill,* June 1987, p. 14 + .

go in publishing private fact that would embarrass any self-respecting person? In a free society, such questions can be answered only by those who are in the business of public communication. The ethical dimension of these questions will be discussed at the end of the chapter.

FALSE LIGHT

False light begins with offensive flattery at one end of the spectrum and merges into libel at the other. It is, in a practical sense, the realm of the communicator who melds fiction with fact. The harm comes in portraying individuals as something other than they are to a point that would be offensive to a person of ordinary sensibilities. The point to remember is that such portrayal need not be defamatory. If it is, courts have held that it should be the subject of a libel action, not a lawsuit for invasion of privacy.

Many of the legal principles that are applied to libel actions also apply to false-light litigation. A person cannot be put in a false light by the truth, so an action for false-light invasion of privacy, like an action for libel, must be grounded in a false assertion of fact. In libel actions, the false assertion of fact must be defamatory. In a false-light action, there is no defamation. There is nothing defamatory about being poor or soured on life, but to portray a person as one or both could result in a lawsuit for false-light invasion of privacy. The Supreme Court has held in two cases that plaintiffs in false-light actions must prove actual malice on the part of media defendants. Because the first of the decisions preceded *Gertz,* and the second clearly involved actual malice, the Court left open the degree of fault that must be proved by a private individual. Lower courts, in some instances, have required all false-light plaintiffs, public or private, to prove actual malice. In the most recent cases, however, courts in some jurisdictions have been distinguishing between public official/public figure plaintiffs and private individuals. The latter have been permitted to prevail on some lesser showing of fault, usually negligence.

Distortion of an individual's personality lies at the heart of a false-light action. A professional communicator who is careful with facts and slow to jump to broad characterizations has little to fear from this branch of the tort. Communicators run a risk only if they are tempted too casually to follow Tom Wolfe and Gay Talese into the kind of writing that purports to portray thought processes and re-create conversations that may not have occurred. To pass muster, such writing must be the product of exhaustive fact gathering, as it is with the writers named above. There must have been sufficient research to ensure that fictionalized passages are true to the character of the persons portrayed.

Time Inc. v. *Hill,* 385 U.S. 374, 87 S.Ct. 534, 17 L.Ed.2d 456 (1967). The first false-light case to reach the Supreme Court, *Time Inc.* v. *Hill,* grew out of a drama review in the old weekly version of *Life* magazine. The play, *The Desperate Hours,* portrayed the experiences of a couple and their two children, who were held hostage in their home by several escaped convicts. The play was based on a book by Joseph Hayes, who said he had taken his inspiration from several such real-life incidents. One of these involved Mr. and Mrs. James Hill and their five children, who had been held hostage in their home in suburban Philadelphia. The three escaped convicts who invaded their home treated the family courteously during a nineteen-hour standoff with the police. When the convicts left the house, two of them were shot and killed by police. The Hills were so shocked that they moved to Connecticut and resisted all efforts to publicize the experience.

When *The Desperate Hours* was playing in Philadelphia on its way to Broadway, an editor for *Life* had what seemed like a bright idea. Why not take the actors to what had been the Hill home and photograph them enacting several of the more dramatic scenes from the play? This would show the magazine's readers that the play was not altogether fiction. The play's producer and the new owner of the house were willing. Three of the resulting photographs accompanied a review of the play in an issue of *Life*. One showed a son being roughed up by one of the convicts. Another showed the daughter biting a convict's hand to make him drop a gun. A third showed the father throwing the gun through a door. None of these things had happened to the Hills, and the copy written by the reviewer did not say that they had. But the editor who prepared the copy for publication changed both the review and the photo captions to make a direct association with the Hill family. He did so, he testified later, to "jazz up" the material. The changes gave readers the impression that the photographs portrayed the Hill family's experiences with the hostages. Hill sued for false-light invasion of privacy, setting in motion a legal yo-yo that remained in motion during more than a decade of litigation.

In the first round of the legal action, the Hills won a $75,000 judgment. An appellate court held that that was excessive. On retrial, they won a judgment for $30,000, which was affirmed on appeal. Time Inc. asked the Supreme Court to consider the case, arguing that its First Amendment rights were involved. The Supreme Court agreed that they were. Holding that the New York courts had not shown a proper regard for freedom of the press, the Court sent the case back for retrial. It said the Hills could win only if they could prove actual malice. At that point, they gave up.

At the time, the effect of the *Hill* decision was open to question. The Court was divided six-to-three, and only three members of the majority endorsed the actual malice standard. Two others would have held that the First Amendment rules out any false light actions. The sixth member of the majority would have permitted the Hills to prevail by proving negligence.

***Cantrell* v. *Forest City Publishing Co.*, 419 U.S. 245, 95 S.Ct. 465, 42 L.Ed.2d 419 (1974).** Seven years after *Hill*, the Supreme Court reviewed a second false-light case, *Cantrell* v. *Forest City Publishing Co.*, and reiterated its actual malice holding, this time with the weight of a majority behind the decision. Mrs. Melvin Aaron Cantrell had been left a widow ten days before Christmas in 1967 when her husband was one of the forty-four victims of the collapse of the Silver Bridge, crossing the Ohio River at Point Pleasant, West Virginia. Several months later, a reporter for the *Cleveland Plain Dealer* decided to do a follow-up story on some of the survivors. He included Cantrell because she had been the focus of one of the prize-winning stories he had written at the time of the disaster. She was not at home, but the reporter did interview several of her minor children. The resulting story, portraying the mother as embittered by broken promises and living in abject poverty, was written as though the reporter had talked with Cantrell. One passage described her as wearing "the same mask of nonexpression she wore at the funeral." *Plain Dealer* editors featured the story in the newspaper's Sunday magazine.

Cantrell sued for invasion of privacy, alleging that she had been placed in a false light. A federal district court jury awarded her a $60,000 judgment. The circuit court of appeals reversed, but the Supreme Court restored the original verdict. Eight justices held that a properly instructed jury had come to the correct conclusion in finding actual malice. There was enough evidence within the story to prove that the reporter's word portrait of Cantrell was false. The story indicated that he had seen her and perhaps had talked with her. He had done neither.

Cantrell was decided about six months after *Gertz*. The majority took note of the latter decision but saw no need to decide whether the reasoning in *Gertz* with respect to private individuals should be applied to Cantrell. Clearly, she was a private individual, but it was also clear that the *Plain Dealer*'s reporter had been caught in a knowing falsehood. Initially, lower courts confronted with false-light cases adopted the *Hill* rationale and required all plaintiffs to prove actual malice. Courts have so held in Arkansas,[51] California,[52] Colorado,[53] Connecticut,[54] Kentucky,[55] and Oregon.[56] A federal district court applied the actual malice standard to a false-light case originating in New York.[57] Courts in other jurisdictions have looked to *Gertz* for guidance and have held that only public official or public figure plaintiffs need prove actual malice: U.S. Court of Appeals for the Fifth Circuit, applying Texas law,[58] and for the Sixth Circuit, applying Michigan law[59]; U.S. district courts in the District of Columbia,[60] the Northern District of Illinois,[61] Kansas,[62] and Maryland[63]; the West Virginia Supreme Court[64]; and an intermediate appellate court in New York.[65]

The Supreme Court of North Carolina held that the First Amendment stands as an absolute barrier against false-light actions. In doing so, it took note of

---

51. Dodrill v. Arkansas Democrat, 590 S.W.2d 840 (Ark. 1979).
52. Fellows v. National Enquirer, 211 Cal.Rptr. 809 (2d Dist. 1985); review granted, 215 Cal.Rptr. 853, 701 P.2d 1171 (Calif. 1985); superseded by 42 Cal.3d 234, 228 Cal.Rptr. 215, 721 P.2d 97 (Calif. 1987).
53. McCammon and Associates v. McGraw-Hill, 12 Med.L.Rptr. 1847 (Colo.Ct.App. 1986).
54. Goodrich v. Waterbury Republican-American, 8 Med.L.Rptr. 2329 (Conn. 1982).
55. McCall v. Courier-Journal, 623 S.W.2d 882 (Ky. 1981).
56. Dean v. Guard Publishing Co., 699 P.2d 1158 (Ore.App.1985).
57. Machleder v. Diaz, 618 F.Supp. 1367, 12 Med.L.Rptr. 1193 (S.D.N.Y. 1985).
58. Wood v. Hustler Magazine, 736 F.2d 1084 (5th Cir. 1984).
59. Bichler v. Union Bank, 715 F.2d 1059; vacated, 718 F.2d 802; affirmed, 745 F.2d 1006 (6th Cir. 1984).
60. Dresbach v. Doubleday, 518 F.Supp. 1285 (D.D.C. 1981).
61. Cantrell v. ABC, 529 F.Supp. 764 (N.D.Ill. 1981).
62. Rinsley v. Brandt, 446 F.Supp. 850 (D.Kans. 1977).
63. Fitzgerald v. Penthouse International, 525 F.Supp. 585 (D.Md. 1981).
64. Crump v. Beckley Newspapers, 320 S.E.2d 70 (W.Va. 1983).
65. Fils-Aime v. Enlightenment Press, 133 Misc.2d 559, 507 N.Y.S.2d 947 (App.Term, 1st Dept. 1986).

changes that have occurred in the practice of journalism since Warren and Brandeis wrote in 1890. The court said:

> Most modern journalists employed in print, television or radio journalism now receive training in ethics and journalism entirely unheard of during the era of "yellow journalism." As a general rule journalists simply are more responsible and professional today than history tells us they were in that era.[66]

The reported false-light actions in other jurisdictions fall into three categories:

1. False material is added to an otherwise accurate news or feature story resulting in a distorted portrayal of the subject of the story.

2. Material, commonly a photograph or videotape, is used in a context that results in a highly offensive portrayal of the subject.

3. Real people, either as themselves or thinly disguised, are used in fictional works.

The classic case illustrating the first of these categories is *Spahn* v. *Julian Messner*,[67] decided by New York's highest court. Warren Spahn was one of the best baseball pitchers of the late 1950s. A winner of baseball's top pitching award, he has long since entered baseball's Hall of Fame. At the height of his career, he became the subject of a biography to be published by Messner. The writer was not content to describe Spahn's career as it was, but said Spahn was a World War II hero, which he wasn't, and generally made him out to be larger than life. The pitcher brought suit for false-light invasion of privacy and eventually was able to win an injunction preventing distribution of the book.

The use of a photograph in a context that would make it highly offensive is illustrated by *Wood* v. *Hustler Magazine, Inc.*,[68] decided by the United States Court of Appeals for the Fifth Circuit. Lajuan Wood and her husband Billy took nude photographs of each other during an outing in a remote section of a Texas state park. They kept the prints in a dresser drawer in their bedroom. A neighbor thought it would be a great joke to send a photo of Lajuan to *Hustler* magazine for its "Beaver Hunt" section. He stole the print long enough to make a copy. The neighbor's wife, pretending to be Lajuan, sent the copy to *Hustler,* along with a letter saying that her secret fantasy was "to be screwed by two bikers." The editors of *Hustler* have a policy of calling persons who submit photos to it to make certain that the sender is who he or she claims to be and does indeed want the photo published. In this instance, the policy was not followed strictly. The call to the neighbor's wife, pretending to be Lajuan, was perfunctory and resulted in a decision to publish.

The Woods learned what had happened when friends began to tease them. Both sued *Hustler* for invasion of privacy. Lajuan said she was so mortified by the experience that she had to have six weeks of psychological counseling. A jury

---

66. Renwick v. News and Observer, 312 S.E.2d 405 (N.Car. 1984).
67. 221 N.E.2d 543 (N.Y. 1966).
68. 736 F.2d 1084 (5th Cir. 1984).

awarded her $150,000 in damages and her husband, $25,000. The court of appeals threw out the award to the husband, holding that he could not collect damages for an invasion of his wife's privacy. But the court said there was no doubt that Lajuan had been put in a false light. It held further that as a private individual she had only to prove that the editors of *Hustler* were negligent in checking the identity of the person who submitted the photograph. That was evident, the court said, from the fact that they had not followed their own procedures.

Because Clarence W. Arrington was unable to prove that a use of his photograph was offensive, he lost a privacy action against the *New York Times*. An issue of the *Times Magazine* featured an article entitled "The Black Middle Class: Making It." The cover was a photo of a well-dressed black man striding along a city street carrying a brief case. Superimposed across the photograph was a promotional box for the featured article. Arrington was not identified in the photo credit lines, nor was he mentioned in the article. In suing the *Times* for invasion of privacy, Arrington argued that his photo was being used for commercial purposes, in violation of a New York statute, and that he had been put in a false light. He said he was associated with the article, parts of which portrayed him as other than he is. The state's court of appeals upheld dismissal of both causes of action.[69] It noted that the photo was used as part of the news content of the magazine and thus was not for a commercial purpose. In dismissing the false-light claim, it held that there was no such cause of action in New York, and even if there were, the photo was not offensive, even if it could be connected with the article.

In one instance, a federal district court held that a television news crew's "ambush" interview not only was an actionable intrusion but put the subject in a false light. A jury awarded the target of the interview, a businessman accused of dumping chemicals on a neighbor's property, $1.25 million. The U.S. Court of Appeals for the Second Circuit reversed.[70] It said there was no intrusion because the interview took place in a semipublic area and the questions were not sufficiently aggressive as to constitute "hounding" the plaintiff. Nor was the businessman placed in a false light. The camera recorded his own words and appearance, which could not be false, even though he was made to seem "intemperate and evasive."

Fictionalization has been a problem largely for television "docudramas," which are mixtures of fact and fiction, with moving pictures, and with novels. The cases indicate that if the subject is a public figure, and the work deals with matters of public concern, courts will protect all but the grossest distortions. Because truth is elusive, and varies with the beholder, the First Amendment gives strong protection to works dealing with public figures and historical events.

Problems have arisen with the portrayal of peripheral figures, with those persons who surround public figures and play the supporting roles. For instance, an attorney who had represented a prominent figure in organized crime was held to

---

69. Arrington v. New York Times, 56 N.Y.2d 284 (N.Y. 1983).
70. Machleder v. Diaz, 801 F.2d 46 (2d Cir. 1986); cert. denied, 479 U.S. 1088, 107 S.Ct. 1294, 94 L.Ed.2d 150 (1987).

have a false-light claim against the publisher of a novel in which his name was used.[71]

Taken as a whole, the reported cases convey a straightforward message. Professional communicators who use words or pictures to portray individuals, and who take care to make certain that their work shows the individuals as they are, have little to fear. Indeed, if the subject of the work is a public figure, or an event of public importance, the law will tolerate material distortion before it will uphold a false-light privacy claim. The critical question is why a professional communicator would want to present a false picture of any individual.

APPROPRIATION AND THE RIGHT OF PUBLICITY

Appropriation, which for years was confined to the taking of a person's name or likeness for advertising purposes, is assuming a different form and taking on new life under what courts are calling "the right of publicity." That right means that individuals, particularly celebrities, have the right to control how others use their names. In effect, the courts are recognizing that a widely known name or likeness is a form of property and has a value that the possessor alone should be permitted to exploit. How far this right of publicity goes is still uncertain. Thus far, courts have found a violation of the right in advertisements, in the televising of a carnival act, in the promotion of feature stories, in film, in a variety show exploiting the memory of Elvis Presley, and even in the name of a company making portable toilets.

The principal and strongest defense against an action for appropriation or violation of the right of publicity is consent, preferably in writing. From the user's point of view, the best consent is written broadly enough to cover any conceivable use of a subject's identity in perpetuity. Short of that, any use of identity for commercial gain should be accompanied by the subject's specific consent. Consent can be implied in some instances, but usually only in connection with a news event, or only if commercial gain is incidental to the use.

Because this branch of invasion of privacy almost always hinges on the user's commercial gain, it is of concern mainly to advertisers, public relations practitioners, and photographers. In only a few instances has news or feature content been at issue in an appropriation or right of publicity action.

Appropriation

In its traditional form appropriation was fairly simple. An unsuspecting person who found his or her name or photograph in a commercial advertisement had a cause of action for damages. Courts usually fixed the award by determining what a model would have received for the same usage. In some instances, an attempt

---

71. Polakoff v. Harcourt Brace, 413 N.Y.S.2d 537 (1st Dept. 1979).

was made to calculate the commercial value of the subject's endorsement. On occasion, appropriation would become intertwined with false light, as when a young woman who posed for an advertisement for sheets found that the photograph had been altered in another usage to make it look as though she were reading a pornographic novel. In such instances, the award for damages might be higher than if appropriation alone were involved.

Kimbrough v. *Coca-Cola/ USA,* **521 S. W. 2d 719 (Tex. 1975).** The experience of John Kimbrough, a former football player at Texas A&M University, illustrates the typical appropriation case. In it, a Texas appellate court held that a jury should decide whether his consent had been exceeded and, if so, how much he should receive in damages. Kimbrough was notified that he had been selected as his school's best former football player. As a result, *Texas Football* magazine and Coca-Cola had commissioned an artist to paint his portrait. He would get the original. One print would go to Texas A&M for permanent display and another would be placed in the Texas Football Hall of Fame. The letter also said in part:

> There is also contemplated use of these paintings [athletes from other Southwest Conference schools were also being honored] in a series of institutional advertisements in behalf of college football in Dave Campbell's *Texas Football* magazine.
> While no endorsement of any product is implied in the institutional nature of the proposed usage, we would not, of course, approach a project of this type without your complete approval.

Kimbrough replied that he was honored at being chosen and would sit for his portrait. Sometime later his daughter called to tell him she had found a reproduction of his portrait in the program for the Southern Methodist-Wake Forest football game—as part of an advertisement for Coca-Cola. Kimbrough reacted by suing everyone connected with the promotion for invasion of privacy. A state district court in Dallas dismissed the action, but an appeals court reversed.

Coca-Cola based its case on two grounds: As a public figure, Kimbrough had lost any claim to a right of privacy, and, in any event, he had given his consent. The court said that while it is true that public figures do surrender much of their privacy, they still are entitled to protection against appropriation for commercial purposes. The court also concluded that the ambiguous wording of the original letter raised a jury question as to whether Kimbrough's consent had been exceeded. Here there was a real possibility that his consent was for noncommercial uses only.

National Bank of Commerce v. *Shaklee Corp.,* **503 F.Supp. 719 (W.D. Tex. 1980).** A case decided by a United States District Court in San Antonio illustrates how complicated an appropriation action can be. The court's decision is of particular value because it illustrates two aspects of appropriation law:

1. The difficulty of determining how far a subject's consent goes.

2. The application of this branch of the law to both advertising and public relations.

For many years, Heloise Bowles wrote a widely syndicated column of sometimes zany household tips, "Hints from Heloise," which since her death has been carried on by her daughter. At the height of its popularity, it was used by 580 to 600 newspapers in the United States and abroad, it had an estimated readership of 30 million, and it generated 4,000 to 5,000 letters a month. Heloise's popularity was aided by two policies from which she never deviated: She never mentioned any product by brand name, and she never published a household tip until she had tried it and found that it worked.

Under a complicated agreement with her syndicate, King Features, she also wrote books, largely collections of her columns, which were published in hardcover by Prentice-Hall and in paperback by Pocket Books. Still another company was involved in bulk and premium sales of some of the books for promotional purposes. Under her contract with King Features, Heloise had to approve any commercial use of her work.

However, without her knowledge, an agent for the bulk sales organization made a deal with Shaklee Corporation, which distributes home care products through a network of independent distributors who deal directly with consumers. Shaklee agreed to buy 100,000 copies of *All Around the House,* one of Heloise's most popular books, for thirty-eight cents each. After it had placed advertising messages on the front and back covers and at the end of each chapter, it offered to resell the books for fifty cents each to its more than 200,000 distributors to use as "door-openers." The front cover proclaimed in large type, "Welcome a new Shaklee Woman," and in even larger type, "Heloise." Two articles in the company's magazine for its distributors hailed Heloise as "an excellent addition to your sales group."

Heloise herself first learned of this promotion when she went to California on a speaking trip. Members of the audience confronted her with questions about when she began to endorse Shaklee products. She testified later that she was "humiliated," and "shocked to death." She also became angry and asked King Features what was going on. It, too, had not been advised. Heloise later testified that when she saw Shaklee's version of her book and the articles promoting it, she "nearly had a heart attack and called Kellis, my lawyer."

Heloise sued Shaklee for invasion of privacy on appropriation grounds, for unfair competition, and for violation of her copyright. During the discovery process, she died, but the suit was pushed forward by the National Bank of Commerce as executor of her estate. Shaklee argued that a dead person has no privacy, but the district court pointed to a section of Texas law that permits an action in torts to survive the death of the person who began it.

Shaklee also argued that because Heloise was a public figure she would have to prove actual malice if she were to prevail. The court rejected that argument.

Nothing false was involved. At issue was simply a blatant use by Shaklee of Heloise's name and good will to promote its products. Thus it was a clear case of invasion of privacy by appropriation.

But, Shaklee argued, there was consent for its use. It had made what it thought was a bona-fide business deal with a bona-fide agent of Heloise, her syndicate, and her publisher. It was doing all of them a favor by buying her book at what it assumed was a profit for them and was using the book to help make a profit for itself. The court held that if that were all that had happened, there would be no case. But when the book was altered to make it look as though Heloise were pushing Shaklee's products, and when the house organ hailed her as a new member of the firm's sales team, the terms of the agreement were exceeded. Therefore, Shaklee was guilty of invasion of privacy by appropriation.

In filing her suit, Heloise had asked for $2 million in actual damages for invasion of privacy, $5 million in special damages as the value of her endorsement, $350,000 for mental and physical pain and suffering, and $5 million in exemplary or punitive damages. Her estate was awarded a total of $135,000 in damages plus the award of profits from the copyright violation.

Consent

Professional advertisers, photographers, and public relations practitioners usually know enough about their business to obtain consent from their subjects. For that reason, as the cases examined above suggest, most appropriation actions are based on attempts to revoke or limit consent or on allegations that the consent was exceeded. Some plaintiffs have learned that consent given too readily and too broadly can not only embarrass the giver but deny him legal relief, as the following episode illustrates.

Shields v. *Gross,* 7 Med.L. Rptr. 2349 (Sup. Ct. N.Y.Co. 1981). When Brooke Shields, the actress and model, was ten years old, she posed for a series of nude photographs taken by Gary Gross for Playboy Press. She was portrayed in and out of a bathtub for a book, *Sugar and Spice,* designed "to depict the woman in the little girl to highlight the sensuality of prepubescent youth." Brooke was photographed with the cooperation of her mother, Mrs. Teri Shields, who signed a standard "model release" and in return received $450. Neither the photos of Brooke nor the book in which they appeared was in any way pornographic. Larger-than-life reproductions of two of the bathtub photos were displayed for weeks in the windows of a Fifth Avenue salon.

Five years later, after Brooke had begun to appear in movies in which she played sensual roles, the nude photos resurfaced. Some appeared in a magazine published in France. Others were used in various American magazines. When "publications of dubious respectability" began proclaiming that they offered photographs of "Brooke Shields Naked," Mrs. Shields tried to buy the negatives from Gross. When that failed, she went to court, asking that the photographer be prevented from selling or using the nude photographs of her daughter. The court granted her a temporary injunction, heard her lawyer's arguments, then turned her down flat, except to put into legal form Gross's agreement not to sell the pho-

Actress Brooke Shields (left) with her mother, Teri Shields, in 1981, when the actress won the Ticket Sellers Union's "Box Office Award." In the same year, Mrs. Shields lost one of several lawsuits in which she and her daughter sought unsuccessfully to stop continued publication of nude photos of Brooke taken with her mother's written consent when the actress was 10 years old. The courts held that because of the consent there was no invasion of privacy. (AP/Wide World Photos)

tos to pornographic magazines or those designed to appeal predominantly to a prurient interest.

Judge Edward J. Greenfield of the New York Supreme Court—a trial court—told Mrs. Shields in blunt language that she could not have it both ways. She could not exploit her daughter's "extraordinary genes," her "exceptional beauty and engaging personality," and then complain when others sought to cash in on the same qualities. He reminded Mrs. Shields that the release she had signed so eagerly, without even reading it, had given Gross an absolute right to use and publish the products of the photo session in any way he liked. She also had waived her right "to inspect or approve" the finished photographs and had agreed to give up any right to recover damages for their use, even if that use "should subject me to ridicule, scandal, reproach, scorn or indignity." In short, she would have to be satisfied with the $450, while Gross was free to sell the photos for whatever the market would offer.

Mrs. Shields proved to be a persistent adversary. She appealed first to the supreme court's appellate division, which found in her favor and gave her part of what she sought, and then to the state's highest court, which rebuffed her by restoring the trial court's order.[72] This litigation took two years to move through the courts, during which time a series of temporary injunctions prevented Gross from further sales of the photographs. When Mrs. Shields lost her last round in the state courts, she went immediately to the United States District Court in New York City. The judge dismissed her suit summarily, accusing her lawyer of abusing the legal system to deny Gross profits that were rightfully his under terms of the consent.[73]

Two contradictory points emerge: Photographers and advertisers who use live models should ask them for the broadest possible terms of consent. Persons who are

---

72. Shields v.Gross, 451 N.Y.S.2d 419 (N.Y.App. 1982); 448 N.E.2d 108 (N.Y. 1983).
73. Shields v. Gross, 503 F.Supp. 533 (S.D.N.Y. 1983).

asked to lend their names and likenesses to others who will try to profit from that use should try to limit the terms of the consent to the specific use. It is a general rule of law, as the New York Court of Appeals reminded Mrs. Shields, that "a defendant's immunity from a claim for invasion of privacy is no broader than the consent executed to him." In short, for purposes of advertising or trade, people have full control over how much of their privacy they are willing to surrender and on what terms.

The Right of Publicity

Until 1977, courts generally held that there could be no appropriation if a person's name or photograph was used primarily for news or feature purposes. Courts were even willing to tolerate some use of a newsworthy person's identity to promote sales of a newspaper or magazine. Courts took the view that publications must make a profit if they are to remain in operation. Editors choose news, feature, photo, and other content with the expectation that it will help the publication prosper. But it does not follow that persons who are featured in such content have been victims of appropriation. For instance, a New York court held that Joe Namath, then a highly successful football quarterback, could not recover from *Sports Illustrated* when his photo was used to promote the magazine.[74] The photo had originally appeared on the cover of one issue of the magazine. That cover was one of several included in the promotional brochure. The court held that Namath's likeness was being used only to show prospective readers the kind of editorial content they could expect to enjoy if they became subscribers.

Zacchini v. *Scripps-Howard Broadcasting,* 433 U.S. 562, 97 S.Ct. 2849, 53 L.Ed.2d 965 (1977).

The nature of appropriation law was changed abruptly in 1977 by the United States Supreme Court's decision in *Zacchini* v. *Scripps-Howard Broadcasting.* The plaintiff, Hugo Zacchini, made his living by being shot out of a huge cannon into a net 200 yards away. When he appeared at the Geauga County Fair in Chardon, Ohio, a crew from WEWS-TV in Cleveland recorded his dramatic flight. Zacchini protested that the station was stealing his act, but that night it was broadcast as part of the news from the fair. Zacchini sued, asking for $25,000 as the value of the performance.

Three Ohio courts came to as many different conclusions as to the merits of his suit, with the state supreme court holding that because the act had news value, the station had a right to show it. Zacchini took his case to the Supreme Court, which reversed, holding that the station had appropriated the act, violating the performer's "right of exclusive control over the publicity given to his performance."

The Court conceded that the station's newscast was protected in its entirety by the First Amendment. It conceded also that there was news value in the fact that Zacchini had performed at the fair. However, Justice White, writing for six members of the Court, held that the First Amendment could not be stretched to

---

74. Namath v. Sports Illustrated, 1 Med.L.Rptr. 1843 (N.Y. 1st Dept. 1975).

justify appropriation of the entire act. He compared the newscast with the usual form of appropriation:

> [T]he broadcast of petitioner's entire performance, unlike the unauthorized use of another's name for purposes of trade or the incidental use of a name or picture by the press, goes to the heart of petitioner's ability to earn a living as an entertainer. Thus in this case, Ohio has recognized what may be the strongest case for a "right of publicity"—involving not the appropriation of an entertainer's reputation to enhance the attractiveness of a commercial product, but the appropriation of the very activity by which the entertainer acquired the reputation in the first place.

The Court's minority argued in vain that the small segment of the newscast devoted to the Human Cannonball's flight contributed little, if anything, to the station's revenue and should be treated as an incidental use. Justice Lewis F. Powell, Jr., predicted that the decision would have unforeseen consequences at the point where news and entertainment meet. His prediction has proved correct, as the next two incidents show.

The television "docudramas" that became popular in the 1970s brought legal problems with them. As noted in the section on false light, when these fictionalized treatments of history dealt with public figures and public events, the persons who were portrayed had little chance of recovery. Courts held that unless the fictionalized portrait was deliberately highly offensive, it was protected by the First Amendment.

The Supreme Court's decision in the *Zacchini* case seems to have given celebrities a new legal weapon against producers of docudramas. When Elizabeth Taylor learned that ABC Television was preparing a movie based on her life, her lawyers set to work to keep it off the air. Using the rationale on which *Zacchini* was based they argued that her life story was a form of commercial property she alone has the right to exploit. She argued that she might some day decide to write or film her autobiography with the expectation of profiting from the work. In her eyes, she told a *New York Times* reporter, ABC, by beating her to the punch, was "taking away from my income."[75] Floyd Abrams, a noted First Amendment lawyer, told the same reporter that if the courts were to adopt Miss Taylor's argument, they would take away some of the freedom of the press. He argued that there is news in the lives of celebrities that serves the public interest, even when some aspects of those lives are fictionalized. To hold otherwise, he said, would not only prevent the telecasting of unauthorized docudramas, but would raise questions about books and articles dealing with the careers of living persons. Nevertheless, confronted with the prospect of going to court to defend its right to show its version of Miss Taylor's colorful life, ABC put the project on hold.

***Cher* v. *Forum International, Ltd.,* 692 F.2d 634 (9th Cir. 1982).** A case decided by the United States Court of Appeals for the Ninth Circuit gave some support to Abrams's concern. In *Cher* v. *Forum International, Ltd.,* the court held that *Forum* magazine

---

75. Tamar Lewin, "Whose Life Is It, Anyway? It's Hard to Tell," *New York Times,* 21 November 1982.

could be held liable for the unauthorized use of a taped interview bought from a free-lance writer.

The writer originally had been hired by *Us* magazine to interview Cher for a cover story. Cher consented, but retained the right to approve any other uses of the material. The interview did not go as Cher expected, and she asked *Us* not to base an article on it. Subsequently, the writer sold copies of the tape to *Forum* and to the publisher of the *Star,* a tabloid sold at supermarket checkout counters. Both magazines prepared articles and promoted them heavily. *Forum* used Cher's photo on the cover, along with promotional copy that said, "There are certain things that Cher won't tell *People* and would never tell *Us.*" The magazine invited readers to "join Cher and *Forum's* hundreds of thousands of other adventurous readers today." The *Star's* cover promotional copy was more direct. It simply said, seeming to quote Cher, "My Life, My Husbands, and My Many, Many Men."

Cher reacted by suing both magazines for violating her right of publicity. A trial court held in her favor and awarded her $600,000. The appellate court cleared the *Star,* but upheld a judgment against *Forum* for $269,117. Although both articles were written in the first person, as though by Cher herself, the court said the *Star's* deceit was not great enough to overcome the news value of the story. However, the court said *Forum* had not only misrepresented the exclusive nature of the interview—Cher had intended it originally for *Us*—but indicated in its promotional material that she endorsed the magazine. This, the court held, amounted to exploitative appropriation of the publicity value of Cher's identity.

Carson v. *Here's Johnny Portable Toilets,* **698 F.2d 831 (6th Cir. 1983).** Courts dealing with right of publicity cases have shown some doubt as to the definition of the identity a celebrity may protect. This is illustrated by a disagreement within a three-judge panel of the United States Court of Appeals for the Sixth Circuit. The suit was brought by John W. Carson, introduced for more than twenty-five years with a drawn-out "Here's Johnny!" to viewers of NBC's "Tonight" show. The owner of a Michigan firm that manufactured and distributed portable toilets admitted he had that introduction in mind when he named his company "Here's Johnny Portable Toilets." Lest there be any doubt, he added to his advertising the phrase, "The World's Foremost Commodian," considering it "a good play on a phrase."

Carson alleged that the firm name infringed the "Here's Johnny" trademark identifying a line of clothing made by a firm in which he held a minority interest. He also said he was embarrassed because he found it odious to be associated with the manufacturer's product. The court rejected both grounds as a basis for suit, but held that the firm clearly was exploiting Carson's identity to its advantage, thus violating his right of publicity. He alone had the right to exploit his name for commercial advantage.

The firm had argued that it was not using Carson's name. It noted that toilets have been known as "johns" for many years. "Here's Johnny," it asserted, is a phrase commonly used, and therefore not subject to protection. The court conceded that the phrase was not strongly enough identified with Carson's line of clothing to become protected as a trademark. But it said each of his appearances since 1957 had been preceded by a distinctive "Here's Johnny," thus indelibly making those words a symbol of his identity. Therefore, the firm's use of "Here's Johnny" in its name violated Carson's right of publicity, and he was entitled to prevent such use or get paid for it.

Judge Cornelia G. Kennedy argued in dissent that the majority went much too far in defining the identity Carson is entitled to protect. She argued that the sentence in question is a part of the public domain, and thus can be used by anyone. She warned that the court's decision could open the way for an almost limitless expansion of a celebrity's identity, leading to many more claims under a right of publicity.

Her warning may have been prophetic. A survey of recent reported cases shows that the right of publicity has become a frequently litigated branch of invasion of privacy. Its potential for expansion has been enhanced by statutes and by court decisions holding that the right survives the death of the individual. States with such laws are California, Florida, Georgia, Nebraska, Oklahoma, Tennessee, Utah, and Virginia. The California law is the most generous, permitting the legal heirs of a celebrity to protect and profit from his or her right of publicity for fifty years after the celebrity's death.

Courts are divided over whether the right of publicity survives death in the absence of a statute. Illustrative of those holding that it does is a decision of the United States Court of Appeals for the Eleventh Circuit. It held, in *Martin Luther King, Jr., Center for Social Change, Inc.,* v. *American Heritage Products, Inc.,*[76] that the right of publicity in the identity of the civil rights leader survived his assassination and, like any other form of property, could be protected by his heirs.

How far the courts will go in expanding on the Supreme Court's decision in *Zacchini* is not clear at this writing. What is clear is that the decision has given celebrities an additional weapon with which to make certain that they control the right to profit from the exploitation of their status. It also is clear that advertisers, photographers, and public relations practitioners no longer are the only likely media targets of actions in appropriation. Movie and television scriptwriters, film and television producers, broadcasting news editors, magazine publishers, and others need to be aware that celebrities have acquired a property right in their identities and that courts will protect it against exploitation by others.

PRIVACY AND GOVERNMENT RECORDS

At one level, the Supreme Court's 1975 decision in *Cox,* followed by *Smith* and *Globe Newspapers,* expanded the media's right to use names and facts. Anything found on the public record can be used without invading someone's right of

---

76.   694 F.2d 674 (11th Cir. 1983).

privacy. But, at another level, the decisions may have restricted information in the public domain. The Court suggested in *Cox* that Georgia might have prevented publication of the name of the rape victim by sealing the records in which it was found. Indeed, at the time that decision was written, federal and state legislative bodies were enacting statutes designed to restrict access to government files containing certain personal information. These statutes took two forms.

One form, exemplified by the federal Privacy Act of 1974, is designed to prevent disclosure by government agencies of personal data about employees and others on whom files are kept. Because such laws restrict media access to information, their effect will be examined in chapter 8, which deals with that topic.

The second form of statutory protection deals with the kinds of information journalists have always considered public—police and court records of adult offenders. In most states, statutes provide that under certain circumstances public records of arrests, and even of convictions, can be either sealed or expunged. These laws vary in their scope, but generally cover arrests that do not result in convictions or guilty pleas, long-past convictions of persons who have gone straight, and records of juvenile offenses. The purposes of these laws, which have been adopted by forty-eight states, the District of Columbia, and Puerto Rico, are to encourage rehabilitation of wrongdoers and to protect the privacy of persons who have been arrested but never convicted. In a sense, they are a legislative adoption of the reasoning used by the California courts in *Melvin* and *Briscoe,* discussed earlier. At some point, a person who was caught in a law violation, but who went straight thereafter, should no longer have to fear having that infraction called to public attention.

Journalists see such laws as restrictions on freedom of the press. Persons have been known to revert to crime after many years of normal life. Should journalists be denied the opportunity to inform the public that one of the candidates for director of a day-care center was once arrested on suspicion of child molesting? Or that a candidate for county auditor had once been convicted of embezzlement? Journalists also argue that they cannot properly assess the performance of police, prosecutors, and judges unless they can get access to all arrest and disposition records. For instance, it would be difficult to check reports that a prosecutor took it easy on men accused of beating their wives or women friends if the records of arrests not resulting in prosecution were sealed.

Expunging or Sealing of Criminal Records

The Illinois statute represents one of the common forms an expungement law takes.[77] The pertinent part states:

> All photographs, fingerprints, or other records of identification so taken shall, upon the acquittal of a person charged with the crime, or, upon his being released without being convicted, be returned to him. Whenever a person, not having previ-

---

77.   Ill.Rev.Stat. 1975, ch. 38, par. 206–5.

ously been convicted of any criminal offense or municipal ordinance violation, charged with a violation of a municipal ordinance or a felony misdemeanor, is acquitted or released without being convicted, the Chief Judge of the circuit wherein the charge was brought, or any judge of that circuit designated by the Chief Judge, may upon verified petition of the defendant order the record of arrest expunged from the official records of the arresting authority.

The Massachusetts law goes further and establishes elaborate safeguards designed to keep anyone but police and courts from having access to criminal dossiers on individuals. The only case testing the law also made clear that it is a limitation on investigative reporting. Under the law, reporters and the public have access only to the day-to-day records of arrests and of public judicial proceedings. Any compilation of records in alphabetical order or any alphabetized index to police or court files is available only to law enforcement officers.

New Bedford Standard-Times Publishing Co. v. *Clerk of Third Dist. Court,* 387 N.E.2d 110 (Mass. 1979).

The *New Bedford Standard-Times* saw the law as an obstacle when it undertook an investigation of individuals believed to be in violation of building, sanitary, or housing laws and regulations. Its reporters were unable to check the records readily to see whether any given individual had been arrested or even convicted at some time in the past. To do so, reporters would have to go through docket books day by day, looking for individual names. The newspapers asked, therefore, to look at an alphabetical case file compiled by the clerk of the Third District Court of Bristol County to make the court's work easier. Cards in that file contained a reasonably complete arrest and disposition record for each offender. When the clerk refused the request, the *Standard-Times* filed suit, arguing that the section of the law barring public inspection of alphabetical files was unconstitutional. The newspaper was rebuffed both by a district court and the supreme judicial court.

The latter viewed the dispute in narrow terms. The only question, it said, was how far the state should go in making it easy for the newspaper to obtain information from public records. The court conceded that the newspaper had difficulty in assembling arrest records, particularly of offenses that had occurred in the distant past. This was as it should be, it concluded, for there is less news value in long-past convictions. In any event, the legislature had decided that the public interest in rehabilitation of offenders requires protection of their privacy. The court held that the right of privacy "weighs more heavily" than the purpose of the newspaper's investigation.

Newspapers, Inc., v. *Breier,* 279 N.W.2d 179 (Wis. 1979).

However, the Supreme Court of Wisconsin held that an interest in the privacy of criminal suspects cannot be carried too far. In *Newspapers, Inc.,* v. *Breier,* it ruled that the Milwaukee police chief could not deny reporters access to his department's daily arrest log or "blotter."

Chief Harold A. Breier took the position that an arrest does not mean that the suspect is guilty. Indeed, the prosecutor may decide there is not enough evidence to take the suspect to court, or, if there is, a court may acquit him or her. Therefore, publication of the details of an arrest, including the name of the suspect, may only result in needless embarrassment of an innocent person. Therefore, the chief adopted a policy of releasing the names of arrested persons only on demand, but even then, police would not release the nature of the charge.

Joseph W. Shoquist, managing editor of the *Milwaukee Journal,* took the chief to court, arguing that arrest records are public records. The trial court would have permitted a forty-eight-hour delay in release of arrest records, but the state's highest court said even that was too much. The power to arrest, it said, "is an awesome weapon for the protection of the people, but it also is a power that may be abused." One way of preventing abuse is to make the people aware of it when it happens. Under the chief's policy, even as modified by the trial court, this could not be done. The supreme court said it would be "a travesty of our judicial and law enforcement system" to report that persons had been arrested, but fail to give the reasons for it.

Bahr v. *Statesman Journal Co.,* **624 P.2d 664 (Ore. App. 1981).**

As of this writing, no reported privacy case has hinged on facts contained in an expunged record, but a libel case decided by an Oregon appellate court did. The decision, in *Bahr* v. *Statesman Journal Co.,* was an interesting victory for the newspaper involved. The Oregon expungement law specifies that a person whose record has been removed from the public files can say, if asked, "I have no criminal record." Les Bahr, a candidate for county commissioner, used that response when a reporter for the newspaper in Salem asked him if he had been convicted of embezzlement several years previously. As a matter of fact, Bahr had been convicted and had served four months in jail. When he had gone three years without committing another offense, he had had his record expunged.

When the reporter, relying on the newspaper's files, reported Bahr's conviction for embezzlement, the candidate sued for libel. The trial court granted the newspaper's request for dismissal, and the appellate court affirmed. A part of Judge Betty Robert's decision for the defendant offers an interesting commentary on Oregon's expungement law:

> The statute does not ... impose any duty on members of the public who are aware of the conviction to pretend that it does not exist. In other words, the statute authorizes certain persons to misrepresent their own past. It does not make that misrepresentation true....
>
> While plaintiff was entitled to deny his conviction ... defendant, in this civil defamation case, was entitled to rely upon the fact that a conviction did occur as a defense.... Because plaintiff admitted in his complaint that he had been convicted, two things follow from the allegations of the complaint and the provisions of [the law]. First, that defendant's statement that plaintiff had been convicted was true, and secondly, that it was true that plaintiff had lied in denying his conviction, despite the fact the lie was authorized by statute.

Juvenile Offenders

All states have laws restricting the release of information that would identify juvenile offenders. In their usual form, the statutes forbid release of such information by the juvenile system unless it is authorized by a judge. The rationale is that young offenders should be given every opportunity to be rehabilitated and should not be haunted for the rest of their lives by the mistakes of their youth. In a few states, courts and legislatures have attempted to protect juveniles further by imposing penalties on the news media for disclosing their names. In two decisions, the Supreme Court has held that such attempts impose an impermissible prior restraint if the juvenile was identified in open court or if the state's only interest is rehabilitation of the offender.

Oklahoma Publishing Co. v. District Court in and for Oklahoma County, 430 U.S. 308, 97 S.Ct. 1045, 51 L.Ed.2d 355 (1977).

One of the cases, *Smith* v. *Daily Mail Publishing Co.,* was discussed earlier in the chapter. In it, the Court struck down a West Virginia law making it a crime for newspapers to disclose the names of juvenile offenders. The asserted state interest was in rehabilitation. The second case, *Oklahoma Publishing Co.* v. *District Court in and for Oklahoma County* struck down a judge's order forbidding publication of the name and photograph of an eleven-year-old boy who was accused of murder. When the boy was taken into custody, the judge permitted reporters to attend the hearing, at which the offender's name was used. When the boy was taken out of the courthouse, newspaper and television photographers recorded the scene. News reports of the arrest in all media identified the suspect.

When the boy was arraigned at a closed hearing four days later, the judge issued an order forbidding the news media to use the name or photograph of any minor child involved in a pending proceeding. Clearly, the order was designed to prevent any further use of the name or photograph of the murder suspect. The news media appealed the judge's edict, arguing that the boy's identity already was common knowledge, owing largely to the court's own actions. Pointing to *Cox* v. *Cohn,* they argued that a name made public during the official proceedings of a court could not later be made private. The Oklahoma Supreme Court rejected that argument, but on further appeal, the United States Supreme Court reversed, issuing only a brief *per curiam* decision. It noted that the news media had obtained their information legally, with the state's implicit approval. Therefore, the judge's subsequent order was a clear violation of the First Amendment's guarantee of freedom of the press.

The Supreme Court's decision in *Cox,* discussed earlier, has cut two ways. Beyond question, it has immunized the media from successful actions for disclosure of facts found in the public records of courts or disclosed in open court. Other court decisions have extended the *Cox* rationale to protect media reliance on facts found in other kinds of public records, if they are obtained legitimately. But in *Cox* a majority of the Court also suggested that courts and legislatures could protect the privacy of rape victims and others by sealing records or closing proceedings in which they are identified. At the time of *Cox,* juvenile records already were sealed in all states. All but two states have also enacted laws providing for expunging or sealing long-past arrest records or even records of convictions. They have done so to encourage rehabilitation and to protect privacy. Courts have upheld such laws, but also have held that they cannot be carried so far as to permit withholding of information about current arrests.

In the *Newspapers* case, the Wisconsin court held that the abuses that could occur if arrests were kept secret outweighed the privacy interest inherent in the fact that charges against many persons arrested by police are dismissed by the prosecutor. An Oregon court held that a person once convicted of a crime could not sustain a libel action against a newspaper which reported that fact after the record had been expunged. What once was true still was true despite a state law permitting the plaintiff to say it wasn't. Finally, the Supreme Court itself has held, in *Oklahoma Publishing,* in *Smith,* and in *Florida Star* that the media can neither be restrained from, nor punished for, publishing the identity of an offender or a victim whose record is sealed, provided the information is obtained legally. That holds true, the Court said in *Florida Star,* even when the information was obtained by mistake.

In the Professional World

When professional journalists get together—whether at formal meetings or informally—few topics arouse more discussion than invasion of privacy. These discussions usually are inconclusive because opinions and practices with respect to the line between private fact and news vary widely. A stake out employed by one newspaper to find out with whom a presidential candidate spent the night was seen as "sneaky snooping" by a former editor of the *New York Times.*[78] An elaborate subterfuge used by another newspaper to catch city employees in the act of taking bribes was condemned as unethical by editors of others.[79] Sometimes the conflict between good journalism and unacceptable ethics occurs in the same individual. One editor said he would nominate for a Pulitzer Prize a photograph he considered a grossly insensitive intrusion into a family's grief.[80]

Codes of ethics adopted by organizations of journalists contain sections on privacy. The code embraced by the Society of Professional Journalists says, "The news media must guard against invading a person's right to privacy." That is followed by a less strongly worded sentence that says, "The media should not pander to morbid curiosity about details of vice and crime." The Associated Press Managing Editors code also advises respect for the individual's right of privacy. The code of the Radio-Television News

---

78. A. M. Rosenthal, "Attack on the Herald," *Louisville Courier-Journal,* 8 May 1987.
79. H. Eugene Goodwin, *Groping for Ethics in Journalism* (Ames: Iowa State University Press, 1983), pp. 135–136, 138–40.
80. Bob Greene, "News Business and Right of Privacy Can Be at Odds," 1985–86 *Journalism Ethics Report,* National Ethics Committee, Society of Professional Journalists, p. 15.

Directors Association is somewhat broader. It says that "broadcast journalists shall at all times display humane respect for the dignity, privacy and the well-being of persons with whom the news deals." Such language obviously leaves the individual professional wide latitude in dealing with questions of privacy.

As we have seen, the law of privacy also gives journalists a wide field in which to work. Courts have shown little sympathy for reporters who trespass or break the law to get a story. In *Dietemann,* two federal courts condemned a reporter's and a photographer's use of deception. However, the decision is clouded by the fact that the deception was used to gain entry to the private sanctuary offered by Dietemann's home. Courts have not condemned other kinds of deception used to obtain news stories. Journalists who are usually quick to condemn the deception of others have on occasion used subterfuge themselves.

In one instance, editors of the *Chicago Sun-Times* asked two reporters to buy and operate a tavern, The Mirage, to investigate tips that city building inspectors were shaking down owners of small businesses. The reporters-turned-barkeepers soon learned that the tips were true. They could not stay open without paying off electrical and plumbing inspectors. Hidden microphones and cameras recorded the transactions. The operation produced stories that ran for weeks.

Were these stories the fruits of unusual enterprise? Or were the unwary officials led into a trap and baited into making demands they might not otherwise have made? If dishonesty was indeed rampant in city officialdom, could it have been exposed only by tactics that were not quite on the level themselves? Those questions were raised by David Halvorsen, then managing editor of the *San Francisco Examiner,* who asked two editors of stature to respond to them.[81] Clayton Kirkpatrick, whose *Chicago Tribune* was scooped by the series, defended his competitor's methods. He said he was convinced there was no entrapment. There are times, he said, when direct, convincing evidence of wrongdoing can be obtained only through the reporter's involvement. He saw The Mirage operation as different only in degree from instances in which reporters posing as ordinary consumers obtain evidence on dishonest television and automobile repair services. Eugene Patterson of the *St. Petersburg Times* disagreed. Like Kirkpatrick, he recognized that on some occasions reporters need not proclaim who they are. A newspaper's restaurant critic can best serve by seeming to be an ordinary diner. Applying what he called "a scale of distinctions," Patterson said his newspaper would not ask reporters to go undercover to investigate conditions in nursing homes. He said he believed that with hard work, open reporting methods could get the same information. He said, "We've inflicted pretty high ethical standards on public and private institutions with our editorials in recent years and I worry a lot about our hypocrisy quotient if we

---

81. *Bulletin of the American Society of Newspaper Editors,* September 1979, p. 12.

demand government in the sunshine and practice journalism unnecessarily in the shade.'' However, he reserved the right to use deception if that proved to be only way to obtain a story of ''vital public interest.''

Where dissemination of private facts is at issue, journalists differ widely. The *Diaz* case represents one extreme. Some editors take the position that people who seek the public's approval, either by entering politics or by becoming celebrities, have little or no right of privacy. A dwindling number of others act on the belief that even persons of prominence are entitled to raise a family, drink, or even philander in private as long as what they do does not affect their duty to the public. In this area, journalistic ethics have changed markedly in the last generation. When John F. Kennedy was president, every Washington correspondent who was halfway alert heard stories of Kennedy's womanizing, but no one reported it. Nor was there anything in the media about Lyndon B. Johnson's ''drinking a quart a day.''[82] The White House correspondents of the time focused their reporting on what both men did as presidents. What they did in private was treated as gossip which the correspondents shared with one another and used to regale their editors on their occasional trips to Washington.

Contrast the easygoing tolerance of that period with what happened to Gary Hart in 1987. On May 1 of that year, Hart was, according to all the polls, the leading contender for the Democratic nomination for president of the United States. That same day, editors of the *Miami Herald,* acting on a telephoned tip from an anonymous source, put a reporter on a flight to Washington, D.C., with instructions to look for an attractive young aspiring actress who supposedly was on her way to spend a weekend with the candidate. That night and the next day, *Herald* reporters kept Hart's Georgetown townhouse under surveillance. They did not try to hide what they were doing. One of them even attempted to interview Hart.

In its editions of Sunday, May 3, the *Herald* proclaimed in a page 1 story that, with his wife in Colorado, Hart had ''spent Friday night and most of Saturday'' at home with a young woman from Miami. On that same Sunday, the *New York Times Magazine's* lead story was a profile of Hart. It portrayed him favorably as a candidate with original ideas for coping with some of the nation's more serious problems. Hart's stature is further attested to by the fact that he was to speak to the American Society of Newspaper Editors on May 5. He kept that date. But by then the editors were far more interested in what he had to say about how he had spent the previous weekend than they were in his ideas for the presidency. Hart denied that he had done anything wrong. He said the reporters' incomplete surveillance had failed to detect the woman's departure through a back door. Nevertheless, before the week was out, Hart had abandoned his campaign for the presidential nomination and returned to Colorado with his wife.

---

82. Patrick J. Buchanan, *Right from the Beginning* (Boston: Little, Brown and Company, 1988), p. 275.

Here's how one widely circulated tabloid played the story of Gary Hart and Donna Rice—after the *Miami Herald* had staked out Hart's Washington, D.C., townhouse and reported that he and the model had spent a night together. At the time, Hart was considered the leading candidate for the Democratic nomination for president in 1988. He dropped out of the race shortly after the *Herald*'s story appeared. Was his privacy invaded? Legally, no. But journalists vigorously debated whether the *Herald* acted ethically. (AP/Wide World Photos)

In retrospect, it is too simplistic to contrast the media's treatment of John Kennedy with that of Gary Hart and conclude that the latter was the victim of sneaky, gossip-mongering reporters. In advance of that fateful weekend, Ellen Goodman, a syndicated columnist for the *Boston Globe,* had written about Hart and "the sex issue."[83] She argued that a candidate's sexual affairs are pertinent to an assessment of character. Noting "the old-boy tolerance of dalliance" that led reporters to ignore JFK's affairs, she said that times have changed. Women have been admitted into the system, bringing with them an awareness that "[y]ou do learn something important about the character of a man from revelations of his sexual behavior." Such behavior, she wrote, is "part of a whole portrait of a man," particularly one who is seeking the nation's highest office. The president is "not just a chief executive, but a chief figurehead, chief role model, chief moral leader—in short, chief American. We ask a great deal. Anyone who runs for the office today has to know that there is no room in the job description for chief womanizer."

She was one of those who wrote after the event to defend the surveillance conducted by the *Herald's* reporters and the newspaper's use of their story. A *New York Times* editorial refused to condone the reporters' methods but said the story served the public interest. The editorial said Hart had

83. Ellen Goodman, "Sex and Politics," *Louisville Courier-Journal,* 21 April 1987.

made himself a special case because of his emphasis on character at a time when members of his own staff were talking about his vulnerability on the womanizing issue.[84] David Broder of the *Washington Post,* whose political columns almost invariably take the high road, also found the methods flawed but justified in this instance. The findings answered important public questions about "Hart's truthfulness, his self-discipline, his sense of responsibility to other people—indeed, his willingness to face hard choices and realities."[85]

Others of equal stature strongly condemned the *Herald*'s methods and their deeper implications. Among them were three *New York Times* columnists, Tom Wicker, William Safire, and A. M. Rosenthal, former executive editor of the newspaper. Wicker and Safire argued that even candidates for high office are entitled to some degree of privacy. Wicker argued that candidates should be judged by their positions on important issues, not on who they may or may not have slept with.[86]

Rosenthal wrote that during his twenty years as a reporter he would have refused an assignment to hide outside a politician's house to find out whether he was in bed with somebody. As an editor for twenty-three more years, he would not have made such an assignment or allowed one of his subordinates to do so. In his opinion, the *Herald*'s editors were mistaken when they ordered the stakeout of Gray Hart's home. Calling for journalists to be as open in gathering news as they expect others to be in carrying out their duties, he concluded:

> In part this is simply a matter of taste. It is not to my taste to hang outside somebody's house in the middle of the night to see who goes in and out. It shows a lack of self-respect, a commodity a journalist does not give up when he gets a press card. It is also a matter of protection of journalism and the First Amendment, both of which have plenty of enemies as it is. If reputable papers such as the *Miami Herald* indulge in sneaky snooping that its editors would never tolerate around their own home, that is bad. But if the rest of the newspaper business justifies it, that's worse. We are begging the nation to treat us as unworthy of respect. In time, without any question, we will lose the support of the American public in the constant struggles against those who would erode the First Amendment. We cannot claim it was designed for voyeurs.[87]

Obviously, many editors, not all of them producing supermarket checkout tabloids, disagree. Stakeouts of the homes of newsworthy people are common in television journalism. Usually such surveillance produces no real news. But in Gary Hart's case, the stakeout did produce news and that news brought down a leading candidate for one party's presidential nomi-

---

84. "More Than Scandal," *New York Times,* 6 May 1987.
85. David Broder, "Too Often, the Media Don't Go Far Enough," Bloomington, Indiana, *Herald-Telephone,* 13 May 1987.
86. Tom Wicker, *Louisville Courier-Journal,* 7 May 1987, and William Safire, "Keyhole Journalism," *Louisville Courier-Journal,* 12 May 1987.
87. "Attack on the Herald," 8 May 1987.

nation. Whether, as Ellen Goodman suggests, he would eventually have fallen victim to his character flaws cannot be known. Nor is any connection established between a political leader's sexuality and his or her ability to govern. As Anthony Lewis, also a columnist for the *New York Times,* observed, eminent statesmen in both Britain and the United States, including Franklin D. Roosevelt, Dwight Eisenhower, and Winston Churchill, have not been saintly Puritans in their private lives.[88]

When private individuals are drawn into the news, the definition of a right of privacy becomes even more difficult. This is illustrated by the experience of John Harte, a photographer for the *Bakersfield Californian,* and his managing editor, Bob Bentley.[89] Harte was present when the body of a five-year-old drowning victim was dragged from a lake. He photographed the victim's father, mother, and older brother at the moment the body bag was opened to reveal the boy's face. The father is crouched over the body, his fists pressed tightly against his eyes. The older brother stands screaming in his mother's arms. Her face is distorted by a sob. The *Californian* used the photograph. In the next two days, the newspaper received more than 500 calls from people protesting what they saw as an invasion of the family's privacy. A bomb threat forced evacuation of the newspaper building. Bentley wrote a column, apologizing to the paper's readers. If he had it to do over, he said, he would not have run the photograph. He told Bob Greene, columnist for the *Chicago Tribune:*

> To me, this case is the strongest validation I've ever seen that newspapers are out of touch with their readers. We did something we thought was right, and the overwhelming majority of our readers thought it was wrong. They told us that by printing the picture, we had violated that child's memory....By running that picture we alienated the hell out of our readers, and if we don't respond to that, we're stupid.

Photographer Harte disagreed. "I'm proud of the shot," he said, adding that it stood as a powerful reminder to others to be careful in the water.

Bentley did not fault the photographer for taking the picture or for being proud of it. He agreed that it was a powerful and dramatic shot, so good that he told Greene he intended to nominate it for a Pulitzer Prize. If he did, it was not among the winners announced in April 1986. However, the winning photographs, taken by Carol Guzy and Michel DuCille of the *Miami Herald,* also portrayed death and grief—that of the victims of mudslides that followed the eruption of Nevado del Ruiz volcano in Colombia.

The dilemmas represented by Bentley's ambivalence are all too common in the professional world. Questions of privacy present more hard decisions than any others. Policies can be adopted and guidelines drafted, but they cannot cover all eventualities.

---

88. *Louisville Courier-Journal,* 6 May 1987.
89. See note 80. above.

Any generalizations about journalism professionals and their attitude toward privacy are likely to be fallacious. And yet one observation may be more valid than not. In recent years, journalists are talking more about ethical considerations than once was the case. In the mid-1980s, both the American Society of Newspaper Editors and the Associated Press Managing Editors Association commissioned credibility studies that were concerned in large part with the ethics of privacy. The Society of Professional Journalists issues annual reports surveying what it sees as the ethical lapses of the media. Each issue of *Quill,* the Society's magazine, has a section on ethics. *Editor & Publisher,* the newspaper trade magazine, has occasional articles on the subject. The list of textbooks designed for college courses on journalism ethics has grown impressively in the last decade. Seminars on journalism ethics are popular with journalists and the general public. All this activity suggests that many journalists are becoming less concerned about how much the law will let them get away with and more concerned with what a sense of compassion tells them they should do. Within the author's experience as a reporter and editor, journalists turned aside requests to keep embarrassing facts out of the paper or off the air with, "I don't make the news, I only report it." During the discussion of APME's credibility study at the association's annual meeting in San Francisco in October 1985, one editor said he now asks, on occasion. "How would I feel if this story were about me, or someone close to me?" That question will not resolve all privacy dilemmas—some embarrassing facts must be reported in the public interest—but it represents another, and welcome, approach.

FOR REVIEW

1. What is meant by "the right of privacy"? Why is the concept of particular interest to journalists?

2. List and define the four branches of invasion of privacy identified by William L. Prosser. Distinguish each from the others in terms of the elements of the offense.

3. How far can a reporter go in gathering news that takes place on private property? In obtaining information from reluctant news sources?

4. Define the limits of a photographer's right to take and use pictures for news purposes. Would the limits be any different if the photographs were to be used for feature purposes?

5. How have the courts defined an "embarrassing private fact"? How far can the news media go in reporting intimate details of a news subject's life?

6. What meaning does *Cox* v. *Cohn* have four journalists? To what extent, if any, was it modified by the Supreme Court's decision in *Florida Star?* Had

you been on the Court, how would you have voted in these cases? On what rationale would your vote have been based?

7. Does the term "public figure" have the same meaning in connection with invasion of privacy as it has in connection with libel?

8. Distinguish between false light and libel. What is the meaning of the *Hill* and *Cantrell* decisions?

9. List and justify a set of rules for use by an advertising agency planning to use identifiable persons in an advertising campaign.

10. What meaning does "the right of publicity" have in law? What hazards does this right raise for television news directors? For writers of magazine articles?

11. Expand on the meaning of newsworthiness, illustrating with examples from cases.

12. Expand on the meaning of consent, illustrating with examples from cases.

13. What is an expungement law? A sealed record? How do they relate to the work of the journalist?

14. In all states, records of juvenile offenders are kept secret unless released by a judge. Does this mean that the news media can be kept from disseminating names of juveniles who have committed crimes? Why or why not?

CHAPTER 6

''Jazz Age journalism'' was born in the 1920s when most U.S. cities had two or more highly competitive newspapers striving for a share of the audience. Sensationalism was considered the key to winning readers, and the era was made to order for it. Prohibition, which spanned the twenties, and the Depression, which ended them, spawned gangland wars and such figures as Al Capone, John Dillinger, Pretty Boy Floyd, and Bonnie and Clyde. Their crimes, and the crimes of others, were the subjects of breathlessly written stories bannered under screaming headlines on page 1. When suspects were arrested, particularly on charges of murder, reporters outdid each other to gather evidence that would prove the suspects guilty. In this trial by newspaper reporters were aided by police officers and prosecutors, eager to win a conviction and get their names in the papers. Defense attorneys, not to be outdone, sought to build backfires by giving reporters any shred of evidence that would help their clients. Most judges looked the other way. Only an occasional libertarian argued that the system violated the suspect's right to a fair trial. Once in a while it was discovered that an innocent

A FAIR AND PUBLIC TRIAL

person had been punished because prejudicial publicity pushed a jury to an improper conviction.

This system began to change about 1960, partly because of changes in journalism. Few cities were left with competitive newspapers, while television, although highly competitive, did not cover crime in detail. College-trained reporters and editors, a minority in most newsrooms prior to World War II, became the rule.

The audience had changed, too. Readers were better educated and more sophisticated in their concept of news. In any event, if they were interested in crime, they could see more of it in prime time television than in the real world—and the film version was a lot more exciting.

But a more important factor in the decline of trial by newspaper was the Warren Court. The term is a tribute to Earl Warren, who was appointed chief justice by President Eisenhower in 1953 and who served until 1969. Under his leadership, the Supreme Court of the United States did more to enlarge and protect the rights of criminal suspects than in any other time in its history. Two of its decisions, *Irvin* v. *Dowd*[1] in 1961 and *Sheppard* v. *Maxwell*[2] in 1966, served notice on judges everywhere that they should not permit prejudicial publicity in the news media to interfere with a suspect's right to a fair trial. The Court found that mandate in the Sixth Amendment:

> In all criminal prosecutions, the accused shall enjoy the right to a speedy and public trial, by an impartial jury of the State and district wherein the crime shall have been committed, which district shall have been previously ascertained by law, and to be informed of the nature and cause of the accusation; to be confronted with the witnesses against him; to have compulsory process for obtaining witnesses in his favor, and to have the assistance of counsel for his defense.

In this chapter, the focus will be on just four words of this amendment: "impartial jury" and "public trial." We will see that, starting with *Irvin*, the Court sought first to define what trial by an impartial jury is. In the process, it established criteria for determining whether a trial has been fair. With the *Sheppard*

1.　366 U.S. 717, 81 S.Ct. 1639, 6 L.Ed.2d 751 (1961).
2.　384 U.S. 333, 86 S.Ct. 1507, 16 L.Ed.2d 600 (1966).

decision five years later, attention was focused on measures judges are expected to take to ensure that a defendant gets a fair trial. In response to *Sheppard,* judges experimented with restraints, popularly called "gag orders," designed to cut off prejudicial information at the source. These took two forms: One was directed at participants in the trial—attorneys for both sides, witnesses, and court employees; the other was directed at reporters covering court proceedings at which prejudicial information was disclosed. Appellate courts have upheld restraint of participants, but only when the threat to a fair trial is clear. The Supreme Court has held that journalists can be subjected to restraint only under conditions that make such a step highly unlikely. However, in so holding, the Court suggested that judges might solve their problem by closing some court proceedings so that highly prejudicial information could be kept from reaching the public. This brought into question the meaning of the Sixth Amendment's guarantee of a public trial. In resolving that issue, the Supreme Court held that the First Amendment implies a right of journalists and the public to attend court proceedings. That right can be overcome only by evidence that the suspect cannot get a fair trial unless some specific part of the process is closed.

Reduced to a brief outline, the Court's twenty-five-year struggle to ensure that trials are both fair and open to the public is stripped of the strong feelings it has aroused. At the height of the struggle, lawyers and judges stood behind the Sixth Amendment, arguing that circulation- and ratings-hungry newspapers and broadcasters were trampling on the rights of criminal suspects. Opposing them, reporters and editors stood behind the First Amendment, arguing that courts and the bar were trampling on the people's right to be informed. Relations between the two sides were so strained at one point that it was news when a press-bar committee was formed in the state of Washington to attempt to reach some middle ground. Skirmishes still are being fought, but there is a middle ground now, and a better understanding on both sides of the accommodations that must be made if defendants are to be assured a fair and public trial, and the people are to be informed. This chapter therefore is a study of what happens when two rights, each directly guaranteed by the Bill of Rights, come into conflict.

Major Cases

- *Chandler* v. *Florida,* 449 U.S. 560, 101 S.Ct. 802, 66 L.Ed.2d 740 (1981).

- *Estes* v. *Texas,* 381 U.S. 532, 85 S.Ct. 1628, 14 L.Ed.2d 543 (1965).

- *Gannett* v. *DePasquale,* 443 U.S. 368, 99 S.Ct. 2898, 61 L.Ed.2d 608 (1979).

- *Globe Newspaper Co.* v. *Superior Court, County of Norfolk,* 457 U.S. 596, 102 S.Ct. 2613, 73 L.Ed.2d 248 (1982).

- *In re Russell,* 726 F.2d 1007 (4th Cir. 1984).

- *Irvin* v. *Dowd,* 366 U.S. 717, 81 S.Ct. 1639, 6 L.Ed.2d 751 (1961).

- *Murphy* v. *Florida,* 421 U.S. 794, 95 S.Ct. 2031, 44 L.Ed.2d 589 (1975).

- *Nebraska Press Association* v. *Stuart,* 427 U.S. 539, 96 S.Ct. 2791, 49 L.Ed.2d 683 (1976).

- *Patton* v. *Yount,* 467 U.S. 1025, 104 S.Ct. 2885, 81 L.Ed.2d 847 (1984).

- *Press-Enterprise Co.* v. *Superior Court of California, Riverside County,* 464 U.S. 501, 104 S.Ct. 819, 78 L.Ed.2d 629 (1984).

- *Press-Enterprise Co.* v. *Superior Court of California, Riverside County,* 478 U.S. 1, 106 S.Ct. 2735, 92 L.Ed.2d 1 (1986).

- *Richmond Newspapers* v. *Virginia,* 448 U.S. 555, 100 S.Ct. 2814, 65 L.Ed.2d 1973 (1980).

- *Rideau* v. *Louisiana,* 373 U.S. 723, 83 S.Ct. 1417, 9 L.Ed.2d 229 (1963).

- *Sheppard* v. *Maxwell,* 384 U.S. 333, 86 S.Ct. 1507, 16 L.Ed.2d 600 (1966).

- *State, ex rel. New Mexico Press Association* v. *Kaufman,* 98 N.M. 261, 648 P.2d 300 (N.Mex. 1982).

- *United States* v. *Dickinson,* 465 F.2d 496 (5th Cir. 1972).

- *United States* v. *Tijerina,* 412 F.2d 661 (10th Cir. 1969).

- *Waller* v. *Georgia,* 467 U.S. 39, 104 S.Ct. 2210, 81 L.Ed.2d 31 (1984).

THREATS TO A FAIR TRIAL

The Legal Process

The trial of a person accused of committing a crime is a ritual, with roots embedded deep in Anglo-Saxon history. However informal the process may sometimes seem, it is surrounded by safeguards designed to prevent the defendant's being railroaded into prison on flimsy evidence or in response to public clamor.

An individual is brought into the criminal justice system in most cases by an *arrest,* which is defined as "the taking of a person into custody for the purpose of charging him with a crime."[3] It is at this point that the nature of the crime and the identity of the suspect become known to the news media because arrests are matters of public record.

This public record is created by a process known as *booking,* that is, the formal entry into the police records system of the date, the time, the nature of the charge, the name of the person arrested, and the name of the arresting officer.

The arrested person is now under custody, and the next step usually is *detention* in jail or a holding cell. If the charge is minor, the suspect may be released on posting bail, or, if he has strong roots in the community, on his own recogni-

---

3. A. C. Germann, Frank D. Day, Robert R. J. Gallati, *Introduction to Law Enforcement and Criminal Justice* (Springfield, Ill.: Thomas, 1976), p. 192.

zance—that is, on his promise that he will show up for such further proceedings as may be scheduled. If the crime is a serious one, the setting of bail may be the subject of a hearing conducted by a judge. If the charge is murder, the suspect may be denied bail as a matter of law.

The next step is the drafting of the *formal accusation,* or *charge.* If the suspect was arrested on a warrant, that step was taken in advance. The formal accusation, which takes varying forms, depending on its origin, is a statement in legal language precisely defining the crime with which the suspect is accused. In federal cases involving serious crimes, the formal accusations must come from a *grand jury,* because the Fifth Amendment so requires. A grand jury is a group of persons whose names have been chosen at random and brought together for the purpose of deciding whether a crime has been committed and, if so, identifying the likely suspect. At the state level, the formal accusation can come from a grand jury or from the prosecutor, acting either on his own or on the basis of complaints from the victim, the police, or others. A formal accusation of crime resulting from a grand jury's investigation is called a bill of *indictment,* sometimes referred to as a ''true bill.'' If the suspect is not already in custody, the indictment may be sealed until he can be arrested.

What happens next varies from state to state and also varies with the manner in which the formal accusation was brought. A prompt *preliminary hearing* is generally required, although this can be waived by the defendant, and usually is if a grand jury has returned an indictment. If the hearing is not waived, the suspect is brought before a judge and the prosecution is required to (1) show that a crime has been committed; and (2) offer sufficient evidence to convince the judge there is a reasonable basis for connecting the accused with the crime. Such hearings are informal. The prosecution is permitted to present evidence that may not be admissible at trial. Because such information may be highly prejudicial to the defendant, the preliminary hearing has become one of the points of contention between the courts and the news media.

If the preliminary hearing results in a finding of ''probable cause,'' the next step is *arraignment.* Again the suspect is brought before a judge. The charge is read and explained, and the suspect is asked how he pleads. If the defendant pleads guilty, all that remains is sentencing. If he pleads not guilty, the next step is the trial.

However, trial is the exception. In most instances, while the steps above are taking place, the prosecutor and the defense attorney will have been engaged in *plea bargaining.* A defendant charged with armed robbery, a serious crime, may balk at pleading guilty to that charge, but may agree, through his attorney, to do so to a lesser charge of simple assault. Or a defendant charged with driving under the influence, and facing a possible loss of his driver's license, may agree to plead guilty to reckless driving. Most cases are disposed of in this way because neither prosecutors' staffs nor the courts themselves could otherwise cope with the large numbers of persons charged with crime.

If the decision is made to go to trial, the defendant may choose to be tried by a judge, or a panel of judges in a serious case, or by a jury. If there is to be a jury, the first day or days of the trial will be concerned with selection of its members. Prospective jurors are chosen by lot from lists of registered voters, taxpayers, or telephone owners, and are supposed to represent a cross section of the community. The judge has the duty of questioning each candidate closely to weed out those who may be prejudiced for or against the defendant. This questioning is called *voir dire*—a French phrase meaning literally, "to say truly." Practically, in the voir dire prospective jurors are questioned closely by the judge, in the presence of the defendant and counsel for both sides. The purpose is to discover any prejudices or personal information that might influence a juror's decision.

Once the jury has been chosen, the trial itself is as rigidly structured as a Bach fugue. Here is a summary of its elements:

THE OPENING STATEMENTS   First the prosecutor and then the defense attorney tells the court his version of the facts and the likely testimony. What is said is argument, not evidence, and the judge will caution the jury to avoid drawing conclusions from it.

THE STATE'S CASE   The prosecutor calls witnesses whose testimony is designed to prove the defendant guilty beyond reasonable doubt. Each witness is subject to cross-examination by defense counsel, who will do all he can to raise doubt about the credibility of each. If the cross-examination produces new information, the prosecutor may follow with redirect examination, which may open the witness to recross-examination.

This process, niggling and repetitive as it may seem, is the heart of the trial. The burden of proof is on the prosecutor, and it is a strong one. He cannot win a guilty verdict unless his evidence can convince each member of the jury beyond a reasonable doubt. In contrast, the defense attorney's job is much simpler. All he must do is raise doubt in the mind of one strong-willed juror. If he can do so, the worst he can get is a hung jury—that is, a jury that cannot agree. A few states permit majority verdicts if the offense is minor, but in most the jury's verdict must be unanimous. If the jury cannot agree, then the state must decide whether to go to the time and expense of another trial, or dismiss the charge.

THE DEFENSE CASE   If the defense attorney thinks the prosecution's case is weak, he will move to dismiss. If the judge agrees, the defendant is freed. If not, the defense presents its case. Its witnesses may merely attack the credibility of the state's case, or they may offer an affirmative defense, such as alibi or self-defense. The defendant is not required to testify. Indeed, if he is a repeat offender, it is unlikely he will be called. If he doesn't testify, the rules of the court forbid any mention of his criminal record. The court operates on the theory that a prior arrest record, or even a term in prison for a similar offense, has nothing to do with proving guilt in the current case. However, if the defendant does choose to testify, the prior record may be introduced by the prosecution to impeach his testimony—that is, to raise doubt in the minds of the jurors as to how far he can be trusted to tell the truth.

REBUTTAL   Witnesses may be offered to respond to allegations made by the defense, or to answer questions raised by it. If the process discloses new evidence, the defense has an opportunity for surrebuttal.

SUMMATION OR CLOSING ARGUMENT   After all the evidence is in, first the defense counsel and then the prosecutor offers his summary of the case. Again, the jury is cautioned that what is said is not evidence. Each attorney summarizes the testimony in a manner calculated to lead the jury to the desired conclusion.

INSTRUCTING THE JURY   The judge is responsible for seeing that the trial is conducted in accord with pertinent law and constitutional safeguards. It is the jury's duty to decide what the evidence means. However, that decision cannot be made without some awareness of the law. The judge may tell the jury, for instance, that it cannot find the defendant guilty if it concludes he was legally insane at the moment the crime was committed. He probably will instruct the jury further on the legal criteria involved in determining insanity. The jury is the ultimate finder of fact. It alone can decide which witnesses to believe, which versions of two or more conflicting stories to accept. The judge also ''charges'' the jury by seeking to impress it with the duty to bring in a verdict based solely on the evidence seen and heard in court.

DELIBERATION   The jury retires to a jury room where it remains until it reaches a verdict. The jurors select one of their number to act as foreman, who seeks to lead them to a verdict. If the judge's instructions on the law permit, the jury may find the defendant guilty of a lesser offense.

MOTIONS   If the defendant is found guilty, motions are in order. Usually at this point, the defense will allege that the judge erred in rulings on points of law raised during the trial. This provides grounds for a possible appeal.

JUDGMENT   The judge issues the decision of the court, making formal the verdict of the jury. Imposition of the penalty usually is deferred pending an investigation designed to guide the judge to a choice of several alternative sentences ranging from release on probation to a long term in prison.

The process is designed to make the state prove its case through valid evidence that goes to the point of the offense with which the defendant is charged. Evidence that does not bear directly on the offense, or that has been obtained in violation of the defendant's rights, is not supposed to be submitted to the jury. For instance, a confession is not admissible as evidence if the defendant had not been advised of his Fifth Amendment right to remain silent and the right to consult a lawyer. Sometimes a hearing on the admissibility of evidence may be the most important element in the criminal process. If a confession is the strongest evidence the prosecution has, a ruling excluding it from the trial may mean that the defendant goes free.

Fair-trial issues are raised when the news media report the existence of evidence that cannot, under the rules, be used at the trial. Jurors are screened at the start of the trial to find out whether they have knowledge of such evidence. Once chosen, they are admonished not to read or listen to news accounts of the trial. But on occasion courts have found that news reports of inadmissible evidence were so pervasive that the jurors could not have been impartial. In such instance, the defendant either must be submitted to a new trial, or go free.

Defining an Impartial Jury

The concern with prejudicial publicity and its presumed effect on the right to a fair trial is not new. Aaron Burr, a former vice-president of the United States, raised the question in 1807 when he was tried for treason because of his alleged part in a conspiracy to set up an independent nation somewhere between the Ohio and Mississippi rivers. He asked that the indictment be dismissed, arguing that inflammatory articles in the *Alexandria* (Va.) *Expositor* and other newspapers had turned the minds of potential jurors against him. The great Chief Justice John Marshall, sitting as a trial judge, rebuffed that argument, setting standards used to this day in selecting juries. He wrote in *United States* v. *Burr*[4]:

> The great value of trial by jury certainly consists in its fairness and impartiality. Those who most prize the institution prize it because it furnishes a tribunal which may be expected to be uninfluenced by an undue bias of the mind. I have always conceived [that]...an impartial jury...must be composed of men who will fairly hear the testimony which may be offered to them, bring in their verdict according to that testimony, and according to the laws arising on it.

Marshall noted the obvious: Persons who have made up their minds in advance about the defendant's guilt or innocence cannot be impartial. This does not mean, he added, that potential jurors must be completely ignorant of the defendant or of the crime. Even in the society of 1807, that would be too much to expect. Therefore, jurors can be considered impartial if they hold "light impressions [as to guilt or innocence] which may fairly be supposed to yield to the testimony...which may leave the mind open to a fair consideration of that testimony...."

An impartial juror, then, is one whose mind is not made up in advance, but who is willing to listen to the evidence and evaluate it fairly. In Burr's case, jurors chosen by Marshall's criteria listened to the evidence for six months and found the defendant not guilty.

The passage of nearly two centuries has not materially changed Chief Justice Marshall's definition of an impartial jury. It is made up of men and women whose minds are open to the testimony offered in court and who will base their decision solely on that evidence. In the America of the early 1800s, sources of information that might prejudice members of a jury were confined largely to the weekly newspapers and to word of mouth. Today, we are surrounded by communications media that use graphic devices, market research, and the latest discoveries of the communications theorists in an attempt to get us to pay attention to them. Not surprisingly, this has raised new questions about the influences that can prevent people from being impartial jurors.

Some of these questions have focused on what makes a potential juror biased. In a University of Chicago study, judges noted that suspects were denied a fair trial because jurors had read or heard about confessions that were made in violation of constitutional safeguards. Other jurors were prejudiced by reading or

---

4. 25 Fed.Cas. 49 (No. 14,692g) (1807).

hearing about the results of lie detector tests, which are not admissible as evidence, the defendant's prior criminal record, or evidence seized in violation of the suspect's right of privacy.[5] By an overwhelming majority, these judges said they believed it "inappropriate" for the news media to publish such information in advance of a trial. However, they also said, as Marshall had many years earlier, they they did not believe jurors needed to be altogether ignorant of the facts of a case in order to be impartial.

Studies of jury performance are inconclusive. One researcher concluded that "the jury is a pretty stubborn, healthy institution not likely to be overwhelmed either by a remark of counsel or a remark of the press."[6] A federal appeals court judge in Chicago once told an audience of newspaper editors that he had learned during his days as a trial judge that most potential jurors hadn't paid much attention to stories of crime. He said very few had made up their minds as to guilt or innocence because of what they read.[7] But the fact remains that in a significant number of cases since 1960 federal and state courts have found that pervasive media publicity given to inadmissible evidence and prior criminal records has caused jurors to come to the trial with their minds not only closed but with their opinion as to guilt or innocence already formed. Thus, they have not been impartial jurors, as required by the Sixth Amendment. As a result of such findings, some criminal defendants have been set free, and others have had to go through new trials with some juries confirming the original verdict and others coming to opposite conclusions.

Causes of an Unfair Trial

A little-noted decision of the Warren Court in 1959 marked the beginning of a new attitude toward trial by newspaper. In *Marshall* v. *United States*,[8] the Supreme Court reversed the conviction of a drug dealer. The Court held that the jurors had been improperly influenced by reading that Marshall had been convicted twice previously. The verdict was of limited interest because the conviction had been in a federal court, so that the decision applied only to the federal court system, which was not heavily involved with criminal cases at the time.

Irvin v. *Dowd,* 366 U.S. 717, 81 S.Ct. 1639, 6 L.Ed.2d 751 (1961).

Two years later, the Court won a great deal of attention with its reversal of a murder conviction that came up to it from the state courts in Indiana. With its decision in *Irvin* v. *Dowd,* the

5. Fred S. Siebert, "Trial Judges' Opinions of Prejudicial Publicity," in Chilton R. Bush, ed., *Free Press and Fair Trial* (Athens: University of Georgia Press, 1970), pp. 2–19. The poll was conducted by the National Opinion Research Center at the University of Chicago.
6. Walter Wilcox, "The Press, the Jury and the Behavioral Sciences," in *Free Press and Fair Trial,* pp. 67–102, quoting Harry K. Kalven, Jr., coauthor with Hans Zeisel of *The American Jury* (Boston: Little, Brown, 1966).
7. "Notable and Quotable," *Wall Street Journal,* 5 May 1976, quoting Judge William J. Bauer of the United States Court of Appeals, Seventh Circuit, in a speech to the American Society of Newspaper Editors.
8. 360 U.S. 310, 79 S.Ct. 1171, 3 L.Ed.2d 1250 (1959).

Court established a principle of constitutional law applicable to all courts, state or federal. The Court held that verdicts reached by jurors who have been influenced by prejudicial publicity violate the Sixth Amendment guarantee of trial by an impartial jury. The *Irvin* decision led to three others in the next five years, making clear the Court's insistence that criminal suspects be tried in the courts rather than in the news media. Each case dealt with a different aspect of media interference with a fair trial. Each also reversed a conviction, leading some editors to accuse the Supreme Court of placing a higher value on the rights of criminals than on a free press.

In *Irvin,* the defendant was Leslie Irvin, who was accused of killing six persons in and near Evansville, Indiana. He showed so little remorse for what he had done that one newspaper story compared his actions to those of a mad dog. Copy editors picked up on that theme, producing headlines about "Mad Dog Irvin." By the time the case came to trial, surveys showed that practically everyone within reach of the Evansville newspapers and broadcasting stations had heard about Irvin and believed him guilty. In an attempt to escape the effects of the publicity, the trial was moved out of Evansville to nearby Gibson County. But there, too, questioning revealed that most prospective jurors knew about the murders. A jury quickly found the defendant guilty and sentenced him to death.

When the Supreme Court agreed to review the verdict, Irvin's attorney offered evidence showing that nine of the twelve jurors had made up their minds as to the defendant's guilt before they had heard any of the testimony. The Court held that in the face of such overwhelming evidence of media-created prejudice a fair trial was impossible.

Irvin was retried in central Indiana, many miles from Evansville and again was found guilty. He was sentenced to a life term and is still in prison.

The next two fair-trial decisions of the Supreme Court involved television coverage, in one instance of a confession made in a jail cell and in the other of the trial itself. In the first case, *Rideau* v. *Louisiana,* the Court held that the inclusion of the confession on three newscasts in two days created an "atmosphere of prejudice" which made selecting an impartial jury impossible. In the second, *Estes* v. *Texas,* the Court speculated that the mere presence of television cameras in the courtroom influenced the participants in such a way as to make a fair trial impossible. In neither case did the Court require evidence, as it had in *Irvin,* that jurors actually were prejudiced against the defendants.

Rideau v. Louisiana, 373 U.S. 723, 83 S.Ct. 1417, 9 L.Ed.2d 229 (1963). In neither case was there much doubt as to the defendant's guilt, and both were convicted when they were tried again. Wilbert Rideau had robbed a bank in Lake Charles, Louisiana. He took three of the bank's employees as hostages on his getaway and killed one of them before he was captured. The morning after his arrest, Rideau was visited in his jail cell by the sheriff, who was followed by a television camera crew. With the sheriff asking the questions, Rideau talked about the robbery, freely admitting that he had killed one of the hostages. When the Supreme Court reviewed his conviction, Justice Potter Stewart wrote that for the tens of thousands of people who had seen the telecasts, Rideau's trial had taken place in his jail cell, and his own words had proved his guilt. The Court held that where there is pervasive exposure to such prejudicial publicity, a trial cannot be fair.

Estes v. *Texas,* 381 U.S. 532, 85 S.Ct. 1628, 14 L.Ed.2d 543 (1965).

Billie Sol Estes was one of the most prominent young businessmen in Texas when he was charged with swindling hundreds of farmers out of millions of dollars. He had made *Time* magazine's man-of-the-year list and was a friend of two presidents of the United States. Under rules of court then in effect only in Texas and Colorado, television and still photographers were permitted in the court room during his preliminary hearing and again during his trial. However, at the trial the photographers operated under restraints that placed them behind a false wall out of sight of most participants and spectators. Nevertheless, five members of the Supreme Court concluded that the jurors may have been distracted by the cameras and their "telltale red lights." Justice Tom C. Clark, who wrote the Court's opinion, cited no evidence to support the majority's belief that

An Associated Press photographer took this photograph of Billie Sol Estes (center) during his 1962 trial on swindling charges. Four years later, the Supreme Court held that the taking of this and other photographs, including the televising of parts of the trial, prevented Estes from getting a fair trial. However, the Court stopped one vote short of holding that photographing trial proceedings would prevent a fair trial in all instances. Consequently, most states now permit some courtroom photography. (AP/Wide World Photos)

the presence of the cameras converted Estes's trial into a theatrical event. How-ever, Clark concluded: "A defendant on trial for his life is entitled to his day in court, not in a stadium, or a city or a nationwide arena. The heightened public clamor resulting from radio or television coverage will inevitably result in preju-dice. Trial by television is, therefore, foreign to our system."

The day was saved for photojournalism by Justice John Marshall Harlan, the fifth member of the majority. He agreed that the presence of cameras had kept Estes from getting a fair trial in this instance. But he was unwilling to conclude, as the other four had, that courtroom cameras would in all circumstances prevent a fair trial. We will see later in this chapter how Harlan's separate concurring opinion was used by a later Supreme Court to uphold the right of photojournalists to record court proceedings.

Sheppard v. *Maxwell,* **384 U.S. 333, 86 S.Ct. 1507, 16 L.Ed.2d 600 (1966).** The Supreme Court's fourth fair-trial case in the 1960s was to become its most celebrated de-cision in this area of law. In *Sheppard* v. *Max-well* the Court not only reversed the murder con-viction of a socially prominent surgeon but went on to tell judges what they must do to prevent prejudicial publicity from interfer-ing with the right to a fair trial. Dr. Sam Sheppard had been found guilty in 1954 of murdering his wife and had served ten years in Ohio State Penitentiary before the Supreme Court accepted his case for review. From the beginning, the doctor asserted his innocence. He said his wife had been beaten to death by a bushy-haired stranger whom he had surprised in the act and who had fled from the house onto a beach along nearby Lake Erie. Because no one else had seen such a stranger, and because it was known that Sheppard and his wife were having marital problems, he quickly became the center of suspicion. When police did not act on that suspicion, Cleveland's three newspapers demanded that they do so.

One headline proclaimed, "Somebody Is Getting Away with Murder." An-other demanded, "Why Isn't Sam Sheppard in Jail?" His arrest followed within hours.

During the weeks leading up to his trial, Cleveland's newspapers and radio and television stations laid down a barrage of stories designed to prove Sheppard's guilt. It was alleged that he had had affairs with a number of women, and that his wife lived in fear of him, but had refused to give him a divorce. One story re-ported as fact that Sheppard had delayed reporting his wife's murder while he washed away a trail of blood leading from the bedroom and disposed of the mur-der weapon. When jurors were chosen for the trial, the newspapers published their names and addresses. All said they received letters and telephone calls from persons trying to influence them. So many reporters wanted to cover the trial that the judge, Herbert Blythin, ordered an extra press table set up inside the bar of the court. It was so close to the defense table that Sheppard had to confer with his lawyers in a whisper to avoid being overheard. Newspaper and radio report-ers took over adjacent courthouse offices. Television cameras kept a vigil on the sidewalk outside the courthouse where interviews were conducted with wit-nesses. The judge would not permit cameras in the courtroom while court was in session, but he made an arrangement with photographers that made the ban a mockery. At each recess, they would burst through the doors, cameras ready, and take their pictures before the witness could leave his chair.

Through more than six weeks of trial, the jurors were permitted to go home each evening. Judge Blythin told them not to read, view, or listen to any reports about the case, but made only the most perfunctory attempts to find out whether his order was being obeyed. If the jurors did disobey him, they read and heard about an altogether different trial from the one conducted in the courtroom. News media, local and national, consistently reported "evidence" from "witnesses" who were not even called to testify. Newscasters of prominence argued on radio that the evidence proved Sheppard guilty long before the trial had ended.

Shortly before Christmas 1954, the jury found Sam Sheppard guilty of the murder of his wife. He was sentenced to life in the penitentiary. He appealed to both the Ohio and U.S. Supreme Courts, arguing that prejudicial publicity had prevented his getting a fair trial. With the *Irvin* decision still seven years in the future, both courts rejected his plea. But in 1964, with the groundwork laid by the *Irvin* and *Rideau* decisions, Sheppard's family hired a prominent defense attorney, F. Lee Bailey, who was able to persuade a newly appointed U.S. district court judge in Dayton, Ohio, to order Sheppard's release on the ground that his conviction was the product of a media "carnival" that not only polluted the atmosphere with inadmissible evidence but violated the serenity of the courtroom. An appeals court disagreed, but the Supreme Court reversed, upholding the district judge's order that Sheppard be subjected to a new trial or set free. In holding that Sheppard had been the victim of a biased jury, the Court reiterated a basic principle of jurisprudence: A judge's first duty is to make certain that a trial is conducted fairly, solely on the basis of admissible evidence.

Justice Clark, writing for seven members of the Court, started with praise for "a responsible press." Over the years, he said, the media have guarded "against the miscarriage of justice by subjecting police, prosecutors, and judicial processes to extensive scrutiny and criticism." Clark endorsed that coverage, noting that the press had been "the handmaiden of effective judicial administration."

He turned next to Judge Blythin's conduct of the trial. Here, he was more critical, holding that the judge had not done as much as he should to protect the jurors from media influences. Indeed, he had permitted the media to turn them into celebrities of a sort by publicizing their names, addresses, and photographs. As a result, the jurors had been exposed "to expressions of opinion from both cranks and friends."

Additionally, by giving reporters and photographers almost free rein in and around the courtroom, the judge had deprived Sheppard of the "judicial serenity and calm to which [he] was entitled." Clark wrote:

> The fact is that bedlam reigned at the courthouse during the trial and newsmen took over practically the entire courtroom, hounding most of the participants in the trial, especially Sheppard....[T]he judge lost his ability to supervise the environment. The movement of the reporters in and out of the courtroom caused frequent confusion and disruption of the trial.

Thus, the Court, which had found television cameras a distracting influence in *Estes,* found reporters and photographers, whatever their medium, to be a problem when they were permitted to take over the courtroom and its environs. Because reporters entered and left the courtroom as they pleased, because photographers congregated in the corridors ready to pounce when the courtroom doors were opened, because witnesses and other participants were fair game for on-the-spot interviews, the ''judicial serenity'' that should have surrounded the trial was lost. Further, by giving publicity to members of the jury, the media had ensured that they would be subjected to pressure from anyone who felt moved to pick up a telephone and call them. All this was in addition to a massive barrage of prejudicial tips, rumors, and speculation pointing to Sheppard's guilt. The Court concluded that a trial conducted under such circumstances could not possibly have been fair. Sam Sheppard's life sentence was set aside. He was entitled to a new trial.

So serious was the problem of prejudicial publicity seen to be that the Court had moved in five years from a holding that convictions in criminal cases should be set aside if the defendant could show that the jury was prejudiced by media publicity to a much looser position. It had held in *Rideau* that convictions might be reversed if the jury was chosen from a locality permeated by prejudicial publicity. With *Estes* and *Sheppard,* courts seemed to be told to decide on a case-by-case basis whether publicity before and during a trial, coupled with distracting conduct on the part of the media, raised a presumption that jurors were prejudiced. If so, there must be a new trial or the suspect must be set free. All four decisions, and the earlier *Marshall* decision as well, accepted as a fact that publicity given to such things as prior criminal records—Irvin had a long one, for example—and inadmissible evidence has an unacceptable influence on jurors. At the time, judges reading the Supreme Court's decisions were acting on the assumption that juror exposure to news stories of any kind dealing with the case at hand made a fair trial unlikely. Given the pervasive penetration of the media in modern society, questions were being raised about the trial system itself. Could not a clever criminal escape punishment by committing a crime on television, as when Jack Ruby shot down Lee Harvey Oswald, the suspected assassin of President John F. Kennedy at Dallas in 1963? What could judges do to ensure that defendants in highly publicized cases were tried in the courtroom rather than in the media?

ENSURING A FAIR TRIAL

The Supreme Court's decision in *Sheppard* went beyond its previous fair-trial decisions in that the Court prescribed steps trial judges might take to counteract prejudicial media publicity. In doing so, it recognized that reversal, and a new trial years after the crime had been committed, did not always lead to justice.

The prescriptions in *Sheppard* began with such basic remedies as a more vigorous voir dire, which always had been part of the jury selection procedure, and change of venue, the moving of the trial to another locality not reached by news stories about the crime and the defendant. These remedies have aroused little controversy, but some of the others have. For instance, some judges reading *Sheppard* have imposed "gag orders." These are orders of the court directing witnesses, lawyers, defendants, and others involved in a trial not to talk to outsiders about the case. Such orders, which are classic prior restraints of the kind discussed in Chapter 2, have also been imposed on journalists who have become aware of prejudicial information through court proceedings. Judges have sought, too, to cut off prejudicial publicity at its source by closing legal proceedings at which prejudicial information might be disclosed or discussed. The latter measures have led to serious conflict between the legal establishment, as it has sought to protect the Sixth Amendment rights of defendants, and journalists, as they have sought to protect First Amendment freedoms. At least half a dozen times in the twenty years after *Sheppard* the Supreme Court has felt compelled to try to resolve various aspects of that conflict.

The Supreme Court Prescribes Remedies

In the Court's *Sheppard* decision, it had concluded that Judge Blythin had lost control of the proceedings. Because he had given reporters and photographers a free rein in and out of the courtroom, he had sacrificed the "judicial serenity and calm" that are essential to a fair trial. Thus, Sam Sheppard was entitled to a new trial at which his right to trial by an impartial jury must be protected.

At that point in the decision, Justice Clark turned to a discussion of remedies that Judge Blythin could have used to ensure a fair trial originally. Clark wrote that the judge had compounded the problems arising from the conduct of reporters and photographers by making no effort to cut off the flood of prejudicial news stories at their source. At the start of the trial, he had announced "that neither he nor anyone else could restrict prejudicial news accounts." He repeated the view many times thereafter. But, said Clark, Blythin looked at the wrong target when he saw the news media as the sources of that problem. What he should have done, and could have done, was to take steps to prevent prejudicial information from reaching the news media. Clark made some specific suggestions:

> The carnival atmosphere at trial could easily have been avoided since the courtroom and courthouse premises are subject to the control of the court....Bearing in mind the massive pretrial publicity, the judge should have adopted stricter rules governing the use of the courtroom by newsmen, as Sheppard's counsel requested. The number of reporters in the courtroom itself could have been limited at the first sign that their presence would disrupt the trial. They certainly should not have been placed inside the bar. Furthermore, the judge should have more closely regulated the conduct of newsmen in the courtroom....
>
> Secondly, the court should have insulated the witnesses. All of the newspapers and radio stations apparently interviewed prospective witnesses at will, and in many instances disclosed their testimony....
>
> Thirdly, the court should have made some effort to control the release of leads, information, and gossip to the press by police officers, witnesses, and the counsel

for both sides. Much of the information thus disclosed was inaccurate, leading to groundless rumors and confusion....

Defense counsel immediately brought to the court's attention the tremendous amount of publicity in the Cleveland press that "misrepresented entirely the testimony" in the case. Under such circumstances, the judge should have at least warned the newspapers to check the accuracy of their accounts....The prosecution repeatedly made evidence available to the news media which was never offered in trial. Much of the "evidence" disseminated in this fashion was clearly inadmissible. The exclusion of such evidence in court is rendered meaningless when the news media make it available to the public....

More specifically, the trial court might well have proscribed extrajudicial statements by any lawyer, party, witness, or court official which divulged prejudicial matters, such as the refusal of Sheppard to submit to interrogation or take any lie detector tests; any statement made by Sheppard to officials; the identity of prospective witnesses or their probable testimony; any belief in guilt or innocence; or like statements concerning the merits of the case....[T]he court could also have requested the appropriate city and county officials to promulgate a regulation with respect to dissemination of information about the case by their employees. In addition, reporters who wrote or broadcast prejudicial stories could have been warned as to the impropriety of publishing material not introduced in the proceedings....In this manner, Sheppard's right to a trial free from outside interference would have been given added protection without corresponding curtailment of the news media. Had the judge, the other officers of the court, and the police placed the interest of justice first, the news media would have soon learned to be content with the task of reporting the case as it unfolded in the courtroom—not pieced together from extrajudicial statements.

...Given the pervasiveness of modern communications and the difficulty of effacing prejudicial publicity from the minds of jurors, the trial courts must take strong measures to ensure that the balance is never weighed against the accused. And appellate courts have the duty to make an independent evaluation of the circumstances. Of course, there is nothing that proscribes the press from reporting events that transpire in the courtroom.

Clark ended by mentioning other steps judges might take in cases like this one, "where there is a reasonable likelihood that prejudicial news prior to trial will prevent a fair trial." The start of the trial can be postponed until the publicity dies down, or the judge can order a change of venue, that is, transfer of the trial to a court not reached by the publicity. If prejudicial publicity continues during the trial, the judge can sequester the jury or declare a mistrial and start over. But Clark emphasized that the cure lies with trial judges, who must "protect their processes from prejudicial outside interferences."

Sam Sheppard was freed from prison and retried late in 1966. Witnesses had died. Memories had faded. A jury acquitted him. Sheppard tried to resume his practice of osteopathy, but was the subject of several malpractice suits. He quit his practice and turned to other things. Immediately after his release from prison, he had married a German immigrant with whom he had corresponded. That ended in divorce. Not long before he died of liver disease in 1970, he became a professional wrestler in the stable of a promoter working out of Columbus, Ohio. He married the promoter's nineteen-year-old daughter, who became his widow.

A book and a television movie later portrayed him as the innocent victim of a vendetta inspired by the *Cleveland Press*.[9] Others remained convinced the first jury was right.

Courts have found ten remedies implicit or explicit in Justice Clark's decision. Six of these either were noncontroversial because they had always been part of the trial process, or have been upheld so firmly by appellate courts that they have become taken for granted. The other four remain controversial. Here is a summary of the ten remedies:

1. Continuance to allow the effect of an initial burst of publicity to subside. However, the Supreme Court has ruled that undue delay violates the speedy trial clause of the Sixth Amendment.[10] Rules of court now require dismissal of cases that do not reach trial within a specified time after arraignment, unless the delay is attributable to the defense. Six months is a common limit.

2. Change of venue, now quite common.

3. Rigorous use of voir dire to screen out prospective jurors who have made up their minds as a result of pretrial publicity.

4. Restrictions on the number of reporters who are permitted to cover trials that attract massive attention in the media, and on the comings and goings of reporters in the courtroom while court is in session.

5. Banishment of photographers from the courtroom and its environs. However, there have been significant changes in attitude on the part of judges in more than half the states, and of the Supreme Court itself, with respect to the photographing of trial proceedings.

6. Sequestration of the jury. Most judges consider this a tool of last resort. Jurors resent being kept virtual prisoners for the duration of a trial, especially if it is a long one.

The remedies that have generated continuing controversy are:

7. Gag orders directed at participants in the trial, including attorneys. These restrictive orders have raised First Amendment questions. However, most appeals courts have upheld the right of trial judges to order participants in the proceedings to refrain from talking to reporters and others, provided that a sufficient need is demonstrated. Some courts require evidence of a clear and present danger to the right of the accused to a fair trial.

   Additionally, attorneys who talk to reporters and disclose prejudicial information are subject to discipline by the bar and the courts. The Code

---

9. Jack H. Pollack, *Dr. Sam: An American Tragedy* (Chicago: H. Regnery Co., 1972). The television movie, *Guilty or Innocent: The Sam Sheppard Murder Case*, was presented by NBC on 17 November 1975.
10. Barker v. Wingo, 407 U.S. 514, 92 S.Ct. 2182, 33 L.Ed. 2d 101 (1972).

of Ethics of the American Bar Association defines the kinds of information likely to be prejudicial and establishes guidelines for the release of information by lawyers involved in criminal cases. Generally, it says that lawyers should confine their public disclosures to factual information of the kind likely to be admitted as evidence without much question at trial. Lawyers are not supposed to talk about such things as confessions, tests, the possibility of a guilty plea, and witnesses and their likely testimony because these are matters to be resolved during the trial process.[11] Occasionally, a lawyer will be punished for violating the guidelines. For instance, F. Lee Bailey, who conducted Sam Sheppard's successful appeal, was suspended from the practice of law in New Jersey for one year for violating state judicial canons against pretrial publicity.[12]

8. Gag orders directed at reporters. This led to a decision of the Supreme Court that makes it difficult, if not impossible, for judges to justify such orders.

9. Closing to the press and public of certain parts of the trial process—preliminary hearings, bail hearings, and hearings on the admissibility of evidence. After four Supreme Court decisions in this area, the controversy continues, but the decisions make clear that court proceedings presumptively are open. They are to be closed only as a last resort to ensure a fair trial.

10. Refusing to release the names and addresses of jurors to the news media.

By applying the above remedies conscientiously, trial court judges have reduced considerably the number of reversals based on prejudicial publicity. As we will now see, they also have generated some notable media-bar confrontations.

Restraining Participants in a Trial

In *Sheppard,* Justice Clark suggested that Judge Blythin should have tried to cut off some of the flood of prejudicial publicity at its source by "proscrib[ing] extrajudicial statements by any lawyer, party, witness or court official...." He acted on the theory that the media don't create news; they only report what sources are willing to disclose. If there are no prejudicial disclosures, there will be no prejudicial stories.

This sometimes is easier said than done. A judge can enforce a gag order only against persons within the jurisdiction of the court. This includes employees of the court; witnesses appearing under subpoena, which is an order of the court; parties to the action, or attorneys representing them. Further, the judge must make a finding, based on evidence, that there is "a clear and present danger, or a reasonable likelihood, of a serious and imminent danger to the administration of

11. American Bar Association Legal Advisory Committee on Fair Trial and Free Press, *The Rights of Fair Trial and Free Press* (1969).
12. "Jersey Suspends F. Lee Bailey from Practice," *New York Times,* 9 February 1971.

justice.''[13] Such findings must be made on a case-by-case basis. For instance, the United States Court of Appeals, Seventh Circuit, rejected an attempt to impose gag orders in all trials through a standing order of the court.[14]

United States v. *Tijerina,* **412 F. 2d 661 (10th Cir. 1969).** In two cases with strong political overtones, federal appeals courts have held that gag orders do not unduly violate the First Amendment rights of participants. The first, *United States* v. *Tijerina,* involved five members of a Spanish-Mexican civil rights group. All were charged with assault on federal forest rangers and damage of government-owned trucks. The five had led an attempt to occupy federal parklands that they contended had been taken illegally from the original native owners. Because feelings were running high, the federal district court judge assigned to the case issued an order forbidding the defendants and other participants in the trial from making any public statement about it.

When the civil rights group conducted a meeting some days later, two of the defendants spoke, urging members to demonstrate against their arrest, which they viewed as political. Police gave the trial judge a tape of the speeches. He found the speakers in contempt for violating his order.

The speakers, Tijerina and Noll, appealed, arguing that they had a right under the First Amendment to plead their case where they wished. They also argued that because the order had been issued to protect their right to a fair trial, they could disregard it if they chose. The United States Court of Appeals, Tenth Circuit, held that they were wrong on both counts. Their proper course was to appeal the gag order, not defy it. In any event, the public also has an interest in insisting on a fair trial. In this instance, that right could be thwarted unless the gag order was obeyed by all to whom it applied, including both the prosecution and the defense. The court observed that the Sixth Amendment requires that the trial be in a courtroom, not in a convention hall, and that the outcome be determined by a jury, not by a mob.

In re Russell, **726 F. 2d 1007 (4th Cir. 1984).** In 1984, in *In re Russell,* the United States Court of Appeals, Fourth Circuit, upheld a gag order imposed on seventeen potential witnesses in the trial of several members of the Ku Klux Klan and the Nazi party. The defendants were involved in a shooting in Greensboro, North Carolina, in 1979 that resulted in the deaths of five persons, most of them members of the far-left Revolutionary Communist Party. The victims were protesting Klan activities. Some of the witnesses had been participants in the protest, and others were related to the victims. Many of the witnesses also were plaintiffs in civil actions related to the shootings. In an attempt to keep highly charged emotional and racial currents from reaching the jury trying the criminal case, the judge imposed a gag order on the witnesses. Not only did he forbid them to talk to reporters, but he forbade them to talk to others with the intent to relay their words to the media.

13.   16 Corpus Juris Secundum, 1981 Supplement, p. 264.
14.   In re Oliver, 452 F.2d 111 (7th Cir. 1971).

In justifying the order, the judge noted that the trial was the "subject of intense local and national publicity." Documents presented to the court showed that the witnesses had strong feelings which led them to make highly prejudicial statements. Some of these already had been in the news. Because the publicity was widespread, and was likely to be repeated wherever the trial might be held, the judge rejected change of venue as a means of ensuring a fair trial. He concluded that the gag order was his only alternative. Arguing that their First Amendment rights were being violated, the witnesses appealed.

The court of appeals upheld the trial court's order, finding that it was drafted narrowly to prohibit only those activities and statements likely to prevent a fair trial. The court concluded:

> The tremendous publicity attending this trial, the potentially inflammatory and highly prejudicial statements that could reasonably be expected from petitioners (and had indeed been openly forecast by their counsel in proceedings before the trial judge), and the relative ineffectiveness of the considered alternatives, dictated the "strong measure" of suppressing speech of potential witnesses to ensure a fair trial.

More recently, gag orders have been imposed on attorneys and others involved in highly publicized cases involving political figures and drug dealers. In one instance, a member of Congress and the Bronx Borough President were accused of accepting bribes to steer government contracts to a manufacturing firm. The U.S. Court of Appeals for the Second Circuit held that if the trial judge had not restrained the trial participants their statements to reporters would have added "fuel to an already voracious fire of publicity" that might have deprived the defendants of a fair trial.[15] A similar order was imposed on participants in the trial of Bess Myerson, a former Miss America who became a cultural affairs commissioner in New York City. She was accused of attempting to influence a judge to reduce the alimony payments of her companion.[16] A federal judge assigned to conduct the trial of a defendant accused of laundering millions of dollars in the United States for the Medellin cocaine cartel imposed a gag order within hours after a federal prosecutor appeared on NBC's *Today* show to discuss the case.[17] The appearance came within a few days after President Bush had appealed to the public to back his war on drugs.

Such instances leave no question about the right of trial judges to impose prior restraints on participants in a criminal trial if the demonstrated need is great enough. There must be a showing that the prejudicial statements are likely to be made by the participants, that the order will prevent prejudicial publicity resulting from such statements, that no other means will ensure a fair trial, and that the order will restrict only that speech likely to create a prejudicial atmosphere.

---

15. Application of Dow Jones & Co., 842 F.2d 603 (2d Cir. 1988); cert. denied 109 S.Ct. 377 (1988).
16. Tamar Lewin, "News Media Battling a Trend of Secrecy in New York's Courts," *New York Times,* 8 February 1988.
17. Ellen Joan Pollack, "In Case of Reputed Medellin Figure, Is a Fair Trial Possible in the U.S.?" *Wall Street Journal,* 12 September 1989.

Restraining the News Media ════════════════════════════

Some trial judges who read *Sheppard* and tried to follow the Supreme Court's mandates concluded that the Supreme Court might condone prior restraint of the media if that were necessary to ensure a fair trial. Headlines culled from *Editor & Publisher,* the newspaper trade magazine, during the mid-1970s indicate media reaction. They include such terms as "gag order," "curb on newsmen," "censorship law," and "more curbs on press." Two decisions from that era remain worthy of note. One prescribes the proper course of action for journalists who may be confronted with an order not to publish prejudicial information. The other makes such an order highly unlikely, although not impossible.

United States v.
Dickinson, **465 F.2d 496**
(5th Cir. 1972).

In the first case, *United States* v. *Dickinson,* a federal district court judge in Baton Rouge, Louisiana, was confronted with a highly charged situation. A young man active in the civil rights movement during the early 1970s was accused of conspiring to kill the mayor of the city. The judge had to conduct a preliminary hearing to determine if there was enough evidence to hold the suspect for trial. He knew that police would offer evidence at that hearing that might not be admissible at the trial, but would point strongly at the young man's guilt. He also knew that reporters would be present, ready to spread that evidence through the city. Thinking ahead to the problem of selecting an impartial jury if the young man were tried, the judge concluded that his only recourse was to cut off harmful publicity at its source. He ordered the reporters present not to publish anything about the hearing except his decision, which was to hold the young man for trial.

Reporters for the two Baton Rouge newspapers consulted their editors, who told them to write stories covering the hearing in full. The editors reasoned that the public was more likely to be inflamed by a lack of fact than by a straightforward account of the evidence presented at the hearing. Without the facts, rumor would take over. When the stories were published, the judge held the reporters in contempt for violating his order and fined each $300. They appealed to the United States Court of Appeals for the Fifth Circuit.

Chief Judge John R. Brown held that "even the merest breeze blowing across the First Amendment" was enough to lead to the conclusion that the gag order was improper. It was a prior restraint, based not on a heavy showing of necessity, but on a series of improbable assumptions—that the suspect would go to trial; that the prejudicial publicity, if any, would be pervasive; and that voir dire would not work. Further, the court held, the public had a right to know as much as the media could learn about a situation as highly charged as that which prevailed in Baton Rouge.

With that said, the court also held that journalists, like everyone else, must obey a judge's order or appeal to a higher court for relief. The First Amendment gives them no special right to disobey a judge, even when they are convinced he is wrong.

On remand, the trial judge stuck to his guns, reimposing the $300 fines. He conceded that his order may have been improper, but reiterated that he would not tolerate defiance. On further appeal, the apppelate court upheld the fines. The Supreme Court refused to review.[18]

Nebraska Press Association v. *Stuart,* 427 U.S. 539, 96 S.Ct. 2791, 49 L.Ed. 2d 683 (1976).

Despite that part of the *Dickinson* decision condemning prior restraint, trial judges persisted in trying to tell reporters what to omit from their stories. The most notable of these attempts took place in a small county seat in western Nebraska in 1975. Erwin Charles Simants had killed six members of the Henry Kellie family and then had confessed to anyone who would listen. One of the victims was a ten-year-old girl, who also had been raped. All this took place in Sutherland, a town with a population of 840 in Lincoln County, which has a population of 36,000, of whom 24,000 live in North Platte, the county seat. The crime was highly publicized by the media in the county and elsewhere.

When Simants was scheduled to appear in court in North Platte for a preliminary hearing, his attorney and the county attorney joined in asking District Court Judge Hugh Stuart to issue an order restricting what could be reported about the case. They said that details highly prejudicial to Simants would be presented at the hearing. They considered these details so inflammatory that it probably would be impossible to select an impartial jury when Simants came to trial. The judge agreed and issued a restrictive order.

The news media, represented by the Nebraska State Press Association, appealed to a higher court in Lincoln, the state capital, for relief. The court noted that the press association and most of the state's media had adopted a set of voluntary guidelines, patterned on the *Sheppard* decision and the American Bar Association guidelines, for the coverage of news of crime and the courts. Media subscribing to these guidelines promised not to publish information that might prejudice a defendant's right to a fair trial. The appellate court said it would make the guidelines mandatory by adopting them as rules of the court. Finding a clear and present danger to Simants's right to a fair trial, the Court issued an order, to be in effect until a jury was chosen, prohibiting media within the trial court's jurisdiction from mentioning the defendant's several confessions. The order also forbade publication of medical information indicating that some of the victims had been sexually assaulted. Finally, the appellate court also ordered the media not to report that they were operating under a gag order.

Appeals were filed in all directions, with the U.S. Supreme Court eventually agreeing to consider the case. Its decision in *Nebraska Press Association* v. *Stuart* erected three high hurdles between courts and a prior restraint of the news media in the interest of ensuring a fair trial. Chief Justice Warren E. Burger wrote for a Court that was unanimous in condemning Judge Stuart's order, but was divided as to whether all such orders violate the First Amendment.

The chief justice began by noting that the drafters of the Bill of Rights guaranteed both freedom of the press and the right to trial by an impartial jury. When

---

18. 476 F.2d 373 (5th Cir. 1973); cert. den., 414 U.S. 979 (1973).

the two rights conflict, how can each be preserved without harming the other? Burger suggested that voluntary press-bar guidelines like those in effect in Nebraska and several other states offered one answer. However, such guidelines may fail when the need for them is greatest. The chief justice noted that "even the most ideal guidelines are subjected to powerful strains when a case such as Simants' arises." Some editors will observe them. Others will not.

Confronted with that fact, Judge Stuart sought to protect Simants's Sixth Amendment right to a fair trial by restraining the media's First Amendment rights. The Court held that he went too far. At the same time, Chief Justice Burger rebuffed those who would resolve the fair-trial issue by holding that First Amendment rights should never be restricted. He wrote:

> The authors of the Bill of Rights did not undertake to assign priorities as between First Amendment and Sixth Amendment rights, ranking one as superior to the other....[I]f the authors of these guarantees...were unwilling or unable to resolve the issue by assigning to one priority over the other, it is not for us to rewrite the Constitution by undertaking what they declined. It is unnecessary, after nearly two centuries, to establish a priority applicable to all circumstances.

The Court proceeded to hold that gag orders could be imposed on the media only as a last resort to ensure a fair trial. Such orders can be imposed, a majority of the Court held, only if three conditions are met. A judge proposing a restraint on the media must offer convincing evidence of these three criteria:

1. There is, or is likely to be, widespread prejudicial publicity.

2. None of the usual methods of ensuring a fair trial—voir dire, change of venue, continuance, and the like—will work.

3. The prior restraint will stop the flow of prejudicial publicity.

The chief justice said that Judge Stuart had satisfied only the first of these criteria. There was ample evidence of widespread prejudicial publicity, and the promise of more. But Judge Stuart could only speculate on the effect of that publicity. There was no evidence to prove that rigorous voir dire or a change of venue could not result in selection of an impartial jury. Nor was there any evidence that a gag order imposed on the media would cut off news of the confessions or of the sordid nature of the crime. Word of mouth, Burger noted, would spread such information quickly through a town of only 840 persons. The news also had been poured into the county by outside broadcasting stations and newspapers. Therefore, Judge Stuart's order was an improper restraint, violating the First Amendment.

Meanwhile, Simants had been tried before a jury in North Platte, with Judge Stuart presiding, and was found guilty of murder. The Nebraska Supreme Court reversed, finding that the Lincoln County sheriff not only had lobbied the jury for a conviction but had played cards with the jurors during the trial. On retrial in Lincoln, with Judge Stuart again presiding, Simants was found not guilty by reason of insanity.

In 1983, a United States District Court judge in California attempted to comply with the *Nebraska Press Association* guidelines in imposing a gag order on CBS News. John DeLorean, a former General Motors executive who organized a British company to build a sports car carrying his name, was about to go on trial for conspiracy to sell cocaine. Federal agents had videotaped him apparently in the act of making the deal. Government prosecutors alleged that he resorted to the cocaine deal to raise money to save his failing automobile business.

A few days before the trial was to begin, KNXT, the CBS affiliate in Los Angeles, broadcast excerpts from the government's videotape. One segment showed DeLorean examining a shipment of cocaine in a hotel room. Another showed FBI agents arresting him. The station said it would show other segments later. Judge Robert M. Takasugi postponed the start of the trial and issued an order forbidding CBS News from broadcasting any part of the tape. He said he feared that the portion already shown would make it difficult for him to find an impartial jury.

This segment of a videotape broadcast or the CBS network shows John DeLorean at the moment of his arrest by FBI agents on charges of conspiring to sell cocaine. A federal judge attempted to block the showing of the tape on the grounds that it would prevent the former automobile manufacturer from getting a fair trial. He was overruled on appeal. A jury later found DeLorean not guilty. (UPI/Bettman Newsphotos)

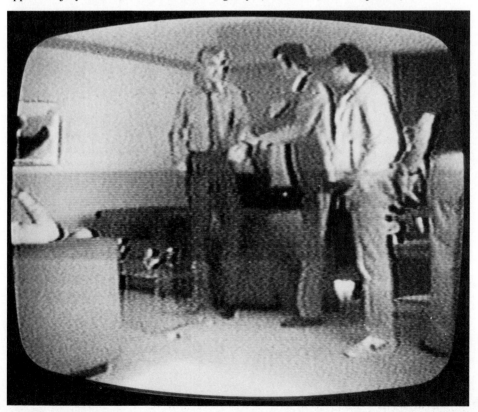

On appeal, the United States Court of Appeals, Ninth Circuit, overruled Judge Takasugi. It held that his gag order was an unconstitutional prior restraint. The court said the judge had failed to prove that further publicity would so distort the views of potential jurors that an impartial panel could not be seated.[19] Events proved that the judge was able to pick a jury, which heard the evidence during many weeks of trial and found DeLorean not guilty. The jury concluded that federal agents had initiated the cocaine transaction and therefore were guilty of entrapment.[20]

The CBS case illustrates the difficulty any court is likely to have in fulfilling the criteria established in *Nebraska Press Association*. It is easy to illustrate the likelihood of prejudicial publicity. But how does a judge prove in advance that such ordinary measures as change of venue and voir dire will not result in finding a dozen persons who can decide the case on its merits? And with satellites, cable, and even the mails bringing in news reports and commentary prepared by individuals who need not come within hundreds of miles of the judge who issues a gag order against the media, how can prejudicial information be cut off by court order? A judge cannot reach out beyond the limits of his jurisdiction, usually limited to a county or district, and punish those who disseminate information he has proscribed. It is for these reasons that any order restricting the media's right to report what is known about a pending criminal case is unlikely to survive an immediate appeal to the next higher court.

Access to Court Proceedings

It was precisely because of the unlikelihood of prior restraint of the media, condemned in *Nebraska Press,* that some courts began using a new technique—the closing of court proceedings at which prejudicial information was likely to be disclosed. Traditionally, trial and other court proceedings were open to the public. The Sixth Amendment guarantees suspects not only the right to trial by an impartial jury but "to a speedy and public trial." In *Sheppard,* Justice Clark had noted, almost as an aside, "Of course, there is nothing that proscribes the press from reporting events that transpire in the courtroom." Nor was there any reason in 1966 to doubt that court proceedings would be conducted in public in all but the most unusual circumstances, usually involving divorce and custody cases or embarrassing testimony in sex crime trials.

By 1976, when *Nebraska Press* was decided, some judges, in their attempt to ensure a fair trial, had begun to experiment with closing pretrial proceedings. The most common closures were of preliminary, sometimes called "probable cause," hearings where police and prosecutors can offer evidence that would not be admissible at a formal trial. The gag order in *Nebraska Press Association* was issued at such a hearing. In his decision in that case, Chief Justice Burger took note of the experiments with closing in a way that seemed to approve them. He wrote:

---

19.   Columbia Broadcasting Systems, Inc. v. U.S. District Court, Central District of California, 729 F.2d 1174 (9th Cir. 1984).
20.   "DeLorean: Not Guilty," *Newsweek,* 27 August 1984, pp. 22–23.

The county court could not know that closure of the preliminary hearing was an alternative open to it until the Nebraska Supreme Court so construed state law; but once a public hearing had been held, what transpired there could not be subject to prior restraint.

Burger was referring to a decision of the Nebraska court holding that the judge who conducted the preliminary hearing, and who imposed the original gag order, might have solved his problem by conducting the hearing in private. Some judges read the first branch of the sentence quoted above and found in it the Supreme Court's endorsement of such closings. One who did was Daniel DePasquale, judge of the Seneca County Supreme Court, a trial court, in upstate New York. He was confronted with the duty of conducting a highly unusual murder case—one without a corpse. The case began when Wayne Clapp, a former police officer, disappeared from his home near Rochester. He had gone fishing in Lake Seneca, forty miles away, with two male companions. When Clapp failed to return, police began a search. His boat, riddled with bullets, was found in Lake Seneca, and his pickup truck was found outside a motel in Jackson, Michigan. Officers arrested Kyle Greathouse and his wife, both sixteen, and David Ray Jones, twenty-one, who were in the motel. The suspects surrendered Clapp's credit cards and a .357 Magnum revolver. They also made statements to police describing how and why they had killed Clapp. Police returned the trio to Seneca County, New York, where the two men were charged with murder.

As the trial date approached, their attorneys filed two motions with the county court. One asked that the statements be suppressed on the ground that they had not been given voluntarily. The other asked for suppression of the credit cards and the revolver. When these motions came up for a hearing, the attorneys made a third motion. Pointing to seven news stories that had appeared in the two Rochester newspapers, they argued that "the unabated buildup of adverse publicity has jeopardized the ability of the defendants to receive a fair trial." They asked that spectators, including reporters, be excluded from the suppression hearing. The district attorney made no objection, and Judge DePasquale granted the request. Only one reporter, Carol Ritter, a correspondent for the Rochester newspapers, was present. She left the courtroom at the judge's request, and the hearing proceeded behind closed doors. Judge DePasquale ruled that the credit cards, the Magnum, and the confessions had been obtained in violation of the defendants' rights and therefore could not be used as evidence. The prosecutor concluded that without such evidence, and without the body of the victim, he could not persuade a jury to convict the suspects of murder. This led to an agreement under which Greathouse and Jones pleaded guilty to lesser offenses and served short terms in prison.[21]

Meanwhile, Gannett's attorney had filed a motion with Judge DePasquale asserting Ritter's right to cover the suppression hearing, even though it had been completed, and asking for a transcript of the proceeding. At the hearing on the motion, DePasquale said he, too, believed the press had a constitutional right of access to court proceedings. He said it was unfortunate that Ritter had not ob-

---

21. Gannett v. DePasquale, 43 N.Y. 2d 373, 396 (N.Y. 1977).

jected at the time the closure motion was made. However, he said her right under the First Amendment was not absolute and would have to be balanced against the right of the defendants to a fair trial. In this instance, he said he would hold that the right to a fair trial outweighed the reporter's right to cover the suppression hearing. He also refused to release the transcript on the ground that it contained information that would make it difficult if not impossible for Greathouse and Jones to get a fair trial. At the time, the prosecutor had not yet agreed to the plea bargain noted above.

Gannett v. *DePasquale,* 443 U.S. 368, 99 S. Ct. 2898, 61 L.Ed. 2d 608 (1979).

Gannett's unsuccessful appeals to New York's higher courts led eventually to the U.S. Supreme Court, resulting in a sweeping decision that divided the justices as have few others and that created a furor in the media and the legal profession. The Court held, five to four, in *Gannett v. DePasquale,* that the judge had acted properly. Gannett based its appeal on the Sixth Amendment's guarantee of "the right to a speedy and public trial," which proved to be a poor choice. Justice Potter Stewart noted that the right to a public trial, like the right to trial by jury, was designed to protect defendants. Defendants who choose to waive a jury trial, or to be tried in private, may do so if the trial judge approves. If such requests are made, Justice Stewart wrote, the Sixth Amendment gives the media and the public no right to object. They may or may not have such a right under the First Amendment. If so, the right is not absolute, and Judge DePasquale fulfilled any duty he may have had under it by listening to Gannett's request for a transcript of the testimony.

Thus, within a few paragraphs a dispute over the right to attend a hearing had been converted into a devastating blow aimed at those who believe justice is more likely to be done in the open than behind closed doors. In the year after *Gannett* was decided, defendants in forty-nine cases asked to have all or parts of their trial closed, and about half the requests were granted.[22]

Justice Harry A. Blackmun, who wrote for the four dissenters, called the decision "an unfortunate one." Even some of the justices who supported Stewart's conclusion wrote to express their doubts about his reasoning. Some argued that the decision should have been grounded in the First Amendment. Others disagreed with Stewart's assumption that a suppression hearing stands on the same constitutional ground as the trial itself.

An indication of the feelings the decision aroused in the news media is conveyed by a bit of doggerel written by Ashton Phelps, president and publisher of the *New Orleans Times-Picayune,* and a lawyer:

Ode to the Gannett Decision

The Burger Court surpassed itself
And reached the height of follies.
The court they should have closed was theirs
Instead of DePasquale's.[23]

---

22. *News Media and the Law,* August/September, November/December, 1979, pp. 7–9, 10–23.
23. "Courts: Pretrial or Trial?" *Presstime,* October 1979, p. 17.

Trials of Criminal Cases

Even as Phelp's "ode" was being published, the Supreme Court seized the opportunity to clarify what it had done in *Gannett*. Since early 1976, a troublesome murder case had been bouncing up and down through the Virginia courts. It began with the stabbing death of a motel manager in Hanover, a hamlet twenty miles north of Richmond. A Hanover County grand jury indicted John Paul Stevenson on a charge of murder, on the basis of the principal piece of evidence connecting Stevenson with the crime, a bloodstained shirt. It belonged to Stevenson, but he contended police had seized it in violation of his rights. The shirt was introduced as evidence at the trial, and a jury found Stevenson guilty of second-degree murder. On appeal, the Virginia Supreme Court ruled that the shirt should not have been used as evidence and ordered a new trial. Two subsequent trials resulted in mistrials. When Stevenson's fourth trial began, his lawyer asked that it be closed to the public. He argued that a member of the victim's family seemed to be coaching the witnesses. The prosecutor made no objections to the closing. The judge noted that the courtroom was not well designed. The jurors could see the spectators and, the judge reasoned, might be influenced by them. When he ordered the courtroom cleared, two reporters for the Richmond newspapers were among those evicted.

At the time, the *Gannett* case had not been decided by the Supreme Court. The Virginia judge acted on his reading of a state law authorizing judges in criminal trials to "exclude from the trial any persons whose presence would impair the conduct of a fair trial, provided that the right of the accused to a public trial shall not be violated."[24]

There is nothing unusual in the statute. As the Supreme Court reminded judges in *Sheppard,* courts have always had a duty to keep prejudicial influences out of the courtroom. However, even a cursory survey of the cases in this area leads to the conclusion that the right to exclude individuals from the courtroom has been used infrequently and limited narrowly. Attempts by judges to stretch the rule into a blanket exclusion order usually were rebuffed.[25]

In the Virginia case, counsel for the Richmond newspapers asked the trial judge later that day for a hearing on the closure order. He agreed to hear the lawyer's argument, listened to him in private, and ruled that the trial would proceed behind closed doors. The trial ended the next day when the judge granted a defense motion to strike the prosecution's case from the record. The judge then found Stevenson not guilty. His written order gave no reason for his decision.

Richmond Newspapers v. *Virginia,* 448 U.S. 555, 100 S. Ct. 2814, 65 L.Ed.2d 1973 (1980).

When the state supreme court rejected an appeal of the closure order, the Richmond newspapers took their case to the U.S. Supreme Court. The petition reached the Court within weeks after *Gannett* had been decided. It seized the opportunity to limit that decision and held, with

---

24. Virginia Code §19.2–266.
25. E. W. Scripps Co. v. Fulton. 125 N.E. 2d 896 (Ohio 1955), and Oliver v. Postel, 282 N.E. 2d 306 (N.Y. App. 1972).

only one dissent, that the Virginia judge had acted improperly. Justice Powell, who had practiced law in Richmond, took no part in the case.

The Court's seven-to-one decision in *Richmond Newspapers* v. *Virginia* was not nearly as unanimous as the vote suggests. While the majority found common ground in holding that the closure was unwarranted, the justices wrote six different opinions to explain why they did so. Some clearly would have preferred to have grounded the decision in the Sixth Amendment guarantee of a public trial. But the leading opinion, written by Chief Justice Burger and signed by Justices Stevens and White, was grounded in the First Amendment. The justices reasoned that because of the historical origins of trials, and a long tradition of openness, trials have become public assemblies where the business of government is conducted. Therefore, the freedom of assembly clause of the First Amendment gives journalists and the public a right to attend trials. It is not an absolute right, but it does give people a right to argue against a motion to close a trial or any part of it, with the presumption in favor of openness.

This represented an important advancement in First Amendment theory. Previously, as Justice Rehnquist had pointed out in *Gannett,* the Court had steadfastly rejected the argument that the right to disseminate news implies a right to gather it. In a few of its previous decisions the Court had spoken in general terms about First Amendment protection for newsgatherers, but it had not upheld any specific right. One aspect of this protection will be the subject of the next chapter.

Chief Justice Burger began his judgment for the Court in *Richmond Newspapers* by putting as much distance as he could between this case and *Gannett.* Using italic type to lend emphasis to his writing, he noted repeatedly that *"pretrial"* proceedings were at issue in *Gannett* while *Richmond* dealt with a "trial."

Burger reviewed the history of trials, quoting from both British and Colonial American documents to make the point that by tradition trials have been open to the public. There are compelling reasons why this should be so, Burger wrote. When spectators are present, they can see for themselves whether the defendant is treated fairly. Witnesses will be less likely to lie. Decisions reached in open court are more likely to command public support than those reached in secret. Public trials also serve as an outlet for community concerns when an especially shocking crime has been committed. The trial will provide an outlet for their anger. If the people see that justice is being done, they are less likely to take the law into their own hands. Burger concluded by observing that "the appearance of justice can best be provided by allowing people to observe it."

The chief justice then made a significant shift in his reasoning. He wrote that "[i]n earlier times, both in England and America, attendance at court was a common mode of 'passing the time.'" Thus, a courtroom was, in a sense, a place of public assembly. People went to court for the drama it offered as well as to observe one branch of their government in action. In more recent times, however, people have come to rely on "the press, cinema, and electronic media" for "the real life drama once available only in the courtroom," Burger wrote. They also rely on the media to cover trials for them. This, Burger said, "validates the media claim of functioning as surrogates for the public." Judges have recognized that role by giving reporters "special seating and priority of entry so that they may report what people in attendance have seen and heard."

Noting that a "core purpose" of the First and Fourteenth Amendments is to assure "freedom of communication on matters relating to the functioning of government," Burger moved to a position he had not previously taken. He concluded that this freedom must imply a right to gather news on the functioning of government. Specifically, he said that because trials are a function of government, and because they have traditionally been open, they are public assemblies that the public has a right to attend. It is not an absolute right, and the chief justice described it as follows:

> What this means in the context of trials is that the First Amendment guarantees of speech and press, standing alone, prohibit government from summarily closing courtroom doors which had long been open to the public at the time that amendment was adopted....
>
> It is not crucial whether we describe this right to attend criminal trials to hear, see, and communicate observations concerning them as a "right of access," or a "right to gather information," for we have recognized that "without some protection for seeking out news, freedom of the press could be eviscerated."... The explicit, guaranteed rights to speak and to publish concerning what takes place at a trial would lose much meaning if access to observe the trial could, as it was here, be foreclosed arbitrarily.
>
> Subject to the traditional time, place, and manner restrictions,...streets, sidewalks, and parks are places traditionally open, where First Amendment rights may be exercised...; a trial courtroom also is a public place where the people generally—and representatives of the media—have a right to be present, and where their presence historically has been thought to enhance the integrity and quality of what takes place....
>
> We hold that the right to attend criminal trials is implicit in the guarantees of the First Amendment; without the freedom to attend such trials, which people have exercised for centuries, important aspects of freedom of speech and "of the press could be eviscerated."

Burger concluded by holding that the Virginia judge had not given enough attention to the remedies recommended in *Sheppard* before he decided to close the courtroom in order to ensure a fair trial. He added:

> Absent an overriding interest articulated in findings, the trial of a criminal case must be open to the public. Accordingly, the judgment under review is reversed.

While Justice White signed Burger's opinion, he could not resist chiding the chief justice for voting with the majority in *Gannett*. If Burger had endorsed the minority view in that case, the Court would have construed the Sixth Amendment "to forbid excluding the public from criminal proceedings except in narrowly defined circumstances." Thus it could have avoided the First Amendment issue.

Justice Stevens, who also put his name on Burger's opinion, wrote separately to expand on White's reservations about the creation of a new First Amendment right of access. Nothing that the Court previously had rejected suggestions that the Amendment implies such a right, he added:

> Today,...for the first time, the Court unequivocally holds that an arbitrary interference with access to important information is an abridgment of the freedoms of speech and of the press protected by the First Amendment.

Even such strong advocates of First Amendment freedoms as Justices Marshall and Brennan seemed worried by the sweep of Burger's position. Writing for both of them, Brennan agreed that there is a First Amendment right of access to trials, and to some other kinds of news as well, but he would have had the Court set limits to that right. He suggested, for instance, that lower-court judges should not read *Richmond Newspapers* as granting a right of access to secret information vital to the nation's security. He would have confined the right of access to information about what Brennan called the "structures" of government. In his view, people have a right to find out how well the institutions of government—of which the courts are one—are functioning.

Even Justice Stewart, who was seeing much of his year-old opinion in *Gannett* reduced to dicta, concurred in the Court's judgment. He said that his earlier decision had left open the question as to whether other parts of the Constitution might guarantee a right of access. That right had now been found in the First Amendment, and he was willing to go along with that. However, Stewart said that right should not be construed as absolute. Judges should be able to "impose reasonable limitations upon the unrestricted occupation of a courtroom by representatives of the press and members of the public."

Justice Blackmun, who had led the dissenters in *Gannett,* made no effort to hide his exasperation with both Stewart and the chief justice. With his position— that the Sixth Amendment gives the public some right of access to court proceedings—rejected, he concurred in the Court's verdict. He wrote that he was happy to see the Court paying some attention to legal history, and added:

> It is gratifying ... to see the Court wash away at least some of the graffiti that marred the prevailing opinion in [*Gannett.*] No less than twelve times in the primary opinion in that case, the Court (albeit in what seems now to have become clear dicta) observed that the Sixth Amendment closure ruling applies to the *trial* itself. The author of the first concurring opinion [Burger] was fully aware of this and would have restricted the Court's observations and rulings to the suppression hearing. Nonetheless, he *joined* the Court's opinion with its multiple references to the trial itself; the opinion was not a mere concurrence in the Court's judgment. And Mr. Justice Rehnquist, in his separate concurring opinion, quite understandably observed, as a consequence, that the Court was holding "without qualification," that "members of the public have no constitutional right under the Sixth and Fourteenth Amendments to attend criminal trials." The resulting confusion among commentators and journalists was not surprising.

Justice Blackmun said he still believed that the right of access to a trial, or to a suppression hearing, lies "where the Constitution explicitly placed it—in the Sixth Amendment." But because he could not persuade a majority of the Court to his position, he wrote that he was driven "to conclude, as a secondary position, that the First Amendment must provide some measure of protection for public access to the trial."

Justice Rehnquist alone remained unconvinced. He believed his colleagues mistaken and he said so bluntly:

In the Gilbert and Sullivan operetta Iolanthe, the Lord Chancellor recites:

"The law is the true embodiment
of everything that's excellent,
It has no kind of fault or flaw,
And I, my lords, embody the law."

It is difficult not to derive more than a little of this flavor from the various opinions supporting the judgment in this case....

...I do not believe that either the First or Sixth Amendments, as made applicable to the States by the Fourteenth, require that a State's reasons for denying public access to a trial, where both the prosecuting attorney and the defendant have consented to an order of closure approved by the judge, are subject to any additional constitutional review at our hands.

However, Rehnquist stood alone. As Stevens emphasized in his concurring opinion, the Court, for the first time, had found in the First Amendment a right of the press and public to attend trials. It is not an absolute right, but the various opinions make clear that it is a right that can be abridged only by a strong showing of evidence that the defendant's right to a fair trial can be protected only by closing the courtroom. Further, representatives of the public and the news media have a right to argue against closing. Because the plurality grounded that right in the First Amendment, the decision implies that there may be other functions of government that historically have been so open that the same reasoning could be applied to them. For that reason Stevens called *Richmond Newspapers* "a watershed case." For that reason Brennan suggested the new right of access be limited to probing the structures of government. And for that reason Blackmun found the decision "troublesome." It is not possible, until courts have had an opportunity to act in properly presented cases, to know how far a First Amendment right of access to government information might reach. The issues of access presented in *Gannett* and *Richmond Newspapers* split the Court as have only two other First Amendment questions: the definition of obscenity and the prior restraint imposed in the Pentagon Papers case. The justices wrote twelve different opinions in the two access cases. However, through all the disagreements and reservations expressed in those opinions, one point comes clear: Eight of the nine justices concluded in varying degree that some right of access to news sources is implicit in the First Amendment and can be applied to the state through the due process clause of the Fourteenth. Rehnquist was the only holdout.

Jury Selection and Pretrial Hearings

Reacting to the confusion created in the minds of judges by its decisions in *Gannett* and *Richmond Newspapers,* the Supreme Court has on four occasions since felt compelled to take cases involving access to criminal justice proceedings. In each instance, the Court has expanded the scope of its holding in *Richmond Newspapers* and greatly restricted the reach of *Gannett.*

In the first of the cases, *Globe Newspaper Co.* v. *Superior Court, County of Norfolk,*[26] decided in 1982, the Court held that a Massachusetts law closing courtrooms during the testimony of certain sex-crime victims violated the First Amendment.

In the second, *Press-Enterprise Co.* v. *Superior Court of California, Riverside County* (Press-Enterprise I),[27] decided in 1984, the Court held that because the voir dire traditionally is part of the trial, it, too, must be conducted in the open unless convincing evidence shows it must be closed to ensure a fair trial.

In the third, *Waller* v. *Georgia,*[28] also decided in 1984, the Court held that a pretrial suppression hearing can be closed over the defendant's objections only if there are compelling reasons to do so. More importantly, the Court held that the people's First Amendment right of access to such proceedings rests on the same factors as the defendant's Sixth Amendment right to a public trial.

In the fourth, *Press-Enterprise Co.* v. *Superior Court of California, Riverside County* (Press-Enterprise II),[29] the Court held that the qualified First Amendment right of access to criminal proceedings extends to preliminary hearings as conducted in California. In that state, such hearings can involve the taking of considerable testimony so as to become, in effect, a preview of the trial. The effect of these decisions has been to reinforce the conclusion that all court proceedings are presumed to be open; that closing, even of nontrial hearings, is the exception; and that each must be justified by evidence showing that a fair trial is unlikely unless the proceeding is closed.

Globe Newspaper Co. v. *Superior Court, County of Norfolk,* **457 U.S. 596, 102 S.Ct. 2613, 73 L.Ed.2d.248 (1982).**

At issue in *Globe Newspaper* was a Massachusetts law that required judges presiding at the trials of certain sex crimes to exclude the public and the media during the testimony of victims under the age of eighteen. The Court held six-to-three that any such arbitrary closing of a courtroom during a trial violates the First Amendment right of access defined in *Richmond Newspapers*.

The law had been invoked during the trial of a man accused of raping three girls, all of whom were under eighteen. When it came time for the victims to testify, the judge closed the courtroom, despite objections by a reporter for the *Boston Globe*. In response to that challenge, the state sought to justify the law on two grounds: It protected "minor victims of sex crimes from further trauma and embarrassment," and it encouraged those victims "to come forward and testify in a truthful and credible manner."

The Supreme Court's majority conceded that both interests were important, but held that they can be served by measures less restrictive than a mandatory law. The court said that while the right of access to criminal trials is not absolute,

> the circumstances under which the press and public can be barred from a criminal trial are limited; the State's justification in denying access must be a weighty one. Where, as in the present case, the State attempts to deny the right of access in order

---

26.　457 U.S. 596, 102 S.Ct. 2613, 73 L.Ed. 2d 248 (1982).
27.　464 U.S. 501, 104 S.Ct. 819, 78 L.Ed. 2d 629 (1984).
28.　467 U.S. 39, 104 S.Ct. 2210, 81 L.Ed. 2d 31 (1984).
29.　478 U.S. 1, 106 S.Ct. 2735, 92 L.Ed. 2d 1 (1986).

to inhibit the disclosure of sensitive information, it must be shown that the denial is necessitated by a compelling governmental interest, and is narrowly tailored to serve that interest.

In this instance, the law swept too broadly. The Court said that Massachusetts could protect minor witnesses through judicial action on a case-by-case basis. In that way, the judge could weigh the interest in privacy and a fair trial against the public's interest in the testimony and reach a suitable decision. Thus, the Court did not rule out the possibility that the courtroom could be closed during the testimony of the young victims, but it could be done only after a hearing at which the media could plead their case. Then the judge would have to conclude, on the basis of clear evidence, that the victims would not testify fully unless reporters and the public were barred.

Press-Enterprise Co. v. *Superior Court of California, Riverside County,* **464 U.S. 501, 104 S.Ct. 819, 78 L.Ed.2d. 629 (1984).**

Press-Enterprise I had its origins in the selection of a jury for the trial of a suspect accused of rape and murder. The crime was the subject of intense media coverage, and the judge took special pains to make certain that the voir dire was as searching as possible. The first three days were conducted in open court. Then the prosecutor asked that the process be closed, arguing that otherwise, the prospective jurors might not respond to questions with sufficient candor to disclose their biases. The judge agreed, and the questioning continued in private for six weeks before a jury was seated.

When the *Press-Enterprise* sought a copy of the transcript of the voir dire, the defendant's attorney objected, arguing that some of it would violate the jurors' right of privacy. The prosecutor joined in the objection, arguing that prospective jurors had answered questions under an "implied promise of confidentiality." The judge upheld the objections, noting that much of the transcript was "dull and boring," and that a few persons had disclosed matters that might prove embarrassing if made public. The *Press-Enterprise* appealed, but was rebuffed by two state appellate courts.

The Supreme Court overruled the California courts, with Chief Justice Burger writing for the majority. Reviewing much of the same historical ground he had covered in *Richmond Newspapers,* he concluded that jury selection, like the trial itself, traditionally has been conducted in public. In his view, open proceedings are more likely to ensure fairness than they are to promote prejudice. The chief justice wrote:

> No right ranks higher than the right of the accused to a fair trial. But the primacy of the accused's right is difficult to separate from the right of everyone in the community to attend the *voir dire* which promotes fairness.

However, the Court stopped short of holding that jury selection never should be conducted in private. It established the following guidelines:

> Closed proceedings, although not absolutely precluded, must be rare and only for cause shown that outweighs the value of openness.... The presumption of openness

may be overcome only by an overriding interest based on findings that closure is essential to preserve higher values and is narrowly tailored to serve that interest. The interest is to be articulated along with findings specific enough that a reviewing court can determine whether the closure order was properly entered.

The passage above has been cited frequently by lower courts seeking guidance in access cases. In one notable instance, the U.S. Court of Appeals for the District of Columbia Circuit held that a district court judge acted improperly in closing the jury selection process for the trial of Michael K. Deaver, a former adviser to President Reagan.[30] Deaver was accused of lying about his lobbying activities after he left the White House. The judge closed the voir dire to protect the privacy of potential jurors who were questioned about their drinking habits. Cable News Network and other media organizations asked the judge to conduct the questioning in open court. He denied their motion. The media plaintiffs appealed to the circuit court for summary reversal. It was granted the same day. The court said the district judge had failed to meet any of the conditions required for closure in Press-Enterprise I.

Waller v. *Georgia,* 467 U.S. 39, 104 S.Ct. 2210, 81 L.Ed.2d 31 (1984).

The Supreme Court itself reiterated the Press-Enterprise I test in its decision in *Waller* v. *Georgia* and went further by holding that the Sixth Amendment, too, gives the press and public a right to argue against closing judicial proceedings. Guy Waller was one of thirty-six persons charged with illegal gambling after police had used court-approved wiretaps to listen to their telephone conversations. In advance of the trial, Waller and several other defendants asked that the wiretap evidence be suppressed. The prosecutor moved that the hearing be closed because it might reveal information that would violate the privacy of persons who had not been charged with gambling. He also said that some of the disclosures might violate the right of other defendants to a fair trial. Over objections from defense attorneys, the judge granted the motion.

The hearing lasted seven days. Only two-and-one-half hours were devoted to playing tapes of the wiretaps. Only one person who had not been indicted was named in court. The judge ruled that about half the evidence seized in response to what police heard on the wiretaps was inadmissible. A jury subsequently found the defendants guilty of gambling. They appealed, arguing that their Sixth Amendment right to a public trial had been violated by the closing of the suppression hearing. The Georgia Supreme Court denied their appeal, holding that the trial judge had acted properly.

The U.S. Supreme Court disagreed. Looking to *Globe, Richmond, Press-Enterprise,* and even to some of the opinions in *Gannett* for guidance, the Court concluded that, although the three most-recent decisions rested primarily on First Amendment grounds, the Sixth Amendment also implies the right of the press and public to attend not only a trial but suppression hearings as well. Indeed, the Court said that the ''need for an open proceeding may be particularly strong with

---

30.   Cable News Network v. United States, 824 F.2d 1046 (D.C. Cir. 1987).

respect to suppression hearings." It noted that a "challenge to the seizure of evidence frequently attacks the conduct of police and prosecutor." Because the public has a "strong interest" in the exposure of police misconduct, suppression hearings generally should be open to public scrutiny, the Court said.

The effect of the decision has been to give the media and the public a right to intervene when a motion is made to close a suppression hearing, even when the motion is based on the defendant's Sixth Amendment right to a fair trial.

Press-Enterprise Co. v. *Superior Court,* **478 U.S. 1, 106 S.Ct. 2735, 92 L.Ed.2d 1 (1986).** With its decision in the second *Press-Enterprise* case in 1986, the Supreme Court completed the undoing of the mischief caused by Stewart's opinion in *Gannett.* In this instance, a trial judge had closed the preliminary hearing of a nurse accused of administering massive and fatal doses of a heart stimulant to twelve persons. The hearing, to determine whether there was enough evidence to bring the nurse to trial, lasted for forty-one days. Journalists not only were denied access to the hearing but were denied access to a transcript after the hearing had been completed. California appellate courts upheld the trial judge, but on further appeal the U.S. Supreme Court reversed, seven to two.

Writing for the majority, Chief Justice Burger noted that more than nine in ten criminal cases are resolved without going to trial. In the usual procedure, the defendant agrees to plead guilty to a lesser charge, as in *Gannett.* As a consequence, Burger wrote, "the preliminary hearing is often the final and most important step in the criminal proceeding,... [and] in many cases provides the sole public observation of the criminal justice system."

The majority held that in this instance the judge's closing of the hearing violated a long tradition "of access to preliminary hearings of the type conducted in California." He concluded, as he had in *Richmond Newspapers* with respect to trials, that such hearings can be closed only if the defendant can prove a compelling reason for doing so. Such proof must demonstrate "a substantial probability that the defendant's right to a fair trial will be prejudiced by publicity that closure would prevent, and [that] reasonable alternatives to closure cannot adequately protect the defendant's fair trial rights." Burger suggested that careful voir dire usually can weed out potential jurors who might have been prejudiced by exposure to pretrial publicity. In any event, he concluded, closure of an entire forty-one-day hearing "would rarely be warranted."

At the time, some observers raised questions about the scope of the decision because Burger repeatedly used the clause "as conducted in California" to describe the kind of preliminary hearing at issue. Those doubts have been dispelled by subsequent lower-court decisions. For instance, the U.S. Court of Appeals for the Second Circuit relied on Press-Enterprise II and *Waller* in holding that journalists had a right of access not only to pretrial proceedings but to papers filed in conjunction with them.[31] The court did so in a case involving Mario Biaggi, a

---

31. New York Times Co. v. Biaggi, 828 F.2d 110 (2d Cir. 1987).

member of Congress, and Meade Esposito, former chair of the executive committee of the Kings County Democratic Committee in Brooklyn. Both were accused of accepting bribes. They sought to suppress introduction of evidence obtained by electronic surveillance. The judge ruled that assertions made in motion papers submitted to him proved that the surveillance had been properly authorized. However, he also ordered the papers sealed to protect the defendants' right to a fair trial and the privacy of persons who had not been indicted. Under challenge from the *New York Times,* the *New York Daily News,* and Associated Press, the judge refused to grant a hearing on his order. The appellate court said he should have done so. It also held that the public's and the media's qualified First Amendment right to attend a trial was extended to nontrial hearings by the Supreme Court's decision in Press-Enterprise II. That right also applies to the inspection of motion papers, the court said. It might well be that release of some parts of the papers would unduly violate the privacy of others. If so, the judge could not so decide without granting the media appellants a hearing, and he would have to justify any decision to keep documents under seal.

Closure of suppression hearings, and even of some part of or all of a trial, to ensure a defendant's right to a fair trial remains an option open to judges in highly publicized cases. However, the Supreme Court has gone to great lengths in its decisions, starting with *Richmond Newspapers* and running through Press-Enterprise II, to make closure an exception, not the rule. The Court also has left no doubt that journalists, or indeed anyone else, have a right to offer an informal motion objecting to closure. If such motions are offered, judges are required to stay the proceeding until a formal hearing can be conducted. Closure then can be ordered only if there is convincing evidence that a fair trial cannot be had otherwise.

On occasion, such evidence has been offered. The U.S. Court of Appeals, Ninth Circuit, held that a federal court judge in Sacramento acted properly when he ordered reporters to leave the courtroom during a suppression hearing but permitted other spectators to stay.[32] The episode occurred four weeks into the trial of seven defendants accused of dealing in narcotics. Other defendants were awaiting trial. The court had not been able to make arrangements for sequestering the jury. Before the judge ordered the reporters to leave the courtroom he tried to reach an agreement with them not to publish prejudicial information that was likely to be disclosed during the hearing. The appellate court said it couldn't understand why the reporters refused to cooperate. It noted that the information could have been published at the end of the trial without harm to anyone. In another instance, the Washington Supreme Court upheld a judge's offer to let reporters remain in the courtroom during a suppression hearing if they would agree to abide by that state's fair trial guidelines.[33] The guidelines, which contained a pledge not to publish prejudicial information while a trial was pending, had been adopted voluntarily by most of the state's news media. When some reporters refused to put their names to that pledge, the judge told them to leave the court-

32.   Sacramento Bee v. United States District Court, 565 F.2d 477 (9th Cir. 1981).
33.   Federated Publications v. Swedberg, 633 P. 2d 74 (Wash. 1981).

room. On appeal, the supreme court said he had acted reasonably in balancing the defendant's right to a fair trial against the journalists' right to be present in the courtroom. In a more recent instance, the U.S. Court of Appeals for the Third Circuit ruled that a trial judge acted improperly when he barred a reporter from the courtroom during the trial of an accused drug dealer and then refused to hear her appeal for access to a transcript of the proceeding.[34] The court said the judge should have given the reporter timely notice of his intent to close the trial and an opportunity to state her objections. However, the court said the trial judge correctly concluded there was grave risk of serious injury to innocent third parties if the proceedings were opened. At risk were the suspect's children, who were in Lebanon.

Protecting Jurors

In its *Sheppard* decision, the Supreme Court said that Judge Blythin had not protected the jurors from the media. The Court said the judge had permitted the media to turn the jurors into celebrities of sorts by publicizing their names, addresses, and photographs. Consequently, the jurors were subjected to pressure from persons who sought to influence the jury's verdict. As a result of the Court's criticism, trial judges have tried various measures, including prior restraint, to protect jurors from the media. Some courts have sought to prevent disclosure of the names and addresses of jurors, and others have forbidden the sketching or photographing of them. Judges also have tried to prevent journalists and lawyers from interviewing jurors after they have reached their verdict.

Orders seeking to ensure the anonymity of jurors are justified on the ground that they will protect the panel from coercion. The few decisions in this area indicate that such orders will be upheld if the probability of coercion is high, if the restraint will indeed protect the identity of the jurors, and if there is convincing evidence that other less restrictive measures will not ensure a fair trial. These tests are derived from the Supreme Court's decision in *Nebraska Press Association*.

State, ex rel. New Mexico Press Association, v. Kaufman, 98 N.M. 261, 648 P.2d 300 (N.Mex. 1982).

In the leading case, the New Mexico Supreme Court held that a trial judge acted improperly when, without notice and without a hearing, he ordered the media not to publish the names and addresses of jurors in the trial of one of several prisoners accused of leading a riot at the state penitentiary. The judge acted at the request of the defendant, who said he was afraid people might try to influence the jury against him. The prosecutor agreed with the request, saying he, too, was afraid of jury tampering, because it had happened in the trial of another of the defendants.

Associations representing the state's newspapers and broadcasters appealed. A unanimous supreme court said that "mere speculation that publishing the

34.   United States v. Raffoul, 826 F. 2d 218 (3d Cir. 1987).

names of jurors might expose them to intimidation'' was not enough. Citing *Richmond Newspapers,* the court held that the trial judge had erred at the start by not giving the media notice of the defendant's request and an opportunity to contest it. Indeed, it said, "[a]nyone present should be given an opportunity to object."

The court then turned to the standards to be applied in deciding whether jurors' names can be kept out of the media. Citing *Nebraska Press Association,* it said the judge should begin by examining "the nature and extent of the evil" that would come from publication. Then the judge should ask if effective alternatives to a gag order are available. The final question is whether the order will work. In this instance, the court said that indeed a great deal of publicity did surround the trial, but no firm evidence indicated that anyone would try to intimidate the jury. The judge himself had recognized that an effective alternative was available when he had considered and rejected a motion to sequester the jury. Finally, no evidence indicated that his order would prevent people from identifying the jurors. Their names had been read in open court. The jury list, including addresses and telephone numbers, was on file in the office of the clerk of courts. Under New Mexico law, the list was a public record.

However, the court stopped short of saying that trial judges could never restrain publication of jurors' names. The court held "that a prior restraint on publication...must be based upon imperative circumstances supported by a record that clearly demonstrates that a defendant's right to a fair trial will be jeopardized and that there are no reasonable alternatives to protect that right."

In some instances, that standard of proof has been met. A federal district court in Nevada held that a judge acted properly in prohibiting the publication of the names of jurors who were called to impose sentence on a man another jury had convicted of murder.[35] But the court emphasized that the case was an exceptional one. The conviction was controversial and had generated much public criticism and discussion. The likelihood that jurors would be subjected to pressure was high. In light of the fact that the judge's order expired with the jury's decision on sentencing, the district court concluded that no public purpose would be served by publication of the names on the first day of the trial rather than the last. This was particularly true, the court said, because the only use the public might make of the names was an improper one—jury tampering.

A Delaware judge went so far as to identify prospective jurors only by number so as to protect them from publicity. He acted after the *Wilmington News-Journal* had published profiles of jurors in another sensational murder case. In that instance, the judge sealed the jury list after the first ten members of the panel said they did not think they could render a fair verdict if they became subject to media attention. After the jury was seated, the judge released the names, but he also lectured the newspapers on what he saw as the hazards of publishing jury profiles.[36] Jury service, he said, is "the heart of American justice," adding: "With all its strengths, it (the jury), like any other human component, is not immune to injury by vivisection. The media's ability to cut often exceeds its ability to repair the damage it may inflict."

---

35. Schuster v. Bowen, 347 F. Supp. 319 (D. Nev. 1972).
36. Bruce W. Sanford, "Jurors in the Spotlight," *Quill,* November 1989, pp. 12–13.

With respect to an order forbidding the televising or sketching of jurors, the Arizona Supreme Court applied the *Nebraska Press* test and concluded an order could not be justified.[37] The court found that the danger posed by televising the sketches—that the jurors would base their verdict on fear—was not grave. The court said an alternative to the restraint was available. Potential jurors who conceded they might be influenced by fear could be excused. Finally, the order was ineffective because it did not apply to publication of sketches by newspapers. However, in another instance, the Fourth Circuit let stand an order forbidding the sketching of prospective jurors in the courthouse.[38]

Appellate courts generally have not looked with favor on attempts by trial judges to prevent reporters and others from talking to jurors about the verdict. In a notable exception, the Fifth Circuit Court of Appeals upheld an order prohibiting reporters from asking jurors how other members of the jury had voted and from making repeated requests for interviews with jurors who had refused to talk.[39] The court said the trial court had not abused its discretion in forbidding the badgering of jurors. Further, the court said that the vote of a juror who refused to be interviewed is information "not available to the public at large." Therefore, there is no violation of First Amendment rights in forbidding reporters to seek such information.

Federal circuit courts, including the Fifth, have held that orders forbidding reporters and others to talk to jurors must be narrowly tailored to serve an important interest if they are to pass First Amendment analysis. The Fifth Circuit ruled that an order forbidding any person to interview jurors without the trial judge's permission swept too broadly.[40] The trial court's order said permission to interview would be granted only on a showing of good cause. The appellate court said that "the First Amendment right to gather news" was reason enough to overrule such a vaguely phrased order. The Tenth Circuit struck down a double-barreled edict forbidding jurors from discussing a highly publicized armed robbery case and ordering everyone, including reporters, to "stay away from the jurors."[41] The court said the judge had failed to meet the heavy burden of proving that the restraint was necessary.

The cases, like the Supreme Court's decision in *Nebraska Press,* leave open the possibility that a judge can issue orders designed to protect jurors from the media. But if the orders are to survive First Amendment scrutiny they must be narrowly drawn and clear evidence must show that the orders will protect the defendant's right to a fair trial that otherwise would be in jeopardy. It is equally clear that if orders protecting the anonymity of jurors are to work, courts also must seal jury lists and conduct the voir dire in such a way as to avoid naming the jurors.

---

37. KPNX Broadcasting Co. v. Maricopa County Superior Court, 139 Ariz. 246, 678 P. 2d 431 (Ariz. 1984).
38. Society of Professional Journalists v. Martin, 556 F. 2d 706 (4th Cir. 1977); cert. denied, 434 U.S. 1022 (1978).
39. United States v. Harrelson, 713 F.2d 1114 (5th Cir. 1983); cert. denied, 465 U.S. 1041 (1984).
40. In re Express-News Corp., 695 F. 2d 807 (5th Cir. 1982).
41. United States v. Sherman, 581 F. 2d 1358 (9th Cir. 1978).

CONDUCTING A FAIR TRIAL

The previous sections of this chapter tell two stories. One is a history of conflict that raged for two decades between the news media and criminal defense lawyers over the right of criminal defendants to trial by an impartial jury. Both sides wrapped themselves in the Bill of Rights. At the height of the conflict, journalists portrayed themselves as beleaguered defenders of the First Amendment and the people's right to know. That a juicy crime also sells newspapers and magazines, or attracts an audience to television news, was treated as beside the point. Lawyers portrayed themselves as the protectors of society's misfits who might be deprived of their liberty or even their lives if the Sixth Amendment could not be used to protect them from prejudicial news stories. That fairness might demand prompt conviction in some instances occasionally was overlooked in the pursuit of a favorable verdict.

The second story is one of accommodation, as courts at all levels, under constant prodding from the Supreme Court, sought to reconcile the conflicting constitutional positions. Judges, literally caught in the middle, have fashioned legal principles that work reasonably well to safeguard the interests protected by both the First and Sixth Amendments. Through their efforts, the conflicts that once led to name calling by both sides now are being resolved in the courts by application of those principles.

Thus, when the media, print and electronic, can and do give saturation coverage to major crime stories, defendants can, even in the most highly publicized cases, get a fair trial. A fair trial is possible in part because the judicial system accepted that not all publicity is prejudicial. Fair trials are possible also because the Supreme Court insisted that court proceedings be conducted in public, accepting that photojournalism has a role in making those proceedings public.

Nonprejudicial Publicity

Need jurors be completely uninformed about the case they are asked to decide? That question has confronted judges since Chief Justice Marshall dealt with it in the *Burr* case. In that instance, he said they need not be completely uninformed, but they do need to have their minds open to the testimony they will hear in the courtroom. He recognized that some defendants, like former Vice-President Burr, might be so widely known that only the least intelligent, or least involved, members of society would have no knowledge of them. Could such persons be entrusted with resolving difficult cases? Would they be likely to understand the issues, or give them serious attention?

Murphy v. Florida, 421 U.S. 794, 95 S. Ct. 2031, 44 L.Ed.2d 589 (1975). To resolve such questions, the Supreme Court twice has accepted for review cases in which defendants were found guilty of highly publicized crimes. In each instance, the Court sustained the convictions, holding that factual information about suspects and the crimes for which they are being tried is not in itself prejudicial. The decisions reinforced the position taken by many judges that impartial jurors need not be uninformed and that rigorous voir dire will eliminate those who have fixed opinions as to guilt or innocence.

The first case involved Jack Murphy, one of the most flamboyant criminals of the mid-century. Murphy first gained media attention in 1964 for his role in stealing the Star of India sapphire from an elaborately protected case in a New York City museum. That episode became the subject of a movie. Later, he went to Miami Beach, where he became known as "Murph the Surf." He was handsome and had a way with women. He used those attributes to gain entry to the homes of the wealthy, from which he took jewels and cash. One such episode resulted in murder, for which Murphy was convicted. All these escapades were given heavy news coverage. When Murphy resumed his criminal career after a prison term, police captured him and three accomplices as they fled from a robbery in a Miami Beach home.

At the trial, Murphy's lawyer argued that news coverage of his client's activities made a fair trial impossible. He supported that position by offering the court a voluminous file of newspaper clippings and transcripts of news broadcasts. The judge conducted a careful voir dire and seated a jury he believed to be impartial. Murphy's lawyer took little part in the trial, resting his case on the belief that any conviction would be reversed on appeal because of publicity given to his client. The jury did indeed convict Murphy. A state appellate court confirmed. Murphy's lawyer turned to the federal courts for relief, arguing that his client was a victim of the news media. When he was rebuffed there, he went to the United States Supreme Court which, in *Murphy* v. *Florida,* affirmed the conviction with only one dissent.

Justice Thurgood Marshall wrote for the Court. He said that the earlier decisions in *Irvin, Rideau, Estes,* and *Sheppard* do not stand for the proposition that juror exposure to factual information about a defendant and his crime is prejudicial on its face. Reasoning as Chief Justice John Marshall had in *Burr,* he wrote that jurors need not come into the courtroom "wholly ignorant of the *facts,* for this would establish an impossible standard." Thurgood Marshall added that voir dire must be used diligently to find out whether exposure to factual information has led a potential juror to a fixed conclusion about the defendant's guilt or innocence. Further, the judge selecting the jury must look beyond the courtroom into the community. Only if the "general atmosphere...is sufficiently inflammatory" should the judge disregard a prospective juror's assertions of impartiality.

The Court found no evidence of such an atmosphere in Miami. Nor could it find anything in the clippings submitted by Murphy's lawyer likely to arouse strong emotions against his client. The news clippings merely recited the facts of a criminal career.

This decision sent a clear message to trial and appeals courts. A mere showing of factual news stories will not alone support the conclusion that an impartial jury cannot be had. Reinforcing a point made by Justice Clark in *Irvin,* the Court emphasized that jurors need not be completely ignorant of a case in order to be fair. Beyond that, the Court was reiterating its faith in the ability of careful, conscientious judges to use voir dire to screen out those potential jurors who would resist the impressions conveyed by the evidence.

Murphy remained in prison until 1986, when he was paroled at the age of forty-eight on condition that he remain on probation for the rest of his life. He said he had undergone a religious conversion and would "make his peace preaching" and his living by lecturing and selling surfing paintings.[42]

Patton v. Yount, 467 U.S. 1025, 104 S.Ct. 2885, 81 L.Ed.2d 847 (1984).

Nearly a decade later, the Court reinforced its decision in *Murphy,* upholding the conviction of a high school teacher, Jon E. Yount, who had twice been found guilty of the stabbing death of a female student. On his arrest, the teacher confessed, then, at trial, pleaded temporary insanity. A jury found him guilty and the judge sentenced him to life in prison. On appeal, the Pennsylvania Supreme Court held that Yount had not been adequately represented by counsel when he made his confession. The court ordered a new trial. All these events were widely publicized.

Because of the publicity, the nature of the crime—the victim had been left in the woods to drown in her own blood, and the small size of the community in which it occurred, virtually everyone called for jury duty in the second trial was familiar with the facts. Nevertheless, the trial judge refused repeated motions for a change of venue. He conducted a thorough voir dire, questioning 163 prospective jurors before settling on a panel that he believed to be free of fixed opinions. That jury, too, found the defendant guilty, and he again was sentenced to life in prison.

Yount, like Sam Sheppard, served ten years of his sentence before he was able to convince a court that publicity had kept him from getting a fair trial. The U.S. Court of Appeals for the Third Circuit noted that the voir dire had disclosed that all but 2 of the 163 persons questioned had heard of the case and more than three-fourths of them had some opinion as to Yount's guilt. These were higher proportions than those that had led the Supreme Court to reverse the conviction in *Irvin*. The court ordered a new trial.

The Supreme Court agreed to review the decision and reversed, six to two. It took the case, it said, "to consider the problem of pervasive media publicity that now arises so frequently in the trial of sensational criminal cases." The majority noted that four years had elapsed between the two trials. Jury selection for the second trial occurred "at a time when prejudicial publicity was greatly diminished and community sentiment had softened." The two newspapers published in the county in which the trial was held had published only a few articles about it, and "many of these were extremely brief announcements." During the voir dire, papers printed daily articles, "but these too were purely factual, generally discussing not the crime or prior prosecutions, but the prolonged process of jury selection." The majority concluded there was neither "the barrage of inflammatory publicity" condemned in *Murphy* nor the "huge...wave of passion," that led to the reversal in *Irvin*.

The majority made much of the passage of time as an antidote for prejudicial publicity, stating that the voir dire had indeed revealed that many of the jurors had held opinions about Yount's guilt, but "time had weakened or eliminated any

---

42. Associated Press, "'Murph the Surf' Is Now Back on Free Turf," *Louisville Courier-Journal,* 11 November 1986.

conviction they had had.'' Nor were old passions revived by the kind of publicity that preceded the second trial. The Court concluded that the judge had used the voir dire reasonably to select those "who had forgotten or would need to be persuaded again."

Thus, in *Patton* as in *Murphy,* the Court said it is not the amount of publicity about a crime, but the nature of that publicity, that determines whether the atmosphere has been so infected with prejudice as to make a fair trial impossible. If the news stories are factual in nature, if there is no attempt on the part of the news media to convict the defendant before trial, a fair trial in the courtroom is possible, even though prospective jurors have read or heard the stories. The law does not expect jurors to be ignorant of the facts. It does require that their minds be open to the evidence and that they base their decision on it. Any less realistic standard would make it virtually impossible for defendants in highly publicized criminal cases to be tried at all.

The Photographer and the Courtroom

The Supreme Court's decision in *Estes* condemned still and television photographers as contributors to an atmosphere of prejudice in the courtroom. The Court came within one vote of holding that their presence would always make a fair trial impossible by denying the defendant the due process guaranteed by the Fifth and Fourteenth Amendments. At that point, in 1965, the future of courtroom photography appeared bleak.

The *Estes* case occurred because at the time Texas, with Colorado, was one of two states that permitted photographers to use their cameras in courtrooms. The decision was, in part, a reaction to the obtrusive nature of the still and television cameras then in use. Photographic equipment was bulky, sometimes noisy, and required special lighting. However, technical advances even then were leading to smaller cameras and to film and videotape that could be used in available light. Justice John Marshall Harlan took note of these advances in writing his concurring opinion in *Estes*. Although he agreed with four other justices in holding that the use of cameras in the courtroom had kept Estes from getting a fair trial, he was not willing to join them in holding that that would always be the case. He argued that further advances in technology might permit unobtrusive photography in the courtroom. Therefore, he wrote, he was unwilling to close the door on future experimentation with courtroom photography.

In time, Florida was one of several states that took up Harlan's invitation to experiment further with photojournalism in courtrooms. The Florida Supreme Court decided, in response to a request from the Post-Newsweek television stations in Jacksonville and Miami, to permit televising of court proceedings on an experimental basis.[43] Reaction was favorable, and the rule was made permanent.[44]

---

43. Petition of the Post-Newsweek Stations, Florida, Inc., 327 So.2d 1 (Fla. App. 1976); 347 So. 2d 402 (Fla. 1976).
44. 370 So. 2d 764 (Fla. 1979).

The guidelines regulating photography in Florida are quite strict.[45] Only one camera and one operator are permitted inside the courtroom. Once placed, the camera cannot be moved during the trial. Nor can the operator change lenses, film, or videotape while court is in session. Sound may be recorded only through the court's own audio pickup system. Operators are forbidden to record conferences between the lawyers, between parties and counsel, and with the judge. The judge can, without being subject to appeal, forbid televising or recording of the testimony of certain witnesses. The jury cannot be filmed under any circumstances. In short, television is limited to covering only what members of the jury can see and hear, and sometimes not all of that. Judges are admonished that their first obligation is to ensure the defendant a fair trial. Judges who conclude that television would prevent that can keep cameras out of the courtroom.

Chandler v. Florida, 449 U.S. 560, 101 S.Ct. 802, 66 L.Ed.2d 740 (1981).

During the experimental period a judge of a Dade County court permitted limited televising of a trial that had attracted a great deal of attention. Two Miami Beach police officers were charged with burglary after an amateur radio operator had heard them talking over their walkie-talkie while they committed the crime. When they were brought to trial, a television camera recorded part of the testimony of the radio operator. It also recorded the closing arguments of counsel for both sides. Only two minutes and fifty-five seconds of videotape was used on the air, and the editor selected only those parts depicting the prosecution's side. When the police officers, Noel Chandler and Robert Granger, were found guilty, they used the presence of the television camera as the basis for an appeal. They got nowhere in the Florida courts, but on further appeal, the Supreme Court took their case. In *Chandler* v. *Florida,* it affirmed the convictions.

The attorney for Chandler and Granger argued that the Supreme Court had held in *Estes* that no televised trial could be fair. Chief Justice Warren Burger, writing for a majority of the Court, rejected that argument. He noted that only four justices had taken that position. The fifth member of the majority in *Estes,* Justice Harlan, confined his reasoning to the facts of that case. While Harlan agreed that the presence of cameras had kept Estes from getting a fair trial, he made a point of noting that smaller, less obtrusive cameras might not interfere with a fair trial in the future. Focusing on Harlan's concurring opinion in *Estes,* Chief Justice Burger said the burden was on Chandler's and Granger's attorney to prove that their trial had not been fair.

The chief justice's conclusions in *Chandler* can be summarized as follows: The Supreme Court has no supervisory authority over state courts. Therefore, they are free to permit photography in the courtroom if they wish. The only limiting provisions at the federal level are that clause in the Sixth Amendment to the Constitution guaranteeing trial by an impartial jury and the clause in the Fourteenth Amendment forbidding deprival of life, liberty, or property without due process of law. As long as the presence of cameras cannot be shown to violate either of those provisions, federal courts have no basis for interfering.

45.　Post-Newsweek Stations, 370 So. 2d 764, at 778–779, 783–784.

There is no firm evidence, Burger continued, to prove that the mere presence of cameras in the courtroom has an effect on the participants. It follows that federal courts cannot ban state experiments with photographic coverage of trials on the mere suspicion that prejudice will somehow occur. Therefore, the Supreme Court had no basis for concluding that the trial of Chandler and Granger had been inherently unfair.

Nor, the Supreme Court concluded, could the defendants offer facts to prove that they had been the victims of a prejudiced jury. Jurors were asked during voir dire whether the presence of cameras would keep them from deciding the case solely on the basis of the evidence. The fact that a jury was seated demonstrated that the judge and lawyers for both sides believed that the jurors could do so.

The Supreme Court's decision in *Chandler* clearly rejected the many assumptions about the effects of television that are found in the leading opinion in *Estes*. The effect of *Chandler* has been to encourage state courts to adopt rules permitting still photographers and television crews to cover their proceedings; and, by 1989, courts in forty-five states had done so.[46] Some have limited photo coverage to appellate courts, which ordinarily do not hear witnesses and take testimony. In all instances, rules of court give the judge broad authority to regulate use of cameras to avoid a disturbance or other interference with the fairness of the proceeding.

Federal rules of criminal procedure continue to forbid photography in federal courts. Alcee Hastings, a federal district court judge in Miami who was accused of accepting bribes, challenged the rules by asking that his trial be covered by television. The Eleventh Circuit Court of Appeals held that only a minimal First Amendment interest would be served by such coverage and rejected his request.[47] Hastings was tried without the presence of cameras and was acquitted. However, he was impeached by Congress, and the Senate voted to remove him from office. On another occasion, the Supreme Court refused to review a decision of the U.S. Court of Appeals for the Sixth Circuit upholding a district judge's refusal to permit photographic coverage of the trial of Teamsters Union officials on embezzlement charges.[48] Television and radio stations and still photographers had argued that photo and audio coverage of the trial would serve an important First Amendment interest. The trial court judge said the ban on such coverage served "the significant government interest of promoting fair and accurate fact-finding by assuring that litigants and witnesses are not distracted by media shyness or showboating."

Thus, although the First Amendment ensures that the public and reporters have a right of access to courtrooms and news of the courts, the Amendment does not go so far as to mandate a right to photograph court proceedings. However, neither the fair trial clause of the Sixth Amendment nor the due process clauses of the Fifth and Fourteenth stand as barriers against photographs. Thus, the Constitution is neutral toward photography in the courtroom as long as the

---

46. Richard D. Heffner, "TV Cameras Don't Belong in the Courts," *Wall Street Journal,* 24 March 1989.

47. United States v. Hastings, 695 F. 2d 1278 (11th Cir. 1983).

48. "Supreme Court Rejects Appeal in Courtroom Camera Case," *Editor & Publisher,* 10 December 1988, p. 25.

judge takes proper steps to ensure a fair trial. Judges remain divided as to whether the presence of cameras, particularly television cameras, distort the conduct of the trial, although by now most seem willing to accept them.

In The Professional World

A criminal trial is not a sporting event, nor is it a television drama. In fact, most trials tend to be more boring than dramatic. They drone to a conclusion, unattended by anyone except a few friends and relatives of the defendant and the victim, and courthouse hangers-on. Only the occasional celebrated case, involving a prominent defendant or victim, or a particularly monstrous crime, attracts full-time attention from the news media. Yet, whether the case is boring or celebrated, it has one common element: The defendant is gambling his freedom, and perhaps even his life, on the outcome. Criminal trials, then, are serious business.

Media professionals treat them as such. With most newspapers, Jazz-Age coverage of the police beat and the courts can be found only in the microfilmed copies of front pages from another era. Police and court beats still are covered on a daily basis, but with an eye for stories that illustrate trends, that will alert the public to problems with a particular kind of crime, or that will serve as a check on the performance of police, prosecutor, and judges. Much of the information is simply reduced to a listing for the record of offenses reported, arrests made, and of court action.

It is that occasional celebrated case that raises tensions between the legal system and the media. Judges who must try such cases are very much aware of the duty imposed by *Sheppard*. They must do all they can to protect the defendant's rights or risk having the verdict overturned on appeal. No judge likes being overruled by a higher court. And prosecutors must be cautious in talking with reporters lest they disclose information that might be seen later as grounds for reversal. If there has been any publicity at all, defense attorneys are under an obligation at the start to seek a change of venue. If that fails, they are likely to appeal a conviction on grounds that the publicity prevented the defendant from getting a fair trial. A defense lawyer who does not raise such questions runs the risk of being accused of offering inadequate counsel. These pressures on the lawyers and the judge may well result in pressures on the news media also, as the cases in this chapter illustrate.

The cases also illustrate that the media are free to publish or broadcast any scrap of information they can learn about the crime, the suspect, the victim, and the possible witnesses. A judge seeking to order the media not to use information in their possession is unlikely to meet the test prescribed in *Nebraska Press Association*. Editors supervising coverage of a celebrated case act in the knowledge that the only restraints are those they impose on themselves.

All of the major professional organizations representing journalists, print or electronic, have adopted codes of ethics. All recognize that prejudicial publicity can interfere with the right to a fair trial and suggest that it be min-imized. However, all of these codes are written in general terms, and jour-nals have resisted attempts to enforce them.

As cases like *Murphy* and *Patton* suggest, much crime and court cover-age is not sensational and prejudicial. It is not unusual for the media to with-hold such information as a defendant's prior criminal record, either until the trial ends or the record has been introduced in court. Many editors under-stand that coverage that results in a change of venue or a reversal of a con-viction only adds to the costs of supporting the courts, costs the taxpayers must bear.

And yet there are limits to the self-restraint of even the most conscien-tious editors. In a competitive market, if one outlet uses leaked information, no matter how prejudicial, others will scramble to get it, too. KNXT's use in Los Angeles of a videotape supposedly showing John DeLorean caught up in a cocaine deal was followed by news stories describing the taped scene in detail.

Nor is competition the only factor that may lead editors to ignore a code of ethics. When someone runs amok, kills several persons, and then talks about it, as in *Nebraska Press Association,* it is illogical to believe that no one will publish or broadcast those facts. As the Supreme Court pointed out, if the facts aren't used by the media, word of mouth not only will cir-culate them, but enlarge on them. The potential for harmful rumor also was a factor in the editor's decision to publish in *Dickinson*. If the police think seriously enough that someone is plotting to kill the mayor so that they make an arrest to prevent it, the public ought to know. In that instance, the editors thought the facts might defuse racial tensions that already were run-ning high. Clearly, there are times when the news media should make every effort to get the facts of a crime and share them with the public.

If the criminal justice system is working as it should, there is not much point in trying cases in the newspapers or on the air. It is doubtful that "scoops" on the police and court beats sell many newspapers or win many ratings points. The public interest is served if the news is reported as it breaks. If the system is not working properly, different considerations come into play. If the police are corrupt, the prosecutor lazy, judges incompetent, the public needs to know. One way to expose such problems is for the news media to dig out the facts pointing to the guilt of suspects who go free or to the innocence of an occasional suspect who is convicted wrongfully. In such situations, editors can hope that, given the facts, the voters will set things right at the next election.

In any event, as the cases in this chapter suggest, whether they are cov-ering the occasional highly newsworthy crime or the routine, professional journalists are aware that someone, at some point, may try to hide things from them. When that happens, professionals usually are quick to assert a right of access, even though they may decide not to use the information. As the earlier cases in this textbook tell us, the First Amendment long has meant that each of us, journalist or not, has a right to decide what in-formation we will share with others. The cases in this chapter also tell us that the First Amendment gives us the right to insist on access to news of the courts.

FOR REVIEW

1. Distinguish between a hearing and a trial. As far as a right of access is concerned, is that difference significant?

2. Plea bargaining sometimes becomes an issue in states where judges and prosecutors are elected. Why might that be?

3. Define "voir dire." What is its purpose?

4. Define "impartial juror." Why is the term important?

5. What kinds of information are considered likely to induce prejudice in jurors?

6. Outline and define the procedures a judge is expected to take to ensure a defendant's right to a fair trial (*Sheppard* v. *Maxwell*).

7. What did the Supreme Court's decision in *Murphy* v. *Florida* contribute to the definition of a fair trial?

8. What is meant by the term "gag order"? Is such an order ever proper?

9. Assess the likelihood that a gag order might be imposed on journalists covering a trial. What should be done if such an order is issued? Why?

10. What is meant by a First Amendment right of access to the courts? How did the Supreme Court rationalize such a right? Why did some justices have reservations about it?

11. You are a photographer confronting a judge who does not permit photography in her courtroom. What arguments would you use in an attempt to persuade her to change her mind? And now you are the judge. Given that you have a principled belief that cameras do not belong in the courtroom, how would you respond to the arguments you have advanced as a photographer? If you were the defendant in a highly publicized criminal trial, what position would you urge your lawyer to take with respect to cameras in the courtroom? Why?

12. You have received a summons to jury duty in the trial of a highly placed cocaine distributor. What position would you take with respect to an open voir dire and release of your name and address to the news media? If you were a reporter covering that trial, what is the likelihood that you could insist and obtain an open voir dire and access to the names and addresses of the jurors? In each of your roles, refer to appropriate legal precedents.

CHAPTER 7

CHAPTER 7

It is a legal principle of long standing that "the public...has a right to every man's evidence," or that courts have legal authority, grounded in the Constitution, to summon as witnesses any persons who may have direct knowledge of a crime or the subject matter of a civil action. The Sixth Amendment, which gives suspects a right to a public trial by an impartial jury, also gives them the right "to have compulsory process for obtaining witnesses" in their behalf. This is a reference to the subpoena power—the power of a court to issue an official order summoning witnesses to appear and testify. This power is available to all who are directly involved in a legal proceeding, civil or criminal, including plaintiffs, defendants, prosecutors, grand juries, and judges. One who refuses to obey an order to appear is in contempt and may be punished by the judge. The subpoena

THE JOURNALIST'S PRIVILEGE: CONFIDENTIALITY

power is based on the theory that a court is more likely to reach a proper verdict if it hears evidence from all who have knowledge of the case in point than it is if some are excused.

Therefore, the courts have been reluctant to grant exceptions to the principle that all should testify. Certain exceptions, called "privileges," have been granted in recognition of special circumstances. The strongest of these is found in the Fifth Amendment, which says, in part: "No person...shall be compelled in any criminal case to be a witness against himself...." It was put there as a guard against the use of torture to force confessions and it means what it says: No matter how guilty a suspect may be, any confession must be completely voluntary and made in full knowledge of the consequences. If the suspect does not want to plead guilty, he has the right to remain silent and make the prosecutor prove the charge against him.

Other privileges have been recognized by decisions of the courts to respect confidential relationships. Some states have written them into rules of court or into statute law. The most common is the husband-wife privilege. Few courts will require one spouse to testify against the other. Other common-law privileges involve lawyer-client, physician-patient, and clergy-penitent relationships. The courts recognize that a lawyer cannot adequately protect a client who tells him less than the truth. A physician may make a wrong diagnosis if the patient withholds information. A priest cannot grant full absolution to a penitent who does not confess fully. In all instances, the receivers of the information are bound by codes of ethics not to disclose it to others without permission. Generally, courts have converted these codes into privileges, but they are not absolute. Physicians, for instance, are required to report suspicious wounds to the police and contagious diseases to the Board of Health.

For years, journalists sought with little success to have courts recognize their confidential relationship with some of their news sources and protect it as privileged. They argued that they served a public purpose when they investigated wrongdoing, particularly on the part of public officials, and called public attention to it. They argued further that some of their information came from sources who would disclose it only on condition that the reporter not identify them. Such sources feared they might lose their jobs or suffer physical harm if their identity became known to anyone other than the reporter. Through the years, the promise to protect a source has become a part of the journalistic code. Journalists asked to identify confidential sources argued that were they to do so, few would trust them again, and their effectiveness would be ended. Until recent times, few courts recognized a privilege for journalists, so some reporters and editors have gone to jail or paid fines rather than break their word to a source.

As far back as 1896, the Maryland Legislature gave enough credence to the journalists' arguments to enact a law defining reporters and giving them a right in some instances to protect their sources. This was the first state shield law. Twenty-five other states now have such laws. They range from near-absolute to limited in their protection.

Journalists served with subpoenas to appear as witnesses also argued for recognition of either a common-law privilege or one grounded in the First Amendment. Until 1972, they did so with little success. In that year, in *Branzburg* v. *Hayes*,[1] the Supreme Court told three reporters that they were like everyone else and would have to honor subpoenas ordering them to appear before grand juries seeking information about possible crime. In doing so, the Court appeared to reject the reporters' argument that the First Amendment should give some protection to their promises to their confidential sources. However, the justices were so divided in their reasoning that most courts now read the decision as creating a limited First Amendment privilege for journalists. Some state courts, reluctant to invoke the First Amendment, are holding that journalists have a common-law right to protect confidential sources and information.

Statutory and court-granted privileges raise four questions:

1. Who is entitled to invoke the privilege? This involves the definition of a reporter and questions as to who is entitled to be considered as one.

2. What is protected? The privilege commonly enables journalists to refuse to identify confidential sources. It may also permit them to protect confidential information.

3. How far does the privilege extend? In the usual context, it can be used to challenge a subpoena, whether to appear before a grand jury or as a witness in a trial. However, courts also have used search warrants and have directed subpoenas at third parties to get information from journalists.

4. To what kinds of situations can the privilege be applied? Most commonly, journalists are asked to testify because they seem to have direct knowledge of a crime or the subject matter of a civil action. But in some instances, as in libel cases, the journalist may be a party to the action.

We will find that the extent of the privilege varies widely and is determined on a case-by-case basis. In a few jurisdictions, it is considered to be absolute. In four states, as of this writing, it has been rejected flatly. Even in states that recognize

---

1.   408 U.S. 665, 92 S.Ct. 2646, 33 L.Ed.2d 626 (1972).

the privilege, journalists may be subjected to punishment if a court rules that it does not apply to their situation. For instance, Richard Hargraves, an editorial writer for the *Belleville* (Ill.) *News-Democrat,* spent three days in jail because he refused to identify his sources.[2] He had written an editorial accusing the chairman of a county board of supervisors of lying and refusing to keep campaign promises. Hargraves's sources became an issue when the chairman sued for libel. When the writer refused to name them, a judge sentenced him to jail until he was willing to do so. The ordeal ended when the chairman's lawyer identified the sources by other means.

Despite wide variations in the application of the privilege, courts generally use three questions when a request is made to quash a subpoena issued to a journalist:

1. Does the journalist have information bearing directly on the case?

2. Can it be obtained from other sources?

3. Is it crucial to the determination of the case?

Major Cases

- *Baker* v. *F & F Investment,* 470 F.2d 778 (2d Cir. 1972).

- *Branzburg* v. *Hayes,* 408 U.S. 665, 92 S.Ct. 2646, 33 L.Ed.2d 626 (1972).

- *Bruno & Stillman* v. *Globe Newspaper Co.,* 633 F.2d 583 (1st Cir. 1980).

- *Commonwealth* v. *Corsetti,* 387 Mass. 1 (Mass. 1982).

- *Grand Forks Herald* v. *District Court,* 322 N.W.2d 850 (N.D. 1982).

- *Greenberg* v. *CBS Inc.,* 419 N.Y.S.2d 988 (N.Y.App. 1979).

- *In re Grand Jury Proceedings, Storer Communications* v. *Giovan,* 810 F.2d 580 (6th Cir. 1987).

- *In re Vrazo,* 423 A.2d 695 (N.J.Super. 1980).

- *Miller* v. *Transamerican Press, Inc.,* 621 F.2d 721 (5th Cir. 1980).

- *Reporters Committee for Freedom of the Press* v. *American Telephone & Telegraph Co.,* 593 F.2d 1030 (D.C.Cir. 1979).

- *United States* v. *Cuthbertson* 630 F.2d 139 (3d Cir. 1980); 651 F.2d 189 (3d Cir. 1981).

- *Zurcher* v. *Stanford Daily,* 436 U.S. 547, 98 S.Ct. 1970, 56 L.Ed.2d 525 (1978).

---

2. Mark Fitzgerald, "Editorial Writer Freed," *Editor & Publisher,* 14 July 1984, p. 10.

THE ORIGINS OF THE PRIVILEGE

Reporters and Grand Juries

The Supreme Court's decision in *Branzburg* v. *Hayes* was widely viewed by journalists as a slap in the face. Three reporters had asked the Court to give them a qualified First Amendment privilege to protect them from grand jury subpoenas, and the Court had turned them down. The leading opinion told them that, like any other persons who were properly summoned, they would have to appear and testify. But that leading opinion was signed by only four justices. The fifth member of the majority in the five-to-four decision invited journalists who felt harassed by the legal process to challenge subpoenas by filing a motion to quash, that is, to request a hearing on the propriety of the subpoena. Three of the four justices in the minority would have granted the reporters a qualified privilege, while the fourth would have made it absolute.

Branzburg v. *Hayes,* **408 U.S. 665, 92 S.Ct. 2646, 33 L.Ed.2d 626 (1972).**

Very quickly, as journalists acted on the invitation to challenge subpoenas, lower courts began reading *Branzburg* as establishing a qualified First Amendment privilege very much like the one the Court had told the three reporters they could not have. Thus, in an ironic way, *Branzburg* v. *Hayes* has become one of the more important decisions expanding the rights of journalists. Although they can't count on it in every instance, it has given journalists additional credibility when they promise sources that their names will not be revealed to authorities.

The three reporters who were brought together in *Branzburg* came from widely separated parts of the country and had only a few things in common—they were investigative reporters; they were interested in people who lived at the fringes of society; they had won the trust of their sources. As a result, they were able to produce stories offering insights into lifestyles that were viewed with distrust by much of the public.

Paul Branzburg was a reporter for the *Louisville Courier-Journal*. He won entry to the subculture of drug abusers in Louisville and Frankfort, the Kentucky capital, and wrote a series of revealing stories for his newspapers in which he sought to describe why the children of middle-class Kentuckians were using narcotics. Earl Caldwell was one of the first black reporters employed by the *New York Times*. Assigned to the newspaper's West Coast bureau, he won the confidence of Black Panthers in the San Francisco area. At a time when that organization was widely believed to be plotting guerrilla warfare against white society, Caldwell was able to explore the forces that moved some blacks to take up arms. He found that the Panthers had some real grievances and sought some positive goals. Paul Pappas was a reporter-photographer for a television station in New Bedford, Massachusetts. In a city torn by racial strife, he, too, won the confidence of a Black Panther group. Members, fearing that police would attack their headquarters and kill them, let Pappas spend a night with them on condition that he would report nothing unless the attack took place. When it didn't, he kept his word.

All three reporters were served with subpoenas by grand juries investigating criminal activity. Branzburg was asked to tell county grand juries in Louisville and Frankfort what he knew about the traffic in illegal drugs. Kentucky had a shield law[3] that protected reporters who refused to identify confidential sources of information. When Branzburg tried to use it, two separate state courts held that he could not. His stories, and the photographs illustrating them, made clear that Branzburg had been present when drug laws were violated. That made him an eyewitness to crime. He was the source of much of the information in his stories, and there was nothing confidential about his identity. Therefore, the courts ruled that he would have to appear before the grand juries and name the persons who had committed crimes in his presence. Caldwell was subpoenaed to appear before a federal grand jury in San Francisco looking into charges that the Black Panthers were plotting to kill President Nixon. He argued that if he were to appear before the jury, he would forever lose the trust of his sources, even though he said nothing. That would cut off important information about the black community, having a "chilling effect" on First Amendment freedoms. Both a federal district court and the Ninth Circuit Court of Appeals were willing to permit Caldwell to refuse to identify his sources, but they were not willing to grant him an absolute right to refuse to meet with the grand jury. Pappas worked in a state that had no shield law. When he was asked to appear before a county grand jury and tell about his night in the Panther headquarters, he asked the courts to excuse him. Massachusetts's highest court held that he would have to honor the summons or be held in contempt.

The Supreme Court took all three cases and treated them as one. Five-to-four it held that the reporters must honor the summonses and tell the grand juries what they knew. But aside from that, the Court's message was not at all clear. The justices wrote four opinions in which they differed sharply over how far the First Amendment should go in protecting newsgathering. Because the justices were split so many ways, and so evenly, in their reasoning, lower courts have been able to read *Branzburg* as both rejecting and supporting the journalist's privilege, with the majority favoring the latter view. To see how that has happened, we need to study the opinions of the justices.

Justice Byron R. White wrote the opinion of the Court, in which he was joined by three others. He began by making an important concession, one that has been quoted frequently in court decisions, most notably in *Richmond Newspapers,* with results examined in the previous chapter. Noting that the reporters had argued that the First Amendment ought to protect them in gathering the news as well as in disseminating it, White wrote that he did not question the Amendment's value to society. He added:

> Nor is it suggested that news gathering does not qualify for First Amendment protection; without some protection for seeking out the news, freedom of the press could be eviscerated.

---

3. Ky. Rev. Stat. 421. 100.

He followed that concession by defining the issue in this case in narrow terms, and by holding that no important First Amendment interests were at stake. He wrote:

> The sole issue before us is the obligation of reporters to respond to grand jury subpoenas as other citizens do and to answer questions relevant to an investigation into the commission of a crime. Citizens generally are not constitutionally immune from grand jury subpoenas; and neither the First Amendment nor any other constitutional provision protects the average citizen from disclosing to a grand jury information that he has received in confidence. The claim is, however, that reporters are exempt from these obligations because if forced to respond to subpoenas and identify their sources or disclose other confidences, their informants will refuse or be reluctant to furnish newsworthy information in the future. This asserted burden on news gathering is said to make compelled testimony from newsmen constitutionally suspect and to require a privileged position for them.
>
> It is clear that the First Amendment does not invalidate every incidental burdening of the press that may result from the enforcement of civil or criminal statutes of general applicability.

White noted that state courts consistently had held that journalists have no right, other than that granted by shield laws, to protect confidential sources and information. He wrote:

> These courts...have concluded that the First Amendment interest asserted by the newsman was outweighed by the general obligation of a citizen to appear before a grand jury or at trial, pursuant to a subpoena, and give what information he possesses.

Grand juries, White noted, play an important role in the criminal justice system. Jurors listen to allegations of wrongdoing and decide whether an individual should be charged with a crime. To help them in getting at the truth, grand juries have broad powers to subpoena witnesses. This authority, White wrote, is essential, but it is not unlimited. If it is abused, it may be restricted by a judge. However, the justice added that the "longstanding principle that 'the public...has a right to every man's evidence,'...is particularly applicable to grand jury proceedings."

At this point, White took notice of the testimonial privileges noted at the start of this chapter—the Fifth Amendment privilege against self-incrimination, and the common-law privileges cloaking marital, physician-patient, lawyer-client, and clergy-penitent relationships. Such testimonial privileges are so deeply rooted, he noted, as to be almost beyond challenge. Then he wrote:

> We are asked to create another [privilege] by interpreting the First Amendment to grant newsmen a testimonial privilege that other citizens do not enjoy. This we decline to do.

In rejecting the reporters' argument, White and the three justices who joined him balanced the public's interest in law enforcement against the journalists' interest in access to sources of news. Because they were not convinced that confidential sources play an important role in newsgathering, the justices came down on the side of law enforcement. They took the position that it is better to do something about crime than to write about it. In their view, anyone, including reporters, with direct knowledge of a crime has a duty to share that knowledge with law enforcement officers.

White further justified the plurality's position by arguing that a testimonial privilege grounded in the First Amendment could be abused. Journalists could use it to "protect a private system of informers..., a system that would be un-accountable to the public, would pose a threat to the citizen's justifiable expec-tations of privacy," and would also protect those tempted for pay or otherwise to "betray their trust to their employer or associates." Under the First Amend-ment, media informants would enjoy a higher degree of protection than do police informants. The latter have no constitutional protection, White noted. If a police informant's testimony is sought by a grand jury, or is needed in court, police ei-ther must identify him or drop the prosecution.

Nor were White and his colleagues willing to grant journalists a qualified priv-ilege based on common law rather than the First Amendment. To do that, they said, would "embark the judiciary on a long and difficult journey to...an uncer-tain destination." Courts would have to determine who would be entitled to claim the privilege. That would put the courts in the position of deciding who is a bona-fide journalist. Such decisions would be made difficult by the fact that the Su-preme Court has held that freedom of the press is a "fundamental personal right not confined to newspapers and periodicals." Lecturers, political pollsters, nov-elists, academic researchers, and dramatists also gather information and offer it to the public.

However, the plurality said it had no objection to legislators attempting to de-fine journalists and grant them a testimonial privilege by statute. Thus, the four justices gave their approval to the shield laws then in effect in seventeen states.

Only at the end did White and his associates temper their strong rejection of a journalist's privilege. They wrote:

> Finally, as we have earlier indicated, news gathering is not without its First Amendment protection, and grand jury investigations, if instituted or conducted other than in good faith, would pose wholly different issues for resolution under the First Amendment. Official harassment of the press undertaken not for purposes of law enforcement but to disrupt a reporter's relationship with his news sources would have no justification. Grand juries are subject to judicial control and subpoenas to motions to quash. We do not expect courts will forget that grand juries must operate within the limits of the First Amendment as well as the Fifth.

Justice Lewis F. Powell, Jr., voted with White and his colleagues to hold that the three journalists had no right to refuse to answer a grand jury's questions. But he wrote separately to enlarge on the point made in the paragraph above. That he did so has proved to be of utmost importance to journalists who receive subpoe-nas, not only to testify before grand juries, but in other legal proceedings, both criminal and civil. The majority of the courts considering challenges to such sub-poenas have found in Powell's concurrence support for a qualified journalist's privilege. Because this is the case, Powell's reasoning merits careful attention.

The justice noted that a majority of the Court had indeed refused to give journalists an absolute privilege that would protect their refusal to testify in any legal proceeding. However, not even the plurality had said that journalists must testify under all circumstances. It had conceded that the right to gather news has some degree of First Amendment protection. Public officials and courts must respect that right, Powell wrote. If they should not, the justice invited journalists to seek redress in court:

> As indicated in the concluding portion of the opinion, the Court states that no harassment of newsmen will be tolerated. If a newsman believes that the grand jury investigation is not being conducted in good faith he is not without remedy. Indeed, if the newsman is called upon to give information bearing only a remote and tenuous relationship to the subject of the investigation, or if he has some other reason to believe that his testimony implicates confidential source relationships without a legitimate need of law enforcement, he will have access to the court on a motion to quash and an appropriate protective order may be entered. The asserted claim to privilege should be judged on its facts by the striking of a proper balance between freedom of the press and the obligation of all citizens to give relevant testimony with respect to criminal conduct. The balance of these vital constitutional and societal interests on a case-by-case basis accords with the tried and traditional way of adjudicating such questions.
>
> In short, the courts will be available to newsmen under circumstances where legitimate First Amendment interests require protection.

Powell thus sought to define how far the First Amendment might go in protecting the right to gather news. He suggested that grand juries ought not subpoena journalists unless there is reason to believe the latter have some substantial knowledge of the subject of the investigation. Further, Powell suggested that grand juries should respect the confidentiality of reporters' sources unless "a legitimate need of law enforcement" requires disclosure. These suggestions were stated with more precision by Justice Potter Stewart, in dissent with two others. The language was blunt:

> The Court's crabbed view of the First Amendment reflects a disturbing insensitivity to the critical role of an independent press in our society. The question whether a reporter has a constitutional right to a confidential relationship with his source is of first impression here, but the principles that should guide our decision are as basic as any to be found in the Constitution. While Mr. Justice Powell's enigmatic concurring opinion gives some hope of a more flexible view in the future, the Court in these cases holds that a newsman has no First Amendment right to protect his sources when called before a grand jury. The Court thus invites state and federal authorities to undermine the historic independence of the press by attempting to annex the journalistic profession as an investigative arm of government. Not only will this decision impair performance of the press' constitutionally protected functions, but it will, I am convinced, in the long run, harm rather than help the administration of justice.

White, in writing for the plurality, had responded to the arguments advanced by Branzburg, Caldwell, and Pappas by focusing on the role of the grand jury.

Stewart and his colleagues focused on the role of the news media. They seized on the majority's recognition that newsgathering has some First Amendment protection and enlarged on that theme:

A corollary of the right to publish must be the right to gather news....

...News must not be unnecessarily cut off at its source, for without freedom to acquire information the right to publish would be impermissibly compromised. Accordingly, a right to gather news, of some dimensions, must exist....

The right to gather news implies, in turn, a right to a confidential relationship between a reporter and his source. This proposition follows as a matter of simple logic once three factual predicates are recognized: (1) newsmen require informants to gather news; (2) confidentiality—the promise or understanding that names or certain aspects of communications will be kept off the record—is essential to the creation and maintenance of a newsgathering relationship with informants; and (3) an unbridled subpoena power—the absence of a constitutional right protecting, in *any* way, a confidential relationship from compulsory process—will either deter sources from divulging information or deter reporters from gathering and publishing information.

It is obvious that informants are necessary to the newsgathering process as we know it today. If it is to perform its constitutional mission, the press must do far more than merely print public statements or prepared handouts. Familiarity with the people and circumstances involved in the myriad background activities that result in the final product called "news" is vital to complete and responsible journalism, unless the press is to be a captive mouthpiece of "newsmakers."

It is equally obvious that the promise of confidentiality may be a necessary prerequisite to a productive relationship between a newsman and his informants. An officeholder may fear his superior; a member of the bureaucracy, his associates; a dissident, the scorn of majority opinion. All may have information valuable to the public discourse, yet each may be willing to relate that information only in confidence to a reporter whom he trusts, either because of excessive caution or because of a reasonable fear of reprisals or censure for unorthodox views. The First Amendment concern must not be with the motives of any particular news source, but rather with the conditions in which informants of all shades of the spectrum may make information available through the press to the public....

...Commentators and individual reporters have repeatedly noted the importance of confidentiality. And surveys among reporters and editors indicate that the promise of nondisclosure is necessary for many types of news gathering.

Finally, and most important, when governmental officials possess an unchecked power to compel newsmen to disclose information received in confidence, sources will clearly be deterred from publishing it, because uncertainty about exercise of the power will lead to "self-censorship."...The uncertainty arises, of course, because the judiciary has traditionally imposed virtually no limitations on the grand jury's broad investigatory powers.

Stewart sought to avoid the uncertainty, and the resulting self-censorship, by proposing a three-point test that must be met before a journalist could be required to testify. He wrote:

Accordingly, when a reporter is asked to appear before a grand jury and reveal confidences, I would hold that the government must (1) show that there is probable cause to believe that the newsman has information that is clearly relevant to a specific probable violation of law; (2) demonstrate that the information sought cannot be obtained by alternative means less destructive of First Amendment rights; and (3) demonstrate a compelling and overriding interest in the information.

This is not to say that a grand jury could not issue a subpoena until a such a showing is made, and it is not to say that a newsman would be in any way privileged to ignore any subpoena that was issued. Obviously, before the government's burden to make such a showing were triggered, the reporter would have to move to quash the subpoena, asserting the basis on which he considered the particular relationship a confidential one.

No doubt the courts would be required to make some delicate judgments in working out this accommodation. But that, after all, is the function of courts of law. Better such judgments, however difficult, than the simplistic and stultifying absolutism adopted by the Court in denying any force to the First Amendment in these cases.

Justice William O. Douglas wrote separately in dissent to advance an absolute view of the First Amendment. He would have held that journalists have a constitutional right to refuse to take part in any legal proceeding. If they chose to testify, they could do so on their own terms. No other member of the Court was willing to go that far.

Judges applying *Branzburg* have found the elements of a First Amendment journalist's privilege in three places:

1. White and the three justices who voted with him recognized that newsgathering has some First Amendment protection. While he was unwilling to convert that protection into a privilege in this case, he warned that "[o]fficial harassment of the press...would have no justification." Where a legitimate interest in coping with crime ends and harassment begins is, of course, a matter of judgment.

2. Powell, whose vote made the decision possible, emphasized White's warning against harassment. He made the further points that journalists ought not to be asked for "information bearing only a remote and tenuous relationship to the investigation," and ought not to be asked to identify confidential sources without good reason.

3. Where White and Powell were vague, Stewart was specific. The former can be read as recognizing that a privilege exists. Stewart had no doubts. The three-part test he suggested for determining when the privilege can be invoked has been adopted almost verbatim by many courts. In most jurisdictions, persons seeking a journalist's testimony must prove that the journalist has firsthand information about the matter at issue, that the information can't be obtained from other sources, and that it is essential to a proper resolution of the case.

The Privilege in the Federal Courts

In reaction to the Supreme Court's decision in *Branzburg,* Congress considered adoption of a federal shield law. But when journalists themselves were unable to agree on how far such a law should go, or even on the need for any law at all, the proposal was dropped.[4] At about the same time, the U.S. Department of Justice adopted guidelines designed to limit the use of journalists as witnesses in federal grand juries and in trials in federal courts.[5]

The guidelines start with the premise the federal law enforcement officers will make no attempt to subpoena journalists until they have made "all reasonable attempts...to obtain information from nonmedia sources." If such attempts fail, the next step is negotiation with the media. If that fails, a subpoena cannot be issued without "the express authorization of the Attorney General."

That authorization is not to be given in criminal cases unless information from nonmedia sources indicates that a crime has been committed and that a reporter has information directly bearing on a suspect's guilt or innocence. Even then, the government is not supposed to issue a subpoena to the reporter unless it has been unable to get that information from nonmedia sources. Questioning of reporters who are subpoenaed is to be limited to verification of published information and to establishing its accuracy. The directive advises government attorneys to avoid the appearance of harassing journalists and to limit their requests to specific kinds of information. The same restrictions apply to civil cases with the added provision that journalists are not to be drawn into such lawsuits unless the issue is "of substantial proportions."

Clearly, the attorney general's guidelines are based on the Stewart-Powell opinions in *Branzburg*. How diligent Justice Department attorneys have been in observing them has been the subject of debate in a committee of Congress,[6] and of a few court cases.

However, whatever their effect, the guidelines have been overshadowed by court decisions interpreting *Branzburg* v. *Hayes*. Seven federal circuit courts have read the decision as giving journalists some First Amendment protection against being subpoenaed as witnesses. Only one, the Sixth, has held that *Branzburg* created no First Amendment privilege for journalists. However, the court tempered its holding by noting that under some circumstances journalists may have a common-law right to ask that their testimony be excluded, using a balancing-of-interests test. The test would balance journalists' interest in freedom of the press against the courts' interest in seeing that justice is done.

This section summarizes the leading federal circuit court decisions interpreting *Branzburg*. We will find that, in the absence of a federal shield law, courts in most circuits recognize a First Amendment testimonial privilege and apply some version of the three-point test proposed by Stewart.

Baker v. F & F Investment, 470 F.2d 778 (2d Cir. 1972). The Second Circuit, comprised of Connecticut, Vermont, and New York, was one of the first to find a First Amendment privilege in *Branzburg*. It did so in *Baker* v. *F & F Invest-*

---

4. Martin Arnold, "Watergate Stalls Press Shield Law Effort," *Louisville Courier-Journal*, 4 July 1973.
5. 28 C.F.R. Part 50.
6. *Newsmen's Privilege:* Hearings, Subcommittee on Courts, Civil Liberties, and the Administration of Justice, Committee on the Judiciary, House of Representatives, 94th Congress, 1st sess., on H.R. 215, 23 and 24 April 1975, pp. 6–36 and 94–102.

ment, a case testing a magazine reporter's right to protect his confidential sources of information. The reporter, Alfred Balk, had written an article on blockbusting for the *Saturday Evening Post.* Relying in part on information obtained from sources who asked not to be identified, Balk described tactics used by some real estate firms to provoke panic selling of homes by white owners when a black family moved into the neighborhood. The real estate firms involved would buy from the white owners at low prices and sell to black families at much higher prices. Baker, representing himself and other black buyers, sued F & F, seeking damages as alleged victims of racial discrimination. Seeking support for his case, Baker asked a federal district court in New York City to compel Balk to identify the sources interviewed for his article. The court refused to do so. Relying on the three-part test advanced by Stewart in *Branzburg,* the court held that Baker had not shown that he could not obtain the information from other sources. That reliance was affirmed on appeal. The circuit court buttressed its verdict by holding that Balk's information did not go to the "heart of the claim" advanced by Baker. The court held further that in a civil action, which *Baker* was, a journalist's First Amendment interest in freedom of the press carries more weight than in a grand jury proceeding, which was at issue in *Branzburg.*

More recently, the Second Circuit has endorsed the application of the Stewart test to a criminal case. In *United States* v. *Burke,*[7] the defendants issued a subpoena for notes, tapes, and other materials in the possession of a reporter who had written a story based on an interview with a key prosecution witness. Their purpose, they said, was to obtain information they could use to cast doubt on the witness's testimony. The trial judge rejected the request, holding that reporters have a qualified First Amendment privilege to protect the methods they use to gather news. Referring to Stewart's dissent in *Branzburg,* the judge said the defendants could defeat that privilege only by making a strong showing of a compelling need for the reporter's notes. The judge further held that in light of other ways in which the defendants could challenge the witness's testimony, they had not made such a showing. The judge noted that the defendants could renew their request after the witness had testified. The judge said that in that event he might be willing to review the reporter's notes in the privacy of his chambers, and he would permit their use in court only it he were convinced they would have a significant noncumulative bearing on the witness's credibility. By that the judge meant that he would not permit the defendants to use the reporter simply to reinforce doubts that other testimony may have raised. On appeal, the Second Circuit affirmed, holding that the standard of review it established in *Baker* for civil cases applies to criminal cases as well.

Other federal circuit courts have recognized a qualified First Amendment privilege as follows:

— The District of Columbia Circuit in libel and privacy actions. In an early case, the court recognized the existence of the privilege but upheld a district court's finding that it must yield to a libel plaintiff's need to identify

---

7. 700 F.2d 70 (2d Cir.); cert. denied, 464 U.S. 816, 104 S.Ct. 72, 78 L.Ed.2d 85 (1983).

a reporter's confidential sources.[8] The court said the identity of the sources went to the heart of the plaintiff's ability to prove actual malice. In the privacy case, the court held that the plaintiff would have to exhaust all available alternative sources before he could question a reporter about who leaked information found in confidential government records.[9]

— The First Circuit in a libel case. The court vacated a district court's order compelling a reporter for the *Boston Globe* to identify his sources of derogatory information about a ship-building firm.[10] The court remanded with instructions that, in effect, asked the trial judge to determine whether the reporter's information was essential to resolution of the dispute and had indeed been obtained in confidence.

— The Third Circuit in both civil and criminal actions. The court reversed a district court's finding that a reporter for the *Delaware County Daily Times* was in contempt because she refused to disclose her sources. She had written that a police officer, who was a candidate for mayor of Chester, Pennsylvania, had been suspended and reprimanded on several occasions although there had been no public announcement of the offenses. The court said the officer would have to show that the identity of the reporter's sources was essential to carrying through the officer's suit against the mayor and others for violating his civil rights.[11] Twice in a criminal case, the court held that CBS News had a right to withhold outtakes—unused sections of videotaped interviews—sought by the defendant in a fraud case. The court said there was no showing that the same evidence could not be obtained from other sources.[12]

— The Fourth Circuit in a criminal action. In applied Stewart's three-part test and ruled that a reporter could testify as to information he had obtained, but did not have to identify his sources.[13]

— The Fifth Circuit in a libel action. But, as the District of Columbia Circuit has done, it held that the privilege must yield when the identity of the reporter's sources is essential to proof of actual malice.[14]

— The Tenth Circuit in a civil rights action brought by the family of a young woman who said she had become contaminated by plutonium radiation while working at a plant processing the material. After her death in an automobile accident, a television producer made her the subject of a documentary. The company she had worked for, the defendant in the lawsuit,

8. Carey v. Hume, 492 F.2d 631 (D.C.Cir. 1974).
9. Zerilli v. Smith, 656 F.2d 705 (D.C.Cir. 1981).
10. Bruno & Stillman v. Globe Newspaper Co., 633 F.2d 583 (1st Cir. 1980).
11. Riley v. City of Chester, 612 F.2d 708 (3d Cir. 1979).
12. United States v. Cuthbertson, 630 F.2d 139 (3d Cir. 1980); 651 F.2d 189 (3d Cir. 1981).
13. LaRouche v. National Broadcasting Co., 780 F.2d 1134 (4th Cir. 1986); cert. denied, 479 U.S. 818, 107 S.Ct. 79, 93 L.Ed.2d 34 (1986).
14. Miller v. Transamerican Press, 621 F.2d 721 (5th Cir. 1980); cert. denied, 450 U.S. 1041, 101 S.Ct. 1759, 68 L.Ed.2d 238 (1981).

asked the producer to identify his confidential sources and to disclose any information that had not been telecast. When the producer moved to quash the subpoena, a district court ruled that he was not a journalist and would have to respond to the company's questions. The Tenth Circuit reversed, holding that television producers are journalists and that the company could get the information only if it met Stewart's three-part test.[15]

In all these instances, the circuit court judges placed emphasis on the reservations in Powell's concurring opinion in *Branzburg,* reading it, and the arguments advanced by the four dissenters, as requiring First Amendment scrutiny of subpoenas issued to journalists. As a consequence, most federal courts, including district courts in circuits not treated above, have been applying a balancing test, on a case-by-case basis, to motions to quash. The essential query in each instance is, "Can the party seeking the journalist's testimony effectively present his or her case without it?"

In re Grand Jury Proceedings, Storer Communications v. *Giovan,* **810 F.2d 580 (6th Cir. 1987).**

The U.S. Court of Appeals for the Sixth Circuit, in *In re Grand Jury Proceedings,* specifically rejected the reasoning outlined above. Upholding a contempt citation that kept a television reporter in jail for twenty-four hours, the court declared flatly that the majority in *Branzburg* "rejected the existence of...a first amendment testimonial privilege." Judge Alan E. Norris, writing for a three-member panel, said he found nothing in Powell's concurring opinion that either limited or expanded the plurality opinion written by Justice White. In his view, "Justice Powell's opinion certainly does not warrant the rewriting of the majority opinion to grant a first amendment testimonial privilege to news reporters."

The reporter in this case was Brad Stone, who worked for a television station in Detroit. He was assigned a story on youth gangs and interviewed several members on camera before he concluded he was learning nothing that was of any use. Subjects told him they would talk candidly only if he promised they could not be identified on the air. Stone's five-part report was edited so as to hide the identity of the youths he interviewed.

The reporter's problems began when a grand jury investigated the murder of a police officer. Several informants told a detective that the assailants were youth gang members who were videotaped when Stone made his first interviews. The informants said they could identify the suspects, but they also said they would not testify. Eyewitnesses to the killing said they could identify the assailants if they were shown photographs of them. The prosecutor issued a subpoena for Stone's outtakes in the belief that they were the key to identifying the officer's killers. The television station filed a motion to quash. The trial judge held that Stone was not protected by Michigan's shield law, which at that time was so written as to protect only reporters for the print media. Nor, the judge said, was he

---

15. Silkwood v. Kerr-McGee Corp., 563 F.2d 433 (10th Cir. 1977).

Television reporter Brad Stone leaves the Wayne County Jail in Detroit after spending twenty-four hours behind bars for refusing to testify to a grand jury. Stone had televised interviews with street gang members on condition that he would not identify them on the air. When some members of the gang became suspects in the murder of a police officer, prosecutors summoned him to appear before the grand jury with tapes that had not been televised. Stone's refusal led to a Sixth Circuit Court of Appeals holding that he was not protected by a journalist's privilege. (UPI/Bettmann Newsphotos)

protected by a constitutional privilege. When Stone again refused to appear before the grand jury with his outtakes, he was found in contempt and was ordered to be jailed either until he did appear or until the grand jury's term expired nearly a year later.[16] Stone was released the next day when he appealed to the federal courts for relief. A district court in Detroit denied his petition, and the Sixth Circuit affirmed.

Stone's lawyers based their appeal on two grounds. They argued that he was protected by a First Amendment privilege created by the Supreme Court in *Branzburg* and recognized at the time by courts in five U.S. circuits. They also argued that the Michigan shield law violated the equal protection clause of the Fourteenth Amendment because it was written to apply only to print journalists. Judge Norris rejected both arguments. In disposing of the first, he quoted from White's opinion in *Branzburg:* "[T]he Constitution does not, as it never has, exempt the newsman from performing the citizen's normal duty of appearing and

---

16. Storer Communications v. Giovan, 13 Med.L.Rptr. 1901 (Mich.Ct.App. 1986).

furnishing information relevant to the grand jury's task.'' In Norris's view, Powell's pivotal concurrence did not question or modify that premise, although he recognized that other judges believe it did. The judge wrote, ''[W]e decline to join some other circuit courts, to the extent that they...have...adopted the qualified privilege balancing process urged by the three *Branzburg* dissenters and rejected by the majority.''

Instead the court relied on a treatise on evidence written by John Henry Wigmore, one of the recognized authorities on the topic.[17] Wigmore's general thesis is that justice is most likely to be done if juries are able to consider all available facts bearing on a case. This means that privileges excusing those who can provide such facts should be kept to a minimum. In Wigmore's view, a privilege can be justified only if it meets a four-point test:

1. The witness must have received the information only by promising that it would be kept confidential.

2. Confidentiality must be essential to maintenance of the relationship between the witness and the source.

3. The relationship must be one which, in the opinion of the community, ought to be respected.

4. The harm to the relationship that would result from violation of the promise of confidentiality must be greater than the contribution the witness's testimony would make to the correct outcome of the litigation.

Although White makes no direct reference to this test in his opinion in *Branzburg,* Judge Norris asserted that ''it is apparent'' that a majority of the Supreme Court concluded that the last three elements are lacking when journalists attempt to claim a testimonial privilege. In short, the Sixth Circuit concluded, as did White, that society has little to gain from protecting a confidential relationship between journalists and their sources.

The court made one concession. Referring to Powell's opinion, it said journalists might be excused from testifying if they could show that a subpoena was issued to ''disrupt their relationship with confidential news sources'' or that a grand jury's inquiry was not being conducted in good faith. The court also pointed out that journalists can be excused if their information has only ''a remote and tenuous relationship to the subject of the investigation'' or would serve no ''legitimate law enforcement need.'' However, the court said these grounds did not create a constitutional privilege. And the court said that, even were it to apply these exceptions to Stone's case, the court would hold that the reporter still must surrender his outtakes because they were essential to identification of the police officer's killer.

---

17. J. Wigmore, *A Treatise on the Anglo-American System of Evidence* § 2286 (J. McNaughton rev. ed. 1940).

Nor did the court find any support for the argument that the equal protection clause required courts to give television journalists the same privilege that the Legislature gave print journalists when it drafted the shield law. The court said that the equal protection of laws guaranteed by the Fourteenth Amendment applies only to "basic, fundamental rights." Because journalists have no constitutional right to refuse to testify when summoned by a grand jury, the equal protection clause simply did not apply to Stone's situation. The court said that if the Legislature wanted to give a testimonial privilege to broadcast journalists, it would have to rewrite the statute. That indeed is what it did at its first opportunity. The Michigan shield law now protects anyone "who is involved in the gathering or preparation of news for broadcast or publication."[18]

The Sixth Circuit's decision in *In re Grand Jury* stands as the precedent for federal courts in Kentucky, Michigan, Ohio, and Tennessee. Courts in a few states also have adopted the same narrow view of *Branzburg* and their own state constitutions' freedom of the press clauses, as we will see.

However, in the majority of the federal circuits and of the states, journalists who move to quash subpoenas can rely on some variation of Stewart's three-part test. The parties seeking their testimony must prove that journalists have admissible evidence, unavailable from other sources, that is crucial to the proper resolution of the litigation.

State Shield Laws

At the time of the *Branzburg* decision in 1972, seventeen states had shield laws granting a testimonial privilege to journalists. In reaction to that decision, nine other states enacted such laws. State courts declared the California and New Mexico laws unconstitutional. California voters used the initiative to write that state's law into its constitution. The New Mexico Supreme Court adopted a rule of court embracing the language of the shield law. The state's legislature also reenacted the law to apply to nonjudicial proceedings. Therefore, as of this writing, twenty-six states have constitutional provisions, statutes, or rules of court defining a testimonial privilege for journalists. They are: Alabama,[19] Alaska,[20] Arizona,[21] Arkansas,[22] California,[23] Delaware,[24] Illinois,[25] Indiana,[26] Kentucky,[27] Louisiana,[28] Maryland,[29] Michigan,[30] Minnesota,[31] Montana,[32] Nebraska,[33]

---

18. Mich.Comp.Laws.Ann. § 767.5a.
19. Ala.Code § 12-21-142 (Cumm.Supp. 1978).
20. Alaska Stat. §§ 09.25.150 − .220 (Cumm.Supp. 1978).
21. Ariz.Rev.Stat.Ann. § 12-2237 (1982); Ariz.Rev.Stat.Ann. § 12-2214 (1982 and Supp.).
22. Ark.Stat.Ann. § 43-917 (1977).
23. Cal.Evid.Code § 1070 (Deering Supp. 1978); California Constitution Art. 1, § 2.
24. Del.Code title 10, §§ 4320-4326 (1974).
25. S.H.A. ch. 110, par. 8-901-8-909 (1983).
26. Ind.Code § 34-3-5-1 (Supp. 1978).
27. Ky.Rev.Stat. 421.100.
28. La.Rev.Stat.Ann. §§ 45:1451-1454 (West Supp. 1978).

Nevada,[34] New Jersey,[35] New Mexico,[36] New York,[37] North Dakota,[38] Ohio,[39] Oklahoma,[40] Oregon,[41] Pennsylvania,[42] Rhode Island,[43] and Tennessee.[44]

The statutes vary widely. All begin by defining the kind of journalist who is eligible for the privilege. The broadest statutes include anyone who gathers information for dissemination to the public through some medium of communication. California's law has been interpreted as not protecting freelance writers.[45] Some laws permit journalists to protect only confidential sources of information. Some of these interpretations are operative only if the information obtained from such sources is published or broadcast. Other statutes protect not only sources, but information, whether or not it is published or broadcast. New York's Court of Appeals ruled that that state's shield law protected only the identity of confidential sources or information provided by such sources. In doing so, it ordered an Albany television station to release outtakes of an interview with a man whose wife had disappeared and later was found murdered.[46] The legislature subsequently amended the law to grant a qualified privilege to reporters' notes, audio or video outtakes, and newsroom files.[47]

A few shield laws are inoperative if the journalist is the target of a libel suit. Other laws require disclosure of information if a judge concludes a fair trial is impossible without it. New Jersey's law, as interpreted by the state's supreme court, may be the strongest. The court held in one instance that it protected a journalist who had witnessed the commission of a nonviolent crime.[48] Pennsylvania's supreme court has observed that that state's shield law is "well nigh absolute."[49] Indiana's law, which is limited to protecting the identity of confidential sources, has been held to be absolute, even when the journalist is a defendant in a libel action.[50] Nevada's law also has been construed as absolute in its pro-

---

29. Md.Cts. & Jud.Proc.Code Ann. § 9-112 (Cumm.Supp. 1978).
30. Mich.Comp.Laws Ann. § 767.5a.
31. Minn.Stat.Ann. §§ 595.021 − .025 (West Supp. 1978).
32. Mont.Code Ann. §§ 26-1-901-903 (1979).
33. Neb.Rev.Stat. §§ 20-144-147 (1977).
34. Nev.Rev.Stat. § 49.275 (1977).
35. N.J.Stat.Ann. §§ 2A:84A-21, −21.1 to 21.8, −21a, −29 (West 1976, Supp. 1977 and 1980 session laws).
36. N.Mex.Stat.Ann. & 38-6-7 (1978 and Supp. 1982), applying to nonjudicial proceedings. In judicial proceedings, a journalist's privilege is defined by Supreme Court rule 514.
37. N.Y.Civ. Rights Law § 79-h (McKinney 1981).
38. N.D.Cent.Code § 31-01-06.2 (1978).
39. Ohio Rev.Code Ann. §§ 2739.04 & 2739.12 (Page 1954 & Supp. 1977).
40. Okla.Stat.Ann. Title 12, § 2506 (West Supp. 1978).
41. Ore.Rev.Stat. §§ 44.510 − .540 (1977).
42. Pa.Stat.Ann. Title 28, § 330 (Purdon Supp. 1977; Pa.Cons.Stat.Ann. § 5942).
43. R.I.Gen.Laws §§ 9-19.1-1 to −3 (Supp. 1977).
44. Tenn.Code Ann. § 24-1-208 (Supp. 1977).
45. In re Van Ness, 8 Med.L.Rptr. 2563 (Cal.Super.Ct. 1982).
46. Knight-Ridder Broadcasting v. Greenberg, 14 Med. L. Rptr. 1299 (N.Y. 1987).
47. "N.Y. Bill Expands Shield Law," *Editor & Publisher*, 22 July 1989.
48. In re Vrazo, 176 N.Y.Super. 455, 423 A.2d 695 (1980).
49. In re Taylor, 412 Pa. 32, 193 A.2d 181 (Pa. 1963).
50. Jamerson v. Anderson Newspapers, 469 N.E.2d 1243 (Ind.Ct.App. 1984).

tection of confidential sources of libelous information.[51] However, the majority of the state shield laws grant qualified privileges which require courts to balance the need for a journalist's evidence against an interest in protecting the journalist's ability to gather news. The applicability of the journalist's privilege in libel cases will be discussed more fully later in this chapter.

As of this writing, courts in twenty-three states and the District of Columbia have looked to *Branzburg,* their own state constitutions, or to common law to find a qualified testimonial privilege for journalists: Alabama,[52] Alaska,[53] California,[54] Connecticut,[55] Delaware,[56] District of Columbia,[57] Florida,[58] Idaho,[59] Indiana,[60] Iowa,[61] Kansas,[62] Maine,[63] Michigan,[64] New Hampshire,[65] New York,[66] North Carolina,[67] Ohio,[68] Oklahoma,[69] Texas,[70] Vermont,[71] Virginia,[72] Washington,[73] West Virginia,[74] and Wisconsin.[75] A comparison of this list with the previous one shows that in nine states journalists can rely on both a shield law and a court-created privilege if they receive a subpoena. Thus forty states have recognized a journalist's privilege to some degree.

Like shield-law protection, court-granted privileges also vary widely in their application. Most are based on a test similar to that proposed by Stewart in *Branzburg.* Florida courts have gone the farthest, granting journalists absolute protection from testifying in civil cases and from identifying their sources of leaks from sealed grand jury records.[76] Journalists in that state also have shown remarkable success in being excused from testifying in criminal proceedings. De-

51. Laxalt v. McClatchy, 14 Med.L.Rptr. 1199 (D.Nev. 1987).
52. Norandal USA v. Local Union No. 7468, 13 Med.L.Rptr. 2167 (Ala.Cir.Ct. 1986).
53. Nebel v. Mapco Petroleum, 10 Med.L.Rptr. 1871 (Alaska 1984).
54. Mitchell v. Marin County Superior Court, 37 Cal.3d 268, 690 P.2d 625, 208 Cal.Rptr. 152 (1984).
55. Conn. Labor Relations Board v. Fagin, 33 Conn.Sup. 204, 370 A.2d 1095 (Super.Ct. 1976).
56. Delaware v. McBride, 7 Med.L.Rptr. 1371 (Del.Super.Ct. 1981).
57. CBS v. Arnold (D.C.Super.Ct.) (unpublished), summarized in *News Media Update,* 30 March 1987.
58. Morgan v. State, 337 So.2d 951 (Fla. 1976).
59. In re Wright, 700 P.2d 40 (1985).
60. In re Stearns, 12 Med.L.Rptr. 1837 (Ind.Ct.App. 1986).
61. Winegard v. Oxberger, 258 N.W.2d 847 (Iowa 1977); cert. denied, 436 U.S. 905 (1978).
62. State v. Sandstrom, 224 Kan. 573, 581 P.2d 812 (1978); cert. denied, 440 U.S. 929 (1979).
63. In re Hohler, 14 Med.L.Rptr., No. 16, News Notes (Maine Super.Ct. 1987).
64. Schultz v. Reader's Digest Association, 468 F.Supp. 551 (E.D.Mich. 1979).
65. Opinion of the Justices, 117 N.H. 386, 373 A.2d 644 (1977).
66. New York v. Korkala, 99 A.D.2d 161, 472 N.Y.S.2d 310 (1st Dept. 1984).
67. North Carolina v. Smith, 13 Med.L.Rptr. 1940 (N.Car. 1987).
68. In re McAuley, 63 Ohio App.2d 5, 408 N.E.2d 697 (Ct.App. Cuyahoga Co. 1979).
69. Taylor v. Miskorsky, 640 P.2d 959 (Okla. 1981).
70. Dallas Oil and Gas v. Mouer, 533 S.W.2d 70 (Ct.Civ.App. 1976).
71. State v. St. Peter, 132 Vt. 226, 315 A.2d 254 (1974).
72. Brown v. Commonwealth, 214 Va. 755, 204 S.E.2d 429 (Va.); cert. denied, 419 U.S. 966 (1974).
73. Washington v. Rinaldo, 102 Wash.2d 749, 689 P.2d 392 (1984).
74. Maurice v. N.L.R.B., 7 Med.L.Rptr. 2221 (S.D.W.Va. 1981); reversed on other grounds, 691 F.2d 182 (4th Cir. 1982).
75. Zelenka v. State, 83 Wis.2d 601, 266 N.W.2d 279 (Wis. 1978); overruled, 103 Wis.2d 228, 307 N.W.2d 628 (1981).
76. Morgan v. State, 337 So.2d 951 (Fla. 1976), and Coira v. Depoo Hospital, 4 Med.L.Rptr. 1692 (Fla.Cir.Ct. Monroe Co. 1978).

fendants seeking to call reporters as witnesses must show that they have evidence unavailable from other sources, that the defendant has been unable to get similar evidence from other sources, and that failure to obtain the journalist's evidence will violate the defendant's right to a fair trial.[77]

At this writing, courts in only four states have refused to recognize a journalist's privilege. They are Colorado,[78] Georgia,[79] Hawaii,[80] and Massachusetts.[81] This leaves six states, Mississippi, Missouri, South Carolina, South Dakota, Utah, and Wyoming, where there are neither shield laws nor cases of record defining or rejecting a journalist's privilege. Two Mississippi trial courts have recognized a privilege in unreported cases, and a Missouri court gave implied recognition to a qualified privilege but found it inapplicable.

The dimensions of the protection granted by state shield laws and by the decisions of state courts will be examined in subsequent sections of this chapter. However, journalists are advised to acquaint themselves with decisions of the courts in the states where they are employed.

QUALIFYING FOR THE PRIVILEGE ═══════════

The Definition of a Journalist ═══════════════════

Shield laws generally define journalists in broad terms so as to include anyone who is able to get an article in print with a recognized publisher, or on the air over a radio or television station. In the past, a few of the laws have extended protection only to persons who are employed by a publisher or broadcaster or who are paid on a free-lance basis. Such laws raise questions as to whether they cover student newspapers, publications produced by community organizations, and other media with nonpaid staffs. The modern tendency is to broaden the laws to cover anyone whose primary purpose is to gather information for dissemination to the public. For instance, the New York law was amended to include free-lancers, still and movie photographers, authors of books, employers of journalists, and persons connected with noncommercial media.[82]

Where the law leaves doubt as to whether the person who receives a subpoena qualifies as a journalist, courts look at the circumstances. If such persons were acting as journalists, and were seeking information for dissemination to the public, then courts have tended to hold that they can invoke the privilege. If not, they may not be protected, as the following three cases illustrate.

---

77. Florida v. Peterson, 7 Med.L.Rptr. 1090 (Fla.Cir.Ct. 1981).
78. Gagnon v. Fremont Dist. Ct., 632 P.2d 567 (Col. 1981) in a libel case, and Pankratz v. Colorado Dist. Ct., 199 Col. 411, 609 P.2d 1101 (1980), where the reporter was a witness to a crime.
79. Hurst v. Georgia, 160 Ga.App. 830, 287 S.E.2d 677 (Ct.App. 1982).
80. In re Goodfader's Appeal, 45 Haw. 317, 367 P.2d 472 (1961).
81. Commonwealth v. Corsetti, 387 Mass. 1 (1982).
82. N.Y. Civ. Rights Law § 79-h (McKinney 1981).

The first case grew out of the discovery process during General William Westmoreland's libel action against CBS News.[83] The general contended that he was defamed by a segment of "60 Minutes," which portrayed him as part of a conspiracy to understate enemy troop strength in Vietnam. When complaints were made about the segment, CBS conducted an internal study, which concluded that some of its news policies had been violated in preparing the report. During pretrial discovery, Westmoreland's lawyers asked for a copy of the study, along with notes and materials used in preparing it. When CBS resisted, the district court ordered the information released, holding that the writer of the study was not engaged in news gathering. Later, the order was modified to exempt sources who had spoken to the writer under promises of confidentiality.

In the second case, an Indiana appellate court denied a claim of privilege under that state's shield law to a part-time reporter. The court held that the reporter was performing as an activist, not a journalist, when she obtained a copy of a confidential Environmental Protection Agency report. As further evidence of her nonjournalistic role, the court noted that she had not used the report in the newspaper to which she contributed articles but had given it to a television reporter. The television station's use of the report led to a libel suit. The court said the woman would have to answer the plaintiff's questions about who had given her the EPA document.[84]

In the third case, the Second Circuit held that the privilege can be invoked only by journalists who begin their news gathering with a demonstrable intent to publish their work. In this instance, the court refused to protect a manuscript produced by a free-lance writer who had no record of previous publication, even though the writer had obtained a contract from a publisher after the project began.[85]

Cases like these are rare. In shield-law states, the definition of a journalist entitled to invoke the privilege is a matter of interpretation of the statutory language. If the statute is broadly written to cover all who gather information for dissemination to the public, the law will protect student journalists and, presumably, communicators who prepare news releases for corporate employers. Such laws also may protect academic researchers. If the statute is written in terms that protect contributors to "bona fide news organizations," student journalists may be protected only if they have an affiliation with a regularly published student newspaper. As the *von Bulow* case indicates, persons who gather information on their own in the hope that they might find a publisher may not be protected. Where the shield is a product of common law or the First Amendment, who is covered is a product of how the judge or judges involved define a journalist. In the landmark case, *Branzburg,* two of the journalists were employed by daily newspapers and the third by the news department of a television station.

83. Westmoreland v. CBS, 97 F.R.D. 703 (S.D.N.Y. 1983), and 596 F.Supp. 1170 (S.D.N.Y. 1984).
84. Northside Sanitary Landfill v. Bradley, 462 N.E.2d 1321 (Ind.App. 1984).
85. Von Bulow v. Von Bulow, 13 Med.L.Rptr. 2041 (2d Cir. 1987).

Defining a Confidential Source

Codes of ethics of all major news organizations caution against the use of anonymous sources. But they also recognize that at times promises of confidentiality must be made—and kept—to obtain news of public importance. The "Statement of Principles" of the American Society of Newspaper Editors puts it this way: "Pledges of confidentiality to news sources must be honored at all costs, and therefore should not be given lightly. Unless there is clear and pressing need to maintain confidences, sources of information should be identified."

In the day-to-day give and take between reporters and their sources, it is not always clear when information is offered in confidence or a source couples an offer of newsworthy information with a request not to be identified. "Don't quote me" slips so easily off the tongue of so many sources that reporters may not even acknowledge it. However, courts interpreting shield laws and applying common-law or First Amendment privileges are insisting that journalists offer evidence that their relationship with their sources was indeed confidential. A few courts are treating an agreement on confidentiality as a contract. Therefore, a key question when journalists seek to quash a subpoena asking for the identity of an anonymous source or for unpublished information is, "Did the journalist and the source reach an agreement on confidentiality before the information was disclosed?"

Bruno & Stillman v. Globe Newspaper Co., 633 F.2d 583 (1st Cir. 1980).

That question was crucial to the First Circuit's decision in *Bruno & Stillman* v. *Globe Newspaper Co.,* referred to earlier. When the *Boston Globe* ran a series of articles commenting unfavorably on fishing vessels made by the company, Bruno & Stillman sued for libel. During discovery, the company asked the reporter for the notes and materials he used in preparing his stories. Discovery is a pretrial process in which lawyers obtain information from participants and potential witnesses in an effort to narrow the issues to be resolved at trial. The newspaper surrendered about 1500 pages of the reporter's handwritten notes, but it refused to disclose the identity of three confidential sources and the unpublished information they gave the paper. A federal district court ordered disclosure of the withheld information.

On appeal, the circuit court remanded with instructions that the district court apply a balancing test before deciding whether to repeat the disclosure order. If the court should again decide that the reporter's information was needed, the court should proceed to an examination of the circumstances under which he obtained it. If the reporter could prove that the information had been obtained under a promise of confidentiality, that promise would be given consideration. Otherwise, disclosure would be ordered. The court made some pertinent points about the nature of news gathering:

> Not all information as to sources is equally deserving of confidentiality. An unsolicited letter may be received with no mention of an interest in anonymity; such

a letter may casually mention the wish for confidential treatment; it may specifically condition use on the according of such treatment; or it may defer communication of any substance until a commitment to confidentiality is received. Oral communications could also range from the cavalierly volunteered to the carefully bargained-for undertaking. . . . In the present case a number of facts need to be sorted out and others need to be developed. For example, although one source sent an unsolicited letter, there was a subsequent promise to protect not only all notes of conversation with the source but the initial letter. Whether and to what extent such a *nunc pro tunc* undertaking merits protection by the court is a matter for its discriminating judgment. The existing record is silent as to the reasonable expectation of confidentiality on the part of the other two sources.

The term *nunc pro tunc* refers to an attempt to modify an existing arrangement, and to proceed on the assumption that the modifications had been in effect from the beginning. In this instance, information about Bruno & Stillman had been offered to the reporter without any request for confidentiality. At a later date, the source and the reporter did enter into a confidential relationship. The question the court raised was whether that relationship could be made retroactive to include the material offered originally.

In a ruling that cited *Bruno & Stillman* as a precedent, a federal district court in St. Louis said a reporter could assert a privilege only on a question-by-question basis.[86] In each instance, it said, the reporter would have to offer a sworn statement as to the circumstances under which a source was promised confidentiality or otherwise show how her ability to gather news would be harmed by responding to questions.

More recently, in a case that did not involve a claim of privilege, Minnesota courts treated two newspapers' identification of their reporters' confidential source as the violation of a contract. A jury ordered the *St. Paul Pioneer Press Dispatch* and the Minneapolis *Star Tribune* to pay Dan Cohen $700,000 after he was identified as the source of derogatory information about a candidate for lieutenant governor.[87] Cohen was working as a public relations consultant to a candidate for governor at the time. Reporters for the two newspapers and two other news organizations agreed not to identify him as the source of documents showing that the opponent's running mate had admitted shoplifting $6 worth of merchandise twelve years earlier. However, the editors of the Minneapolis and St. Paul newspapers overruled the reporters and identified Cohen. The *Star Tribune* also denounced him in an editorial.[88] Cohen was fired by the advertising agency for which he worked, and the candidate he represented lost by a large margin.

Cohen sued the newspapers for damages, arguing that the papers had violated an oral contract. A jury in Hennepin County court agreed, awarding him $200,000 in actual damages and $250,000 from each newspaper in punitive damages.

---

86. Continental Cablevision v. Storer Broadcasting Co. 583 F.Supp. 427 (E.D.Mo. 1984).
87. "Source Identified by Papers Awarded $700,000 by Jury," *Wall Street Journal*, 23 July 1988.
88. Albert Scardino, "When the Press Breaks a Promise," *New York Times*, 31 July 1988.

On appeal, the Minnesota Court of Appeals voted two to one to uphold the award of actual damages but overturned the award of punitive damages.[89] The majority held that the reporters' promise of confidentiality was a contract which could be enforced without violating the newspapers' First Amendment rights. Judge Marianne Short wrote: "Were we not to enforce the newspapers' promises of confidentiality, confidential sources would have no legal recourse against unscrupulous reporters or editors. Ultimately, news sources could dry up, resulting in less newsworthy information to publish."

The Minnesota Supreme Court reversed, but it also acknowledged that there may be instances when a confidential source can seek damages for a broken promise.[90] Thus, pledges of confidentiality should not be made casually, as the "Statement of Principles" of the ASNE suggests. Indeed, some news organizations now have a policy which requires approval of a supervising editor before a source can be promised confidentiality, and others have forbidden reliance on confidential sources in all but the most unusual of circumstances.

Who Controls the Privilege?

When a privilege is granted, either by statute or by a court, can the privilege be waived, and, if so, by whom? Most courts that have considered the matter have held that the privilege can be waived, but only by the journalist or news organization protected by it. Two decisions, one by the U.S. Third Circuit and the other by the New Jersey Supreme Court, illustrate the majority position with respect to control over the right to waive the privilege.

United States v. *Cuthbertson* 630 F.2d 139 (3d Cir. 1980); 651 F.2d 189 (3d Cir. 1981).

In *United States* v. *Cuthbertson,* the Third Circuit held that CBS retained control over its outtakes even though the government obtained waivers from witnesses who appeared in some of them. Further, no evidence indicated that any of the interviews had been conducted under a promise of confidentiality. The outtakes were videotapes of interviews not used in a "60 Minutes" episode examining complaints about Cuthbertson's franchising of Wild Bill's Family Restaurants. Later, a federal grand jury indicted Cuthbertson on charges of conspiracy and fraud. A month before the date set for the trial, Cuthbertson's lawyers issued a subpoena to CBS News asking for all the outtakes rejected in preparing the program. The lawyers did so in the belief that the unused tape included interviews with persons who might appear as witnesses for the government and that it might be helpful in impeaching their testimony. At the same time, the government obtained waivers from all its witnesses agreeing to release of the outtakes.

---

89. Mark Fitzgerald, "Confidentiality Is a Contract," *Editor & Publisher,* 9 September 1989, p. 11.
90. "Contract Status Is Denied for Vow of Confidentiality by Reporters," *Wall Street Journal,* 23 July 1990.

When CBS moved to quash the subpoena, the trial judge ruled that the news organization would have to let him review any outtakes in which the government's witnesses appeared. If he concluded that any of the footage might be helpful to the defense, he would turn those parts of the outtakes over to Cuthbertson's lawyers. CBS rejected the request. The judge found the network in contempt and ordered it to pay a fine of a dollar a day until it complied with his order.

On appeal, the Third Circuit reversed. It held that, despite the waivers from many of the persons appearing in the outtakes, CBS retained control over them. They were subject to subpoena, but need be made available only if Cuthbertson's lawyers proved they could not otherwise get the information they contained. The decision's importance lies in the protection the court gave the news-gathering process. It said:

> The compelled production of a reporter's resource materials can constitute a significant intrusion into the news gathering and editorial processes....Like the compelled disclosure of confidential sources, it may substantially undercut the public policy favoring the free flow of information to the public that is the foundation of the privilege....Therefore, we hold that the privilege extends to unpublished materials in the possession of CBS.

In *New Jersey* v. *Boiardo,*[91] that state's supreme court came to a similar conclusion. In this instance, a key government witness in a criminal case had written a letter to a reporter, apparently complaining that the prosecutor had reneged on a promise of leniency offered in return for the witness's cooperation. During the trial, the witness testified as to the contents of the letter. However, when the defendant's attorney sought to subpoena the letter in the belief that it might help him raise questions about the witness's truthfulness, the reporter moved to quash. The defendant's lawyer argued that the witness waived any privilege that might have protected the letter when he testified as to its contents. The supreme court said that made no difference. The state's shield law grants a testimonial privilege only to journalists. Therefore, the privilege cannot be waived by anyone else, including the person who provided the privileged information.

Courts have held that journalists can waive their privilege involuntarily by agreeing to testify as to some aspect of the protected information. In a few instances, judges have held that reporters waived the privilege simply by testifying that they wrote the story in question and believed it to be accurate.[92] Journalists who choose, for whatever reason, to respond to a subpoena and testify about some aspects of a story based on confidential information or derived in part from confidential sources are advised to seek a stipulation as to what they can say without being held to have forfeited their privilege.

---

91. 83 N.J. 350, 416 A.2d 793 (N.J. 1980).
92. In re Corsetti, 387 Mass. 1 (Mass. 1982), and Bunting v. Municipal Court, unpublished (Cal.Super.Ct. 1982).

Because some shield laws are written in terms that grant a privilege both to journalists and to news organizations, a California court held that the *National Enquirer* waived, in part, a privilege claimed by two of its reporters.[93] The reporters had interviewed the woman who was with John Belushi, a comedian and actor, when he died of a drug overdose. When the reporters were summoned by a grand jury, they agreed to answer some questions but refused to say whether the woman was sober when they talked to her or whether they had paid her for the interview. However, the editors of the weekly tabloid already had given the grand jury copies of tape recordings made by the reporters and a transcript of the interview. The court held that by doing so the editors had waived the reporters' privilege with respect to all information in the tapes and transcript. However, the court also ruled that the reporters could safely refuse to testify about "a considerable quantity" of unreleased notes and investigative material not disclosed by their employer.

THE SCOPE OF THE PRIVILEGE

Journalists in Criminal Proceedings

Journalists who break the law are treated like any other violators: They are subject to arrest, and, if arrested, they have no more, and no less, protection than anyone else. The only privilege available to a journalist who is accused of committing a crime is that offered by the Fifth Amendment's right to remain silent.

However, in most jurisdictions, journalists who have knowledge of crimes committed by others are treated differently from other kinds of witnesses. They usually can avoid testifying, if they want to do so, whether they be summoned by a grand jury or as a witness for the defense or the prosecution. In federal proceedings, the right to avoid testifying is grounded in the First Amendment interpretation of *Branzburg*. In state courts, that right may be grounded in the First Amendment, in the freedom-of-press clause of the state's constitution, in a shield law, or in common law. Because of the varying sources of the privilege, it varies widely and is granted or denied on a case-by-case basis. Therefore, the cases chosen for treatment in this section can be considered only as illustrative.

Grand Jury Subpoenas

A review of recent cases in which reporters have contested subpoenas ordering them to testify before grand juries shows that reporters are least likely to be excused if they have witnessed a crime. However, they have prevailed in a few instances by arguing that the jury must prove an overriding need for their testimony or that they are exempted by the language of a state shield law. The following case is illustrative.

---

93.   In re Brenna, 8 Med.L.Rptr. 2561 (Cal.Super.Ct. 1982).

In re Vrazo, 423 A.2d 695
(N.J.Super. 1980).

Fawn Vrazo, a reporter for the *Philadelphia Bulletin,* had written a series of stories on corruption in government in southern New Jersey.

A grand jury was asked to look into the allegations, and it summoned Vrazo to testify. Her stories had relied heavily on confidential sources, but it also appeared that the reporter had been present when illegal acts were committed. Vrazo moved to squash the summons, citing New Jersey's strong shield law. The prosecutor argued that the law did not protect reporters who were eyewitnesses to a crime. He argued further that Vrazo had waived any claim to privilege with respect to information by publishing some of it. In *In re Vrazo,* the state's Superior Court rejected both arguments. It held that the eyewitness exception applied only to crimes involving physical violence or property damage. Further, the law defines a journalist's privilege as protecting both sources and information. The court held it could not be waived so far as the grand jury was concerned by disclosing privileged information in the newspaper. Vrazo was not required to testify.

The absolute nature of New Jersey's shield law was reaffirmed by that state's supreme court in an instance in which a prosecutor sought testimony from a *New Jersey Herald* reporter.[94] A lower-level appellate court had held that Evan Schuman would have to appear in court and answer questions about a story reporting an interview with a murder suspect. The supreme court reversed, holding that the New Jersey Legislature had made clear its intent to give journalists absolute protection for their sources and for information obtained from them.

In a New York case, *In re Grand Jury Investigation,*[95] a public official had violated a state law by giving a sealed report to a television reporter. The reporter might also have been subject to prosecution as a witness to an illegal act. A special grand jury, called to look into the release of the report, issued a subpoena to the reporter. A motion to quash ultimately was upheld by the Court of Appeals, New York's highest court. It held that the shield law was written to give journalists an absolute right to protect the identity of their confidential sources, even when the journalist might be involved in the crime. Since the reporter had obtained the sealed document under a promise not to identify the source, he could not be compelled to testify, the appeals court held, even though a guilty public official might go unpunished as a result.

Reporters who have not seen a crime committed, but who have talked to those who have, may have to testify if they are summoned by a grand jury. Here, too, much depends upon the existence of a shield law.

The experience of Paul Corsetti, a reporter for the *Boston Herald,* illustrates the worst that can happen when a journalist bases a story on a conversation with a criminal. Corsetti talked by telephone with a man suspected of murder. He wrote that the man had confessed to the crime. A grand jury summoned Corsetti to testify about the interview. Corsetti filed a motion to quash, arguing that the

---

94. "N.J. Supreme Court Makes Shield Law Protection Absolute," *Editor & Publisher,* 4 February 1989.
95. 460 N.Y.S.2d 227 (N.Y.Co.Ct. 1983); rev'd. Beach v. Shanley, 466 N.Y.S.2d 725 (3d Dept. 1983), rev'd motion granted, 476 N.Y.S.2d 765 (N.Y. 1984).

grand jury could get the same information from a police officer. A judge concluded that Corsetti's testimony would indeed duplicate the officer's, but ordered the reporter to testify anyway. Massachusetts had no shield law. On appeal, the state's highest court ruled that because the grand jury had completed its work, there was no reason to decide the case.[96] That did not end Corsetti's problems, as we will see shortly.

Reporters whose stories disclose a direct knowledge of a crime or the suspect open themselves to the possibility of a grand jury subpoena. If one is issued, reporters have three options: They can agree to testify without qualification, or they can hire a lawyer who may advise either the filing of a motion to quash or an attempt to reach an agreement as to the limits of the reporter's testimony. The purpose of a motion to quash is to obtain an order excusing the reporter from testifying. However, if the accuracy of the reporter's story is at issue, a motion to quash may leave the court with the impression that the reporter is unwilling to defend it. In such instances, the best course may be an attempt to limit the reporter's testimony to rule out questions about confidential sources or information.

Denial of a motion to quash can be appealed. If that, or an attempt to limit the testimony, fails, reporters are confronted with difficult alternatives. One is to seek permission to identify their confidential sources or to testify as to information imparted in confidence. The other is to defy the court and be held in contempt. That holding, too, is subject to appeal. At that stage, the cases show that some reporters have escaped punishment because the grand jury's investigation was dropped or completed, as in Corsetti's case, or it obtained enough information from other sources to support an indictment.

As Prosecution Witnesses

Reporters whose stories disclose knowledge of a crime run a risk not only of being summoned by a grand jury, but of being called as a witness by the prosecution. In such instances, recent reported cases show that reporters have a fifty-fifty chance of getting the subpoena quashed. Again, much depends upon the existence of a shield law and the degree of privilege recognized by the court involved.

Commonwealth v. *Corsetti,* 387 Mass. 1 (Mass. 1982). Paul Corsetti's experience, which began with a summons to testify before a grand jury, was renewed when the murder suspect with whom he had talked was brought to trial. The prosecutor subpoenaed the reporter as a witness. Corsetti appeared in court as ordered, but testified only as to the fact that he had written the story that appeared in the *Boston Herald*. When he was pressed for details of his interview with the suspect, Corsetti said he had promised that he would not testify in court as to the substance of the conversation. The judge found Corsetti

---

96. *Corsetti v. Commonwealth,* 411 N.E.2d 466 (Mass. 1980).

in contempt and sentenced him to ninety days in jail, the maximum permitted by law. On appeal, the Supreme Judicial Court indicated, in *Commonwealth* v. *Corsetti,* that it might be willing to recognize a common-law journalist's privilege, but had no need to do so in this instance. Corsetti had identified his source, and had disclosed much if not all of the information, when he wrote the article. Therefore, he had waived any claim to a privilege. Corsetti spent about a week in jail before the governor commuted his sentence to time served and ordered his release.

In a Maryland case, neither the state's shield law nor the court's recognition of a qualified privilege protected a television station served with a subpoena. A reporter for WBAL-TV had interviewed a suspected criminal. Part of it was used in the station's news programs. An assistant state's attorney who was preparing for the suspect's trial issued a subpoena to the station for its outtakes, the portions of the videotape not used on the air. The station resisted, arguing that the fact that the suspect had already been convicted in a federal court proved that whatever might be on the outtakes was not needed as evidence. When the attorney insisted, a trial court judge looked at the videotape in the privacy of his office and ruled that it was needed. When the station persisted in its refusal to surrender the videotape, the judge found it in contempt. On appeal, the Maryland Court of Appeals, in *WBAL-TV Division, The Hearst Corporation* v. *Maryland,*[97] upheld the trial court judge's order. The court said the videotape offered evidence ''frozen in time'' that could be duplicated in no other way. Thus, despite the court's recognition of a three-prong test similar to that advanced by Stewart in *Branzburg,* the court said the state's need for the tape was overriding.

However, reporters involved in two separate cases in Florida were the victors under that state's common-law privilege. In *Florida* v. *Taylor,*[98] the reporter had talked to a suspect at the scene of the crime. When the prosecutor summoned the reporter as a witness, the reporter filed a motion to quash, which was upheld by a state circuit court. It held that the prosecutor had failed to show the reporter's evidence was relevant, that it could not be obtained from other sources not protected by the First Amendment, that the prosecutor had tried in vain to get the evidence from other sources, and that there would be a miscarriage of justice if the reporter was not compelled to testify. In the second case, *Tribune Co.* v. *Green,*[99] a state appellate court applied a shortened version of the same test and held that the reporter, who also had interviewed a suspected criminal, should not be required to testify.

Journalists who are subpoenaed as prosecution witnesses in other states should not place too much reliance on the Florida decisions. That state does not have a shield law, but its courts have forged one of the strongest privileges for journalists in effect anywhere.

The California Supreme Court held that the state's shield law, which is a part of the state constitution, does not offer absolute protection to journalists who

---

97. 477 A.2d 776 (Md.App. 1984).
98. 9 Med.L.Rptr. 1551 (Fla.Cir.Ct. 1982).
99. 440 So.2d 484 (Fla.Dist.Ct.App. 1983).

have witnessed a crime.[100] If what they saw or heard is essential to a defendant's case, they must testify or be in contempt. A reporter and a photographer for the *Los Angeles Times* were present during a drug and theft investigation when police made an arrest in a shopping mall. An officer searched the suspect, found a set of brass knuckles, and charged him with carrying a concealed weapon. At trial, the public defender argued that the charge should be dismissed because the search was made without the suspect's consent. Police said consent was given. When both the prosecutor and the defender summoned the reporter to resolve the dispute, she refused to testify, even though no promise of confidentiality had been made. The judge ordered her jailed and fined her $100 a day. She spent six hours in a cell before she was released on $1000 bond. An appellate court upheld the judge's order. In a separate proceeding, the photographer also was found in contempt. The supreme court affirmed the appellate court's decision, noting that the suspect's defense "will rise or fall" on whether he consented to the search. The court held that what the journalists saw and heard was neither confidential nor sensitive. Nor would their testimony "even remotely" hinder their ability to gather information in other instances. "All that is being required of them is to accept the civil responsibility imposed on all persons who witness alleged criminal conduct."

As Defense Witnesses

When a reporter is believed to have evidence that will help prove a criminal defendant not guilty, two constitutional rights may come into conflict. A clause in the Sixth Amendment gives a criminal defendant a right "to have compulsory process for obtaining witnesses in his favor." That process is exercised through the subpoena power. Despite the amendment's guarantee, courts in many jurisdictions are applying a balancing test when defendants seek testimony from journalists. As a consequence, some journalists have been excused from testifying, but others have not.

An early decision of an Ohio appeals court in *People* v. *Monica*[101] is illustrative of the majority position. A reporter for the *Cleveland Plain Dealer* had written that a murder was arranged by Mafia chieftains. When a suspect in the murder was brought to trial in California, he sought a subpoena to compel identification of the reporter's confidential sources and information. He argued that the information would show that he was not the Mafia figure who had arranged for the murder. An Ohio trial court judge refused to issue the subpoena and the appeals court affirmed. It held that the defendant had failed to prove that the reporter was a necessary and material witness. The court said that the reporter's First Amendment privilege could be overcome only if the defendant were able to show that: (1) the material sought from the reporter would help establish guilt or innocence; (2) alternative sources of helpful information had been exhausted; (3)

---

100. "Shield Law Clarified in California Ruling," *Editor & Publisher,* 12 May 1990, p. 27.
101. Ohio Court of Appeals, 8th Dist., No. 39950 (1979).

an effort had been made to obtain the reporter's testimony as to nonconfidential information; and (4) a request had been made to a judge to examine confidential information in private to determine if it was relevant.

The Oregon Court of Appeals held that the *Portland Oregonian* did not have to release seventy unpublished photographs sought by lawyers defending three women who were arrested during an antinuclear demonstration.[102] The court reversed a contempt order issued when a county district judge fined the paper $300 and ordered its editor jailed for refusing to surrender photographs taken during a demonstration in Portland's Pioneer Square. Judge John Butler noted that the women had made no attempt to explain how the photos might work in their favor. Therefore, the defendants had not complied with the terms of Oregon's shield law, which protects unpublished information unless it is needed by the defendant to ensure a fair trial.

In two California cases, courts upheld the right of reporters to refuse to testify on behalf of criminal defendants. In one instance, a Superior Court judge in Santa Cruz Country held that a reporter for the *San Jose Mercury News* and the paper's editor could not be required to surrender notes and tapes of an interview with a key witness in a murder trial.[103] The materials had been sought by the defendant's attorney. The judge said that the state's shield law and constitution place a high priority on the journalist's privilege. The judge added that the reporter's information was not essential to the case, was available from other sources, and would not be a determining factor in acquittal or conviction.

In the second case, the Court of Appeals, First Appellate Circuit, overturned a superior court's contempt order that could have sent Erin Hallissy of the *Contra Costa Times* to jail. Hallissy had interviewed a suspected murderer and reported that he had told her he had killed other persons than those named in the charges against him.[104] The suspect's attorney issued a subpoena for Hallissy's notes, saying that he needed them to show contradictions and inconsistencies in his client's statements, which were the principal evidence against the suspect. When Hallissy refused to surrender her notes, a judge found her in contempt. The appellate court held that the attorney had not proved that Hallissy's notes contained evidence necessary to his case. The court's decision also noted that the suspect had made similar admissions to other persons who could be called as witnesses.

However, the balancing test can go against journalists. The U.S. Court of Appeals, First Circuit, ruled that a trial judge acted properly when he ordered NBC News to let him examine outtakes of an interview with a prospective key witness in the trial of Lyndon LaRouche, a right-wing activist accused of political campaign irregularities. LaRouche's attorney had argued that some of the material in the outtakes might help him in cross-examination of the witness. The judge asked

---

102. "Paper Does Not Have to Release Photos," *Editor & Publisher*, 19 September 1987, p. 32.
103. M. L. Stein, "Reporter's Jailing to Be Reviewed by Appeals Court," *Editor & Publisher*, 5 December 1987, p. 30.
104. M. L. Stein, "Appeals Court Overturns Reporter's Contempt Ruling," *Editor & Publisher*, 7 May 1988, p. 14.

to look at the materials to see if that indeed was the case. NBC appealed the order, which was upheld. The appellate court recognized that "there is a lurking and subtle threat to journalists and their employers if disclosure of outtakes, notes, and other unused information becomes routine and casually compelled," but the court held that in asking to review the materials himself rather than ordering them handed over in their entirety to LaRouche's attorney, the district court judge had shown "proper sensitivity" to the competing constitutional interests.[105]

The most celebrated loser in a contest with defense attorneys was Myron Farber, a reporter for the *New York Times*. He spent forty days in jail in 1978 rather than let a New Jersey state court judge examine his notes on a murder investigation.

Farber had written a series of stories about the deaths of several patients in a New Jersey hospital. As a result, a grand jury indicted a former physician at the hospital on a charge of murder. The physician's lawyer subpoenaed Farber as a witness, alleging that he had information that would help the defendant's case. Subpoenas also were issued for Farber's notes and for any memoranda in the newspaper's files bearing on the investigation. The judge was willing to examine the materials in private to see whether any of them would indeed help the physician. When Farber and the *Times* refused his offer, the judge found both in contempt, sending the reporter to jail and fining the newspaper $5000 a day until each complied with his order.[106] Farber's jail term and the *Times's* fine ended when a jury found the physician not guilty. Governor Brendan Byrne pardoned Farber and the newspaper. He also returned $101,000 of the fine.

As a result of Farber's ordeal, the New Jersey Legislature greatly strengthened the state's shield law, and state courts have construed it as near absolute in its effect, as noted earlier.

The cases in the preceding sections make several points for journalists who cover the crime beat. If a reporter's investigations point to a crime for which no arrests have been made, the reporter faces the possibility of being summoned by the prosecutor or a grand jury to tell what she or he knows. If police have made an arrest and a reporter's stories contain information the police do not have or raise doubts about a defendant's guilt, the reporter faces the possibility of being summoned as a witness by one or both sides if the case goes to trial. Reporters who see a crime committed or who are present when police make an arrest are particularly vulnerable to a summons. Reporters whose crime stories are based on information from confidential sources may be asked to identify those sources. Although the recent reported cases indicate that reporters who contest subpoenas prevail in most instances, there is no certainty that they will do so. Reporters have gone to jail or been fined for refusing to disclose information sought by the criminal justice system. Each case, even in strong shield-law states such as California, Florida, and New Jersey, is decided on its own set of facts, and the outcome cannot be predicted with certainty. A journalist's worst course is to ignore

---

105. U.S. v. LaRouche Campaign, (1st Cir.) No. 87-2054, 9 March 1988.
106. In re Farber, 394 A.2d 330 (N.J. 1978).

Myron Farber, a *New York Times* reporter, spent 40 days in a New Jersey jail in 1978 because he refused to let a judge examine his notes. Farber's stories in the *Times* had led to the indictment on murder charges of a physician accused of giving fatal injections to hospital patients. A jury acquitted the physician. (UPI/Bettmann Newsphotos)

a subpoena. That will lead inevitably to a contempt citation. But where a proper challenge is mounted, courts are balancing the reporter's First Amendment or shield-law claim of privilege against the public's interest in justice. Key questions in striking the balance are:

— Does the reporter indeed have evidence bearing on the case?

— Can similar evidence be obtained from other sources?

— If it cannot, is the reporter's evidence crucial to proper resolution of the case?

Journalists in Civil Actions

Judging from the large number of cases in point, a journalist is far more likely to be summoned in connection with a civil action than a criminal proceeding. The decisions make clear that most courts not only recognize, but respect, a journalist's privilege in civil lawsuits. Litigants seeking a journalist's testimony are likely to have to prove that the journalist has information essential to their case and that it cannot be obtained from other sources. This is true even when the government is one of the parties to the civil action. The following cases exemplify the majority holdings.

When five states brought a civil antitrust action against seventeen oil companies, they acted on the theory that price movements were coordinated through a trade publication, *Platt's Oilgram Price Report.* Consequently, the states obtained a subpoena directing the newsletter and two of its reporters to provide the names of their confidential sources of price information. In response to a motion to quash, a U.S. District Court judge in New York ordered disclosure. One reporter gave the court four names. The other refused. The court held the newsletter's publisher, McGraw-Hill, in contempt and imposed a fine of $100 a day until its order was complied with. On appeal, the U.S. Court of Appeals, Second Circuit, reversed. Its decision in *In re Petroleum Products Antitrust Litigation* was emphatic.[107] The court said journalists could not be forced to identify confidential sources unless there was "a clear and specific showing that the information is highly material and relevant, necessary or critical to the maintenance of the claim, and not obtainable from other available sources." In this instance, the court said the states had offered no evidence that the newsletter was involved in any price fixing scheme. It was not enough to suggest that the reporters may have been unknowing conduits for information through which the oil companies fixed prices.

Playboy magazine was able to invoke California's shield law when it was caught in the middle of a dispute between the comedy team of Cheech and Chong and their former accountants. The comedians sued the accounting firm for damages, charging it with fraud. While the case was pending, a *Playboy* reporter interviewed the comedians. In the course of the interview, Richard ("Cheech") Marin allegedly made statements about the accountants. When the interview was published, two things happened. The accountants subpoenaed *Playboy,* asking for all notes and tape recordings taken in connection with the interview. They were seeking information that could be used to cast doubt on Marin's testimony at trial and to support their side of the case. Also in response to publication of the article, Marin said he had not made some of the statements attributed to him. *Playboy* moved to quash the subpoena. A state appeals court ordered the subpoena dismissed except for one element: The magazine would have to give the accountants the address and telephone number of the reporter. Otherwise, the appeals court ruled that California's shield law protected any unpublished information known to the interviewer or any unpublished information in documentary form. The accounting firm did not have an interest strong enough to overcome the shield's protection.[108]

A few courts have balked at excusing journalists who are asked to testify in civil actions, but have held that they could assert a privilege on a question-by-question basis. This is illustrated by a federal district court's decision in *Continental Cablevision, Inc.* v. *Storer Broadcasting Corp.*[109] The two firms were

107. 680 F.2d 5 (2d Cir. 1982).
108. Playboy Enterprises, Inc. v. Superior Court, 201 Cal.Rptr. 207 (Cal.App. 1984).
109. 583 F.Supp. 427 (E.D.Mo. 1984).

competitors for a cable television franchise in Florissant, Missouri, a suburb of St. Louis. When Continental's bid was rejected by the city council, the firm sued Storer for libel, based on a written statement given to members of the council. As a part of its pretrial discovery, Continental issued a subpoena to a *St. Louis Globe-Democrat* reporter who had written a story about Storer's statement. She moved to quash, arguing that she was protected by a federal common-law privilege. The court held that because the plaintiff and defendant were from different states, the common-law privilege was not applicable. Nor did the base states of the parties—Massachusetts and Missouri—have shield laws. The court then relied on First Amendment principles. It held that the reporter would have to respond to the subpoena and submit to questioning by Continental's lawyer. At that point, the balancing test proposed in *Branzburg* would come into play. With help from her lawyer, the reporter would decide which questions she would answer and which she would not, following detailed guidelines set by the court.

Grand Forks Herald v. District Court, 322 N.W.2d 850 (N.D. 1982). When a litigant in a civil action seeks a newspaper's unpublished photographs neither a shield law nor a journalist's privilege may be of much help if other courts follow the example of the North Dakota Supreme Court. In *Grand Forks Herald* v. *District Court,* that state's highest court denied a motion to quash a subpoena for unpublished photographs. The newspaper's photographer had taken several pictures of an accident, which became the subject of an action for damages. Only one of the photos was published. One of the parties to the damage suit sought the others, thinking they might help his case. When the newspaper resisted, the supreme court ruled against it, noting that the litigant had tried without success to find other photographs of the accident. Further, it held there was nothing confidential involved. The photographer had taken the pictures in a public place. His editors might have selected any one, or all of them, for publication. Further, the photos offered evidence that would not be presented in any other way. Finally, surrender of the photos would be less intrusive into First Amendment rights than requiring the photographer to testify as to what he had seen at the site of the accident.

Grand Forks Herald is an exceptional case. Most attempts to draw journalists into civil actions as witnesses have resulted in rulings that the evidence should be sought from other sources. In several instances, cases have been continued for as long as a year while alternative sources were sought.

Libel and Confidential Sources

When journalists' reliance on confidential sources subjects them to a libel suit, courts vary widely in their treatment of such sources. Some will not permit defendants to use information from such sources as part of their defense. A few have instructed juries to decide cases on the assumption that the source did not exist. More recently, courts have begun to apply balancing tests similar to Justice Stewart's three-part test in *Branzburg*.

The first two of these three approaches can be traced to the Supreme Court's 1979 decision in *Herbert* v. *Lando,*[110] which is summarized in Chapter 4. In that case, the Court held that journalists who are sued for libel do not have a privilege to protect their editorial processes. These are the decisions that go into the shaping of a story—to include some facts while omitting others, and to believe some sources more than others. In *Herbert,* the court held that libel plaintiffs can ask detailed questions about such decisions during discovery leading up to trial and during the trial itself. It did so, it said, to avoid making it impossible, or nearly so, for plaintiffs to prove the requisite degree of fault.

Some courts have read that decision to apply not only to the editorial process, but to the identity of confidential sources. This has led these courts to impose harsh restrictions on media defendants in libel actions growing out of stories in which confidential sources were used. One of these approaches, to deny the defendant the use of any information obtained from such sources, has been applied in shield-law states. The following case is illustrative.

Greenberg v. *CBS Inc.,* **419 N.Y.S.2d 988 (N.Y.App. 1979).** A segment of "60 Minutes" entitled "Over the Speed Limit" included an interview with an unidentified woman who said a Dr. Greenberg had prescribed more than eighty pills a day to help her lose weight. When the physician sued for libel, CBS tried to verify the patient's allegation by offering affidavits from other unidentified sources. It acted in the belief that New York's shield law gave it absolute protection against being required to identify its sources. Both sides moved for summary judgment. The trial court rejected CBS's motion, and the appeals court affirmed. It conceded that because of the shield law, it could not make CBS identify any of the sources. But it held that when the case went to trial, CBS would have two options. It could continue to stand behind the shield law. In that instance, it could use none of the evidence it had obtained from confidential sources. Or it could waive the shield law, identify its sources, and use their evidence to refute Greenberg's assertion that CBS was grossly negligent.

The second approach, to instruct the jury to assume no source existed, has been taken by appellate courts in California and New Hampshire. It is equivalent to a holding that the reporter acted in actual malice. The California case, *Rancho La Costa, Inc.* v. *Penthouse,*[111] was based on a story in *Penthouse* alleging that the owners of a luxury golfing resort had ties to organized crime. The owners sued for libel and asked the magazine to identify confidential sources on whom it had relied for part of its information. *Penthouse,* relying on California's strong shield law, refused to do so. The trial judge conceded he had no means of compelling the magazine to name its sources. But he said that when the case came to trial, he would instruct the jury to act on the assumption they did not exist. On appeal, the appellate court modified the form of the order without changing its effect. It said the judge should tell the jury that *Penthouse's* only sources were those it was willing to identify in court.

---

110.   441 U.S. 153, 99 S.Ct. 1635, 60 L.Ed.2d 115 (1979).
111.   165 Cal.Rptr. 347 (Cal.Super.Ct. 1980).

The New Hampshire case is *Downing* v. *Monitor Publishing Co.*[112] Downing, a police chief, was the subject of a newspaper article in which an unidentified source said he had failed a lie detector test. When Downing sued for libel, he said he could not prove actual malice unless he knew who the source was. The newspaper insisted on keeping its source confidential. Although the state had no shield law, the New Hampshire Supreme Court said it would not compel disclosure until the chief had offered proof that the story was false. Holding that he already had done so, the court said that if the reporter chose to go to jail rather than identify the source, the trial judge should proceed on the assumption that none existed.

More commonly, courts have shown a willingness to look past *Herbert,* if the key issue is identity of a source, and apply a balancing test. One element of such tests was applied by the New Hampshire court in *Downing.* It would not act to compel disclosure of the source's identity until the plaintiff had established that he was the target of a defamatory falsehood. Other courts have held that the plaintiff must prove that his suit is not frivolous or brought for purposes of harassment. *Bruno & Stillman,* discussed earlier, illustrates how such threshold tests are applied.

Miller v. Transamerican Press, Inc., 621 F. 2d 721 (5th Cir. 1980). The United States Court of Appeals, Fifth Circuit, carried balancing still further in *Miller* v. *Transamerican Press, Inc.* A trade publication reported that Miller, a trustee of the Teamsters' pension fund, had mishandled the fund's assets. The article was based on information from a confidential source. Miller sued the magazine for libel and sought, during discovery, to learn the identity of the source. On three occasions, a federal district court ruled that Miller could not compel discovery from the writer or the magazine's editor until he could prove that the information was not available from other sources. One of Miller's fellow trustees gave him a sworn statement saying he knew nothing to indicate the fund's assets had been mishandled. Miller gave the court a sworn statement asserting that the article was false. At that point, the trial judge ruled that Miller could not prove actual malice unless he knew who the source was. Because that went to the heart of his case, the judge ordered Transamerican to name its source. On appeal, the Fifth Circuit court modified the order, limiting disclosure to Miller's lawyer. On rehearing, the circuit court said its order would not go into effect until Miller had proved that the article was false and defamatory, that he had made reasonable, but unsuccessful, efforts to identify the source on his own, and that his case could not proceed unless the source were identified.

However, in several more recent cases judges have interpreted shield laws as protecting reporters who refused to identify confidential sources of defamatory information. An Indiana court held that that state's shield law created "an absolute privilege" for the news media.[113] In a libel action brought by a former police chief, the court rejected the argument that the law unconstitutionally impaired the plaintiff's right to protect his reputation. It also rejected the chief's argument

---

112.   415 A.2d 683 (N.H. 1980).
113.   Jamerson v. Anderson Newspapers, 469 N.E.2d 1243 (Ind.Ct.App. 1984).

that the reporter's refusal to identify the source should be construed as an admission he had no source. The newspaper eventually won the lawsuit. A federal court interpreting Nevada's shield law held it to be the strongest in the country.[114] In a case brought against the McClatchy newspapers of California by a former U.S. senator from Nevada, Paul Laxalt, the court said the plaintiff could not require the newspapers' reporters to disclose their sources of derogatory information about him. However, the court also ruled that the reporters could not testify about the reliability of their confidential sources unless they waived their privilege. A Pennsylvania court, reversing a $4.5 million libel judgment against the *Philadelphia Inquirer,* held that the trial judge had acted improperly in prohibiting the newspaper from presenting information provided by confidential sources.[115] The court, noting that the Pennsylvania shield law protects the identity of confidential sources, said the judge should have let the jury decide whether to believe what the reporters said about information obtained from those sources.

Thus, in civil actions as in criminal, reporters run a risk when they seek to be excused from testifying about confidential information or identifying confidential sources. However, in applying the balancing test that has evolved from Stewart's dissent in *Branzburg,* courts seem more inclined to rule in the journalist's favor in civil cases than in criminal.

SEARCH WARRANTS AND THIRD-PARTY SUBPOENAS

Thus far, this chapter had dealt with instances in which grand juries, courts, and participants in judicial proceedings have used their subpoena powers in an attempt to compel journalists to testify. As the numerous cases suggest, a subpoena directed to individuals who are assumed to have direct knowledge of a crime or the substance of a civil action is the most common method of seeking testimony from reluctant witnesses. There is no need for a subpoena if witnesses testify voluntarily.

Courts, prosecutors, and police agencies also have other methods of obtaining information, two of which have seen limited use against journalists. One method is the search warrant. The other is a subpoena directed at third parties who have information that might identify a journalist's sources. Search warrants are authorized by the Fourth Amendment, which was drafted to protect people's property and possessions from arbitrary seizure by police. The amendment says that searches of private property can be made only if authorized for good cause by a magistrate. Usually, warrants are issued only to seize evidence of a crime, such things as a stash of drugs, stolen property, or weapons believed to have been used in committing a crime. Third-party subpoenas sometimes are served on banks to obtain financial information about a suspected criminal, or on the telephone company to obtain records of a user's long-distance calls.

---

114. Laxalt v. McClatchy, 14 Med.L.Rptr. 1149 (D.Nev. 1987).
115. Sprague v. Walter, 13 Med.L.Rptr. 1177 (Pa.Super.Ct. 1986).

The Privacy Protection Act of 1980

Until the advent of photojournalism, search warrants seldom were a problem for the news media. Few journalists have been involved in crime, and most newsrooms are unlikely hiding places for criminal contraband. The era of political activism that reached a climax during the latter years of the Vietnam War brought police search teams into newsrooms in disturbing numbers. Usually, they were seeking unpublished photographs, still or video, that would help them identify persons who had caused personal injury or property damage during riots. The most notable of these searches saw police rummaging through desk drawers and wastebaskets in the office of the *Stanford* (Cal.) *Daily,* a student newspaper. They were seeking photographs that would help them identify students and others who had occupied the Stanford University Hospital, and who had severely beaten several police officers. The searchers found nothing that would help them, but their actions led first to a significant Supreme Court decision and then to congressional enactment of the Privacy Protection Act of 1980. The latter has made it unlikely that police again will search a newsroom.

Zurcher v. *Stanford Daily,* **436 U.S. 547, 98 S. Ct. 1970, 56 L.Ed.2d 525 (1978).**

The Supreme Court decision, in *Zurcher* v. *Stanford Daily,* was seen at the time as a serious blow to First Amendment freedoms. The editors of the newspapers had reacted to the search by filing suit against those responsible, alleging violation of freedom of the press and abuse of the search warrant provision of the Fourth Amendment. They argued that because there was no evidence that anyone on the *Daily* had been involved in a crime, the police should have used a subpoena, not a search warrant, to obtain the unused photographs. Lower federal courts found in the students' favor, but the Supreme Court took the case and reversed.

Justice White, writing for a majority of the Court, noted that search warrants had been used on other occasions to seize printed materials. His reference was to instances, mainly during the Cold War era after World War II, when police seized books and pamphlets alleged to be subversive. The court held that any First Amendment interest in protecting the newsroom from police intrusion had been taken into account by the magistrate who issued the search warrant.

White noted further that the Fourth Amendment requires only that the warrant described specifically "the place to be searched." He found nothing in that language exempting newsrooms. If police believe helpful evidence can be found in a place, and if they further believe that a subpoena would result in destruction of that evidence, issuance of a search warrant is justified. The First Amendment, in the Court's view, cannot create sanctuaries beyond the reach of the police.

The decision encouraged police and prosecutors to conduct twenty-three other newsroom searches in ten states within the year after it was handed down.[116] It also helped persuade Congress to enact the Privacy Protection Act of 1980.[117] The law, which applies to federal, state, and local law enforcement agencies,

---

116. News Media Update, 19 October 1981.
117.   42 U.S.C. §§2000aa-2000aa-12.

strictly limits the circumstances under which a warrant can be issued to search for the "work products" and "documentary materials" of persons "engaged in First Amendment Activities." Translated from legal jargon, the Act protects photographs, audio and video tapes, notes on interviews, drafts of articles, and notes used in preparation of articles.

The law does not raise absolute barriers against newsroom searches. A warrant can be issued to seize any materials if there is probable cause to believe a journalist is using them to commit a crime, or if seizure is necessary to prevent death or serious injury. Further, such things as photos, tapes, and notes on interviews can be seized if there is reason to believe they would be destroyed in response to a subpoena or if they have not been handed over in response to a court order and further delay would stand in the way of justice.

As of this writing, there have been no cases testing the limits of the Act.

Limitation on Privacy

In the 1970s and in 1980, a few journalists learned that Justice Department attorneys had been studying a listing of their long-distance calls. The listings, showing the telephone numbers of persons called by the journalists, had been obtained under subpoena to the telephone companies serving the reporters' homes and offices. The attorneys sought the records in an attempt to find out who gave the Pentagon Papers to the *New York Times,* how Jack Anderson obtained copies of a classified report on relations between the United States, India, and Pakistan, and on how the *Times* obtained an income tax audit and access to secret grand jury proceedings.

Reporters Committee for Freedom of the Press v. American Telephone & Telegraph Co., 593 F. 2d 1030 (D.C. Cir. 1979). Believing that such subpoenas were both an invasion of privacy and a violation of First Amendment freedoms, a group of journalists challenged the practice in court. However, the United States Court of Appeals for the District of Columbia Circuit upheld the Justice Department's position. Its decision, in *Reporters Committee for Freedom of the Press* v. *American Telephone & Telegraph Co.,* rejected both grounds for the lawsuit.

The court said that the search warrant provision of the Fourth Amendment implies a right of privacy that will be protected as long as people stay on their own property. But when people venture off their property, or even use the telephone to call others, they give up some of their privacy. In this instance, the telephone company had made records of long-distance calls for billing purposes. Those records belonged to the company, not to the callers. Because the callers gave up their expectations of privacy when they placed the calls, they could not prevent the phone company from surrendering its records to the government under subpoena.

The circuit court referred to White's opinion in *Branzburg* in rejecting the reporters' First Amendment argument. The government's purpose in seeking the long-distance billing records was to investigate a crime. In this instance, it seemed likely from their stories that journalists had sought information from persons who had committed crimes. As long as the investigation was conducted in good faith, the subpoena for the long-distance records did not violate the journalists' First Amendment interests.

However, in 1980, the Justice Department adopted guidelines that reduced the likelihood of further subpoenas for records of journalists' long-distance calls.[118] Except in unusual circumstances, department attorneys are expected to seek the journalist's consent to obtain the records. If that fails, a subpoena can be issued only with the attorney general's approval. The department can proceed in criminal cases if it has "reasonable grounds to believe, based on information obtained from nonmedia sources, that a crime has occurred, and that the information sought is essential to a successful investigation." Subpoenas also may be issued in a civil action if the case is of "substantial proportions" and there is reason to believe the information is "essential to [its] successful completion."

As of this writing, in no known recent instances has the Justice Department sought subpoenas for reporters' long-distance telephone records. However, President Bush's attorney general, Dick Thornburgh, asserted on a network news program that the Justice Department might do so to find out who leaked word that a member of Congress was being investigated by the FBI to determine whether he was misusing federal funds.[119] Thornburgh said his department had no intention of prosecuting reporters who used the information but would act against those who had supplied it. In the face of protests from the media, no subpoenas were issued.

In the Professional World

Journalists who investigate wrongdoing by public officials or others enter a legal and ethical minefield. If they do their work well, they may win a Pulitzer Prize for meritorious public service. That's what the *Washington Post* did for showing that a burglary at Democratic headquarters was linked to President Nixon's personal staff. Without the help of a still-unidentified source known as "Deep Throat," that connection might not have been traced. That same newspaper had to return a Pulitzer Prize when its editors discovered that one of its reporters had made up a touching story about a young boy who was being injected with heroin by his mother and her boyfriend. That story, too, was based on reports from anonymous sources. When Washington police began looking for the boy to save him from almost certain death, the reporter still refused to identify him and her editors backed her up. Only when the story won the prize was the deception discovered.

They were not the first, nor the last, editors to be duped. Editors at the *New York Times,* the *New York Daily News,* and *The New Yorker* magazine have run as fact stories later discovered to be part fiction because quoted

---

118. 28 C.F.R. §50.10.
119. *Meet the Press*, NBC Television Network, 20 August 1989.

sources did not exist. No doubt other editors have been taken in, too. The temptation to make a good story better, to achieve superficial balance, or to cover for a missing fact is more than some writers can resist. Unfortunately, there is more than a little truth in the cynical newsroom advice, ''Never let the facts stand in the way of a good story.''

It is because of such temptations that both professional editors and the courts have looked askance at stories based on anonymous sources. When Carl Bernstein and Bob Woodward were developing their prize-winning Watergate stories for the *Washington Post,* no fact obtained from a confidential source was published unless it was corroborated by at least two other sources. Stylebooks for both wire services caution against using material from sources who do not wish to be identified. Many newspaper editors permit the use of anonymous sources only if their information serves an important public purpose and cannot be obtained on the record. Professionals are aware that not all sources who insist on anonymity are motivated by the highest principles of public service. Many are self-serving and are engaged in nothing more noble than an attempt to use the news media to get even for a real or imagined wrong.

The threshold question, then, for journalists is whether and to what extent they will rely on confidential sources. Some news organizations advise reporters to promise confidentiality only with an editor's approval. This approval is usually based on evidence that the story can't be obtained otherwise. Even then, information obtained from confidential sources is treated with care and may not be used unless it can be confirmed by on-the-record sources. As the cases discussed in this chapter indicate, courts are more likely to grant the journalist's privilege when they are convinced that the source and the reporter reached a clear agreement on confidentiality. However, the experience of Richard Hargraves also suggests that there should be room for reconsideration if the reporter is cited for contempt. It is one thing to break a good story. It is another to become a martyr for it.

If a journalist's investigation, with or without the help of confidential sources, does uncover evidence of wrongdoing, new ethical and legal problems arise. Once the story or stories have been published, does that end the journalist's responsibility to society? As this chapter makes clear, shield laws in some of the states and court decisions in others answer that question with a qualified yes. They do so, in most instances, in recognition of the fact that if a reporter, working without the subpoena power, can uncover wrongdoing, police, prosecutors, and grand juries, with all the resources at their command, ought to be able to do so, too. This is especially true if the journalist has done a thorough reporting job. Since the purpose of journalism is public exposure, all the facts that police need ought to be in the newspaper or magazine, or in the televised newscast. However, as the cases in this chapter again suggest, that is not always true. Drug pushers made sales and converted marijuana into hashish in Paul Branzburg's presence. They would not knowingly do so in a police officer's presence. When the reporter may be the only witness to a crime, does his or her duty to society end with the production of a no-names story? That question clearly troubled Justice

White when he wrote his opinion in *Branzburg*. In his view, "The crimes of news sources are no less reprehensible and threatening to the public interest when witnessed by a reporter than when they are not." In fashioning testimonial privileges, courts think of the worst possible "what ifs": "What if a reporter was the only person who knew who shot the governor—and for whatever reason chose not to testify?"

The other side of the coin is illustrated by the *Farber* case. There, Myron Farber's stories for the *New York Times* resulted in revival of a long-dormant murder investigation and the arrest of Dr. Mario E. Jascalevich. The stories relied heavily on unidentified sources and may or may not have revealed all that the reporter knew about the case. Acting on the theory that the identity of some of the sources and unpublished information might help his client, Dr. Jascalevich's lawyer issued a subpoena for Farber, his notes, and such notes as the *Times* itself might have. Standing on First Amendment principle, Farber and the *Times* resisted to the point of being held in contempt. Farber spent forty days in jail and the *Times* was fined heavily to defend a principle. In the end, the jury found the doctor not guilty. But what if Farber had been hiding the only evidence that would have proved his innocence?

As this brief look at the ethical dilemmas suggests, professional journalists tend not to nod politely when a potential news source says, "Don't quote me, but..." or "This is off the record." They react by trying to find out why such a request is made and the subject matter that prompts it. Promises of confidentiality are not made lightly.

Sophisticated news sources and reporters have developed commonly understood terms that convey degrees of meaning with respect to confidentiality. "Off the record" means that the source does not want to see the information in print or hear it on the air. The reporter is expected to use it only for guidance to avoid misstating the thrust of the news. Information offered "for background only" is designed to help the reporter understand a complex situation and may be reflected, but not directly included, in the story. If the source offers information "not for attribution," he or she wants to see it in print or hear it on the air, but does not want to be connected with it. Public officials sometimes use this means "to float a trial balloon," that is, to disclose a policy option and see how the public reacts to it before making it official. If the policy is shot down, it is the reporter, not the official, who takes the flak.

Journalists are of two minds about confidential sources and information. The Jack Andersons, and other commentators on the political labyrinth that is the federal government, could not survive without them. Indeed, we would not know as much as we do about the inside doings of government at any level if it were not for good reporters' "informed sources." Part of the art of reporting is knowing who to go to for the straight story when the official, on-the-record version is laced with doubletalk.

There also are reporters who receive all off-the-record requests with skepticism or even distrust. They are afraid of being used, and they don't want to have their hands tied if they can get the same information on the record. This difference of opinion among journalists is part of the reason there is no federal shield law. Reporters and editors who testified before committees of Congress not only could not agree on how far the law should go, but on whether there should be one at all. Also a factor in Congress's failure to act was the fact that Woodward and Bernstein's Watergate stories were written without the protection of a shield law.

The opinions written by Justices White and Stewart in *Branzburg* reflect the differences among journalists. In White's view, confidential sources play a minor role in journalism. To him, it was incredible that a press that had flourished for more than 150 years without the ability to protect its sources suddenly had need for a First Amendment privilege. To Stewart, that was a "crabbed view" that might reduce the news media to serving as a transmission belt for the official views of official spokesmen. In his view, confidential sources are important simply because now and then one of them does help the news media expose incompetence, mistaken policies, or outright wrongdoing on the part of public officials. In Stewart's eyes, the possibility for abuse is a small price to pay for the public benefit that might flow from even a limited journalist's privilege.

FOR REVIEW

1. What is the journalist's privilege? Is it comparable with other testimonial privileges recognized by the courts?

2. What did the Supreme Court decide with respect to the three journalists who were involved in *Branzburg* v. *Hayes?* Identify the elements in that case that can be construed as creating the journalist's privilege.

3. List and discuss arguments for and against the journalist's privilege. What is your opinion? Why?

4. What is a shield law? If your state has one, what are its terms?

5. Has your state recognized a privilege for journalists other than that established by a shield law? If so, what are its terms?

6. Assess the likelihood that a newsroom will be searched by police.

CHAPTER 8

CHAPTER 8

As its Preamble declares, the Constitution established a government of the people. It is easy to postulate, then, that there must have been some intent on the part of the authors of that document to provide for access to information about government. After all, if the people are to make wise decisions about how they are to be governed, they must have access to information about the performance of government and government officials. This idea is embodied today in the phrase ''the right to know.''

However, if the founders intended that there be public access to government information, they did not write that intention into the Constitution. Nor did they act as if they believed government should be conducted in the open. The Constitutional Convention itself was conducted in secrecy. Once the finished product had been announced to the public and the new government established, the Senate met behind closed doors for the first five years of its exis-

THE RIGHT TO KNOW

tence.[1] Only two paragraphs in the Constitution mandate any degree of openness on the part of the federal government. Both are found in Article I, which established the Congress and defines its powers:

> Each House shall keep a journal of its proceedings, and from time to time publish the same, excepting such parts as may in their judgment require secrecy; and the yeas and nays of the members of either House on any question shall, at the desire of one-fifth of those present, be entered on the journal. [Section 5, paragraph 3]
>
> No money shall be drawn from the Treasury, but in consequence of appropriations made by law; and a regular statement and account of the receipts and expenditures of all public money shall be published from time to time. [Section 9, paragraph 7]

The first requirement is met by publication of the *Journal,* a summary listing of actions taken by both houses of Congress, and, in an expanded form, by the *Congressional Record.* The second requirement is met by publication of the annual budget, which includes actual receipts and expenditures by categories in the last previous fiscal year, an estimate for the current year, and planned spending for the next year. That is all the information the Constitution requires the government to give its people. Until 1966, citizens who approached government officials in quest of information had to be content with what they got. Vance Trimble, a reporter for the Scripps-Howard News Service, learned in 1959 that even the First Amendment was no help to him when he tried to find out whether members of the Senate were violating the law by putting relatives on their office payrolls.[2] He had won a prize for distinguished reporting with a series of articles naming House members who illegally funneled tax money to their relatives. But when he sought the same information from the clerk of the Senate, Felton Johnston turned him down flat. When Trimble went to the United States District Court for the District of Columbia for an order directing Johnston to let him examine the Senate payroll, Judge Alexander Holtzoff told him the court could not create a duty where neither the Constitution nor Congress had established

---

1. Robert A. Diamond, ed., *Origins and Development of Congress* (Washington, D.C.: Congressional Quarterly, 1976), pp. 178–80.
2. Trimble v. Johnston, 173 F. Supp. 651 (D.D.C. 1959).

one. The First Amendment, he said, would protect Trimble in publishing any news he might find, but it could not be used to pry news from reluctant officials. Nor would Article I, section 9, paragraph 7 help him. The Senate payroll, in total amount—without names—was in the budget, as that paragraph required.

A present-day Vance Trimble still would find himself unable to compel a congressional employee to let him look at the Senate payroll. But if he looked elsewhere for information about how the government functions he could obtain help from two sources that were not available in 1959. Trimble thought he could use the First Amendment to gain access to government information. A judge told him he was mistaken. But in 1980, the Supreme Court held in *Richmond Newspapers* v. *Virginia*[3] that the First Amendment does give reporters and the public a right to attend trials. The decision was summarized in Chapter 6. Since 1980, lower courts have interpreted that decision as granting a right of access to other kinds of judicial proceedings and some court records that previously were kept confidential. However, courts have been reluctant to stretch the First Amendment into a general right of access to government information.

Nevertheless, reporters seeking information from federal administrative agencies have a powerful tool at their command: the Freedom of Information Act, passed by Congress in 1965 and strengthened by amendments in 1974. The Act established as policy that records of the federal government shall be available to the public on demand unless they fall within one or more of nine exemptions. The law applies to all federal agencies except the Office of the President, the courts, and the Congress. Its limits have been established by hundreds of court decisions. Today, journalists, scholars, business firms, and the general public use it routinely to obtain records that once might have been withheld at an official's whim.

This chapter begins with a survey of the decisions in which the courts have ruled on a claimed First Amendment right of access to government information. The major part of the chapter examines the court decisions defining the limits of the Freedom of Information Act, with particular attention to the nine exemptions. We will see that the exemptions have given agencies rather wide discretion to withhold information sought by journalists and others and that the courts have supported them more often than not. Courts have shown a particular reluctance to order release of information deemed to invade an individual's privacy. Congress also has adopted a "Government in the Sunshine" Act, which requires that administrative decision-making bodies meet and act in public.

The latter part of the chapter deals in a general way with the open records and open meetings laws in effect in all fifty states. Although these laws vary in detail, all are based on the same principle as the federal law—that government be conducted in the open so that the people can check the performance of those who hold public office.

---

3.   448 U.S. 555, 100 S.Ct. 2814, 65 L.Ed.2d 973 (1980).

Major Cases

- *Butterworth* v. *Smith,* 494 U.S. _ _ _, 110 S.Ct. 1376, 108 L.Ed.2d 572 (1990).

- *Chrysler Corp.* v. *Brown,* 441 U.S. 281, 99 S.Ct. 1705, 60 L.Ed.2d 208 (1979).

- *Consumer Product Safety Commission* v. *GTE Sylvania, Inc.,* 447 U.S. 102, 100 S.Ct. 2051, 64 L.Ed.2d 766 (1980).

- *Department of Justice* v. *Reporters' Committee for Freedom of the Press,* 489 U.S. _ _ _, 109 S.Ct. 1468, 103 L.Ed.2d 774 (1989).

- *Department of the Air Force* v. *Rose,* 425 U.S. 352, 96 S.Ct. 1592, 48 L.Ed.2d 11 (1976).

- *Federal Bureau of Investigation* v. *Abramson,* 456 U.S. 615, 102 S.Ct. 2054, 72 L.Ed.2d 376 (1982).

- *Forsham* v. *Harris,* 445 U.S. 169, 100 S.Ct. 978, 63 L.Ed.2d 293 (1980).

- *Kissinger* v. *Reporters Committee for Freedom of the Press,* 445 U.S. 136, 100 S.Ct. 960, 63 L.Ed.2d 267 (1980).

- *Public Citizen* v. *United States Department of Justice,* _ _ _ U.S. _ _ _, 109 S.Ct. 2558, 105 L.Ed.2d 774 (1989).

- *Seattle Times Company* v. *Rhinehart,* 467 U.S. 20, 104 S.Ct. 2199, 81 L.Ed.2d 17 (1984).

- *United States Department of Justice* v. *Tax Analysts,* 492 U.S. _ _ _, 109 S.Ct. 2841, 106 L.Ed.2d 112 (1989).

- *United States Department of State* v. *Washington Post Co.,* 456 U.S. 595, 102 S.Ct. 1957, 72 L.Ed.2d 358 (1982).

THE RIGHT OF ACCESS TO GOVERNMENT INFORMATION

In 1959, a federal judge surveyed the Supreme Court's First Amendment decisions and told Vance Trimble he could find in them nothing to require government officials to divulge information they wished to withhold. Twenty years later, Justice William H. Rehnquist, writing in *Gannett* v. *DePasquale*,[4] said that neither he nor the Court could find anything in the First Amendment that gives the public a right of access to news of government. One year later, a majority of the Court held in *Richmond Newspapers* that the First Amendment does give the

---

4. 443 U.S. 368, 99 S.Ct. 2898, 61 L.Ed.2d 608 (1979).

public a right of access to the courts and to any news that is generated there. Justice John Paul Stevens hailed the decision as "a watershed case." He said, "[T]he Court unequivocally holds that an arbitrary interference with access to important information is an abridgment of the freedoms of speech and of the press protected by the First Amendment."

As of this writing, the dimensions of a constitutional right of access to the news are still undefined. If it has not been carried as far as Justice Stevens suggested it might go, neither is it nonexistent, as Justice Rehnquist averred. This is evidenced by the 1981 decision of a U.S. District Court in New York City in *United States* v. *Carpentier*[5] The court held that the First Amendment grants a right of access to audio tapes made by police during an investigation of a crime. The tapes at issue had been made by the Federal Bureau of Investigation during the events that led to the "Abscam" cases. The investigation produced evidence that seven members of the House of Representatives, a United States senator, and several local government officials were willing to take bribes to do favors for foreign nationals who, in reality, were FBI agents. Voice recordings of one transaction were admitted in evidence during the trial, but they were not played in court. At the end of the trial, the defendants' attorney moved to seal the tapes for sixty days. The *New York Times* and the *New York Daily News* objected. Looking at a line of Supreme Court cases ending with *Richmond Newspapers*, the court found "an emerging right of the public to know what happens in court." It ordered the tapes released.

Five years later, a panel of the U.S. appeals court in Boston surveyed *Richmond's* progeny,[6] and found that the "emerging right" seen by the New York district court has moved in two directions. In one direction, courts have found a strong right in the First Amendment for the news media and the public to insist that judicial procedures be conducted in public. The Supreme Court's decision in *Richmond* dealt only with criminal trials, but subsequent decisions have opened the doors to other proceedings associated with trials. These include jury selection, preliminary hearings, hearings on the admissibility of evidence, and hearings on the setting of bail. Access to such proceedings is important because fewer than 10 percent of the persons accused of serious crimes are subjected to a trial. This aspect of the First Amendment right of access to the news was discussed in the chapter on fair trial.

But the appellate court panel found that the Supreme Court's decision in *Richmond* had added very little to the long-standing common-law right of access to records generated by court proceedings. Under common law, decisions of judges, transcripts of testimony given in open court, and any exhibits admitted as evidence in a trial are public records open to inspection by anyone, with important exceptions. Information gathered to guide judges in sentencing convicted criminals has been kept confidential. So have reports on the conduct of criminals released on probation. Rules of court at both the state and federal levels permit sensitive court records to be sealed "for good cause shown" at the request of

---

5. 7 Med.L.Rptr. 2332 (S.D.N.Y. 1981).
6. Anderson v. Cryovac, Inc. 805 F.2d 1 (1st Cir. 1986).

either party with the approval of the judge. Typically a "good cause" could be to protect national security, privacy, or trade secrets, or to safeguard an ongoing criminal investigation. Once records are sealed, they cannot be released to anyone without an order of the court. Such "protective orders," as they are called, are prior restraints because their effect is to prevent information from reaching the public. Restraint is most likely to be used to prevent release of information collected in preparation for a trial but not yet presented in open court.

The news media and others have had mixed results in arguing that the First Amendment implies a right of access to court records of the kinds listed above. The most serious defeat was suffered when the Supreme Court held, in *Seattle Times* v. *Rhinehart,* that in some instances protective orders "do not offend the First Amendment." The decision is noteworthy not only because it condones prior restraint but because it imposes a limit on the First Amendment right of access to court news established in *Richmond Newspapers.* And if the *Richmond* decision is seen as establishing a broad right of access to newsworthy information, as Justice Stevens's comment quoted at the beginning of this section seemed to imply, the *Richmond* decision is at odds with five earlier cases in which the Supreme Court found no First Amendment right of access to the news.

Seattle Times Company v. *Rhinehart,* 467 U.S. 20, 104 S.Ct. 2199, 81 L.Ed.2d 17 (1984)

In *Seattle Times,* the Court was confronted with the question of access, in an action for libel, to records produced during discovery. In complicated cases, as most libel suits are, it can produce thousands of pages of information, much of which may never be submitted to a court. Some of it may be highly newsworthy—if the media can gain access to it. In this instance, a judge in Washington state had ruled that the newspaper could not use discovery documents as a source of news. Ironically, those documents were compiled by the *Times*'s own lawyers in the process of defending it against a libel suit. The action was brought by Keith Rhinehart, the leader of a small religious group, the Aquarian Foundation. He contended that a series of articles in the *Times* describing the group's activities had subjected him and his followers to ridicule and scorn. Rhinehart asked for $14.1 million in damages. Part of that sum was based on the claim that donations to the Aquarians had declined sharply after the newspaper articles appeared.

The claim gave the newspaper's lawyers an opening which they sought to exploit. As a part of the pretrial process of discovery, they asked Rhinehart to give them the names and addresses of the group's members and of any other persons who had given money to him or the Aquarians. The lawyers took the position that such data would prove or disprove the Aquarians' alleged losses. The process also would give the lawyers names of people who could be questioned to find out whether they had indeed left the church because of what they read in the *Times.*

Rhinehart's lawyer resisted the newspaper's request. He noted that editors of the *Times* had said they would continue their investigation of the Aquarian Foundation. He argued that any significant information the group provided during discovery would be published. Therefore, if the names, addresses, and contributions of Rhinehart's followers were made the subject of discovery, this would not only lead to an invasion of their privacy but interfere with the freedoms of association and religion protected by the First Amendment. He pointed to the fact that some members already had been harassed by people who found their views objectionable.

The judge supervising the discovery process concluded that the newspaper's lawyers needed access to the membership and contribution lists if they were to prepare their defense properly. But he said such information was to be used only by them and was not to be given to their client for publication. However, he said the newspaper was free to publish the names of members or contributors if it could get them from sources other than the discovery documents.

Neither party to the libel action was pleased with the order. The Aquarian Foundation did not want to release the lists even with the protective order. The newspaper contended that it was the subject of a prior restraint in violation of its First Amendment rights. Both sides appealed to the Washington Supreme Court, which affirmed the judge's order.[7] The newspaper took its case to the U.S. Supreme Court, which ruled against it unanimously.

The *Times*'s lawyers argued that information gathered through the civil discovery process is like any other information and therefore is "protected speech" for First Amendment purposes. In their view, the newspaper could be restrained only if the judge could prove convincingly that his order served an overriding public interest. In this instance, the lawyers argued, the public interest favored the newspaper because the people had a right to know how the religious group functioned.

Justice Lewis F. Powell, Jr., writing for the Court, did not agree. He focused the Court's decision narrowly on the nature of discovery and its purpose. It is conducted under rules of court to expedite the judicial process. Through discovery, lawyers gather information that will help them prepare for trial or reach a settlement. At times, Powell noted, discovery touches privacy interests that need protection to ensure candor. The majority concluded that "pretrial depositions and interrogatories [components of the discovery process] are not public components of a civil trial." In a footnote, the Court said, "Discovery rarely takes place in public." Because pretrial questioning must be arranged to suit the convenience of the witness and the lawyers for both sides, such questioning quite often takes place in a law firm's conference room with a legal stenographer as the only outsider present. The process is informal and may produce information with only a remote bearing on the issues being readied for trial.

The Court noted that rules of court in the federal system and in some states require that discovery documents be filed with the clerk of the court. But in those jurisdictions, the Court said, the rules also give trial courts authority to order that certain records not be filed or to seal those that are. Such orders, the Court added, "are not a restriction on a traditionally public source of information."

In the end, the Supreme Court gave no comfort whatsoever to those who believe that the sealing of pretrial documents is a prior restraint to be imposed only

---

7. 654 P.2d 673 (1982).

after strict analysis of the public's First Amendment interest in access to them. Powell said that a Washington rule of court, which gives judges authority to issue protective orders "for good cause shown," "requires, in itself, no heightened First Amendment scrutiny." A similar rule is in effect in the federal court system and in a majority of the states. In upholding those rules, Powell wrote: "...The trial court is in the best position to weigh fairly the competing needs and interests of parties affected by discovery. The unique character of the discovery process requires that the trial court have substantial latitude to fashion protective orders." In any event, Powell concluded, the judge had not tried to extend his order to prevent the *Times* from publishing information it was able to gather on its own. Therefore, "it does not offend the First Amendment."

Since then, several courts have held that there is little, if any, First Amendment right to challenge orders sealing discovery documents.[8] The U.S. Court of Appeals for the Fifth Circuit extended the principle, holding that several news organizations had no right of access to the transcripts of proceedings conducted to find out whether jurors had been paid off in the trial of a former governor. The governor had been twice acquitted on fraud and racketeering charges, and a juror in one of the trials had wondered out loud how much jurors were paid for their verdict.[9] The court also held that the news organizations had no right to obtain the jurors' names. The judge who conducted the hearing said he sealed the records to protect the attorney-client privilege and to prevent needless embarrassment of the jurors. He said he considered the remark that led to the investigation a joke.

The U.S. Court of Appeals for the Sixth Circuit upheld a district judge's decision not only sealing the records of a fourteen-day secret summary trial but also imposing a gag order on the six jurors who decided it. The Supreme Court refused to review the circuit court's ruling.[10] The trial was conducted as part of the process leading to a settlement of a dispute between three Ohio electric power companies and General Electric over the safety of parts provided for a nuclear generating plant that was abandoned during construction. To resolve the questions at issue, the parties agreed to submit them to a U.S. district court jury in Cincinnati for optionally binding decisions. Under rules in effect in sixty-five federal court districts in twenty-one states, such trials are conducted in closed courtrooms. Records of the proceedings, including the names of the jurors, are sealed. Two months after the trial ended, the parties announced they had reached agreement on a settlement. General Electric issued a press release saying the jury had

---

8. See, for example, Anderson, cited in note 6; Cippolone v. Liggett Group, Inc. 785 F.2d 1108 (3d Cir. 1986); Worrell Newspapers of Indiana, Inc. v. Westhafer, 739 F.2d 1219 (7th Cir. 1984), Tavoulareas v. Washington Post Co., 737 F.2d 1170 (D.C.Cir. 1984), and Courier-Journal and Louisville Times Co. v. Marshall, No. 86-5741 (6th Cir. 1987). All these deal with discovery in civil actions. A Florida appellate court cited *Seattle Times* in upholding an order denying access to discovery in a criminal case, Palm Beach Newspapers, Inc. v. Burk, 471 So.2d 571 (Fla.App. 4 Dist. 1985).
9. Garry Boulard, "Louisiana Newspapers Lose Appeal to Unseal Jury Transcripts," *Editor & Publisher*, 29 August 1987, p. 31.
10. George Garneau, "Supreme Court Upholds Sweeping Secrecy," *Editor & Publisher*, 4 March 1989, p. 22.

not found it liable on any of the claims made against it. Newspapers in Cincinnati, Dayton, and Columbus sued to obtain access to the trial records, citing *Richmond Newspapers*. The district court judge dismissed the action. He conceded that the proceeding indeed had seemed to be a trial, but in reality it was only a part of the procedure leading to a settlement. Such procedures, he said, are not open to the public but are private actions between the parties. The court of appeals agreed, holding that the First Amendment "does not attach to summary trial proceedings."

Two actions, one by the U.S. Ninth Circuit Court of Appeals and the other by the Texas Supreme Court, stand in sharp contrast to the line of cases above. The Ninth Circuit broke new legal ground when it decided in *United States* v. *Schlette*[11] that journalists have a right to examine documents prepared to guide a judge in sentencing a convicted criminal and to probation reports prepared when a convict is released before the end of his sentence. Previously, such records had been confidential. In this instance, Roland Schlette had threatened to kill the prosecutor who was responsible for sending him to prison for twenty years for arson. Years later, when Schlette was released on probation, he carried out the threat, then took his own life. The *Marin* (California) *Independent Journal* and the victim's family asked to examine court and probation records on Schlette to see if there was anything in them that should have led officials either to keep him in prison or warn the prosecutor. The request was refused. An appeal was taken to a federal judge who happened to be the same one who had approved Schlette's release. She denied the request, ruling that such records are prepared only for the judge's guidance. On further appeal, the Ninth Circuit panel reversed, holding, "The newspaper has a legitimate interest in explaining to a concerned public the means by which sentencing decisions are made."

In the second instance, the Texas Supreme Court modified its rules to limit the sealing of records in civil suits that are ended by a settlement rather than by trial.[12] Records in such cases can be sealed at the request of either party with the approval of the judge. Such requests are made to prevent others from finding out how much money, if any, was involved in the settlement, or to prevent public access to facts learned during discovery that might reflect unfavorably on either party. Justice Lloyd Doggett of the Texas Supreme Court said such requests were being made and approved almost routinely to the detriment of the public. Under the new rules, anyone requesting the sealing of civil case records must post a public notice. The court involved must schedule a hearing within two weeks. Even if no one objects, the new rules say judges are expected to keep papers available to the public if they concern matters with "a probably adverse effect upon general public health or safety, or the administration of public office, or the operation of government." The amounts of monetary settlements still may be kept secret as can records filed in divorce cases. The rules are expected to have their greatest impact on environmental and products liability suits.

---

11.   No. 87-1106 (9th Cir.) March 31, 1988.
12.   "Texas High Court Cuts into Secrecy in Civil Suits," *New York Times*, 23 April 1990.

Despite actions like those above, still in effect are four Supreme Court cases that run counter to any assumption that *Richmond Newspapers* can be stretched to create a general First Amendment right of access to the news. In 1978, the Court held in *Nixon* v. *Warner Communications, Inc.*[13] that several news and entertainment organizations could not copy the famous Nixon Watergate audio tapes even though they had been admitted as evidence in the trial of several of the president's top aides. The Court concluded that Nixon was justified in his fears that the tapes, secretly made recordings of conversations in his Oval Office, might be exploited for commercial purposes. The Court said that the trial judge's orders sealing the tapes did not restrict the public's right to know because transcripts of the tapes had been widely distributed.

The other Supreme Court decisions on the First Amendment and a right of access dealt with requests by journalists to visit prisons and interview prisoners. In *Pell* v. *Procunier*[14] and *Houchins* v. *KQED*,[15] the Court held that journalists have no more right to visit jails or prisons than does anyone else. The Court said there is no First Amendment right of entry to places where prisoners are kept. In *Saxbe* v. *Washington Post Co.*[16] the Court held there is no right to interview prisoners, even when they are willing to be interviewed. The Court said the principal duties of prison officials are to maintain order and encourage rehabilitation. Therefore, if prison officials conclude that an interview would detract from these duties, the officials can forbid it.

Thus, such right of access to government information as may be implicit in the First Amendment seems limited primarily to the right to attend trials and other associated court proceedings. In a few instances, courts have upheld a limited right of access to some court documents. At this writing, the watershed seen by Justice Stevens in *Richmond Newspapers* in 1980 seems to have produced no more than a trickle of information.

THE FREEDOM OF INFORMATION ACT

Governments at all levels both acquire and create vast amounts of information. Much of it is routine and of little interest to anyone. Only the police care, for instance, who has been issued which license plate number, and then only if they are trying to trace a hit-and-run driver or a stolen car. Some records are highly personal. The federal government has tax files showing the reported income of everyone who files a return. Many business firms and journalists might find such information interesting, and even helpful, but it is kept secret by law. Other kinds of information are classified as secret by executive order because disclosure

---

13. 435 U.S. 589, 98 S.Ct. 1306, 55 L.Ed.2d 570 (1978).
14. 417 U.S. 817, 94 S.Ct. 2800, 41 L.Ed.2d 495 (1974).
15. 438 U.S. 1, 98 S.Ct. 2588, 57 L.Ed.2d 553 (1978).
16. 417 U.S. 843, 94 S.Ct. 2811, 41 L.Ed.2d 514 (1974).

might harm national security. The Defense Department, no doubt, has contingency plans covering such things as another outbreak of war in the Middle East or any one of a dozen other trouble spots. It would be interesting to know what those plans are, but exposure would ensure our defeat if one of them had to be used.

Government files also hold vast amounts of information that might serve a public interest if released. Government agencies collect information on the safety of products ranging from face creams to prescription drugs to automobiles. The Department of Agriculture assesses periodically the expected annual production of farm crops and the number of animals being readied for market. Other agencies collect voluminous data measuring every aspect of the economy. The kinds of information above are released routinely. As any Washington correspondent will attest, federal agencies release a torrent of information every day, far more than any one news medium can keep up with.

Without question, the government of the United States is one of the most open in the world. And yet aside from the kinds of information for which the need for secrecy is apparent, there have been times when the public has been denied access to data in which it has had a legitimate interest. Usually, such information is withheld because it would point to inefficiency, stupidity, or outright wrongdoing on the part of government officials. Until 1966, reporters seeking such information had no legal means of getting access to it. Their alternative was to cultivate sources in Congress or in the agencies who might be willing to "leak" the desired data. Even then, reporters would never know whether they got the full story or only that part serving the source's purposes. Then Congress passed the Freedom of Information Act (FOIA),[17] which declared as a policy of government that the public should have access to information in the files of government agencies.

How helpful the law was to journalists in its early years is open to debate. No doubt, its mere existence did some good. However, government officials found that the nine exemptions written into the Act by Congress gave them a new reason to refuse release of information they might previously have made public. Some of the exemptions seemed justified, such as those covering documents classified as secret by the defense and state departments. But there also was a broadly drawn exemption for investigatory records, which the Federal Bureau of Investigation and the Central Intelligence Agency used to deny virtually all FOIA requests. When, during the Nixon presidency, some agencies used the exemptions to withhold records sought by members of Congress,[18] pressure built up that led to significant changes in the law. Amendments designed to effect a greater degree of openness were passed over President Gerald Ford's veto and took effect in 1975.

The Act requires that federal agencies make available for inspection and copying the decisions of administrative tribunals, policy statements, and staff manuals of instructions affecting the public. To make the search for information easier, each agency must publish an index to its files and update it every three months.

---

17. 5 U.S.C. § 552.
18. Environmental Protection Agency v. Mink, 410 U.S. 73, 93 S.Ct. 827, 35 L.Ed.2d 119 (1973).

In response to FOIA requests, agencies may delete information that clearly would invade an individual's privacy but must explain such deletions in writing. The agency also may refuse to release information that it believes to be covered by one of the nine exemptions which survive, in a modified version, in the existing law. However, even when documents are withheld, the agency is required to describe them in a general way and give its reasons for denying access to them. This requirement was mandated by the U.S. Court of Appeals for the District of Columbia Circuit in *Vaughn* v. *Rosen*.[19] Appropriately, such a report is called a *Vaughn* index.

Requests for information do not have to be justified and must be disposed of within ten working days. If the agency decides not to release information, the seeker is entitled to appeal to an agency review officer, and the appeal must be granted or denied within twenty working days. Thus, the maximum delay, if the law is observed, is limited to thirty working days, or six weeks. However, because some agencies have been swamped with large numbers of requests, or with requests for huge volumes of documents, the law permits a ten-day extension. The seeker must be notified of the delay in writing and must be given a reason.

If the time limits are not met, or if the seeker meets a final refusal, the next step is appeal to a federal district court. Such appeals must be given expedited treatment. If the plaintiff wins, the government must pay all costs, including attorneys' fees. However, in some recent cases, judges have refused to award legal fees to plaintiffs who have obtained information that will aid them in their businesses. Business firms have become major users of the Freedom of Information Act.

Agencies are permitted to charge fees for providing copies of records, but the law says these must be reasonable and limited to recovery of direct costs. If a request is deemed in the public interest, the agency can reduce its fees or even waive them altogether.

The act defines the covered agencies:

> [T]he term "agency"...includes any executive department, military department, Government corporation, Government controlled corporation, or other establishment in the executive branch of the Government (including the Executive Office of the President), or any independent regulatory agency.

The language above includes all but three parts of the government. The Freedom of Information Act cannot be used to obtain documentary information in the possession of the following:

— The president and his immediate advisers

— Congress, its committees, and the few agencies under its direct control, principally the Library of Congress and the General Accounting Office

— The federal judicial system

---

19. 484 F.2d 820 (D.C.Cir. 1973); cert. denied, 415 U.S. 977, 94 S.Ct. 1564, 39 L.Ed.2d 873 (1974).

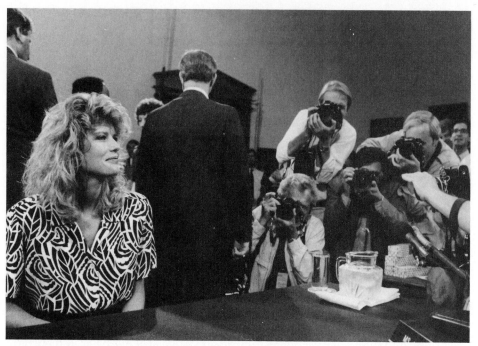

Although Congress exempted itself and its agencies from the Freedom of Information Act, most of its proceedings are open to both reporters and photographers. Here cameras are focused from close range on Fawn Hall as she testified before a joint session of the House-Senate Iran-Contra investigating committees. As Marine Lt. Col. Oliver North's secretary, she said she helped Reagan's then national security aide remove possibly incriminating documents from his office. (AP/Wide World Photos)

The revised version of the Act continues the nine exemptions written into the original. However, exemptions 1 and 7 were modified to provide some degree of access to classified documents and investigatory records. The exemptions are as follows:

1. Materials properly classified under executive order "to be kept secret in the interest of national defense or foreign policy."

2. "Internal personnel rules and practices of an agency."

3. Materials exempted from disclosure by a specific statute worded in such a way as to leave no doubt of the intent of Congress.

4. "Trade secrets and commercial or financial information obtained" with the assurance that it will be kept confidential.

5. "Inter-agency or intra-agency memorandums or letters" that would not ordinarily be available to outsiders except in connection with a lawsuit.

6. "Personnel and medical files and similar files the disclosure of which would constitute a clearly unwarranted invasion of privacy."

7. "Investigatory records compiled for law enforcement purposes." However, the law requires disclosure of records that will not interfere with an ongoing investigation, identify confidential sources or methods of gathering information, invade privacy, interfere with a fair trial, or endanger lives.

8. Materials bearing on the operating conditions, regulation, or supervision of financial institutions.

9. "Geological and geophysical information and data, including maps, concerning wells."

It needs to be emphasized that the Freedom of Information Act does *not* apply to state and local governments. These are covered by their own laws, which vary from state to state and city to city. However, the federal law does cover local branches of federal agencies, several of which are to be found in any city of any size.

One other limit on access to information at the federal level needs to be noted. The Privacy Act of 1974[20] applies directly to the Freedom of Information Act. It seeks to limit access to personal files collected by government. Such files are defined as those that link an individual's name with "his education, financial transactions, medical history, and criminal or employment history..."

The Act is a product of concern over the possibilities for abuse inherent in computerized record-keeping systems. It establishes procedures under which each of us can examine any files kept on us by the federal government and correct errors found there. It also establishes civil and criminal procedures that can be used to prevent or punish invasions of privacy resulting from misuse of personal records kept by the government. The law forbids agencies of government to keep records bearing on how an individual uses First Amendment rights, unless such information is pertinent to a bona-fide law enforcement activity. It also forbids sale of names and addresses to compilers of mailing lists.

There is no question that the revised version of the Freedom of Information Act has greatly increased public access to the files of government agencies. So many requests are made, in fact, that some agencies have been unable to keep up with them. The FBI and five other units of the Department of Justice have come under criticism for failing to meet the Act's deadlines. The General Accounting Office reported that the FBI was taking an average of 139 calendar days to process requests for information, and other units of the Justice Department were taking four to fifteen months to process complex requests.[21]

Differences of opinion over the scope of the Act have led to hundreds of lawsuits, more than twenty of which have reached the Supreme Court. The Court

---

20. 5 U.S.C. §552a.
21. "Report Raps Justice on FoI Requests Delays," *Editor & Publisher,* 11 June 1983, p. 30.

has held that the exemptions in the Act should be construed as written, in line with traditional rules of statutory interpretation. As a consequence, a majority of the lower court decisions during the decade after the Act was revised ran against the seekers of access to information.[22] However, the large volume of court decisions helped define the exemptions with such precision that by 1985, the number of appeals had declined significantly. Both agency officials and those who made requests for information seemed content, with occasional exceptions, to work within those limits. Time also has brought about changes in users of the FOIA. The Act originally was championed by journalists. The Act has provided considerable help to them, allowing the news media to expose some shortcomings of government that once might have remained hidden. But in recent years business firms seeking information about government purchases and about competitors have became major users of the Act. So, too, have law violators who have used the Act in large numbers in an attempt to find out how much the FBI and the Drug Enforcement Administration know about their activities.[23]

INTERPRETING THE FREEDOM OF INFORMATION ACT

Court decisions interpreting the Act have fallen into three categories:

1. Defining an "agency record." This is the first hurdle facing a seeker of information from the government. The requested information must be contained in an identifiable record legally in the agency's possession. Otherwise, it cannot be obtained.

2. Defining the ability of third parties, usually business firms that have supplied information to the government, to prevent disclosure of an agency record.

3. Defining the nine exemptions. By far the largest number of cases is in this category. In line with the judicial rules of statutory interpretation, the Supreme Court has insisted that the language of the exceptions must be interpreted literally and in accord with the intent of Congress.

Defining an "Agency Record"

The Supreme Court has held in two instances that the Freedom of Information Act can be used only to obtain records in the physical possession of an agency. In a third instance, the Court held that an agency must hand over documents ob-

---

22. Author's compilation from case summaries reported in *West's Federal Case News.*
23. U.S. Congress, House Subcommittee on Government Operations, *Freedom of Information Act Oversight,* 97th Cong., 1st sess., 15 July 1981, p. 165. Assistant Attorney General Jonathan C. Rose testified that 40 percent of the requests received by the Drug Enforcement Administration were believed to come from prisoners and another 20 percent from law violators not yet in custody.

tained from other agencies, even though the person making the request might also have obtained them from the originating agencies.

As a result of these decisions, the threshold question in any attempt to use the FOIA is, "Does the document being sought meet the criteria defining an 'agency record'?" To do so, it must legally be in the agency's physical possession, and its subject matter must be pertinent to the agency's mission.

Kissinger v. *Reporters Committee for Freedom of the Press*, 445 U.S. 136, 100 S.Ct. 960 63 L.Ed.2d 267 (1980)

In the first of the three Supreme Court cases, journalists sought access to notes of telephone conversations made while Henry Kissinger was serving, first, as foreign policy adviser to President Nixon, and later as secretary of state. The Supreme Court held that neither set of notes need be released. The Court ruled that the notes made while Kissinger was an adviser to the president were not subject to the FOI Act because the president and his immediate advisers are exempt from its terms. Ordinarily, notes made of the secretary of state's conversations would be subject to disclosure because the Department of State is an "agency" within the scope of the Act. However, in this instance, the notes had been transferred to the Library of Congress under terms that gave Kissinger strict control over their release. Kissinger, who left office before the legal action began, had acted in good faith in consigning his official papers to the Library, but a recently enacted law had made his action illegal. The Reporters Committee pointed to this fact in asking a federal district court to compel the State Department to regain custody over the former secretary's papers. The district court issued such an order and was upheld by a circuit court of appeals.

The Supreme Court held that both courts were wrong. There is nothing in the Freedom of Information Act, the Supreme Court ruled, that requires an agency to sue a third party to recover records no longer in its possession, even though the transfer to that third party may have been illegal. The Act, the Court held, applies only to records in the physical possession of an agency. The Act's terms cannot be used to compel an agency to release records it does not have. Nor, the Court held, does the law give persons outside of government a right to sue to compel an agency to return documents it might be holding illegally. Only the attorney general can initiate such action. In this instance, he did not choose to do so. Nor could the reporters obtain Kissinger's notes from the Library of Congress without his permission because as an agency of Congress it is not covered by the FOI Act. One effect of the decision was to prevent other authors from using information that Kissinger chose to disclose in his memoirs, the first volume of which was published while this case was making its way through the courts.[24]

The second case, *Forsham* v. *Harris*, involved an attempt to gain access to raw data collected by a private organization hired by the government to study thousands of diabetes pa-

Forsham v. *Harris*, 445 U.S. 169, 100 S.Ct. 978, 63 L.Ed.2d 293 (1980).

---

24. Henry Kissinger, *White House Years* (Boston: Little, Brown, 1979). The second volume, *Years of Upheaval*, was published in 1982.

tients. The focus of the study was on the side effects of drugs used to control the disease. Under its contract, the research organization was required to summarize its findings and report periodically to the Department of Health, Education and Welfare. Although the department had the right to obtain the raw data gathered during the study, it did not do so.

When the summaries indicated that the oral medicines commonly used as alternatives to injected insulin might cause heart disease, the study became a subject of controversy. The committee on the Care of the Diabetic and other groups resorted to the FOI Act to compel the Department of Health, Education and Welfare to obtain and release the raw data so that other researchers could analyze it and come to their own conclusions. When HEW refused to do so, the groups went to court. The department's decision was upheld.

The Supreme Court ruled that a private organization, even one working under a $15 million contract with the government, is not an "agency" as defined by the FOI Act. Nor can that Act be used to compel a federal agency to obtain data from a private contractor if it does not choose to do so.

U.S. Department of Justice v. *Tax Analysts,* 492 U.S. _ _ _, 109 S.Ct. 2841, 106 L.Ed.2d 112 (1989). More recently, the Supreme Court held that U.S. district court opinions and orders received by the Department of Justice in litigating tax cases become agency records. Therefore, they must be made available for copying on request by individuals or business firms even though the documents also can be obtained directly from the clerks of the district courts. This ruling, in *U.S. Department of Justice* v. *Tax Analysts,* was of direct benefit to the publisher of a weekly magazine, *Tax Notes,* sold to tax attorneys, accountants, and economists. The publisher also provides full texts of the decisions in microfiche and publishes a daily electronic data base including summaries and full texts of federal court tax decisions.

The publisher sought the decisions from the Justice Department because it did not always receive prompt service from the clerks of the federal courts and from lawyers involved in tax cases. The department rejected the request, arguing that the decisions were not agency records because they were not prepared by it but were obtained from the courts, which are not covered by the Freedom of Information Act. Justice Thurgood Marshall, joined by seven others, said the Supreme Court's decisions have established that an "agency record" is one either created or obtained by an agency subject to the FOIA. Once a document becomes an "agency record," it cannot be withheld, if requested, unless it is subject to one of the nine exemptions. The fact that Tax Analysts could have obtained the decisions directly from the courts was not relevant. Marshall said an agency cannot meet its obligations under FOIA "simply by handing requesters a road map and sending them on scavenger expeditions throughout the Nation."

In accord with *Kissinger* and *Forsham,* lower courts consistently have held that information sought from an agency subject to the FOIA must be in a document, report, or letter in the physical possession of the agency. In two decisions, the U.S. district court in Chicago has gone further. It held in one instance that the subject matter of the document must be pertinent to the agency's work.[25] In a more recent decision, the court held that an agency could not be compelled to release records to which it had no legal right, even though they were in its possession.[26] The case was of more than usual interest because the records involved were medical reports on "Infant Doe," a child who was permitted to die in a Bloomington, Indiana, hospital. The child was born with Down's Syndrome and a blocked esophagus. The child's parents, concluding that a child so badly handicapped never could attain a tolerable quality of life, decided, with the advice of their obstetrician, to let the child die. Indiana courts upheld their right to make that decision. The Office of Civil Rights of the Department of Health and Human Services conducted an investigation to determine whether laws forbidding discrimination against handicapped persons had been violated. In connection with the investigation, the office obtained copies of the infant's hospital records, even though the Privacy Act of 1974 prohibits dissemination of such records. The office was able to obtain the records because it promised to keep them confidential. The case reached the federal district court when a lawyer for a group representing the handicapped filed an FOI request with HHS for its records bearing on the decision to let the child die. When the agency refused the request, the lawyer appealed to the district court, which held that Infant Doe's hospital record was not an agency record because the agency had no legal right to it. On appeal, the circuit court avoided that question by holding that the record was protected by the privacy exemption of the FOIA.

Defining the Ability of Third Parties to Prevent Release of Information

In an action brought by Chrysler Corporation, the Supreme Court held that the nine exemptions contained in the Act can be enforced only by the government. In order to obtain a weapons contract, Chrysler *Chrysler Corp.* v. *Brown,* had to file data with the Defense Department **441 U.S. 281, 99 S.Ct.** showing that it did not discriminate against **1705, 60 L.Ed.2d 208** women and minorities. When a labor union **(1979).** sought release of the data under the FOI Act, Chrysler filed suit, arguing that disclosure was forbidden by Exemption 4, which protects trade secrets and commercial and financial information. It said that the employment figures could be used unfairly by the unions representing its employees or by its competitors. Chrysler won a partial victory in the lower courts, but the Supreme Court reversed, holding that it was seeking a remedy in the wrong forum and with the wrong means. The purpose of the FOI Act, the Court said, is to encourage release of information. And

---

25. Illinois Institute for Continuing Education v. U.S. Department of Labor, 545 F.Supp. 1229 (N.D.Ill. 1982).
26. Marzen v. U.S. Department of Health and Human Services, 632 F.Supp. 785 (N.D.Ill. 1986); aff'd on other grounds, 825 F.2d 1148 (7th Cir. 1987).

while it does exempt certain kinds of information from disclosure, language in the Act is permissive, not mandatory. Thus, if an agency in its discretion decides to release information arguably subject to one of the exemptions, it can do so. If, as in this instance, a corporation or an individual believes it would be harmed by such release it should first seek relief through the agency's administrative procedures. Only if that fails can the victim resort to the courts. However, the Supreme Court said that such action would have to be based on some law other than the FOI Act.

The decision conveys two messages to government officials and to users of the FOI Act. In the narrower sense, the decision said that third parties cannot invoke the Act to prevent release of information they have given to a covered government agency. In the broader sense, the Court also told government officials that the exemptions are not mandatory. If officials decide to release information within the scope of one of the exemptions, they can do so, provided some other restrictive law does not apply. There is no way of finding out whether many officials have read the *Chrysler* decision and have been moved by it to release information subject to one of the exemptions.

Defining the Nine Exemptions

The nine exemptions were crafted with two objectives: (1) to permit the government to protect secrets it must keep if it is to carry out its functions; (2) to protect the privacy of government employees and of persons or business firms who provide information to the government. The first objective covers such things as secrets bearing on national security, current investigations by law enforcement officers, the working papers of government lawyers, and memoranda proposing government policies. The second covers such things as personnel records, medical records, trade secrets, financial data used in compiling economic statistics, tax returns, and other kinds of information obtained in confidence. What follows is a sampling of the decisions interpreting seven of the nine exemptions. There are no media-related cases involving the last two, which pertain to the regulation of financial institutions and to geological data concerning wells.

CLASSIFIED INFORMATION   In a world bristling with political, economic, and religious animosities, it is obvious that government must try to keep some secrets. The Defense and State Departments particularly generate information every day that other governments would dearly love to have. The ultimate responsibility for keeping such information limited to those who must have it rests with the president. By executive order, each president in modern times has established guidelines to be followed in deciding what kinds of information need to be safeguarded by being classified as "Confidential," or "Secret." In general, access to such information is limited to those who must have it so that they can carry out their duties. It is a crime for a person authorized to have access to restricted materials to disclose them to an unauthorized person.

Until the Freedom of Information Act was revised in 1975, restricted information was treated like the holiest of holies, protected by the most fearsome taboos. Judges could not even examine restricted documents to determine whether they had been classified properly, or to sort out of a packet of classified documents those that contained no secrets whatsoever.[27]

Since 1975, the FOI Act has permitted courts to examine documents withheld under Exemption 1 to determine whether they were classified properly. However, an examination of the cases shows that this has not resulted in widespread release of sensitive information dealing with foreign policy and defense. In some instances, courts have upheld a refusal to release information that on the face of it seemed to have more to do with history than current events.[28] In determining whether documents have been classified properly, courts give great weight to affidavits offered by government officials asserting a need for secrecy. However, judges can, and have, examined documents in the privacy of their chambers to resolve doubts. That process was used in *Alfred A. Knopf, Inc.* v. *Colby,*[29] which was discussed in Chapter 2. The message implicit in that decision is that declassification of secret documents is a job for experts, not for judges who may not be widely informed in foreign policy or the intricacies of national defense.

More recently, the Supreme Court upheld the view that great weight must be given to the claims of officials who assert a need for secrecy. In *Weinberger* v. *Catholic Action of Hawaii/Peace Education Project,*[30] the Court upheld the navy's refusal to prepare an environmental impact statement for a weapon storage area in Hawaii. The only claimed environmental impact was that which would come from an accidental detonation if the navy decided to store nuclear weapons in the facility. By law, the location of nuclear weapons storage depots is classified. The mere filing of an impact statement, which would be open to inspection under the Freedom of Information Act, would confirm supposition about the depot's purpose. Thus, Justice Rehnquist wrote, the Court would have to take the navy's word for its claim that it had complied with environmental protection law "to the fullest extent possible." Any more than that was "beyond judicial scrutiny" for security reasons.

Reporters and others seeking access to classified documents do not face an impossible task, but most of the assumptions work against them. This is illustrated by a sampling of Exemption 1 cases reaching federal courts in the 1980s. The decisions were ten-to-three against disclosure, with partial disclosure in another case. In the most notable instance, the U.S. District Court for the District of Columbia upheld the refusal of the State Department to release records bearing on an alleged plot by exiled French Secret Army terrorists to assassinate President Kennedy.[31]

INTERNAL PERSONNEL INFORMATION   Every agency of government has a body of rules to guide its employees as they carry out the duties imposed on them

27. Environmental Protection Agency v. Mink. See note 18 above.
28. Miller v. Casey, 730 F.2d 773 (D.C.Cir. 1984), in which the U.S. Court of Appeals, District of Columbia Circuit, upheld the CIA's refusal to disclose information on alleged attempts to infiltrate potential guerrillas into Albania between 1945 and 1953.
29. 509 F.2d 1362 (4th Cir. 1975).
30. 454 U.S. 139, 102 S.Ct. 197, 70 L.Ed.2d 298 (1981).
31. Shaw v. U.S. Department of State, 559 F.Supp. 1053 (D.D.C. 1983).

by law. Some may be so picayune as to limit what may be stacked on desks. Others may detail procedures to be followed in auditing income tax returns. Each agency also maintains files on its employees, which include such things as educational background, work history, and pertinent medical data. The question is, how far does Exemption 2 go in shielding the internal operations of an agency from public view?

Department of the Air Force v. *Rose,* 425 U.S. 352, 96 S.Ct. 1592, 48 L.Ed.2d 11 (1976).

The Supreme Court dealt with that question when it decided *Department of the Air Force* v. *Rose,* an access suit brought by the student editors of the *New York University Law Review.* In preparing an article on disciplinary procedures at the service academies, the editors asked for summaries of honor and ethics hearings. These are informal proceedings, conducted by the students themselves, to look into allegations that cadets have lied, cheated, or otherwise broken the strict code of conduct governing them. The air force refused to hand over summary reports of these proceedings at the Air Force Academy even with the names of the offending cadets deleted. It argued that the offenders still might be identifiable, with consequences that would haunt them the rest of their lives. Disclosure, the air force contended, would violate Exemptions 2 and 6. The latter permits agencies to withhold records that would pose "a clearly unwarranted invasion of personal privacy."

Lower courts disagreed on withholding, but the Supreme Court ruled that the summaries should be released without the names. Justice William J. Brennan, Jr., wrote that neither exemption should be read as an absolute barrier against disclosure. Each requires a balancing of the public's interest in the requested information against the agency's or the individual's interest in withholding it.

In the present instance, the Court held, the public had an interest in cheating and dishonesty in the service academies. Some cadets had been discharged. Others were being disciplined. The summaries in question were posted routinely on bulletin boards within the living areas of all three service academies. Clearly, rumor abounded. Therefore, release of the facts, carefully edited to protect individual cadets, was in the public interest.

With this decision as their guide, lower courts have ordered release of such things as manuals used to guide internal revenue service agents in approving or disallowing certain deductions. In most recent Exemption 2 decisions, courts have required those seeking access to agency rules to prove that an important public interest will be served by disclosure.

INFORMATION EXEMPTED BY LAW   In about a hundred instances, Congress has written provisions into federal law prohibiting disclosure of certain kinds of information. In many such instances, the intent is to protect an individual's privacy. Thus, there is considerable overlap between Exemption 3 and Exemption 6, which permits agencies to withhold information to protect privacy. Recent court decisions interpreting both exemptions show a reluctance by both federal agencies and the courts to release data that would permit others to intrude into an individual's private life.

Consumer Product Safety Commission v. GTE Sylvania, Inc., **447 U.S. 102, 100 S.Ct. 2051, 64 L.Ed.2d 766 (1980).**

However, the one Exemption 3 case that has reached the Supreme Court did not involve privacy. At issue was an attempt by Consumers Union, publisher of *Consumer Reports* magazine, to obtain government data on possibly dangerous television sets. The magazine's editors learned that the Consumer Product Safety Commission was investigating reports that some people had been injured when the picture tube of their television set had exploded. When *Consumer Reports* asked the agency for its data, the commission was willing to release it, but some television manufacturers objected. Led by GTE Sylvania, Inc., they went to court, arguing that the law under which the Consumer Product Safety Commission operated forbade disclosure. The United States District Court in Delaware agreed and issued an order forbidding the commission from releasing the data sought by *Consumer Reports*. The magazine countered by filing suit to compel release of the data in compliance with the Freedom of Information Act. Both actions reached the Supreme Court.

In *Consumer Product Safety Commission* v. *GTE Sylvania, Inc.,* the Court upheld the Delaware court's order forbidding release of the information. It noted that the law establishing the commission put restrictions on the release of information reflecting unfavorably on a product. Under the law, such information cannot be released until the manufacturer has been notified and given an opportunity to defend its product. The commission's news release describing the problem is required to include the manufacturer's response. Nor can the commission issue any release until it is satisfied that its report is accurate "and that disclosure is 'fair in the circumstances and reasonably related' " to the purpose of the law, which is to protect consumers from hazards. The Supreme Court held that the commission had not complied with the law when it expressed its willingness to give *Consumer Reports* unfavorable information about television sets.

The commission reminded the Court that it had held in the *Chrysler* case that agencies of government are permitted to release information covered by the exemptions if they choose to do so. In some instances, that could be done, Justice Rehnquist replied, but not here. The law establishing the commission specifically limited the circumstances under which it could release information. That law must be obeyed. Therefore, the injunction issued by the district court was proper.

In recent years, most Exemption 3 cases decided by the courts have involved Section 6102 of the Internal Revenue Code, which forbids release of tax return information to a third party. Courts will permit release of such information only if the data are presented in a way that will not identify individual taxpayers.

TRADE SECRETS AND OTHER CONFIDENTIAL DATA   The Supreme Court has not ruled directly on this exemption. In the *Chrysler* case, it conceded that release of trade secrets may have been involved, but advised the company to seek a remedy through the administrative processes of the Defense Department. The Circuit Court of Appeals for the District of Columbia held that a consumer advocacy group was not entitled to Food and Drug Administration records on intraocular lenses because the records contained trade secrets.[32] The lenses are implanted in patients' eyes to correct vision after cataract operations. Earlier, a federal district court upheld the refusal of the Federal Aviation Administration to give aircraft certification records to the Air Line Pilots Association.[33] The court held that disclosure would result in considerable competitive harm to the McDonnell-Douglas Corporation.

MEMORANDA   Stripped of its legal terminology, Exemption 5 applies primarily to working papers used in preparing a legal case, or to memoranda exchanged by government officials in laying the groundwork for decisions on policy. If release of such information would give persons in litigation with the government, or persons subject to a proposed governmental policy, an unfair advantage, withholding is justified. In recent years, Exemption 5 has been the subject of more than twenty-five federal court decisions, almost all of which have upheld an agency's refusal to release memoranda. Three cases have reached the Supreme Court. In all three, that Court supported an agency's refusal to release information.

The first of these decisions, *Federal Open Market Committee* v. *Merrill*,[34] permits the Federal Reserve Board to delay for one month the public disclosure of its decisions on buying or selling government securities. Such decisions, made monthly, have an effect on interest rates, the availability of credit, and the value of the dollar in foreign exchange. The Supreme Court agreed with the Federal Reserve Board's contention that prompt release of its buying and selling plans would thwart their purpose, which is to keep the economy on an even keel.

The second Supreme Court decision, in *Federal Trade Commission* v. *Grolier, Inc.*,[35] protects the working papers of government lawyers. The commission had sued Grolier, alleging that its sales representatives were using deceptive methods to sell encyclopedias. The lawsuit was dismissed before it reached trial. Grolier then filed a request under the Freedom of Information Act for memoranda prepared by FTC lawyers in preparation for trial. The firm's admitted purpose was to find out how much the agency had learned about sales methods through its surveillance of Grolier's sales representatives. Two lower courts ordered disclosure of the data on grounds that the litigation had ended, thus ending any need to protect strategy planned for the trial. The Supreme Court overruled them, holding that the wording of Exemption 5 says nothing about the status of litigation. It protects the working papers of government lawyers at all times.

The third decision, in *United States* v. *Weber Aircraft Corp.*,[36] upheld the air force's refusal to disclose statements obtained during investigation of an aircraft accident. The pilot, who suffered serious injuries, sued Weber, manufacturer of

---

32. Public Citizen Health Research Group v. Food and Drug Administration, 704 F.2d 1280 (D.C.Cir. 1983).
33. Air Line Pilots Association v. Federal Aviation Administration, 552 F.Supp. 811 (D.D.C. 1982).
34. 443 U.S. 340, 99 S.Ct. 2800, 61 L.Ed.2d 587 (1979).
35. 462 U.S. 19, 103 S.Ct. 2209, 76 L.Ed.2d 387 (1983).
36. 465 U.S. 792, 104 S.Ct. 1488, 79 L.Ed.2d 814 (1984).

As this photo attests, photographers can get close enough to take pictures of downed military aircraft, in this case an Air Force Phantom II fighter jet that crashed in North Carolina during a training mission. The crew ejected and escaped injury. Reporters also can gather and report whatever facts the Air Force may release. But the Supreme Court has held, that because of an exemption in the Freedom of Information Act, the public may not be able to learn why the crash occurred. (UPI/Bettmann Newsphotos)

the plane's ejection seat, for damages. To support his case, he sought access to the data collected by air force investigators. The air force readily released factual information gathered under oath during its attempt to find the cause of the crash, but it refused to surrender supplementary data gathered in an attempt to prevent similar accidents in the future. Much of that data was gathered under assurances that the identity of the sources would not be made public. The Supreme Court held that confidential statements gathered in an attempt to formulate safety regulations clearly are intra-agency memoranda of the kind Congress sought to protect when it approved Exemption 5. Therefore, they did not have to be released.

While Exemption 5 applies only to administrative agencies, it is similar in principle to the claim of executive privilege advanced by presidents since George Washington to protect their communications with advisers. The privilege is based on the assumption that some advisers might not be completely candid with a president if they thought their advice would be made public. On numerous occasions, presidents have invoked the privilege to justify their refusal to release information sought by Congress. Courts have respected that privilege, as they have Exemption 5, but have reserved the right to decide when the privilege has been invoked properly. That right was reasserted by the U.S. Court of Appeals for the District of Columbia Circuit in *Public Citizen* v. *Burke*.[37] The court held that Attorney General Edwin Meese III was mistaken when he told the General Services Administration (GSA) to honor all claims of executive privilege made by former presidents whose records are under the agency's control. The principal beneficiary of the order was Richard Nixon, who had been attempting to prevent release of some of the many records accumulated during his presidency. The court said that claims to executive privilege must be asserted and decided on a case-by-case basis. The court also told GSA that, as archivist for the government, it has an affirmative duty to disclose information.

DISCLOSURES THAT INVADE PERSONAL PRIVACY   The concern for individual privacy written into Exemption 6 is not absolute. It erects a barrier only against "a clearly unwarranted invasion of personal privacy," thus requiring agencies and the courts to balance an individual's interest in privacy against the public interest served by release of data. Increasingly in recent years, courts have upheld a refusal to release information on privacy grounds.

United States Department of State v. *Washington Post Co.*, **456 U.S. 595, 102 S.Ct. 1957, 72 L.Ed.2d 358 (1982).**

The leading case interpreting Exemption 6 is *United States Department of State* v. *Washington Post Co.*, decided by the Supreme Court in 1982. It began when a reporter for the *Post* received a tip that two officials prominent in Iran's revolutionary government held valid United States passports. The *Post* asked the State Department for information in its files that would prove or disprove the tip. The department refused, citing Exemption 6. While passport data did not qualify as "personnel or medical files," the department's lawyers argued that it qualified as "similar files the disclosure of which would constitute a clearly unwarranted invasion of personal privacy." When lower federal courts rejected that argument, the State Department took its case to the Supreme Court.

Writing for the Court, Justice Rehnquist noted that Exemption 6, unlike the other eight, is written in general rather than specific terms. This means, he reasoned, that Congress intended that agencies and courts give special consideration to protecting data bearing on personal privacy. The general purpose of Congress, Rehnquist wrote, "was to provide for the confidentiality of personal matters."

In this instance, the Court gave great weight to the State Department's claim that disclosure of any information about the two Iranians might very well sign their death warrants. Not long after the *Post* made its original request, the Khomeini government's rabid anti-Americanism had led to capture of the United States Embassy in Teheran and the taking of its employees as hostages. The Supreme Court directed the district court to conduct another hearing on the *Post's* request, at which it should consider the danger to the Iranians' lives. Such danger, the Court said, was an important element in determining whether "similar files" contained private information that ought to be withheld from the public.

---

37. (C.A.D.C.) No. 87-5194, April 12, 1988.

Court reports show no further action on the *Post's* request, but lower courts have been citing *Department of State* in expanding the scope of "similar files" entitled to privacy. United States courts of appeals in two instances have upheld refusals to disclose information that would identify investigators and thus open them to possible harassment.[38] In another instance, a federal appeals court upheld the refusal of the Veterans Administration to disclose details of VA-guaranteed loans on homes in Cleveland Heights, Ohio.[39] A community organization sought the information so that it might check allegations that loans were being steered to whites and blacks in such a way as to resegregate the city. The court ruled that the borrowers' interest in privacy outweighed the organization's interest in promoting racial integration. Decisions in two circuits have upheld an agency's refusal to disclose the mailing addresses of individuals. In one instance, a labor union asked for the addresses of Social Security employees so that it might solicit them as members.[40] In the other, a resort owner was refused the names and addresses of persons who had obtained government permits to boat on a stretch of scenic river on which his resort was situated.[41]

However, the U.S. Court of Appeals for the District of Columbia ordered release to a reporter of the names and amounts of prescription drugs supplied to the Office of the Attending Physician of the Congress.[42] The reporter was investigating allegations that members of Congress were obtaining undue amounts of prescription medicines commonly used by drug abusers. Because the Office of the Attending Physician obtained its supply from the National Naval Medical Center, records of the center were subject to the FOI Act. The center refused the reporter's request, arguing that specific drug orders might be traceable to individual members of Congress. The appellate court ruled that possibility was too remote to overcome the public interest in knowing what quantities of various medicines were being dispensed to members of Congress.

INVESTIGATORY RECORDS   Because the battleground over the meaning of Exemption 7 lies in the terms under which disclosure can be denied, a reading of its full text, 5 U.S.C. § 552(b)(7), is essential. The exemption permits withholding of

> records or information compiled for law enforcement purposes, but only to the extent that the production of such law enforcement records or information (A) could reasonably be expected to interfere with enforcement proceedings, (B) would deprive a person of a right to a fair trial or an impartial adjudication, (C) could reasonably be expected to constitute an unwarranted invasion of personal privacy, (D) could reasonably be expected to disclose the identity of a confidential source, including a State, local, or foreign agency or authority or any private institution which furnished information on a confidential basis, and, in the case of a record or infor-

---

38. Kiraly v. Federal Bureau of Investigation, 728 F.2d 273 (6th Cir. 1984), and New England Apple Council v. Donovan, 725 F.2d 139 (1st Cir. 1984).
39. Heights Community Congress v. Veterans Administration, 732 F.2d 526 (6th Cir. 1984).
40. American Federation of Government Employees, AFL-CIO, Local 1923, v. U.S. Department of Health and Human Services, 712 F.2d 931 (4th Cir. 1983).
41. Minnis v. U.S. Department of Agriculture, 737 F.2d 784 (9th Cir. 1984).
42. Arieff v. U.S. Department of the Navy, 712 F.2d 1462 (D.C.Cir. 1983).

mation compiled by criminal law enforcement authority in the course of a criminal investigation or by an agency conducting a lawful national security intelligence investigation, information furnished by a confidential source, (E) would disclose techniques and procedures for law enforcement investigations or prosecutions, or would disclose guidelines for law enforcement investigations or prosecutions if such disclosure could reasonably be expected to risk circumvention of the law, or (F) could reasonably be expected to endanger the life or physical safety of any individual....

What all these words boil down to is this: Investigatory agencies, foremost among them the FBI, have been given many reasons to withhold information from the public. They can do so to protect confidential sources, to protect the right of suspects to a fair trial, to prevent disclosure of techniques that might help persons evade arrest, to protect the privacy of persons named in records, and to protect the lives of law enforcement officers or informants.

The language of the exemption, which has been changed twice since the FOI Act was adopted, has led to four Supreme Court cases. In one of them, the Court held that the protection of privacy found in Exemption 7 is stronger than that found in Exemption 6. The latter provides for release of records unless such release would result in "a clearly unwarranted invasion of personal privacy." But Exemption 7 gives investigatory agencies authority to refuse release of any record that "could reasonably be expected to constitute an unwarranted invasion of personal privacy." Although it may sound like a quibble over words, the Court held, as we shall see, that an official's reasonable expectation of an invasion of privacy is more likely to justify secrecy than is the need to prove that release of information would lead to a "clearly unwarranted" denial of privacy.

The first of the Supreme Court's Exemption 7 cases, *National Labor Relations Board* v. *Robbins Tire and Rubber Co.*,[43] grew out of a labor dispute. Robbins Tire was defending itself in an NLRB hearing against charges that it treated its workers unfairly. In preparing its case, Robbins Tire asked the agency for transcripts of staff interviews with employees who were to testify at the hearing. The board refused the request. The Supreme Court upheld the refusal, citing subsections (A) and (B) of the exemption. The Court said that disclosure might lead to coercion of the witnesses, thus interfering with the proper resolution of the dispute.

The most recent, *John Doe Agency* v. *John Doe Corp.*,[44] clarified the meaning of "records compiled for law enforcement purposes." In that case, the Court held that records become subject to the strict limitations of Exemption 7 once they have been acquired by an investigatory agency. At issue was an attempt by a defense contractor to obtain records of an audit conducted by the Defense Contract Auditing Agency some years previously. At the time, the audit was routine. But when the contractor became suspected of fraud, the records were transferred to the FBI. The contractor asked for copies to use in its defense, arguing that the records were subject to release under the FOIA because they had not originally been made for law enforcement purposes. A U.S. circuit court agreed. The Su-

---

43.   437 U.S. 214, 98 S.Ct. 2311, 57 L.Ed.2d 159 (1978).
44.   493 U.S. _ _ _, 110 S.Ct. 471, 107 L.Ed.2d 462 (1989).

preme Court reversed, saying that the language of the Act speaks only of records "compiled for law enforcement purposes." A compilation "is something composed of materials collected or assembled from various sources or other documents." The law says nothing about a record's original purpose. Once information becomes part of a file assembled as part of an investigation, that information is subject to Exemption 7. In this instance, the Court said release might interfere with enforcement proceedings and told the company it would have to rely on the discovery process to obtain information it needed to prepare its defense.

Federal Bureau of Investigation v. *Abramson*, 456 U.S. 615, 102 S.Ct. 2054, 72 L.Ed.2d 376 (1982).

The other two Exemption 7 cases directly affected the ability of journalists to gather news. The first, *Federal Bureau of Investigation* v. *Abramson*, was brought by a journalist who was investigating allegations that President Nixon had used federal agencies for political purposes. Specifically, the journalist, Howard Abramson, had been told that Nixon had asked the FBI to collect information on people whose only crime was that he considered them his political enemies. Abramson asked the FBI to give him all data in its files that pertained to such individuals. The FBI rejected the request, stating that release of such data would be an unwarranted invasion of privacy and thus could be withheld under both Exemption 6 and Exemption 7(C). When Abramson appealed to a U.S. district court for help, the FBI gave him 84 pages of information, from which some names and facts had been deleted.

However, the reporter did not get what he wanted most—63 pages of data on eleven political figures, which were contained in a memorandum sent personally by J. Edgar Hoover, for years chief of the FBI, to John D. Ehrlichman, one of the president's closest aides. When Abramson again went to court, he was rebuffed, but the court of appeals reversed, holding that because the White House is not involved in law enforcement the memorandum at issue could not have been compiled for law enforcement purposes. Therefore, the FBI had no justification for withholding it.

On further appeal, five justices of the Supreme Court disagreed with the circuit court's reasoning. They held that the court had lost sight of the origins of the data in the memorandum and thus had been led into error. It was true, the five conceded, that the document sent to the White House was not an investigatory record, nor had it been compiled for law enforcement purposes. But the information it contained had been collected by the FBI, a law enforcement agency, presumably for investigatory purposes. Congress had written the exemption to protect information, not pieces of paper conveying information. Because all the information on the pieces of paper sent to Ehrlichman had been compiled for law enforcement purposes, it was protected by Exemption 7. Further, no one had argued during the proceedings in the courts that the data would not invade privacy. Therefore, the FBI was correct in concluding that its release might reasonably lead to an unwarranted invasion of privacy.

In *Abramson*, one might also reasonably conclude that few, if any, of the people on Nixon's enemies list were law violators. Their only crime, if indeed it was one, was that the president didn't like them and was looking for information that could be used to embarrass them. But in a more recent case, the Supreme Court held that Exemption 7(C) justified the FBI's refusal to release to the news media compilations of arrests and convictions on bona fide criminals. Such compilations are known to law enforcement officers and journalists as "rap sheets." For years, the Justice Department has shared such compilations with police agencies and courts. On occasion, it also has released them to the public.

Department of Justice v. *Reporters Committee For Freedom of the Press,* ___ U.S. ___, 109 S.Ct. 1468, 103 L.Ed.2d 774 (1989).

However, the Supreme Court held unanimously in *Department of Justice* v. *Reporters' Committee for Freedom of the Press* that reporters have no right under the FOIA to obtain rap sheets from the Justice Department if it decides to withhold them. Justice John Paul Stevens, writing for the Court, said Justice Department officials were correct in concluding that disclosure "could reasonably be expected to constitute an unwarranted invasion of personal privacy."

The decision ended an eleven-year effort on the part of the Reporters Committee and CBS correspondent Robert Schakne to obtain the rap sheet on Charles Medico, whose Medico Industries allegedly obtained defense contracts in exchange for contributions to the late Daniel J. Flood, a Democratic member of the House of Representatives from Pennsylvania. The FBI released rap sheets on Medico's three brothers after they died but withheld its compilation on Charles, prompting the lawsuit that led to the Supreme Court.

In upholding the Justice Department's decision, Stevens focused on what he saw as the purpose of the FOI Act. He wrote that its "central purpose is to ensure that the *government's* activities be opened to the sharp eye of public scrutiny, not that information about *private citizens* that happens to be in the warehouse of the government be so disclosed." He noted that the FBI has rap sheets on 24 million persons and that they are kept up to date and on file until the subject dies or reaches the age of eighty. Conceding that much of the information could be found elsewhere, Stevens said that the federal government's computerized record system has created "a vast difference" between its files and the public records of county courts and police stations. At the heart of that difference is the federal government's ability to collect and bring together vast amounts of information on any one individual. As the Court saw it, that ability has a potential for abuse that could be invasive of privacy rights. Thus, Stevens concluded, the decision to withhold Medico's rap sheet was supported by Exemption 7(C). All that was required was a finding that disclosure "could reasonably be expected to constitute" an invasion of privacy. Had the Justice Department chosen to rely on Exemption 6, it would have had to find that disclosure "would constitute" a "clearly unwarranted" invasion of privacy.

To further support the Court's decision, Stevens noted that the Privacy Act forbids disclosure by government of personal records without the consent of the individual involved. He saw this as further evidence that individuals have a significant privacy interest even in their criminal histories. The Court concluded: "The privacy interest in a rap sheet is substantial. The substantial character of that interest is affected by the fact that in today's society the computer can accumulate and store information that would otherwise have surely been forgotten long before a person attains the age of eighty."

Jane Kirtley, executive director of the Reporters Committee, said she saw two "very troubling" results flowing from the decision.[45] In her view, the Court was saying that when information taken from readily available paper records is compiled in a computer it is altered in nature and becomes private. She said, "If they can find this transformation happens to something that is so obviously of public interest—like a conviction—I don't think there is any limit on where they will find a privacy interest on an individual." Her second concern was with the purpose Stevens ascribed to the FOIA. She said that if his view is accepted it could cut off access to great bodies of data gathered by government but not directly concerned with its operation.

The decision has proved particularly troublesome because the government, like business organizations and newspapers, is relying increasingly on computers to file and maintain information that once filled reams of paper tucked away in filing cabinets. In some instances, investigative reporters have been able to obtain from some agencies copies of magnetic tapes containing vast amounts of data and have used them to develop stories. But in other instances, agencies have argued that their tapes also contain electronic mail or other messages, which are exempt from disclosure. That position has been challenged in a lawsuit filed by the American Civil Liberties Union, the National Security Archive, the American Historical Association, and the American Library Association.[46] The suit was inspired in part by an order issued in the closing days of the Reagan administration asking all administrative agencies to clear their electronic mail files. A committee of Congress began hearings in 1989 on whether the FOI Act needs to be amended to more clearly define what constitutes a record.

"GOVERNMENT IN THE SUNSHINE"

In 1976, Congress enacted what it called the "Government in the Sunshine" Act.[47] It was a straightforward attempt to open most of the decision making of federal administrative agencies to the public. Generally, it has served that purpose, and courts have had to deal with few cases alleging that its terms have not been met.[48] Therefore, it is enough simply to note its major provisions.

The law applies to

> any agency...headed by a collegial body composed of two or more individual members, a majority of whom are appointed to such position by the President with the advice and consent of the Senate, and any subdivision thereof authorized to act on behalf of the agency.

---

45. George Garneau, "Locked Away from Public View," *Editor & Publisher,* 1 April 1989, p. 9.
46. Tess Chichioco, "Making It Hard to Get Records," *Editor & Publisher,* 31 March 1990, p. 16.
47. 5 U.S.C. §552b.
48. 5 U.S.C.A., 1981 supplement, pp. 125–26.

The list of such agencies is long. It includes some obvious ones, like the Federal Communications Commission and the Federal Trade Commission, along with some obscure ones, like the Harry S. Truman Scholarship Foundation and the Overseas Private Investment Corporation.

In effect, a meeting takes place any time a quorum gets together to discuss or act on any item that is properly the business of the agency. No such meetings are to be held without prior notice to the public.

There are exceptions, of course. These roughly parallel the exemptions contained in the Freedom of Information Act. The Sunshine Act also outlines highly detailed procedures that must be followed if a meeting is to be closed. A decision to close must be accompanied by a written explanation. The agency must keep detailed minutes of closed meetings and make an edited version available as soon as possible. All agencies subject to the law have been required to draft regulations applying to their meetings and publish these in the *Federal Register*.

Public Citizen v. *U.S. Department of Justice, ___ U.S. ___, 109 S.Ct. 2558, 105 L.Ed.2d 377 (1989).*
Federal courts have been asked in only a handful of instances to interpret the Sunshine Act, and only one of these led to a Supreme Court decision. In *Public Citizen* v. *U.S. Department of Justice,* the Court held that the American Bar Association's Standing Committee on Federal Judiciary is not an "advisory committee" within the meaning of the Federal Advisory Committee Act.[49] Therefore, it is exempt from the provisions of both the Government in the Sunshine Act and the Freedom of Information Act.

For more than thirty years, presidents and the Senate Judiciary Committee have relied on the bar group to screen nominees for federal judgeships and to assess their competence. In 1986, the Washington Legal Foundation, joined later by Public Citizen, sought access to meetings of the Bar Association's Standing Committee and to its records. When they were rebuffed on grounds that the committee is a private group not subject to federal access laws, they asked a federal district court to hold that it is a federal advisory committee. In part, the statute defines an advisory committee as any regularly constituted group "utilized by the President." Had they succeeded, at least some parts of the committee's deliberations might have been opened to public scrutiny.

When the case reached the Supreme Court, all eight justices who participated in the decision agreed that the Standing Committee is outside the reach of the Federal Advisory Committee Act. But they disagreed profoundly in their reasoning. Justice Brennan, writing for himself and four others, went through an exercise in statutory interpretation. Conceding that in the common usage of the term, the president and the Department of Justice do indeed "utilize" the committee in reaching decisions on judicial appointments, Brennan said that was not the end of the matter. When the literal reading of a statute would "compel an odd result," courts must look to the legislative history to find out what Congress really meant. Brennan did that, starting with an Executive Order issued by President Kennedy

---

49. 5 U.S.C.App. § 1 *et seq.* (1982 and Supp. V.).

in 1962. His conclusion was that "there is scant reason to believe that Congress desired to bring the ABA Committee within FACA's net." Brennan said he chose this route to his goal to avoid deciding constitutional questions raised by the Act. Three other justices would have preferred to face those questions, which have to do with the president's power to appoint judges and other high-level federal officials. In their view, the Constitution gives the president sole power to make such appointments, subject only to the advice and consent of the Senate. If presidents want to consult others, including the bar association's Standing Committee, it's their business and is protected by executive privilege.

Earlier, the Court of Appeals for the District of Columbia Circuit held that the Chrysler Loan Guarantee Board was not an agency subject to the law. While it was true that each of its members was an official appointed by the president and confirmed by the Senate, it also was true that the appointments were to other positions within the federal government.[50]

There remain times, of course, when even the most dedicated government officials, acting in full awareness of the law's commitment to openness, feel compelled to sound the waters before embarking on a potentially stormy sea of public controversy. There is no way of checking on telephone calls that are made from one board member to others in advance of a public meeting. Nor does the law forbid members of an administrative tribunal from talking with one another if they meet at a cocktail party or at lunch. On occasion, reporters have argued that because they saw a majority of a board's members having lunch together they were holding an unlawful meeting, but such complaints seldom get far. The fact remains that, taken together, the Sunshine Act and the Freedom of Information Act stand as remarkable commitments to public access to the activities and files of the federal government.

ACCESS TO STATE AND LOCAL DECISION MAKING

Problems of access to government information are not confined to the labyrinthine colossus that is the federal government. Reporters who cover the lowest levels of local government engage in a daily battle to find out what's going on. Increasingly, according to the cover story in the November 1988 issue of the ASNE Bulletin,[51] reporters must go to court to gain access to important records and to meetings at which touchy issues are being discussed. The story quoted Charles Rowe, editor and publisher of the *Free Lance-Star* of Fredericksburg, Virginia, as saying, "We seem to be ALWAYS tied up in some kind of FOI brawl." His experience seems to be typical. Most issues of *Editor & Publisher*, the weekly magazine covering the newspaper business, report one or more freedom-of-access cases involving state and local agencies of government.

---

50. Symons v. Chrysler Loan Guarantee Board, 7 Med. L.Rptr. 2363 (D.C.Cir. 1981).
51. Craig Klugman, "Freedom of Information Skirmishes Spreading at the Local Level," *ASNE Bulletin*, November 1988, pp. 4–11. Klugman is editor of the Fort Wayne (Ind.) *Journal-Gazette* and vice-chair of ASNE's Freedom of Information Committee.

Reporters often find that the day-to-day reality of seeking newsworthy information from government officials is at odds with the policy of openness written into law by the legislatures of each of the fifty states. Recently modified statutes in all the states give reporters and the public access to most state and local records and to meetings of deliberative bodies, including such agencies as city and county councils, school boards, and the boards of trustees of state universities. Further, there is a long history of common-law access to public records and meetings. Courts long have recognized that certain kinds of information must be readily available. If we are to know what the law is, we must have access to statutes enacted by legislatures, ordinances passed by city councils, and regulations adopted by administrative agencies. People also need access to court decisions interpreting the law. If government is to be kept honest, records of money spent and received should be open to inspection. So should detailed election results. No prudent person would buy property without a rigorous title search. If taxes are owed on the land, or if it is subject to an unpaid mortgage, the would-be purchaser needs to know. All the kinds of information listed above, customarily and as a matter of legal right have long been freely available. Indeed, in some states, laws require that local governments buy newspaper advertising space once a month to list their receipts and expenditures.

Other kinds of records—such as birth and death certificates, complaints filed with police, accident reports, welfare rolls—may or may not be freely available for public inspection. It depends on whether a law defines them as public records, or whether courts, applying common law, have defined them as such. Because the common-law definition of a public record has been incorporated into the statutes of some states, it is worth a look. *Corpus Juris Secundum,* a legal encyclopedia, states that definition as follows:

> A public record is one required by law to be kept, or necessary to be kept in the discharge of a duty imposed by law, or directed by law to serve as a memorial and evidence of something written, said or done, or a written memorial made by a public officer authorized to perform that function, or a writing filed in a public office.[52]

The problem with the common-law definition was that it required a study of each record sought by a journalist or others to determine whether it qualified as a public record. Sometimes such a determination required weeks of litigation. The public records statutes now in effect in each state attempt to define and classify state and local records, listing those that are freely available, those that may be made available at an official's discretion, and those that are not to be made public because they might invade an individual's privacy, interfere with an investigation, or lead to other kinds of harm.

At common law, there was also a right of access to most meetings of governmental bodies. State legislatures traditionally have opened their sessions to the public, although some committees may meet in secret occasionally. City and

---

52. 76 C.J.S., Records, §1, p. 112.

county legislative bodies usually have met in public, as have school boards. However, at the local level, governing bodies have made a practice of going into "executive session" to discuss, and even come to conclusions on, sensitive matters. The term is a euphemism for secret meeting. Such sessions usually involve sensitive issues that the members don't want to discuss in public.

The open-meetings laws now in effect in every state have been enacted in an attempt to end the practice of conducting public business behind closed doors. Such laws require legislative and administrative bodies to meet in public, with closed meetings permitted only for limited purposes. Most such laws define a public agency in broad enough terms to include any agency spending public funds. To enforce openness, they provide that any final action taken during an executive session is null and void. They also provide for use of the injunction to mandate openness.

An open-meeting law is of limited use if agencies can call special meetings with little or no notice. Therefore, most such laws require adequate advance notice of such meetings, usually forty-eight hours. News organizations that want to receive notice of special meetings provide agencies with addressed postcards that can be used for this purpose. Open-meetings laws also require posting a notice of special meetings, including the topic to be considered.

Open-meetings laws narrowly restrict executive sessions. The Indiana law, for instance, requires forty-eight-hour notice of such meetings and a statement, in general terms, of the topic to be discussed. Subject matter considered proper for closed meetings is limited to such things as the strategy to be followed in collective bargaining, or in a pending legal action. The law also permits executive sessions to discuss possible purchase of land or buildings, or to interview industrial or commercial prospects who may be thinking of locating in a community. Most such laws permit confidential discussion of personnel matters, including complaints against individual employees. But any action taken on matters discussed in executive session must take place at a subsequent open meeting.

Experience in two states, California and Ohio, indicates that exceptions written into open meetings laws can be abused. California's original open meetings law, like those in many other states, permitted local governing agencies to go into closed sessions to discuss legal strategy with an attorney. The Legislature amended the provision to limit it to discussion of pending litigation.[53] The California Newspaper Publishers Association strongly backed the change because member newspapers concluded that agencies were calling in their attorneys to justify closed discussions of issues that were not involved in lawsuits. A decision by the Ohio Supreme Court virtually wiped out provisions of the Cleveland city charter that permitted members of the City Council to discuss business in private.[54] The court held that a meeting, as defined by the charter, is any gathering of a majority of the Council or its committees at which public business is

---

53. M. L. Stein, "Bill Limiting the Closing of Public Board Sessions to Become Law," *Editor & Publisher*, 24 October 1987, p. 32.

54. State, ex rel. Plain Dealer Publishing Co. v. Barnes, 38 Ohio St.3d 165 (Ohio 1988).

discussed. The decision overruled lower-court decisions holding that the state's open meetings law did not apply to cities with home-rule charters.

No law, no matter how strongly worded, will ensure that the public's business is conducted in public or that records compiled by government agencies are open to public inspection. The ASNE FOI report mentioned earlier lists more than twenty recent instances in which newspapers had to go to court to obtain access to meetings or records. Each issue of *Quill,* the magazine of the Society of Professional Journalists, contains an FOI "roundup" prepared by The First Amendment Center in Washington, D.C.[55] These roundups list instances in which journalists have had to take legal action to obtain information. Such reports demonstrate that the right to know, however it is defined, does not come easy. An editor's note in the November 1988 *ASNE Bulletin* called the effort to obtain information a "cold war" that "shows no signs of a truce any time soon."

The constant struggle against secrecy reflected in the reports mentioned above can lead us to the wrong conclusion. The many FOI actions, formal and informal, do not prove that public officials as a lot are contemptuous of the public they serve. A few are. But every day, newspapers and broadcasters offer a torrent of information that was given to them freely by public officials. When public officials seek to withhold information, they do so, in some instances, in the belief that they are complying with exemptions provided by law. Court decisions demonstrate that at times public officials act correctly. At other times, the officials' concern, legitimate or not, is with protecting privacy. Sometimes, too, officials, being human, would prefer not to be bothered. James Derk, a reporter for the *Evansville* (Ind.) *Press,* who has used the federal Freedom of Information Act more than fifty times, said he frequently encounters the "unofficial 10th Exemption, known as the 'forget it' exemption."[56] The computerization of records seems to have encouraged the use of the unofficial exemption. When a "record" exists only in a computer memory, an official can resist a request for access by saying it would take too much time away from ongoing work to search for the requested information. Finally, some officials at all levels of government don't know that they are supposed to conduct the public's business in public. That has been the experience of the Wisconsin Freedom of Information Council, which, for more than ten years, has been educating officials as to the meaning of that state's access laws. Dave Zweifel, editor of the *Madison* (Wisconsin) *Capital Times* and president of the council, reported that it's a job that seems to have no end.[57] The council, representing print and broadcast journalists, tries to resolve access problems informally. Frequently it is able to do so simply by having a member meet with local officials and explain the law to them.

---

55. The Center, funded by the Sigma Delta Chi Foundation, is a clearing house for reports of attempts to limit access to government information or First Amendment freedoms. Its address is 1093 National Press Building, Washington, D.C. 20045. The telephone number is (202) 393-0133.
56. James Derk, "It Takes a Lot of Persistence to Make the Freedom of Information Act Pay Off," *ASNE Bulletin.* November 1988, pp. 10, 11.
57. Dave Zweifel, "Statewide Council Helps Head Off FOI Firefights," *ASNE Bulletin,* November 1988, p. 7.

SPECIFIC PROBLEMS IN JOURNALISTIC ACCESS

When records are clearly public and customarily open to inspection by anyone, journalists have no problems. But when records are not clearly defined as public, or when a journalist makes an unusual request for information, questions can arise. The most common of these are dealt with in the following part of the chapter.

Do Journalists Have a Special Right of Access to Records and Meetings?

Legally, no. Public records laws define a right of access for all persons, including journalists. However, by earning the trust of their sources, reporters may be able to obtain access to records that the law defines as available only at the discretion of an official, or even to records defined as nonpublic.

Nor do reporters have any special legal right of access to meetings of government agencies. However, as a courtesy, and in the interest of ensuring a greater degree of accuracy, governing bodies usually provide special seating for reporters where they can see and hear all that goes on. Governing bodies also commonly give reporters copies of proposed legislation and other documents scheduled for consideration. Reporters who are going to do more than cover the surface of events also seek to gain the confidence of individual members of government agencies. Only by doing so can they learn about the wider, and sometimes hidden, interests that mold government policy at all levels.

Do Journalists Have a Right to Inspect Police Records?

It depends on the kind of record sought, state law, and the terms of the state constitution. The police agencies' policies also are a factor. In all states, arrest records of adults are required to be kept by law. Therefore, they are public records and anyone can inspect the log, or "book," in which arrests are listed. While the fact that the police have made an arrest is noteworthy, it is not the end of the matter. All arrests are subject to review by prosecutors or district attorneys who may dismiss the preliminary charge if they conclude there is not enough evidence to prove guilt beyond a reasonable doubt.

Police also receive and investigate many complaints that may or may not result in an arrest. Officers file written reports of such activities. Reporters may or may not be given access to these reports, depending on a variety of factors. How much journalists can do to force disclosure of information when police use their discretion and withhold it depends on state law. Unless there is a law requiring disclosure of specific police records, or defining complaints recorded by police as public records, there is little journalists legally can do to gain access.[58] With some notable exceptions, the recent tendency has been for both state legislatures and courts to provide for greater access to police records. For instance, an Indiana law effective in 1984 mandates access to most pertinent information "if an agency maintains a daily log or record that lists suspected crimes, accidents, or complaints." Most police departments do maintain such records. Information that might interfere with an investigation or violate a right of privacy is exempt from disclosure. However, the Indiana law says that if "a public record contains disclosable and nondisclosable information, the public agency shall separate the material that may be disclosed and make it available for inspection and copying."[59] In practice, a police records officer may agree to meet reporters at a designated time each day and either read parts of the record to them or let them inspect all or part of the file. Police justify such arrangements by asserting that any more liberal policy would interfere with their processing of the records.

Texas and Florida courts have held that there is a limited constitutional right of access to police records. The Texas decision came in an action brought by the *Houston Chronicle* after police had interpreted the exemptions in a Texas open records law as justifying the withholding of some information previously made public.[60] The Florida decision grew out of an investigation by the *Lakeland Ledger* of the activities of a local sheriff. The sheriff responded by instructing his employees not to talk to reporters for the newspaper. The paper sued, charging that the sheriff had violated its constitutional right of access and that he had destroyed public records. The court found for the newspaper.[61]

The Ohio Supreme Court twice has issued decisions narrowing the scope of the exemptions in that state's law opening police records to public inspection. In one case, the court ruled that records of investigations conducted by the Cleveland police into shootings by police officers were not exempt as either "trial-preparation records" or "investigatory work product."[62] In the other case, the court ruled that the city of Middletown must allow access to records of an investigation into allegations of misconduct by the city's former police chief.[63] The chief had resigned in exchange for a promise that the city would not release the results of its investigation. The Georgia Supreme Court ordered the Atlanta police department to open part of its files on Wayne B. Williams, who is serving time for murder. Williams was accused of killing twenty-nine young blacks but was tried and found guilty on only two counts. The disclosure order was limited to the two convictions, and the court said police could withhold information identifying people not charged with a crime.[64]

---

58. See, for example, Gallagher v. Marion County Victim Advocate Program, Inc. 401 N.E.2d 1362 (Ind.App. 1980).
59. Indiana Code 5-14-3, §§ 5(c) and 6.
60. Houston Chronicle Publishing Co. v. City of Houston, 531 S.W.2d 177 (Civ. App. 14th Dist. 1975).
61. Klugman, "Freedom of information," p. 9.
62. State, ex rel. NBC v. City of Cleveland, 38 Ohio St.3d 79 (Ohio 1988).
63. Barton v. Sharpe, 37 Ohio St.3d 308 (Ohio 1988).
64. "Lawyer Asks Judge to Clarify Order," *Editor & Publisher*, 4 July 1987, p. 22.

But other decisions indicate that courts at the state level are not willing to open all the criminal justice process to public inspection. The Florida Supreme Court held that newspapers in that state have no right of access to depositions obtained in criminal cases unless the depositions become part of the public record of a trial court.[65] The ruling affirmed a decision by an appellate court, which relied heavily on the U.S. Supreme Court's decision in *Rhinehart* discussed earlier in this chapter. The lower court held that reporters have no right to attend the taking of depositions, nor do they have a right to inspect depositions unless the transcript becomes a part of a trial court's record,[66] which rarely happens unless the deposition is admitted as evidence. The newspapers that sought access to the depositions argued that in some instances they contain newsworthy information that might not come to light if the case ends with a plea bargain, as more than 90 percent do. The appellate court was not impressed. It said, "All who have taken discovery depositions know that it entails fishing on a dangerous and uncharted sea." The presence of reporters might inhibit that fishing, the court said. And disclosure of the contents of a deposition could result in dissemination of false allegations which could harm innocent people.

The *Lawrence* (Massachusetts) *Eagle-Tribune* was denied access to the evaluative records of a state prison inmate who was destined to become an issue in the 1988 presidential campaign. The inmate was Willie Horton. He had been released on furlough and had gone to Maryland in violation of its terms. When he was accused of raping a woman there, the *Eagle-Tribune* wanted to know why he had been released. Horton's lawyer argued that the prisoner's right to maintain the privacy of his records outweighed the public's right to know what was in them. Both the state Department of Corrections and the Privacy Council agreed.[67]

The instances described above are only a small sample of the actions, formal and informal, taken by the media to get access to police news. The examples cited serve as a reminder that police and courts reporters need to become familiar with their state's access laws and should not hesitate to use them.

Do Journalists Have a Right of Access to Juvenile Court Proceedings?

In general, journalists do not have a right of access to juvenile court proceedings, although many states give judges of such courts wide discretion over access to their proceedings. The juvenile justice system is a product of the idealism that suffused this country in the early part of the century. It is based on the theory that youngsters go wrong not because they are evil, but because they have not been shown the right way to go. Therefore, the purpose of the system is seen as educational rather than punitive. Offenders are put on probation. If that doesn't work, they are sent to "reform schools." They are held in "detention facilities"

---

65. "Fla. Papers Have No Right to Pretrial Information," *Editor & Publisher*, 2 May 1987, p. 66.
66. Palm Beach Newspapers, Inc. v. Burk, 471 So.2d 571 (Fla.App. 4 Dist. 1985).
67. "Mass. Paper Cannot Get Info on Inmate," *Editor & Publisher*, 4 July 1987, p. 22.

rather than in jails. Traditionally, the system has been cloaked in secrecy on the theory that publicity for juvenile offenders would stigmatize them and make it more difficult for them to go straight.

The theory on which the juvenile justice system is based has been tested sorely in the latter part of the twentieth century. In 1985 for instance, 17 out of every hundred arrests were of a boy or girl under eighteen years old.[68] For crimes of violence against people or property, the proportion was 26 out of one hundred. To give these figures their full meaning, it needs to be noted that the census of 1980 found that only nine of each one hundred persons was in the fifteen-to-nineteen-year-old age group.[69] Given, then, the fact that young people account for more than their share of crime, pressures have been generated to force some aspects of the juvenile justice system into the open.

Thus, in the case of particularly vicious crimes, a juvenile court judge may order offenders tried as adults in the regular court system. When that happens, there is no question about a right of access to the records and disposition of that particular offense. Legislatures also have given judges of juvenile courts authority to open some of their own proceedings and records to inspection. In some states, juvenile courts are releasing edited versions of their proceedings, designed to show the nature of the offense and the disposition by the court, but to protect the identity of the offender. In part, such arrangements are a response to accusations that nothing happens to punish persistent offenders.

State laws designed to protect juveniles from publicity usually apply only to the courts, leaving police free to release names if they wish. In other states, the statutory cloak extends even to police records. However, the Supreme Court has held that neither a judge's order nor a state law can prevent publication of a juvenile offender's name, if it has been acquired legally.[70]

Do Journalists Have a Right of Access to the Scene of a Crime?

It depends. The police investigation takes first priority. Whether the crime took place on public or private property, the police have a duty to protect the scene while evidence is being gathered. Thus, they can prevent access in the interest of preserving evidence. If a crime or accident takes place on public property, there is nothing to prevent reporters and photographers from coming as close as the police will permit. And, while it is not uncommon for police to attempt to forbid photography of particularly gruesome scenes, or of situations that may make them look bad, they have no legal right to do so. An officer who grabs the camera of a photographer who is not interfering with an investigation, or who shoves him or her, has committed an assault. The news media can take prompt legal action in all such cases.

---

68. Uniform Crime Report, Federal Bureau of Investigation.
69. *1980 Census of Population and Housing,* U.S. Bureau of the Census.
70. Oklahoma Publishing Co. v. District Court of Oklahoma County, 430 U.S. 308, 97 S.Ct. 1045, 51 L.Ed.2d 355 (1977); Smith v. Daily Mail Publishing Co., 443 U.S. 97, 99 S.Ct. 2667, 61 L.Ed.2d 399 (1979).

If the crime or accident takes place on private property, there is no right of access except that granted by whoever is in control of the property. Courts in Florida and Indiana have held that if police or firefighters are in control of the property, and are willing to admit reporters and photographers, they may do so.[71]

All police forces of any size have policies regulating actions by officers at the scene of a crime. Usually these state that the news media shall be given information and permitted to take photographs as long as there is no interference with the investigation.[72] However, reporters and photographers who refuse to obey a valid order by police in charge of the scene of a crime or accident risk arrest. For instance, the Wisconsin Supreme Court upheld a reporter's conviction for disorderly conduct based on his refusal to obey a police order to stay away from the scene of an airplane crash.[73]

Do Journalists Have a Right to Find Out What Grand Juries Are Doing?

Journalists do have a right to find out what grand juries are doing, a right that has been affirmed by the U.S. Supreme Court. But that right still is hedged by limitations, both legal and ethical.

The grand jury is almost as old as English common law and had its origins in a need to temper the sometimes harsh and arbitrary authority of the king and his minions. Present-day grand juries are made up of persons chosen by lot whose duty is to hear evidence indicating that a crime has been committed. If the jurors find reasonable cause to believe that a named individual has violated a specific law, they put their names to an indictment, or "charge." If the individual is not already in custody, the indictment serves as a warrant for that person's arrest. Under the Fifth Amendment, no person can be charged with a "capital, or otherwise infamous crime" except by a grand jury. In federal courts, all felony charges must come from a grand jury. Most states give prosecutors authority to file charges without first submitting evidence to a grand jury. But if the evidence is in doubt, or the case carries political freight, prosecutors may prefer to let a grand jury make the decision.

Since at least 1681, grand juries have met in secrecy. All states and the federal government prescribe secrecy for grand jury proceedings, either by statute, rule of court, or common law.[74] There are several reasons for this. Grand juries operate informally, and, at the state level, have broad authority to look into what they will. They are not bound by the strict rules of evidence prevailing in the courts. Witnesses are free to report unfounded gossip, voice their suspicions, or even express views based on hatred or malice. Grand juries also may hear from witnesses whose lives would be in peril or who would be ostracized by their

---

71. Fletcher v. Florida Publishing Co., 319 So.2d 100 (Fla. App. 1st Dist. 1975); quashed as Florida Publishing Co. v. Fletcher, 340 So.2d 914 (Fla. 1977); cert. den., 97 S.Ct. 2634 (1977); *Bulletin,* Hoosier State Press Association, No. 26, 28 June 1976.
72. The Indiana State Police policy statement issued in 1975 is typical.
73. City of Oak Creek v. King, No. 87-1305, 23 February 1989.
74. Yale Kamisar, Wayne R. LaFave, and Jerold H. Israel, *Modern Criminal Procedure,* 4th ed. (St. Paul, Minn.: West Publishing Co., 1974), pp. 884–93.

friends if word of their testimony became public. Secrecy also protects jurors from those who might try to influence them and protects those who have been investigated and cleared. Finally, if a grand jury does decide to indict a person who is not in custody, secrecy may be essential to keep him or her from fleeing.

Secrecy is enforced through an oath given to members of the grand jury and to those stenographers or officers of the court who work with it. The record of the jury's deliberations, including the testimony it hears, is sealed. Thus, a juror who talks to a reporter about the proceedings, or an official who leaks all or part of a transcript, faces punishment for contempt if caught. Some reporters have been punished for contempt, not for publishing information leaked from a grand jury, but for refusing to identify the source of the leak.

Butterworth v. *Smith,* **494 U.S. _ _ _, 110 S.Ct. 1376, 108 L.Ed.2d 572 (1990).** However, when a Florida prosecutor summoned reporter Michael Smith as a grand jury witness and then told him he could be jailed under state law if he ever published any part of his own testimony, the U.S. Supreme Court ultimately told the prosecutor that he and the state had gone too far. The effect of the order was to prevent Smith and his newspaper, the *Charlotte Herald-News,* from complete coverage of its own investigation into allegations of misconduct in the offices of the Charlotte County State Attorney and the Sheriff. The newspaper's investigation had led to the calling of the grand jury.

At issue was a Florida law making it a crime for "any person knowingly to publish, broadcast, disclose, divulge, or communicate to any other person...any testimony of a witness examined before the grand jury, or the content, gist, or import thereof" unless it had been disclosed in court.[75] Smith, planning a book based on his investigation, asked a U.S. district court to declare the law unconstitutional. The court held that the legislature acted within its powers in deciding that a permanent ban on disclosure of testimony is essential to proper functioning of the grand jury. The Eleventh Circuit Court of Appeals reversed, and the Supreme Court affirmed unanimously. However, the decision was a narrow one, applying only to the provision prohibiting a witness from disclosing his own testimony after the term of the grand jury has ended.

Chief Justice Rehnquist noted that on several occasions the Court has upheld grand jury secrecy. But he also noted that there is a point at which such secrecy can impinge on freedoms guaranteed by the First Amendment. The complete ban imposed by the Florida law reached one of those points. He said the state's interest in protecting witnesses ought not overcome their own judgment as to what they might choose to reveal to the public. Nor was the state's interest in protecting the reputations of persons who may be accused of, but not charged with, criminal activity sufficient to justify a prior restraint. Further, as it was applied in this instance, the law was subject to abuse because it could be used "to silence those who know of unlawful conduct or irregularities on the part of public officials." Justice Antonin Scalia would have gone further. In a concurring opinion he expressed doubt that a witness can be prevented, even while a grand jury is

---

75. Section 905.27, Florida Statutes.

still sitting, from talking about what he knew before he entered the grand-jury room.

Fourteen other states have laws similar to Florida's, the Court noted. Twenty-one states have directly or indirectly exempted witnesses from the secrecy that cloaks the jurors and the investigative process. The remaining fourteen have remained silent on the issue.

A week after the Supreme Court's decision in *Butterworth*, the Indiana Supreme Court held, three to two, that two reporters for the Hammond *Times* were not in contempt of court when they questioned former grand jurors two years after the grand jury had concluded an investigation. Although the majority's reasoning and its conclusion closely paralleled the *Butterworth* decision, a footnote indicated the case had no effect on the court's deliberations.[76] The Lake County prosecutor had asked that the reporters be held in contempt for attempting to induce the grand jurors to violate their oath of secrecy. A trial court rejected the request, but a state court of appeals ruled that the reporters should be found in contempt. In reversing, the supreme court endorsed the need for grand jury secrecy but held that with the passage of time the need to protect that secrecy diminishes. However, the court cautioned that its decision did not establish a blanket rule. The majority said courts would have to decide on a case-by-case basis whether reporters' attempts to question grand jurors might interfere with the administration of justice.

Thus reporters are free to proceed with caution in their attempts to learn what grand juries were told. Nothing prevents reporters from waiting outside the grand jury room and trying to talk to witnesses as they emerge. Nor is there anything to prevent reporters from identifying the individuals or offices under investigation and going after the news on their own. But in the states that impose an oath of secrecy on grand jury witnesses, reporters may risk being held in contempt if they induce witnesses to violate that oath before the grand jury's term ends. In any state and in the federal courts, reporters run a risk of being cited for contempt if they attempt to induce grand jurors to violate their oaths of secrecy.

One further note of caution: If a grand jury does not return an indictment, reporters who have produced stories about the investigation cannot rely on privilege as a defense if they are sued for libel. The record of the testimony will remain sealed and therefore unavailable for use as evidence to support the accuracy of the story.

In the Professional World

While there is no question that the Freedom of Information Act has opened many previously closed federal agency files to public inspection, the Act is by no means a magic key. Doug Lee, writing in the 1985–1986 *Freedom of Information Report* of The Society of Professional Journalists, said

---

76. David J. Remondi, "Court Clears Reporters for Quizzing Ex-Jurors," *Indianapolis Star,* 28 March 1990.

reporters who use the Act must persist in their quest for information.[77] He said first-time users of the Act can expect to encounter delay and then may obtain only a heavily edited document. Despite the seemingly rigid timetable written into the Act, release of requested data may be delayed for as long as six months, depending on the agency's backlog. Reporters also told Lee that the agencies' interpretation of the exemptions seems arbitrary and inconsistent.

Reporters who seek information from a federal agency are advised to telephone the agency's FOIA officer to get an estimate of the likely delay. The next step is to consult the agency's index to identify the documents in which the needed information is likely to be found. This search may also uncover documents containing other helpful information. When the documentary sources have been identified, the next step is the filing of a formal request, which should be in writing. It should state that the request is being made under the terms of the Freedom of Information Act, it should list the documents requested, and it should suggest some limit to the search and copying fees the requester is prepared to pay.[78] The law mandates that such fees be "reasonable," but in instances where large numbers of documents are sought they can run into thousands of dollars.

At the state and local level, access procedure usually is less formal. In part this is because the volume of requests is not as great. Reporters also are more likely to have frequent contact with the officials controlling release of the documents. Ready access also is related to the fact that many state press associations, individual publishers and broadcasters, and the Society of Professional Journalists have shown a willingness to go to court to enforce the terms of state open-records and meeting laws.

Because reliance on legal procedures can be slow, experienced reporters also continue to cultivate sources. Any controversy has losers as well as winners. The losers in an intra-agency battle over policy may be willing to carry an appeal to the public through a trusted reporter. Inefficiencies, and even corruption, in public agencies have been brought to light because a conscientious employee was willing to give information to journalists under a promise of confidentiality. In such instances, access laws can be used to obtain supporting or supplementary data. The writer has talked with many editors who say they meet any denial of access, either to meetings or to records, by asking the newspaper's lawyer to file an FOIA lawsuit. Usually that will be enough to pry loose the sought-after information.

Beyond question, today's journalists have greater access to government meetings and information at all levels than at any time in history. As the *Progressive* episode, discussed in Chapter 2, attests, this freedom includes the right to publish the nation's most highly guarded secrets, if they can be

---

77. Doug Lee, "The Many Benefits of the FOIA," *Freedom of Information*, 1985–86 Report of the Society of Professional Journalists, Chicago, 1986, p. 9.
78. A suggested request letter is included in the report in note 77 above and in "How to Use the Federal FOI Act," a publication of the FOI Service Center, 800 18th St., N.W., Washington, D.C. 20006.

obtained. Nor is the right to publish restricted information confined to the workings of a hydrogen bomb or the labyrinths of foreign policy, as in the Pentagon Papers case also discussed in Chapter 2. At the local level, the Supreme Court has held that journalists can publish the names of juvenile offenders, even when state laws say that those names aren't to be released. And, as the 1988 presidential campaign demonstrated, the media are free to poke as far as they can into the private lives of candidates for public office. A weekend rendezvous, staked out by reporters, ended Gary Hart's run for the presidency. Senator Joseph Biden dropped out when reporters disclosed that one of his most effective campaign speeches was taken almost word for word from a candidate for the British Parliament. Some newspapers reported unsubstantiated claims that the Reverend Jesse Jackson had been expelled from the University of Illinois for plagiarism. Reporters demanded that Indiana University release Vice President J. Danforth Quayle's law school grades and would not believe that the Privacy Act of 1974 prevented their disclosure to anyone without Quayle's permission. After the election, a Washington, D.C., magazine published what it said was his law school point average.

Does anything go? Most editors say not. Most, for instance, do not publish the names of juvenile offenders unless the crime involved the taking of a life or serious injury. Nor do many publications use the names of rape victims. Newspapers in Indiana did not publish the names of the parents of the severely retarded and deformed "Infant Doe" who was allowed to die in Bloomington Hospital, although many residents of the community knew who they were. Increasingly, editors are questioning long-established policies which required full identification, including age and address, of the victims of crimes, and the publication of the name and address of every person arrested by police. Some newspapers that continue to publish arrest records also routinely advise readers that an arrest does not mean that the person is guilty of a crime. Other editors are waiting until arrestees have been brought to court before reporting their names.

The critical legal question is not whether government information of any sort can be published but whether that information is made available to the public on request. Statutes in all states and at the national level say that most government information should be made available. That leaves journalists with the ethical questions of how much of the torrent of government information should be published and how it should be published. The public's right to know means little if the media fail to insist that the right of access be honored, if they fail to share significant information with the public, or if they become propagandists, either for government or for their own view of what should be.

FOR REVIEW

1. What is meant by a "First Amendment right of access"? How far does it seem to go?

2. What is the significance, with respect to a constitutional right of access, of the Supreme Court's decision in *Seattle Times Company* v. *Rhinehart?* Discuss the possible consequences if the Court's decision had gone the other way.

3. What is the Freedom of Information Act? What are its strengths? Its limitations?

4. Good reporters pride themselves on their ability to get information that government and other sources would prefer not to disclose. Why, then, should there be laws mandating access to most government records?

5. Define an "agency record." Why is the term important?

6. Discuss the significance of the case in which the *Washington Post* sought access to the State Department's passport records.

7. Assess the right to obtain copies of records of investigatory agencies. To what kinds of records can journalists reasonably hope to gain access?

8. To what degree is there a right of access to police records? Given that most such records deal with incidents that are embarrassing to at least some of the participants, how much right of access to them should the public have?

9. How far can the media go in publishing information about juvenile offenders? How far should it go?

10. Should reporters respect the secrecy that cloaks the proceedings of grand juries? Why or why not? What legal problems may arise from attempts to penetrate grand jury secrecy?

11. If you could define an ideal relationship between journalists and government officials, what would it be? What does the public have a right to know? Who or what can best fulfill that right?

PART 3

LEGAL
REGULATION
OF THE MEDIA

CHAPTER 9

SUPREME COURT ATTEMPTS TO DEFINE OBSCENITY

RAW SEX OR REDEEMING SOCIAL IMPORTANCE?

COMMUNITY STANDARDS OF OBSCENITY

OBSCENITY LAW SINCE MILLER AND PARIS

Refining the Definition of Obscenity / Defining Child Pornography
/ Defining and Limiting the Use of Zoning Laws

LIMITING THE USE OF PRIOR RESTRAINT

The urge to censor portrayals of human sexuality has run deep in American society since colonial times. Courts have upheld such censorship as a necessary step to protect public morality in the belief that obscene publications lie outside the realm of ideas protected by the First Amendment. That belief was reinforced by the Supreme Court's 1931 decision in *Near* v. *Minnesota*[1] in which Chief Justice Charles Evans Hughes wrote that "the primary requirements of decency" may permit prior restraint to prevent circulation of obscene materials.

The problem with the suppression of obscenity has been in defining what it is. Through most of America's history, until after World War II, any description of sexual activity, no matter how delicately phrased, was likely to draw a censor's frown. James Joyce's *Ulysses,* now studied as a classic, was banned as obscene until a federal judge held in 1933 that it was literature, not pornography.[2] *Lady Chatterley's Lover,* the novels of Henry Miller, and Edmund Wilson's *Memoirs of Hecate County* were among the works that drew official disapproval. Even Norman Mailer had to be wary of the censor when he wrote *The Naked and the Dead,* a realistic account of small-unit combat in World War II. To avoid having his work labeled as obscene, he invented the word "fug" to substitute for one of the two most common epithets of the war. The four-letter version did not win

---

1. 283 U.S. 697, 51 S.Ct. 625, 75 L.Ed. 1357 (1931).
2. United States v. One Book Entitled "Ulysses," 5 F. Supp. 182 (D.N.Y. 1933).

OBSCENITY

the Supreme Court's approval until 1971.[3] By that time, the Court had lowered the barriers against literary and pictorial portrayals of sexual activity, but it had not abolished them.

Over the years, persistent attempts to suppress obscenity have pitted religious groups against civil libertarians, citizens' groups fearing human degradation against citizens' groups fearing suppression of healthy sexual expression, and prosecutors against a multibillion-dollar industry that makes and sells explicit sexual movies, videotapes, printed materials, and devices. This says nothing of the even larger flood of materials, including advertising, that exploits sex appeal short of the limits set by obscenity law. Recently, feminists have entered the fray, arguing that much explicit sexual material encourages rape by portraying women as inviting and enjoying the most degrading kinds of sexual assault. Cases requiring courts to interpret obscenity laws have divided judges as have few other issues.

As we enter the last decade of the twentieth century, the legal attempt to suppress pornography shows no signs of abating, although some evidence indicates that the public demand for sexually explicit materials may be. Production of sex videos peaked in 1986 and declined thereafter. Sex titles, which accounted for about 15 percent of videocassette rentals in 1984, had declined to about 9 percent in 1989. One researcher speculated that people had outgrown porn. Another attributed the decline to the wide availability of simulated sexual activity in movies, on music video, and on cable television. A decrease in the supply of new materials was attributed in part to increased awareness of the hazards of AIDS, which made it difficult to assemble casts to make films.[4]

The controversy over the enforcement of obscenity laws centers on the fact that prosecutors seeking a conviction need not prove that anyone has suffered physical harm. The crime is one of the few that is committed in the mind. The

---

3. Cohen v. California, 403 U.S. 15, 91 S. Ct. 1780, 29 L.Ed.2d 284 (1971), held that the four-letter word avoided by Mailer was protected speech when it was printed on the back of a man's jacket to show his opposition to the Vietnam War. Hess v. Indiana, 414 U.S. 105, 94 S.Ct. 326, 38 L.Ed.2d 303 (1973), held that the same word was not actionable when it was directed at a deputy sheriff during an antiwar demonstration.
4. Jennifer Steinhauer, "Prosecute Porn? It's on the Decline." *Wall Street Journal,* 28 December 1989.

Supreme Court has held that material is obscene if it "appeal[s] to a prurient interest in sex" by portraying "sexual conduct in a patently offensive way."[5] Traced to its Latin roots, "prurient" means literally "to itch," therefore, figuratively, "to yearn for, to be lascivious." As the courts use it, the word means that material is considered obscene if a jury concludes that it arouses an obsessive or morbid interest in sex. Since virtually all humans feel, and even welcome, an interest in sex at some point, the critical determination is when an interest becomes obsessive.

Those who oppose the traffic in obscenity argue that it degrades society by corrupting the morals of persons who are exposed to it, particularly young people. Critics of stature have argued that the ready availability of magazines, moving pictures, and videotapes devoted to infinite varieties of sexual gratification encourages sexual permissiveness and weakens the bonds that hold society together.[6] Scientific evidence to support such conclusions is harder to come by. In 1970, the President's Commission on Obscenity and Pornography concluded that there was no relationship between exposure to erotic materials and antisocial behavior.[7] More recently, Edward Donnerstein and Daniel Linz, psychology professors at the University of Wisconsin, reported that there is evidence to support the conclusion that "exposure to even a few minutes of sexually violent pornography, such as scenes of rape and other forms of sexual violence against women, can lead to antisocial attitudes and behavior."[8]

However, courts generally have chosen to sidestep the question of harm in dealing with allegedly obscene materials. They have focused on the idea of content—or lack of it—of sexually explicit matter. In *Roth* v. *United States*,[9] the Supreme Court of the United States held that obscenity can be suppressed because it is devoid of idea content and therefore "not within the area of constitutionally protected speech or press." Materials are obscene, the Court said, if their dominant purpose is to arouse a prurient interest in sex. However, the Court added that "sex and obscenity are not synonymous." Materials dealing with sexuality in a responsible way are protected because they do deal in ideas. The Court has since clarified its position, holding in *Miller* v. *California* that portrayals of sexual activity are not obscene if they have "serious literary, artistic, political, or scientific value." What constitutes such values is for a jury to determine, subject to review by the court, applying a standard of reasonableness.

This chapter will trace the development of obscenity law, focusing on the *Roth* and *Miller* decisions. Although the Supreme Court has decided numerous obscenity cases in the past thirty-five years, these are the landmarks. In them, the Court established, as precisely as words can do, the line at which sexually explicit ma-

---

5.   Miller v. California, 413 U.S. 15, 93 S.Ct.2607, 37 L.Ed.2d 419 (1973).
6.   Edwin McDowell, "The Critics Descend on Pornotopia," *Wall Street Journal*, 15 May 1973.
7.   1970 *Report of the Presidential Commission on Obscenity and Pornography* (New York: Bantam Books, 1970).
8.   Edward Donnerstein and Daniel Linz, "Sexual Violence in the Media: A Warning," *Psychology Today*, January 1984, p. 14 + .
9.   354 U.S. 476, 77 S.Ct. 1304, 1 L.Ed.2d 1498 (1957).

terials leave the realm of ideas and can be suppressed because they are obscene. We will find that the line is not a sharp one, nor can it be fixed with certainty. This is because the Supreme Court held in *Miller* that juries must apply their notion of community standards in determining whether sexually explicit materials are obscene. Thus, it is possible that magazines, movies, and the like condemned as obscene in one community may be freely available in another a few miles away.

A word on meanings before we proceed further. Many students, and even some professors, attempt to distinguish between obscenity and pornography. There is, indeed, a shade of difference between the two terms, but many courts, including the Supreme Court, use the terms interchangeably. "Pornography" is of Greek origin, where its original meaning was "writing about prostitutes." In its current meaning it applies to any portrayal of explicit sexual behavior. "Obscenity" is of Latin origin and is the broader of the two terms. In its primary meaning, it encompasses whatever may be offensive to accepted standards of decency or modesty. In its secondary meaning, "obscenity" applies to matter that incites lustful feelings or to lewdness. The latter term has both sexual and scatological connotations. In their decisions dealing with sexually explicit materials, the Supreme Court justices use the term "obscene" to define matter that lies outside the protection of the First Amendment. It is in that sense that the term is used in this chapter.

Major Cases

- *Fort Wayne Books, Inc.* v. *Indiana,* 489 U.S. _ _ _, 109 S.Ct. 916, 103 L. Ed.2d 34 (1989).

- *FW/PBS* v. *City of Dallas,* 493 U.S. _ _ _, 110 S.Ct. 596, 107 L.Ed.2d 603 (1990).

- *Hamling* v. *United States,* 418 U.S. 87, 94 S.Ct. 2887, 41 L.Ed.2d 590 (1974).

- *Jenkins* v. *Georgia,* 418 U.S. 153, 94 S.Ct. 2750, 41 L.Ed.2d 642 (1974).

- *Miller* v. *California,* 413 U.S. 15, 93 S.Ct. 2607, 37 L.Ed.2d 419 (1973).

- *New York* v. *Ferber,* 458 U.S. 747, 102 S.Ct. 3348, 73 L.Ed.2d 1113 (1982).

- *Paris Adult Theatre I* v. *Slaton,* 413 U.S. 49, 93 S.Ct. 2626, 37 L.Ed.2d 446 (1973).

- *Pope* v. *Illinois,* 481 U.S. 497, 107 S.Ct. 1918, 95 L.Ed.2d 439 (1987).

- *Roth* v. *United States,* 354 U.S. 476, 77 S.Ct. 1304, 1 L.Ed.2d 1498 (1957).

- *Stanley* v. *Georgia,* 394 U.S. 557, 89 S.Ct. 1243, 22 L.Ed.2d 542 (1969).

SUPREME COURT ATTEMPTS TO DEFINE OBSCENITY

Congress enacted its first obscenity law in 1873 at the urging of Anthony Comstock, who came out of Union Army service in the Civil War as a one-star general to devote the rest of his life to the suppression of vice. The law, which bears his name, is still in effect. It prohibits, subject to a fine of up to $5000 and up to five years in prison, the mailing of "every obscene, lewd, lascivious, indecent, filthy or vile article, matter, thing, device or substance."[10]

An examination of the language of the law illustrates the difficulty in defining the crime of obscenity. Murder can be defined as the act of taking the life of another person. Obscenity is defined with other words, each of which involves a value judgment as to what might be offensive or arouse sexual excitement, neither of which need result in an overt act.

The vagueness of the language of the Comstock Law did not keep it from being enforced. For decades, trial courts translated its generalities by applying a standard borrowed from England. In 1868, in *Regina* (the Queen) v. *Hicklin*,[11] Lord Chief Justice Cockburn ruled that a work is obscene if "the tendency of the matter...is to deprave and corrupt those whose minds are open to such immoral influences and into whose hands a publication of this sort might fall."

In the United States, the test was made even stronger by rulings that it could be applied to isolated passages, even if they were taken out of context. A few lurid passages in any book, no matter how serious its overall purpose, could condemn the work as obscene. Obscenity laws in every state supplemented the Comstock Law. Their combined effect was to drive the traffic in sexually explicit materials under the counter. Few tried to argue that a First Amendment issue might be at stake.

The first break in the high barriers against sexually explicit materials came in 1957 when, for the first time, the Supreme Court accepted two obscenity convictions for review. One of the cases, *Butler* v. *Michigan*,[12] involved a bookseller who had been fined $100 for violating that state's obscenity law. The judge had held that the book in question contained "obscene, immoral, lewd, lascivious language, or descriptions tending to incite minors to violent or depraved or immoral acts, manifestly tending to the corruption of the morals of youth." The Supreme Court found two things wrong with the judge's decision: (1) the book had been sold to an adult police officer, not a minor, and (2) the Michigan law, by defining obscenity in terms of material that would corrupt minors, would reduce the people of the state "to reading only what is fit for children." The Court added, "Surely this is to burn the house to roast the pig."

Roth v. *United States,* 354 U.S. 476, 77 S.Ct. 1304, 1 L.Ed.2d 1498 (1957).

Later that year, the Court decided two cases as one and, for the first time, applied First Amendment theory to materials considered obscene. One case came out of New York City

---

10.   18 U.S.C.A. §1461.
11.   6 L.R. 3 Q.B. 360 (1868).
12.   352 U.S. 380, 77 S.Ct. 524, 1 L.Ed.2d 158 (1957).

where Samuel Roth had been found guilty in U.S. District Court of violating the federal law forbidding the sending of obscenity through the mails. The other case came out of Beverly Hills, California, where David S. Alberts was found guilty in a state court of "lewdly keeping for sale obscene and indecent books," in violation of state law. Roth's name appeared first in the Supreme Court's decision and thus he has achieved a sort of immortality by lending his name to the test still being used to determine obscenity.

Justice William J. Brennan, Jr., wrote for himself and four others in upholding the convictions of both men. He began by asking "whether obscenity is utterance within the area of protected speech and press":

> Although this is the first time the question has been squarely presented to this Court, either under the First Amendment or under the Fourteenth Amendment, expressions found in numerous opinions indicate that this Court has always assumed that obscenity is not protected by the freedom of speech and press.

Brennan reviewed the history of laws curbing speech and came to the usual conclusion: The First Amendment is not absolute. He also concluded that the purpose of the amendment is to protect "unfettered interchange of ideas" designed to bring about social and political change. He elaborated on that theme:

> All ideas having even the slightest redeeming social importance—unorthodox ideas, controversial ideas, even ideas hateful to the prevailing climate of opinion—have the full protection of the guarantees, unless excludable because they encroach upon the limited area of more important interests. But implicit in the history of the First Amendment is the rejection of obscenity as utterly without redeeming social importance. This rejection for that reason is mirrored in the universal judgment that obscenity should be restrained, reflected in the international agreement of over 50 nations, in the obscenity laws of all of the 48 states, and in the 20 obscenity laws enacted by the Congress from 1842 to 1956.... We hold that obscenity is not within the area of constitutionally protected speech or press.
>
> It is strenuously urged that these obscenity statutes offend the constitutional guarantees because they punish incitation to impure sexual *thoughts,* not shown to be related to any overt antisocial conduct which is or may be incited in the persons stimulated to such *thoughts.*

The Court said the answer to that argument lies in the finding that a work is obscene. Once that finding has been made, the consequences that might flow from the work are irrelevant. The point is that once material has been found obscene, it carries no First Amendment protection whatsoever. The Court then turned to defining the obscene:

> However, sex and obscenity are not synonymous. Obscene material is material which deals with sex in a manner appealing to prurient interest. The protrayal of sex, *e.g.,* in art, literature and scientific works, is not itself sufficient reason to deny material the constitutional protection of freedom of speech and press. Sex, a great and mysterious motive force in human life, has indisputably been a subject of ab-

sorbing interest to mankind through the ages; it is one of the vital problems of human interest and concern.

With that passage, Brennan made clear his belief that sex in itself is not obscene. In some of its aspects, sex is a matter of public concern that requires public discussion. Such discussion is within the realm of ideas protected by the First Amendment. Courts, then, must be on guard lest the prosecution of obscenity intrude into the realm of protected speech. If the material in question "does not treat sex in a manner appealing to prurient interest," it must be safeguarded. Brennan noted that some American courts had adopted the *Hicklin* rule under which a work was judged by the effect an isolated excerpt might have on particularly sensitive persons. He wrote:

> [L]ater decisions have rejected it and substituted this test: whether to the average person, applying contemporary community standards, the dominant theme of the material taken as a whole appeals to prurient interest.

Brennan footnoted that sentence to a series of recent decisions in federal and state courts. It is not found in so many words in any of them. His formulation has come to be known as the *Roth* test, and, despite many subsequent decisions, it remains the key to a finding that a work is obscene. Although the test did not exist until Brennan wrote it in *Roth*, the Court held that it had been applied properly by the juries that convicted Roth and Alberts.

Brennan's decision for the Court established a precedent that lower courts were required to follow. However, the concurring and dissenting opinions in *Roth* are worth attention because they embody the deep differences that would divide the Court on obscenity cases for the next two decades.

Chief Justice Earl Warren sought to avoid having the Court decide whether materials are obscene. He argued that the critical test should be the suppliers' conduct. If they "were plainly engaged in the commercial exploitation of the morbid and shameful craving for materials with prurient effect," they should be charged with pandering. Justice John Marshall Harlan would have upheld Alberts' conviction under California law, but he would have reversed Roth's conviction under federal law. He would have done so because he wanted to avoid adoption of a national standard for obscenity. Nor was Harlan comfortable with Brennan's willingness to let juries decide what might appeal to a prurient interest. He wrote that he could accept a jury's banning a book in one state—if it had any value, people still could buy it elsewhere—but he was not willing to run the risk of having a *Ulysses* or the *Decameron* outlawed everywhere in the United States. Jury decisions on obscenity, he argued, should be reviewable by a judge to avoid suppression of such works.

Only Justices William O. Douglas and Hugo L. Black would have reversed both convictions. In a vehement dissent, Douglas raised questions that persist in obscenity cases to this day. He wrote:

> The tests by which these convictions were obtained require only the arousing of sexual thoughts. Yet the arousing of sexual thoughts and desires happens every day in normal life in dozens of ways. Nearly 30 years ago a questionnaire sent to college

and normal school women graduates asked what things were most stimulating sexually. Of 409 replies, 9 said "music"; 18 said "pictures"; 29 said "dancing"; 40 said "drama"; 95 said "books"; and 218 said "man." Alpert, Judicial Censorship of Obscene Literature, 52 Harv. L. Rev. 40, 73.

The test of obscenity the Court endorses today gives the censor free range over a vast domain. To allow the State to step in and punish mere speech or publication that the judge or the jury thinks has an *undesirable* impact on thoughts but that is not shown to be part of unlawful action is drastically to curtail the First Amendment.

Douglas also deplored Brennan's willingness to let a jury determine a community's standards for tolerating portrayals of sexual activity. In his view, that would give jurors a free hand to "censor, suppress, and punish what they don't like."

Despite Douglas's protests, the decision in *Roth* settled one question: Materials found to be obscene do not have First Amendment protection. Because Roth and Alberts properly had been found guilty of selling such materials, they had to take their punishment. The decision also established a test for obscenity: "[W]hether to the average person [a jury], applying contemporary community standards, the dominant theme of the material taken as a whole appeals to prurient interest." Further, the material must be, in Brennan's words, "utterly without redeeming social importance." The Court held that materials that fail the *Roth* test are outside the realm of ideas and therefore outside the realm of the First Amendment. The test does not require any proof that the materials in question harmed anyone. Indeed, Brennan noted that obscenity laws "punish incitation to impure sexual thoughts." He was willing to accept punishment of thought, he said, because the effect of the materials is beside the point. If a work is obscene, that is enough. It can be condemned out of hand, and those who traffic in it can be punished.

RAW SEX OR REDEEMING SOCIAL IMPORTANCE?

Experience was to prove that the Supreme Court's decision in *Roth* raised more questions than it answered. Producers of sexually oriented materials studied the decision and found a challenge. How far could the producers go in linking portrayals of sex with ideas before crossing the line into a raw appeal to prurient interest?

The producers of these materials soon found that they could go a long way. The decision came when attitudes toward sexual activity, and portrayals of sexuality, were becoming more relaxed. Hugh Hefner founded *Playboy* magazine in 1953, four years before the Court decided *Roth*. It was one of the first magazines of general circulation to feature photographs of bare-breasted young women. A nude Marilyn Monroe, photographed from the side and rear, was the subject of its first centerfold. Soon it had many imitators which went far beyond it in portraying not only nudity but sexual activity. Explicit sexual movies once seen only at clandestine all-male gatherings came out from under the counter and onto the-

Hugh Hefner's *Playboy* was one of the first magazines to take advantage of the Supreme Court decision holding that nudity and portrayals of sexual activity are not necessarily obscene. By its thirtieth anniversary in 1982, it had begun to lose circulation. Hefner sought to change with the times by producing video cassettes featuring the same kinds of materials that had made the magazine popular. (AP/Wide World Photos)

ater screens in the 1960s. So-called adult bookstores became thriving businesses. The proliferation of sexually oriented materials led to more than a dozen Supreme Court obscenity decisions in the fifteen years after *Roth*. Few of them are of more than historical interest because rarely could as many as five of the justices agree on any one point of law.

One, *Memoirs* v. *Massachusetts*,[13] was important at the time because it greatly expanded the scope of permissible sexual portrayals. At issue was that durable classic of erotic literature, John Cleland's *Memoirs of a Woman of Pleasure*, commonly known as *Fanny Hill*. Although the book contains no four-letter words, it abounds in descriptions of many kinds of sexual activity. *Memoirs* was the subject of this nation's first reported obscenity decision,[14] and, in the mid-1960s, Massachusetts courts again condemned it as obscene. The U.S. Supreme Court reversed that finding, but no more than three justices could agree on any one reason for doing so. The leading opinion, written by Brennan, tried to define the role of "redeeming social value" in the test used to measure obscenity. He said a jury could not find a work obscene unless the prosecution proved it to be "utterly without redeeming social value." In this instance, several professors at esteemed New England universities had testified that *Memoirs* was "a minor work of art," having "literary merit" and "historical value." One witness said it

---

13.   383 U.S. 413, 86 S.Ct. 1975, 16 L.Ed.2d 1 (1966).
14.   Commonwealth v. Peter Holmes, 17 Mass. 336 (Mass. 1821).

was redeemed by its moral, as expressed by Fanny toward the end of the book, that sex in marriage is more desirable and enjoyable than sex in a brothel.

The Court's decision seemed to signal a virtual end to successful prosecutions for obscenity, provided care was taken in offering sexually explicit materials to the public. Within a year, that conclusion was reinforced by the *per curiam* decision in *Redrup* v. *New York*[15] reversing the convictions on obscenity charges of the operators of adult bookstores in several states. In doing so, the Court seemed to take the advice offered by Chief Justice Warren in *Roth*. It looked at the vendors' conduct and found that none had offered their wares to minors. The vendors had not thrust sexually explicit materials on unsuspecting adults. Nor was there any evidence of pandering. In short, the vendors simply were catering to the tastes of adults who knew what they were after when they entered the stores.

Thereafter, courts in many jurisdictions read *Memoirs* and *Redrup* as virtually wiping obscenity laws off the books, particularly if sexually explicit materials were offered behind doors that were open to consenting adults but closed to minors. In its next major obscenity decision, the Supreme Court went a step further, holding that laws making possession of obscene materials a crime are unconstitutional. The Court said that whatever people choose to see or read in the privacy of their homes is their business. The decision retains its importance because of the number of sexually oriented videocassettes available for sale or for rent.

Stanley v. Georgia, 394 U.S. 557, 89 S.Ct. 1243, 22 L.Ed.2d 542 (1969). The unwilling protagonist in the case was Robert E. Stanley, a suspected bookie. Police obtained a search warrant authorizing them to enter his home to look for evidence that he was accepting bets on sporting events. The search found no such evidence, but in a desk drawer in Stanley's bedroom, an officer found three reels of eight-millimeter film. Using Stanley's projector and screen, police spent about fifty minutes looking at the film. That was enough to convince them it was obscene. Unable to make a gambling arrest, police arrested Stanley for possessing an obscene film, a crime under Georgia law. A county court found him guilty. The Supreme Court agreed to review the decision and reversed.

Writing for a majority of the Court, Justice Thurgood Marshall held "that the mere private possession of obscene matter cannot constitutionally be made a crime." Applying First Amendment principles to the facts of Stanley's arrest, Marshall found absolute protection for the "right to receive information and ideas." That protection is such that it forbids "state inquiry into the contents of a person's library." Marshall wrote: "If the First Amendment means anything, it means that a State has no business telling a man, sitting alone in his own house, what books he may read or what films he may watch. Our whole constitutional heritage rebels at the thought of giving government the power to control men's minds."

At that point, the Court had held that the First Amendment prevents officials from punishing people who choose to view obscene materials in their homes. The

---

15. 386 U.S. 767, 87 S.Ct. 1414, 18 L.Ed.2d 515 (1967).

Court also had reversed the convictions of several adult bookstore operators, although the Court had written no new law in doing so. And a plurality of the Court had held that materials could not be considered obscene unless they were proved to be "utterly without redeeming social value," whatever that might be. It is not surprising, then, that some authorities were predicting an end to obscenity prosecutions.[16] A commission appointed by President Johnson to study the traffic in obscenity recommended in 1970 that the government give up its attempts to censor what adults might see or read. Twelve of the eighteen members said they had been unable to find any link between explicit sexual materials and sexual arousal, to say nothing of a link to antisocial behavior.

Richard Nixon, who was elected president while the commission was conducting its study, refused to accept its report. In his first years in office, he appointed four conservative justices to the Supreme Court: Warren E. Burger, who replaced Warren as chief justice of the United States, Harry L. Blackmun, Lewis F. Powell, Jr., and William H. Rehnquist. Shortly after Burger's appointment, a *Wall Street Journal* reporter wrote that one of the chief justice's goals was to use the obscenity issue to "reverse a major decision of the Warren Court,"[17] and thus signal a more conservative approach to First Amendment law.

The prediction proved to be accurate. Three years later, Burger found an obscenity case behind which he could muster a majority of the Court. The decision, which he wrote, specifically repudiated *Memoirs* and *Redrup* and narrowed the scope of *Roth*.

COMMUNITY STANDARDS OF OBSCENITY

In the late 1960s, the young manager of a restaurant in Newport Beach, California, was opening the day's mail while his mother stood near. He opened an envelope and found it stuffed with advertising brochures that were not like the usual "junk" mail. These brochures described a film, *Marital Intercourse,* and four books, *Intercourse, Man-Woman, Sex Orgies Illustrated,* and *An Illustrated History of Pornography.* The brochures were illustrated with photographs leaving no doubt that the materials offered for sale portrayed sexual activity.

The manager and his mother gave the brochures to the police, who arrested Marvin Miller, the sender, on a charge of mailing unsolicited sexually explicit material, a violation of state law. A trial court found him guilty, and a state appeals court affirmed. A further appeal was taken to the U.S. Supreme Court. Chief Justice Burger had found the case on which he could muster a majority. For the first time since *Roth,* sixteen years earlier, five justices would agree on a definition of obscenity.

---

16. See, for instance, Charles Rembar, *The End of Obscenity* (New York: Bantam Books, 1968). Rembar was counsel for G.P. Putnam's Sons in *Memoirs.*
17. Louis M. Kohlmeier, "High Court to Review Post Office's Power to Ban Obscence Materials from the Mails," *Wall Street Journal,* 3 March 1970.

Miller v. *California,* 413 U.S. 15, 93 S.Ct. 2607, 37 L.Ed.2d 419 (1973).

Like the decision in *Roth,* the new decision was to be laced with irony. The Court had upheld Roth's conviction. But its decision was to clear the way for others to do legally what Roth was punished for doing illegally. Now the Court would find that Miller's conviction was improper because the California courts had used the wrong standard to determine obscenity. But in doing so, the majority would write a decision making it even easier to obtain future convictions.

The chief justice himself wrote the decision in *Miller* v. *California.* He was joined by the three other Nixon appointees—Blackmun, Powell, and Rehnquist—and by Byron R. White, who had been appointed in 1962 by President Kennedy. The majority began by focusing on the origins of the case. "Aggressive sales action" had been used to thrust "sexually explicit materials" on an unwilling recipient. Burger wrote:

> This Court has recognized that the States have a legitimate interest in prohibiting dissemination or exhibition of obscene material when the mode of dissemination carries with it a significant danger of offending the sensibilities of unwilling recipients or of exposure to juveniles.

This was a reference to the Court's decision in *Redrup.* Burger turned next to a review of the decisions in *Roth* and *Memoirs,* noting that the latter had imposed a nearly impossible burden of proof on prosecutors in obscenity cases. They were required to prove a negative, that is, "that the material was '*utterly* without redeeming social value.'" He noted that the *Memoirs* decision, like all other obscenity decisions since *Roth,* had been the product of a divided court. At no time had a majority of the Court endorsed the "redeeming social value" test. Nevertheless, it had been widely used by lower courts, including, Burger said, the California court that had convicted Miller. Then came his clincher: "But now the *Memoirs* test has been abandoned as unworkable by its author, and no member of the Court today supports the *Memoirs* formulation."

That was the truth, but a somewhat misleading one. Brennan was the author of the plurality opinion in *Memoirs.* He had also written the *Roth* test. In *Miller,* he wrote a strong dissent in which he indeed abandoned the *Memoirs* formulation. But that did not mean that he wanted to make it easier for prosecutors to obtain obscenity convictions. On the contrary, he had moved close to the absolute position of Black and Douglas. In part, this was out of revulsion against the Court's role as a "Supreme Board of Censors," which required it to look at sleazy books, photographs, and films to decide whether they would appeal to prurient interest. Brennan, joined by Marshall and Potter Stewart, urged the Court to adopt the decision in *Redrup* as its sole guide, thus making the test of obscenity the conduct of the vendors rather than the content of their wares.

The majority chose another course. It rejected the *Memoirs* test, and then wrote its own three-part test to be applied by lower courts in future obscenity prosecutions. One of its purposes was to hand back to the states the major responsibility for controlling the traffic in pornography. States could do this without infringing on First Amendment freedoms, Burger wrote, if they acted under statutes specifically defining obscenity. Such statutes would have to be "carefully limited" and confined to "works which depict or describe sexual conduct." Further,

> A state offense must also be limited to works which, taken as a whole, appeal to the prurient interest in sex, which portray sexual conduct in a patently offensive way, and which, taken as a whole, do not have serious literary, artistic, political, or scientific value.

Within a paragraph, a majority of the Court had rewritten the law of obscenity. Lest that point be missed, Burger set down three guidelines for juries to apply:

> (a) whether "the average person, applying contemporary community standards," would find that the work, taken as a whole, appeals to the prurient interest,
> (b) whether the work depicts or describes, in a patently offensive way, sexual conduct specifically defined by the applicable state law, and
> (c) whether the work, taken as a whole, lacks serious literary, artistic, political, or scientific value.

The newly proclaimed three-point test retained Brennan's formulation in *Roth,* but rejected his plurality opinion in *Memoirs.* Henceforth, purveyors of sexually explicit materials could avoid an obscenity conviction only if they could prove that the items in question had some serious value to society.

The Burger majority offered advice to state legislatures in drafting statutes that would comply with the new test and to courts interpreting them. It listed "a few plain examples" of the kinds of works that would be obscene under "the standard announced in this opinion":

> (a) Patently offensive representations or descriptions of ultimate sexual acts, normal or perverted, actual or simulated.
> (b) Patently offensive representations or descriptions of masturbation, excretory functions, and lewd exhibition of the genitals.

The majority expanded on these examples:

> Sex and nudity may not be exploited without limit by films or pictures exhibited or sold in places of public accommodation any more than live sex and nudity can be exhibited or sold without limit in such public places. At a minimum, prurient, patently offensive depiction or description of sexual conduct must have serious literary, artistic, political, or scientific value to merit First Amendment protection.... For example, medical books for the education of physicians and related personnel necessarily use graphic illustrations and descriptions of human anatomy. In resolving the inevitably sensitive questions of fact and law, we must continue to rely on the jury system, accompanied by the safeguards that judges, rules of evidence, presumption of innocence, and other protective features provide, as we do with rape, murder, and a host of other offenses against society and its individual members.

The majority proceeded to give the jury a central role in obscenity cases. Jurors were to determine the standard of decency prevailing in their communities and decide what kinds of materials violated it. At the same time, the Court adopted the position Harlan had taken in *Memoirs,* rejecting the idea of a national standard for measuring obscenity. The standard would vary from community to community. Burger wrote:

> Under a National Constitution, fundamental First Amendment limitations on the power of the States do not vary from community to community, but this does not mean that there are, or should or can be, fixed, uniform national standards of precisely what appeals to the "prurient interest" or is "patently offensive." These are essentially questions of fact, and our Nation is simply too big and too diverse for this Court to reasonably expect such standards could be articulated for all 50 States in a single formulation, even assuming the prerequisite consensus exists. When triers of fact [a jury] are asked to decide whether "the average person, applying contemporary community standards" would consider certain materials "prurient," it would be unrealistic to require that the answer be based on some abstract formulation. The adversary system, with lay jurors as the usual ultimate fact-finders in critical prosecutions, has historically permitted triers of fact to draw on the standards of their community, guided always by limiting instructions on the law. To require a State to structure obscenity proceedings around evidence of a *national* "community standard" would be an exercise in futility....
>
> It is neither realistic nor constitutionally sound to read the First Amendment as requiring that the people of Maine or Mississippi accept public depiction of conduct found tolerable in Las Vegas, or New York City....People in different States vary in their tastes and attitudes, and this diversity is not to be strangled by the absolutism of imposed uniformity.

Thus, the Court sought to define "community" as the place from which a jury is drawn to hear an obscenity case. It also sought to define the "community standard" as the jurors' collective estimate of the level of sexual candor tolerated by them, their friends, and their neighbors.

Justice Douglas, writing in dissent, protested that the majority was giving juries of lay citizens a task that even Supreme Court justices had shown remarkably little talent for doing; that is, determining what is obscene. In his view, the new test "would make it possible to ban any paper or any journal or magazine in some benighted place." Douglas's protest had no effect. The Court returned the case against Miller to the California courts for retrial under the new standard.

Paris Adult Theatre I v. *Slaton,* **413 U.S. 49, 93 S.Ct. 2626, 37 L.Ed.2d 446 (1973).**

On the same day, the Court decided *Paris Adult Theatre I* v. *Slaton,* an obscenity case aimed at an adult theater operator in Georgia. Again Chief Justice Burger was able to muster a majority, this time to repudiate the Court's *per curiam* decision in *Redrup.*

Lewis R. Slaton, district attorney of Fulton County, Georgia, had brought a civil action to prevent the showing in an adult theater of two films, *Magic Mirror* and *It All Comes Out in the End,* which a judge had declared obscene. However, the judge had held that he could not prevent the theater from showing them because it operated within *Redrup* guidelines, that is, it excluded minors and unsuspecting adults, and it did not pander. The Georgia Supreme Court overruled him, and the U.S. Supreme Court affirmed that decision.

The chief justice moved directly to the attack on *Redrup:*

> We categorically disapprove the theory, apparently adopted by the trial judge, that obscene, pornographic films acquire constitutional immunity from state regulation simply because they are exhibited for consenting adults only....Although we have often pointedly recognized the high importance of the state interest in regulating the exposure of obscene materials to juveniles and unconsenting adults,...this Court has never declared these to be the only legitimate state interests permitting regulation of obscene material. The States have a long-recognized legitimate interest in regulating the use of obscene material in local commerce and in all places of public accommodation, as long as these regulations do not run afoul of specific constitutional prohibitions....
>
> In particular, we hold that there are legitimate state interests at stake in stemming the tide of commercialized obscenity....These include the interest of the public in the quality of life and the total community environment, the tone of commerce in the great city centers, and possibly, the public safety itself....
>
> If we accept...the well nigh universal belief that good books, plays, and art lift the spirit, improve the mind, enrich the human personality, and develop character, can we then say that a state legislature may not act on the corollary assumption that commerce in obscene books, or public exhibitions focused on obscene conduct, have a tendency to exert a corrupting and debasing impact leading to antisocial behavior?

Lawyers for the theater had pointed to the Court's decision in *Stanley,* arguing that it established a right of privacy protecting the viewing of obscene materials. Burger replied that the decision in *Stanley* clearly confines that right to the home:

> The idea of a "privacy" right and a place of public accommodation are, in this context, mutually exclusive. Conduct or depictions of conduct that the state police power can prohibit on a public street do not become automatically protected by the Constitution merely because the conduct is moved to a bar or a "live" theatre stage, any more than a "live" performance of a man and woman locked in sexual embrace at high noon in Times Square is protected by the Constitution because they simultaneously engage in a valid political dialogue.

At that point, *Redrup* and the broader implications some had seen in *Stanley* had been torn to ribbons. States and localities might permit so-called adult bookstores and films if they wanted to, but if states chose to ban obscenity, the makers and the sellers of it could not look to the United States Supreme Court for help. If the materials in question portrayed explicit sexual or excretory activity, and did so in a manner that a jury found patently offensive, they could be condemned as obscene, unless they were redeemed by serious literary, artistic, political, or scientific value. Nor could obscene materials find sanctuary behind doors marked "adults only." If state officials chose to do so, they could prosecute purveyors of obscenity if a state law defined the crime in terms of specific sexual conduct.

OBSCENITY LAW SINCE
MILLER AND *PARIS*

In the immediate aftermath of the *Miller* and *Paris* decisions, two currents worked at cross purposes. Police and prosecutors moved against obscenity with renewed vigor. But some judges, reading *Miller,* were finding state statutes unconstitutional because they did not define obscenity in terms of explicit sexual conduct. For instance, a federal district court in Alabama ruled that the state's obscenity law was unconstitutional in a case involving *Last Tango in Paris,* which starred Marlon Brando.[18] In another case, the Minnesota Supreme Court struck down that state's law, which included, word-for-word, the formulation in *Roth.*[19] Pointing to *Miller,* the court said the law was flawed because it did not describe sexual conduct in specific terms.

It also quickly became apparent that with its decisions in *Miller* and *Paris* the Court had not succeeded in ridding itself of obscenity cases. In the years since, it has decided at least one, and as many as four, in several of its terms. It also has refused to review many others. The Court has felt a need to deal with problems in several areas, which are summarized and categorized below.

Refining the Definition of Obscenity

Brennan had predicted that local juries would condemn as obscene works that were seen elsewhere as art. Even as he wrote that passage in *Miller,* a case bearing out his prediction was on its way to the Court. A jury in Albany, Georgia, had found the movie *Carnal Knowledge* obscene. The exhibitor was fined $750 and placed on probation for a year. The film, starring Jack Nicholson, was a serious look at the sexual fantasies and later hangups of college friends who go their separate ways into early middle age. Most reviewers found it an honest look at the process and problems of maturing. Some thought well enough of it to place it on their lists of the ten best films of the year. After the Georgia Supreme Court had upheld the Albany jury, the *Miller* decision came down. In light of that verdict, the Supreme Court of the United States agreed to review.

Jenkins v. *Georgia,* **418 U.S. 153, 94 S. Ct. 2750, 41 L.Ed.2d 642 (1974).**

In its decision in *Jenkins* v. *Georgia,* the Court reiterated two points it had made in *Miller:*

1. The Georgia Supreme Court was correct in holding that a jury need not be told to apply a state-wide standard. Local standards of sexual candor are to be used in determining whether a film is obscene.

2. However, local juries do not have "unbridled discretion" in deciding what is obscene. Material can be obscene only if it depicts or portrays "patently offensive 'hard core' sexual conduct."

---

18.   United Artists Corp. v. Wright, 368 F.Supp. 1034 (M.D.Ala. 1974).
19.   State v. Welke, 216 N.W.2d 641 (Minn. 1974).

Therefore, *Carnal Knowledge* was not obscene. Justice Rehnquist explained why:

> While the subject matter of the picture is, in a broader sense, sex, and there are scenes in which sexual conduct including "ultimate sexual acts" is to be understood to be taking place, the camera does not focus on the bodies of the actors at such times. There is no exhibition whatsoever of the actors' genitals, lewd or otherwise, during these scenes. There are occasional scenes of nudity, but nudity alone is not enough to make material legally obscene under the *Miller* standards.

On the same day, in *Hamling* v. *United States,* the Court upheld prison terms imposed on two men who had used the mails to distribute 55,000 brochures advertising *The Illustrated Presidential Report of the Commission on Obscenity and Pornography.* The sample illustrations used in the brochure showed a wide variety of heterosexual and homosexual activity, and of humans engaged in sexual activity with animals. The convictions had taken place in a federal district court and had been upheld by the court of appeals before *Miller* was decided. The Court held that in such instances convicted defendants were entitled to any help *Miller* might give them but concluded that in this instance it gave them none.

Hamling **v.** *United States,* **418 U.S. 87, 94 S.Ct. 2887, 41 L.Ed.2d 590 (1974).**

Three points emerged from the decision:

1. Although federal laws define obscenity in general terms, they were made specific by the Supreme Court's decision in *Miller*. Under well-established principles of constitutional law, statutes mean what the courts say they mean. Thus, the federal law must be interpreted and applied in the light of the "few plain examples" provided by Chief Justice Burger in *Miller*.

2. Juries deciding obscenity cases brought under federal law are not required to apply a national standard. They are to draw on their knowledge of the standard of sexual candor prevailing in the communities from which jurors are selected.

3. Nor are jurors required to pay any attention to expert witnesses who testify as to what they believe the standard is. The jurors are considered the experts.

The effect of *Hamling* has been to strengthen the role of the locally drawn jury in determining what is obscene. The jury's discretion is limited only by the proviso, reinforced by *Jenkins*, that the material at issue must portray, in words or pictures, specific sexual activity lacking "serious literary, artistic, political or scientific value."

Pope **v.** *Illinois,* **481 U.S. 497, 107 S.Ct. 1918, 95 L.Ed.2d 439 (1987).**

However, in a more recent case the Supreme Court held that the standards of the average person in any given community are not the measure of such values. Rather, presumably there is an absolute scale reasonable persons can apply to determine whether material has "serious value." The case, *Pope* v. *Illinois,* came to the Court from Rockford, Illinois, where judges in two separate obscenity trials had instructed juries that they could find materials obscene if the average person in the community would believe them lacking in serious literary, artistic, political, or scientific value. Defendants in both trials were found guilty, and the convictions were upheld by the Illinois Court of Appeals. The Illinois Supreme Court denied review. The U.S. Supreme Court took the case and reversed, five to four.

Justice White, writing for a majority, said there is "no suggestion in our cases that the question of the value of an allegedly obscene work is to be determined by reference to community standards." In *Miller,* White continued, the discussion of contemporary community standards was linked with prurient interest and patent offensiveness, but not to the value of the material. In that decision, the Court said that the First Amendment protects any allegedly obscene works "which, taken as a whole, have serious literary, artistic, political, or scientific value, regardless whether the government or a majority of the people approve of the ideas these works represent." Such value does not vary from community to community and is not "based on the degree of local acceptance it has won. The proper inquiry is not whether an ordinary member of any given community would find serious literary, artistic, political, or scientific value in allegedly obscene material, but whether a reasonable person would find such value in the material."

The effect of the decision is to invite expert testimony as to a work's value and to place the ultimate decision as to whether that value is serious with judges rather than juries. Presumably, judges are in a better position than jurors to discern whatever national standard reasonable people might use to measure the "serious literary, artistic, political, or scientific value" of a book, magazine, or film.

In another case, *Splawn* v. *California,*[20] the Court upheld a California judge who had told a jury it could consider the seller's methods in coming to the conclusion that two reels of film were obscene. This revived and affirmed the pandering test first proposed by Chief Justice Warren in *Roth* and endorsed by the Court nine years later in *Ginzburg* v. *United States.*[21] The decisions mean that a seller who tells customers his materials will arouse their prurient interest is likely to be taken at his word if an obscenity prosecution results.

Defining Child Pornography

Some adults see children as exciting sexual objects who can be exploited because of their immaturity. Such adults are willing to pay well for photographs of children engaged in sexual action. In 1977, the traffic in such materials led to passage by Congress of a law providing for prosecution of persons who make or sell such photographs.[22] Under its terms, violators can be sentenced to as long as ten years in prison for a first offense. All fifty states have similar laws.

---

20. 431 U.S. 595, 97 S.Ct. 1987, 52 L.Ed.2d 606 (1977).
21. 383 U.S. 463, 86 S.Ct. 942, 16 L.Ed.2d 31 (1966).
22. Protection of Children Against Sexual Exploitation Act of 1977, 18 U.S.C. §§2251–2253.

Most such laws describe the crime of child pornography in terms of specific sexual acts. Even an isolated portrayal of a proscribed act is subject to prosecution if it involves a minor. For that reason, the laws do not precisely fit the *Roth-Miller* mold, which requires that a work charged with being obscene must be looked at as a whole.

New York v. Ferber, 458 U.S. 747, 102 S. Ct. 3348, 73 L.Ed.2d 1113 (1982). In *New York* v. *Ferber*, the Supreme Court upheld that state's child pornography law. The Court said that in protecting children from sexual exploitation, states can go beyond the limits imposed by *Miller*. It held flatly that there is no First Amendment protection for portrayals of specifically described sex acts performed by boys or girls under sixteen years of age. Justice White said the Court could find no value whatsoever in encouraging children to engage in sex. On the contrary, it would uphold the legislature in its conclusion that "the use of children as subjects of pornographic materials is harmful to the physiological, emotional, and mental health of the child. That judgment, we think, easily passes muster under the First Amendment."

The decision is of further interest in that all nine justices agreed that Ferber should be punished. However, four of them wrote opinions in which they differed with White on some elements of his reasoning. Justices John Paul Stevens and Brennan, for instance, did not join that part of the decision holding that all depictions of minors engaged in sexual activity are without First Amendment protection. They would have held open the possibility that sometime, somehow, a work portraying sexual activity by teenagers might be a work of art.

More recently, the Supreme Court upheld an Ohio statute which makes mere possession of child pornography, even in the privacy of one's home, a crime.[23] In doing so, the Court said it was not repudiating the rationale it had used in *Stanley*. In that case, the Court said the First Amendment protects the right of individuals to read or view pornography, even that which might be legally obscene, in the privacy of their homes. But it said there is no First Amendment interest protecting child pornography, even though it may not be obscene by *Miller* standards. Referring to *Ferber*, the Court said the suppression of child pornography is justified by the state's interest in protecting minors from exploitation. Thus, the purpose of laws criminalizing the traffic in child pornography is to cut off such materials at their source. In the immediate aftermath of that decision, a bill was introduced in the U.S. Senate to make the viewing or possession of child pornography a federal crime.[24] Violators could be sent to prison for as long as ten years.

The law upheld in *Ferber* makes the sellers of sexually oriented photographs responsible for proving that the persons portrayed in them are of legal age. That requirement was upheld by the Ninth Circuit Court of Appeals,[25] but a federal district court held that the law swept too far in requiring everyone involved with

---

23. Osborne v. Ohio, _ _ _ U.S. _ _ _, 110 S.Ct. 1691, 109 L.Ed.2d 98 (1990).
24. S. 2481, the Anti-Child Pornography Possession Act of 1990. 136 Cong.Rec. S4730 (No. 44).
25. United States v. U.S. District Court, Central District of California, Los Angeles, 858 F.2d 534 (9th Cir. 1988).

such photographs to keep records on the ages of the participants.[26] The court acted at the request of the American Library Association and eight other organizations who argued that the provision would have made librarians reluctant to circulate works on sexuality or art books in which nudity is portrayed.

Defining and Limiting the Use of Zoning Laws

Zoning laws can be used to confine adult theaters and bookstores to specified parts of a city, but they cannot be used as a subterfuge to ban all such establishments. The Supreme Court's decisions in this area point up the variety of approaches to obscenity law made possible by *Miller*. In some states, or even in parts of states, anything goes. Either there is no law making obscenity a crime, or, if there is a law, local prosecutors do not bother to enforce it. Some states, formally or informally, condone establishments that operate within the *Redrup* guidelines. In still other states and localities, obscenity laws are enforced and juries return convictions. In states that continue to apply *Redrup,* some local authorities have turned to zoning laws to control the location of adult establishments.

In *Young* v. *American Mini Theatres,*[27] the Supreme Court upheld a Detroit ordinance that confined adult bookstores and theaters to commercial areas of the city. Its terms were held to be a reasonable restriction of time, place, and manner on First Amendment activities. But in *Schad* v. *Borough of Mount Ephraim,*[28] the Court said a New Jersey community went too far when its zoning law forbade live entertainment. The law's target was an adult bookstore in which a woman danced in the nude behind a glass screen. The Court said the law also could be used to restrict other forms of expression. In *City of Renton* v. *Playtime Theatres, Inc.,*[29] the Supreme Court expanded on its holding in *Young*. It upheld a zoning ordinance that prohibited adult theaters from locating within a thousand feet of any dwelling, church, park, or school. Thus, zoning laws may be used to concentrate sexually oriented businesses in a particular part of a city and to prevent them from expanding into designated neighborhoods.

However, the U.S. Court of Appeals for the Sixth Circuit held that the city of Ann Arbor, Michigan, went too far when it adopted an ordinance that would have confined sellers of sexually explicit materials to less than six-hundredths of a square mile, or to about one city block.[30] The court said the city acted unreasonably in confining adult establishments to such a small part of the city, especially when it offered no valid reasons, such as preventing urban blight, for doing so.

LIMITING THE USE OF PRIOR RESTRAINT ══════

As the cases above suggest, the Supreme Court has been of two minds about obscenity. For more than half a century, starting with *Near* v. *Minnesota,* the

---

26. Milo Geyelin, ''Publishers Gain as Court Strikes Down Key Aspects of a Child Pornography Law,'' *Wall Street Journal,* 18 May 1989.
27. 427 U.S. 50, 96 S.Ct. 2440, 49 L.Ed.2d 310 (1976).
28. 452 U.S. 61, 101 S.Ct. 2176, 68 L.Ed.2d 671 (1981).
29. 475 U.S. 41, 106 S.Ct. 925, 89 L.Ed.2d 29 (1986).
30. Christy v. City of Ann Arbor, 824 F.2d 489 (6th Cir. 1987).

Court has said that materials found to be obscene are not protected by the First Amendment and may be subjected to the ultimate in prior restraint. Obscene materials can be seized by police and destroyed. But the Court also has said that obscenity is not to be defined arbitrarily. As with other kinds of trash, items some find fit only for burning may be treasured by others. The task of separating one from the other is made difficult because obscenity is found in books, magazines, photographs, films, and videotapes, all media of communications protected by the First Amendment. Thus, the Supreme Court has been required over the years not only to establish criteria for determining what is obscene but to establish procedures to prevent arbitrary seizure and destruction of materials believed, but not proved, to be obscene. In doing so, the Court has on several occasions found itself at odds with police, prosecutors, and others who have applied their own standards to justify seizing and destroying sexually oriented materials.

Officials have used various weapons against allegedly obscene materials. These weapons have included licensing, the forced closing of businesses found guilty of purveying obscenity or seen as creating public nuisances, and, more recently, the use of racketeering laws to justify seizure of the assets of adult establishments.

With respect to licensing, the landmark case is *Freedman* v. *State of Maryland*.[31] At issue was that state's film censorship law. The Court held that the decision to grant or deny a license must be made promptly and be subject to "expeditious judicial review." In the event of a decision to deny, a film can be suppressed only if the state goes to court and proves it to be obscene beyond reasonable doubt. In other contexts, the Court has used *Freedman* to remind zealous police and prosecutors that they cannot confiscate sexually explicit materials without first going to court and proving them obscene.

FW/PBS v. *City of Dallas*, 493 U.S. _ _ _, 110 S.Ct. 596, 107 L.Ed.2d 603 (1990). When officials in Dallas, Texas, adopted an ordinance providing for strict licensing and inspection of "sexually oriented businesses," the Court referred to *Freedman* in finding parts of it unconstitutional. The ordinance was aimed at a variety of businesses whose principal purpose was to offer the public entertainment or materials featuring "specified sexual activities." The ordinance defined the latter in terms drawn from *Miller*. The target included adult book and video stores, adult theaters, cabarets, escort agencies, nude model studios, "sexual encounter centers," and motels renting rooms for fewer than ten hours. Justice Antonin Scalia saw the law as "one of an increasing number of attempts throughout the country...to prevent the erosion of public morality."

However, when a variety of challenges to the ordinance reached the Supreme Court, the Court held that the licensing provision violated the *Freedman* guidelines, although a majority could not agree on the extent to which it did so. Under the ordinance, police were supposed to reach a decision on whether to grant or refuse a license within thirty days. But the police could not issue one until the

---

31.   380 U.S. 51, 85 S.Ct. 734, 13 L.Ed.2d 649 (1965).

premises had been approved by the fire and health departments and had been found by a building official to be in compliance "with applicable laws and ordinances." Because no time limit was fixed for completion of these approvals, the Court said the ordinance imposed an unconstitutional restraint on those businesses offering printed matter and films subject to First Amendment protection. Justice Sandra Day O'Connor, writing for herself and two others, noted that simply by delaying any one of the required inspections, the city could deny a license indefinitely. Therefore, the ordinance violated that part of the *Freedman* guidelines requiring a prompt decision on the licensing of First Amendment activities. However, she said that because the license applied to the right to do business rather than to "the content of any protected speech," the city would not have to go to court to justify the denial of a license.

Justice Brennan, writing for himself and two others, disagreed. In his view, denial of a license would indeed serve as a prior restraint on arguably protected speech. Therefore, the city should be required to prove to a court's satisfaction that a denial was justified. Three justices found no First Amendment problems with the licensing scheme and, therefore, no need to refer to *Freedman*. Scalia took the most extreme position. In his view, the businesses covered by the ordinance were engaged in pandering to a prurient interest in sex and therefore could simply have been outlawed.

Despite these differences of opinion, the effect of the decision was to declare the licensing provision unconstitutional so far as it applied to businesses selling or displaying books, magazines, videotapes, movies, and other materials protected by the First Amendment.

In another line of cases, the Court has held that performances cannot be forbidden merely because some authority thinks they might be obscene. One involved a ruling by Chattanooga, Tennessee, city officials preventing a performance of the rock musical *Hair* in a municipal auditorium.[32] Although the musical contains one scene in which the cast strips on stage, the production had not then been held obscene by any court anywhere. Nor has it been since. In another case, the Court struck down an ordinance of the city of Jacksonville, Florida, forbidding outdoor theaters to show movies containing nudity. The Court pointed out that nudity in itself is not obscene.[33]

The Texas Legislature sought to combat obscenity by enacting a law permitting authorities to close theaters in which an obscene film had been shown. The Court said it couldn't do that because the fact that a theater had shown one movie found to be obscene did not mean that it would show others.[34] However, in another decision the Court upheld a California court's order closing an adult theater for one year on the grounds that it had become a public nuisance.[35] The decision was not based on a judgment of the kinds of films the theater offered but on the

---

32. Southeastern Promotions v. Conrad, 420 U.S. 546, 95 S.Ct. 1239, 43 L.Ed.2d 448 (1975).
33. Erznoznik v. City of Jacksonville, 422 U.S. 205, 95 S.Ct. 2268, 45 L.Ed.2d 125 (1975).
34. Vance v. Universal Amusement Co., 445 U.S. 308, 100 S.Ct. 1156, 63 L.Ed.2d 413 (1980).
35. Cooper v. Mitchell Brothers' Santa Ana Theater, 454 U.S. 90, 102 S.Ct. 172, 70 L.Ed.2d 262 (1981).

type of patrons attracted and their effect on the neighborhood. The Court said the authorities can act under a state's police powers to abate a nuisance.

More recently, authorities have been using racketeering laws, enacted originally to combat organized crime and the traffic in drugs, to justify attempts to close businesses dealing in sexually oriented wares. Under these laws, officials can impose heavy penalties on individuals involved in a "pattern of conduct" pointing to repeated illegal activity. More importantly, the laws permit officials to seize at the time of arrest any assets earned by or associated with that activity. Typically, a "pattern of conduct" can be established by as few as two prosecutions for specified criminal offenses. In federal statutes and in at least fifteen states,[36] violations of obscenity laws are included among the predicate offenses. The criminal version of such laws is known as the Racketeer Influenced and Corrupt Organizations Act, or RICO. Some states provide also for civil actions to forfeit property under laws known as Civil Remedies for Racketeering Activity Acts.

Fort Wayne Books, Inc. v. Indiana, **489 U.S. _ _ _, 109 S.Ct. 916, 103 L.Ed.2d 34 (1989).**

In the first RICO obscenity cases to reach the Supreme Court, the Court found no problem with the enhanced penalty provisions of the law. Nor did the Court find anything wrong with defining the traffic in obscene materials as racketeering, the Court did say that RICO laws cannot be used to justify wholesale seizure of an adult bookstore's stock in trade even though the requisite "pattern of conduct" has been established. Justice White, writing for a unanimous Court, noted that "this Court has repeatedly held that rigorous safeguards must be employed before expressive materials can be seized as 'obscene.'" At a minimum, an adversary proceeding must be held, meaning a jury trial, applying the *Miller* standards. The materials cannot be taken out of circulation unless, and until, that proceeding results in a finding that the materials are obscene. "It is 'the risk of prior restraint' that motivates this rule," White wrote.

However, the Court did not say that RICO's seizure provisions could never be used in obscenity cases. It assumed without deciding that bookstores and their contents can be forfeited like yachts and bank accounts where proper proof of their link to law violation can be established. But in this instance, the Court was not convinced that such a link had been established. Not only had authorities cleaned out the contents of the offending bookstore, they had padlocked the building. It was likely, White wrote, that some of the contents were protected by

---

36. 18 U.S.C. § 1961(1) (1982 ed., Supp. IV); Ariz.Rev.Stat.Ann. § 13-2301(D)(4)(u) (Supp. 1988–1989); Colo.Rev.Stat. § 18-17-103(5)(b)(VI) (1986); Del.Code Ann., Tit. 11, §§ 1502(9)(a), (9)(b)(7) (1987); Fla.Stat. § 895.02(1)(a)(27) (1987); Ga.Code Ann. § 16-14-3(3)(A)(xii) (1988); Idaho Code § 18-7803(8) (Supp. 1988); Ind.Code § 35-45-6-1 (Supp. 1987); N.J.Stat.Ann. § 2C:41-1(e) (West Supp. 1988–1989); N.C.Gen.Stat. § 75D-3(c)(2) (1987); N.D.Cent.Code § 12.1-06.1-01(2)(d)(17) (Supp. 1987); Ohio Rev.Code Ann. §§ 2923.31(I)(1), (I)(2) (1987); Okla.Stat., Tit. 22 § 1402(10)(v) (Supp. 1988); Ore.Rev.Stat. §§ 166.715(6)(a)(T), (6)(b) (1987); Utah Code Ann. § 76-10-1602(4)(fff)-(iii), (zzz) (Supp. 1988); Wash.Rev.Code § 9A.82.010(14)(s) (Supp. 1988).

the First Amendment. Books cannot be taken out of circulation simply because police officers have probable cause to believe a crime has been committed. He concluded with the warning that "the State cannot escape the constitutional safeguards of our prior cases by merely recategorizing obscenity violations as 'racketeering.'"

Despite that aspect, the decision was generally viewed as a victory for prosecutors who have been using RICO laws to combat obscenity.[37] A majority of the Court held that obscenity convictions can be considered racketeering. The majority also found nothing offensive to the Constitution in the fact that penalties for racketeering may involve longer prison terms and steeper fines than those for dealing in obscenity. The majority did not close the door on using the law to seize the assets of dealers in obscenity, saying only that if those assets include materials arguably protected by the First Amendment, they cannot be seized until a jury has found them obscene.

In the last third of this century, few aspects of media law have led to more Supreme Court decisions than obscenity. And no aspect of media law has divided the Court as obscenity has. The differences began with *Roth,* the first true obscenity case accepted by the Court. Only four other justices, a bare majority, agreed with Justice Brennan's definition of obscenity, which reads almost like a mathematical formula: "Whether to the average person, applying contemporary community standards, the dominant theme of the material taken as a whole appeals to a prurient interest."

As of this writing, Brennan is the only survivor from the *Roth* Court. But although the cast has changed, the divisions have persisted. In his dissenting opinion in *Fort Wayne Books,* Brennan argued that it is anything but "well established" that "delivery of obscene messages to consenting adults may be prosecuted as a crime."[38] He reminded his colleagues that in none of its cases, covering a thirty-two-year span, have more than five justices agreed with that proposition. In four of those cases, four justices signed opinions saying that "criminal prosecution for obscenity-related offenses violates the First Amendment."

The Court's persisting disagreement over obscenity obviously reflects a similar disagreement in our society. That there continue to be cases like *FW/PBS* and *Fort Wayne Books* is evidence that catering, or pandering, to the public's demand for sexually explicit entertainment and reading matter is a profitable business. Such cases also are evidence that police and prosecutors are reacting to the belief that the traffic in sexually explicit materials poses a threat to society. Chief Justice Burger referred to that belief in his opinion in *Paris Adult Theatre.* If we believe that "good books, plays, and art lift the spirit, improve the mind, enrich the human personality, and develop character," the state may act on the assumption that obscenity has "a tendency to exert a corrupting and debasing impact leading to antisocial behavior."

---

37. Stephen Wermiel, "Tactic to Fight Pornography Is Upheld," *Wall Street Journal,* 22 February 1989.
38. 109 S.Ct. 916, 931, n. 1.

As noted earlier, a majority of the commission appointed by President Johnson to study the effects of pornography found no evidence of such a tendency. More recently, a commission appointed by Edwin Meese, III, then President Reagan's attorney general, came to an opposite conclusion.[39] It concluded that exposure to certain kinds of pornographic materials, including those portraying physical abuse of women, causes an "increase in the incidence of sexual violence." This was based in part on testimony from law enforcement officers, who said they invariably found pornographic materials in the possession of sexual offenders, and on interviews with convicted offenders, half of whom said they were incited by such materials. Social scientists recommended to the commission by Surgeon General C. Everett Koop concluded that pornography changes values, especially if sexual aggression is portrayed "as pleasurable for the victim." But the commission also acknowledged "that scholarly comment generally agrees with the dissenters," who argued against restrictions on the ability of consenting adults to obtain explicit sexual materials.

However, some scholars believe there is a link between pornography and the continuing problem of male assaults on women. Among them are Edward Donnerstein, Daniel Linz, and Steven Penrod, psychologists at the University of Wisconsin, whose experiments are summarized in *The Question of Pornography*.[40] That view is shared by feminist organizations who were able to persuade city councils in Minneapolis and Indianapolis to adopt ordinances treating obscenity as a violation of women's civil rights. The ordinances defined obscenity as the "graphic sexually explicit subordination of women," which was considered a form of discrimination against women. The mayor of Minneapolis vetoed that city's ordinance, acting in the belief that it was unconstitutional. That belief was confirmed by experience with the Indianapolis ordinance. Challenged by the American Booksellers Association, the ordinance was declared unconstitutional by a federal district court and affirmed on appeal.[41] The court recognized that the government has an interest in preventing sexual discrimination, which is the subject of both federal and state laws. But the court also said that in light of the Supreme Court's specific guidelines in *Miller,* the city could not define as obscene materials what some see as promoting such discrimination.

Thus we are left with another version of a vexing question that has arisen throughout this book. Given the First Amendment's treatment of free speech and a free press as basic rights, what limits can be imposed on these rights? A considerable body of opinion holds, as it has since writing began, that some kinds of speech and publication are harmful to society and to individuals. Speech attacking the state has been punished as sedition. Speech harmful to the reputation of individuals is punished as libel. In our time, there is increasing uneasiness with speech that attacks individuals on the basis of their race, religion, gender, or sex-

---

39. Attorney General's Commission on Pornography, *Final Report* (July 1986).
40. Free Press, 1986.
41. American Booksellers Association v. Hudnut, 598 F.Supp. 1316 (S.D.Ind. 1984); 771 F.2d 323 (7th Cir. 1985). The Supreme Court affirmed, six to three, without writing an opinion, 106 S.Ct. 1172 (1986).

ual preferences. Commentator Andy Rooney was suspended by CBS News and columnist Jimmy Breslin by *Newsday* because of slighting remarks about homosexuals in one instance and Asian women in another. In this chapter, we have explored the tensions between those who believe the portrayal of sexual activity is debasing to society and should be suppressed and those who believe such portrayals must be permitted because sexual activity is a form of human expression. Sexuality has been the subject of artistic works in every medium as far back as such works have endured. In our time, a collection of Robert Mapplethorpe's photographs, including some of an homoerotic nature and others of nude children, was considered of sufficient artistic stature to be exhibited in several of the nation's leading art galleries with the help of funding from the National Endowment for the Arts. The exhibit also led to the arrest of the director of a Cincinnati art gallery on a charge of obscenity.

With obscenity, as in the other areas of controversial expression noted above, the Supreme Court has taken the middle ground. The Court's decisions have held that at some point the portrayal of sexual activity can be punished or even suppressed, but only after a court has found the portrayal obscene, as the Court has

Demonstrators stand outside the Hamilton County Courthouse in Cincinnati urging police and the prosecutor to prevent the exhibition of Robert Mapplethorpe's photographs in one of the city's art gallerys. Police temporarily seized several of the photos and charged the gallery's director with obscenity. A court order permitted the exhibition to remain open pending trial. The exhibition attracted record crowds. (AP/Wide World Photos)

defined that term. The limits set by the Court strike some as being well beyond the point at which pornography can be harmful, but the Court has held here, as it has with sedition and libel, that some harm must be tolerated to avoid suppression of speech that may contribute to the advancement of ideas.

In the Professional World

When the Supreme Court handed down its decision in *Miller,* a *New York Times* reporter talked to several major writers of fiction and found uneasiness among them.[42] Kurt Vonnegut, Jr., Hoosier-born author of best-selling satire on middle-class mores, was one of several who thought it possible that some jury, somewhere, might find one of their works obscene. Joyce Carol Oates predicted that the decision would lead to repression of the arts. Such fears have proved groundless. A Georgia jury found *Carnal Knowledge* obscene but was soon overruled by a unanimous Supreme Court. Since then, no professional communicators of any stature have been condemned as purveyors of obscenity. One has only to read some of the best-selling fiction, go to an R-rated movie, or watch cable television to know that it is highly unlikely that any will be. For most professional communicators, a prosecution for obscenity is not an issue.

However, anyone who is moderately aware of events knows that the portrayal of sex in the mass media is an issue. And so, to a perhaps lesser extent, is the portrayal of violence. The short-lived ordinances in Minneapolis and Indianapolis, and the experiments of Edward Donnerstein and colleagues, indicate that still other issues are raised when sex and violence are linked. Professional communicators ranging from reporters through advertising and public relations practitioners to recording artists deal with one or both in a variety of situations, sometimes without much thought for the consequences, at other times after calculating them closely. A short discussion cannot deal with all the questions raised by portrayals of sex and violence in the mass media. It can only point to some of the problems.

The spectrum begins with the treatment of words considered profane or vulgar. The Supreme Court has held that even the "strongest" of such words is protected by the First Amendment.[43] However, the *Associated Press Stylebook* advises journalists not to use "obscenities, profanities, vulgarities" "unless they are part of direct quotations and there is a compelling reason for them."[44] Many editors have learned that it may not be advisable even then. When the *Louisville Courier-Journal* ran an unexpurgated version of a report on the causes of the riot in Chicago during the Democratic National Convention in 1968, Norman Isaacs, executive editor, said he

---

42. Robert A. Wright, "Broad Spectrum of Writers Attacks Obscenity Ruling," *New York Times,* 21 August 1973.
43. See note 3 in the introduction to this chapter.
44. Christopher W. French, ed., *The Associated Press Stylebook* (New York: The Associated Press, 1987), p. 155.

wrote hundreds of letters of apology to protesting readers.[45] They were offended by the report's frequent use of variations on the vulgarism for sexual intercourse. When one federal employee directed the same kinds of words at another in the federal courthouse in Dayton, the target of his abuse shot him to death. The publisher of the *Dayton Journal Herald* thought the newspaper's readers should know the words that provoked a public employee to such violence. Publication of them provoked protests from enough readers to get the publisher fired.[46] More recently, the wives of several highly placed federal officials formed a nationwide organization—Parents Music Resource Center—to protest the use of explicit sexual language and hatefulness in rock recordings.[47] For awhile, some record companies voluntarily advised buyers they might find some of the language objectionable, but by the end of the decade punk rockers had made such language commonplace in music directed at teenagers. However, public reaction against such lyrics had become so strong that by 1990 most record companies were putting warning labels on raunchy albums, and some stores were refusing to sell such recordings to minors.

Questions of another kind are raised by portrayals of sex designed to sell products or attract viewers to a form of entertainment. It is a truism of both the advertising and entertainment worlds that sex sells, despite the fact that some church groups have organized campaigns against what they consider television's overexposure of women's breasts and buttocks.

When the owner of a weekly newspaper in rural southern Indiana announced that he was going to install a cable television system to serve his community, he said he was the target of two questions, "You are going to show R-rated movies, aren't you?" and "You aren't going to show R-rated movies, are you?" He said he decided he wouldn't.[48] Four years later, under another owner, the system was offering—at a premium—channels that included R-rated movies.

One of the many valid questions about sex in the media is, "To what extent does it contribute to reinforcing stereotypes about sexual roles?" What of the brewers' television ads that show trim, virile young men trooping off the job into a bar where they have a great time ordering beer by the pitcher? The only women in sight either are looking at the men adoringly or are waitresses, who not only serve the men but are the objects of their playful pranks. Or consider the plight, in another beer ad, of two young men condemned to live forever among a bevy of scantily clad women bearing their favorite brew. True, some brewers also are advising their customers to "know when to say when," but is there a connection with the party atmosphere that pervades many university campuses? Or with the sexual assaults that are a problem at most universities?

---

45. Interview with Norman Isaacs.
46. Interview with the former publisher.
47. Michael Cieply, "Records May Soon Carry Warning that Lyrics Are Morally Hazardous," *Wall Street Journal*, 31 July 1985.
48. Conversation with the author.

Clearly, the professional world shows no clear limits as to how far media managers will go in the exploitation of sex. Few newspapers carry cigarette advertising, but for years many carried advertising for X-rated movies. Many accept advertising from topless bars or for "escort services." Some newspapers have stopped publishing photographs and the dimensions of topless performers. Others use photographs of seminude performers but use an airbrush to clothe them within the limits of decency. There is no way of knowing whether such delicacy is dictated by ethical considerations or by an unwillingness to offend some portion of the newspaper's subscribers.

Whatever their standards with respect to the treatment of sex, very few of the mainstream mass media will show the act that creates life. Even today, allusions to it are treated delicately in most newspapers and general interest magazines. However, a syndicated column written by June Reinisch, director of the Kinsey Institute at Indiana University, has brought to many newspapers a straightforward approach to such once-taboo topics as oral sex and impotency. So has the necessity to inform readers about the more likely means of transmitting the human immunodeficiency virus, which causes AIDS, from one person to another. Some publishers have discovered that their newspapers will survive publication of the word "condom."

It still is a crime to engage in public sexual intercourse, whether "at high noon in Times Square," as Chief Justice Burger wrote in *Paris,* or elsewhere. But there are questions about the logic of his conclusion that the criminal nature of the act justifies making its public portrayal a crime if that portrayal serves no serious purpose. Author Ross Macdonald, in the *Times* article referred to above, noted the inconsistency in the chief justice's logic. Murder also is a crime, whether committed in Times Square at high noon or in private. Further, murder occurs more frequently in the United States, by most measures, than in any other nation except those racked by religious or ethnic strife. In 1987, about 20,000 persons in the United States had their lives taken by another person.[49] As a cause of death, murder ranked twelfth in frequency, just behind suicide.[50] Murder has become a leading cause of death among male teenagers. And yet with respect to the portrayal of violent death—whether on television, in the movies, or in books—there is no outcry comparable to the outcry over the portrayal of sexual activity. Murder has been a staple of drama and fiction from earliest times. Homer's *Odyssey,* written three thousand years ago, describes in gory detail the manner in which Odysseus killed his wife's suitors when he returned home in disguise after the siege of Troy. And any well-done version of Shakespeare's *Macbeth* literally drips blood.

However, it is only in recent times that filmmakers and television scriptwriters have produced works in which violence as violence plays the leading role. Special-effects technicians have become experts in showing

---

49. Federal Bureau of Investigation, Index of U.S. Crime, 1987, *The World Almanac 1989,* p. 819.
50. National Center for Health Statistics, U.S. Department of Health and Human Services, *The World Almanac 1989,* p. 808.

what happens when a chain saw cuts through flesh and bone, an ax cleaves a skull, or a bullet smashes through a brain. Films like *Texas Chainsaw Massacre, Maniac,* and *The Slumber Party Massacre* have become cult movies for younger people. Television producers, responding to pressure from some groups, have cleaned up their scripts somewhat from the days when viewers could see twenty or so persons killed in one evening's prime time,[51] but dramas featuring various kinds of skullduggery continue to dot the upper levels of the Nielsen ratings. Statistics measuring the effects of violence in the media probably are no more reliable than statistics measuring the effects of sexually explicit materials. And yet there are research studies showing that people who watch a lot of television tend to believe crime is more prevalent than it is,[52] and that exposure to filmed violence, especially when it is linked with sex, tends to desensitize the members of the audience toward sex crimes.[53] This is not to suggest, in a textbook devoted in large part to First Amendment freedoms, that obscenity laws should be broadened to include portrayals of violence. It is to suggest that professionals in a position to control what the media offer to the public may need to think beyond a consideration of what sells as entertainment or what will sell a product. Sex and death are inescapable realities. Treated with respect, sex can unite two persons like no other force. Treated with respect, death can be a sublime escape, or a tragedy reminding the survivors that life is too precious to waste. Trivialized, both sex and the taking of life can become meaningless acts.

FOR REVIEW

1. Outline the arguments for and against restrictions on obscenity.

2. What is the nature of the crime of obscenity?

3. How did the Supreme Court define obscenity in *Roth* v. *United States?*

4. List and explain the changes in obscenity law resulting from the Court's decision in *Miller* v. *California.*

5. Outline and explain the role of the jury in obscenity cases. Is it true that a jury has unbridled discretion in determining what is obscene? Why or why not?

6. What is the "community" in an obscenity case? How are its standards of sexual candor determined?

7. Some people in your community become upset over two developments: The offering for rent of sexually explicit videotapes by video stores and a cluster

---

51. Author's count during one evening as a relative's captive audience in the 1960s.
52. George Gerbner et al., "The 'Mainstreaming' of America: Violence Profile No. 11," *Journal of Communication,* vol. 30, 1980, No. 3, pp. 10–29.
53. Donnerstein et al. n. 40.

of massage parlors that are widely believed to be fronts for prostitution. The stores that rent the videotapes do not advertise them, nor are scenes from them visible to the customers who come to the stores to rent other kinds of cassettes. The sexually explicit videos are kept in a locked room which is opened only at the request of a customer known to the manager. The city council is asked to adopt an ordinance placing strict license requirements on both kinds of enterprises. One provision in the proposed ordinance would give the police chief authority to revoke a license if the holder of it was believed to be in the business of purveying obscenity. You are asked to advise the council in drafting the final form of the ordinance. What advice would you give?

8. Let us assume that a licensing ordinance has been adopted. Let us also assume that the manager of one video rental store has twice been arrested for violating its terms. The police chief consults the prosecutor and concludes that under your state's law the store can be padlocked and its contents seized as the fruits of racketeering. Is that conclusion correct? Why or why not?

9. Make the same assumptions as in question 8 with respect to one of the massage parlors. How, then, would you answer the two questions in question 8?

CHAPTER 10

CHAPTER 10

In the last decade of the twentieth century, one news medium remains subject
to control by the federal government. That medium is broadcasting, both radio
and television, and its close relatives, cable and satellite television. The degree of
control is much less than it was in 1980, when President Carter initiated a program of deregulation that was carried forward and expanded by presidents
Reagan and Bush. But as this is being written, committees of Congress are considering legislation that would restore some control over public affairs programming on radio and television and over the rates charged by cable television operators. Even during the period of deregulation, remaining controls, combined
with pressure from influential members of Congress, have affected broadcast
public affairs programming, including the presentation of news. Under existing
law, broadcasting stations are the only news media that can be required to sell or
give time to candidates for public office. Such stations also are the only media

whose right to operate depends, at least in theory, on how well they serve what the Communications Act calls "the public interest, convenience and necessity."

Broadcasters are subject to control because theirs is the only medium of mass communication that operates under licenses granted by the federal government. Radio stations are licensed for periods of seven years, television stations, for five.[1] Although renewal is not automatic, it is nearly so. Holders of broadcast licenses must live with the possibility, however remote, that some individual or organization may challenge the holder's right to continue to operate. If such challenge occurs, and is taken seriously by federal regulatory officials, the holder must prove that it has operated in the public interest. If the holder cannot do so, it must surrender the license.

Licensing has been in effect since 1927, when Congress passed the first Radio Act. Congress did so at the request of broadcasters and the public to end competition for frequencies that had brought chaos to the fledgling industry. Commercial radio began in the early 1920s and soon became a popular form of entertainment, but because station operators could use any AM band frequency they pleased, with whatever power they could afford, electronic interference frequently made it impossible for listeners to hear the station of their choice.[2] Congress responded by creating the Federal Radio Commission (FRC) and giving it authority to license broadcasters, requiring them to operate on an assigned frequency. The commission also specified the power, or wattage, with which they could operate.

Congress rationalized its actions by adopting a theory that has made it possible to impose rules on broadcasters that in any other medium would be considered a violation of the First Amendment. The theory is based on the assumption that the electronic spectrum, made up of electromagnetic frequencies, belongs to all the people. Further, those frequencies are a scarce commodity because they are limited in number. Therefore, government, acting on behalf of the people, has a right to assign frequencies to operators who will best serve the public interest. One federal appeals court ruled that the right to use a frequency is a public trust,

---

1. Omnibus Budget Reconciliation Act of 1981, § 1241 (a), 47 U.S.C. 307(c) (1982).
2. E. Barnouw, *A History of Broadcasting in the United States*, Vol. 1, *Tower of Babel* (1966).

which carries with it an obligation to offer public affairs programming serving all elements of the station's audience. If the holder of a frequency does not do so, listeners who feel they have been poorly served have a right to challenge renewal of its license.[3]

In the beginning, the government's main interest in broadcasting was the regulation of frequencies to prevent interference. But the focus soon shifted to ensuring variety in programming and to preventing broadcasters from becoming propagandists. During the 1930s, when Adolf Hitler used radio to help him rise to power in Germany, broadcasting was recognized as a powerful means of reaching people and persuading them to a point of view. In response to that recognition, the Federal Communications Commission, which supplanted the FRC in 1934, adopted rules designed to prevent one political candidate, or one point of view on public issues, from dominating the airwaves. Although these rules raised serious First Amendment questions, the rules were upheld by the courts, acting on the theory that diversity of opinion reaching the audience is more important than license holders exercising unrestricted freedom of speech. Thus, it became legally established that owners of broadcasting stations do not enjoy the same editorial freedom as owners of newspapers and magazines. For instance, the FCC ruled during World War II that editorializing by broadcasters was not in the public interest.[4] That ruling since has been changed, although most broadcasters choose not to present formal editorials.

For decades, broadcasting prospered under the federal regulatory regime. Although the number of daily newspapers has remained stable at around 1750, broadcasting stations have proliferated. By 1990, about 10,700 radio stations were almost equally divided between the AM and the FM bands. Television, which did not become commercially feasible until the 1950s, reached almost all the people through about 675 VHF stations and 775 UHF.[5] VHF stations, which are capable of delivering a clearer picture over a longer distance with less power than are UHF stations, operate over the air on channels 2 through 13; UHF, on channels 14 through 69.

As this is written, long-established patterns in broadcasting, including relationships with the advertisers who pay for the programming, are undergoing severe strain. Cable television, which began in 1948 to bring programming from distant stations to a few residents of Mahoney City, Pennsylvania, has become a giant, reaching 50 million subscribers, or about 56 percent of the homes with television sets.[6] Cable systems began simply by retransmitting the programs of commercial television stations to viewers whose home antennas could not clearly pick up over-the-air signals. Today cable systems offer not only commercial stations,

---

3. Office of Communication of the United Church of Christ v. FCC, 359 F.2d 994 (D.C.Cir. 1966).
4. In re Mayflower Broadcasting Corp., 8 F.C.C. 338 (1941).
5. The number of broadcasting stations licensed by the FCC is listed regularly in *Broadcasting* magazine.
6. Paul Kagen Associates, as reported in "Untangling the Debate over Cable Television," *Wall Street Journal,* 19 March 1990, and Nielsen Media Research, as reported in "The '80s: Plugged in to TV," *USA Today,* 1 December 1989.

both local and regional, but news, sports, movies, music, documentaries, discussion, weather, the arts, and other programming not available over the air, including complete coverage of Congress. Cable stations also have become a means through which powerful independent stations in Atlanta, Chicago, New York, and Los Angeles can reach nationwide audiences. One result has been to fragment the television market: In 1982, the three major television networks—ABC, CBS, and NBC—reached 83 percent of the nation's viewers. At the end of 1989, that share had decreased to 67 percent and was continuing to drop.[7]

The rapid proliferation of electronic media, coupled with a change in the political climate in the 1980s, raised challenges to the federal regulatory system. Are broadcasting frequencies still a scare commodity requiring government intervention to ensure variety in programming? The line-of-sight signal distance on the FM band makes it possible for any given frequency to be assigned to stations in many cities scattered across the country. Although AM radio has become only marginally profitable, the FCC is considering extending both ends of the commercial AM band to accommodate more stations. Cities of less than 100,000 population commonly have at least one AM station and as many as four FM stations. Thus, the owner of even a cheap, portable radio can tune to any one of a dozen or more stations in most localities. Even without cable, most television set owners can pick up five or more stations. With cable the number of available channels can reach fifty or more. In contrast, fewer than two dozen cities still have fully competitive newspapers, and, in most markets, avid readers may have a choice of no more than six or eight local, regional, and national newspapers.

Federal Communications Commission studies begun during the last year of the Carter administration led in 1981 to the lifting of most programming requirements from commercial radio.[8] Three years later, commercial television stations were given similar relief.[9] In 1985, the FCC released a report in which it concluded that the fairness doctrine—a central tenet of broadcast regulation since 1949—no longer served the public interest.[10] Four years later, that conclusion was upheld by a federal appeals court.[11] The first two steps in this progression were challenged by groups acting in the belief that the quality of public debate on the air would decline and that easier license renewal procedures would make it more difficult for minority groups to acquire broadcasting licenses. Critics of deregulation also decried the disappearance of wholesome children's programming and a decrease in public affairs programming, particularly on radio. Supporters of the changes, including some members of the FCC, argued that market forces are more likely to move broadcasters to offer programming in the public interest than

---

7. Nielsen Media Research.
8. Report and Order (BC Dkt. No. 79–219), 84 F.C.C.2d 968; reconsidered, 87 F.C.C.2d 797 (1981).
9. Report and Order (BC Dkt. No. 81-496), F.C.C. 84-294, 22 August 1984.
10. *Inquiry into Alternatives to the General Fairness Obligations of Broadcast Licensees,* 102 F.C.C.2d 143 (1985).
11. Syracuse Peace Council v. Federal Communications Commission, 867 F.2d 654 (D.C.Cir. 1989).

are decrees from a federal agency. Powerful members of Congress decried the passing of the fairness doctrine, but several attempts to write it into law foundered under the threat of a presidential veto.

Because in several vital areas the state of broadcast law can best be described as somewhere between limbo and chaos, this chapter attempts to focus on fundamentals. We will begin by looking at history to see why broadcasting evolved as a regulated medium. We will examine the major cases upholding regulations that still are in effect, including the licensing procedure. We will find, as suggested earlier, that broadcasting, particularly television, is perceived as an especially powerful medium. For that reason, its use by candidates for public office is carefully regulated.

Broadcasters also are more restricted than owners of print media in their right to present sexual materials or language some people consider offensive. They can be censured, fined, or in extreme cases, lose their licenses for broadcasting programs that are indecent, even though they are not obscene by *Miller-Roth* standards.

Major Cases

- *Branch* v. *Federal Communications Commission*, 824 F.2d 37, (D.C.Cir. 1987).

- *CBS, Inc.* v. *Federal Communications Commission*, 453 U.S. 367, 101 S.Ct. 2813, 69 L.Ed.2d 706 (1981).

- *Federal Communications Commission* v. *Pacifica Foundation*, 438 U.S. 726, 98 S.Ct. 3026, 57 L.Ed.2d 1073 (1978).

- *Miami Herald Publishing Co.* v. *Tornillo*, 418 U.S. 241, 94 S.Ct. 2831, 41 L.Ed.2d 730 (1974).

- *National Broadcasting Co.* v. *United States*, 319 U.S. 190, 63 S.Ct. 997, 87 L.Ed. 1344 (1943).

- *Office of Communication, United Church of Christ* v. *Federal Communications Commission*, 359 F.2d 994 (D.C.Cir. 1966).

- *Paulsen* v. *Federal Communications Commission*, 491 F.2d 887 (9th Cir. 1974).

- *Red Lion Broadcasting Co.* v. *Federal Communications Commission*, 395 U.S. 367, 89 S.Ct. 1794, 23 L.Ed.2d 371 (1969).

- *Sable Communications of California* v. *Federal Communications Commission*, 492 U.S. _ _ _, 109 S.Ct. 2829, 106 L.Ed.2d 93 (1989).

- *Syracuse Peace Council* v. *Federal Communications Commission*, 867 F.2d 654 (D.C.Cir. 1989).

- *Telecommunications Research and Action Center* v. *Federal Communications Commission*, 801 F.2d 501 (D.C.Cir. 1986).

LICENSING IN THE PUBLIC INTEREST

The Regulation of Broadcasting

There is no doubt about the government's authority to regulate broadcasting in the public interest. The legal challenges to that authority were met and overcome more than fifty years ago.

The first questions were raised in the 1920s, when the government, in cooperation with Canada and Mexico, adopted an orderly process for assigning frequencies, prescribing limits on transmitter power, and setting hours of operation. Ninety-six of the 107 channels on the AM band were reserved for stations in the United States. Forty of these were set aside for clear-channel operation; that is, for the exclusive use of one powerful station. The rationale was that the clear-channel stations could reach out, especially at night, and provide news and entertainment for listeners in even the most remote parts of the country. The remaining fifty-six channels were assigned to low-power local stations on a zoned basis. The result was supposed to be a system of broadcasting that would serve the entire nation with a minimum of electronic interference.

Stations that were forced to change frequencies or reduce power if they were to retain their licenses challenged the government's authority. This led to court decisions holding that broadcasters were engaged in interstate commerce and therefore were within the reach of federal regulation.[12] Owners threatened with loss of their licenses because they refused to comply with the new regulations argued that the government was taking their property without due process of law, thus violating the Fifth and Fourteenth Amendments to the Constitution. Courts held that a broadcasting license was not a form of property belonging to the station owner. It was only a token of the station owner's right to use a frequency belonging to the people. That right was valid only as long as the station owner served the "public interest, convenience, and necessity." However, a broadcaster faced with nonrenewal or revocation of his license was entitled to a hearing before the Federal Radio Commission. If the commission then acted within its powers in deciding not to renew or to revoke, the due process requirement was met.[13]

Can a refusal to renew a broadcasting license violate the station owner's First Amendment right to freedom of speech? That question was raised in *Trinity Methodist Church, South* v. *Federal Radio Commission,*[14] decided by the U.S. Court of Appeals for the District of Columbia Circuit in 1932. Radio station KGEF in Los Angeles was owned by the church, whose pastor, Rev. R. P. Shuler, used it as an extension of his pulpit. He was an opinionated, outspoken preacher who mixed politics with religion and became one of few persons held in contempt of court for statements made over the air.[15] His targets included gamblers, bootleggers, labor unions, judges, the bar association, Jews, and Roman

---

12. United States v. American Bond & Mortgage Co., 31 F.2d 448 (N.D.Ill. 1929).
13. Technical Radio Laboratory v. Federal Radio Commission, 36 F.2d 111 (D.C.Cir. 1929).
14. 62 F.2d 850 (D.C.Cir. 1932).
15. Ex parte Shuler, 292 P. 481 (Calif. 1930).

Catholics. As he saw it, all were involved in ungodly immorality, and he said so in strong terms, using the station to spread his views. When KGEF's license came up for renewal in 1930, some listeners objected. After hearing more than ninety witnesses, the FRC refused to renew. The church appealed, arguing that the commission's action was a prior restraint of the kind the Supreme Court recently had condemned in *Near* v. *Minnesota*.[16]

The Court of Appeals rejected that argument, holding that the commission was acting within its powers when it refused to renew the license. The court said that a license to broadcast did not give the holder an unlimited right to spread hatred "from one corner of the country to the other." If licensees could do so, "then this great science, instead of a boon, will become a scourge, and the nation a theater for the display of individual passions and the collision of personal interests." The court said the commission's action was "neither censorship nor previous restraint," nor was it "a whittling away of the rights guaranteed by the First Amendment." It was simply an exercise of the FRC's authority to make certain that the airwaves were used in a way that served the public interest. It was in the public's interest to deny use of one of those frequencies to spread Dr. Shuler's strong opinions.

These early lower-court decisions, handed down when broadcasting was in its infancy, proved influential in shaping judicial attitudes. They established that broadcasters must obtain a license from the federal government before they can go on the air. To obtain a license, they must promise to serve the public interest. To retain it, broadcasters must prove that they have done so. No matter how much broadcasters may invest in buildings and equipment in order to go on the air, they do not own the license that permits them to do so. The license is merely a permit to use a frequency that belongs to the people as a whole, a permit that may not be used at the whim of the holder. If it should be used in a one-sided way to spread a message that violates the public's concept of decency and fair play, the right to use a frequency can be taken away. This has not happened often. But the possibility has been there since 1932 and has had an effect on broadcasting for sixty years.

Thus, almost from the beginning, the courts have applied a different set of rules to broadcasters than to other media. A newspaper publisher's right to express a point of view is limited only by the willingness of the people to keep on buying the publication. As we have seen, the courts have given publishers and film makers wide latitude to say what they please, particularly about public issues. Broadcasters have not enjoyed that same degree of freedom because they must go to government for a license that gives them a right to use an assigned frequency on which to transmit their messages to the public.

Broadcasting and the Supreme Court

Radio came to maturity in World War II. Germany's conquest of Poland, France, Denmark, and Norway under direction from Adolf Hitler was brought to

---

16.   283 U.S. 697, 51 S.Ct. 625, 75 L.Ed. 1357 (1931).

Americans step by step through shortwave transmissions that were rebroadcast over networks of domestic stations. The voice of Hitler himself came directly from his carefully orchestrated Nazi party rallies. Correspondents such as William L. Shirer, H. V. Kaltenborn, and Edward R. Murrow broadcast dramatic accounts of these and other events. When London came under massive German air attacks in 1940, Americans sitting in their living rooms could hear by radio the crack of antiaircraft guns, the wail of air raid sirens, and the thud of bombs, while a reporter described the action.

Radio also served other purposes. During the Great Depression it became the only source of entertainment for many who no longer could afford to go to the movies. Networks of local radio stations were formed by the National Broadcasting Company and the Columbia Broadcasting System to carry entertainment and news across the country. So great was the demand for such programming that NBC broke its network into two, called the Blue and the Red networks. Radio also provided a nationwide audience for championship boxing matches, college football, and the World Series of baseball. A ruckus over the broadcasting of the latter event gave the Supreme Court its first opportunity to review the powers of the Federal Communications Commission, which had replaced the Federal Radio Commission in 1934. With the change in name came broadened responsibilities, not only for radio, but for interstate telephone and telegraph systems.

In 1938, the FCC became concerned enough about the growth of network broadcasting to conduct seventy-three days of hearings, spread over more than a year. While it was pondering the mass of evidence gathered by the hearings, a new network, Mutual, bid for and obtained the right to broadcast the World Series of 1939 between the New York Yankees and the Cincinnati Reds. Because Mutual stations were relatively few, baseball fans in some parts of the United States were unable to hear the games. Stations affiliated with CBS and NBC were willing to air the games in areas not served by Mutual affiliates, but were blocked by terms of their network contracts. The resulting furor was reflected in the chain broadcasting regulations drafted by the FCC to take effect in 1941.

National Broadcasting Co. v. United States, **319 U.S. 190, 63 S.Ct. 997, 87 L.Ed. 1344 (1943).** The Federal Communications Commission conceded that it could not regulate the networks directly because they did not require a license to operate. However, it proceeded on the theory that it could regulate network practices by imposing restrictions on the affiliated stations. The new rules said that any station that was a party to a network contract containing certain prohibited conditions would not have its license renewed. NBC and CBS joined forces in asking a federal court to nullify the rules. The court dismissed their plea. In *National Broadcasting Co.* v. *United States,* the Supreme Court affirmed. It held that to protect the public interest, the FCC can impose reasonable regulations on broadcasters consistent with the powers given it by Congress.

The Court began its analysis by noting that NBC and CBS had gained an almost complete monopoly over programming, especially at night. Together, they controlled more than 85 percent of the night-time wattage, a measure of a station's ability to reach its audience. The Court also took note of the fact that this control had prevented persons in some parts of the country from hearing the 1939 World Series.

Justice Felix Frankfurter, writing for five members of the Court, proceeded to an examination of each of the eight abuses found by the FCC and that it sought to correct:

1. A station affiliated with NBC or CBS could not broadcast a program originated by any other network. The effect of this restriction was to make it difficult for other networks to be formed. It also had the effect of denying certain programming to persons in some parts of the country. The FCC proposed to correct this by refusing to renew the license of any station signing an exclusive affiliation agreement.

2. Both networks had agreed not to sell programs to any other station in an area covered by an affiliate. Thus, if a local station chose for some reason not to carry a network offering, no other station in the same area could pick it up. The FCC rules would permit other stations to carry such rejected programming.

3. Affiliation agreements were for five-year periods. The FCC wanted to limit them to two years, or one year less than the three-year license period then in effect.

4. All three networks required their affiliates to take a certain number of hours of network programming each day, thus limiting the time available for local programming. These required hours included prime time, when the station's potential audience was the largest. The FCC proposed cutting back this mandatory time.

5. Affiliates were restricted in the number of network offerings they could refuse. Thus local stations were captives of the networks, which, in turn, let their advertisers dictate program content. The public, then, was being offered programming over which local license holders had little, if any, control. The FCC saw this as an abdication of the public interest role of broadcasting. The proposed regulations gave local stations the right to refuse any network program.

6. The networks also were becoming station owners. NBC owned ten; CBS, eight. These included some of the most powerful stations in the country, operating on the most desirable frequencies. The FCC said that if it could start over, it would not license any stations owned by a network. Since it could not do that it would simply limit a network to one station in any given market and reserve for later the decision as to the maximum number a network might own.

7. NBC operated two networks out of the same studios in Rockefeller Center in New York City. The FCC said this was one too many, but took no action on a recommendation that NBC be required to sell one of them. Later, the FCC adopted the recommendation, and one of NBC's two networks became the American Broadcasting Company.

8. NBC went so far as to control the local advertising rates its affiliates might charge for commercials inserted into network programs. The FCC would leave local stations free to charge what they would for advertising.

The networks argued that these proposals went beyond the powers Congress had given the Federal Communications Commission. If they were carried into effect, the government would violate the networks' First Amendment freedoms. The majority of the Court disagreed. In doing so, it adopted and amplified the public interest theme that had run through the lower-court decisions summarized in the first section of this chapter.

Reviewing the history of radio, Frankfurter said that the old FRC was brought into existence not merely to act as a sort of scientific traffic officer, policing frequencies and transmitter power, but to make certain that the new medium operated in the "public interest, convenience, and necessity." These words, he wrote, were not an empty litany, but a grant of power authorizing the commission to use its judgment in coping with the medium's complications. He continued:

> The "public interest" to be served under the Communications Act is thus the interest of the listening public in "the larger and more effective use of radio."
>
> The avowed aim of the Communications Act of 1934 was to secure the maximum benefits of radio to all of the people of the United States. To that end Congress endowed the Federal Communications Commission with comprehensive powers to promote and realize the vast potentialities of radio.

Thus the Court gave its endorsement to a principle that had emerged more than a decade earlier. Broadcasting is regulated so that it will serve the public in the broadest possible way. Those who are fortunate enough to obtain a license must use it first to serve their audiences and then to serve their own interests.

But surely, the networks argued, this mandate did not extend to them. They were not licensed. They merely provided needed programming to stations that were.

Frankfurter reminded the networks that their practices had denied some of that programming to people who had wanted it very badly. Thus, the FCC had intervened properly to make certain that the networks, too, served the public interest. To ensure that radio does serve the public, he wrote, Congress "gave the Commission not niggardly but expansive powers." This included authority to impose special rules on stations "engaged in chain broadcasting."

Frankfurter turned next to the argument that the regulations proposed by the FCC would abridge the networks' freedom of speech. He wrote: "If that be so, it would follow that every person whose application for a license to operate a station is denied by the Commission is thereby denied his constitutional right of free speech."

But that is not the case, the justice continued. Radio is not like newspapers or magazines. It operates in a medium that imposes physical limits on the number of stations that can use the available frequencies. It is not open to all who have the desire and the money to erect a transmitter. Some who would like to go on the air must be turned down. Congress gave the authority to make such choices to the

Federal Communications Commission, acting for the people as a whole. Frankfurter said that if the FCC were to use the authority ''to choose among applicants upon the basis of their political, economic or social views, or upon any other capricious basis,'' it would violate its trust.

But that was not the case in this instance, Frankfurter concluded. The FCC was using its licensing powers to strike down restrictive network rules that clearly had prevented member stations from serving the public interest. In doing so, he said, it had acted well within the authority given to it by Congress. The reasonable use of that authority did not violate the First Amendment.

The Court's decision was a solid victory for the Federal Communications Commission. Its proposed network regulations were put into effect and have carried over into the television era. But, in a broader sense, the *National Broadcasting Co.* decision has become a part of the foundation of the commission's power. The Court said that its grant of authority from Congress is to be construed broadly. The commission's authority is to be used to ensure that broadcasters serve the public, in the full meaning of that term. When broadcasters raise First Amendment questions, courts look first at the interests of the audience. Because not everyone who wants to do so can go on the air, those who are able to get a license must bow to the free-speech needs of those who cannot.

Licensing Procedures and Policies

Only rarely these days is a new frequency made available to potential licensees, although some frequencies allocated to smaller markets have not been claimed because of doubt that a station can make a profit. More commonly, individuals or organizations wanting to get into broadcasting either must buy a station, and the right to its frequency, from a licensee, or launch a challenge to renewal of a license. The latter course is the more difficult because licensees who are deemed to have operated in the public interest are given preference by the FCC. To be successful a challenger not only must offer convincing proof that the holder has not operated in the public interest but must convince the FCC that the challenger is likely to do so and is financially able to keep the station on the air for at least a year.[17] Radio licenses are granted for seven-year periods; television, for five.

Obtaining a License

Although the government charges nothing more than a modest filing fee for a broadcast license, the successful applicant obtains a right that can be quite valuable. In 1989, the average AM station grossed $361,000; the average FM station, $1.4 million.[18] Prices of AM stations sold that year ranged from $100,000 to $26 million; FM stations ranged from $1.5 million to $100 million. Sale prices of television stations ranged upward from the latter figure to more than $500 million.

---

17. Television Deregulation, 98 F.C.C.2d at 1091-96. 56 P & F Rad.Reg.2d at 1017-20 (1984).
18. Geraldine Fabrikant, ''Struggling Stations in Search of a Niche,'' *New York Times*, 20 May 1990.

Despite the fact that there is no charge for use of the frequency, getting a station on the air can be expensive. If there is competition for a new frequency, applicants will have to pay thousands of dollars in legal fees and, if successful, additional sums for studios, offices and a transmitter. Such costs can run well into six figures for an FM station in a city of 100,000.

Persons or organizations seeking a broadcasting license in a competitive proceeding must convince the FCC that they are best qualified to use the available frequency in the public interest. Several factors govern the commission's deliberations[19]:

1. Diversity in the marketplace of ideas. The commission's policy encourages competitive points of view. An applicant who owns no other media properties in the same area will be favored over one who does. In the most favored position is an applicant who owns no other stations. Since 1975, daily newspapers have been barred from acquiring broadcasting stations within their own circulation area.[20]

2. Owner participation in the station's operation. The commission's policy assumes that owners who live in the same community and who take part in the station's operation are more likely to focus on local issues than are absentee owners.

3. Ownership by minorities and women. Starting in 1978, the commission gave a priority to blacks (other than Hispanics), Asians or Pacific Islanders, American Indians or Alaskan natives, Hispanics, and women. In 1985, a federal appeals court held that in granting a preference to women, the FCC exceeded its authority.[21] Congress granted that authority in 1987. Challenges to both racial and gender preferences were overruled by the Supreme Court in 1990.[22]

4. The past broadcast record of the applicants. Evidence of exceptional public service as a broadcaster is a plus factor; evidence of poor service, a minus. Average performance is not counted.

5. Programming. A prospective licensee must have a plan to offer programming that will serve the needs of the station's audience.

6. Efficiency of operation. This is a technical factor involving the quality of the station's signal.

7. The character of the owners. The keys here are honesty and candor. Because the FCC's enforcement procedures rely to a great extent on reports prepared by station management, and endorsed by the owner or owners, any proven record of sharp dealings probably will disqualify an applicant.

19. Policy Statement on Comparative Broadcast Hearings, 1 F.C.C.2d 393 (1965).
20. "Multiple Ownership of Standard, FM and Television Broadcast Stations," 50 F.C.C.2d 1046 (1975).
21. Steele v. Federal Communications Commission, 770 F.2d 1192 (D.C.Cir. 1985).
22. George Will, "Court Ruling Liberates Reverse Discrimination," *Herald-Times,* Bloomington, Indiana, 5 July 1990.

In a few instances, such a record also has resulted in refusal to renew or in renewal for less than the full license term.

8. Financial stability. Prospective broadcasters not only must prove they have funding to obtain a studio and erect a transmitter, but must be able to fund the first year's operation.

The FCC has held repeatedly that diversity is the most important of the factors listed above. This means that, all other factors being equal, an applicant who has a financial interest in no other media is most likely to be granted a new license. *In re Santee Cooper Broadcasting Co.*[23] offers an interesting example of the fine lines the FCC draws when it decides who is going to get a potentially valuable broadcasting license. At issue was an FM frequency assigned to an area including the rapidly growing, up-scale resort community of Hilton Head, South Carolina. At the time, Hilton Head was directly served by one FM and one AM station owned by the same company.

Eighteen individuals or organizations applied for the new license. The FCC's staff winnowed these down to five: an individual, Jesse N. Williams, Jr.; a partnership, Reginald Taylor and G. Troy Mattox, doing business as Calibogue Sound; and three corporations, Women's Broadcasting Coalition, Heritage Broadcasting Corp., and Plantation Broadcasting Corp. One of the losers in the final rounds was Santee Cooper, which dropped out of contention after an administrative law judge noted that its principal stockholder owned a radio station within a two-hour drive of Hilton Head.

The corporations were carefully put together to fit the FCC's list of preferences. Women's Coalition was made up of three women who owned no other businesses. However, the husband of one of the women and the father of a second, along with other family members, owned the telephone company serving Hilton Head. That company also owned a cable television system serving three communities within a hundred miles of Hilton Head. One of the women said she would make a seventy-mile round trip each day to serve as manager of the proposed FM station. Another would make the same commute to serve as sales manager. The third would be its operations manager. One of the women was an office manager for the family telephone company. None had any radio experience, although one noted in her application that she had once visited a radio station. All three said they did not plan to move to Hilton Head but listed activities in fraternal and business organizations with connections to the island.

The major stockholders in Heritage were a husband and wife who also were stockholders in corporations operating radio and television stations in Texas and South Carolina. The wife, who would become the general manager of the new station, had been living in Hilton Head for several years and was vice president of her husband's firm, which was engaged in media investment analysis and brokerage. She was active in a several organizations, including a Parent-Teachers Association and the Hilton Head Island Historical Society. Ten percent of Heritage's stock was assigned to a black couple. The man, who received a Bronze

---

23.   99 F.C.C.2d 781 (1984); 100 F.C.C.2d 469 (1985).

Star for valor in the Vietnam War and who currently was manager of an FM station in Sumter, South Carolina, would become station manager. The woman would become the business manager.

Plantation was entirely owned by a woman who lived in North Carolina. Her application said she had no ownership interest in any other media. It also said she would become full-time manager of the station, although her application listed less than a year's experience in business. Her husband, the FCC noted, owned 30 percent of a television station in Greensboro, North Carolina, and was an officer of two FM stations, one of them in another South Carolina resort city, Myrtle Beach.

One of the partners in Calibogue owned an FM station in Blackshear, Georgia. The other, a black, was a teacher and guidance counselor in the public schools there. He also was a member of the city council and had been honored by being chosen Outstanding Citizen of the Year and Outstanding Teacher of the Year. Although he had no broadcast experience, the application said he would work twenty-five hours a month at the station during the school year and full-time during the summer selling advertising and announcing.

The individual applicant, Williams, a black, was chief investigator for the public defender in Charleston, South Carolina, about fifty-five miles from Hilton Head. He had worked part-time on two radio stations, primarily as an announcer of gospel music programs. He also was a promoter of gospel music concerts. Other than that, neither he nor his wife had any media interests. He said running the station would become his full-time occupation.

During the hearing, there was considerable controversy over whether the members of the Women's Coalition were indeed free of ties to other communications media. The FCC examiner concluded that they were involved in ownership of the telephone company and its cable television subsidiary, leaving Williams as the only applicant who had no other media interests. That gave him a clear preference over the others. However, the two came out even, and ahead of the others, in their commitment to devote full time to operating the station. Williams was given "substantial enhancement credit because of his 100 percent minority ownership" and a further enhancement for the experience he had gained by conducting his radio gospel program. However, the other applicants argued that the experience should be discounted because, in their opinion, Williams had used the program to plug the gospel concerts he promoted. He conceded that on occasion he had signed off by saying, "The concert is tonight. Don't forget. I will see you there." The examiner concluded that the infraction was innocent in intent and therefore should detract only minimally from Williams's otherwise strong position. Therefore, he was awarded the construction permit, with the Women's Coalition coming in second.

Williams, with the help of a partner who was not mentioned in his original application, followed through and built his station, WIJY-FM, on Hilton Head Island, getting it on the air in 1988. In the following year, he sold it to Cookerly Communications for $2.2 million.[24]

---

24. Interview with Monty Jett, general manager of WIJY-FM, 15 June 1990.

License Renewal

Until the early 1980s, licensees had to be ready at renewal time to prove they had operated their stations in the public interest. Station owners were required to poll community leaders and identify controversial issues of public importance. They were expected, then, to schedule programming that would air all sides of those issues. Federal Communications Commission rules established rigid quotas for news and public affairs programming, including time devoted to interviews with public officials, religious programming, and cultural events. As proof of compliance, broadcasters had to compile, and submit along with the application for renewal, detailed logs showing how each on-the-air hour was used. These logs gave both the broadcaster and the FCC a precise measurement of the time devoted to the public interest. The logs did not measure the quality of such programming, of course, nor did it seem to matter that most stations aired their serious discussions of local issues during the early hours of Sunday morning.

Deregulation ended such mechanical measurements of "public service."[25] The rules still require broadcasters to devote "reasonable time" to public issues, but what is reasonable is not strictly defined. Stations in large markets can meet their obligation by focusing on issues of concern to their particular audience. Thus, a station offering programming for blacks or Hispanics can meet its public affairs obligation by focusing on issues of importance to the black or Hispanic communities.

Although the FCC no longer mandates procedures broadcasters must use to identify controversial public issues, radio license holders must show that they have made a reasonable attempt to identify such issues. They also must place in their "public file" a listing of five or ten issues that have been the subject of public affairs programming. Television license holders must compile on a quarterly basis a list of five or more issues that the stations featured during the quarter and report how they covered them.

Normally, license renewal is automatic, or nearly so. The licensee need only send a postcard form to the FCC.[26] However, 5 percent of the television and radio licensees are selected at random for more intensive scrutiny. Stations in this sample must submit program audit forms designed to show how they operated in the public interest. They also are subject to on-site inspection of their public file, in which they supposedly have placed evidence of their public service, along with copies of complaints from viewers and listeners, and their responses thereto.

Licensing and Affirmative Action

One factor considered in license renewals has been little affected by deregulation: Broadcasters must show that they not only hire minorities and women but promote them to positions of leadership. The only exemptions are for small stations in areas in which minorities make up less than 5 percent of the population.

---

25. *Report and Order on Deregulation of Radio*, 50 R.R.2d 93 (1981), and *Report and Order*, MM Dkt. No. 893-670 F.C.C. 84-293 (1984).
26. Memorandum Opinion and Order, 46 Fed.Reg. 26236 (1981).

The FCC's goal for broadcasters is employment equity, that is, a station staff that mirrors the racial and sexual patterns of the community.[27] The required annual affirmative action reports to the commission indicate that the policy is having an effect. Women make up 44.5 percent of the work force; minorities, 20.5 percent. In 1986, women held 37.4 percent of the jobs in broadcasting, and minorities, 16 percent.[28] Among the higher-level positions—officials and managers, professionals, technicians, and sales workers—women held 29.2 percent of the jobs. Members of minority groups held 15.4 percent of such positions.

Broadcasters seem content with that aspect of FCC policy, but policies designed to promote station ownership by minorities and women have come under fire. As noted earlier, the commission gives a preference in licensing to ownership entities including minorities and women. Promulgated in 1978, the policy has had some success. When it was adopted, fewer than 1 percent of the radio and television stations were minority owned. By 1989, the figure was 3.5 percent. That figure was not higher because of a variety of factors, starting with the fact that by 1978 most of the economically viable frequencies had been claimed. Also, policies governing license renewal greatly favor the current holder. It is no easy matter to prove that a station that has been operating profitably under the same owner for five, seven, or more years is not serving some version of the public interest. In addition, the asking price for successful stations can be an obstacle: Money-losing AM stations can be had for as little as $100,000, but to most minority aspirants that is a lot of money to put up for the prospect of perhaps losing still more.

To counter these factors, the FCC adopted a policy permitting owners of "distressed" stations to sell them at a discount and to obtain some tax relief if the sale is to a minority-controlled entity. A station is considered "distressed" if its owner is in danger of losing its license because of infractions of broadcasting regulations. Such owners can avoid loss of the license, and a consequent drastic reduction in the value of the property, by agreeing to sell to a minority owner for 75 percent of the combined fair-market value of the station and the license. From the provision's adoption in 1978 to April 1989, thirty-eight such sales took place; at that time, a divided appeals court panel held that the policy violated the equal protection clause of the Fifth Amendment.[29] The court did so in a case involving a UHF television station in Hartford, Connecticut. The station operator had been charged with fraud, and the station was on its way to an FCC revocation. When two attempts to sell the station at a distress price failed, a white male computer consultant sought to buy the station. Instead, the FCC approved a transfer to a company headed by an Hispanic. The consultant appealed to the District of Columbia Circuit Court for relief. Two of the three judges held that the FCC had not proved a link between minority ownership and program diversity, which was the

27. "Nondiscrimination in the Employment Policies and Practices of Broadcast Licensees," 60 F.C.C.2d 226 (1976).

28. "Women, Minorities Gain in Cable, Broadcast Jobs," *Wall Street Journal,* 11 March 1987.

29. Mary Lu Carnevale, "FCC Program on Minorities Dealt Setback," *Wall Street Journal,* 3 April 1989.

stated goal of the policy.[30] Nor had the FCC established that neutral alternatives, such as equal employment opportunity rules, would not further its goal. As it stood, the judges concluded, the policy discriminated against innocent non-minorities.

Six weeks later, another panel of the same court, ruling in a Florida case, upheld the preference given to minorities and women in the granting of new licenses.[31] At issue was the granting of a license to a company 90 percent owned by Hispanics to operate a UHF television station in Orlando. One of the losing companies was 20 percent owned by blacks and the other by whites. The majority said it was bound by a 1984 decision in the same circuit upholding minority set-aside programs for public works contracts.

The Supreme Court accepted both cases for review. The Court held that the court had ruled correctly in the Orlando case and mistakenly in the Hartford case.[32] By a five-to-four vote in each instance, the Court held that Congress may authorize affirmative action to promote racial and ethnic diversity and that the FCC had acted reasonably in concluding that encouraging diversity in station ownership would lead to greater diversity in programming.

Challenging License Renewal

Obviously, the Federal Communications Commission and its staff cannot subject each request for license renewal to strict scrutiny to determine whether the holder has operated in the public interest. Nor does the FCC try. And for many years it was not willing to listen, in a formal way, to people who might not be satisfied with the way a station served their particular public interest. It was not until the 1960s, and then only under orders from a federal court, that the FCC permitted public interest groups and others to offer testimony at renewal time on a station's programming. At the time, stations were required by a policy known as the "fairness doctrine" to identify controversial issues and present a balanced version of competing points of view.

Office of Communication, United Church of Christ v. Federal Communications Commission, 359 F.2d 994 (D.C.Cir. 1966).

On television station WLBT in Jackson, Mississippi, during the early years of the civil rights movement, the station readily aired the arguments of those favoring continued racial segregation but refused time to groups seeking to present the case for integration. When the station's network presented programs in which black and white entertainers were together, WLBT's viewers saw only a sign saying, "Sorry, cable trouble." The Office of Communication of the United Church of Christ joined local civil rights groups in monitoring the station's programming to build a record against it.

30. Astroline Communications Co. v. Shurberg Broadcasting of Hartford, 876 F.2d 902 (D.C.Cir. 1989).

31. Mary Lu Carnevale, "Appeals Court Unit Upholds FCC Policy Of Minority Preference on New Licenses," *Wall Street Journal,* 24 April 1989.

32. Metro Broadcasting v. Federal Communications Commission, _ _ _ U.S. _ _ _, 110 S. Ct. 2997, 111 L.Ed.2d 445 (1990).

However, when the groups sought to present their evidence to the FCC at license renewal time, they were told they lacked standing to do so. Under its rules, the FCC said, it heard evidence only from station operators who could show either electronic interference or unfair economic competition from the license holder seeking renewal. The Office of Communication took its case to the U.S. Court of Appeals for the District of Columbia Circuit. Judge Warren E. Burger, then three years away from becoming chief justice of the United States, overruled the commission. He reasoned that if viewers could intervene at license renewal time, broadcasters would have an additional incentive to be "responsive to the needs of the audience."

The broadcaster argued that if viewers were given a voice in programming decisions, the station's own right to control content would be diminished. If Burger's principle were followed to its extreme, broadcasters could be required to carry whatever programs were demanded by some segment of the audience. Burger said his decision did no go that far. It simply stood as a reminder that when a "broadcaster seeks and is granted the free and exclusive use of a limited and valuable part of the public domain," she or he accepts a "franchise... burdened by enforceable public obligations." Further, he said that by giving viewers a right to be heard on the quality of programming, his decision would diminish the FCC's role in assessing a station's performance. In the future, its role would be that of an impartial umpire, passing judgment on complaints about a station's service. No longer would it have to be both prosecutor and judge.

On remand, the commission listened to complaints from the Office of Communication and civil rights groups, then renewed WLBT's license. Again there was an appeal. Judge Burger rebuked the commission, withdrew WLBT's license, and invited new applicants for the frequency.[33]

The episode is unique in broadcasting history and has had one lasting effect. Licensees are required to announce well ahead of the expiration date that they will seek renewal and to invite public comment. Normally, nothing happens. But on occasion an individual or an organization will be unhappy enough with some part of a station's operation to intervene either by seeking to obtain the license to start up a new station or by filing a petition to deny.

If a challenger offers evidence of fraudulent operations, or of a gross abuse of the broadcaster's public service obligation, the FCC may require the station to defend itself in a hearing. Rarely do such challenges succeed, but the expense involved in preparing for a hearing can cut deeply into a licensee's profit. Two close observers of the FCC's performance have noted, "Designating a license renewal for hearing is considered by both key staff people and most commissioners almost as drastic as taking a license away."[34]

Why this is so is not evident on the record. Between 1982 and 1989, about 11,000 broadcast licenses came up for renewal. Only sixty were challenged by a competing applicant, and twenty of these were dismissed. Aside from thirteen of

---

33. Office of Communication, United Church of Christ v. Federal Communications Commission, 425 F.2d 543 (1969).

34. B. Cole and M. Oettinger, *Reluctant Regulators* (Reading, Mass.: Addison-Wesley, 1978), p. 213.

the challenges, which will be discussed more fully later in this section, only four resulted in the FCC's revoking the license. Two licenses were forfeited because the holder failed to provide the FCC with requested information, and two other cases resulted in negotiated settlements with the challengers.[35]

Despite all the emphasis in broadcast law on serving the public interest, the fact is that a licensee's character and business practices are far more likely to get him or her in trouble with the FCC than are deficiencies in programming. A study of the sixty-four revocations or failures to renew between 1970 and 1978 showed that lying to the commission was the most common reason for the action. Only eleven of the revocations or failures to renew were for departures from promised programming.[36] A recent refusal to renew the license of WBUZ, the only AM station in Fredonia, New York, is illustrative.[37] Owner Harry Serafin's troubles began in 1981 when three local groups filed a Petition to Deny. They acted after he had refused to hire a black woman applicant for a secretarial position. According to testimony in an FCC hearing, Serafin asked the referring agency, "Don't you have any white girls to send me?" The commission also held that in one of the station's contests, Serafin had kept the grand prize—a stereo receiver and tape unit. Beyond that, the commission said that Serafin had followed a "pattern of deliberate misrepresentations" in his relations with it. It added that the bias issue and the mishandling of the contest "only reinforced the conclusion" that the owner was not qualified to hold a broadcast license.

Earlier, the FCC had acted to revoke the licenses of two prominent station owners who had become embroiled in controversy. One action was aimed at RKO General, which was forced to give up its license to operate a Boston television station in 1982.[38] The other was aimed at Ivan Boesky, who pleaded guilty to violating rules against insider trading in securities and was sentenced to prison.[39] In Boesky's case, the commission voted to conduct a formal hearing on his request to transfer his majority stake in an Oklahoma City television station to his wife. The question at issue was whether his integrity was such as to support his claim to a broadcasting license.

RKO's troubles with the FCC began in 1965 when a group of investors challenged renewal of its license for KHJ-TV in Los Angeles, alleging that the station did not serve the public interest. That challenge failed, but it led to others, and, in 1980, the FCC voted to revoke RKO's licenses for WOR-TV in New York, WNAC-TV in Boston, and KHJ-TV. It did so because RKO's parent company, General Tire & Rubber Co., had been found guilty of paying bribes to obtain overseas business. The FCC held that RKO's failure to include notice in its renewal application of its corporate parent's infraction was a breach of faith justi-

---

35. Michael A. McGregor, "Assessment of Renewal Expectancy in FCC Comparative Renewal Hearings," *Journalism Quarterly,* Summer 1989, p. 295 +
36. Weiss, Ostroff, and Clift, "Station License Revocations and Denials of Renewal, 1970–78," 24 J.Broadcasting 69 (1980).
37. "FCC Denies New License for a Small Radio Station," *Wall Street Journal,* 23 February 1989.
38. John E. Yang and Gregory Stricharchuk, "FCC Aide Acts to Strip RKO of 14 Licenses," *Wall Street Journal,* 12 August 1987.
39. Bob Davis, "FCC to Delay Computer Access Fee, Votes Inquiry on Boesky Family's TV Station," *Wall Street Journal,* 25 November 1987.

fying revocation of its licenses. That action led to loss of the license for the Boston television station and in transfer of the license for WOR-TV from New York
City to a company that would operate it from Secaucus, New Jersey. When a
new revocation order aimed at RKO's remaining thirteen radio and television stations was filed in 1987, the company decided to get out of the broadcasting business. The following year, the FCC approved sale of KHJ-TV to Walt Disney
Company and of an AM radio station in Memphis to Flinn Broadcasting for about
two-thirds of their purchase price.[40] The FCC, concluding that RKO had been
punished enough, said its policy was to encourage sale of the company's remaining properties at something less than three-quarters of their purchase price, the
level set for distress sales to minorities.

Programming Quality and License Renewal

Theoretically, at least, a broadcaster's devotion to serving the public interest
is the justification for its right to possess a valuable portion of the people's airwaves. In reality, the FCC has wobbled all over the lot in trying to assess programming quality and to apply such assessment to licensing proceedings. As we
noted earlier, it was the U.S. Court of Appeals for the District of Columbia, not
the FCC, which held, in *United Church of Christ,* that a station should forfeit its
license because its programming ignored its sizable black audience.

During the 1970s, judges of that court and the commissioners sparred regularly
over the role of programming in license renewal and the transfer of a license from
one owner to another. One case grew out of Zenith Radio's decision to sell its
FM station in Chicago. Under Zenith's ownership, the station broadcast classical
music. The new owner announced it would offer contemporary sound. Listeners
appealed to the FCC to disapprove the transfer, arguing that they would be left
without access to classical music on radio. The FCC ruled that they were not
entitled to a hearing. The listeners took their case to the court of appeals, which
held that if a proposed format change causes "public grumbling of significant proportions," the FCC must conduct a hearing.[41] Two years later, a new challenge
to a station's change in format gave the FCC an opportunity to adopt a policy
toward the problem.[42] It took the position that programming changes beyond the
news and service elements then required are best left to the forces of the market.
Again, the court of appeals disagreed. However, the Supreme Court held that the
FCC's policy reflected the intent of the Communications Act: The commission's
role in seeking to influence the quality of programming should be minimal.[43]

That decision, coming when the FCC commissioners and the presidents who
appoint them were committed to deregulation, accelerated a hands-off policy toward broadcast programming. One step was the elimination of limits on commer-

---

40. Bob Davis, "FCC Approves Sale of Two Stations by GenCorp's RKO," *Wall Street Journal,*
     21 July 1988.
41. Citizens Committee to Save WEFM v. Federal Communications Commission, 506 F.2d 246
     (D.C.Cir. 1974).
42. "Changes in the Entertainment Formats of Broadcast Stations," 41 Fed.Reg. 32950 (1976).
43. Federal Communications Commission v. WNCN Listeners Guild, 450 U.S. 582, 101 S.Ct.
     1266, 67 L.Ed.2d 521 (1981).

cial time. Another, as already noted, was the elimination of fixed quotas for time devoted to news, public affairs, and public service announcements. However, the commission continued a policy that rewards, in contested renewals, licensees who have provided "meritorious or substantial service." Such reward is known as a renewal expectancy and, in practice, has proved virtually impossible for a challenger to overcome.[44] In one instance, the commission rewarded a station's "local community orientation," its "responsiveness to community needs," and its "reputation in the community."[45] The commission also looked favorably on the amount of time the station devoted to news, public affairs, and discussions of local topics.

The decade since that decision was affirmed has seen obvious changes in the "quality" of programming on radio and less obvious changes on television. A group founded by Ralph Nader surveyed TV listings in fifty markets in 1988 and concluded that public affairs programming had been cut in half since 1981. Some stations no longer offered any local public affairs programming.[46] An FCC spokesperson was quoted as saying the report "sounds terribly bogus." Nevertheless, even a casual listener to radio or viewer of television can note some changes. FM radio stations in particular have adopted formats that have them playing one kind of music—country western, contemporary, various kinds of rock, golden oldies—around the clock, occasionally interrupted for a minute or so of news provided by a satellite service. Many AM stations, which cannot match the quality of stereo sound of their FM competitors, invite listeners to call in to discuss the problem of the day with an announcer. Others offer an opportunity to talk sports.

One of the early casualties of deregulation on commercial television stations was educational children's programming. CBS cut back Bob Keeshan's *Captain Kangaroo* from 30 minutes, five mornings a week to weekend spots and then eliminated it altogether. All three networks canceled educational children's programming that had been developed under pressure from the activist-minded FCC of the early 1970s. Interviewed by a reporter from the *Wall Street Journal,* Mark Fowler, a Reagan-appointed chairman of the FCC, conceded that deregulation might not be best for children. But he said he did not think it the role of the commission to order the networks to do a better job. The policy adopted at his urging, he said, marked the end of "regulation by raised eyebrow." His reference was to a period when the FCC used its powers subtly—and sometimes overtly—to influence the nature of programming, in its opinion, for the better.

In 1988, Congress attempted to mandate a return to better children's programming, with fewer commercials, but ran into a veto by President Reagan.[47] He said

---

44. McGregor, "Assessment of the Renewal Expectancy."
45. Cowles Broadcasting, 86 F.C.C.2d 993, 49 R.R.2d 1138 (1981), aff'd sub nom. Central Florida Enterprises v. Federal Communications Commission, 683 F.2d 503 (D.C.Cir. 1982); cert. denied, 460 U.S. 1084 (1983).
46. Jay Arnold, Associated Press, "Group Claims Drop in Public Affairs Shows," *Indiana Daily Student,* 6 April 1989.
47. "Measure to Limit Ads during Children's TV Killed by Pocket Veto," *The Wall Street Journal,* 7 November 1988.

he could not reconcile the bill with the First Amendment. Congress acted after a federal appeals court had held that the FCC went too far when it permitted stations to air children's programs that were, in effect, commercials for toys.[48] The programs were produced by toy manufacturers and distributed to television stations in exchange for free advertising time. Stations also were permitted to sell commercial time within the programs to other advertisers. The court said that the FCC's consent to the arrangement violated the intent of Congress.

Any attempt by an agency of government to set standards for "quality" programming or to assess a station's performance in terms of "quality" raises obvious questions. Some of us know, or think we know, that there is "quality" in the presentation of serious drama, serious music, and serious discussion of public affairs, leavened by the whimsy of a Garrison Keillor and the satire of a Mark Russell. One can find such quality seven days a week on public radio and television stations. But that's not where one finds the big audiences. The masses watch Roseanne Barr, or funny home videos, or Vanna White flip the letters on "Wheel of Fortune." For more than a decade, enough people sought enlightenment of a sort on Sunday evenings to make "60 Minutes" a consistently top-rated program. Sizable numbers of people in some age groups listen to MTV, to rock radio, to the Nashville Network, or to golden oldies, meaning the music Elvis and the Beatles helped make popular in the 1960s. Whose standards, then, should Congress or the FCC use in determining whether the people's airwaves are used in the public interest? Should a station's service be measured by what interests the public or what should interest the public—as determined by the collective taste and wisdom of five political appointees? If the latter, who is to foot the bill if the programming does not attract a large enough audience to win the advertising revenue needed to keep the station on the air? Even some public television stations have had to resort to reruns of Lawrence Welk to woo the public donors needed to erase the deficit between government funding and the station's expenses.

One thing is certain in the last decade of the twentieth century. The electronic media offer us a wider variety of entertainment and information than was available to the most wealthy seekers of culture and diversion in earlier generations. Over-the-air broadcasting stations, supplemented in more than half the homes by multichannel cable or satellite delivery systems, offer something for every taste and interest. News, weather, sports events, frothy sitcoms, soap operas, World War II documentaries, nature films, travelogues, mysteries, simulated sex, music of every kind from rap to classical, comedy, tragedy, drama, movies new and old, are offered most places on some channel every hour of the day. And if you can't find what you want on the air, you can rent videotapes from your supermarket or video store. With such variety, the problem that preoccupied regulators for decades is no longer pressing. When many people could get only a few broadcasting stations, it made sense for government to use its power to require all stations to present a broad variety of programming and even to show some concern about its quality. Today, broadcasters have so much competition that

---

48. Bob Davis, "FCC Ruling That Gave Toy Companies Anonymity on TV Shows Is Overturned," *Wall Street Journal*, 30 September 1987.

the best hope for survival lies in appealing to some segment of the audience in sufficient numbers to be attractive to advertisers. That is what the FCC means when its members talk about ''regulation by the market.''

Limitations on Chain Ownership

For more than thirty years, FCC rules forbade any one entity from owning more than seven stations in each of three categories—television, AM radio, and FM radio. The purpose of the rule was to prevent chain ownership of broadcasting stations, particularly by the networks. This has prevented the rise of broadcasting empires akin to Gannett, Knight-Ridder, Thomson, Cox, Scripps-Howard, and other chain newspaper owners. In 1984, over opposition from some members of Congress and groups representing minorities, the FCC expanded its rules to permit one entity to own as many as twelve stations in each category. The rule also says that no one entity can own television stations reaching more than 25 percent of the national television audience. However, if the entity includes at least two stations controlled by minorities, it can own up to fourteen stations reaching no more than 30 percent of the national market. If the chain includes UHF television stations, they are counted as covering only half their potential audience.[49]

Broadcasting, which began in the 1920s as a scarce commodity operating almost as by magic on the people's airwaves, has become a pervasive force. In its beginning, the new medium literally cried out for regulation by government so that its messages could reach the people unmarred by electronic interference. In response, Congress created the Federal Radio Commission, later the Federal Communications Commission, and gave it broad powers to license broadcasting in the public interest. With the Supreme Court's 1943 decision in *National Broadcasting,* regulators became more than electronic traffic cops. They were told that they could use their licensing power to require stations to offer public affairs programming and to serve as forums for discussion of local problems. In time, the commission adopted elaborate rules designed to help measure which of competing applicants for the same frequency was most deserving of the license to use it. These rules also were applied when licenses were renewed. In the eyes of the commission and the federal courts, a broadcasting license was a public trust whose holder could be required to meet certain obligations to the public.

In recent times, those obligations have come to include the hiring of minorities and women in proportions that mirror the composition of the community a station serves. The commission also has sought, with indifferent success, to encourage station ownership by minorities and women. One means of doing so is to permit an owner faced with revocation of a broadcast license to sell the station to a minority or female owner at 75 percent of the combined value of the physical plant

---

49. Multiple Ownership (12-12-12 Reconsideration), 100 F.C.C.2d 74, 57 R.R.2d 967 (1985).

and the license. That policy has survived challenge on equal protection grounds and been upheld by the Supreme Court. However, the reality is that few licenses have been revoked and therefore made eligible for a distress sale. Renewal is not automatic, but preferences granted for better-than-average performance have made it nearly so. Unless a licensee is caught lying to the commission or has been dishonest in conducting the station's business operations, renewal is almost certain. Rarely has the commission or a court found that a station was not offering programming in the public interest.

LEGAL RESTRAINTS ON BROADCAST CONTENT

The Equal Opportunities Law

Beginning with the Radio Act of 1927, the statutes have contained language designed to prevent radio, and now television, from being dominated by any political candidate or party. Currently, §315 of the Broadcasting Act defines what is known as the equal opportunities requirement. Under its terms, a station that permits any candidate for public office to use its facilities to reach an audience must stand ready to permit equivalent use by the candidate's opponents. "Use" is defined in terms that exclude "bona fide" newscasts, documentaries, news events, and news interviews. As a practical matter, then, a political "use" is limited to paid messages in which the candidate is a participant, and to appearances in non-news programming, whether it be entertainment or a talk show not normally devoted to newsworthy issues. Under §315, no station is required to permit itself to be used by any candidate. If it does so, it cannot censor the content of the candidate's message. And, of course, if it permits a use, paid or free, by one candidate, the equal opportunities provision comes into effect with respect to that candidate's opponents.

Other provisions of §315 require stations that elect to sell time to political candidates to do so at the lowest rate offered commercial advertisers. "Broadcasting stations" are defined to include cable television systems.

A subsection of §312, not §315, requires broadcasting stations to sell "reasonable amounts of time" to candidates for federal elective offices. Refusal to do so can result in loss of license. Thus broadcasting stations must make themselves available for use as a public forum by candidates for president, the House of Representatives, the Senate, and a few other elective federal offices, if they can pay for the time. Obviously, §§312 and 315 imposed on broadcasters both duties and restrictions with respect to political campaigns that are not imposed on newspapers and magazines.

Broadcasters have chafed at these duties and restrictions. They have argued that they could do a more meaningful job of covering political campaigns if they did not have the FCC looking over their shoulders and applying a stopwatch to each use by a candidate.

To qualify for access to air time under §315, a candidate must meet three criteria[50]:

1. He or she must be eligible for election to the office sought. In one instance, the FCC held that a thirty-one-year-old was not a legally qualified candidate for president because the Constitution says a president must be at least thirty-five.

2. He or she must be an announced candidate.

3. He or she must have taken the steps required by law to qualify for a place on the ballot. Candidates who seek write-in votes must show that they are conducting a campaign.

These criteria apply equally to primary and general elections. A primary is a preliminary election at which members of a political party select their candidates for office. If nominations are made by convention or caucus, the candidate must make a serious showing of an effort to win the nomination.

In legal terms, a political spot announcement is a ''use'' if the candidate or the candidate's voice is identifiable in it. On the other hand, a political commercial of any length is not a ''use'' if the candidate's likeness or voice is not a part of it. The key to a use that will trigger §315 is the candidate's identity. If the candidate can be recognized by the viewer or listener, and the appearance is not covered by one of the four exemptions listed in the Act, it is a ''use.'' If the candidate or his backers did not pay for such a use, then his or her opponents are entitled to a similar free use if they ask for it. It makes no difference if the original candidate's use had nothing to do with politics.

''Equal opportunities'' goes beyond a counting of minutes. It starts there—if one candidate for governor buys thirty minutes of air time, the station must be willing to sell thirty minutes to his opponent—but also takes into account the potential audience. Thus, thirty minutes at 1 A.M. is not equal in opportunities to thirty minutes at 8 P.M. Usage must be scheduled so that each candidate can reach approximately the same number of persons. If a station offers help to one candidate in preparing for a use—in staging, graphics or whatever—it must offer the same help to his or her opponents. However, none of these provisions is self-triggering. A candidate who is seeking to balance an opponent's use, free or paid, must apply to the station within seven days of that use.

The equal opportunities provision balances paid time against paid time, free time against free time. There is no crossover between the two. If one candidate is able to buy a great deal of time, and the other can afford little or none, the station is under no obligation to balance the scales by giving the latter free time. If it were to do so, it would be obligated to give the first candidate free time if he or she asked for it, as almost certainly would happen.

---

50. Material in this section and the next is drawn from *The Law of Political Broadcasting and Cablecasting,* Federal Communications Commission, 43 *Federal Register* 36342-36399, 16 August 1978.

The FCC has been quite liberal in defining bona fide news programs subject to the four exemptions. Any station's regular news programs are exempt from equal opportunities requirements. Even in an instance in which one candidate for office was interviewed on a newscast five days in a row, the FCC ruled that §315 could not be invoked.[51] It has held that NBC's "Today,"[52] and CBS's "60 Minutes"[53] are bona fide news programs.

To qualify as a "bona fide news interview," the interview must take place during a regularly scheduled, continuing series of programs devoted to newsworthy topics. Thus, such long-established programs as "Meet the Press," "Face the Nation," and "Issues and Answers" are exempt from the equal opportunities requirement.[54] A call-in show has been held to be exempt if it is regularly scheduled and is under the control of the station's news department.[55] But talk shows not primarily devoted to newsworthy topics do not qualify for exemption from §315. The commission looked at one such program and found that its content had ranged from "monsters in films to sexual fantasies to psychic healing and TV soap operas." Therefore, it held, a candidate's appearance on the program had not resulted in a "bona fide news interview,"[56] and therefore was a "use."

There has been little dispute over the meaning of a "bona fide news documentary." If such programs are under the control of a station's or network's news department and are devoted to a newsworthy topic, they qualify for exemption.

However, there has been considerable dispute over the meaning of "on-the-spot coverage of bona fide news events." Some complaints have grown out of broadcasts by presidents to announce or comment on news events when they were candidates for reelection. In such instances, the commission generally has upheld the broadcaster's "reasonable, good-faith judgment" that the occasion was newsworthy. Debates among candidates for the same office are considered bona fide news events, even when they are arranged by a broadcaster, and may be covered without triggering the equal opportunities requirement.[57] Press conferences held by candidates for public office also are considered news events.

The FCC's interpretation of the bona fide news exemptions written into §315 has given broadcasters considerable leeway to cover political campaigns as they see fit. Usually, this means that news coverage focuses on the candidates of the two mainstream political parties, Democrat and Republican. During the 1988 presidential campaign, the television networks and Cable News Network gave daily coverage to George Bush and Michael Dukakis. The debates between them were treated as major news events. But only the most diligent students of presidential campaigns are likely to know that seventeen other candidates aspired to

---

51. Letter to Citizens for Reagan (WCKT-TV), 58 F.C.C.2d 925 (1976).
52. Lar Daly, 40 F.C.C. 314 (1960).
53. Letter to CBS, 58 F.C.C.2d 601 (1976).
54. Letters to Andrew J. Easter, 40 F.C.C. 307 (1960); Lar Daly, 40 F.C.C. 310 (1960); Hon. Frank Kowalski, 40 F.C.C 355 (1962), and telegram to Yates for U.S. Senator Committee, 40 F.C.C. 368 (1962).
55. Socialist Labor Party, 7 F.C.C.2d 857 (1967).
56. Socialist Workers Party, 65 F.C.C.2d 234 (1976).
57. *The Law of Political Broadcasting and Cablecasting: A Political Primer—1984 Edition,* 100 F.C.C.2d 1476.

the presidency that year, even though one of them, carrying the banner of the Libertarian Party, was on the ballot in forty-seven states. That candidate, Ronald E. Paul, received 432,000 votes, or less than one-half of one percent of the total. A second candidate, Lenora B. Fulani of the New Alliance Party, was on the ballot in thirty-five states and won only about half as many votes as Paul. They and the other also-rans received little or no media coverage because editors dismissed them as having no chance of winning. Therefore, they were not considered newsworthy. The equal opportunities law did not require broadcasters to cover them.

Paulsen v. *Federal Communications Commission,* **491 F.2d 887 (9th Cir. 1974).**

Few cases interpreting the equal opportunities provision have reached the courts. Two of the more interesting raised the question: Should persons who earn their living performing on radio or television have to give up their jobs if they decide to run for office? In one instance, Pat Paulsen, a comedian, argued that no one else must give up his or her occupation when he becomes a candidate. As he saw it, §315 discriminates against TV and radio performers. Paulsen's problem began in 1972 when he entered the New Hampshire primary as a candidate for the Republican nomination for president. His purpose was to poke fun at the news media's heavy focus on a mid-winter primary usually involving fewer than 200,000 voters. Shortly before his flirtation with politics, he had signed a contract with Walt Disney Productions to appear in a TV series, "The Mouse Factory." One episode would be telecast during the primary campaign. When the producer learned of Paulsen's candidacy, he asked the FCC whether that would raise equal opportunities problems. The FCC ruled that it would. When Disney canceled Paulsen's contract, the actor appealed first to the FCC and then to the U.S. Court of Appeals for the Ninth Circuit. In *Paulsen* v. *Federal Communications Commission,* the court upheld the producer and the FCC.

The Court said the purpose of §315 was to require broadcasters to treat all candidates alike. Paulsen argued that he should be treated differently because his appearance in "The Mouse Factory" would be nonpolitical, he would have no control over the script, and, because he already was well known, the program would have no effect on his candidacy. The court said that if it were to accept his arguments, it would plunge the FCC into passing judgment on program content to distinguish between political and nonpolitical appearances. Further, it also would open a loophole that ingenious candidates could exploit by creating entertainment programs for no other purpose than to help them win election.

Nor did Paulsen get anywhere with his argument that §315 discriminates against TV and radio actors, thus denying them the equal protection of law guaranteed by the Fourteenth Amendment. The court held that the interest of Congress in "preventing unfair and unequal use of the broadcast media" for political purposes was important enough to outweigh such discrimination as might result.

Branch v. *Federal Communications Commission,* **824 F.2d 37, (D.C.Cir. 1987).**

More recently, the U.S. Court of Appeals for the District of Columbia Circuit used similar reasoning in holding that a Sacramento television reporter would have to stay off the air if he chose to run for town council. William Branch, a general assignment reporter for KOVR, argued that his appearances on his station's newscasts were part of bona fide news events and therefore should not be considered a use as defined in §315. Whenever he reported such events, he was simply doing his job as a reporter, not campaigning for office. KOVR's management, seeking to avoid equal opportunities requests, told Branch he'd have to chose between his job and his political aspirations. The reporter appealed to the FCC, which told him the same thing.

In rejecting Branch's further appeal, the circuit court said Congress had amended §315 in 1959 to remove any doubt about its application to on-the-air journalists. Their job is to cover bona fide news events. If a political candidate is involved in the event, his or her appearance on the air is not considered a use. But reporters who cover the event are not a part of it, the court said, "for the event would occur without them and they serve only to communicate it to the public. . . . There is nothing at all 'newsworthy' about the work being done by the broadcaster's own employees, regardless of whether any of those employees happens also to be a candidate for public office."

The court, echoing the Ninth Circuit's decision in *Paulsen,* also rejected the argument that §315 unduly interfered with Branch's right to run for office. The court said he could run for office if he wished, but he could not remain on the air unless the station's management was willing to provide time on request to his opponents, adding, ". . . [N]obody has ever thought that a candidate has a right to run for office and at the same time to avoid all personal sacrifice."

Political Candidates and Censorship

Section 315 flatly forbids broadcasters to censor a political candidate's use of their stations. Until 1984, the commission and the courts interpreted that provision to mean exactly what it says, no matter how crude or libelous the candidate's remarks. In that year, an unusual candidate, Larry Flynt, publisher of *Hustler* magazine, who proposed an unusual campaign message, led to an FCC staff conclusion that broadcasters could not be required to use obscene political advertisements.[58] The staff analysis pointed to another section of the Communications Act that makes it a crime to air obscenities. Short of that, broadcasters can exercise no control over the content of a political use, as is illustrated by an FCC ruling and a Supreme Court decision.

In 1972, one of the candidates in the Democratic primary for governor of Georgia was J.B. Stoner, an ardent segregationist. He made a series of spot announcements for radio and television in which he made blatant and vulgar attacks on blacks, vowing to "put them in their place" if he were elected. He used the epithet "nigger" repeatedly. The Atlanta unit of the National Association for the Advancement of Colored People, arguing that airing of the commercials was likely to incite racial violence, appealed to the FCC to ban them. The commission ruled that the stations could not keep them off the air unless they could show a

---

58. "Stations Needn't Show Political Ads with Obscenities," *Wall Street Journal,* 26 January 1984.

"clear and present danger of imminent violence,"[59] which they could not do. The commercials were broadcast on Georgia stations throughout the campaign. Most stations preceded and followed them with an advisory explaining that by law, and under orders from the FCC, they could not censor political broadcasts. Some stations also told listeners to direct complaints to the Stoner campaign headquarters or to the FCC rather than to the station.

During the 1980 presidential campaign, Barry Commoner, candidate of the Citizens Party, caused a brief stir by authorizing use of a radio spot announcement containing what the *New York Times* called "a barnyard expletive."[60] An announcer twice used the word to describe the political rhetoric of President Carter and his leading opponents, Ronald Reagan and John Anderson. The commercial was broadcast on the CBS and NBC radio networks, producing an immediate reaction. The networks and the Federal Communications Commission reported receiving thousands of letters and telephone calls from persons objecting to the use of the expletive. With the Stoner precedent firmly behind it, the FCC didn't bother to make a formal ruling. A press officer announced that §315 forbids broadcasters "from exercising any censorship on the use of air time by bona fide candidates." Bill Zimmerman, campaign director for Commoner, noted an irony in the attention the commercial received. He said the media had paid more attention to it than to the candidate's repeated attempts to deal seriously with the major problems facing the country. Commoner received about 234,000 votes in the District of Columbia and the thirty-two states where his name appeared on the ballot.

The Supreme Court held in 1959 that a station cannot be sued for a libel spoken during a political use. Ruling in *Farmers Educational and Cooperative Union of America* v. WDAY,[61] the Court said lawsuits must be directed at the candidate. The case grew out of an equal opportunity demanded by a minor candidate for United States senator from North Dakota after WDAY had given time to the two major-party candidates. The speaker devoted part of his time to an attack on the Farmers Union, accusing it of trying to establish "a Communist Farmers Union Soviet right here in North Dakota." The Union, which was a farmers' cooperative marketing organization and a strong political force in the state, sued both the candidate and the station for libel. When state courts dismissed the suit against the station, the Supreme Court agreed to take the case. It upheld the state courts, five-to-four. The majority noted that in writing §315 Congress had given broadcasting stations no option. If they gave or sold time to one candidate for political office, they had to be willing to give or sell time on request to his or her opponents. The law also said they could not censor a candidate's remarks.

The "Reasonable Time" Requirement

Section 312(a)(7) of the Communications Act requires broadcasters to sell reasonable amounts of time to candidates for federal offices. Congress adopted the

59. Atlanta N.A.A.C.P., 36 F.C.C.2d 635 (1972).
60. Bernard Weinraub, "One Word Is Worth a Thousand Speeches to Obscure Presidency Hopeful," *New York Times*, 16 October 1980.
61. 360 U.S. 525, 79 S.Ct. 1302, 3 L.Ed.2d 1407 (1959).

provision because broadcasters in some large cities, where there are a number of congressional districts, had refused to sell time to candidates for the House. In 1981, the Supreme Court upheld the law and an FCC interpretation of it.

CBS, Inc. v. *Federal Communications Commission,* **453 U.S. 367, 101 S.Ct. 2813, 69 L.Ed.2d 706 (1981).**

In October 1979, the Carter-Mondale Presidential Committee asked all three networks to sell it thirty minutes of air time during the first week of December. The purpose was to announce the start of President Carter's reelection campaign. For various reasons, including the assertion that it was too early to start the 1980 political campaign, the networks refused to sell the requested time. The committee complained to the FCC, which ruled that the networks had violated §312(a)(7) by denying reasonable access to the airwaves. The networks took their case to the court of appeals, which affirmed the FCC's ruling. On further appeal, the Supreme Court did likewise.

Chief Justice Burger, writing for six members of the Court, held that the networks did not have the right to determine when a political campaign ought to begin. That is a decision to be made by politicians. However, the majority held that stations could refuse time to candidates for federal offices if they acted on some rational basis. It offered guidance as follows:

> In responding to access requests...broadcasters may also give weight to such factors as the amount of time previously sold to the candidate, the disruptive impact on regular programming, and the likelihood of requests for time by rival candidates under the equal opportunities provision....These considerations may not be invoked as pretexts for denying access; to justify a negative response, broadcasters must cite a realistic danger of substantial program disruption—perhaps caused by insufficient notice to allow adjustments in the schedule—or of an excessive number of equal time requests. Further, in order to facilitate review by the Commission, broadcasters must explain their reasons for refusing time or making a more limited counteroffer. If broadcasters take the appropriate factors into account and act reasonably and in good faith, their decisions will be entitled to deference even if the Commission's analysis would have differed in the first instance. But if broadcasters adopt "across-the-board policies" and do not attempt to respond to the individualized situation of a particular candidate, the Commission is not compelled to sustain their denial of access.

The Court brushed aside CBS's argument that the reasonable access provision violated its First Amendment rights. The section was written, Burger said, to enhance the ability of candidates for federal office to present their views to the voting public. Thus it served the more important First Amendment interests of the people in receiving "information necessary for the effective operation of the democratic process."

The Fairness Doctrine

From the earliest days of federal regulation of broadcasting, critics of the medium, members of Congress, and others have been both awed and troubled by its

During the Vietnam war, daily television coverage of antiwar demonstrations on college campuses helped convey the impression of a nation also at war with itself. Here, Ohio National Guard troops move against students at Kent State University on May 4, 1970. Moments later, the guardsmen turned and fired, killing four students. The event provoked protests that temporarily closed classes at colleges and universities throughout the United States. (UPI/Bettmann Newsphotos)

potential as a mass medium of communication. In a way that carries more impact than words on paper, it can convey a message from Maine to California, Florida to Washington state, instantly, and with whatever emotional content the sender desires. Television has enhanced the impact, because the spoken word can be supported by pictures and graphic devices that carry the ring of truth. Television has shown the ability to pull the nation together, as it did with its 24-hours-a-day coverage of the assassination of President Kennedy and its aftermath. Or it can contribute to forces that have seemed to tear the nation apart, as with its coverage of the Vietnam War and the violent reaction to it on the nation's college campuses. Every president in modern times has resorted, first, to radio, as with Franklin D. Roosevelt, and then to television to go over the heads of the print media to reach the people.

The *Trinity Methodist Church* case was an early manifestation of concern over the power of broadcasting to inflame public passions. That same concern was evidenced in 1941, during intense debate over whether the United States should enter World War II, in the FCC's ruling in *Mayflower Broadcasting Corp.*[62] The

---

62. 8 F.C.C. 333 (1941).

commission ruled that broadcast license holders could not use their stations to air their own views on public issues. But after the war ended, the FCC changed its mind. In its 1949 Report on Editorializing by Broadcast Licensees,[63] it held that broadcasters could argue a point of view, provided that air time also was made available to persons holding other points of view. This led to a series of commission rulings that formulated what has come to be known as "the fairness doctrine." In 1959, Congress gave the doctrine official sanction by amending §315(a) of the Communications Act to include this sentence:

> Nothing in the foregoing [the equal opportunities provision] shall be construed as relieving broadcasters, in connection with the presentation of newscasts, news interviews, news documentaries, and on-the-spot coverage of news events, from the obligation imposed upon them under this Act to operate in the public interest and to afford reasonable opportunity for the discussion of conflicting views of issues of public importance.

For thirty years that doctrine shaped and, its critics say, limited the way in which radio and television stations presented news, documentaries, and discussions of public events. Under threat of losing their licenses—although that seldom happened—broadcasters were required (1) "to provide coverage of vitally important controversial issues of interest" in their communities, and (2) "to provide a reasonable opportunity for the presentation of contrasting viewpoints on such issues."[64]

So pervasive was the mandate created by the fairness doctrine—broadcasters must make a conscious effort to balance the discussion of any controversial issue—that the television networks and most local station news directors continue to observe the mandate despite the FCC's conclusion, supported by two appellate court decisions, that it no longer serves the public interest. Powerful members of Congress disagree with that conclusion, but, despite several efforts, as of this writing they have been unable to enact the doctrine into law.

Because of the uncertainty about the fairness doctrine, this section will summarize both the major decisions supporting it and the decisions that led to, and upheld, its official demise.

We start with the essential elements of the fairness doctrine. Unlike the equal opportunities requirement, which applies only to specifically defined "uses" of air time by candidates for public office, the fairness requirement applied to every element of a station's programming, particularly to its coverage of news and public affairs. Station management had to be prepared to show that it had identified controversial public issues and had presented, over a reasonable period, a balanced version of the points of view bearing on the issues' resolution. Stations could sell time to advocates of a particular point of view, but the stations had to be willing to give time to advocates of opposing views if the latter were unwilling or unable to buy time. If broadcasters exercised reasonable news judgment and showed good faith in carrying out their fairness obligations, they could anticipate

---

63. 13 F.C.C. 1246 (1949).
64. *Report Concerning General Fairness Doctrine Obligations of Broadcast Licensees,* 102 F.C.C.2d 143, 146 (1985).

no problems at license renewal time. The system was policed through complaints filed with the FCC, and the record shows that few even resulted in a letter of inquiry to the station. One study showed that, in a three-year period, the commission sustained only 13 of 15,189 fairness doctrine complaints.[65]

The doctrine was a product of the same principles that underlie all government regulation of broadcasting. Broadcasters reach the public by sending signals through an electronic spectrum that belongs to the people. The government, acting for the people, must decide who can use the scarce frequencies in that spectrum and on what terms. From the beginning, regulators and the courts have held that holders of those frequencies must use them to serve the public interest. A most important public interest is "'uninhibited, robust, wide-open' debate on public issues."[66] If such issues are to be resolved logically, broadcasters must give truth and falsehood a fair chance to grapple by opening the microphones to all shades of opinion. Thus the fairness doctrine is based on an affirmative theory of the First Amendment, which recognizes a responsibility on the part of government to encourage freedom of expression.

Ironically, that line of reasoning has resulted, as we have already noted, in a system of licensing and regulation that leaves owners and operators of broadcasting stations with a lesser degree of First Amendment freedom than is granted owners and managers of any other medium. The Supreme Court has erected high barriers against attempts by government to prevent newspaper and magazine editors from publishing what they please, even when they choose to publish secret government documents or tell how a hydrogen bomb works.[67] Further, when the Florida Supreme Court upheld a law that required newspapers to give a right of reply to persons who felt they had been treated unfairly, the U.S. Supreme Court reversed, holding that the law imposed a form of prior restraint, violating the First Amendment. And yet the same court held in another case that the First Amendment permitted the FCC to order broadcasting stations to give a right of reply to persons who felt they had been treated unfairly. These cases will be examined next.

A Right of Reply and the Supreme Court

As interpreted by the Federal Communications Commission, the fairness doctrine protected persons who were targets of personal attacks growing out of the discussion of controversial public issues. Victims of such attacks had to be notified by the station carrying the offending broadcast. They also had to be given a tape or transcript of the offending remarks and offered time, without charge, for a reply.

---

65. David Burnham, "F.C.C. to Examine Fairness Doctrine," *New York Times,* 12 April 1984.
66. New York Times v. Sullivan, 376 U.S. 254, quoted in the Introduction to the *Fairness Report,* 48 F.C.C.2d 1 (1974).
67. New York Times Co. v. United States, 403 U.S. 713, 91 S.Ct. 2140, 29 L.Ed.2d 822 (1971), and the failure of the government to take further action to prevent several newspapers and *The Progressive* from publishing stories on the mechanism of a hydrogen bomb after it had won an injunction preventing publication of the magazine's original story. See Chapter 2.

A legal challenge to the personal attack rule was launched in 1964 when Fred J. Cook, a journalist and author, learned that he was the target of a fifteen-minute radio broadcast carried by more than three hundred stations. The speaker was the Rev. Billy James Hargis, a radio and television evangelist, who bought time to broadcast his "Christian Crusade." In the Rev. Mr. Hargis's eyes, Cook was twice a sinner. He had written a campaign tract highly critical of Barry Goldwater, a conservative Republican who ran for president in 1964, and he had written an article attacking J. Edgar Hoover, for years director of the Federal Bureau of Investigation. Hargis denounced Cook as a Communist sympathizer. The author considered filing a libel suit, then decided it would cost less to seek redress under the personal attack rule of the fairness doctrine. With the help of his daughter, he wrote to each of the stations carrying the Hargis broadcast asking for reply time. Some offered time without question, but WGCB, in the small town of Red Lion, Pennsylvania, was among those that sent Cook a rate card. The station manager took the position that because Hargis had paid for his time, Cook should have to pay for his response. Cook appealed to the FCC for an order requiring the station to give him time without charge. The FCC issued the order.

***Red Lion Broadcasting Co.* v. *Federal Communications Commission,* 395 U.S. 367, 89 S.Ct. 1794, 23 L.Ed.2d 371 (1969).**

WGCB appealed to the U.S. Court of Appeals for the District of Columbia Circuit. At about the same time, the Radio-Television News Directors Association brought suit in the Seventh Circuit Court of Appeals in Chicago asking it to declare the personal attack rule in violation of broadcasters' First Amendment freedoms. That court did so, also holding that the fairness doctrine itself was unconstitutional. The Supreme Court accepted both cases for review, combining them under the *Red Lion* title. The seven justices who heard the cases unanimously upheld the District of Columbia Circuit's decision in *Red Lion* and reversed the Seventh Circuit's decision in RTNDA.

Justice Byron R. White, writing for the Court, said lawyers for WGCB and RTNDA were mistaken in arguing that the personal attack rule, and the fairness doctrine of which it was a part, violated the First Amendment rights of broadcasters. Because broadcast frequencies are scarce, and belong to all the people, the First Amendment interests of successful applicants for a radio or television license are subordinate to those of the viewers and listeners. White wrote:

> Because of the scarcity of radio frequencies, the Government is permitted to put restrictions on licensees in favor of others whose views should be expressed on this unique medium. But the people as a whole retain their interest in free speech by radio and their collective right to have the medium function consistently with the ends and purposes of the First Amendment. It is the right of the viewers and listeners, not the right of the broadcasters, which is paramount.... It is the purpose of the First Amendment to preserve an uninhibited marketplace of ideas in which truth will ultimately prevail, rather than to countenance monopolization of the market, whether it be by the Government itself or a private licensee.... It is the right of the public to receive suitable access to social, political, esthetic, moral and other ideas

and experiences which is crucial here. That right may not be constitutionally abridged either by Congress or the FCC.

With that decision the Court endorsed the view, first advanced in *Trinity Methodist Church, South,* more than thirty years earlier, that owners of broadcasting stations are not to use them to promote their own political, social, or economic views. Rather they are to operate their stations as a sort of community smorgasbord, laden with points of view and political arguments designed to appeal to all segments of the audience. No one position is to be advanced over another, but all arguments are to be given a reasonable airing, leaving the viewers and listeners to decide which they will accept and which they will reject. And if some individual should be verbally assaulted—treated unfairly—during the debate, that individual must be given a reasonable amount of time to set the record straight.

Miami Herald Publishing Co. v. *Tornillo,* **418 U.S. 241, 94 S.Ct. 2831, 41 L.Ed.2d 730 (1974).** Less than five years later, Pat Tornillo, a candidate for the Florida Legislature, felt he had been treated most unfairly—and personally attacked—by an editorial in the *Miami Herald,* Florida's most widely circulated newspaper. The paper noted that Tornillo, an officer of a teachers' union, had called a strike in defiance of a law forbidding such actions. Its editorial called him a "czar" and a lawbreaker. Relying on Florida's long unused right-of-reply law, Tornillo asked the newspaper to publish his defense of his actions. When the editors refused, he asked a county court to order them to do so. That court turned Tornillo down, holding that the law violated the newspaper's First Amendment rights. On appeal, the state Supreme Court reversed. On further appeal, a unanimous U.S. Supreme Court held that the right-of-reply law was unconstitutional.

Chief Justice Burger, who wrote for the Court, endorsed the idea that the media should fairly reflect conflicting points of view. But he noted that any attempt to force the media to do so "necessarily calls for some mechanism, either governmental or consensual." If government provides that mechanism, "this at once brings about a confrontation with...the First Amendment." Burger offered four reasons why any attempt by government to force newspapers to publish material their editors would reject violates the Constitution:

1. In many previous decisions, the Court held that an attempt to force publication of "that which 'reason' tells [editors] should not be published" violates the First Amendment. The chief justice added, "A responsible press is an undoubtedly desirable goal, but press responsibility is not mandated by the Constitution and like many other virtues, it cannot be legislated."

2. Compelled publication is a form of prior restraint. If editors are forced to put something into a newspaper, they will be forced to leave out something else. "Governmental restraint on publishing need not fall into familiar patterns to be subject to constitutional limitations."

3. The alternative to leaving something out is to increase the number of pages to accommodate the material mandated by government. This increases the publisher's costs for paper, ink, and composing time, thus imposing an economic penalty amounting to a taking of property in violation of the Fifth Amendment.

4. Finally, the factors might lead some editors to "conclude that the safe course is to avoid controversy and...political and electoral coverage would be blunted or reduced."

At the time, the Court had no reason to note that some of the reasoning it used in *Tornillo* applied with equal force to the facts at issue five years earlier in *Red Lion*. The fairness doctrine, like the Florida personal attack rule, sometimes required broadcast news directors to air assertions that their news judgment rejected as fallacious, repetitive, or even trivial. Further, air time is even more restrictive than the page count of a newspaper. If several major news stories break on the same day, a publisher can add two or more pages to permit full coverage of the events. Try as they might, station owners cannot add even a second to the time available in any hour or any day. Time devoted to a reply or to fulfill a fairness obligation inevitably crowds off the air matter that an editor might consider more newsworthy. Finally, one of the arguments long advanced against the fairness doctrine was that some station owners advised their news staffs to steer clear of controversy so that the station would not have to air unpopular points of view.

But the FCC and some lawyers representing broadcasters did note the parallels between *Red Lion* and *Tornillo*. Ten years later, in response to a rising tide of discontent with the fairness doctrine, the FCC invited comment on it.[68] A year later, the FCC dropped a bombshell.[69] The commission reported that, as a result of its inquiry, it had concluded that the fairness doctrine no longer served the public interest. Rather than encouraging debate, the doctrine actually inhibited it. Further, the doctrine gave government officials an opportunity to intimidate broadcasters. The inquiry was told that President Nixon directed his staff on twenty-one occasions to "take specific action relating to what could be considered unfair news coverage."[70] An official in a Democratic administration said its strategy "was to use the fairness doctrine to challenge and harass the right-wing broadcasters and hope that the challenges would be so costly to them that they would be inhibited, and decide it was too expensive to continue."[71]

Nor was that all. Referring directly to *Tornillo*, the report said that decision had cast doubt on the constitutional validity of the doctrine. Those doubts had been reinforced more recently by the Supreme Court's decision in *Federal Com-*

---

68. *Notice of Inquiry*, Gen. Docket No. 84-282, FCC 84-140, 49 Fed.Reg. 20317, 14 May 1984.
69. *Report Concerning General Fairness Doctrine Obligations of Broadcast Licensees*, 102 F.C.C.2d 143 (1985).
70. Memorandum to H.R. Haldeman from Jeb S. Magruder, "The Shot-gun Versus the Rifle," 17 October 1959, reprinted in D. Bazelon, "FCC Regulation of the Telecommunications Press," 1975 Duke L.J. 213, 247-251 (1975).
71. *Report Concerning General Fairness Doctrine Obligations*, p. 54.

munications Commission v. *League of Women Voters of California.*[72] The Court noted in that decision that the constitutional permissibility of the fairness doctrine is based on an assumption that the doctrine enhances coverage of controversial issues. The Court said it would have to reevaluate the doctrine if the commission demonstrated the falsity of that assumption.[73] The Court also noted that "[t]he prevailing rationale for broadcast regulation based upon spectrum scarcity has come under increasing criticism."[74] The Court added:

> Critics, including the incumbent chairman of the FCC, charge that with the advent of cable and satellite television technology, communities now have access to such a wide variety of stations that the scarcity doctrine is obsolete. [Citation omitted.] We are not prepared, however, to reconsider our longstanding approach without some signal from Congress or the FCC that technological developments have advanced so far that some revision of the system of broadcast regulation may be required.

With its report, the FCC clearly sent that signal. What the commission needed was a case on which to act. As it happened, two were already in process, and, prodded by the U.S. Court of Appeals for the District of Columbia Circuit, the commission ultimately declared the fairness doctrine dead.

The Demise of the Fairness Doctrine

A major question standing between the Federal Communications Commission and abolition of the fairness doctrine was, "Did the FCC have the authority to act?" If the doctrine was a product of the FCC's policy-making authority, the commission could abolish it with a good reason for doing so. But if the doctrine had been written into law by Congress, then an act of Congress was needed for repeal. At issue was the language of §315(a) as amended by Congress in 1959. That language, which was quoted at the beginning of our discussion of the fairness doctrine, says that nothing in the equal opportunities law relieves broadcasters from the obligation "to operate in the public interest and to afford reasonable opportunity for the presentation of conflicting views on issues of public importance." In the eyes of some, that made the fairness doctrine a part of the Communications Act and therefore beyond the reach of an FCC bent on eliminating it.

The test of the commission's authority came about in an unusual way. In the late 1970s, several agencies began experimenting with an interactive communications system, known as "teletext," that operated in the intervals between the "pulses" of conventional television signals. Among the experimenters were two newspaper giants, Knight-Ridder and the *Los Angeles Times*. Subscribers were provided with a device that permitted them to receive text and graphics on their television screens. The service included news, sports, weather, community events, the full texts of some government documents, airline schedules, shopping

---

72. 468 U.S. 364, 104 S.Ct. 3106, 82 L.Ed.2d 278 (1984).
73. 104 S.Ct. 3106, n. 18.
74. 104 S.Ct. 3106, 3117, n. 12.

services, and whatever else the originating agency thought might be of value to its audience. Through a keyboard, subscribers could decide which items to call up for viewing. No sound was provided with the service.

In 1981, the FCC served notice that it was considering rules under which teletext services could operate and invited public comment. Two years later, the commission issued its report.[75] It concluded that none of the political access rules, including the fairness doctrine, should be applied to teletext. The conclusion was based on the view that the service was more like a print medium than it was like conventional broadcasting. Thus a candidate could not "appear" on the system, constituting a "use" as defined by §315. To apply the fairness doctrine to the medium would not serve the public interest, the FCC felt. In reaching that conclusion, it took the position that the doctrine was an FCC policy, not statute law.

Telecommunications Research and Action Center v. *Federal Communications Commission*, **801 F.2d 501 (D.C.Cir. 1986).**

Two organizations, Telecommunications Research and Action Center and Media Access Project, asked the U.S. Court of Appeals for the District of Columbia Circuit to review the order. That court held that teletext was broadcasting as defined in the Communications Act. Therefore it must comply with the equal opportunities law.

But the commission acted reasonably when it decided not to require teletext to offer access to candidates for federal office or abide by the fairness doctrine. With respect to access, the court said a television station carrying teletext as an ancillary service could meet the requirement by providing access to regular broadcasts.

With respect to the fairness doctrine, the court held that if the FCC followed a policy it had first defined in 1949,[76] teletext providers would be bound by the doctrine. However, the court said the commission could change that policy unless, as Telecommunications contended, the policy had been made law by Congress. The court said that had not happened: "We do not believe that language adopted in 1959 made the fairness doctrine a binding statutory obligation; rather, it ratified the Commission's longstanding position that the public interest standard authorizes the fairness doctrine."

Thus, in 1959 Congress had done nothing more than recognize the FCC's authority to impose the fairness doctrine on broadcasters. That left the commission free to exempt teletext from the fairness requirement if it had good reasons for doing so. It offered two:

1. The commission said its reading of Supreme Court decisions led it to believe that, because of the textual nature of teletext, any attempt to regulate its content would violate the First Amendment.

2. The commission further concluded that "the burdens of applying the fairness doctrine might well impede the development of the new technology."

---

75. *Report and Order,* 53 Rad.Reg.2d (P & F) 1309 (1983).
76. *Editorializing by Broadcast Licensees,* 13 F.C.C. 1246 (1949).

Rather than risk the expense of fighting fairness doctrine challenges, teletext providers either would steer clear of controversy or abandon their experiment.

The court held that those two reasons were sufficient to support the FCC's finding that application of the fairness doctrine to teletext would not serve the public interest. The Supreme Court refused a request to review the decision.[77]

Meanwhile, a direct challenge to the fairness doctrine was proceeding on another track. That challenge began in 1982 when television station WTVH in Syracuse, New York, ran a series of advertisements arguing that a nearby nuclear power plant was a "sound investment for New York." The Syracuse Peace Council complained to the FCC that the station's owner, Meredith Corporation, had not adequately presented opposing viewpoints. The commission found that comments favorable to nuclear power outnumbered opposing arguments by ten to one and gave Meredith twenty days to tell it how it would even the balance.[78] Meredith asked the FCC to reconsider. While reconsidering, the FCC issued its 1985 Fairness Report in which it concluded that the fairness doctrine no longer served the public interest.

Notwithstanding, the FCC fudged on the Syracuse case. It refused to address constitutional questions raised by Meredith and held that the fate of the doctrine should be left up to Congress and the courts. Meredith took its case to the U.S. Court of Appeals for the District of Columbia Circuit, which reversed and remanded.[79] In doing so, the court reminded the commission that in *Telecommunications* it had held that the fairness doctrine was not mandated by Congress. The court also said the commission could not "blind itself" to the constitutional questions raised by Meredith. In response to this prodding, the FCC broadened its inquiry by asking for public comment on its 1985 Report. The result was a decision in Meredith's favor.[80]

Syracuse Peace Council v. *Federal Communications Commission,* **867 F.2d 654 (D.C.Cir. 1989).**

This time the Syracuse Peace Council appealed to the District of Columbia Circuit. The court held that the commission acted within its authority in holding that the fairness doctrine no longer serves the public interest. But despite its earlier chastisement of the FCC for dodging the First Amendment issues raised by the doctrine, the court did likewise. It based its decision solely on its finding that, in abandoning the doctrine, the FCC was neither arbitrary nor capricious, nor had it abused its discretion. The Supreme Court refused a request to review the decision.[81]

The FCC's justification for rejecting the Peace Council's fairness complaint was drawn directly from its 1985 report, which was based on four points, all of which the court found reasonable. They are:

---

77.   482 U.S. 919, 107 S.Ct. 3196, 96 L.Ed.2d 684 (1987).
78.   Syracuse Peace Council, 99 F.C.C.2d 1389 (1984).
79.   Meredith Corp. v. FCC, 809 F.2d 863 (D.C.Cir. 1987).
80.   Syracuse Peace Council, 2 F.C.C.Rcd. 5043 (1987); reconsideration denied, 3 F.C.C.2d 2035 (1988).
81.   cert. denied, _ _ _ U.S. _ _ _, 110 S.Ct. 717, 107 L.Ed.2d 737 (1990).

1. The growth in the number of broadcast outlets has made the scarcity rationale obsolete, thus reducing any need for the fairness doctrine. The number of radio stations increased by 30 percent between 1974 and 1985. The number of FM stations increased by 60 percent. Television coverage also increased dramatically. By 1984, 96 percent of the television households received five or more over-the-air stations, and nearly two out of three could get nine or more. When cable was factored into the equation, the availability of alternative channels brought the networks' share of the television audience down from 90 percent in 1982 to 76 percent in 1984. That share since has dropped to 67 percent.

2. Rather than enhancing broadcast coverage of public issues, the fairness doctrine "often worked to dissuade broadcasters from presenting *any* treatment of controversial viewpoints." Faced with the expensive possibility of defending themselves against fairness doctrine complaints, the cost of granting free air time to opposing views if a violation was found, and the reputational harm resulting from even a frivolous complaint, some broadcasters chose to ignore controversy. The FCC documented more than sixty such instances. This "chilling effect often fell on the expression of unorthodox or 'fringe' views on controversial issues."

3. Enforcing the doctrine put the government "in the doubtful position of evaluating program content." The FCC was compelled "to evaluate broadcasters' decisions concerning the importance of given viewpoints," opening the possibility that it could be put in the position "of favoring one type of opinion over another."

4. By its existence, the fairness doctrine gave the president, his administration, and members of Congress "an opportunity to abuse it for partisan purposes." Some of the evidence of that abuse was summarized at the start of this section.

Even before the court had endorsed the FCC's decision, Congress reacted by trying to add the doctrine to the Communications Act. President Reagan vetoed the bill, and the Senate could not muster enough votes to override. When Congress sought to add the measure to a "veto-proof" bill extending government funding into a new fiscal year, Reagan served notice he would find no bill containing the fairness doctrine exempt from his veto. Congress backed off. Although powerful members of both houses of Congress continue, on occasion, to talk about reimposing the fairness doctrine, no formal action to do so was taken in 1988, 1989, or 1990.

One element of the fairness doctrine escaped the FCC's deregulatory fervor. The doctrine still applies to broadcast coverage of issues submitted to voters for resolution at the polls. On such issues, broadcasters are supposed to provide reasonable coverage of all points of view. A report prepared by two groups seeking enactment of a fairness law said some broadcast news editors seemed unaware of the requirement.[82] The U.S. Public Interest Research Group and the Safe Energy

---

82. "Fairness Doctrine Study Details Non-Compliance," *Wall Street Journal,* 10 February 1989.

Communication Council said they had found that 14 percent of radio and television stations refused to give free air time to opposing viewpoints on ballot issues in the November 1988 election. The study sampled broadcaster response to requests for time on six issues involving insurance rates, bottle recycling, and nuclear power. In all instances, industry groups bought time to present their positions. When opponents asked for free reply time, they were told in about a third of the instances they would not get time because the fairness doctrine had been abolished. After negotiation, just over half of those stations offered time. Robert Baker, a senior attorney at the FCC, said the commission had received only a few complaints of a lack of fairness in coverage of ballot issues and had found none valid.

Indecent Programming

Although the courts have enhanced the First Amendment rights of broadcasters by upholding the FCC's abolition of all but a remnant of the fairness doctrine, the courts have upheld a law forbidding indecent programming. The Supreme Court has defined "indecency" to include matter that falls short of the obscenity standard established in *Miller* v. *California*.[83] Thus, broadcasters can be punished, up to the point of revocation of their licenses, for airing language or sexual portrayals that would be protected by the First Amendment in print, in a theater, or in a nightclub. This, then, is another area in which broadcasters have a lesser degree of freedom of speech and press than are enjoyed by other communications media.

Federal Communications Commission v. *Pacifica Foundation*, **438 U.S. 726, 98 S.Ct. 3026, 57 L.Ed.2d 1073 (1978).**

The case upholding the right of the Federal Communications Commission to punish indecent broadcasts began when a disc jockey on the Pacifica Foundation's FM radio station in New York City played all twelve minutes of a George Carlin monologue entitled "Filthy Words." It was recorded before a nightclub audience that howled in appreciation as Carlin repeated in many contexts "the curse words and swear words...you couldn't say on the public, ah, airwaves, um, the ones you definitely wouldn't say." He proceeded to say them, and the station put them on the airwaves in the middle of a weekday afternoon. One listener, who was riding in his automobile with his small child when the words came spilling out of the radio, was not amused. He complained to the FCC.

The commission reprimanded Pacifica, holding that the Carlin monologue violated 18 U.S.C. §1464, which forbids use on the air of any "obscene, indecent, or profane language." Although a reprimand is a mild form of censure, its potential harm lay in the fact that it would become a part of the station's file and would be a negative factor if someone were to challenge renewal of its license. Pacifica took its case to the courts. There it argued that the controlling word in §1464 is "obscene." It further argued that despite the sexually and scatologically explicit

---

83. 413 U.S. 15, 93 S.Ct. 2607, 37 L.Ed.2d 419 (1973).

words in the monologue, it was not obscene, because the Court itself had held that such words do not in themselves appeal to a prurient interest.[84] A badly divided Supreme Court agreed that "Filthy Words" was not obscene, but it rejected Pacifica's first argument, upholding the FCC's reprimand, five to four.

Justice John Paul Stevens, writing for himself and two other members of the majority, said that the three elements of §1464 must be looked at separately, not as a unit. Thus, a station could be punished if it broadcast matter that is indecent or profane, without being obscene. Upholding the commission's finding that the monologue was indecent, the plurality defined "indecent" as "nonconformance with accepted standards of morality." The commission also made much of the fact that the recording was put on the air at a time when children were likely to be in the audience.

Pacifica offered two other arguments: (1) Section 1464 imposes a form of censorship, directly violating §326 of the Communications Act, which forbids censorship of broadcasting stations by the FCC. (2) The Court's definition of "indecent" was so broad that it might well include matter protected by the First Amendment.

The Court rejected both. When sections 1464 and 326 are looked at together, they mean that the FCC can't prevent stations from broadcasting "obscene, indecent, or profane" language, but the FCC can punish stations if they do broadcast such material. The Court granted that there might be some First Amendment values in indecent language, even in Carlin's monologue, but, Stevens wrote, "surely [they] lie at the periphery of First Amendment concern." Such value as there might be was not enough to overcome the fact that "of all forms of communication it is broadcasting that has received the most limited First Amendment protection."

Stevens offered two reasons for upholding the FCC's right to punish indecent broadcasts:

1. Unlike other forms of communication, broadcast messages come directly and unannounced into the privacy of one's home "where the individual's right to be let alone plainly outweighs the First Amendment rights of an intruder." Because viewers and listeners tune in and out of stations at will, "prior warnings cannot completely protect the listener or viewer from unexpected program content. To say that one may avoid further offense by turning off the radio when he hears indecent language is like saying that the remedy for an assault is to run away after the first blow."

2. "[B]roadcasting is uniquely accessible to children, even those too young to read." The Court has upheld the right of government to assist parents in protecting their children from exposure to indecent materials.[85]

The plurality ended by emphasizing the narrowness of its decision. It said it had no intention of making it impossible for a station to broadcast unexpurgated

---

84. Cohen v. California, 403 U.S. 15, 91 S.Ct. 1780, 29 L.Ed.2d 284 (1971), and Hess v. Indiana, 414 U.S. 105, 94 S.Ct. 326, 38 L.Ed.2d 303 (1973).
85. Ginsberg v. New York, 390 U.S. 629, 88 S.Ct. 1274, 20 L.Ed.2d 195 (1968).

versions of Shakespeare's more earthy comedies. Nor was it saying that a taxi company could be punished if a frustrated driver uttered a curse into an open microphone. It was simply reminding broadcasters that their medium entered homes where children and unsuspecting adults might be listening. Therefore, discretion is in order. To many, the Carlin monologue would be a nuisance, which Justice George Sutherland had once described as "a right thing in the wrong place—like a pig in the parlor instead of the barnyard." To which Stevens added: "We simply hold that when the Commission finds that a pig has entered the parlor, the exercise of its regulatory power does not depend upon proof that the pig is obscene."

In *Pacifica,* the Court spoke to broadcasters at two levels. At one level, it was merely telling them that they run a risk at license renewal time if they persist in airing sexually oriented material when children are likely to be in the audience. While the Supreme Court was deciding this case, the Court of Appeals for the District of Columbia reinforced that warning with its decision in *Illinois Citizens Committee for Broadcasting* v. *Federal Communications Commission.*[86] The Committee had objected to an FCC order fining Sonderling Broadcasting Corporation $2,000 for airing material the commission considered obscene. The host for an afternoon call-in show had encouraged his female listeners to talk about their experiences with oral sex. The appeals court held that the Committee had a right to be heard, but also that the FCC was correct in holding that the program violated 18 U.S.C. §1464.

At another level, the Court's decision gave support to those who believe that because of broadcasting's intrusive nature, and because of its potential for influencing conduct, government must retain some control over broadcasting content. That belief is as old as the decision in *Trinity Church, South,* and as current as attempts to prevent the broadcasting of the lyrics of sexually explicit rap songs. Broadcasters read the *Pacifica* decision as permitting them to broadcast raunchy material between 10 p.m. and 6 a.m., when children are assumed to be in bed. For more than a decade, the FCC apparently gave the decision the same reading.

Then, in 1987, reacting to more than 20,000 complaints a year, the FCC issued regulations forbidding the broadcast of obscene and offensive material at any time.[87] It said studies show children may be watching at any hour.

Later that same year, the commission relaxed its policy to permit television and radio stations to broadcast indecent material between midnight and 6 a.m. But it reiterated that it had no intention of sanctioning the broadcast of obscenity at any time.[88] Less than a year later, the District of Columbia Circuit Court told the FCC to reconsider its policy.[89] The court said the agency had not demonstrated that such a limitation is necessary to protect children. However, the court said if the FCC was able to make such a showing, it could restrict indecent programming.

---

86.   515 F.2d 397 (D.C.Cir. 1974).
87.   Caroline E. Mayer, Washington Post Service, "FCC Cracks Down on Dirty Talk, Lyrics on Radio, Television," *Louisville Courier-Journal,* 17 April 1987.
88.   Bob Davis, "FCC Limits Shows of Raunchy Nature to after Midnight," *Wall Street Journal,* 25 November 1987.
89.   Bob Davis, "Appeals Panel Rejects FCC Ruling Curbing Indecent-Broadcast Hours," *Wall Street Journal,* 1 August 1988.

The Federal Communications Commission's crackdown on indecent programming caused problems for groups like 2 Live Crew, shown here in a performance at a club in Miami Beach. Officials in several cities charged that Crew's actions and the lyrics of some of its rap songs were both indecent and obscene. (David Walters/The Miami Herald)

At that point, Congress entered the fray, enacting legislation requiring the commission to punish licensees for indecent broadcasts. The commission announced that it would comply with the law.[90] In doing so, the FCC refined its definition of "indecent speech." Sanctions would be limited, the FCC said, to "language or material that, in context, depicts or describes, in terms patently offensive, as measured by contemporary community standards for the broadcast medium, sexual or excretory activities or organs." The definition is based on the language used by the Supreme Court in *Miller* to define obscenity, but with three important differences. The community is that of the broadcast medium, not the whole community. Further, there is no requirement that the broadcast in question be looked at as a whole. The inference is that a broadcaster could be punished for airing an isolated outburst of profanity or a brief sexually explicit scene. Finally, the commission's definition does not require that the material appeal to a prurient interest in sex. Commissioner Patricia Diaz Dennis said she had "serious doubts whether our new rule will pass constitutional muster." Broadcasters said they would challenge the directive in court.

---

90. "FCC, Following New Law, Bans Indecent Broadcasts," *Wall Street Journal,* 22 December 1988.

As of this writing, courts have not ruled on the policy. The FCC has invited a challenge by asking three radio stations to respond to complaints about indecent programming.[91] They are WLUP-AM, Chicago; KSJO-FM, San Jose, California; and WFBQ-FM, Indianapolis. All the complaints involved sexually explicit talk during daytime hours.

Thus, in principle, and with the backing of both Congress and the Supreme Court, the Federal Communications Commission can punish broadcasters for airing indecent programming. But aside from the Supreme Court's condemnation of George Carlin's "Filthy Words," there is little to tell us what kind of programming will meet the FCC's disapproval. The commission has adopted a definition, based on *Miller* and *Pacifica,* but few concrete findings flesh it out. Nor has a station lost its license for broadcasting indecency. Thus, this area of broadcast regulation, like others, must be characterized as more bark than bite, as more threat than action. However, broadcast frequencies, even if no longer deemed to be scarce, have a value that investors in studios and transmitters will not lightly risk by testing the limits of the Communications Act as established in FCC policy and court decisions.

"Dial-a-Porn"

The same considerations that led Congress and the Federal Communications Commission to act against indecent broadcasting resulted in an attempt to outlaw "dial-a-porn" services. Such services offer sub-

Sable Communications of California **v.** *F.C.C.,* **492 U.S. _ _ _, 109 S.Ct. 2829, 106 L.Ed.2d 93 (1989).**

scribers an opportunity to dial a 900 number and, for a fee charged at so much a minute, listen to sexually explicit talk. Although the FCC hedged the offering of such services with restrictions designed to prevent children from using them, Congress went further and sought to outlaw them, relying on the Supreme Court's decisions in *Pacifica* and *New York* v. *Ferber,*[92] the child pornography case. The Supreme Court ruled on First Amendment grounds that Congress could not ban talk on the telephone that is merely indecent, but it could act against messages found to be obscene.

The effect of the decision was to uphold administrative restrictions imposed by the FCC to make it difficult for children to dial porn services. These restrictions include requirements that the message be scrambled so that it can be heard only through a device obtained by an adult telephone subscriber. As a further safeguard, users are provided with a coded access number.

Sable Communications, a provider of "dial-a-porn" in Los Angeles, argued that because it provided a nationwide service, a ban on obscene messages amounted to imposing a national standard for measuring obscenity, something the Supreme Court had said in *Miller* could not be done. Sable said if the law was

---

91. Jay Arnold, Associated Press, "FCC Warn's Indy's WFBQ to Clean Up 'Bob and Tom Show,' " *Indiana Daily Student,* 25 August 1989.
92. 458 U.S. 747, 102 S.Ct. 3348, 73 L.Ed.2d 1113 (1982).

upheld, Sable would have to tone down its messages to fit the standards of the most conservative communities. Six justices of the Supreme Court said the Court had found no constitutional problems with federal laws forbidding the mailing or interstate transportation of obscene materials and had none with the ban on obscene telephone calls. The Court suggested the providers of the talk services could protect themselves by identifying the communities in which the callers reside and tailoring their messages accordingly.

A unanimous Court agreed that the ban on "indecent" messages swept too broadly. Borrowing a phrase from *Butler* v. *Michigan*,[93] the Court said that to limit adult telephone users to sexual talk considered fit for children "would burn the house to roast the pig." It rejected the government's argument that the precedent established in *Pacifica* should control this case. *Pacifica* grew out of a radio broadcast to which anyone, including children, might tune inadvertently and be assaulted by an unwanted sexual message. In this instance, the Court said, people who dial porn message services know what they are seeking. There are no unwilling listeners. The Court conceded that children still might be able to find a way to dial such services but that nothing in the record showed that the rules imposed by the FCC will not work.

In the Professional World

Rapid technological change has done far more than alter the nature of the electronic media. It also has changed the way news is presented on television. Electronic newsgathering techniques have made it possible for minicameras to go almost anywhere and, with the help of microwave links sometimes bounced off satellites, put news on the air as it is happening. The live remote has become a staple of television news in the last decade.

When the space shuttle Challenger exploded seconds after liftoff in 1986, television viewers shared the shock and surprise of the event. They also shared the intrusion into the privacy of the next of kin of the astronauts as the cameras shifted focus to record their stunned reaction to the tragedy. In the hours that followed, viewers who stayed tuned also shared the tedium as the networks strove to fill time between interviews with officials speculating on what went wrong, or with persons who wanted to talk about the victims. The live coverage of that event and others reinforced the observation once made by Elmer Lower, a retired president of ABC News and a veteran of service with all three networks. He said, "We are the only journalistic medium that does its reporting and editing right in front of the audience."[94]

Television's ability to present the news raw, before it can be tested and refined to an approximation of truth by the checking and rechecking of skilled reporters and editors, raises special ethical considerations that apply

---

93. 352 U.S. 380, 77 S.Ct. 524, 1 L.Ed.2d 158 (1957).
94. Richard D. Yoakam and Charles T. Cremer, *ENG: Television News and the New Technology* (New York: Random House, 1985), p. 248.

to no other medium. So, too, does the ring of truth television conveys by giving viewers the sense of being present as news is made. When a newspaper or magazine presents one version of a news event and television another, it is difficult to argue with the viewer who says, "I saw it with my own eyes." And yet television professionals live with the knowledge that their medium has an infinite capacity to distort the news. Tom Pettit, an award-winning television newsman and executive vice-president of NBC News, wrote, "Today, technology permits producers to speed up or slow down actual events, actual voices. This is alteration of reality akin to forging a check."[95]

To forestall such forgery, the news divisions of all three networks and of many local television stations have adopted codes of ethics that are more detailed than that of their professional organization, the Radio-Television News Directors Association. That code starts with the assertion that the primary purpose of broadcast journalists is "to inform the public of events of importance and appropriate interest in a manner that is accurate and comprehensive." That purpose, the code says, overrides all others. The code also says that stories should be given sufficient background to make them meaningful and should not be sensationalized. Further, it says broadcast journalists "shall at all times display humane respect for the dignity, privacy and the well-being of persons with whom the news deals."

It is at this point that the code seems to part company with the realities generated by the intense competition among television news organizations. The television reporter who thrusts a microphone at the grieving survivors of disaster victims to catch their response to "How do you feel?" has become a cliché. That approach to news, and the ambush interview used on ABC's "20/20" and other news shows, have contributed to the public's perception that reporters are callous invaders of privacy. There is enough truth in that perception to make some journalists sensitive about it, but it may in part be a factor of what is not seen on the air. The more detailed codes of ethics adopted by CBS and NBC news advise against interviewing survivors on the air unless their permission is obtained in advance. And even with permission, the codes say that such interviews should be used only if they produce information essential to a proper telling of the story.

Fred Friendly, a former president of CBS News who became a professor at Columbia University, once told WBBM-TV that the ambush interview "is the dirtiest trick department of broadcast journalism."[96] In such interviews, a subject suspected of having something to hide is confronted suddenly in front of a live camera and is asked a question akin to "Why don't you stop beating your wife?" Even persons with nothing to hide are likely to look as though they have. Producers of television news shows are divided

---

95. Ibid., p. xi.
96. Interviewed on "Watching the Watchdog" documentary, WBBM-TV, Chicago, 20 April 1981.

in their opinions as to the propriety of such interviews.[97] All concede they can be abused. Most prefer not to use an ambush interview with people who are not generally in the news. But all feel there are times when it should be used with public officials and others who are accountable to the public for their performance.

More recently, Friendly used even stronger language to condemn a much more serious lapse in broadcast journalism ethics. ABC News used an actor to portray a U.S. diplomat passing a briefcase to a Soviet KGB agent, also an actor. The videotape, as shown on the evening news with Peter Jennings, was grainy, as hidden-camera tape or video often is. It included an electronic time code and cross hairs. The tape was labeled "Exclusive" and was introduced by Jennings as "a harsh reminder that secrecy sells." Nothing was said about the whole episode's being a reenactment of an event that may never have happened. Four days later, Jennings apologized on the air for not labeling the tape as a reenactment. He attributed the lapse to a "production error." At any event, the diplomat, who was named in the story—and in many other news accounts—has not been charged with any offense, let along espionage.

Friendly called the ABC News episode a "fraud," which it was, and "an outrageous demonstration of shameful journalism."[98] It, and the stories in other media, was based on leaks from the State Department, the FBI and other government agencies. Using the information at all was questionable ethics, but to stage an event as though it had actually happened and pass it off as news, Friendly said, could "not be excused as dramatic license." But ABC was not alone in treating news as a form of drama. For a brief period all three networks offered simulations of news events in lieu of the real thing. ABC did it on *Prime Time Live,* featuring Diane Sawyer and Sam Donaldson; CBS News, on *Saturday Night with Connie Chung;* and NBC, on *Yesterday, Today and Tomorrow,* starring Maria Shriver, Chuck Scarborough, and Mary Alice Williams.[99] These experiments in recreating what the cameras did not see—and in most cases could not have seen—were greeted with a storm of professional criticism and with complaints from viewers who said they could not tell where reality ended and fiction took over. NBC soon announced that it would stop using reenactments,[100] and CBS said it was scaling back their use on Connie Chung's show and might end them altogether.[101] ABC said it had reprimanded the employees

---

97. H. Eugene Goodwin, *Groping for Ethics in Journalism* (Ames: Iowa State University Press, 1983), pp. 181–82, 301.
98. Fred W. Friendly, New York Times News Service, "Has Television News Crossed the Line?" *Sunday Herald-Times,* Bloomington, Indiana, 6 August 1989.
99. Kevin Goldman, "TV Network News Is Making Re-Creation a Form of Recreation," *Wall Street Journal,* 30 October 1989.
100. Bill Carter, "NBC News Decides to Stop Using Dramatizations," *New York Times,* 21 November 1989.
101. Kevin Goldman, "CBS Scales Back Use of Re-Enactments on Connie Chung's Prime-Time Show," *Wall Street Journal,* 13 November 1989.

who produced the spy film and had adopted a policy of using no more re-enactments. But the episode serves as a reminder that cameras, like word processors, can manipulate and distort the news. What we see on the television screen with our own eyes may be no closer to the truth than the words of a skilled propagandist. The episode also illustrates that the challenge to get a more dramatic version of the news than is available to the competition can lead even the best broadcast news directors down ethical byways.

Television journalists also live with the knowledge that because their reporting methods are more obtrusive than those of their colleagues in the print media, television reporters may distort the news simply by being there when it happens. Print reporters carry nothing more noticeable than a tape recorder, and these are usually so small they can be slipped into a pocket or purse. Television reporters are part of a team. At the very least, a camera operator will be in evidence, and somewhere nearby there will be a technician to see that the words and pictures get back to the studio. Although cameras have become small enough to carry in one hand, they are difficult to hide. Even in the fifth decade of the television era, a camera tends to draw a crowd. As John Premack, a prizewinning photojournalist with WCVB-TV in Boston, said, "We must recognize that a television camera tends to create its own reality. Part of our job as photojournalists is to understand that our mere presence can inflame, incite, initiate, and otherwise alter events we wish to cover.[102] Everyone in the news business is very much aware that some events, including press conferences, are staged solely in the expectation that cameras will be there. When all television news was recorded in advance and edited before it appeared on the air, such events could be cut to a size commensurate with their importance, or even ignored. Today, when television news producers emphasize "live from the scene" reports, there is little opportunity to screen out the exhibitionists. Their possible presence requires a higher degree of awareness on the part of the reporter on the scene, the camera operator, the electronic coordinator, the anchor, and the news director to detect the point at which the news event is taken over by someone with an ax to grind or a personal score to settle.

No other medium can bring news into the home with the impact of television. No words, no still picture, could duplicate television's portrayal of the awful moment when Challenger disappeared behind a glistening white cloud of smoke. But television news has its shortcomings, too. It tends to magnify stories high in emotional content and visual impact. The taking of hostages by anyone, anywhere, for whatever purpose, seems more important on television than it does reduced to a few paragraphs in a newspaper—especially if the hostages are interviewed in front of cameras. Stories of far greater importance may pass almost unnoticed because they are complex or do not lend themselves to pictorial treatment. It is difficult to simplify and

---

102. Yoakam and Cremer, *ENG*, p. 261.

glamorize a revision of the tax code or a proposal to reduce the federal deficit. If the latter must be explained in forty-five seconds, it is apt to come out in terms of what it might do to a mother of two small children who fears that reduction of her rent subsidy will drive her into the streets.

Despite its shortcomings, polls indicate that some people get all their news from television. For most of us, television and radio are the first to bring us breaking news. All of us rely on it for such impression as we have of the world's newsmakers. Television professionals are aware that theirs is a serious and important business demanding more thought and care than time sometimes permits.

FOR REVIEW

1. What is the rationale for the regulation of broadcasting?

2. Compare and contrast the First Amendment rights of broadcasters and of print publishers.

3. What did the Supreme Court say in *National Broadcasting Co.* v. *United States* with respect to the powers of the Federal Communications Commission?

4. List the principal provisions of the equal opportunities sections of the Communications Act. To whom do they apply? Under what circumstances? How much discretion does a station owner have in deciding whether to grant time to a candidate for public office? Can a station owner exercise control over the content of political usages? Why or why not?

5. What was the fairness doctrine? What was its purpose?

6. List arguments for and against reinstatement of the fairness doctrine. Rank them according to your estimate of the validity and importance of each. Defend your assessment of the arguments. If you were in Congress, how would you vote? Why?

7. Polls show that some people think newspapers are unfair to some people in the news and in their treatment of controversial issues. How would the same arguments you used above apply to a proposed fairness doctrine for newspapers?

8. Describe the factors considered by the Federal Communications Commission in determining which of competing applicants will be granted a broadcast license.

9. If you were a member of the FCC, how would you determine whether a broadcasting station is serving the public interest? If you owned a station, what factors would you want the FCC to consider in determining whether you were operating in the public interest? As a listener and a viewer,

which of the stations you listen to or watch regularly best serves the public interest? Justify your answers to each branch of this question.

10. On what rationale did the Supreme Court decide the *Pacifica* case? On the basis of your exposure to radio and television, give examples of what you might consider indecent programming.

11. Compare and contrast the Supreme Court's decisions in *Pacifica* and *Sable Communications*.

CHAPTER 11

CHAPTER 11

THE CABLE COMMUNICATIONS POLICY ACT

Restrictions on Channel Usage and System Ownership /
Franchising / Regulation of Services and Facilities / Modification
and Renewal of Franchises / Other Requirements

The Cable Policy Act and the Courts
The Cable Policy Act Reconsidered

CABLE SYSTEMS AND THE FIRST AMENDMENT

Cable Systems and Antitrust Law
Must-Carry Programming
Public Access Channels
Sexually Oriented Programming

When the first community antenna television system (CATV) brought signals from Philadelphia stations into Mahoney City, Pennsylvania, less than half a century ago, the new technology was welcomed as a helpful servant. To viewers in mountain valley towns and other remote areas, CATV was seen as a handy tool, giving them access to the entertainment and sports offered by the few VHF television stations then on the air. The owners of those stations saw CATV as a means of extending their audiences, thus making the stations more attractive to advertisers. Sponsors of network programming saw such systems as a means of extending the reach of their advertising messages. The only grumblers were the creators of television programming, who saw the fledgling cable systems as freeloaders, dodging payment of copyright royalties. But when United Artists Television sued to force antenna systems in Clarksburg and Fairmont, West Virginia, to pay for picking up movies it had licensed to the television networks, the U.S. Supreme Court turned it down.[1] The Court held that CATV was simply an extension of the individual viewer's television set, doing "no more than enhance the viewer's capacity to receive the broadcaster's signal." Clearly, the Court

---

1. Fortnightly Corp. v. United Artists Television, 392 U.S. 390, 88 S.Ct. 2084, 20 L.Ed.2d 190 (1968).

472

CABLE TELEVISION SYSTEMS

acted on the theory that cable systems were passive in nature, doing no more than delivering signals from over-the-air television stations to viewers who might not otherwise be able to pick them up.

At the time, that was true. In 1965, fewer than 1400 cable systems served a small percentage of the homes with television sets.[2] Only about 10 percent of those systems originated programming. But in a little over two decades, the once-humble extension of home antennas has become a pervasive force, reaching more than 53 million subscribers, nearly 58 percent of the households with television sets.[3] Further, cable networks originate more programming, both in variety and in quantity, than the over-the-air networks. As a consequence, cable, with help from VCR and satellite dish receivers, has whittled away at the networks' share of the audience, reducing it to about two-thirds of the viewers tuned in at any one time.[4] The money taken in by cable systems has grown accordingly, rising from $3 billion in subscriber fees in 1980 to an estimated $15 billion in 1990.[5] Cable's income from advertising, once anemic, has passed $2 billion a year.

In the beginning, both the Federal Communications Commission and Congress treated cable as the Supreme Court had in *United Artists*. But in the 1960s, as cable operators began charging viewers for special programming, mainly sports events and movies, the climate changed. Over-the-air broadcasters came to see cable systems as competitors for both audience and advertising. At the time, such regulation as there was came primarily from local governments. Cable systems, like the telephone and the electric companies, could provide service only from stringing wires over or under public streets or through easements obtained from owners of private property. This made cable subject to franchises granted by local governments. In return for the right to operate in a community, local officials could and did impose conditions the system must meet. Typically, the franchise might specify the quality of service and the number of channels to be offered, the fee to be charged subscribers, and particular stations that must be carried. Bid-

---

2. Thomas Whiteside, "Onward and Upward with the Arts: Cable—1," *The New Yorker*, 20 May 1985, p. 45 + .
3. "Summary of Broadcasting & Cable," *Broadcasting*, 2 July 1990, p. 61.
4. Nielsen Media Research, as reported in *USA Today*, 1 December 1989.
5. Paul Kagan Associates, "Cable's Growth," *Wall Street Journal*, 19 March 1990.

ding for the right to serve a community sometimes became intensely competitive and tinged with politics. Payoffs were not uncommon.

Beginning in 1965, the FCC assumed some control over cable systems even though they did not use the people's airwaves to deliver their service. The commission acted on the same rationale it had used in the 1940s to bring the broadcasting networks under its supervision. Because virtually all cable programming came from licensed broadcasters, cable operators were treated, at least in part, as though they were broadcasters, too. The FCC required cable systems to carry all local stations with ''significant'' numbers of viewers in the area covered by the system. They also were required to meet the FCC's standards for hiring and promoting minorities and women. Cable operators who initiated their own programming were required to comply with the equal opportunities law with respect to political candidates, the fairness doctrine, and the ban on indecency.

Although cable operators complained that local franchising agencies kept rates too low to be profitable, the demand for service grew steadily during the 1970s. The number of subscribers reached 10 million by the end of the decade, producing revenue of about $3 billion. That growth also brought changes in the legal status of cable. Congress revised the Copyright Act in 1976, imposing licensing fees on cable television systems and authorizing the Copyright Royalty Tribunal to allocate the revenues among originating programmers. In 1984, Congress passed the Cable Communications Policy Act ''to establish a national policy concerning cable communications.''[6] The Act permitted local governments to continue to franchise cable systems, but it limited the fees they could charge and took away their ability to mandate programming. More importantly, effective in 1987, the Act ended, in most instances, the power of local governments to control the rates cable systems could charge their customers. Consequently, rates for basic cable service increased by nearly 50 percent in the next 3 years, accompanied by some increase in the number of channels included in that service.[7] One effect of the Act was to greatly increase the value of cable systems.[8] Another was to create pressure that, as of this writing, may result in new restrictions on cable systems, including a cap on rate increases.[9] Early franchising agreements gave the winning cable operators a monopoly within their assigned territories and a presumption of renewal. In effect, cable systems were seen as public utilities, like the telephone and the electric companies. That view came under attack from companies that were denied franchises in Los Angeles, resulting in a Supreme Court decision holding that the city's refusal to permit competitive service violated the First Amendment.[10] However, in other instances, courts are treating cable systems like public utilities, holding that they must be permitted to use ease-

6. Pub.L. 98-549, 98 Stat. 2779, codified in scattered sections of 47 U.S.C., starting with §521 (1984).
7. Rep. Lee Hamilton, ''The Changing Television Industry,'' newsletter to his 9th Indiana District constituents, 11 July 1990.
8. Laura Landro, ''Market for Cable TV Systems Heats Up,'' *Wall Street Journal,* 9 March 1988.
9. ''Cable Takes a Hit in the House,'' *Broadcasting,* 2 July 1990.
10. City of Los Angeles v. Preferred Communications, 476 U.S. 488, 106 S.Ct. 2034, 80 L.Ed.2d 480 (1986).

ments granted other utilities to gain access to real estate developments, condominiums, and apartment complexes.[11]

This chapter summarizes the major statutes and court decisions pertaining to the regulation of cable television.

Major Cases

- *American Civil Liberties Union* v. *Federal Communications Commission,* 823 F.2d 1554 (1987).

- *City of Los Angeles* v. *Preferred Communications,* 476 U.S. 488, 106 S.Ct. 3034, 80 L.Ed.2d 480 (1986).

- *City of New York* v. *Federal Communications Commission,* 486 U.S. 57, 108 S.Ct. 1637, 100 L.Ed.2d 48 (1988).

THE CABLE COMMUNICATIONS POLICY ACT

As cable television systems grew and became more powerful during the middle years of this century, the cable companies found themselves in the middle of a battle among titans for control of a communications system some deemed capable of changing the very nature of society. The contenders included telephone companies, newspapers, broadcasters, local governments, providers of computerized data bases, and advertisers.

In the early going, telephone companies enjoyed a significant advantage. They already were wired to most homes in their service areas. With upgrading to coaxial cable or fiber optics, they could deliver not only telephone messages but other services—particularly their valuable Yellow Pages—to their subscribers. Subscribers who chose do to so could attach a keyboard to their television screen and let their fingers do the walking into electronic offerings of goods and services that could be updated whenever the advertiser wished. At that point, newspaper publishers, fearing loss of their equally valuable classified advertising, stepped into the fray. With help from Congress and from cable operators, they were able to persuade a federal court to bar the American Telephone & Telegraph Co., and the regional telephone companies that had been a part of it, from providing electronic information services. Judge Harold Greene, approving the consent decree that broke up the Bell system, wrote that if AT&T was "permitted to engage both in the transmission and generation of information there would be a substantial risk not only that it would stifle the efforts of other electronic publishers but that it would acquire a substantial monopoly over the generation of news in the more

---

11. Centel Cable TV Co. of Fla. v. Thos. J. White Development Corp. (11th Cir. 1990) No. 89-5318, June 5; Centel Cable Television Company of Florida v. Burg & Divosta Corp., 712 F.Supp. 176 (S.D.Fla. 1988); Cable TV Fund 14-A v. Property Owners Association Chesapeake Ranch Estates, 706 F.Supp. 422 (D.Md. 1989).

general sense." Were that to happen, he said, it would "strike at a principle which lies at the heart of the First Amendment: that the American people are entitled to a diversity of sources of information."[12]

There was more here than met the eye. By the early 1980s, far-seeing newspaper publishers knew that their delivery system—carriers toting many pages of newsprint to subscribers' homes—was the most inefficient part of their operation. Technology then in sight, the electronic publishing systems mentioned by Judge Greene, pointed to the possibility of using cable to deliver a customized newspaper that could be printed in each subscriber's home. Arthur Ochs Sulzberger, chairman of the New York Times Company, was one of several publishers who urged repeal of the political restrictions applied to broadcasting because, "the line between print and electronic journalism is thin at best and getting thinner."[13] If at some time in the future newspapers did have to use cable systems to deliver information, their First Amendment freedoms would be diminished if cable still were regulated by the FCC on the same terms as broadcasters.

Cable operators wanted the rules changed, too. They felt squeezed between the demands of local franchising authorities, which kept their fees up and rates down, and their subscribers, who wanted more and better service.

Congress reacted in 1984 by adopting legislation to establish "a national policy concerning cable communications."[14] One of the law's goals was to "assure that cable communications provide and are encouraged to provide the widest possible diversity of information sources and services to the public," echoing Judge Greene. On a more mundane level, the law established "an orderly process for franchise renewal which protects cable operators against unfair denials of renewal." The law did so by establishing standards for quality of service which, if met, would ensure renewal.

The major provisions of the act are summarized below.

Restrictions on Channel Usage and System Ownership

The Act permits authorities to require operators to set aside channels for public, educational, or government use. If they do so, the operator is forbidden to exercise editorial control over the content of those channels. Further, systems that offer more than thirty-six channels must set aside some of them for commercial use by others, which could include newspaper publishers. Cable operators can charge reasonable fees for such use but are forbidden to exercise editorial control over the content. However, franchising authorities may forbid programming that is obscene or "is in conflict with community standards in that it is lewd, lascivious, filthy, or indecent or is otherwise unprotected by the Constitution." Another section of the Act provides for stiff penalties for use of a cable system to transmit obscene materials.

---

12. U.S. v. American Tel. & Tel. Co., 552 F.Supp. 131 (D.D.C. 1982); affirmed, Maryland v. U.S., 460 U.S. 1001, 103 S.Ct. 1240, 75 L.Ed.2d 472 (1983).
13. "Sulzberger, Paley Call for End of the Equal Time Rule," *Editor & Publisher*, 27 November 1982, p. 10.
14. 47 U.S.C. § 521.

Owners of television stations are forbidden to own cable systems serving the same area but can own systems serving other areas. Franchising authorities cannot reject an applicant because "of such person's ownership or control of any media of mass communications or other media interests." However, the FCC was given authority to prevent the owners of other media, such as newspapers, from owning a cable system serving the same community. Common carriers, i.e., telephone companies, are forbidden to own cable systems except in areas where delivery of video programming by cable "demonstrably could not exist" unless the telephone company provided it.

Franchising

Local governments retain the authority to grant and renew franchises. However, they are not permitted to treat cable systems as common carriers for purposes of regulation. This exempts them from rate-setting procedures with which public utilities must comply. The Act requires franchising authorities to "assure that access to cable service is not denied to any group of potential residential cable subscribers because of the income of the residents of the local area in which such group resides."

Local governments also retain the authority to require cable operators to pay a franchise fee for the privilege of doing business. However, § 542 limits that fee to 5 percent of a system's annual gross revenues from its cable operations. If a fee set at less than 5 percent is increased, operators are permitted to bill subscribers for the difference. Any decrease must be passed through.

The Act took from local governments, effective in 1987, all authority to regulate rates charged for cable service except in those few areas where cable systems have no competition either from over-the-air stations or from another cable system. This has proved to be one of the most significant changes made by Congress. Rates have increased, as already noted. But so has the number of channels offered by cable systems. Profits also have increased, making cable systems much more valuable to investors. In 1985, $1500 per subscriber was considered "a dangerously high price" to pay for a cable system.[15] In 1989, New York Times Co. sold its cable TV unit, serving suburban communities around Cherry Hill, New Jersey, for between $2500 and $3000 a subscriber.[16] A system in Broward County, Florida, sold for $2878 a subscriber.

Regulation of Services and Facilities

Section 544 took away from local governments all authority over services, facilities, and equipment of cable operators. It gave the Federal Communications Commission authority to establish technical standards for equipment and thus for the quality of the video pictures delivered to subscribers. Section 544 also took

---

15. Laura Landro, "Market for Cable TV Systems Heats Up," *Wall Street Journal,* 9 March 1988.
16. Laura Landro, "Sales of Two Cable Firms Set for $2 Billion," *Wall Street Journal,* 10 January 1989.

from local governments authority to require operators to carry specified "video programming or other information services." At the time, the authority to require cable systems to carry specific channels—"must carry" rules—was believed to reside in the FCC. However, a federal appeals court since has held that such rules violate the First Amendment rights of cable operators.[17] There is more on this later.

Modification and Renewal of Franchises

Cable operators are permitted to change the terms of their franchise if they can demonstrate that it is "commercially impracticable" to continue to comply with them. This means that operators may propose to drop a channel if the fee charged by the provider is raised, or if subscriber fees drop below the break-even point. However, such proposals must be submitted to a public hearing.

If local governments are dissatisfied with a cable operator's service and therefore not likely to renew its franchise, they must schedule a hearing 3½ years prior to the termination date. At that time, officials must identify the future cable-related needs and interests of the community and review the performance of the current operator. If the operator seeks renewal, its request must be granted unless further hearings result in an adverse finding in one or more of four areas:

1. The operator has not "substantially complied with the material terms" of the existing franchise.

2. The quality of service, "including signal quality, response to consumer complaints, and billing practices," is unsatisfactory.

3. The operator is unable because of financial, legal, or other problems to provide the service called for in the franchise.

4. The operator's proposal for meeting the community's needs, as identified in the earlier proceeding, is unreasonably inadequate or expensive.

A local government that decides not to renew the franchise must issue a written decision giving the government's reasons for not doing so. That decision is subject to appeal to the courts. The law says "the court shall grant appropriate relief" if the franchising authority failed to comply with the prescribed procedures or if its findings in any of the four areas above are "not supported by a preponderance of the evidence." The language of the section creates a strong presumption that franchises are to be renewed.

If the franchise is not renewed, the law requires the franchising authority or the new franchisee to pay the operator the "fair market value" of the physical property "valued as a going concern." No value is to be allocated to the franchise itself. If a franchise is revoked for cause, the new owner is required to pay

---

17. Century Communications Corp. v. Federal Communications Commission, 835 F.2d 292 (D.C.Cir. 1987).

"an equitable price." The difference between that and "fair market value" is not explained.

Other Requirements

Cable operators who obtain personal information about their subscribers are forbidden to disclose it to others. This section is designed to protect the privacy of people who subscribe to interactive systems, which have not caught on with the general public. A related section gives franchising agencies authority to require prescribed levels of customer service. This covers such things as signal quality and restoration of service interrupted by technical problems.

The law provides a maximum fine of $1000 for unauthorized tapping into a cable system and more severe penalties, including a prison term, if the unauthorized tap is used for commercial purposes.

Cable systems employing more than five persons are bound by the same equal employment opportunities provisions applying to broadcasters.

The Cable Policy Act and the Courts

Municipalities, which saw themselves as losers in the struggle for control over cable systems, promptly challenged the provisions of the Cable Policy Act. They were joined by others, including the American Civil Liberties Union, Cable Television Access Coalition, the National League of Cities, and some cable system owners. Their principal targets were the cap on franchise fees and the Federal Communication Commission's rules defining the level of competition required to exempt cable systems from control over the rates charged their subscribers. Both provisions were upheld by the U.S. Court of Appeals for the District of Columbia Circuit. Another lawsuit attacked the technical standards for quality of service established by the FCC under authority given it by the Policy Act. The latter led to a Supreme Court decision affirming the commission's authority.

American Civil Liberties Union v. *Federal Communications Commission*, **823 F.2d 1554 (1987).**

The more comprehensive decision came in *American Civil Liberties Union* v. *Federal Communications Commission*, which included the attack on the rate and fee sections of the act. It was one of eight cases consolidated for decision by the District of Columbia Circuit. The court dealt first with the rules adopted by the FCC to define "effective competition." Section 623(b)(1) authorizes the FCC to prescribe regulations under which a franchising authority can set rates "for basic cable service in circumstances in which a cable system is not subject to effective competition." The agency ruled that such competition exists if three off-the-air stations are available in the cable community, even though reception of any or all of them may be poor.

The FCC's next step was to define the terms under which a franchising authority could regulate rates in areas, which it conceded were few, lacking effective competition. The law permits regulation of the rate charged for "basic cable service," which it defines as "any service tier which includes" local over-the-air television channels. The FCC narrowed the definition to include only "the tier of service regularly provided to all subscribers that includes" all "must-carry broadcast television channels." Within that tier, the FCC rules said, cable operators could automatically pass through to their subscribers any additional fees charged by the providers of the services, including any increase in copyright royalties. Some cable operators offer such services as ESPN, the sports network, or CNN, Ted Turner's 24-hour news service, as part of their basic package. In 1989, CNN charged operators 30 cents a subscriber a month; ESPN, 32 cents. CNN's charge had doubled since 1983; ESPN's had more than tripled.

The ACLU and others argued that the commission had acted arbitrarily in defining effective competition and in limiting the authority of local governments to control rates. The court disagreed, upholding the FCC's rate regulation rules "in all respects" save for three exceptions. It held that the FCC had acted arbitrarily in establishing the criteria for determining "effective competition" and in permitting operators an automatic pass-through for increased costs. It further held that the FCC had ignored the clear intent of Congress in redefining the "basic tier of services."

The court instructed the commission to refine its criteria for determining whether an over-the-air station reaches a community. At the least, a significant number of viewers must be able to receive a clear picture. The court also told the

ESPN, a 24-hours-a-day cable sports service, began with a reputation for its willingness to cover sports events of any kind, no matter how trivial. It has become the prime carrier for college basketball, and also has won the right to cover professional football and baseball games. As a consequence, by 1989 it was able to triple the rate it charges cable operators for the right to present its programming. (Courtesy ESPN. Photo by Tom Maguire)

FCC that it was bound by the Act's clear and unambiguous language defining "basic cable service." That language, it said, leaves cable operators free "to structure their service tiers in whatever way they wish."

In striking down the automatic pass-through rule, the court said the law contains procedural safeguards adequate to protect operators from a franchising authority's arbitrary denial of rate increases needed to cover increased costs. In addition, the court noted that the law permits operators to raise rates by 5 percent each year at their discretion. The court concluded that in drafting the Cable Policy Act Congress had created "an elaborate scheme for automatic rate increases" and needed no further help from the FCC.

City of New York v. *Federal Communications Commission,* **486 U.S. 57, 108 S.Ct. 1637, 100 L.Ed.2d 48 (1988).**

The case that reached the Supreme Court was brought by New York City, joined by several other cities and the National League of Cities. While the lawsuit was aimed only at § 544(e), which gave the FCC permissive authority to establish technical standards for cable systems, it posed a challenge to the Act itself. The question was, "Can the FCC preempt local control over cable systems?" The Supreme Court saw the case as "yet another development in the ongoing efforts of federal, state, and local authorities to regulate different aspects of cable television over the last three decades." In this instance, the Court held unanimously that the FCC did not exceed its authority by preempting state and local technical standards governing the quality of cable television signals.

The cities complained that the technical standards established by the FCC were too low. They argued that they should be able to hold cable operators to higher standards, thus assuring viewers of a higher quality of service. The Supreme Court looked to the Supremacy Clause of the Constitution for its answer.[18] Under that clause, laws enacted in compliance with the Constitution are "the supreme Law of the Land." It long has been established, the Court said, that the clause applies not only to acts of Congress, but to regulations adopted by administrative agencies under authority given them by Congress. Here, the authority was clear, leaving only the question whether the FCC acted reasonably in setting technical standards. The Court held that it had. In establishing the standards, the commission had said that if standards were permitted to vary from community to community they would "create potentially serious negative consequences for cable system operators and cable consumers in terms of the cost of service and the ability of the industry to respond to technological changes." As of this writing, then, the Cable Policy Act, and the FCC regulations fleshing it out, govern cable systems everywhere in the United States. Local franchising authorities are limited in the fees they can collect from cable systems. Except for those few parts of the country where systems have no effective over-the-air competition, local authorities have no control over fees charged subscribers. Nor can they refuse to renew an operator's franchise unless they can document compelling reasons for doing so.

---

18. Art. VI, cl. 2.

The Cable Policy Act Reconsidered

Beyond question, the Cable Policy Act of 1984 has been good for cable system operators. But five years after it took effect, powerful members of Congress were asking whether it was good for cable system subscribers, for over-the-air television stations, and for other competitors in the information and entertainment sectors. Some charged that one effect of the cable act was creation of a powerful monopoly that needs taming in the public interest.[19] In mid-1990, both houses of Congress were considering legislation to bring cable systems under a greater degree of regulation, particularly with respect to the rates they can charge their subscribers.[20] Witnesses told the Senate Commerce Committee that rates in some Tennessee cities had increased by more than 100 percent in three years. The average monthly rate for basic service has risen from about $7.50 in 1980 to $16 in 1990.

Both the House and Senate versions would give the Federal Communications Commission authority to deal with "unreasonable or abusive" rates or rates that are "significantly excessive." Neither would restore local control over rates. Nor would they raise the 5 percent cap on franchise fees. Other provisions of the bills would:

1. Seek to prevent cable operators from monopolizing programming sources or discriminating against programmers who refuse to give them a financial interest in programs.

2. Restore rules requiring cable operators to carry in preferred channel locations local commercial and noncommercial stations.

3. Limit the size of cable systems.

4. Permit local franchising authorities to impose higher technical standards than those established by the FCC.

CABLE SYSTEMS AND THE FIRST AMENDMENT

Although cable systems have been the subject of court decisions for more than thirty years, courts have reached no firm position as to cable systems' First Amendment status. At times, courts have given cable no more First Amendment protection than they have given broadcasters. At others, they have suggested that cable systems have more in common with newspapers than with broadcast-

---

19. Jack J. Valenti, "Is Cable Monopolizing Television? How Congress Created a Cable Monster," *New York Times,* 24 May 1987; Mary Lu Carnevale, "Congress Seeks to Rein In Cable TV," *Wall Street Journal,* 11 December 1989; and Dennis Kneale, "Why Viewers Would Like to Zap Their Cable Firms," *Wall Street Journal,* 19 March 1990. Valenti is president and chief executive officer of the Motion Picture Association of America.
20. "Cable Takes a Hit in the House," *Broadcasting,* 2 July 1990, p. 19 + .

ers. This uncertainty was the subject of a seminar in 1982 that brought together more than sixty educators, lawyers, journalists, broadcasters, cable system operators, government administrators, scientists, and members of special interest groups.[21] The assignment was to visualize the future of information delivery systems and to think about the rules that ought to regulate them. Those convened assumed that in the not-too-distant future cable would be the principal means of bringing news, information, and entertainment into most homes. Although the participants differed on many topics, they agreed on two points:

1. "The First Amendment bars, and ought to bar, 'content regulation' in any form, for print or broadcasting or any combination of the two."

2. Print publishers who move into electronic transmission of text materials should retain the same degree of First Amendment freedom they now enjoy.

Courts have not yet fully embraced those two points. The present tendency is for courts to treat cable systems as offering a mixture of speech—the programming—and conduct—the system itself. In theory, then, this makes cable television a form of symbolic speech. The leading case in that area of First Amendment law is *United States* v. *O'Brien*,[22] in which the Supreme Court established a four-part test for determining when government may regulate speech laced with conduct. Many courts are holding that a specific restriction can be imposed on a cable system only if

1. It is within the constitutional power of the government. Whatever the restriction is, it must be something that the government unit involved has authority to do.

2. It furthers an important or substantial government interest. The government must be acting to advance some goal that will benefit significant numbers of people.

3. The government interest is unrelated to the suppression of free expression. Government can't impose restrictions on a cable system for no other purpose than to prevent expression of unpopular ideas.

4. The incidental restriction on alleged First Amendment freedoms is no greater than is essential to the furtherance of that interest. Government cannot ban all sexually oriented programming from cable systems to prevent the possibility that some of it might be obscene.

That test has been used in decisions attacking the granting of exclusive franchises to cable systems, rules requiring cable systems to carry designated sta-

---

21. First Amendment Congress, "Special Report," The Newspaper Center, Washington, D.C. (1982).
22. 391 U.S. 367, 88 S.Ct. 1673, 20 L.Ed.2d 672 (1968).

tions, public access requirements, and state and local laws forbidding indecent programming. Court decisions pertaining to each of these areas are discussed in the next four sections.

Cable Systems and Antitrust Law

By their very nature, cable systems tend to be monopolies. Stringing coaxial cable, even in densely populated neighborhoods, costs a considerable amount of money per subscriber. To protect their investment, cable operators sought and obtained exclusive franchises to serve a community or a well-defined part of a community. Early court decisions upheld such franchises on the ground that the "apparent natural monopoly characteristics of cable television provide...an argument for regulation of entry."[23]

City of Los Angeles v.
Preferred
Communications, **476**
U.S. 488, 106 S.Ct. 3034,
80 L.Ed.2d 480 (1986).

However, in 1986 the U.S. Supreme Court held, in an antitrust case originating in Los Angeles, that cable systems engage in activities that "plainly implicate First Amendment interests," which limit a city's authority to grant an exclusive franchise to a cable operator. But because the case reached the Court on a motion to dismiss rather than after a trial to resolve factual issues, the Court did not say how strong those interests are. In its analysis, the Court seemed to endorse the argument that cable systems are closer to newspapers than to broadcasters in the First Amendment hierarchy.

The case began when Preferred Communications sought to install a cable system in a part of Los Angeles already served by another operator franchised by the city. The city and its Department of Water and Power refused to let Preferred use poles or underground conduits to string its cable, although both agreed that there was space to install another service. Preferred appealed to a U.S. district court for relief, arguing that its rights had been violated under the First Amendment and federal antitrust law. The court granted the city's motion to dismiss. The court of appeals affirmed the dismissal of the antitrust complaint but reversed on First Amendment grounds, holding that the city's grant of an exclusive franchise in an area where existing pole systems could support more than one cable restricted freedom of speech. The Supreme Court affirmed, but remanded the case to the trial court to resolve disputed questions of fact.

In its argument to the Court, Preferred compared cable television service with newspapers and magazines. Its business, like theirs, it said, is to provide subscribers with a mixture of news, information, and entertainment. And, like newspapers, it does so by using some of its space to retransmit material provided by others and at the same time originating content on its own. Justice William H. Rehnquist, writing for the majority, gave partial endorsement of that argument:

---

23.   Omega Satellite Products v. City of Indianapolis, 694 F.2d 119 (7th Cir. 1982).

...[T]hrough original programming or by exercising editorial discretion over which stations or programs to include in its repertoire, respondent seeks to communicate messages on a wide variety of topics and in a wide variety of formats. We recently noted that cable operators exercise "a significant amount of editorial discretion regarding what their programming will include."[24] Cable television partakes of some of the aspects of speech and the communication of ideas as do the traditional enterprises of newspaper and book publishers, public speakers and pamphleteers. Respondent's proposed activities would seem to implicate First Amendment interests as do the activities of wireless broadcasters, which were found to fall within the ambit of the First Amendment in [*Red Lion*], even though the free speech aspects of the wireless broadcasters' claim were found to be outweighed by the government's interests in regulating by reason of the scarcity of frequencies.

Three justices concurred in the Court's decision but wrote separately to note their understanding that, because the factual basis for the dispute had not been resolved by the courts below, the First Amendment status of cable was left open. It still is.

The unresolved facts, required for an *O'Brien* analysis, involved the interests the city sought to protect by granting exclusive cable franchises. It said it sought to minimize the demands cable systems make on the use of public property, prevent "a permanent visual blight" resulting from Preferred's stringing of "nearly 700 miles of hanging and buried wire," and avoid traffic delays caused by cuts in city streets.

Three years later, Preferred's owners still were waiting for the district court judge to set a trial date. City officials continued to oppose the company's ten-year effort to bring competitive cable to Watts and other nearby areas largely populated by blacks. Nor had competition caught on in many other places. A senior analyst with Paul Kagan and Associates, a media research firm, estimated that only two or three dozen communities have allowed second companies to compete for cable subscribers.[25]

The U.S. Court of Appeals for the Eighth Circuit read the Supreme Court's decision in *Preferred* as permitting exclusive franchises in smaller cities where the size of the market makes competing systems impractical.[26] In such instances, the court said, the First Amendment interest in a competitive marketplace for ideas can be served by opening a franchise for competing bids at the end of the current holder's term. A U.S. district court judge in California held that the scarcity rationale used by the Supreme Court in *Red Lion* clearly does not apply to cable systems because they have "the potential of providing a virtually limitless number of channels."[27] Therefore, "unless cable television differs in some material respect from the print media, the First Amendment standards that apply to

---

24. The quotation is from United States v. Midwest Video Corp., 406 U.S. 649, 92 S.Ct. 1860, 32 L.Ed.2d 390 (1972).

25. John R. Emshwiller, "Prying Open the Cable-TV Monopolies," *Wall Street Journal*, 10 August 1989.

26. Central Telecommunications v. TCI Cablevision, 800 F.2d 711 (8th Cir. 1986).

27. Group W Cable v. City of Santa Cruz, 669 F.Supp. 954 (N.D.Cal. 1987).

newspapers apply with equal force to cable." The court concluded that the city of Santa Cruz could not grant an exclusive franchise to one cable operator but could require that a potential competitor prove its financial ability to install and maintain a system.

Must-Carry Programming

In the 1960s, as cable systems emerged as competitors to broadcasters, the Federal Communications Commission imposed various restrictions on programming. Some were designed to prevent systems from bringing in distant stations whose programming might draw viewers away from the fare offered by local stations. Others were designed to protect UHF stations whose signal quality often was significantly poorer than that offered by cable. By 1980, most protective rules had been abandoned, leaving only requirements that cable systems must carry any local station or any station "significantly viewed," if it requested carriage. The principal beneficiaries were public television stations and independent UHF stations, which were assured of an opportunity to reach cable subscribers.

In 1980, Turner Broadcasting System asked the Federal Communications Commission to start rule-making procedures leading up to abandonment of the must-carry rules. It said that the First Amendment and changes in the broadcast and cable businesses required such examination. At about the same time, a cable system in Quincy, Washington, appealed a $5000 fine imposed by the FCC because the system had ignored an order to carry television stations in Spokane, Washington. The U.S. Court of Appeals for the District of Columbia Circuit combined the two cases and ruled in *Quincy Cable TV* v. *Federal Communications Commission*[28] that the must-carry rules violated the First Amendment rights of cable system operators. Applying the *O'Brien* test, the court concluded that the FCC had not proved that a substantial government interest was furthered by requiring cable systems to carry designated stations.

Broadcasters and interest groups representing television viewers protested. They feared that cable operators would drop poorly viewed local stations, including public television stations, to show more popular fare. The National Cable Television Association entered into negotiations with broadcasters to seek agreement on a revised set of must-carry rules both sides could live with. With a push from Congress, the FCC adopted the resulting compromise. It was challenged almost immediately, leading to an appellate court decision in *Century Communications Corp.* v. *Federal Communications Commission,*[29] again holding that the rules violated the First Amendment. Dennis Patrick, then FCC chairman, said the decision justified the commission's reluctance to renew the must-carry rules. "It's difficult to square the First Amendment with any must-carry regime in the

28. 768 F.2d 1434 (D.C.Cir. 1985).
29. 835 F.2d 292 (D.C.Cir. 1987).

absence of actual evidence of harm,'' he said.[30] Nevertheless, Congress has continued its study of bills designed to reinstate must-carry rules.

Public Access Channels

About 1500 communities require their cable systems to provide a public access channel open without charge to anyone who wants to try to reach the public with a noncommercial message. The cable operator is required to provide a studio, video camera, and other assistance needed to get the message on the air. Some cable operators cover such events as high school athletic awards dinners, band concerts, and service club speakers, presenting them either as they happen or on a delayed basis. The original idea was that the channel could become a public forum for the airing of opinion on local issues.

The channels also have been discovered by such groups as the Ku Klux Klan, American Nazis, ''skin heads,'' and other fringe groups. Some of these have produced taped programs and offered them through their members to public access channels on a regular basis.[31] The presumption is that such channels are public forums which must be open to all points of view, no matter how offensive to some members of the community. The Cable Act forbids censorship except to prevent obscene programming. Some communities have reacted to hate broadcasts by organizing discussion groups to present arguments rebutting the racists.

The city council in Kansas City, Missouri, took another course to counteract cable use by the Klan. It abolished the public access channel called for in its franchise with American Cablevision. The Klan, helped by the American Civil Liberties Union, sued on grounds that it was being denied freedom of speech. Although there are no cases directly in point, the city's lawyers concluded they could not win the lawsuit. The council voted to restore the channel.[32] Representatives of the city's minorities protested. A spokesperson for the cable company said it was concerned that the Klan's messages might offend some of its 152,000 subscribers. However, the legal status of public access requirements is still unresolved.

Sexually Oriented Programming

As we saw in the previous chapter, the Supreme Court has upheld the authority of the Federal Communications Commission to punish radio and television stations for airing indecent programming. There is no similar restriction on cable

---

30. Bob Davis, ''Court Throws Out FCC's Requirement That Cable-TV Carry Broadcast Outlets,'' *Wall Street Journal*, 14 December 1987.
31. Charles McCoy, ''White Supremacists Find a TV Platform via Public Access,'' *Wall Street Journal*, 12 July 1988.
32. ''Kansas City Restores Cable Outlet to Which the Klan Sought Access,'' *New York Times*, 16 July 1989.

systems. Indeed, the Supreme Court has affirmed without opinion lower court decisions striking down a Utah law aimed at limiting the sexual content of cable television programs.[33] Although the law closely followed standards the Court established in *Pacifica* and *Miller,* a U.S. district court in Salt Lake City held that the law violated the First Amendment. The lower courts held that the definition of indecency was so broadly written that cable operators would have no clear idea as to which programs might be found offensive.

The law gave state and local governments the right to file civil actions seeking a fine for cable operators who broadcast indecent material, defined as matter "patently offensive" as measured against the community's standards. The time at which the material was broadcast was a factor in the determination. The state attorney general interpreted the law to mean that programs considered indecent, but not legally obscene, could be shown only between midnight and 7 a.m. The state argued that the limitation was a reasonable means of furthering the state interest in protecting minors and the privacy of unwilling adults. Attorneys general in ten other states filed friend of the court briefs supporting Utah's position.

With the rejection of that position, the only legal restriction on sexually explicit programming delivered by cable is that found in §559 of the Cable Policy Act. That section provides for a fine of not more than $10,000 or imprisonment of not more than two years, or both, for the transmission of obscene programming. A second restriction has arisen in some instances through public pressure. A grand jury in Cincinnati indicted the Warner Amex cable system serving part of that city on a charge of pandering obscenity because the system had offered its subscribers programming provided by Playboy Enterprises.[34] The charge was dismissed in exchange for Warner's promise not to offer X-rated programming, which it had not offered in the first place. The Playboy channel included nudity but not the sexual activity required to meet the *Miller* standard. Warner had dropped it before the grand jury returned its indictment.

In the Professional World

From humble beginnings, within two generations cable television has become a pervasive force. Once welcomed by over-the-air broadcasters as an extension of their reach, it has slowly devoured their audiences so that by 1990 stations affiliated with ABC, CBS, and NBC were being viewed in less than two-thirds of the television homes. The networks also had lost their exclusive rights to professional football and baseball games, which they now share with ESPN, a sports service designed specifically for distribution by cable, and others.

---

33. Community Television of Utah v. Wilkinson, 611 F.Supp. 1099 (D.Utah 1985); aff'd as Jones v. Wilkinson, 800 F.2d 989 (10th Cir. 1986); aff'd without opinion, 489 U.S. 986, 107 S.Ct. 1559, 94 L.Ed.2d 753 (1987).
34. "Warner Amex Cable Unit in Cincinnati Indicted for Obscenity," *Wall Street Journal,* 15 June 1983.

The Supreme Court has endorsed the view that the First Amendment mandates competition among cable operators, if pole and conduit space permits the threading of more than one wire. Despite that ruling, lower courts have almost universally recognized an economic reality. Installation costs and profit margins make effective competition a near impossibility. Thus, entrenched cable systems are a natural monopoly, like public utilities. Also like public utilities, cable systems can be counted on to return a profit in good times and bad. Consequently, cable systems have proven attractive to investors, who have bought local systems from local owners and made them part of multi-billion-dollar corporations. In 1990, the five largest cable operators reached just under 50 percent of the homes subscribing to a cable system.[35] The largest operator, Tele-Communications, reached about 11 million subscribers. The other four large cable firms are Time Warner, Comcast, Continental Cablevision, and Cox Cable Communications. Time Warner is a product of a union between Time, Inc., the magazine publisher, and Warner Brothers, a major producer of movies and television programs. Cox is affiliated with Cox Newspapers and Cox Broadcasting, owners of newspapers and television stations in Ohio, Georgia, Arizona, Colorado, and Texas. Cablevision has a 50-50 cable programming partnership with General Electric Co., owner of the National Broadcasting Co.[36] Obviously, cable systems have reached full stature among the multimedia giants.

There is more to come. In 1990, National Broadcasting Co., Hughes Communications, Rupert Murdoch's News Corp., and Cablevision Systems announced plans to invest $1 billion in Sky Cable, which is being formed to deliver news and information by satellite directly to viewers' homes, starting in 1993.[37] Three of the companies involved also create programming, some of which will be offered by Sky Cable. Murdoch's News Corp. owns Twentieth Century Fox and Fox Broadcasting. News Corp. also operates Sky Television, which provides satellite service to homes in Europe. Cablevision and NBC provide programming for Consumer News and Business Channel, Bravo, Sports Channel America, and ten regional sports channels. NBC also is part owner of the Arts & Entertainment Network. At the heart of the new system will be a Hughes-built satellite transceiver so powerful that its signals can be picked up by a 12-by-18-inch receiving antenna. The satellite will have a capacity of 108 channels and will be able to deliver high-definition television and digital sound. Officials of the companies said they will direct their marketing toward the 20 million U.S. homes not now reached by cable systems.

Separately, General Electric's GE American Communications announced that it was entering a joint venture with nine cable operators to

---

35. Paul Kagan Associates.
36. Laura Landro, "Direct-Broadcast TV May Be Getting Off the Ground," *Wall Street Journal,* 21 February 1990.
37. Paul Richter, "New Satellite-to-Home TV Service Due in 1993," *Los Angeles Times,* 22 February 1990.

In a little more than a generation, cable television has become a pervasive force, reaching nearly two-thirds of the homes with television sets. Because of the costs of installing cable, it also has become a monopoly in the areas it serves. However, new technology, represented by this unobtrusive antenna perched on a window ledge, makes it possible for digital signals, bounced off a satellite, to deliver more than 100 high-quality television and audio channels to receivers anywhere. (Courtesy of Hughes Communications)

deliver ten channels of programming from a GE satellite directly to homes. Its offerings will include some of the superstations now given nationwide distribution by cable.

Whether such systems will remain nothing more than a means of reaching areas cable cannot economically reach remains to be seen. The antenna required to pick up signals from the satellite will cost about $300, compared to the $2000 to $3000 cost of the six-foot dishes now in use in a few million homes. Users of those dishes must buy a decoder to unscramble some signals, and they are supposed to pay a monthly fee for the services they pluck out of the air. The starting rate for basic service on Sky Cable is estimated at $25 a month, compared to the present average rate of about $16 a month for basic cable service. Given current trends in the price of the latter, the figures might well be comparable by 1993.

There are other aspects of cable television that some find troubling. Once a family plugs into a cable system, it is not likely to use the set to bring in television stations through the air. The Federal Communications Commission has pending a rule that would require cable systems to provide subscribers with a switch that would permit them to choose between cable and over-the-air reception at will, but this assumes that homeowners will be willing to maintain an antenna. Thus, cable systems have the potential to become monopolists in another way. Given the studies that show the average person spending six or more hours a day watching television, and only thirty minutes or less with a newspaper, cable operators conceivably can shape our view of our surroundings. If at some time cable's hundred or so channels are used to carry high-fidelity, stereophonic music in several varieties, movies on demand, classified advertising, catalog shopping services, and an around-the-clock news service, will people need any other sources of entertainment and information? Could not cable be the only medium in town?

But, in another sense, cable is a fragmenting medium, as conventional broadcasters are discovering to their sorrow. Subscribers to the basic channels on a small cable system have their choice at any one time of a bewildering array of programming. As this is being written, the cable television system serving our small south-central Indiana community offers access to five movies, a pot-boiler comedy, a classic crime drama from the 1970s, a John Wayne classic, a mystery thriller from the 1950s, and a filmed Broadway musical; reviews of current movies, including clips of some of the best scenes; sports, including the British Open golf tournament live from St. Andrews in Scotland, a stock car race from Pennsylvania, a baseball game from Chicago, and a roundup of the sports highlights of the previous week; a profile of the Baka Pygmies in Cameroon; news, including Turner Broadcasting's Cable News Network and its Headline service, a discussion of a civil rights bill recently passed by the U.S. Senate, and the expectation of a top-of-the-hour news capsule from an Indianapolis station; a profile of a renowned ballerina, with excerpts from her work; music, both the colorful, pulsating contemporary rock of MTV, and the country-western fare of the Nashville Network; for children, reruns of *Lassie;* for older children and the futuristic minded, a fanciful look at the not-so-distant twenty-first century; an uplifting look at life from the Christian Broadcasting Network; two channels that huckster jewelry, clothing, and gadgets; and a weather service confirming that this is indeed a rainy day with more to come in the next five days. All of this on an early Sunday afternoon in midsummer.

The point of such variety is that cable allows people to use their leisure time to immerse themselves in the fare of their choice, to the exclusion of all else. Those who are turned off by the world's troubles need, if they choose, never be troubled by them. They can create their own world from the choices available on cable, supplemented by a rented cassette from their neighborhood video store or supermarket if need be. A study conducted in 1990 by the Times Mirror Center for The People & The Press discovered such a lack of interest in national and international news among young people that the report was entitled "Age of Indifference."[38] The survey showed

---

38. Debra Gersh, "Age of Indifference," *Editor & Publisher,* 7 July 1990, p. 10 + .

that the younger generation "knows less, cares less, and reads newspapers less. It is also a generation that votes less and is less critical of its leaders and institutions than young people in the past." Other than a reference to MTV as a possible influence on attention-span, the report made no connection between television viewing habits and its findings. Nor does this author. Nevertheless, the findings offer material for discussion.

The survey was conducted in the immediate aftermath of the overturn of Communist governments in eastern Europe, climaxing in the breaching of the Berlin Wall. For older people who had spent their lives thinking of the Soviet Union and communism as powerful forces shaping twentieth-century history, those events were breathtaking. And yet the study found that only 42 percent of the sample under 30 years old said they were interested in the story of the Wall, and only 19 percent said they were interested in news about the execution of the Communist dictator and his wife in Romania. News of subsequent events in east Europe attracted as few as one in twenty young people. In contrast, 58 percent of the sample over 50 followed the news about the Berlin Wall, and a third said they were "engaged" by stories from Romania. The study also found that people aged 30 to 49 "are almost as likely to be tuned out" to news about domestic and international political matters as are younger people. Young people showed significant interest only in sports events, major catastrophes, and news about the attempts to make abortions illegal again.

The study examined surveys conducted by other polling organizations since 1944 to discover whether indifference to political and governmental news among young people is a recent phenomenon. The authors concluded that it is. Surveys conducted after Watergate—the White House-directed burglary of Democratic headquarters that led to President Nixon's resignation in 1974—showed that young people expressed "considerably less interest in serious news subjects" than they had previously. This declining interest was reflected in a decrease in newspaper readership and in the viewing of television news programs. In 1965, a Gallup poll reported that 67 percent of adults under 35 said they had read a newspaper yesterday. The Times Mirror survey found only 20 percent who said they had. Viewing of television news fell from 52 percent in 1965 to 41 percent in 1990.

The survey asked young people about the 1988 presidential campaign between George Bush and Michael Dukakis. After studying the answers, the authors concluded: "The 30-second commercial spot is a particularly appropriate medium for the MTV generation.... Sound-bites and symbolism, the principal fuel of modern political campaigns, are well-suited to young voters who know less and have limited interest in politics and public policy. Their limited appetites and aptitudes are shaping the practice of politics and the nature of our democracy."

What that shape and nature will be cannot be known.

FOR REVIEW

1. List reasons for giving local franchising authorities the sole right to regulate cable television systems, for giving the Federal Communications Commission that right, for exempting cable television systems from government regulation. On balance, what degree of regulation, and by whom, strikes you as fair?

2. Outline the major provisions of the Cable Communications Policy Act of 1984.

3. Under that Act, could newspapers use cable systems to distribute news and opinion with the same degree of First Amendment freedom they now enjoy?

4. What happened when the rate sections of the Cable Policy Act were challenged in the courts?

5. On what rationale did the Supreme Court act when New York and other cities challenged the Federal Communications Commission's authority to control the technical standards cable systems are required to meet?

6. Describe the First Amendment status of cable system operators as defined by court decisions.

7. Some cable system operators have argued that they are more like newspapers than broadcasters for regulatory purposes. Are they? Explain. Why is this distinction important?

8. What have the courts said about cable systems as monopolies? Is the position taken by the courts realistic? Why or why not?

9. Cable television systems should be required to offer public access channels open to all who wish to use them. Agree or disagree? Explain.

CHAPTER 12

Advertising, after word of mouth, is the most pervasive means of communication. It makes up a substantial part of the content of newspapers and magazines. Without advertising, radio and television would not exist in their present form. Makers of commercial products, providers of services, and advocates of causes spend in excess of $130 billion a year to catch the public's attention. A major part of this amount supports the news media.

ADVERTISING

Despite this intimate relationship, until recent times advertising had little or no legal protection except that afforded by the law of contracts and commercial transactions. As far as the First Amendment was concerned, advertising was in exile, along with obscenity, fighting words, sedition, and other kinds of speech condemned by courts as lacking in valid idea content. Thus advertising, unlike news and opinion, could be subjected to prior restraint and other legal punishments with little hindrance.

This is not to say that advertising suffered from many restrictions. Any history student who has scanned the advertisements in turn-of-the-century newspapers has noted that any claim, no matter how preposterous, could be, and was, made for products like patent medicines. Until well into this century, the rule in advertising was "anything goes," reflecting the age-old rule of commercial transactions—*caveat emptor* ("Let the buyer beware"). The law assumed that buyers and sellers, advertisers and their audiences, were of equal intelligence. Anyone who was stuck with a bad bargain or taken in by a flowery ad was out of luck. It was assumed that victims of sharp practices would learn from their experience and not be taken in the next time. Not until 1906 did Congress take a first small step toward control of deceptive advertising. In that year it passed the Pure Food and Drug Act, which gave a federal agency authority to regulate claims made on package labels. This was followed in 1914 by the Federal Trade Commission Act. One of the duties of the commission was to regulate advertising claims. The Federal Trade Commission has become one of several weapons used against deceptive advertisers.

This chapter deals with four major themes of advertising law:

1. The Supreme Court's recognition in the 1970s that advertising is commercial speech entitled to limited First Amendment protection. That protection extends to advertisements for legal products and services as long as the ad is not deceptive. Government can regulate protected advertising only if it can demonstrate an overriding public interest in doing so, and even then only if the regulation is narrowly drawn to advance that public interest without restricting other kinds of speech.

2. The role of the Federal Trade Commission in regulating advertising to prevent deception. This role peaked in the 1970s in response to consumer ac-

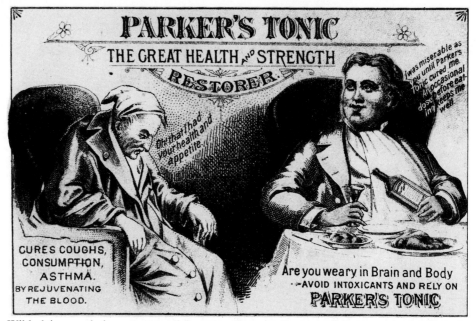

Wild claims made by patent medicine advertisers at the turn of the century contributed to adoption of the Pure Food and Drug Act in 1906. Eight years later the Federal Trade Commission was created and was given authority to regulate deceptive advertising. (The Bettmann Archive)

tivism and declined in the 1980s as a part of the government's move toward deregulation of business. At the end of the decade, state attorneys general reacted to the decline in federal regulation by cooperating in actions aimed at advertising by airlines, car rental agencies, and others. Further, some firms have gone to court to combat allegedly deceptive advertising by competitors.

3. The media's right to refuse advertising, whether it be for a commercial product or to persuade others to adopt a point of view on a public issue. Courts generally have rejected the argument advanced by Jerome Barron and others that people should have a right under the First Amendment to compel the media to carry their messages. However, courts have held that media under direct control of state officials can be required to accept advertising advocating a point of view on public issues, if the medium has been serving as a public forum. This applies mainly to public high school newspapers that are not part of the school's course work in journalism and to college newspapers owned by state universities. The Supreme Court has held that municipalities may forbid outdoor advertising for aesthetic or safety reasons but not because of objections to the content.

4. The right of corporations to spend corporate funds on advertising intended to influence opinion on a public issue. The Supreme Court has held that

corporations may advertise a point of view even when the issue will not have a direct effect on their business. It also has held that utility companies can advocate a point of view in their mailings to their customers and cannot be compelled to distribute messages prepared by others.

Major Cases

- *Bates* v. *State Bar of Arizona,* 433 U.S. 350, 97 S.Ct. 2691, 53 L.Ed.2d 810 (1977).

- *Central Hudson Gas & Electric Corp.* v. *Public Service Commission,* 447 U.S. 557, 100 S.Ct. 2343, 65 L.Ed.2d 341 (1980).

- *First National Bank of Boston* v. *Bellotti,* 435 U.S. 765, 98 S.Ct. 1407, 55 L.Ed.2d 707 (1978).

- *Metromedia, Inc.* v. *City of San Diego,* 453 U.S. 490, 101 S.Ct. 2882, 69 L.Ed.2d 800 (1981).

- *Posadas de Puerto Rico Associates* v. *Tourism Company of Puerto Rico,* 478 U.S. 328, 106 S.Ct. 2968, 92 L.Ed.2d 266 (1986).

- *Shuck* v. *The Carroll Daily Herald,* 247 N.W. 813 (1933).

- *Virginia State Board of Pharmacy* v. *Virginia Citizens Consumer Council,* 425 U.S. 748, 96 S.Ct. 1817, 48 L.Ed.2d 346 (1976).

- *Zauderer* v. *Office of Disciplinary Counsel of Supreme Court of Ohio,* 471 U.S. 626, 105 S.Ct. 2265, 85 L.Ed.2d 652 (1985).

THE DOCTRINE OF COMMERCIAL SPEECH

Advertising and the First Amendment

Not until 1941 did the Supreme Court have occasion to consider the argument that advertising might be protected by the First Amendment. And when it did, in *Valentine* v. *Chrestensen,*[1] it seemed to reject that argument out of hand. The issue involved was picayune. Police in New York City had arrested F. J. Chrestensen for violating an ordinance forbidding distribution of commercial handbills on city streets. But the ordinance did not forbid distribution of handbills promoting a cause. Chrestensen had bought a submarine and was selling admission to it. He advertised by passing out handbills to people on the streets. When police told him he was breaking the law, he sought to avoid arrest by printing two-sided handbills. On one side was a message protesting the city's refusal to let

---

1. 316 U.S. 52, 62 S.Ct. 920, 86 L.Ed. 1262 (1942).

him dock his submarine at one of its piers. On the other was a message informing people where the submarine was docked, the hours it was open to visitors, and the price of admission. The city's police and courts were not impressed. As they saw it, he still was using the city's streets to distribute advertising for his submarine. Chrestensen was ordered to pay a fine. He appealed all the way to the U.S. Supreme Court.

That Court was not impressed either. A unanimous Court noted that the streets long have been considered proper forums for the communication of ideas, subject only to reasonable time, place, and manner restrictions. But with respect to commercial messages, the Court added: "We are equally clear that the Constitution imposes no such restraint on government as respects purely commercial advertising. Whether, and to what extent, one may promote or pursue a gainful occupation in the streets...are matters for legislative judgment."

In short, the Court said, state and local governments could decide for themselves how far they wanted to go in permitting commercial advertisers to use public property. If they wanted to forbid such use altogether, as New York City had, there was nothing in the Constitution to hinder them. For more than twenty years thereafter, legislators and judges assumed that the Court had held that "purely commercial advertising" was not the kind of speech protected by the First Amendment, putting it in the same category as "fighting words" and obscenity.

The first doubts about that assumption were raised in 1964 by the Supreme Court's decision in *New York Times* v. *Sullivan,*[2] which is discussed in Chapter 3. The basis for that case was an advertisement urging readers to support students at Alabama State College who were demonstrating against racial segregation. Lawyers for Sullivan cited *Chrestensen* in their brief, arguing that because the assertions allegedly defaming their client appeared in a paid advertisement they were not protected by the First Amendment in any way. The Supreme Court disagreed. But it was careful to draw a line between the advertisement at issue in *New York Times* and other kinds of advertising. The former argued a cause of vital interest to the nation's welfare. People who might not be able to reach the public through other means had bought space in a leading newspaper to air their grievances. That their views appeared in an advertisement was beside the point. But it was to the point that publishers be encouraged to accept cause advertising. For that reason, the Court held that ads expressing opinions on public issues are fully protected by the First Amendment. Otherwise, publishers fearing libel suits might turn away other groups seeking to buy space to argue a cause.

However, the Court was silent on "purely commercial speech." It appeared, then, that the Court had divided paid communication into two classes, depending upon the purpose of the ad. If the purpose was to sell an idea, the ad was protected by the First Amendment. If the purpose was to sell a product, or a service, it was not.

This neat classification persisted for nearly a decade before another aspect of the civil rights movement raised questions about it. In the early 1970s, the Pitts-

---

2.   376 U.S. 254, 84 S.Ct. 710, 11 L.Ed.2d 686 (1964).

burgh newspapers got into trouble with the city's Human Relations Commission because of the way they presented employment advertising. The newspapers said they were doing readers a service by listing some ads as of "male interest," others as of "female interest," and still others as "male-female." The commission disagreed. It held that the categories perpetuated male-female stereotypes and encouraged sexual discrimination in violation of a recently enacted city ordinance. When the newspapers were cited for violating that ordinance, they argued that editorial judgments were involved in deciding how to categorize the ads. Therefore, any attempt by the city to tell the newspapers how to label the ads would violate the First Amendment. Neither the commission nor a county court bought that argument. The newspapers were ordered to comply with the law. The newspapers carried their case to the Supreme Court, which upheld the lower court's verdict.

However, in reaching its decision in *Pittsburgh Press Co.* v. *Pittsburgh Commission on Human Rights,*[3] the Supreme Court avoided the First Amendment question. The Court upheld the view that the newspapers' sexually oriented labels furthered discrimination on the basis of gender. Because such discrimination was illegal, the ads thus promoted an illegal act, making the newspapers law violators, too. However, in reaching its conclusion, the Court's majority conceded that "[u]nder some circumstances,...a newspaper's editorial judgments in connection with an advertisement" might be protected by the First Amendment. The degree of such protection would hinge on the content of the ad. In this instance, there was no protection because the ads fostered an illegal purpose. Taken in context, the court's reasoning raised questions. What kind of advertising content might be protected? In *New York Times,* the ad in question discussed political and social issues. Are such issues the only kinds protected by the First Amendment? What about economic issues, which frequently are resolved in the marketplace? Is there not a public interest in knowing which goods and services are available and at what price?

Within two years, the Court was offered an opportunity to clarify the questions raised by *Pittsburgh Press.* In 1975, the Court took a case that had been in and out of state and federal courts for four years. The dispute began when the *Virginia Weekly,* an "underground newspaper" at the University of Virginia, accepted an advertisement for an abortion clinic in New York City. At the time, which was before the Supreme Court's decision in *Roe* v. *Wade*[4] made abortions a matter of constitutional right, abortions were legal in New York but illegal in Virginia. Furthermore, a Virginia law made it a crime to advertise abortion services. The weekly's editor, Jeffrey Bigelow, was found guilty of violating that law and was fined. Ultimately, the case reached the Supreme Court, which held, in *Bigelow* v. *Virginia,*[5] that the advertisement was protected by the First Amendment. Therefore, Bigelow could not be punished for publishing it. The service offered was legal in New York. Virginia could not punish women who went to New York to obtain an abortion. Therefore, it could not punish Virginia media

---

3. 413 U.S. 376, 93 S.Ct. 2553, 37 L.Ed.2d 669 (1973).
4. 410 U.S. 113, 93 S.Ct. 705, 35 L.Ed.2d 147 (1973).
5. 421 U.S. 809, 95 S.Ct. 2222, 44 L.Ed.2d 600 (1975).

for advertising legal abortion services. But again the Court stopped short of saying that all ads for legal goods or services contain ideas that the First Amendment will protect. Instead, the Court's majority rationalized its decision by focusing on what it saw as the abortion ad's informational content. By informing Virginia readers that other states had legalized abortions, the ad contributed to the debate on the issue.

Virginia State Board of Pharmacy v. *Virginia Citizens Consumer Council,* 425 U.S. 748, 96 S.Ct. 1817, 48 L.Ed.2d 346 (1976).

Within a year, the Court took another Virginia advertising case and this time held without apology that people find helpful ideas in straightforward product and price advertising. With that decision, in *Virginia State Board of Pharmacy* v. *Virginia Citizens Consumer Council,* the Court established the doctrine that even "purely commercial advertising" enjoys First Amendment protection if it is for a legal product. At issue in this case was the right of pharmacies to post the prices of prescription drugs. Under Virginia's laws regulating the practice of pharmacy, price advertising was banned as being unprofessional. This meant that a patient who required a prescription drug was, in effect, a blind buyer forced to pay whatever price was charged at the time of purchase. If all drug stores charged the same price for the same drug, there would be no problem. The reality is that prices vary greatly from store to store. The case report notes that the price of a commonly prescribed antibiotic ranged from $1.20 to $9 for the same number of capsules. Unless individuals had the time and persistence to go from store to store asking about prices, or could use the telephone, they had no way of knowing where to get the most for their money.

In its eight-to-one decision, the Court left no room for doubt about the status of advertising with respect to the First Amendment. It wrote:

> Here, in contrast [to the earlier cases], the question whether there is a First Amendment exception for "commercial speech" is squarely before us. Our pharmacist does not wish to editorialize on any subject, cultural, philosophical, or political. He does not wish to report any particularly newsworthy fact, or to make generalized observations even about commercial matters. The "idea" he wishes to communicate is simply this: "I will sell you the X prescription drug at the Y price." Our question, then, is whether this communication is wholly outside the protection of the First Amendment.

The answer was a resounding no. Justice Harry A. Blackmun, who wrote the decision, rationalized that in inflationary times, when prescription drug purchasers, many of them elderly pensioners, were being squeezed financially, price information became significant. Indeed, he wrote, the consumer's interest in prices "may be as keen, if not keener by far, than his interest in the day's most urgent political debate." When he had finished writing, the doctrine of commercial speech had been established. At the least, the Court said, that doctrine means that the First Amendment protects the right to advertise any legal product or service.

But important questions remained unanswered. Chief Justice Warren E. Burger endorsed the Court's conclusion that pharmacies have a constitutional right to advertise the prices of prescription drugs. But he wrote separately to serve notice that he did not believe other professionals, especially lawyers and physicians, had a right to advertise. Justice Potter Stewart, also concurring in the result, wondered whether Blackmun had written so broadly as to nullify laws regulating deceptive advertising. Would the actual malice rule born in *New York Times* permit advertisers to stretch the truth about their products? With the Court's ruling that price advertising for legal products and services is protected by the First Amendment, were state and local governments left without authority to regulate advertising?

Defining the Doctrine's Scope

For decades, lawyers and judges can move serenely along, unaware that a given area of law may offer legal or constitutional problems. All the questions seem to have been answered. Then some court will be persuaded to accept and decide a case that challenges the comfortable assumptions of the status quo. The case will not quite square with precedents long taken for granted, and a bold court will strike out in a new direction. Soon, other courts will be persuaded to explore that new direction, leading to further expansion of the law. So it has been with commercial speech cases. A doctrine grudgingly recognized by the Supreme Court in the mid-1970s has expanded so rapidly that seldom has a Court term passed since without producing one or more advertising cases. We will start by looking at what has become the leading case defining the boundaries of the commercial speech doctrine and then see what has developed in three areas:

1. Advertising by professionals, particularly lawyers

2. The regulation of signs and billboards

3. The advertising of products that are themselves subject to regulation, notably cigarettes, alcoholic beverages, and gambling casinos.

Middle Eastern Arab countries, exasperated by United States policy toward Israel, cut off oil exports to this country in 1973. The resulting temporary shortages of petroleum products caused more irritation than hardship, but they did serve to focus attention on oil as a dwindling resource. New York's Public Service Commission reacted by forbidding all advertising by electric companies promoting the use of electricity. Its rationale was straightforward. Most of the electrical generating plants in the state burned fuel oil. If the companies sold less electricity, they would need less oil. Therefore, they should not be advertising to obtain more customers, or to urge their present customers to buy appliances that would use more electricity. The Arab embargo was lifted in March 1974, but the New York advertising ban remained in effect.

Central Hudson Gas & Electric Corp. v. Public Service Commission, **447 U.S. 557, 100 S.Ct. 2343, 65 L.Ed.2d 341 (1980).** The Central Hudson Gas & Electric Corp., acting for itself and other New York state electric companies, asked a state court to end the ban. Looking at the Supreme Court's commercial speech cases, the utilities argued that it violated their First Amendment right to advertise.

The state court disagreed, holding that there was a continuing need for oil conservation, which was great enough to justify the restriction. When state appeals courts affirmed, Central Hudson carried its case to the Supreme Court. In *Central Hudson Gas & Electric Corp.* v. *Public Service Commission,* it reversed, with only one dissenting vote.

Justice Lewis F. Powell, Jr., writing for the Court, reviewed the commercial speech cases and found in them protection even for advertising that ''communicates only an incomplete version of the relevant facts.'' The First Amendment, he said, ''presumes that some accurate information is better than no information at all.'' Therefore, the state cannot prohibit all commercial speech, even though the Constitution gives it less protection than it does most other kinds of speech. The degree of protection for commercial speech, Powell wrote, ''turns on the nature both of the expression and of the governmental interests served by the regulation.'' The Court has brought the First Amendment into play to protect ''the informational function of advertising.'' Thus, if a commercial message does ''not accurately inform the public about lawful activity,'' it may even be suppressed, as in the *Pittsburgh Press* case.

But if the commercial message does not mislead, and it concerns lawful activity, the government's power to regulate it is limited. Here, Powell outlined the points that must be taken into consideration in determining whether such regulation is proper:

> The State must assert a substantial interest to be achieved by restrictions on commercial speech. Moreover, the regulatory technique must be in proportion to that interest. The limitation on expression must be designed carefully to achieve the State's goal. Compliance with the requirement may be measured by two criteria. First, the restriction must directly advance the state interest involved; the regulation may not be sustained if it provides only ineffective or remote support for the government's purpose. Second, if the governmental interest could be served as well by a more limited restriction on commercial speech, the excessive restrictions cannot survive.

Powell wrote that the state cannot impose regulations that only indirectly advance its interests. Nor can it regulate commercial speech that poses no danger to a state interest. He concluded:

> In commercial speech cases, then, a four-part analysis has developed. At the outset, we must determine whether the expression is protected by the First Amendment. For commercial speech to come within that provision, it at least must concern lawful activity and not be misleading. Next, we ask whether the asserted governmental interest is substantial. If both inquiries yield positive answers, we must determine whether the regulation directly advances the governmental interest asserted, and whether it is not more extensive than is necessary to serve that interest.

Powell applied this four-step analysis to the New York commission's regulation and concluded that it violated the utility company's First Amendment rights. Clearly, Central Hudson's proposed advertising was not inaccurate, nor did it promote unlawful activity. But the utilities commission argued that Central Hudson, like all electric companies, was a monopoly. If people in its territory wanted electricity, they had to get it from Central Hudson. The New York courts had looked at that fact and concluded there was little point to advertising by electric companies. Therefore, such advertising was of little First Amendment value and must yield to a larger state interest in conservation.

Powell said the lower courts had looked at the issue too narrowly. For some purposes, fuel oil and natural gas are in direct competition with electricity. And even in uses where there is no competition, advertising serves some purpose. The electric company may wish to offer new services, or inform its customers of new terms of doing business. Further, it might also wish to advertise new lines of appliances that use less energy than those now in use. Powell concluded that there are substantial reasons why electric companies should be permitted to advertise.

The state of New York had argued that it was serving two important interests by banning advertising: It was encouraging conservation of a scarce resource, and it was keeping rates lower than they otherwise would be. If the companies' advertising led to increased use of electricity, they would have to build new plants to meet peak demands. These building costs would be reflected in higher rates.

Powell conceded that both interests were substantial. But he dismissed the latter with a few sentences:

> The link between the advertising prohibition and [Central Hudson's] rate structure is, at most, tenuous. The impact of promotional advertising on the equity of [the company's] rates is highly speculative. . . . Such conditional and remote eventualities simply cannot justify silencing [its] promotional advertising.

He took the conservation argument more seriously, noting a direct link between promotional advertising and increased use of electricity. But it is well established, Powell said, that a restriction on speech cannot go beyond what is needed to protect a vital state interest. New York's ban was not limited to promotional advertising. It applied to all advertising by electric utilities. This swept too broadly and thus was in violation of the First Amendment. The utilities commission had made no showing that it could not encourage conservation by some more limited restriction. Therefore, its broad ban on advertising must fall.

Powell made the four-part test look neater than it has proved to be. Even the first two parts of the test, which seem to be the most precise, have presented some problems. We can buy corn flakes, television sets, and clothing without breaking any laws. These products and thousands of others can be, and are, advertised freely. But it is against the law to sell marijuana. Therefore, a publication that accepts an ad for "Acapulco Gold," as some college newspapers have, is courting trouble. That much with respect to the first part of the test is reasonably simple. But beer, guns, and cigarettes also are legal products. However, all of them are subject to regulation by government. Further, all of them can be misused so as to break the law, and cigarettes have been held to be a major health hazard. Does this mean that advertising for such products can be regulated or even forbidden? Courts have differed in their answers to that question, depending upon the product, but a recent decision by the Supreme Court seems to say that if the government can regulate a product or service it can regulate the advertising for it.

The second part of the test, whether an ad is deceptive, presents frequent problems. The Federal Trade Commission and other agencies at both the federal and state levels have procedures that are used to determine whether advertising has a capacity to mislead unwary consumers. If those procedures lead to the conclusion that an ad is deceptive, it may be banned, or the advertiser may be subject to other penalties.

Many problems in defining the scope of the doctrine have risen in connection with the last two prongs of the *Central Hudson* test. At what point does a state interest in regulating advertising become substantial enough to justify a restriction on the advertiser's First Amendment right to promote a product or a service? Some people believe that the advertising of alcoholic beverages promotes overindulgence. Other people are offended by ads for condoms. Is this enough to support laws banning such advertising? If the state interest in forbidding or controlling advertising is great enough, how narrowly must the law be tailored to prevent its harming other kinds of speech? These are questions on which courts have disagreed frequently.

Advertising by Professionals

In the *Virginia Pharmacy* case, then Chief Justice Burger agreed that it was proper for professional pharmacists to advertise the price of prescription drugs, but he said he did not think it proper for physicians and lawyers to advertise their services. At the time he wrote, the codes of ethics of both professions condemned advertising as unprofessional. A listing by name in the Yellow Pages of the telephone directory was permitted, as was a discreet newspaper advertisement announcing the opening of an office or the formation of a partnership. But anything beyond that was seen as fee grubbing. Lawyers seeking clients had to make themselves visible by joining luncheon clubs or fraternal organizations, by going into politics, or by engaging in volunteer community work. Lawyers who were too overt in seeking clients ran a risk of being disciplined by their peers and could even be disbarred.

The low profile maintained by most lawyers for many decades came under challenge when the 1960s brought an explosive increase in the number of people applying for admission to law schools. Among them were women and minorities seeking entry to a profession long dominated by white males. The pressure led to increased enrollments and, inevitably, to an increase in the number of lawyers admitted to practice. In the resulting competitive atmosphere, the old ways of attracting clients no longer were good enough. John R. Bates and Van O'Steen, fledgling lawyers in Phoenix, Arizona, were among the first to challenge those methods. They did so by placing an ad in the *Arizona Republic* that went straight to the point. "DO YOU NEED A LAWYER?" it asked in big, bold type. In smaller type it proclaimed, "Legal Services at very reasonable fees." Under an illustration representing the scales of justice, the ad listed prices for half a dozen services, including uncontested divorces and bankruptcy. What the lawyers did flew in the face of the canons of the American Bar Association and of the rules of court embedded in Arizona statutes. The president of the state bar himself filed charges alleging that Bates and O'Steen were soliciting clients in violation of the code of ethics. A hearing committee recommended that they be suspended from the practice of law for not fewer than six months. On appeal, the state supreme court reduced the penalty to censure. The lawyers took their case to the Supreme Court, which held, only a year after the *Virginia Pharmacy* decision, that even censure was too much. Under the doctrine of commercial speech, lawyers could advertise as long as they did not mislead the public as to what they could do for their clients.

Bates v. *State Bar of Arizona,* 433 U.S. 350, 97 S.Ct. 2691, 53 L.Ed.2d 810 (1977).

The decision, in *Bates* v. *State Bar of Arizona,* struck at the foundations of the legal system by opening the way for radical changes in the way lawyers do business. For that reason, Justice Blackmun, who wrote for the Court, devoted a great many words to a discussion of the nature of the practice of law. What they boil down to is the conclusion on Blackmun's part that by remaining aloof from the marketplace lawyers may have made themselves too remote and mysterious. Their clients tended to be corporations or persons of wealth who relied on their advice to keep out of trouble or to get them off the hook if worse came to worst. Not long before this decision was handed down, the Supreme Court had held that poor folk who are accused of crime must have a lawyer at public expense. Congress also had established legal aid societies to help the poor with civil court actions. But, in Blackmun's view, the great middle classes had hesitated to seek legal advice, perhaps out of ignorance as to what such advice could do for them or fear that a lawyer might charge them more than they could afford. Blackman reasoned that ads like that run by Bates and O'Steen could help such persons defend their legal rights when they need to do so. As it had in its earlier cases, the Court resorted to the rationale that whatever its commercial ends, the ad in question conveyed valuable information: "You, too, can afford a lawyer."

Blackmun also dealt with Stewart's reservation—in *Virginia Pharmacy*—that the doctrine of commercial speech might condone misleading advertising. He wrote:

> Advertising that is false, deceptive, or misleading of course is subject to restraint....Since the advertiser knows his product and has a commercial interest in its dissemination, we have little worry that regulation to assure truthfulness will discourage protected speech....And any concern that strict requirements for truthfulness will undesirably inhibit spontaneity seems inapplicable because commercial speech generally is calculated. Indeed, the public and private benefits from commercial speech derive from confidence in its accuracy and reliability. Thus, the leeway for untruthful or misleading expression that has been allowed in other contexts has little force in the commercial arena.

In other words, Blackmun was serving notice that there was no room in the doctrine of commercial speech for the *New York Times* rule. The First Amendment protection given to commercial advertising does not contain the "breathing space" for falsehood enjoyed by speech commenting on the activities of public officials and public figures.

In context, Blackmun was trying to assure the chief justice and all other old-school lawyers that the *Bates* decision would not open the way for lawyers to make wild promises in order to attract clients. It also was a bow in the direction of those who believe that the practice of law is indeed a profession and not a trade like plumbing or a service like the preparation of tax returns. Plumbers and tax preparers make no bones about soliciting customers. At the time of the *Bates* decision, strict rules in effect in every state and in the federal courts prohibited lawyers from soliciting clients. But isn't advertising, even of the kind approved in *Bates*, a form of solicitation? How far can lawyers go in advertising their services without running afoul of the rules against solicitation? How far can they go without misleading prospective clients? To what extent can state bar associations or state courts regulate lawyer advertising without running afoul of the First Amendment?

These have proved to be particularly vexing questions. Between 1978 and 1990, the Supreme Court decided six cases in which it sought to define how far lawyers may go in advertising for clients. The answer is: They can go pretty far, as anyone who watches television can testify. At this writing, the decisions seem to say that lawyers can solicit clients if they do so through the airwaves, in printed advertisements, or by letter, but they cannot do so in a face-to-face encounter—if they get caught.

It took less than a year for the first two post-*Bates* cases to reach the Supreme Court. One of them, *In re Primus*,[6] grew out of a letter from a lawyer, Edna Smith Primus, to a female Medicaid patient who had been sterilized without her consent. Primus, who was affiliated with the American Civil Liberties Union, spoke to a group of such patients and advised them they had a right to sue. She then wrote a letter to one of the women telling her that the ACLU would be willing to represent her without fee in a suit against the doctor who had performed the operation and the hospital that had permitted it to be done. The state bar association found Primus guilty of unprofessional conduct in soliciting clients and reprimanded her. The Supreme Court held that the First Amendment protected what Primus had done. Her letter was not an in-person solicitation. She would not profit from representing the woman. Justice Thurgood Marshall wrote separately to commend Primus. He said she was acting "in accordance with the highest standards of the legal profession" by offering her services without charge to a woman who otherwise would have been unable to win redress against those who violated her rights.

On the same day, the Court decided another client solicitation case, *Ohralik* v. *Ohio State Bar Association*,[7] but with the opposite result. Albert Ohralik had not written a letter or advertised. When he learned that a young woman with whom he was acquainted had been in an automobile accident, he telephoned her par-

---

6.   436 U.S. 412, 98 S.Ct. 1893, 56 L.Ed.2d 417 (1978).
7.   436 U.S. 447, 98 S.Ct. 1912, 56 L.Ed.2d 444 (1978).

ents, learned she was in the hospital, and went to the hospital to see her. While he was there, he offered to represent the young woman on a contingency fee basis. Learning that the woman had a friend who also had been injured in the same accident, Ohralik called on her, too, and made a similar offer. The attorney tape-recorded both conversations and, when one of the women tried to dismiss him and accept an offer for settlement, used the recording as evidence in a suit for breach of contract. The state bar association charged Ohralik with unprofessional conduct. The Ohio Supreme Court held that Ohralik's direct solicitation of clients warranted an indefinite suspension of his right to practice law. Without dissent, the U.S. Supreme Court affirmed.

The decisions in *Primus* and *Ohralik* drew a line through the field on which lawyers can seek clients. On one side, represented by *Ohralik,* is personal solicitation. Lawyers who get caught at it invite severe punishment. On the other side, represented by *Primus,* are other methods of seeking clients. *Bates* and *Primus* outlined a small field in which lawyers could operate. In *Bates,* the Court approved lawyers' use of factual, unadorned newspaper advertising calling attention to services they are willing to perform and even listing fees for such things as uncontested divorces and the filing of bankruptcy petitions. In *Primus,* the Court said it is acceptable for lawyers to talk to groups about their legal rights and even to write letters to prospective clients, provided that the service is being offered without charge to the client through an organization such as the American Civil Liberties Union. Since 1978, the Court has considerably expanded the *Primus* side of the line.

In 1982, in *In re R.M.J.*,[8] the Court struck down a Missouri Supreme Court rule narrowly restricting the content of advertisements placed by attorneys. A lawyer was facing disbarment because his listing of practice areas did not use precisely the words prescribed by the rules. The intent of the Missouri courts in prescribing a list of words lawyers might use in indicating their preferred practice areas was to prevent deception. But a unanimous Supreme Court said Missouri, to prevent possible deceptions, could not prevent lawyers from describing areas of speciality in their own terms. The Court said that the state's authority to regulate the content of an attorney's advertising is limited to actual instances of deception.

Zauderer **v.** *Office of Disciplinary Counsel of Supreme Court of Ohio,* **471 U.S. 626, 105 S.Ct. 2265, 85 L.Ed.2d 652 (1985).** Three years later, the Supreme Court again struck down an attempt to prescribe the content of attorney advertising. Ohio's rules regulating the practice of law said that lawyers could not use illustrations in their advertisements. Philip Q. Zauderer, a lawyer practicing in Columbus, had defied that rule by using a drawing of a Dalkon shield, a birth control device, in a newspaper ad seeking clients who had suffered harm from its use. Large type immediately beneath the drawing asked, "DID YOU USE THIS IUD?" The text of

---

8.   455 U.S. 191, 102 S.Ct. 929, 71 L.Ed.2d 64 (1982).

the ad described the harm that some women said they had suffered because of their use of the device. The ad concluded with Zauderer's offer to represent Dalkon shield clients on a contingency fee basis, that is, for a percentage of such damages as a client might be awarded. The last sentence said, "If there is no recovery, no legal fees are owed by our clients." The ad, placed in thirty-six newspapers, proved to be highly successful, drawing more than 200 inquiries. Zauderer filed lawsuits in behalf of 106 of the women who wrote to him. The ad also attracted the attention of the Office of Disciplinary Counsel, which filed a complaint against him. The Ohio Supreme Court found Zauderer in violation of its rules on advertising and subjected him to a public reprimand. On appeal, the U.S. Supreme Court held that all but the last sentence in the ad was protected by the First Amendment. In so holding, the Court specifically struck down that part of the Ohio rules forbidding the use of illustrations. Writing for himself and five other Justices, Byron R. White said:

> ...The use of illustrations or pictures in advertisements serves important communicative functions: it attracts the attention of the audience to the advertiser's message, and it may also serve to impart information directly. Accordingly, commercial illustrations are entitled to the First Amendment protections afforded verbal commercial speech: restrictions on the use of visual media of expression in advertising must survive scrutiny under the *Central Hudson* test.

By that, White said he meant that the visual element in the ad must not be misleading. If illustrations or photographs used in advertising, including that by lawyers, are not misleading, then they cannot be regulated unless the state can demonstrate some overriding interest in doing so. In this instance, there was no such interest.

However, the Court said the last sentence in Zauderer's ad was misleading because it implied that clients would not have to pay him anything if he was unable to win a settlement or judgment for them. In reality, clients who retain lawyers on a contingency fee basis may have to pay certain expenses incurred in preparing their case and may be responsible for court costs. The Court said that if the ad were to be completely honest, it should make clear the distinction between a lawyer's fees and costs which usually are passed on to the client.

In 1988, the U.S. Supreme Court held that lawyers who write factual letters to potential clients advertising their services are protected by the First Amendment from being disciplined for improperly soliciting business. Further, in *Shapero* v. *Kentucky Bar Association*,[9] it held that those letters could be directly addressed to individuals believed to be in need of specific legal services. At issue were letters attorney Richard D. Shapero of Louisville drafted for mailing to people whose home mortgages were being foreclosed.

This decision so broadened the field established by *Primus* that three justices protested. Sandra Day O'Connor, writing for Chief Justice William H. Rehnquist, Associate Justice Antonin Scalia, and herself, said the decision could strip away

---

9.   486 U.S. 466, 108 S.Ct. 1916, 100 L.Ed.2d 475 (1988).

the safeguards that make the practice of law a profession rather than a "trade or occupation like any other." As they saw it, there is little difference with respect to solicitation of clients between a personalized letter and a face-to-face encounter.

The majority, led by Justice William J. Brennan, Jr., held otherwise. Relying on the precedents established in *Zauderer,* Brennan said there is no difference between a newspaper advertisement aimed at a specific group of potential clients and a letter sent to identified members of such a group. In either instance, the targets of the solicitations have the option of ignoring the appeal. In a portion of the decision in which he was joined by only three of his colleagues, Brennan wrote:

> The pitch or style of a letter's type and its inclusion of subjective predictions of client satisfaction might catch the recipient's attention more than would a bland statement of purely objective facts in small type. But a truthful and nondeceptive letter, no matter how big its type and how much it speculates can never "shou[t] at the recipient" or "gras[p] him by the lapels," as can a lawyer engaging in face-to-face solicitation.

The partial quotations are from the Court's decision in *Bates.* Brennan wrote the paragraph to distinguish the kinds of solicitation that are condoned by the decisions in *Primus, R.M.J., Zauderer,* and *Shapero* from that condemned in *Ohralik.*

In 1990, the Court held that three lines of type on an Illinois lawyer's letterhead did not deceive prospective clients.[10] Gary E. Peel, who practiced in Edwardsville, had tried to verdict more than 100 jury trials and had taken courses on trial advocacy. His letterhead included this information:

> Certified Civil Trial Specialist
> By the National Board of Trial Advocacy
> Licensed: Illinois, Missouri, Arizona

On a complaint from the Illinois Attorney Registration and Disciplinary Committee, the state supreme court censured Peel, ruling that he was holding himself out to be a certified legal specialist in violation of a section of the Illinois Code of Professional Responsibility. The court said the ad was misleading because the court had never recognized any certification process. Further, the court said that taken together the three lines could lead the general public to believe that Peel had been licensed as a civil trial specialist in three states. By five to four, the U.S. Supreme Court overruled the Illinois court.

Noting that in 1973 then Chief Justice Warren E. Burger had urged specialized training and certification for trial advocates, the Court said that the National Board of Trial Advocacy was established in 1977 for that purpose. It has set rigorous standards of experience and additional training which lawyers must attain if they are to be certified. Certificates are issued for five-year periods and cannot

---

10. *Peel v. Attorney Registration and Disciplinary Commission of Illinois,* _ _ _ U.S. _ _ _, 110 S.Ct. 2281, 110 L.Ed.2d 83 (1990).

be renewed without an additional course of training. The Court concluded that the certificate has meaning and that Peel was simply stating a fact in noting that he had been certified. The majority further held that the third line also stated a fact. Nor did it believe that people who are thinking of hiring a lawyer are unable to distinguish between a certificate and a license. The letterhead's potential to mislead some consumers was not great enough to "satisfy the State's heavy burden of justifying a categorical prohibition against the dissemination of accurate factual information to the public."

The decisions leave bar associations and courts with the power to discipline lawyers only if they use deceptive advertising or direct face-to-face solicitation to gain clients. Further, deception must be proved on a case-by-case basis. In *Zauderer,* the Court found deception in a sentence that did not explain the difference between the fee a lawyer charges for his services and the costs he incurs on a client's behalf.

A survey of lower court decisions shows a few instances in which specific advertisements by lawyers and other professionals, such as dentists, chiropractors, or physicians operating primary care clinics, have been found to be deceptive. A New York appellate court held that it was deceptive for a lawyer to advertise under the title "The People's Law Firm."[11] The court said the term was misleading in that it implied that the firm was controlled by the public or provided services on a nonprofit basis.

The Regulation of Signs and Billboards

Shortly before the Supreme Court held in *Bates* that advertising by lawyers is protected by the First Amendment, the Court was asked to decide whether outdoor advertising enjoys similar protection. The Court held, in *Linmark Associates* v. *Township of Willingboro,*[12] that outdoor advertising does, but the Court also held that signs can be regulated if government can demonstrate a compelling need to do so. In this instance, the government could not.

Willingboro, a New Jersey township, had forbidden posting of "For Sale" or "Sold" signs in residential neighborhoods. It had done so to halt the flight of white homeowners from racially integrated neighborhoods. The Court ruled the law unconstitutional. In doing so, it noted that homeowners traditionally have used yard signs to tell others that their houses are for sale. There are other ways of doing so, but all are more expensive and may not be as effective. If homeowners can be prevented from using the most direct way to tell others their house is for sale, Justice Marshall wrote, "then every locality in the country can suppress any facts that reflect poorly on the locality, so long as a plausible claim can be made that disclosure would cause the recipients of the information to act 'irrationally.'"

That decision, inconsequential as it seemed at the time, was the first of a series of decisions in which the Supreme Court has sought to define how far communi-

11. Matter of Sullivan, 92 A.D.2d 978, 459 N.Y.S.2d 633 (A.D. 1983).
12. 433 U.S. 350, 97 S.Ct. 2691, 53 L.Ed.2d 810 (1977).

ties can go to regulate or even ban outdoor advertising. The results have been mixed because the justices have been divided on the issue.

Metromedia, Inc. v. *City of San Diego,* 453 U.S. 490, 101 S.Ct. 2882, 69 L.Ed.2d 800 (1981).

The second outdoor advertising case to reach the Court, *Metromedia, Inc.* v. *City of San Diego,* led the justices to so many differing views that a majority could agree on only one conclusion: San Diego's ordinance banning most billboards was unconstitutional. But no more than three justices could agree on any one reason, leading Justice Rehnquist to call the decision "a virtual Tower of Babel," a reference to the story in the Old Testament that purports to explain why the peoples of the world speak so many different languages. The decision is significant because all the justices agreed on one point: Local governments can regulate or even ban outdoor advertising if they do so in an evenhanded way and have a persuasive reason for doing so.

San Diego had enacted the ordinance "to eliminate hazards to pedestrians and motorists brought about by distracting sign displays" and "to preserve and improve the appearance of the city." The California Supreme Court had held that those interests were important and that the city's decision to ban billboards was a reasonable means of carrying them out. Three justices of the U.S. Supreme Court said they could not disagree with that conclusion. However, they held that the ordinance was fatally flawed by the fact that it did not ban all signs and billboards. Under its terms, businesses could erect signs on their own premises advertising the goods or services they offered. A second set of exemptions permitted erection of historical plaques, religious symbols, informational signs at bus stops, and signs displaying time, temperature, or news. As the plurality saw it, the ordinance placed a higher value on some commercial speech—on-premise advertising signs—than on noncommercial speech, that is, signs advocating a cause, for which the ordinance made no provision. Further, the law was flawed because it permitted some kinds of noncommercial speech—time, news, and temperature signs—but not others. Therefore, the law was not content neutral, nor did it leave open adequate alternative channels of communication.

Two other justices agreed that San Diego could have banned all signs and billboards to promote traffic safety or the city's aesthetic values. But Brennan, joined by Blackmun, said the city had not proved that "billboards actually impair traffic safety" or that there was a substantial interest in promoting aesthetics in the city's commercial and industrial areas.

Three justices found no problem with the ordinance. Then Chief Justice Burger found the plurality's position a "bizarre" example of "the long arm and voracious appetite of federal power—this time judicial power—with a vengeance, reaching and absorbing traditional concepts of local authority." Justice John Paul Stevens, like Justice Brennan, treated the ordinance as a total ban on signs and billboards. Unlike Brennan, he thought the city had proved its case. Justice Rehnquist said that aesthetic grounds alone justified the city's attempt to ban billboards.

Within a year, the justices were able to reconcile their differing views and uphold a Los Angeles ordinance forbidding the posting of signs on public property.

The case began when Roland Vincent, a candidate for city council, sued the city because his campaign signs were removed from utility poles by city employees. He took his case to the Supreme Court, which held, in *Members of City Council v. Taxpayers for Vincent,*[13] that the city has a right to protect aesthetic values by prohibiting advertising signs on public property as long as the ban applies to all signs. Vincent argued that the Court had held on several occasions that political speech, as exemplified by his campaign signs, lies at the heart of the values the First Amendment protects and therefore cannot be restricted. The Court responded that his interest in posting his signs on public property could prevail only if he could demonstrate that he had no other effective means of advancing his candidacy. The Court concluded that he had offered no such proof.

A survey of recent outdoor advertising cases finds that courts are looking to *Metromedia* for guidance despite the fragmented nature of the decision. Laws regulating billboards and other signs are being upheld if they apply in an even-handed way to all signs and if the rationale is sufficiently convincing. Courts are upholding restrictions based on aesthetic considerations. For example, the Supreme Court of Arkansas upheld ordinances regulating the size and placement of billboards despite testimony that the rules would increase the costs to the advertisers by more than 50 percent.[14] The court found that the regulations directly advanced substantial state interests in traffic safety and aesthetics. However, a Michigan appellate court struck down an ordinance of the city of Wyoming, Michigan, limiting the display of temporary signs to sixty days a year.[15] The city advanced a number of reasons for the limit, including elimination of traffic and fire hazards and preservation of the city's aesthetic values. The court held that the ordinance not only discriminated between temporary and permanent signs but was based on considerations that could be corrected by means other than the sixty-day limit. The U.S. Court of Appeals for the Second Circuit held that Needham, Massachusetts, could not prevent residents from erecting political signs on their own property.[16] The town argued that the Supreme Court's decision in *Taxpayers for Vincent* supported the ban. The appellate court said that reliance was mistaken. In *Vincent,* the Los Angeles ordinance banned all signs on all public premises. The Needham ordinance permitted some kinds of signs, including "For Sale" signs, on private property. Therefore, it was discriminatory in that it gave commercial speech a greater degree of protection than political speech. The court conceded that communities can forbid signs on private property, but only if the ban directly advances a compelling public interest.

The Advertising of Products Subject to Regulation

For various reasons, government has seen fit to regulate the sale of certain products, or even to prohibit their sale altogether. Alcoholic beverages are a con-

13.   466 U.S. 789, 104 S.Ct. 2118, 80 L.Ed.2d 772 (1984),
14.   Donrey Communications v. City of Fayetteville, 280 Ark. 408, 660 S.W.2d 900 (1983); cert. den., 466 U.S. 959 (1984).
15.   Risner v. City of Wyoming, 147 Mich.App. 430, 383 N.W.2d 226 (Mich.App. 1986).
16.   Matthews v. Town of Needham, 764 F.2d 58 (2d Cir. 1985).

spicuous example. During the early part of this century, enough people became alarmed by the excessive consumption of such beverages to force adoption of a constitutional amendment outlawing their manufacture or use.[17] The amendment was so commonly violated that it was repealed by another constitutional amendment, the Twenty-first, in 1933. However, that Amendment reserved to each state the power to continue prohibition, as some did until recent times, and to regulate the conditions under which beer, wine, and liquor can be sold. Because the right to regulate alcoholic beverages is grounded in the Constitution, courts have held that advertising for such beverages can be regulated more strictly than other kinds of commercial speech. Other products and services considered harmful have not been the subject of a constitutional amendment but have been regulated nevertheless. These include tobacco products, guns, gambling casinos, and houses of prostitution.

A decade before the Court held that commercial advertising is protected by the First Amendment, the surgeon general of the United States concluded that cigarette smoking causes serious health problems. At that time, tobacco companies were major television advertisers, spending about $250 million a year on commercials. A young lawyer in New York City, John W. Banzhaf, reasoned that the surgeon general's ruling made cigarettes the subject of a public controversy, as indeed it did. Banzhaf's persistence in his belief led in 1967 to a ruling by the Federal Communications Commission that the fairness doctrine, as it then was defined, required broadcasters to balance cigarette advertising by carrying public service messages calling attention to the health hazard.[18] These messages led to a significant drop in cigarette sales. Two years later, when Congress adopted a law banning cigarette advertising on "any medium of electronic communication subject to the jurisdiction of the FCC," the tobacco companies did not oppose it.[19] The only legal challenge to that law resulted in a federal district court decision upholding the law.[20] The court acted on the then prevailing assumption that commercial advertising is not protected by the First Amendment. It also noted that because broadcasters are licensed by the government, they are especially subject to regulation in the public interest. Also dating from that era is a federal law mandating that all cigarette advertising in the print media, on billboards, and even on cigarette packages carry a warning that smoking is hazardous to one's health.

Although the Supreme Court has not directly ruled on cigarette advertising, the Court has decided cases involving advertising for alcoholic beverages and gambling casinos. The latter is the more significant because some authorities have read the decision as condoning legislation banning in any medium advertisements for a regulated product.[21]

---

17. The Eighteenth Amendment, ratified in 1919.
18. WCBS-TV, 8 F.C.C.2d 381 (1967); aff'd, Applicability of the Fairness Doctrine to Cigarette Advertising, 9 F.C.C.2d 921 (1967); sustained, Banzhaf v. F.C.C., 405 F.2d 1082 (D.C.Cir. 1968).
19. Public Health Cigarette Smoking Act, 15 U.S.C. § 1335 (1969).
20. Capital Broadcasting Co. v. Mitchell, 333 F.Supp. 582 (D.D.C. 1971); aff'd without opinion, Capital Broadcasting Co. v. Acting Attorney General, 405 U.S. 1000 (1972).
21. P. Cameron De Vore and Robert D. Sack, "Advertising and Commercial Speech," *Communications Law 1987* (New York: The Practising Law Institute, 1987) vol. 1, pp. 76–78.

With respect to the advertising of alcoholic beverages, courts generally have held that the Twenty-first Amendment sanctions strict controls both on the sale of alcoholic beverages and on advertising for them. In a frequently cited case, *Queensgate Investment Co.* v. *Liquor Control Commission,*[22] the Ohio Supreme Court held that the Twenty-first Amendment and a state interest in minimizing the consumption of alcohol justified a regulation prohibiting off-premises advertising of the prices of alcoholic beverages. Thus, the Amendment condones prior restraint, which the U.S. Supreme Court has condemned in many other circumstances.

However, when the state of Oklahoma attempted to forbid advertising of any alcoholic beverage stronger than 3.2 percent beer, the state encountered problems. Newspapers and other print media located in the state had to comply with the law. Broadcasting stations located within the state were required to refuse beer and wine advertising from local outlets but carried network programming that did include such commercials. So did broadcasters in adjoining states whose programs could be seen or heard in Oklahoma. Newspapers and magazines published elsewhere and distributed within the state also carried liquor advertising. Cable systems presented a particularly vexing problem. They had offices in the state but routinely retransmitted programs, many of them containing beer and wine commercials, originating in distant states. Further, the rules under which they operated required them to pass along distant programming in its entirety, including commercials. For awhile, state authorities required over-the-air broadcasters to block out beer and wine commercials, but made no attempt to police cable systems. When the state attorney general ruled that those systems, too, would have to comply with the law, broadcasters and cable operators combined to challenge the law in court.

A district court judge held that the law was unconstitutional, but, on appeal, the circuit court reversed.[23] Citing the Twenty-first Amendment and *Queensgate,* it said the state's interest in discouraging consumption of alcoholic beverages was sufficient under the *Central Hudson* test to overcome any First Amendment values the advertising might have. On further appeal, the U.S. Supreme Court reversed with respect to cable systems but did so without reaching the First Amendment issue.[24] The Court noted that cable systems are regulated under federal law. That law requires them to retransmit in their entirety all programs the systems choose to carry. The Court held, applying long established constitutional principles, that a state cannot impose its will in an area of law preempted by the federal government.

A year later, Oklahoma broadcasters, joined by the state's newspapers, went to court again and succeeded in having the law ruled unconstitutional in its continued application to them.[25] The court said that by then the law had so many holes in it that the remaining prohibitions violated the equal protection clause of the Fourteenth Amendment. In reaching that conclusion, the court listed twenty-

---

22. 69 Ohio St.2d 361, 433 N.E.2d 138; appeal dismissed, 459 U.S. 807 (1982).
23. Oklahoma Telecasters Association v. Crisp, 699 F.2d 490 (10th Cir. 1983).
24. Capital Cities Cable, Inc. v. Crisp, 467 U.S. 691, 104 S.Ct. 2694, 81 L.Ed.2d 580 (1984).
25. Oklahoma Broadcasters Association v. Crisp, 636 F.Supp. 978 (W.D.Okla. 1986).

seven ways through which beer, wine, and liquor advertising reached Oklahoma residents. Therefore, the court said, it was unfair to continue to enforce the ban against only two kinds of media. At the same time, however, the court reiterated that the Tenth Circuit's holding with respect to alcoholic beverage advertising and the First Amendment still is valid. The clear inference is that a regulation applying to all media would be upheld. The Fifth Circuit took that position in 1983 in upholding a Mississippi law forbidding liquor advertisements originating within the state.[26] That court rejected an argument that the law violated the equal protection clause.

Posadas de Puerto Rico Associates v. *Tourism Company of Puerto Rico,* 478 U.S. 328, 106 S.Ct. 2968, 92 L.Ed.2d 266 (1986).

In 1986, the Supreme Court held in a widely disputed decision that advertising for a regulated service, in this instance casino gambling, can be prohibited in any medium under a relaxed application of the *Central Hudson* test. A tobacco company executive, in a speech to a newspaper advertising group, said the decision opened "a good-sized can of worms" and predicted it would be used to justify attempts to ban advertising for any product considered harmful.[27] Advocates of a federal law to ban tobacco advertising in the print media have based their arguments on the case. However, other commentators have argued that because the decision involved Puerto Rican law, its effect may be limited to the situation that brought it about.[28] Puerto Rico is a commonwealth which is joined to the United States under different legal conditions than apply to the states.

The Supreme Court was divided five to four in its decision in *Posadas de Puerto Rico Associates* v. *Tourism Company of Puerto Rico,* with Justice Rehnquist writing for the majority. At issue was a Puerto Rico statute and regulations forbidding advertising of casino gambling aimed at residents of Puerto Rico. The law, as construed by Puerto Rico authorities, permitted advertising of casinos in media directed at tourists and in hotels associated with the casinos. Posadas, operator of a Holiday Inn, had twice been fined for violating the law and asked Puerto Rico courts to declare it unconstitutional. The commonwealth's courts held that the law, as modified by the Tourism Company, was constitutional. The U.S. Supreme Court took the case on appeal. Rehnquist applied the *Central Hudson* test and concluded:

1. The advertising was for a legal product and was neither deceptive nor misleading. Therefore, it qualified for First Amendment protection.

2. The state's purpose in enacting the law was to reduce the demand for casino gambling among residents of Puerto Rico. "We have no difficulty in concluding that the Puerto Rico Legislature's interest in the health,

---

26. Dunagin v. City of Oxford, Miss., 718 F.2d 738 (5th Cir. 1983); cert. den., 467 U.S. 1259, 104 S.Ct. 3553, 82 L.Ed.2d 855 (1984).
27. Debra Gersh, "Cigarette Company Exec Sounds Off on Ad Censorship," *Editor & Publisher,* 26 October 1986, p. 45.
28. *Communications Law 1987,* p. 77.

safety, and welfare of its citizens constitutes a 'substantial' governmental interest.''

3. As modified by the Tourism Company, so as to permit advertising in the kinds of materials resort hotels provide for their guests, the law swept no further than necessary to serve the government's interest.

The majority noted that the commonwealth's legislature could have banned casino gambling altogether. That it chose instead to discourage such gambling by Puerto Rico residents was within its powers. The Court took note of the fact that several other kinds of gambling also are legal in Puerto Rico and that the law made no attempt to limit advertising for them. Residents of Puerto Rico may bet on horse races and cock fights, wager on games of chance at fiestas, or play the commonwealth's lottery. Rehnquist distinguished these forms of gambling from casino gambling by noting the trial court's holding that the former "have been traditionally part of the Puerto Rican's roots." Casinos are a recent development aimed at tourists from the mainland United States. Rehnquist said that the Legislature's concern that most Puerto Ricans might not be able to cope with the more sophisticated games of chance offered by casinos was sufficient justification to meet the state interest requirement of *Central Hudson*.

The dissenters were troubled by the majority's willingness to tolerate a prior restraint on advertising for a legal activity and to condone seemingly arbitrary regulations that permit such advertising in one medium while banning it in others. Justice Brennan said he did not believe Puerto Rico could "suppress truthful commercial speech in order to discourage its residents" from engaging in only one of the several forms of gambling available to them. Justice Stevens also was struck by the inconsistencies implicit in the law. He wrote:

> . . . Unless the Court is prepared to uphold an Illinois regulation of speech that subjects *The New York Times* to one standard and *The Chicago Tribune* to another, I do not understand why it is willing to uphold a Puerto Rico regulation that applies one standard to *The New York Times* and another to the *San Juan Star*.

So far, there is little to indicate that the decision in *Posadas* did more than reinforce the principles embodied in the *Central Hudson* test, even though it applied them less strictly than it has in cases involving advertising for products or services that are not subject to regulation. In other cases, the Court has held that advertising can be regulated and even prohibited if the state interest justifying such restrictions is strong enough and the regulation does not sweep more broadly than necessary to achieve its purpose. The corollary that had begun to emerge even before *Posadas* is that an interest sufficient to support regulation of a product or service probably is sufficient to justify regulation of the advertising for it. The Court held in 1982 in *Village of Hoffman Estates* v. *Flipside, Hoffman Estates*,[29] that communities can regulate "head shops" and the advertising associated with them in order to discourage use of illegal drugs. In that instance, the

---

29. 455 U.S. 489, 102 S.Ct. 1186, 71 L.Ed.2d 362 (1982).

Court said authorities could look to the nature of advertising messages and even to the editorial content of publications offered for sale as guides to the purposes for which certain items were being sold. Justice Marshall, writing for the Court, pointedly noted that speech promoting an illegal purpose may be regulated or banned entirely. In *Posadas,* the Court stretched that principle to cover a service that had not been made illegal but which could have been made so.

Conversely, the Court struck down laws carried over from more prudish times forbidding advertisements for condoms. Until the middle of this century laws in many states forbade sale of condoms and other birth control devices. Federal law reflected those times by forbidding the mailing of condom advertising. It was not until 1983 that the Court recognized reality by holding in *Bolger* v. *Youngs Drug Products Corp.*[30] that the federal law violated the doctrine of commercial speech. Postal authorities argued that some persons might be offended if they opened their mail and found an advertisement for birth control devices. Justice Marshall responded by saying that if so, they could close their eyes and drop the ad in the wastebasket.

Looked at too closely, the cases summarized in the preceding sections seem to point in several conflicting directions. However, a common thread runs through them: If the sale of a product or service can be regulated or prohibited, the advertising for it likewise can be regulated or prohibited. That conclusion was implicit in earlier commercial speech decisions of the Supreme Court and was made explicit by the majority in *Posadas.* With respect to cigarettes, the long-standing prohibition against radio and television commercials is based in part on the fact that those media are themselves subject to federal regulation. With respect to alcoholic beverages, the power to regulate advertising is reinforced by the Twenty-first Amendment. However, one federal circuit has held that attempts to prohibit the advertising of alcoholic beverages must apply to all media or run afoul of the equal protection clause of the Fourteenth Amendment. The Supreme Court has not yet directly addressed that question.

Advertisements That May Lead to Harm

In 1988, a federal district court jury in Houston held that a classified advertisement in *Soldier of Fortune* magazine had led to a woman's murder by a hired gunman. The court ordered the magazine to pay her parents and teen-age son $9.4 million in damages.[31] The court acted on the theory that the magazine was negligent in accepting an advertisement that implied an offer to commit a crime. The advertisement, similar to others carried by *Soldier of Fortune,* said: "EX-MARINES-67-69 'Nam Vets, Ex-DI, weapons specialist—jungle warfare, pilot, M.E., high risk assignments, U.S. or overseas." It was placed by John Wayne Hearn. Subsequently, Robert Black of Bryan, Texas, offered Hearn $10,000 to kill Black's wife, Sandra. Hearn did so. He was arrested and was convicted. He

---

30.   463 U.S. 60, 103 S.Ct. 2875, 77 L.Ed.2d 469 (1983).
31.   Eimann v. Soldier of Fortune Magazine, 680 F.Supp. 863 (S.D. Texas 1988).

said the murder of Sandra Black was the third he committed in nineteen days. Robert Black was found guilty of hiring Hearn to kill his wife.

A year later, the U.S. Court of Appeals for the Fifth Circuit reversed without addressing the First Amendment defense offered by the magazine. Relying solely on Texas law governing products liability actions,[32] the court said newspapers and magazines cannot be held to the same liability standards as manufacturers and other business firms. The court said the news media do have a duty to use "reasonable care" in screening ads for possible harm. In this instance, the court said *Soldier of Fortune* had met that standard because the wording of the ad was too ambiguous to be read as a solicitation for criminal employment.

This was not the first time *Soldier of Fortune* had been sued because of its advertising content. In 1987, a federal district court judge in Fayetteville, Arkansas, rejected a motion to dismiss an action brought by a man who said several attempts to injure or kill him had been made by persons hired through ads in the magazine.[33] At issue were two advertisements, each carrying the heading, "GUN FOR HIRE." The magazine's lawyer argued that the ads were fully protected by the First Amendment. The court ruled that they were entitled only to the lesser degree of First Amendment protection given commercial speech. It ruled further that "a reasonable juror could find that [the] advertisements...had a substantial probability of causing harm to some individual." Therefore, the plaintiff was entitled to take his claim for damages to a jury. The record does not show whether that happened.

THE REGULATION OF ADVERTISING ════════

The Rise of the Federal Trade Commission ════════

When the Federal Trade Commission was established in 1914, its mission was to protect business firms from each other. It did so in part by seeking to stop deceptive advertising, which was held to give the offending firm an unfair advantage over its more honest competitors. This focus on unfair competition was reinforced by the Supreme Court in 1931 when it held in *Federal Trade Commission* v. *Raladam*[34] that the law creating the commission did not give it the authority to act to protect consumers. Not until 1938 was the law changed to permit the FTC to act to protect consumers from deceptive advertising.

Even with that change, the Federal Trade Commission (FTC) was destined to labor in obscurity for more than thirty years. It was limited on one side by anemic budgets and on the other by news media that usually ignored its work. Its occasional findings that certain advertisements were deceptive and would have to be withdrawn or changed went largely unreported except in a few consumer-oriented magazines of limited circulation.

---

32.   Christi Harlan, "Magazine Liability Rejected on Appeal in $9.4 Million Case," *Wall Street Journal,* 21 August 1989.
33.   Norwood v. Soldier of Fortune Magazine, Inc., 651 F.Supp. 1397 (W.D.Ark. 1987).
34.   283 U.S. 643, 51 S.Ct. 587, 75 L.Ed. 1324 (1931).

That began to change in the 1960s when the same ferment that produced the civil rights and anti-Vietnam War movements also produced a consumer movement. In the beginning, it was largely the work of one man, Ralph Nader, who made himself highly visible by taking on such giants as General Motors. Nader's book *Unsafe at Any Speed*[35] documented charges of engineering and design problems that led GM to stop production of its rear-engined Corvair. The consumer movement gathered strength from several other sources. Inflation, which became an uncomfortable factor of American life in the late 1960s, made everyone more conscious of value. It also was a time when authority generally was being questioned. Young people particularly were asking why those who were in charge of business firms and other institutions couldn't do things right. The media, particularly television, contributed to the questioning mood. For years, most people took it for granted that there was a certain amount of puffery in print ads. But even children could see that there sometimes was a considerable difference between the way a product performed in a television commercial and the way it performed in actual use. In 1969, the American Bar Association appointed a committee headed by Miles Kirkpatrick to study the FTC's role in policing advertising. The result was a scathing expose' of the agency's ineffectiveness accompanied by recommendations for reform.[36] President Richard M. Nixon followed up by appointing Kirkpatrick to the commission. Congress responded by increasing the FTC's budget.

Thus began in the early 1970s a decade of what one observer called "trench warfare" between the FTC and the advertising business.[37] By 1982, the FTC was under attack on four fronts—from business, the Congress, President Ronald Reagan, and even from its own chairman. James Miller, appointed by Reagan, asked a Senate committee to limit the agency's power to challenge ads as deceptive. He said it operated under such broad authority that "virtually any ad can be found to be deceptive."[38]

A look at the FTC's rulings in the early 1980s might lead one to that conclusion. A sampling of the files shows the following:

— Kroger Co.'s "price patrol" advertising, featuring the results of comparison shopping, was held deceptive in 1981 because it was not based on a broad enough sampling.[39]

— Sterling Drug Co. ads for Bayer, Bayer Children's Aspirin, Cope, Vanquish, and Midol were found to promise more than they could deliver in the way of headache and tension relief.[40]

35. Ralph Nader, *Unsafe at Any Speed* (New York: Grossman, 1972).
36. *Facts on File*, vol. 29, no. 1507, 11–17 September 1969, p. 597; vol. 30, no. 2556, 20–26 August 1970, p. 608.
37. Bruce Fohr, "War: FTC v. Advertisers," Freedom of Information Center Report No. 535, School of Journalism, University of Missouri at Columbia, June 1976.
38. "New Chief of FTC Urges Congress to Limit Commission's Authority to Challenge Ads," *Wall Street Journal*, 19 March 1982.
39. "FTC Says Kroger's Ads Were Deceptive; Company Comparing Food Prices to Competitors'," *Wall Street Journal*, 1 October 1981.
40. "Sterling Drug, Inc., Gets Big Headache from an FTC Judge," *Wall Street Journal*, 11 February 1981.

— Standard Brands agreed to stop advertising that "every 15 seconds, a doctor recommends Fleischmann's" margarine. It could not produce valid survey results supporting the claim.[41]

— Control Data Corp. ads for its computer-programming courses were found to be misleading. The ads had said a college education was not an advantage in getting a job in the computer field.[42]

— Mobil Corporation agreed to warn users of its Mobil 1 oil, touted as reducing oil consumption up to 25 percent, that it might actually increase oil usage in some kinds of cars.[43]

These instances could be multiplied many times. Other targets of FTC deceptive advertising rulings during the decade included AMF bicycles and tricycles, Litton microwave ovens, Sears appliances, Bristol-Myers pain relievers, Sanka, Fresh Horizons, Wonder and Profile breads, Geritol tonic, Warner-Lambert's Listerine, STP oil treatment, and the most common acne remedies. As the list suggests, the FTC managed to step on some very important toes in the business world.

It would be misleading, however, to suggest that the FTC was working wonders in that era. Its budget had been increased, but it was still minute in comparison with expenditures on advertising. It was receiving a great deal of attention in newspapers, many of which routinely covered FTC actions. But in many of the instances above, the advertising campaigns held to be deceptive had been discontinued months or even years before the finding was issued. Under its administrative procedures, the commission was always operating after the fact. That is, it could do nothing, of course, until an allegedly deceptive advertising campaign had come to its attention. Then its investigation, and the hearings designed to meet the need for due process, would take still more time. Meanwhile, the advertisements in question would continue in use either until the campaign ran to its scheduled end or was terminated just ahead of an adverse commission ruling. The Kroger price patrol campaign, for instance, ended two years before the FTC held it deceptive. One of the concerns of the revitalized commission was to find procedures that would either forestall deception or permit it to be attacked and ended at an early stage.

Any action by the Federal Trade Commission begins by determining whether the advertisement has a capacity to deceive. If the commission's staff concludes that it does, that sets in motion a chain of procedures designed to end the problem.

Deceptive Advertising

Over the years, the Federal Trade Commission has used varying standards to determine whether an advertisement has the capacity to deceive consumers. At

---

41. Margaret Gerrard Warner, "Standard Brands Settles FTC Charges over Margarine Ads," *Wall Street Journal,* 7 January 1981.
42. "Control Data Settles with FTC on Claims for Computer Courses," *Wall Street Journal,* 9 October 1980.
43. "Mobil Agrees to Warn Consumers on Results of Synthetic Motor Oil," *Wall Street Journal,* 19 September 1980.

one point, ads were considered deceptive if they could mislead "the ignorant and unthinking and credulous, who, in making purchases, do not stop to analyze but too often are governed by appearances and general impressions."[44] However, the standard used in more recent years was written into a policy statement adopted by the commission in 1983:

> The Commission will find an act or practice deceptive if there is a misrepresentation, omission or other practice, that misleads the consumer acting reasonably in the circumstances, to the consumer's detriment.[45]

This standard is known as the "reasonable person" test. Such persons are assumed to know enough about the ways of advertisers to tolerate a bit of puffery as long as the claims are not demonstrably false.[46]

The law under which the FTC operates is so written as to give the staff considerable leeway in determining what might be deceptive. When the staff decides to act on a complaint, it looks not merely at the words of the ad, but at the overall impression it might convey. The basic test is the capacity, or tendency, to deceive. There need be no proof that the ad has deceived anyone. The FTC staff is not required to survey consumers, either for evidence of deception or to determine how the ordinary person perceives the ad. Thus, the staff has the initial authority to decide that an ad is deceptive. The law assumes that staff members are experts in the field, and their findings are to be given great weight.[47]

An advertisement can be literally true and still be considered misleading. Truth can be used, for instance, to create a misleading impression, to promise more than the product will deliver. If the ad conveys a misleading innuendo, it is in trouble. If a statement can be read two ways, one perfectly proper but the other misleading, the ad is to be judged by the latter interpretation. Finally, it makes no difference what the advertiser intended. Intent is not a factor in determining whether deception is present. The test is of the ad, and the meaning found in it by the staff of the FTC.

The catalog of deceptive advertising listed in such legal reference works as *American Jurisprudence* and *Corpus Juris Secundum* is long and interesting.[48] Courts have held that widely advertised "free gifts" had costly hidden strings attached; that a product advertised at a ridiculously low price is bait designed to lure customers into the store so that salespersons can try to switch them to a higher priced model, and that encyclopedia salespersons should not pose as pollsters. The decisions show that some "diet breads" have fewer calories per slice, not because of their ingredients, but because the slices are thinner than with regular bread. Courts also have held that despite advertising claims, no golf club in itself will convert a duffer into a crack golfer; that "shockproof, waterproof" watches should not be worn in a shower (to say nothing of a snorkeling expedition), and that some "Havana" cigars were made in Pennsylvania after Fidel Castro came to power in Cuba. There is much, much more.

---

44. United States v. 95 Barrels of Vinegar, 265 U.S. 438, 44 S.Ct. 529, 68 L.Ed. 1094 (1924).
45. CCH Trade Regulation Reports (Current) ¶50,455, p. 56,079.
46. Kircher, 63 F.T.C. 1282 (1963).
47. This paragraph and the next are based on 55 Am. Jur.2d 740, pp. 51–53.
48. 55 Am. Jur.2d 750–76, pp. 56–75; 87 C.J.S. 92–120, pp. 325–405.

This is not to say that all advertising is deceptive. The great bulk of it is not. Advertising and public relations agencies subscribe to codes of ethics and usually follow them. Newspapers, magazines, broadcasting stations, and television networks have codes of acceptance designed to turn away fraudulent or misleading advertising. The problems occur at the fringes where sharp operators are to be found in any business, and in a genuine difference of opinion over the meaning of "deception" and as to whether a given ad has a capacity to deceive. The Federal Trade Commission takes a literal view of those terms. If a product is advertised as capable of removing "even the most stubborn sink stains with a single application," then it must do so, or the ad is subject to being ruled deceptive. But the FTC has been unwilling to find deception in ads that portray a mouthwash's ability to combat bad breath as the key to romance, even though most users will not be kissed by the next attractive man or woman they meet. Even in its most active period, the commission rejected suggestions that psychological manipulation of people's anxieties and desires might be a form of deceptive advertising. And, in light of the First Amendment decisions discussed earlier in this book, it is clear that the FTC has no authority over political advertising, no matter how distorted or deceptive it may be.

Even within the rather narrow range in which it operates, the Federal Trade Commission's authority to rule ads deceptive is limited by several safeguards. Staff findings are subject to review by administrative law judges, who in turn are subject to review by the commission itself. Beyond that, an advertiser displeased by the commission's verdict can go to the United States Courts of Appeals for further review.

Coping with Deceptive Advertising

The Federal Trade Commission is made up of five members, appointed by the president, subject to confirmation by the Senate, for seven-year terms. No more than three can be members of the same political party. The president designates one of the members to serve as chairman. Although the term of each member spans almost two presidential terms, each president in recent times has been able to appoint enough members to have an influence on the commission's approach to its duties. By the fifth year of the Reagan administration, that approach was to let the competitive forces of the marketplace carry the burden of coping with deceptive advertising.[49]

The commission had concerns in two major areas. Its Bureau of Competition is concerned with antitrust law violations and with restraint of trade. The Bureau of Consumer Protection is concerned with deceptive advertising and unfair trade practices. Therefore, the commission is able to devote only a little more than half its budget, which was $69 million in 1989, to deceptive advertising. The FTC's spending for all purposes in that year was less than one-tenth of 1 percent of the $140 billion spent on advertising. Each of the top 100 advertisers spent far more

---

49. John Koten, "More Firms File Challenges to Rivals' Comparative Ads," *Wall Street Journal*, 12 January 1984.

on its attempts to sell its products than the FTC's entire annual budget.[50] Thus, staff and budget limitations require the agency to act largely in response to complaints.

If the staff decides a complaint is worth investigation, it notifies the advertiser. At that point, the commission may be willing to settle for a *letter of compliance,* which is simply a written promise that the advertiser will change its ads to remove the alleged deception. This does not involve an admission of deception on the part of the advertiser.

If the advertiser decides to contest the action, it is entitled to a hearing before an administrative law judge. The procedure is informal. The judge's conclusions are drafted as a *consent agreement,* outlining what the advertiser must do, if anything, to comply with the law. If the advertiser is willing to accept its terms, that ends the matter. Again, acceptance does not involve a confession of wrongdoing. It can mean no more than unwillingness to go to the expense of further litigation. Or it can mean that the campaign in question has ended.

There are compelling reasons that both the advertiser and the FTC try to avoid going beyond the consent agreement level. For an advertiser, further attempts at vindication not only become expensive but can result in protracted unfavorable publicity. For the government, the prospect of a court action can raise its level of proof from capacity to deceive to a showing that the advertisement at issue actually has deceived consumers. Circuit courts have varied on this point.[51] However, whatever the reasons, about three-quarters of the actions begun by the FTC do not go beyond the consent agreement level.

Advertisers who do elect to proceed begin to risk penalties. The next step up the enforcement ladder leads to the possibility that the commission will issue a *cease and desist order.* This is precisely what the name implies. The advertiser who gets such an order has only two courses open: immediate compliance or an appeal to the U.S. Court of Appeals. Failure either to comply or appeal can lead to an injunction and fines.

Working within this simple framework, the FTC has relied on an early decision of the Supreme Court[52] to devise a wide variety of remedies designed to cope with deceptive advertising. Congress further strengthened its hand in 1975, at the height of the consumer movement, with passage of the Magnuson-Moss Warranty-Federal Trade Commission Improvement Act.[53] Some of its remedies are examined below.

---

50. The FTC's budget figure is from the summary of the U.S. budget for fiscal 1988 published in the *World Almanac, 1990* (New York: World Almanac, 1989), p. 75. The top 100 advertisers are listed on p. 371 of the *Almanac.* Philip Morris led the list with about $1.5 billion in advertising expenditures. Ameritech, a midwestern telephone company, was number 100 with $83 million. Total annual advertising expenditures, with a breakdown of the amounts spent with various media, are reported each year by the American Newspaper Publishers Association and summarized in "Facts about Newspapers," available from the ANPA, The Newspaper Center, Box 17407 Dulles Airport, Washington, D.C. 20041.

51. National Commission on Egg Nutrition v. Federal Trade Commission, 517 F.2d 485 (7th Cir. 1975); Federal Trade Commission v. Simeon Management Corp., 391 F. Supp. 697 (D. Calif. 1975); aff'd, 532 F.2d 708 (9th Cir. 1976).

52. Jacob Siegel Co. v. FTC, 327 U.S. 374, 66 S.Ct. 758, 90 L.Ed. 888 (1946).

53. 15 U.S.C. §§2301–12, 2345–58.

Broadened Cease and Desist Orders

The traditional order merely forbade repetition of a specific deception by a single advertiser for a single product. As a result of the Supreme Court's decision in *FTC* v. *Colgate Palmolive Co.*[54] in 1965, the commission has been able to issue cease and desist orders covering a specific deceptive practice but applying to all advertisers who might be tempted to use it. Such orders have had their greatest effect on television commercials. If a product is demonstrated, it must be shown as is and under conditions of normal usage. If there is a time lapse between the application of that new, improved detergent and the disappearance of the "ring around the collar," the announcer must say so, or a graphic must indicate it.

Affirmative Disclosure

Sometimes a truth is not the whole truth. For years, the J. B. Williams Co. advertised Geritol as the great rejuvenator of the aging. For that tired feeling, brought on by "iron-poor blood," there was no better remedy than regular doses of iron-rich Geritol. There were truths in the commercials. People do tend to tire more easily as they grow older. And persons who suffer anemia, an iron deficiency, will tire more easily than others. However, most tiredness has nothing to do with iron deficiency. For such persons, the only "pickup" they might find in Geritol would be in its alcohol content. The FTC found the Geritol ads deceptive and ordered J. B. Williams to state in future advertising that iron-poor blood is only rarely the cause of tiredness.[55] This affirmative disclosure was required to supply the element of truth that the advertiser had left out of the original message.

This principle has been applied in other contexts. Many stores will sell a person an appliance on a deferred-payment schedule. However, most merchants don't carry their own accounts. They sell their installment contracts to banks or finance companies. Thus a purchaser of a faulty product may try to force the seller to make repairs by withholding payments, only to find this has no effect except for a nasty letter from the holder of the note. There was a time when stores did not have to tell customers what they did with their notes. The FTC now requires affirmative disclosure of the sale of installment contracts to financial institutions.[56]

Affirmative Acts

Sometimes the fault lies not in the advertising, but in the advertisers' willingness to do what they promised to do. In such instances, the FTC has ordered specific performances to carry out the terms of an ad. This remedy has been applied most commonly to promotional games and contests, including the multitude of major prize offers that are sent to millions of persons through the mails. The

---

54. 380 U.S. 374, 85 S.Ct. 1035, 12 L.Ed.2d 904 (1965).
55. J.B. Williams Co. v. FTC, 381 F.2d 884 (6th Cir. 1967).
56. See, for example, Seekonk Freezer Meats, Inc., 82 F.T.C. 1019 (1973).

FTC concluded that such promotions were being abused. For instance, winning numbers might be distributed only in cities where the promoter was hard pressed by competitors. Or the list of winners might be posted in an inconvenient place, so that most prizes would not be claimed.

In the late 1960s, the FTC looked into a promotion conducted by the McDonald's hamburger chain. Advertisements said the chain would give away 15,610 prizes worth $500,000. The FTC learned that only 227 prizes worth about $13,000 were claimed by McDonald's customers.[57] However, a divided commission rejected the staff's conclusion that advertising for the sweepstakes was deceptive. The majority concluded that if one accepted the literal meaning of the ads, McDonald's had not promised to give away all of the prizes.

However, the investigation of that and similar sweepstakes led to adoption of a Trade Regulation Rule for Games of Chance in the Food Retailing and Gasoline Industries.[58] This requires that customers be notified of the exact number of prizes to be given away in each category and the approximate odds against winning. If the sweepstakes continues more than thirty days, participants must be told how many prizes remain. Winning tickets must be distributed solely by chance, and the list of winners must be made available.

In addition, as a result of a case involving the *Reader's Digest* sweepstakes, the FTC held that if advertising promises that all prizes will be awarded, drawings must be continued until they are.[59]

Corrective Advertising

In the early 1970s, a group of law students at George Washington University in Washington, D.C., came up with a brilliantly original remedy for deceptive advertising: Why not require advertisers to confess and correct their deceptions? They were outraged at television commercials for a new line of Campbell's Soups—Chunky Soups, so thick with meat and vegetables that the solid ingredients stuck up through the liquid in the bowl. What the camera didn't show was the layer of marbles on which the meat and vegetables rested. The FTC staff accused Campbell's of misleading advertising.

Into the fray charged the law students, calling themselves Students Opposing Unfair Practices, or SOUP. Why, they argued at the hearing, should Campbell's, or anyone else, be permitted to profit from the impression left by a misleading ad campaign? Why not require an errant advertiser to erase the impression by confessing his sin in subsequent commercials? This would be a form of penance that would indeed carry a sting likely to make other would-be sinners mend their ways. The commission, by a three-to-two vote, rejected the need for corrective advertising in this instance, but a majority agreed that it was an idea worth looking into.[60] Chairman Caspar W. Weinberger wrote

---

57. McDonald's Corp. 78 F.T.C. 606 (1971).
58. 16 C.F.R. §419, 17 October 1969.
59. Reader's Digest Association, 79 F.T.C. 696 (1971); modified, 83 F.T.C. 1356 (1974).
60. Gerald J. Thain, "Corrective Advertising: Theory and Cases," N.Y. Law Forum, 19:1–34, Summer 1973.

We have no doubt as to the Commission's power to require such affirmative disclosure when such disclosures are reasonably related to the deception found and are required in order to dissipate the effects of that deception.... All that is required is that there be a "reasonable relation to the unlawful acts found to exist."[61]

Very shortly, the FTC began to carry the idea into effect. Several companies were even willing to accept consent orders requiring them to run corrective advertising. One of the notable pioneers was ITT Continental Baking Co., bakers of Profile bread, widely touted in advertising as an aid in weight reducing. A series of television commercials featured slender young women, who were being admired by handsome young men while an announcer extolled the virtues of Profile bread. Eat two slices, of it, plain or toasted, before lunch and dinner, the announcer said, and you, too, can lose weight. The FTC staff held that the ads conveyed the misleading impression that Profile bread had fewer calories than other kinds of bread and had some special value in taking off weight. In reality, bread is bread, and all brands of a given kind of bread contain essentially the same number of calories an ounce. If Profile had any value in a weight-reducing program it was because it was sliced thinner than other breads and therefore had about four and a half fewer calories a slice.

ITT Continental agreed to a consent order requiring it to include a corrective statement in all of its advertising for the next year. It was required to spend not less than 25 percent of its advertising costs on messages proclaiming that "Profile is not effective for weight reduction, contrary to possible interpretations of prior advertising."[62] The effect was sobering. Sales of Profile bread dropped 20 to 25 percent. Some store owners relegated it to the least favorable shelf positions.[63] Such an effect was noted by other prospective targets for corrective advertising. Foremost among these was the Warner-Lambert Co., makers of Listerine antiseptic mouthwash, which fought the FTC all the way to the Supreme Court. The case was a straightforward test of the authority of the FTC in light of the doctrine of commercial speech.

Warner-Lambert Co. v. FTC, **562 F.2d 749 (D.C. Cir. 1977).** Listerine had been on the market since 1879 with a formula that remained unchanged for a hundred years. Starting in 1921, it had been advertised as beneficial in preventing colds and sore throats, and in alleviating their symptoms. It became one of the most widely sold mouthwashes. Several times, the FTC had studied Listerine's advertising claims and had taken no action.[64] But in 1972 it began another study that led to a formal complaint. Warner-Lambert asked for a hearing, which lasted four months and produced four thousand pages of testi-

---

61. Campbell Soup Co., 77 F.T.C. 664, at 668 (1970).
62. ITT Continental Baking Co., Inc., 79 F.T.C. 248 (1971).
63. John Holusha, "Baking Firm Beats False Ad Charge," *Louisville Courier-Journal,* 2° ber 1972. The headline referred to a subsequent FTC staff finding that ITT Contir⌐ntal had misrepresented the nutritional qualities of Wonder Bread and Hostess Snack C⌐кes. This time, ITT fought it out and an administrative law judge found in its favor.
64. Listerine's advertising was reviewed by the FTC in 1932, 1940, 1951, 1958, and 1962. Warner-Lambert Co. v. FTC, 562 F.2d 749, at 763, n. 70 (D.C.Cir. 1977).

mony. The administrative law judge upheld the complaint as did the full commission in 1975.

The commission found that Listerine did indeed kill millions of bacteria in the mouth and throat, but it left many millions more. However, this had no effect on colds, because colds are caused by viruses, which are immune to the ingredients in Listerine. The commission therefore ordered Warner-Lambert to cease and desist from all advertising that claimed or implied that its mouthwash would cure colds or sore throats, or help its users avoid either. Further, it ordered the company to include in future advertising a corrective sentence: "Contrary to prior advertising, Listerine will not help prevent colds or sore throats or lessen their severity." It was to do so until it had spent on such advertising a sum equal to its average annual expenditures on Listerine advertising during the preceding ten years. This was about $10 million.

Warner-Lambert appealed to the Court of Appeals for the District of Columbia Circuit, arguing in part that the First Amendment protected its claims for Listerine and that the penalty was excessive. The result was a nearly complete victory for the FTC. In *Warner-Lambert* v. *FTC,* a divided court held that the commission had not exceeded its powers in ordering corrective advertising. Nor could it find any relief for Warner-Lambert in the First Amendment. In the commercial-speech cases decided up to that time, the Supreme Court had said several times that false or misleading advertising does not merit First Amendment protection. Warner-Lambert tried to take its case to the Supreme Court, but was denied certiorari.[65]

Long before the decision was handed down, Warner-Lambert had shifted the thrust of its advertising campaign for Listerine. It was being touted as the perfect remedy for bad breath, because it kills the bacteria that produce unpleasant odors in the mouth. The corrective sentence was incorporated as part of this new approach.

Relying on the *Warner-Lambert* decision, the FTC ordered other firms to use corrective advertising in 1980 before the advent of the Reagan administration led to a general relaxation of its campaign against allegedly deceptive advertising. Among them were two marketers of products designed to treat acne. Both were ordered to stop advertising their products until they had agreed to run specific corrective advertising. Hayoun Cosmetique of New York City had been advertising a kit offering four of its products as a cure for acne. It was ordered to stop suggesting that the products would eliminate the blemishes associated with the teenage affliction. Nor could it advertise in any way unless for the next six months its advertising clearly proclaimed, "No product can cure acne."[66] AHC Pharmacal of Miami, marketer of AHC Gel and Dr. Fulton's Acne Control Regimen, was the target of an even more specific order. The FTC said it could not advertise further until it had run ads in Sunday newspaper supplements in six cities proclaiming in 48-point type, "No product can cure acne." The prescribed type is two-thirds of an inch high.[67]

---

65. 435 U.S. 950, 98 S.Ct. 1575, 55 L.Ed.2d 800 (1978).
66. Hayoun Cosmetique, Inc., 95 F.T.C. 794 (1980).
67. AHC Pharmacal, Inc., 95 F.T.C. 528 (1980).

Substantiation of Advertising Claims

Advertisers who make performance claims for products must be prepared to back them up. Advertising of gasoline mileage claims for automobiles offers one example. Because mileage can vary greatly with the way a car is driven, automobile manufacturers lean heavily on the ratings the federal government requires for all new cars. But because these figures are products of laboratory tests, the FTC requires that their use in advertising be qualified by the notice that actual mileage will depend on the individual driver, road conditions, and weather.

Advertisers who claim that their product tastes better than others must be able to support that claim with data collected from a representative sampling of consumers. Because such sampling is costly, and is certain to show that some portion of the sample did not like the product, television has seen the rise of the blind taste test. The viewer sees the blinding sleeve come off the can of beer or cup of cola, and the look of surprise as the drinker recognizes that he or she has just been a traitor to a favorite brand. No mention need be made of how many samplers made the wrong choice.

Since 1971, the FTC has insisted that any claims for product performance be backed by valid survey results. It has taken a dim view of surveys conducted exclusively among dealers for a product, or by the manufacturer of a product. The Kroger-conducted price survey, mentioned earlier, is one example.

Until 1984, the FTC periodically asked all major companies in certain industries to send the agency their data supporting advertising claims. These were studied by agency staff members looking for discrepancies. After five thousand hours of study over several years produced not a single case, FTC Chairman Miller proposed that the substantiation program be dropped. After hearing from protesters, the agency agreed to continue to require advertisers to collect data to support their claims, but it no longer requires that the data be submitted routinely. The agency will seek supporting data only as part of a specific investigation.[68]

Trade Rules

All the above remedies share a common problem. None can be imposed until a complaint has been made and an investigation conducted by the FTC staff. If the advertiser resists, there is further delay until a hearing can be scheduled and conducted by an administrative law officer. Further resistance can lead to a hearing before the full commission and thence into the federal courts. In the Listerine case, the procedure took six years. Thus, all remedies, except for corrective advertising, amount to little more than locking the garage door after the car has not only been stolen, but has been stripped and the remains sent to the crusher. Many television advertising campaigns, for instance, run for no more than thirteen weeks.

---

68. ''Running the Government Right,'' *Wall Street Journal,* 27 March 1984; ''FTC Reaffirms Policy Requiring Advertisers to Prove Their Claims,'' *Wall Street Journal,* 30 July 1984.

The FTC began in the early 1970s to establish trade regulation rules (trade rules) with the idea that they could be used to bring quick action against errant advertisers. Doubts about the commission's authority to do this were resolved by Section 18 of the FTC Improvement Act of 1975. However, the history of trade rules has been an uneven one. The procedure works as follows:

The FTC staff tries to identify misleading practices on an industrywide basis. Then it proposes a set of rules designed to cope with such practices. These are published in the *Federal Register* and distributed within the affected industry with a request for comment. A hearing is scheduled. When all sides have been heard, the proposed trade rules are put in final form. These, too, are published and distributed. From that point on, the FTC acts on the theory that all of those involved know what the rules are and should be expected to obey them. Thus, an infraction is considered willful. If one occurs, the FTC can move at once with a cease and desist order backed by the ability to impose an injunction or fines that can run up to $10,000 a day.

In some areas, trade rules have met with little objection. In others, they have been fought. The oil industry, for instance, fought a trade rule requiring the posting of octane ratings on gasoline pumps. It lost.[69] The clothing industry, on the other hand, accepted a rule that requires placement of a cleaning instruction label in garments.[70]

But when the FTC tried to establish trade rules for the advertising of over-the-counter drugs, it ran into a storm of protest that led it, six years later, to retreat from the field.[71] At one point, the agency proposed that drug advertisers be required to use approved medical terms. Thus, a cough remedy would have to be described as an "antitussive." A mint tablet designed to quell digestive gases would have to be described as an "antiflatulent." Ads no longer could offer "relief for that burning sensation due to hyperacidity," nor could they present a remedy for "that bloated feeling due to excess gas."[72] After years of argument, the FTC abandoned the proposed regulation, in part because of its patent absurdity and in part because the drug industry and its advertising agencies resisted vigorously.

An attempt to write rules regulating nutritional claims for food came to the same end after another six-year effort.[73] However, the agency was able to write rules for claims that a food is "natural." That term can be used only for foods that contain no artificial ingredients and have been subjected to no processing other than what could be done in a home kitchen.[74]

During the decade of the 1980s, the deregulation of business by government, begun by President Carter, was carried forward by President Reagan. In keeping

---

69. National Petroleum Refiners Association v. FTC, 482 F.2d 672 (D.C.Cir. 1973); cert. den., 415 U.S. 951, 94 S.Ct. 1475, 39 L.Ed.2d 567 (1974).
70. Care Labeling of Textile Wearing Apparel, 16 C.F.R. §423, 3 July 1972.
71. FTC Kills Proposal on Ads for Drugs Sold over Counter," *Wall Street Journal,* 12 February 1981.
72. Burt Schorr, "How the FTC Plans to Cure Synonymity (Or Is It Synonymy?)," *Wall Street Journal,* 13 February 1978.
73. "FTC to End Six-Year Bid to Write a Rule on Nutrition Claims in Food Industry," *Wall Street Journal,* 3 April 1980.
74. "U.S. Issues Rules for Advertising 'Natural' Foods, *New York Times,* 13 October 1980.

with the policy, Federal Trade commissioners showed little interest in pursuing deceptive advertising claims. Work on trade rules stopped and, in one instance, was reversed. In 1988, the commission voted to repeal a requirement, in effect since 1971, that supermarkets keep enough stock on hand to meet the demand for advertised items.[75] The commission concluded that shortages of advertised items no longer are much of a problem and that the rule served little purpose other than to increase food stores' costs. Under the new rule, supermarkets can offer rain checks or substitute items, which most already do. Or, if the ad states that supplies are limited, an item may be advertised without the need to offer an alternative. When the rule was adopted, studies showed that as much as 10 percent of advertised items weren't on the shelves.

However, it should be noted that, active or not, the trade commission, and the law under which it operates, survives. So do the remedies designed to check deceptive advertising. The commission has the authority to order advertisers to substantiate claims made for their products. And, in the first week of the Bush administration, the commission used that authority in a manner designed to signal a new period of action. It charged that Campbell Soup Co. told something less than the truth when it advertised that chicken noodle and "most of" its other soups are low in fat and cholesterol and thus helpful in fighting heart disease.[76] The FTC said the ad failed to disclose that "soups are high in sodium and that diets high in sodium may increase the risk of heart disease." That failure made the ad deceptive, the commission charged. John MacLeod, director of the Bureau of Consumer Protection, said, "This case stands for the proposition that when you advertise a particular quality or characteristic of your product, you should disclose facts that tend to undermine or refute the specific claim that you have made. The message here is that the commission takes health claims seriously and will police the advertising of these claims."

Other Means of Coping with Deceptive Advertising

Federal Agencies Other than the FTC

Although the Federal Trade Commission has been the most visible and most active agency dealing with deceptive advertising, the FTC is not alone in the field. Other federal agencies have some control over certain kinds of advertising. Agencies involved in financing housing and enforcing civil rights have adopted guidelines for real estate advertising placed in newspapers[77] to prevent discrimination based on race, religion, color, sex, or national origin of the buyer or renter.

---

75. "FTC Votes to End Supermarkets Rule on Advertised Items," *Wall Street Journal,* 22 April 1988.
76. Alix M. Freedman, "FTC Alleges Campbell Ad Is Deceptive," *Wall Street Journal,* 27 January 1989.
77. *Publication Guidelines for Compliance with Title VIII of the Civil Rights Act of 1968,* 37 Fed.Reg. 6700 (1 April 1972); 45 Fed.Reg. 57102 (22 September 1980).

The Securities and Exchange Commission (SEC) imposes narrow limits for advertisements of securities. In 1988, the SEC extended its control to include automated messages reporting yield data by telephone.[78] The action was taken to bring the guidelines for such messages in compliance with uniform reporting rules imposed on print advertising for mutual funds. In general, the guidelines require that yield data be reported for specified periods ranging from thirty days to ten years, depending on the nature of the fund. The purpose is to prevent reporting a current rate of return that might not accurately reflect performance over time. The telephone rule does not apply to live conversations with brokers.

Also at the federal level, agencies regulate the labeling of foods and drugs; of alcoholic beverages; and of potentially dangerous tools, machinery, and appliances. The Food and Drug Administration took the unusual step in 1987 and 1988 of issuing statements alleging that advertisements for a prescription antihistamine and for aspirin might be misleading. Normally, advertising for such products is policed by the FTC, not the FDA, which is concerned with product labels. The FDA said it was moved to action because the ads might lead to misuse of the products.

In one instance, the FDA released a letter it had sent to Sandoz Pharmaceuticals Corp. charging that full-page newspaper advertisements for its prescription antihistamine, Tavist-1, were "false and misleading."[79] The full-page ads, which had appeared in major newspapers, had been cleared in advance by the FDA. But an agency official said its drug-advertising branch was not aware "that some statements in the ad had been rejected as unproven by the FDA's medical-reviewing division." At issue was a claim that the product was less likely to cause drowsiness than other prescription antihistamines.

In the second action, the FDA expressed concern over aspirin advertisements calling attention to a study indicating that daily doses of aspirin may help prevent heart attacks in some persons.[80] FDA officials said they feared that some persons might take too many aspirins and that others who have conditions for which aspirin can be harmful might take the drug. An FDA official noted that normally the FTC has jurisdiction over such advertising, but he said the FDA could take action against the aspirin ads because they suggest "an intended use for which adequate directions are not given on the product label." The FDA's inquiry led to an agreement with aspirin makers to exercise voluntary restraint with respect to advertising aspirin as a heart-attack preventive until more data are available.

State Agencies

Two other methods of combating deceptive advertising moved to the fore in the 1980s. State attorneys general, coordinating their activities through the National Association of State Attorneys General, moved against major advertisers.

---

78. Michael Siconolfi, "SEC Restricts Phone Messages That Cite Yields," *Wall Street Journal*, 27 May 1988.
79. Michael Waldholz, "FDA Calls Some Newspaper Ad Claims for Sandoz Drug 'False and Misleading,'" *Wall Street Journal*, 26 October 1987.
80. Ronald Alsop, "Aspirin Makers Face FDA Scrutiny for Heart-Attack Prevention Ads," *Wall Street Journal*, 1 February 1988.

Their targets included airlines, car rental agencies, insurance companies, McDonald's, and Sears. The vigor of the campaigns led to a protest from an FTC commissioner who accused the attorneys general of "misdirected regulatory zeal" and of moving into an area best left to federal regulators.[81] The decade also saw an increase in the number of civil actions in which business firms sought damages from competitors whom they accused of deceptive advertising.

State attorneys general moved into the national spotlight when more than forty states announced that they had adopted standards for airline advertising of discount fares and frequent-flier programs. The actions were coordinated through the officials' national organization and were soon followed by the adoption of standards applying to other kinds of advertising. The association said it took action because funding restrictions and deregulatory policies had left the FTC unable or unwilling to regulate advertising likely to mislead consumers. In the case of the airlines, the Department of Transportation had fined several carriers for lapses in their dealings with passengers, and Congress was considering an airline consumer-protection bill when the attorneys general made their move.[82] They issued standards including ten limitations on airline advertising. One such limitation required that restrictions on bargain fares be stated in type at least one-third the size of the largest type in the ad. Another limitation, applied to television commercials, required that restrictions be described orally rather than be reduced to a printed message briefly flashed across the screen. The limitations imposed by the state officials were more restrictive than those imposed by federal agencies.

The airlines complained that the restrictions were such as to discourage their attempts to publicize price competition. The director of the Bureau of Consumer Protection of the FTC agreed with the complaint. He said that as a result of the state actions airline price advertising had decreased. But the Oregon attorney general, David Frohnmayer, said that state guidelines had led to a "demonstrable increase in clarity" in airline advertising, thus enabling consumers to make a more informed choice among competing carriers.

Insurance companies, particularly those using celebrities in pitches directed at the elderly, were the next major target.[83] Attorneys general in California and Washington took the lead, challenging television commercials featuring Tennessee Ernie Ford, Art Linkletter, Ed McMahon, Dick Van Dyke, and the late Lorne Greene. Some of the celebrities promoted low-cost life insurance for the elderly. Others were selling medical care and hospitalization insurance. State insurance regulators said they had received many complaints about the policies being offered. As a result of the challenges, some of the commercials were taken off the air by court order. Insurance companies modified or withdrew others.

---

81. Andrea Rothman, "Attorneys General Draw Fire of FTC in Turf War on Ads," *Wall Street Journal,* 15 December 1988.
82. Jonathan Dahl, "States Agree to Crack Down on Airline Ads," *Wall Street Journal,* 14 December 1987.
83. Ken Wells, "Insurance Ads Starring Celebrities Are Target of Crackdown by States," *Wall Street Journal,* 5 May 1988, and Paul M. Barrett, "Attorneys General Flex Their Muscles: State Officials Join Forces to Press Consumer and Antitrust Concerns, *Wall Street Journal,* 13 July 1988.

In Pennsylvania, a pharmaceutical company agreed, under prodding from state officials, to end an advertising campaign promoting Ascriptin brand of aspirin as "beneficial in the prevention of first-time heart attacks."[84] New York State's attorney general won agreement from the Kellogg Co. that it would stop implying that the B vitamins in its Rice Krispies give consumers added vigor and energy.[85] In New York City, an action charging Sears with misleading price-cutting advertising led to an agreement on the phrasing of future ads.[86] In all three instances, the companies agreed to pay the costs incurred in bringing the complaints against them.

However, at the end of 1988, lawsuits filed in two federal courts challenged the authority of the states to regulate national advertising. One of the actions led to an order in January 1989 restraining the Texas attorney general from further enforcement of rules regulating airline advertising.[87] An attorney for the airlines predicted that the ruling would be used as a precedent to restrain states from acting against other kinds of national advertising. However, because the judge based his decision on the Federal Aviation Act, which specifically gives the Department of Transportation authority to determine when an airline is engaging in practices harmful to a competitor, other lawyers said the decision may have only a limited effect.

Civil Actions Brought by Business Firms against Competitors

Business firms moved into the void left by FTC inaction by filing civil court actions against competitors. Plaintiffs have asked courts to order competitors to stop or modify allegedly deceptive advertising campaigns. Some also have sought damages. In two notable decisions courts have upheld the complaints. One of the legal actions involved charges and countercharges between Johnson & Johnson, the maker of Tylenol, and American Home Products, the maker of Anacin-3 and Advil, all highly advertised over-the-counter pain relievers. A U.S. District Court judge in New York ruled that both firms were making exaggerated advertising claims for their products.[88] He went so far as to suggest how Johnson & Johnson could advertise Tylenol without being misleading: "For mild to moderate pain, you can't buy a more effective pain reliever without a prescription." The court ordered both companies to refrain from further deceptive advertising but awarded no damages. The ruling came after four years of litigation. At about the same time, another federal district court in New York City ruled that Warner-Lambert Co. made false and misleading advertising claims for its "new improved

84. "Aspirin Unit Agrees to Stop Using Ad on Heart Attacks," *Wall Street Journal,* 13 July 1988.
85. Alex Kotlowitz, "Kellogg Agrees It Won't Run Some Cereal Ads," *Wall Street Journal,* 29 August 1988.
86. Robert Johnson and John Koten, "Sears Has Everything, Including Messy Fight over Ads in New York," *Wall Street Journal,* 28 June 1988; Robert Johnson, "Sears Drops Suit, Agrees to Change Ads in New York," *Wall Street Journal,* 10 January 1989.
87. Joanne Lipman, "Ruling May Clarify If the U.S. or States Should Regulate Ads," *Wall Street Journal,* 2 February 1989.
88. William Power, "A Judge Prescribes a Dose of Truth to Ease the Pain of Analgesic Ads," *Wall Street Journal,* 13 May 1987.

e.p.t. Plus'' home pregnancy kit.[89] The lawsuit was brought by Tambrands Inc., maker of a competitive home-testing kit. The court imposed a permanent injunction forbidding future claims that users of the kit can know ''in as fast as ten minutes'' whether they are pregnant. The judge said that the test requires at least thirty minutes to give accurate results for most women. Also forbidden were further claims that the kit provides a ''one-step'' test and that it is the fastest test. The judge also ordered Warner-Lambert to pay Tambrand's legal expenses.

The examples summarized above are only a sampling of the lawsuits and state actions taken against allegedly deceptive advertising. This section serves as a reminder that attempts to control the content of advertising come from many sources. In the 1970s, the most notable control came at the national level from the Federal Trade Commission. When that agency retreated from the field in keeping with the deregulation policies of the Carter and Reagan administrations, state governments and civil actions moved in. Although business firms argued in some instances that their advertising was protected by the First Amendment, courts reminded them that the Supreme Court has held that deceptive advertising does not qualify for such protection. The challenge facing those who prepare advertising is to know what the limits on puffery are and to work within them.

ACCESS TO THE MEDIA

The Right to Refuse to Refuse Advertising

The news media, with few exceptions, are supported by advertising. Therefore, in the normal course of events, it can be assumed that the purpose of the advertising department of a newspaper, magazine, or broadcasting station is to sell as much advertising as possible. Yet there are times when management feels compelled to refuse an ad. Most broadcasting stations, for instance, won't accept advertising for hard liquor. Some newspapers won't print cigarette advertising. Others won't advertise X-rated movies. Some have rules against advertising that is used to attack another business or an individual. Some won't accept advertising on topics considered too controversial.

As long as advertising was considered to be without First Amendment protection, there was little question about the right to refuse advertising. Publishers could point to article I, section 10, paragraph 1 of the Constitution which states in part: ''No State shall...pass any bill of attainder, ex post facto law, or law impairing the obligation of contracts.''

Advertising is sold under contract. If a state can't impair a contract already made, it certainly can't force an unwilling party to enter into one. That ended the matter as long as most towns of any size had competing newspapers. With the advent of one-newspaper towns in mid-century, efforts were begun to change the

---

89.   Tambrands, Inc. v. Warner-Lambert Co., 673 F.Supp. 1190 (S.D.N.Y. 1987).

rule. The argument was advanced that the news media are like common carriers—a bus line, the telephone company, or a ferry. If a newspaper was the only carrier of advertising in town, then it ought to be required to accept an ad from anyone who could pay the established price. One low-level Ohio court accepted that reasoning in 1919 in *Uhlman* v. *Sherman*,[90] but no other court has done so.

Shuck v. *The Carroll Daily Herald,* **247 N.W. 813 (1933).**

The classic case in this area is *Shuck* v. *The Carroll Daily Herald,* decided by the Supreme Court of Iowa in 1933. In that instance, the newspaper's agent went so far as to accept money for an ad brought in by the owner of a dry cleaning store. The publisher decided not to publish it, and returned the money. The dry cleaner, Shuck, sued to force the publisher to run the ad. The trial court refused, and the state supreme court affirmed unanimously. Rejecting the common-carrier argument advanced by Shuck and supported by reference to the *Uhlman* case, the court held:

> The newspaper business is an ordinary business. It is a business essentially private in its nature—as private as that of the baker, grocer, or milkman, all of whom perform a service on which, to a greater or lesser extent, the communities depend, but which bears no such relation to the public as to warrant its inclusion in the category of businesses charged with a public use. If a newspaper were required to accept an advertisement, it could be compelled to publish a news item. If some good lady gave a tea, and submitted to the newspaper a proper account of the tea, and the editor of the newspaper, believing that it had no news value, refused to publish it, she, it seems to us, would have as much right to compel the newspaper to publish the account as would a person engaged in business to compel a newspaper to publish an advertisement....
>
> Thus, as a newspaper is a strictly private enterprise, the publishers thereof have a right to publish whatever advertisement they desire and to refuse to publish whatever advertisements they do not desire to publish.

The many decisions since have added nothing to the principle. They have established that publishers can classify advertisements as they see fit,[91] or can change an ad to meet their standards of acceptability.[92] However to avoid conflict over whether a contract is in force, the wording of advertising contracts should reserve to the publisher or advertising director the final right of approval and should state the kinds of advertising that are unacceptable. Any prospective advertiser should be given a copy of the terms at the first inquiry.

With respect to newspaper advertising, courts generally have recognized that some common acts signal acceptance of an ad. If an ad is received by telephone, as much classified advertising is, the copy is accepted at the end of the conversation. If copy for an ad is brought to a counter at the newspaper, the ad is con-

---

90. 31 Ohio Dec. 54 (1919).
91. Staff Research Associates v. Tribune Co., 346 F.2d 372 (7th Cir. 1965).
92. Camp-of-the-Pines v. New York Times, 53 N.Y.S.2d 475 (S.Ct., Albany Co. 1945).

sidered accepted when the employee or the customer leaves the counter. If the copy is received by mail, the ad is not accepted until it has been verified or the advertisement has been published.[93] If there is doubt as to whether an ad is acceptable, employees who take the copy should tell the customer that the copy cannot be used until the employee has checked with a supervisor. If the copy is deemed not acceptable, the customer should be told that the paper does not intend to use it. Lawyers recommend that in such instances, the less the employee says to the customer, the better. Any attempt at explanation may be used in court if a lawsuit should result.

What can happen if the terms of the contract are not clearly understood is illustrated by an Indiana Court of Appeals decision in *Herald-Telephone* v. *Fatouras*.[94] A candidate for a local school board paid for an ad that was to be run on the day before the election. She submitted the copy late, and the newspaper bent its normal deadlines to accept it. When the publisher's representative reviewed the copy, he rejected it on the ground that it made serious charges against persons who would have no opportunity to respond before voting began. The candidate persuaded a county judge to hold court on Sunday evening to hear her argument that the publisher not only had refused to honor a contract, but had violated her First Amendment rights. Deciding that a contract had been reached when the candidate's money was accepted and the copy delivered to the newspaper, the judge ordered the ad run the following day. The newspaper did so. The court of appeals eventually held that if a newspaper imposes conditions on the acceptance of advertising copy, advertisers must be told about them in advance.

The right to refuse advertising also is subject to antitrust law. The landmark case in this area is *Lorain Journal Co.* v. *United States*.[95] It grew out of an attempt by the publisher of the *Lorain Journal* to freeze out a newly established radio station in an adjoining city. The publisher ordered the newspaper's advertising department to monitor the station and cancel the advertising contract of any Lorain merchant who bought time on the station. Because the newspaper's circulation reached 97 percent of the households in the area, and the station could demonstrate nowhere near such coverage, this was a potent threat. The Supreme Court held there was no doubt that the purpose of the policy was to preserve the newspaper's monopoly, and therefore it was a violation of the law.

However, barring a pattern of refusal that points to an intent to harm a competitor, any news medium may refuse commercial advertising for reasons of policy or for no reason. The three major commercial television networks said they were complying with long-established policy when they refused advertising for birth control pills.[96] At the time some women had stopped using the pills because of reports that their use increased the risk of heart disease. An organization of health professionals and a major maker of the pills wanted to make the point that

93. Peter J. Caruso, "Your Right to Refuse Ads," *Editor & Publisher*, 12 May 1984, p. 48.
94. 431 N.E.2d 171 (Ind.App. 1982).
95. 342 U.S. 143, 72 S.Ct. 181, 96 L.Ed. 162 (1951).
96. "Major Networks Won't Air Ads for Birth Control Pills," *Providence Journal*, 3 November 1987.

the pill has been improved to reduce its potential risks and the likelihood of pregnancy. Some individual television stations did accept the commercials.

Who May Refuse Cause Advertising?

What happens if people have a serious grievance against society, or a great idea for saving the world, but can't get a reporter to listen? If the media are to be a true marketplace of ideas, shouldn't they be required to carry all points of view? During the civil rights and anti-Vietnam War disturbances of the 1960s, Jerome Barron, a professor of law at George Washington Law School, pondered those questions and concluded there should be a right of access to the media. He first argued his thesis in the *Harvard Law Review* in 1967[97] and expanded it into a book published six years later.[98] He also acted as counsel in several cases testing his theory. However, courts at every level, including the Supreme Court, have rejected his argument as it applies to privately owned media.

Briefly summarized, Barron's argument is as follows: The news media have become big businesses engaged in pursuit of an audience. This pursuit makes the managers of the media cautious. They don't want to make people angry, lest they lose part of their audience and their advertisers. The results of this caution are bland media that largely ignore the ills of society. As Barron saw it, the violence of the 1960s was in part a reaction to the media's indifference. Frustrated groups of individuals resorted to public demonstrations to call attention to their grievances.

Barron read *New York Times* v. *Sullivan* and found in its grant of First Amendment protection to cause advertising a mandate that such ads should be accepted by publishers. He also found support for his belief in the fairness doctrine, which then required broadcasters to present news and public affairs programming on controversial topics of public interest. Barron argued that if the First Amendment is to have any real meaning in the modern world, it must be changed from a passive defense for matter already published to an active weapon for forcing all shades of opinion into the media. Otherwise, the concept of the marketplace of ideas is a mockery. Barron wrote:

> At the very minimum, the creation of two remedies is essential—(1) a nondiscriminatory right to purchase editorial advertisements in daily newspapers, and (2) a right of reply for public figures and public officers defamed in newspapers. These remedies could be instituted by either legislative or judicial action. They represent the very least of what ought to be done to broaden public participation in the press.[99]

Despite the facts and logic Barron used to support his thesis, courts generally have held that he has failed to overcome two barriers, both grounded in the Constitution.

---

97. "Access to the Press—A New First Amendment Right," 80 Harv. Law Rev. 1641 (1967).
98. *Freedom of the Press for Whom?* (Bloomington, Ind.: Indiana University Press, 1973).
99. Ibid., pp. 6–7.

1. Most media are privately owned. This is true even of broadcasting, the one medium that is regulated by government. Thus, any attempt by government to tell an owner that an article or an ad must be accepted and used could be a taking of property without due process of law, violating the Fifth Amendment.

2. Further, an attempt by the state to tell media owners that they must accept an article or an ad violates the freedom of the press protected by the First Amendment.

Privately Owned Newspapers

Although Barron's arguments appeal to those who embrace an expansive, positive view of the First Amendment, lower-level courts have rejected attempts to force privately owned newspapers and magazines to accept cause advertising, and the Supreme Court has refused to review any of the decisions. The Supreme Court has struck down on First Amendment grounds a state law mandating a right of reply for public officials and others who believed they had been treated unfairly by newspapers.[100] Because the law rejecting a right of access to privately owned media seems well settled, the pertinent decisions will be summarized briefly.

When Chicago's newspapers refused to publish an advertisement urging consumers to boycott stores selling imported clothing, a labor union asked a federal district court to compel the papers to do so. The union advanced two arguments. One compared newspapers to places of public accommodation, which are forbidden by law to refuse service on racial or religious grounds. The union said that the newspapers' refusal to accept its ad was a form of discrimination made illegal by the First Amendment protection given to cause advertising by *New York Times* v. *Sullivan*. The second argument was based on the thesis that newspapers enjoy so many favors from government that they have become a part of government. The union noted that local governments are required to advertise certain of their activities in newspapers. State and local governments at the time commonly gave newspaper reporters office space in police headquarters, city hall, county courthouses, and state capitols. In many cities, newspapers are the only product that legally can be sold on public streets and sidewalks.

A federal district court judge rejected both arguments.[101] With respect to the first, he said the Supreme Court's purpose in *New York Times* was to encourage newspapers to publish cause advertising by offering them a high degree of protection against successful libel actions. It did not intend to stretch the First Amendment "to include the right to use the other fellow's presses." With respect to the second, the court said that government and its officials make news, but

---

100. Miami Herald Publishing Co. v. Tornillo, 418 U.S. 241, 94 S.Ct. 2831, 41 L.Ed.2d 730 (1974), summarized in Chapter 10.
101. Chicago Joint Board, Amalgamated Clothing Workers of America, AFL-CIO v. Chicago Tribune Co., 307 F.Supp. 422 (N.D.Ill. 1969); aff'd, 435 F.2d 470 (7th Cir. 1970); cert. den., 402 U.S. 973 (1971).

they do not publish it. "[T]here is no state press, no American equivalent to *Izvestia* or *Pravda*." His reference was to the government-controlled newspapers in the Soviet Union. In the United States, the judge added, "the press has long and consistently been recognized as an independent check on governmental power." His decision was upheld by the circuit court of appeals, and the Supreme Court rejected a request for a review of the decision.

Government-Owned Media and the Right of Access

The First Amendment stands as a barrier against government interference with media carrying news and opinion, and, to a lesser extent, with the advertising content of such media. As written, the amendment forbids Congress to make laws abridging freedom of speech and press. Since the 1920s, the Supreme Court has interpreted the language of the Fourteenth Amendment as applying the First Amendment to any attempts by state and local governments and their officers to abridge freedom of speech and press. How that came about is discussed in Chapter 2. However, First Amendment rights are not protected absolutely against either federal or state action, as this text illustrates. Further, the First Amendment has no application to decisions by private individuals that may prevent widespread public dissemination of someone's point of view. Nor does that Amendment require that people in a position to decide what is published or broadcast be fair, responsible, or even honest. When editors decide not to use something, the decision is an editorial judgment, protected by the First Amendment. With rare exceptions, government officials cannot second-guess editors and force them to publish what their judgment has led them to reject. Because there are many editors, with many points of view, making decisions as to the content of all kinds of media, most ideas or events of even remote significance reach some part of the public.

However, when media are owned by government, the application of First Amendment law changes. In the eyes of the law, many public high school and state university student newspapers are government-owned media. So is advertising space sold by public transit systems. When decisions on the content of such media are made by a government official, the power of government is brought into play. Thus, courts have held that an official's decision preventing publication of cause-oriented content in some kinds of government-owned media under some circumstances is a form of prior restraint condemned by the First Amendment. The preceding sentence is phrased as carefully as it is because the Supreme Court's decision in *Hazelwood School District* v. *Kuhlmeier*[102] casts doubt on some of the earlier decisions holding that administrators and teachers could not control the content of public school newspapers. The *Hazelwood* decision is discussed in Chapter 2. At this writing, it appears that a right of access to a public school or university newspaper, or any other government-owned medium of communication, depends upon the answers to three questions:

---

102. 484 U.S. 260, 108 S.Ct. 562, 98 L.Ed.2d 592 (1988).

1. If the publication is a public school newspaper, is it published independently, or as part of the staff's course work in journalism?

2. Whatever the medium, is it considered a public forum?

3. What is the status of the individual who makes decisions as to content?

In *Hazelwood*, the Supreme Court said clearly that if a high school newspaper is published as part of the school's course work in journalism, the teachers involved and the school principal have authority to determine its editorial content. Presumably, that authority also would apply to the right to reject cause-oriented advertising. The preceding sentence must be qualified as it is because, in *Hazelwood*, the Court avoided deciding whether the paper was a public forum. If the newspaper is not tied to journalism courses, the rules seem to be different. In recent decisions, courts have held that if state-owned media customarily carry views on controversial public issues they are public forums. If so, a state employee's decision to reject content is subject to challenge on First Amendment grounds. Teachers and school administrators are considered to be state employees. If the medium involved is a public school newspaper published independently of course work in journalism, the student editor has authority to reject both editorial content and advertising. These principles emerge from the cases summarized below.

The U.S. Court of Appeals for the Ninth Circuit ruled that a public high school governing board violated the First Amendment by refusing to accept an ad from an organization opposing registration for the draft.[103] The court held that the board had created a limited public forum by permitting the general public to buy advertising space in the school newspaper. It pointed specifically to armed forces recruiting advertisements as evidence that the board had opened its forum to speech by nonstudents which is "both political and commercial with respect to at least one important and highly controversial topic—military service." Scattered earlier decisions by lower-level courts were to the same effect.[104] When student editors act on their own, without coercion from state employees, courts have upheld their right to make decisions on content. An editor can refuse to publish an article submitted by a would-be contributor.[105] Student editors also have been upheld when they rejected cause advertising. In *Mississippi Gay Alliance* v. *Goudelock*,[106] the Fifth U.S. Circuit Court took note of the fact that the decision to reject an ad offering counseling and legal aid to gay students at Mississippi State University was the student editor's alone. The majority quoted from *Tornillo* to support the conclusion that government ought not interfere with editorial decisions made by someone other than a state official.

---

103. San Diego Committee against Registration and the Draft v. The Governing Board of Grossmont Union High School District, 790 F.2d 1471 (9th Cir. 1986).

104. See, for instance, Lee v. Board of Regents of State Colleges, 306 F.Supp. 1097 (W.D.Wis. 1969); aff'd, 441 F.2d 1257 (7th Cir. 1971), and Zucker v. Panitz, 299 F.Supp. 102 (S.D.N.Y. 1969).

105. Avins v. Rutgers, State University of New Jersey, 385 F.2d 151 (3d Cir. 1967); cert. den., 88 S.Ct. 855 (1968).

106. 536 F.2d 1073 (5th Cir. 1976); cert. den., 97 S.Ct. 1678 (1977).

In several instances, courts have held that transit companies created public forums by accepting political advertising. Therefore, they could not reject advertising offered by controversial political organizations. A federal district court in New York State held that the Niagara Frontier Transit Authority could not deny space to an abortion rights group.[107] New York City's Metropolitan Transportation Authority was told that it could not deny *Penthouse* access to subway walls for an advertising poster.[108] The poster depicted Walter Mondale, then the Democratic presidential candidate, in a seminude pose.

However, if no public forum has been created, public transit systems can reject cause advertising, the Supreme Court held in *Lehman* v. *City of Shaker Heights*.[109] The five-justice majority noted that the Court has been "jealous to preserve access to public places for purposes of free speech" but held that the system's buses were not public forums. Therefore, the city did not violate the First Amendment when it limited car card advertising to commercial messages.

It seems, then, that a right of access to state-owned media is limited and rests on a narrow base. If the medium makes itself a public forum by accepting cause advertising, or even politically tinged advertising such as recruiting messages for the armed forces, the medium cannot refuse other such advertising if the decision is made by an agent of the state. However, in the case of student newspapers, student editors can make decisions as to content, whether it be an article or a cause ad. But if the medium is not a public forum, it cannot be opened up to political advertising as long as the ban on such ads is absolute.

Corporate Cause Advertising

Because political speech lies at the core of First Amendment concerns, it enjoys almost absolute protection. The Supreme Court took note of that fact in 1978 when it held, in *First National Bank of Boston* v. *Bellotti*, that corporations have a right to spend their stockholders' money to advertise a position on a public issue. In doing so, the Court struck down a Massachusetts law that made it a crime for a corporation to spend its funds to influence the outcome of a referendum unless the issue submitted to the voters would materially affect the corporation's business, property, or assets. In 1976, Massachusetts residents were asked to change the state constitution to permit a graduated income tax. As it stood, the constitution required that all persons be taxed at the same rate. Officers of many financial institutions, including First National Bank of Boston, believed the proposal mistaken and sought to use corporate funds to oppose it. But because the tax measure would not have a material effect on the institutions themselves, the law stood in their way. First National took the lead in

First National Bank of Boston v. *Bellotti*, **435 U.S. 765, 98 S.Ct. 1407, 55 L.Ed.2d 707 (1978).**

---

107. Coalition for Abortion Rights and against Sterilization Abuse v. Niagara Frontier Transportation Authority, 584 F.Supp. 985 (W.D.N.Y. 1984).
108. Penthouse International Ltd. v. Koch, 599 F.Supp. 1338 (S.D.N.Y. 1984).
109. 418 U.S. 298, 94 S.Ct. 2714, 41 L.Ed.2d 770 (1974).

asking state courts to declare the law unconstitutional, but they upheld it. The Supreme Court agreed to take the case.

The Massachusetts courts had acted on the theory that the Supreme Court's commercial-speech cases gave the state the right to restrict corporate speech. They had held that there was an overriding public interest in preventing corporations from spending funds to influence the outcome of a referendum. The Supreme Court said that was a misreading of the commercial-speech doctrine. At the heart of the issue, the Court said, was the nature of the speech in question. Its subject, in this instance, was taxation, a central concern of every citizen. Corporations, like other citizens, have a right to speak on public issues, through advertising or by other means. They do not have to prove, any more than a real person would, that the issue in question would have a material effect on them.

Two years later, in *Consolidated Edison Co.* v. *Public Service Commission*,[110] the Supreme Court expanded on that holding. At issue were bill inserts used by Consolidated Edison to argue its case for nuclear power. The Natural Resources Defense Council argued that the company should be compelled to permit it to prepare inserts arguing against nuclear power. When that failed, the council succeeded in persuading the public service commission to ban all bill inserts of a political nature. The commission rationalized that utility customers hold widely divergent views and should not be made a captive audience for a company's opinions. The Court decided the case by direct application of the *First National Bank* precedent. It held that the state could regulate the time, place, and manner of corporate speech, but it could not do so on the basis of the content of that speech. As long as Consolidated Edison did not lie to its customers, it could offer them its views on any subject.

In 1986, the Court carried the protection of corporate speech an additional step, nullifying a California rule requiring public utility companies to distribute bill inserts prepared by consumer groups.[111] In response to complaints about a newsletter mailed by Pacific Gas & Electric Co. with its bills, the state's Public Utilities Commission ordered the company to include four times a year messages prepared by an organization opposing its rate increase requests. Four of the five justices voting to strike down the order held that corporations, like individuals, can't be compelled to associate themselves with views with which they disagree. However, the fifth justice focused narrowly on the company's envelopes, seeing them as private property to which it could deny access by others.

The effect of the three decisions is to place corporate messages advocating a position on public issues at a higher level in the First Amendment hierarchy than messages designed to sell a product or service. The latter lie outside the realm of First Amendment protection if they promote an illegal product or promote a legal product in a deceptive way. Nondeceptive advertising for legal products is protected by the First Amendment, but still is subject to regulation if an overriding state interest requires it. But, in the three cases discussed in this section, the Su-

---

110. 447 U.S. 530, 100 S.Ct. 2326, 65 L.Ed.2d 319 (1980).
111. Pacific Gas and Electric Co. v. Public Utilities Commission of California, 475 U.S. 1, 106 S.Ct. 903, 89 L.Ed.2d 1 (1986).

preme Court held that states cannot restrict a corporation's right to express a point of view on public issues, whether the corporation does so by placing advertisements in the media or by mailings to its customers. In the most recent case, the Court also held that states cannot compel corporations to become unwilling distributors of messages prepared by others.

However, in 1990, the Supreme Court upheld a Michigan law prohibiting corporations from using their general funds to support or oppose political candidates. Ruling in *Austin* v. *Michigan Chamber of Commerce*,[112] the Court said the state's interest in preventing corporations from using "resources amassed in the economic marketplace" to obtain "an unfair advantage in the political marketplace" was sufficient to justify the restriction on First Amendment rights. Corporations are permitted to support or oppose candidates with segregated funds collected for political purposes. Three dissenting justices called the decision "an Orwellian announcement." They said it is "incompatible with the absolutely central truth of the First Amendment: that government cannot be trusted to assure, through censorship, the 'fairness' of political debate."

In the Professional World

It would be misleading in the extreme to leave the impression that advertising claims are held in check only by the forces of law. This is no more true than the belief that the news staffs of the various media would engage in unbridled libel and invasion of privacy were it not for fear of lawsuits. Virtually all advertisers and media that accept advertising police themselves, applying professional standards of honesty and ethics that are products of experience and training. The several professional organizations representing people who prepare advertisements have codes of fair practices. As one example, the Direct Mail Marketing Association not only publishes a fourteen-page booklet, "Guidelines for Ethical Business Practices," but has a full-time director of ethical practices whose job is to investigate complaints.[113] Newspapers, magazines, and broadcasters have adopted standards designed to screen out ads that are deceptive, fraudulent, or considered to be in bad taste. Because of these checks, perhaps no more than 3 percent of the millions of advertisements published or broadcast in any year raise bona-fide legal questions.[114]

To an extent unequaled by any other medium of expression, advertising operates in a fishbowl. The purpose of advertising is to call attention to a message designed to sell a product or service. Thus, advertising is likely to have more of an impact on more people than all but the most important news stories or commentary. If a reporter misstates a fact about an action taken by a city council, few aside from the persons immediately involved

112. ___ U.S. ___, 110 S.Ct. 1391, 108 L.Ed.2d 652 (1990).
113. Direct Mail Marketing Association, Inc., 6 E. 43d St., New York, NY 10017.
114. S. Watson Dunn and Arnold M. Barban, *Advertising, Its Role in Modern Marketing*, 4th ed. (Hinsdale, Ill.: Dryden Press, 1978), p. 84.

will know or care. If an advertiser makes overblown claims for a product, every dissatisfied user will know and care, and may take the further step of buying no more of that product or of any other products made by the same company. It is not surprising, then, that the guidelines adopted by the various advertising organizations focus on honesty and clarity. A typical code advises advertisers to be able to substantiate any claims made for a product, to avoid unfair disparagement of other products, and to give full price information. If gifts are offered as inducements, any conditions attached to the offer should be stated clearly. Because such codes are voluntary, they are not observed by all advertisers all of the time, but, measured strictly in terms of literal accuracy, the rate of compliance is high, as is indicated by the figure above.

Honesty is not solely a matter of ethics. There are good business reasons for it, as Eugene S. Pulliam, publisher of the *Indianapolis Star* and *News,* noted. He quoted with approval a statement made by Leonard S. Matthews, president of the American Association of Advertising Agencies, in the organization's newsletter.[115] Matthews wrote: "We ought to examine every ad from the standpoint of 'Would my mother believe it?' or, 'Would I recommend this product to my friends?'" In Matthews's opinion, advertising "is much more honest than it has ever been." He gave four reasons for this, the first of which was that honesty is good business. He also took note of the role played by "a much brighter consumer of advertising," the higher ethical standards of the media, and advertising's own self-regulation program.

Even a superficial survey of the literature leaves little doubt that advertising professionals are committed, with Don Quixote, to the belief that honesty is the best policy. However, the same survey leaves no doubt that advertising, because of its pervasiveness and the role it therefore is believed to play in shaping society, remains controversial. Many of the questions raised probe at the professional's ethics. These questions lie in a realm where beliefs are strong, facts are evasive, and conclusions subject to heated debate. The major points at issue can only be noted, not resolved, in a text of this kind.

One of the most persistent ethical questions is: At what point does advertising become offensive? For years, television networks refused ads for vaginal deodorants but had no qualms about ads for underarm deodorants, or products designed to quell digestive gases. Media of all kinds commonly use advertisements holding out the promise of intimate romance to the users of the right shaving lotion, shampoo, makeup, or lingerie. It is a truism in the trade that sex sells. But when Revlon planned an advertising campaign to promote its Charlie perfume, the *New York Times Magazine* ruled that one of its ads was so sexy as to be in bad taste.[116] It featured a photograph of a young man and a young woman standing with their backs to the camera. The woman has her right hand on the man's left buttock. Both are not

---

115. Eugene S. Pulliam, "Publisher's Memo: Advertising," *Indianapolis Star,* 29 December 1985.
116. "Ad Too Cheeky," *Indianapolis Star,* 31 July 1987.

only fully clothed, but obviously expensively and conventionally clothed. The caption over the photo says, "She's very Charlie." In rejecting the ad, the *Times*'s advertising executives reasoned that readers would object if the ad showed a man patting a woman on the rear. Revlon said the ad "equalizes the gesture." Eleven women's magazines found it acceptable. The generally conservative *Indianapolis Star* ran the photo three columns wide by 9 inches deep—as news—with its article reporting the *Times*'s rejection.

This is but one example of sex-oriented advertising. An executive with Planned Parenthood in New York City estimated that each year, the three television networks broadcast 20,000 sexually explicit references in their

Editors of the *New York Times Magazine* found this attempt by Revlon to "equalize the gesture" too raunchy to use. Editors of eleven women's magazines did not. Some newspapers used it as a newsphoto to illustrate a story about the *Times*'s rejection. (AP/Wide World Photos)

This is one of two versions of an advertisement some magazine editors found offensive. But it was published in *USA Today* and *New York* magazine. The AIDS epidemic has made television, magazines, and newspapers more receptive to condom advertising and to discussions of sexual practices once considered taboo. (Courtesy of Ansell International)

programs and commercials. But when the agency prepared a thirty-second commercial for its services, which started, "Four out of five young women who don't use birth control get pregnant before they want to," the city's three network-affiliated TV stations rejected it.[117]

The AIDS epidemic of the late 1980s brought about some changes in advertising policies with respect to the use of condoms for prevention of that disease if not for birth control. But even when condoms were presented as a means of preventing AIDS, one advertisement failed to pass muster with

---

117.   Alfred F. Moran, executive director of Planned Parenthood of New York City, in "TV Advertising and Hypocrisy," a letter to the editor of the *Wall Street Journal*, 18 September 1987.

some media. Della Femina, Travisano & Partners created two versions of a condom ad with an AIDS prevention theme. The print version showed the frightened face of a young woman. The copy said, "I enjoy sex, but I'm not ready to die for it. AIDS isn't just a gay disease, it's everybody's disease. And everybody who gets it dies." The ad suggested that smart women protect themselves by buying the advertiser's brand of condoms. In addition to promoting its business, the advertiser believed it was performing a public service. Acceptance executives at *Time, Newsweek,* and *People* magazines turned the ad down as offensive. *USA Today* and *New York* magazine used it. A television commercial based on the same theme was rejected by all three networks. Ad agency Chairman Jerry Della Femina commented, "What the networks are saying is, 'We don't care if people die. We have our policy.'"[118]

Does advertising reinforce stereotypes—about the young, the elderly, women, and others? When the women's movement came to the fore in the 1960s, the National Organization of Women listed ten advertisements it considered most insulting to women. These portrayed women as homebodies whose greatest fear was that their husbands might find their coffee bitter, whose greatest concern was avoiding ring around the collar, and who lived in the kitchen, preparing food and washing dishes. Such ads appear on television with lesser frequency, but might there also be a stereotype in the well-groomed, physically attractive young woman who is always on the go, always involved in making major business decisions? The American Association of Retired Persons has objected to commercials portraying the elderly as frail, somewhat befuddled people who putter around until someone offers them a glass of lemonade, a powerful painkiller for their arthritis, or a bowl of hot oatmeal. Only recently have advertisers begun to discover that people over sixty do more traveling for pleasure than any other segment of the population.

Closely related to the above is the question as to whether advertising influences behavior. Its purpose, of course, is to influence buying decisions. But what else does it do? What, for instance, are the consequences of portraying young men as eager to get off work so they can troop to the nearest bar? If there are any women in those bars, they either are staring adoringly at the young men or are serving them beer by the pitcher. The men are laughing, chattering, clapping each other on the back in great camaraderie. Is there any connection with the fact that alcohol has become a major problem on college campuses or that driving under the influence has become a major cause of motor vehicle accidents?

Interestingly, beer advertising on television showed significant changes as the decade of the 1980s moved to a close. Beer still was associated with partying, but some ads also suggested that smart drinkers "know when to say when." Further, one beer maker experimented with ads that did a switch on the time-honored macho male beer drinker theme. Coors commit-

---

118. Joanne Lipman, "Controversial Product Isn't an Easy Subject for Ad Copywriters," *Wall Street Journal,* 6 December 1986.

ted $500,000 of its $75 million advertising budget in 1987 to magazine ads showing sweaty women softball players opening a cold beer after a game. The campaign was called the first of its kind.[119]

But if beer advertisers were showing some awareness of the need to discourage abuse of their product and to chip away at the stereotypes, automobile advertisers were moving in the opposite direction. Mercedes-Benz ran a series of television commercials in which its car was driven at speeds in excess of 100 miles an hour. Presumably, the commercials were made in Germany, where such speeds are legal, but the message was clear—this car is built for high speed. Other makers showed their high-performance cars breezing through the curves on mountain roads, threading obstacles, or coming to panic stops inches short of the engineers who designed them. The fine-print message advising viewers not to try to duplicate the maneuvers was on and off the screen in seconds. There is no way, of course, of telling which came first, commercials that encourage speeding and reckless driving or the prevalence of such driving. As one advertising executive noted, America's love affair with speed goes back to the time when people rode horses.

The 1988 presidential campaign raised anew questions as to whether advertising distorts the political process. That campaign, to a greater extent than any other, was largely an advertising campaign, with millions of dollars poured into spot commercials on radio and television. Both candidates built their campaigns around simple themes that not only lent themselves to use in commercials but could be converted into a sentence or two likely to appeal to television news directors. Such snippets came to be called "sound bites." "Read my lips," used by George Bush to emphasize his "no new taxes" theme, was one such. It became a fad expression that carried over into the first months of his administration, where it had a constraining effect on policy. Indeed, the nature of the campaign raised serious questions about the application of the principles of product marketing to the political process. Both candidates steered clear of the substance of controversial issues, even those of such magnitude as the nation's annual budget and trade deficits. Thus, when the $100 billion savings and loan crisis surfaced in the first weeks of the new administration, it seemed a surprise, although it had been developing through changes in the law and lax regulation of the industry for a decade. It is tempting to dismiss politicians as egotistical seekers of personal power and attention. Obviously, many of us do, judging from the fact that almost half the people who could have voted in 1988 chose not to do so. But the fact remains that government officials have tremendous power over our lives. Government programs affect everything from the quality of prenatal care to medical care for the elderly. Tens of millions of people depend on government for all or part of their income. Government policies determine how much a dollar is worth, either in terms of purchasing power in the domestic market or our ability to buy imported automobiles, stereo equip-

119. Marj Charlier, "New Print Ads for Coors Beer Target Women," *Wall Street Journal,* 2 June 1987.

ment, videocassettes, or computers. In short, the power of government is prevasive, and how that power is used affects us all. Further, the issues involved in deciding what government shall do and how it will do it usually are highly complex, are rooted in history, and affect various elements of society in quite different ways. The ethical question confronting both politicians and advertisers is whether the public is well served when discussion of those issues is reduced to the simple terms suitable for a thirty-second commercial or a sound bite on the evening news. A few advertising professionals have concluded that the answer is no. Some agencies refuse to prepare any political campaign advertisement that runs fewer than five minutes on the grounds that it is impossible to deal with any issue of substance in a shorter time.[120]

Other ethical questions deal with the propriety of direct comparisons with other products, with the manipulation of the fears and desires that we all share, with the selling of useless or even marginally harmful products, and with the influence of advertising on media content. In connection with the latter, one frequently asked question is whether magazines that rely heavily on cigarette advertising have downplayed the hazards of smoking. In another connection, there still are newspapers that report "grand reopenings" of advertisers who have done no more than remodel a store's front windows. There was a time when advertisers might also keep a story out of the paper by threatening to withdraw their ads. But today, when most communities are served by only one newspaper, and when shopping malls have made it difficult for one retailer to hold a dominant position, advertiser pressure on an editor is likely to be shrugged off.

Thus, while there is no reason to doubt the assertion that advertising "is much more honest than it has ever been," there also is no doubt that the questions do not end there. Advertising professionals, like their editorial counterparts, are aware that beyond the question "Is it legal?" lies the harder question "Is it right?"

FOR REVIEW

1. What is the meaning of "the doctrine of commercial speech?"

2. Explain the significance of the *Pittsburgh Press* case. On what rationale was it decided?

3. What common thread ran through the Supreme Court's early commercial speech decisions? Is the rationale on which those cases were decided the same rationale that underlies the most recent decisions? Why or why not?

4. Outline the four-part test established by Justice Powell in *Central Hudson Gas* to determine when a commercial advertisement is protected by the

---

120. Dunn and Barban, *Advertising,* p. 93.

First Amendment. With reference to one of the cases in the text, explain how each branch of the test is applied.

5. If you were advising a law firm that wanted to start an advertising campaign, what would you tell it? What could you do for the firm? What should you not do?

6. You are in the outdoor advertising business. Your community is considering an ordinance restricting signs and billboards. Can the community adopt such an ordinance? Why or why not?

7. Under what rationale can government regulate the advertising of legal products or services? How far can such regulation be carried? Can you make a case for regulating advertising for a legal product or service that is not now regulated? Conversely, can you make a case for the argument that the First Amendment forbids regulation of nondeceptive advertising for any legal product or service?

8. Should advertising media be held responsible for harm attributed to the content of an advertisement? Why or why not?

9. What makes an ad deceptive? What standards are used by the Federal Trade Commission to determine whether an ad is deceptive? Illustrate.

10. Define each of the following and assess its effectiveness: "broadened cease and desist order," "affirmative disclosure," "affirmative acts," "corrective advertising," "advertising substantiation," "trade rules."

11. How can the Federal Trade Commission's power to order corrective advertising be harmonized with the *Central Hudson* decision?

12. State attorneys general and lawsuits among competing advertisers can cope with deceptive ads more effectively than can the Federal Trade Commission. Agree or disagree? Discuss.

13. Explain the rationale that permits a medium of communication to refuse commercial advertising.

14. If you were adviser to a public high school or state university newspaper, what advice would you give the staff with respect to the public's right to place cause, or editorial, advertising in the publication?

15. You are public relations director of a large corporation whose stock is owned by millions of shareholders. The company's board of directors is convinced that a bill pending in the legislature would hurt the firm's business. You are asked to supplement your usual lobbying efforts with an advertising campaign explaining the effect of the bill to the general public. Can you carry out such a campaign? Why or why not? Given that you are spending money that might otherwise go to the stockholders in dividends, should you endorse such a campaign?

CHAPTER 13

CHAPTER 13

The drafters of the Constitution recognized that persons who work with
words—and with other means of expression—have a right to be paid for their efforts. They included this provision among the powers of Congress listed in Article I, section 8: "To promote the progress of science and useful arts, by securing
for limited times to authors and inventors the exclusive right to their respective
writings and discoveries."

Since 1790, that mandate has been carried into effect, in part, by a series of
Copyright Acts, the last adopted in 1976 and amended in 1980 and 1984 to include
computer programs and semiconductor chips, through which computers function.
Copyright law sets the conditions under which those who have creative talent in
any field of expression can protect their work from unauthorized copying. The
purpose is to protect their right to profit from their talent and thus encourage its
use. The law does so by granting them a monopoly for a fixed period over the
uses that can be made of a protected work.

In a sense, then, copyright law complements the First Amendment. There
might not be a vigorous marketplace of ideas if those with a talent for words,

COPYRIGHT LAW

pictures, or other means of expression could not be sure of payment for their work. By protecting the right to profit from one's creative talents, the law encourages discussion in the public interest.

Looked at from another point of view, copyright law can be seen as placing limits on the free marketplace of ideas. Publishers, broadcasters, and film producers cannot freely use any work they please in preparing their own offerings. If they are going to make substantial use of copyrighted works produced by others, they must be prepared to pay a reasonable fee for such use.

Although copyright is grounded in the Constitution, it is defined by statute. Therefore, we will begin with an overview of the Copyright Act. Generally, the law protects any original work that can be fixed in some tangible means of expression. If the work is an article, a book, a poem, or some other form of written expression, the copyright covers the exact arrangement of words, phrases, sentences, and paragraphs. Courts have held that ideas, theories, historical incidents, and news cannot be copyrighted, but an author's account of them can be. However, copyright protection is not limited to words. Photographs, drawings, graphic devices, paintings, musical compositions, dance routines, and even pantomime can be protected from copying. The televised version of such major sports events as the Superbowl, the World Series, and the Masters Golf tournament is copyrighted by the originating network.

The Copyright Act gives the creators or owners of copyrighted works complete control over their use by others. Thus, a copyright is a form of property and can be sold, assigned, or inherited like any other kind of real property. However, the law also recognizes that in the everyday world, every author cannot research every work back to original sources. Some copying of someone else's work is inevitable, especially in such well-explored fields as history, biography, public affairs, and the various academic disciplines. If copying is minimal, and does not detract unduly from the commercial value of the original work, the law allows it as a "fair use." But if copying is substantial, or if it detracts from the commercial value of the original, it becomes an "infringement." This means that the copier can be required to pay damages to the owner of the original copyright. The law also authorizes prior restraint to keep the offending work off the market.

The First Amendment plays only a peripheral role in copyright law. Alleged infringers have argued in some instances that the work in question served a public interest of such importance that it was protected by the First Amendment. In 1985, in *Harper & Row, Publishers, Inc.* v. *Nation Enterprises*,[1] the Supreme Court of the United States rejected that argument. It held that whatever First Amendment interest there is in the copying of a protected work was taken into consideration by Congress when it defined "fair use."

This chapter also examines copyright questions raised by copying machines, cable television, and video recorders, and two topics that are closely related to copyright: trademarks—those words or symbols that are a part of the identity of many businesses and their products—and misappropriation. The latter involves the systematic copying by one news outlet of news gathered by a competing medium of communications.

The subject matter of this chapter has applications not only to persons working in all media of communications but to public relations practitioners and the entertainment business. Anyone who works a with tangible means of expression runs a risk of copyright infringement. Advertisers and public relations people deal not only with materials subject to copyright but also with trademarks.

Major Cases

- *Allen* v. *Men's World Outlet*, 679 F.Supp. 360 (S.D.N.Y. 1988).

- *Carpenter* v. *United States*, 484 U.S. 19, 108 S.Ct. 316, 98 L.Ed.2d 275 (1987).

- *Community for Creative Non-Violence* v. *Reid*, _ _ _ U.S. _ _ _, 109 S.Ct. 2166, 104 L.Ed.2d 811 (1989).

- *Harper & Row, Publishers* v. *Nation Enterprises*, 471 U.S. 539, 105 S.Ct. 2218, 85 L.Ed.2d 588 (1955).

- *Hoehling* v. *Universal City Studios*, 618 F.2d 972 (2d Cir. 1980).

- *Iowa State University Research Foundation* v. *American Broadcasting Companies*, 621 F.2d 57 (2d Cir. 1980).

- *Jason* v. *Fonda*, 526 F.Supp. 774 (C.D.Calif. 1981); aff'd, 698 F.2d 966 (9th Cir. 1982).

- *Maxtone-Graham* v. *Burtchaell*, 803 F.2d 1253 (2d Cir. 1986).

- *Rosemont Enterprises* v. *Random House*, 366 F.2d 203 (2d Cir. 1966); cert. denied, 385 U.S. 1009, 87 S.Ct. 714, 17 L.Ed.2d 546 (1967).

- *Salinger* v. *Random House*, 811 F.2d 90 (2d Cir. 1987); reh. denied, 818 F.2d 252 (2d Cir. 1987); cert. denied, 108 S.Ct. 213 (1987).

- *Time Inc.* v. *Bernard Geis Associates*, 293 F.Supp. 130 (S.D.N.Y.1968).

---

1. 471 U.S. 539, 105 S.Ct. 2218, 85 L.Ed.2d 588 (1985).

■ *Universal City Studios* v. *Sony Corporation of America,* 465 U.S. 1112, 104 S.Ct. 1619, 80 L.Ed.2d 1480 (1984).

COPYRIGHT

The Copyright Act

So widespread is the knowledge that original compositions in any form may be protected that the Copyright Act is one of the few laws summarized in detail in the *World Almanac,* a popular reference work.

Since 1978, copyright has been governed only by federal law.[2] Under that law, the creator of any original work in any medium has a copyright on it from the moment it is put into tangible form. However, if the work is to be offered to the public, the originator needs to take two steps to protect his or her rights fully.

1. A notice of copyright should be placed on the work. The form of such notice is a *C* with a circle around it, followed by the date of first publication and the owner's name. The word "Copyright" or its abbreviation, "Cop.," may also be used.

2. The work should be registered with the Copyright Office at the Library of Congress. Forms may be obtained for the asking from the office. To fully complete a copyright, a copy of the work, with or without registration, must be sent to the Library of Congress.

Registration need not be immediate. However, without registration, an owner's right to recover damages is limited if an infringement should occur.

A copyright is in effect for the life of the author and 50 years thereafter. If the work is done for hire, the copyright belongs to the employer, not the author, unless the terms of employment provide otherwise. If the copyright is owned by the employer, it is valid for 100 years from the date of creation, or for 75 years from the date of publication, whichever is shorter. During the term of the copyright, the holder has the exclusive right to control the use of the composition by others. In the case of author-held copyrights, control passes to the author's heirs.

Because a copyright is a form of property, it may be bought and sold, or, if it is held by an individual, be made the subject of a bequest in a will. In many instances, the right to obtain a copyright belongs to the creator or originator of the work. But if the creator or originator is an employee, and the work is done under the direction of the employer, the employer has the right to copyright the work. In any event, the rights guaranteed by copyright law can be defined by a contract.

---

2. This section is based on Title 17, Copyrights, United States Code.

*Community for Creative
Non-Violence* v. *Reid,*
_ _ _ **U.S.** _ _ _, **109 S.Ct.
2166, 104 L.Ed.2d 811
(1989).**

In light of a Supreme Court decision in a 1989 case, freelance creators should insist on a contract with individuals or organizations who commission their work. The Court held in *Community for Creative Non-Violence* v. *Reid* that in the absence of a contract the common law of agency governs whether such creators are employees or independent contractors. The distinction is the controlling factor in determining who is entitled to royalties from the work.

The case had unusual origins. In the fall of 1985, the Community for Creative Non-Violence, an organization calling attention to the plight of the homeless, decided to participate in the annual Christmas Pageant of Peace in Washington, D.C. Mitch Snyder, a trustee of the organization, conceived the idea of creating a work of sculpture that would dramatize his organization's cause. The trustees agreed to depict a modern nativity scene in which two adult figures and an infant would appear huddled on a street side steam grate. James Earl Reid, a sculptor with a studio in Baltimore, agreed to create the work for not more than $15,000 to cover his expenses. There was no written contract. Reid, Snyder, and other

"Third Word America" was created by sculptor James Earl Reid at the request of activist Mitch Snyder, in the background at the right, to dramatize the plight of Washington, D.C.'s homeless. When Snyder proposed that the sculpture be taken on tour to raise money for the homeless, Reid objected, leading to a dispute over copyright ownership that had to be resolved by the Supreme Court. (Hugo Wessels/Photopress)

members of the organization agreed on details of the design, which would portray the figures reclining on the grate, as homeless persons do to keep warm. The work was to be called "Third World America." During the two months Reid took to complete the sculpture, Snyder and others went frequently to his studio to check on its progress and to coordinate the building of the base, which was in the form of a steam grate.

The work was delivered on Christmas Eve and remained on display as part of the pageant for a month. At the end of that time, Snyder proposed that the sculpture be taken on a tour of several cities to raise money for the homeless. Reid objected. He said the material he had used would not stand such a trip. The figures were returned to Reid's studio for repair of minor damage that had occurred during their display.

In March 1986, Snyder asked Reid to turn the sculpture over to him and the Community. Reid refused. He filed an application for a copyright in his name and announced plans for a more modest tour than Snyder had suggested. Snyder countered by seeking copyright registration in behalf of his organization. He also filed suit in a federal district court asking for return of "Third World America" and a resolution of the copyright dispute. The district court ruled that Reid had been hired to create the sculpture and therefore had no right to copyright it. On appeal, the U.S. Court of Appeals for the District of Columbia Circuit held that the arrangement between Reid and the Community for Creative Non-Violence did not make the sculptor an employee as defined by section 101 of the Copyright Act. However, it sent the case back to the district court, suggesting that a closer look at the evidence might justify a conclusion that Reid and the Community jointly created the disputed work, thus permitting them to share ownership of the copyright. On further appeal, the Supreme Court unanimously upheld the circuit court's decision.

The Supreme Court took the case to resolve conflicting circuit court opinions as to the meaning of section 101. In its first part the section defines a "work made for hire" as a "work prepared by an employee within the scope of his or her employment." But the second part of the section attempts to define the circumstances under which "a work specially ordered or commissioned" will be considered as a "work for hire." The language is so limited that it leaves many kinds of commissioned works, such as the Community's "Third World America," in limbo. The Court noted that how "work for hire" is defined has "profound significance for freelance creators—including artists, writers, photographers, designers, composers, and computer programmers—and for the publishing, advertising, music, and other industries which commission their works."

After examining several cases in which it had distinguished between employees and independent contractors, the Court concluded that the test most likely to bring about uniformity is that found in the common law of agency. Under that law, the examination begins with "the hiring party's right to control the manner and means by which the product is accomplished." It proceeds to a study of the skill required to produce the work, the source and ownership of the tools and equipment used by the producer, the place at which the work is done, the duration of the relationship between the parties, whether the hiring party has a right to assign other duties to the producer, how much control the producer has over hours of work, the method of payment, the producer's control over the hiring and paying of assistants, whether the work is part of the regular business of the hiring party, and, indeed, whether the hiring party is in any business, the extent of employee benefits, if any, and the tax treatment of the hired party.

When those criteria were applied to the arrangement between Reid and the Community for Creative Non-Violence, clearly the sculptor was an independent contractor, not an employee. Snyder and other trustees of the organization had conceived the idea and had provided occasional supervision, as well as the funding to cover Reid's expenses. But that ended it. As a sculptor, Reid was in a highly skilled vocation. He used his own tools and worked in his own studio. He was retained for about two months, a relatively short period. The Community had no right to expect him to do additional projects for it. He alone decided when and how long he would work as long as he met the deadline. His payment was for a specific job. He alone decided to hire two assistants and how much he would pay them. The Community was not in business and certainly was not regularly engaged in creating works of sculpture. Finally, the organization provided Reid with no benefits and paid no taxes on his behalf. Therefore, the organization had no right to copyright "Third World America."

Two early cases defined the rights of photographers. A photographer who was hired to take pictures of a newsworthy boxer found that the promoter who hired him not only had the right to copyright his work but owned the negatives.[3] However, a photographer who arranged to take pictures of members of a high school graduating class in the hope that he could sell enough of them to make a profit held a valid copyright on the class photograph.[4]

More recently, the U.S. Court of Appeals for the Fourth Circuit held that an advertiser who asks a newspaper to prepare an advertisement and then exercises no control over the creation of the ad loses the right to copyright it.[5] The court said that under the current definition of "work done for hire," in such situations the right to copyright belongs to the newspaper unless a written agreement specifies otherwise. In this instance, the newspaper used its ownership of the copyright to prevent the advertiser from placing the ad in a competing newspaper.

Some newspapers are copyrighted. This means that the publisher controls the right to sell to others any staff-produced articles or photographs, unless the terms of employment state otherwise. The terms under which magazines buy articles from freelance authors generally include the right to copyright the articles. However, an author of stature may be able to retain the copyright. An author who contracts with a publisher to write a book may find that under the terms of that contract the publisher owns the copyright. Federal employees who produce reports, or judges who write decisions, cannot copyright their work. What they write is in the public domain and can be used by anyone.[6] But professors at state

---

3.   Lumiere v. Robertson-Cole Distributing Corp., 280 F. 550 (2d Cir. 1922).
4.   Altman v. New Haven Union Co., 254 F. 113 (D.Conn. 1918).
5.   Brunswick Beacon v. Schock-Hopchas Publishing Co., 810 F.2d 410 (4th Cir. 1987).
6.   17 U.S.C. § 105.

universities, who are required to publish if they want to gain tenure or win promotions, are permitted by custom to copyright their writings. They also may enter into contracts with publishers entitling them to earn royalties on works copyrighted by the publisher. Theoretically, the professors are writing for themselves. The university hires them to teach.

Copyright, then, is a function of statute law and valid only if the procedures prescribed by statute are followed. Although all original works are copyrighted when they are put in tangible form, the originator's rights can be protected fully only if at some time the work is registered with the Copyright Office and a copy filed with the Library of Congress.

What Copyright Protects

Section 102 of the Copyright Act describes the kinds of works that can be protected against copying. Because the section is written in legal language, it can be made more understandable by looking at each of its elements separately.

It is basic that the work in question must be original with the creator. If the work borrows from others, say by quoting extensively from the Bible or from Shakespeare, the copyright does not cover the borrowed quotations. Further, the original work must be expressed in some tangible form "now known or later developed." This means that a writer must put words on paper or onto a computer disk; a photographer must take a picture; a choreographer must diagram the positions of the dancers; a composer must take the notes pecked out on a piano and enter them onto a score. Whatever the form, it must make possible the communication of the work to others, because it is at that point that the work becomes vulnerable to copying. For illustrative purposes, §102 lists seven categories of "works of authorship." They are:

1. Literary works

2. Musical works, including any accompanying words

3. Dramatic works, including any accompanying words

4. Pantomimes and choreographic works

5. Pictorial, graphic, and sculptural works

6. Motion pictures and other audiovisual works

7. Sound recordings

These categories apply to the completed form taken by the specific work or composition. The ideas, discoveries, or processes embodied in that completed form are not covered by copyright. However, thanks to the words "now known or later developed" found in §102, the forms of expression protected by copyright are almost infinitely variable. For instance, a federal court held in 1981 that a tiny silicon chip used to translate an operator's commands into computer language is a form of expression protected by copyright.[7] Printed on the chip was a minute replica of the computer program that made the translation possible. That, the court held, made the chip "a tangible medium of expression" within the meaning of the copyright statute.

However, federal courts have issued conflicting decisions as to whether software makers can copyright the way their programs display information on the screen. Some judges have held that screen displays are nothing more than reflections of ideas that could not be expressed in other ways. Therefore, there is nothing uniquely original that can be protected by copyright. But other courts have held that the placement, arrangement, and design of words and other elements on a screen are original means of expression that can be protected by copyright.[8] In 1988, the Copyright Office sought to resolve the differences by issuing an advisory. The office said it had determined that all copyrightable expression owned by the same claimant and embodied in a computer program, including computer screen displays, is a single work and should be registered on a single application form. In addition, the office said, in order to clarify copyright claims in computer screen displays, applicants can if they wish deposit visual reproductions of computer screens along with identifying materials for the computer code.[9]

The Copyright Office stepped into another controversial issue in 1987 by ruling that computer coloring of black-and-white movie films is entitled to copyright protection. The colored versions, the office said, are "derivative works" within the meaning of the law. Such protection gives a studio the right to distribute a colored version of a movie through broadcast and cable television outlets and to sell videotape copies. The studio also can collect damages from firms that copy colored films. Whether classic black-and-white films should be converted to color aroused hot debate between those who said colored films sell better and those who said that coloring destroys the director's original creation.[10]

The news of the day cannot be copyrighted. Neither can the notable events of an individual's life, or the facts of history. No news medium can gain the sole right to exploit a given news event by copyrighting its presentation of it. But a newspaper can copyright its particular account of a news event. Television networks can, and do, copyright their news programs. An author who conducts research into an individual's life can copyright his version of the events that made the individual of interest to the public. The *World Almanac* comprises facts, many of them taken from the public domain, but this does not prevent the Newspaper Enterprise Association from getting a copyright on each year's edition. It is entitled to protect the work it did in compiling those facts, and its particular presentation of them. But its copyright cannot prevent others from using the facts the Almanac contains.

---

7. Tandy Corp. v. Personal Micro Computers, Inc., 524 F. Supp. 171 (N.D.Calif. 1981).
8. Peter Waldman, "Software-Copyright Laws Are in State of Confusion," *The Wall Street Journal,* 21 March 1988.
9. *Federal Register,* vol. 53, no. 112, p. 21817, 10 June 1988.
10. *Federal Register,* vol. 52, no. 121, p. 23691, 24 June 1987. Bob Davis, "Computer-Colored Films Are Entitled to Copyright Protection, Agency Rules," *The Wall Street Journal,* 22 June 1987.

Hoehling v. *Universal City Studios, Inc.,* **618 F.2d 972 (2d Cir. 1980).**

Separating an idea from its expression frequently is difficult. Is a theory of history, for instance, an idea or a form of expression? The U.S. Court of Appeals for the Second Circuit held that it is an idea, not subject to copyright.

The explosion and fire that destroyed the German dirigible *Hindenburg* at Lakehurst, New Jersey, in May 1937, with the loss of thirty-six lives, has been the subject of considerable speculation. The official verdict is that the fire probably was caused by static electricity that ignited the dirigible's highly flammable hydrogen. However, A. A. Hoehling spent years investigating the tragedy and came to a different conclusion. He concluded that a rigger, Eric Spehl, had planted a timed explosive device in one of the gas cells, intending to blow up the balloon after its passengers had disembarked. His purpose was to impress his girlfriend, an anti-Hitler Communist, in Germany. However, a thunderstorm delayed the ship's arrival, and Spehl was among those killed when his bomb went off. Hoehling described his theory in a book that had a limited market in 1962.

Ten years later, Michael Mooney took Hoehling's thesis and developed it into a fictionalized version entitled *The Hindenburg.* Universal City Studios bought the rights to Mooney's book and converted it into a motion picture released in 1975. Hoehling sued Universal for copyright infringement, and lost. In upholding the district court's summary dismissal of the suit, the court of appeals said:

> [T]he protection afforded the copyright holder has never extended to history, be it documented fact or explanatory hypothesis. The rationale for this doctrine is that the cause of knowledge is best served when history is the common property of all, and each generation remains free to draw upon the discoveries and insights of the past. Accordingly, the scope of copyright in historical accounts is narrow indeed, embracing no more than the author's original expression of particular facts and theories already in the public domain. As the case before us illustrates, absent wholesale usurpation of another's expression, claims of copyright infringement where works of history are at issue are rarely successful.

The court held that Hoehling's thesis was not subject to copyright. His conclusion that Spehl had planted a bomb was simply one of many possible interpretations of historical data. The court added:

> To avoid a chilling effect on authors who contemplate tackling an historical issue or event, broad latitude must be granted to subsequent authors who make use of historical subject matter, including theories or plots.

The court said its ruling would not excuse verbatim copying by one author of another's copyrighted work. But in this instance, it held, each author had developed the material in an individual way. In effect, the court sanctioned Mooney's and Universal's stealing of Hoehling's idea but would not have sanctioned the taking of the language Hoehling used to express that idea.

More recently, the U.S. Court of Appeals for the Seventh Circuit used the same reasoning in upholding the dismissal of a lawsuit seeking $10.5 million in damages from the producers of the television series *Simon and Simon*.[11] At issue was an episode in which the father and son detective team investigated the murder of a retired FBI agent who believed John Dillinger, a one-time public enemy number 1, was not killed by police outside the Biograph theater in Chicago in 1934. Jay Robert Nash sued CBS Inc., MCA Inc., Universal City Studios and others alleging that they had violated his copyright on several books in which he maintained that Dillinger learned of the trap police set for him and induced a small-time hoodlum to take his place. The court concluded that the producers had indeed based the episode on Nash's books but ruled that the author's analysis of historical events is not protected by copyright. The court wrote: "The first person to conclude that Dillinger survived does not get dibs on history. If Dillinger survived, that fact is available to all."

Because today's news is tomorrow's history, the principles applied in the cases above also apply to the coverage of news events. A reporter who reads about a newsworthy disclosure in another publication, or sees an account of it on television, is not prevented from developing the same story. Reporters are free to go to sources mentioned in another's story and learn from them what they can. Reporters also can seek out other sources who know something about the event. As long as the resulting story does not quote substantially from the original story, or paraphrase it without offering new information or insights, there is no risk of being penalized for copyright violation.

The importance of research, not only for journalists, but for all creators of copyrightable works, cannot be overemphasized. One who does research, or who possesses unique creative talent in any medium, has the capacity to produce original works. By definition, the purpose of copyright law is to protect original works. However, the law also recognizes that on occasion even the most creative persons cannot present something new without borrowing from an existing work. This recognition originally was established by the courts as the doctrine of fair use. Since 1978, that doctrine has been a part of the statute itself.

The Doctrine of Fair Use

Fair use, as defined in section 107 of the Copyright Act, permits one author, composer, or artist to borrow limited amounts of material from another without seeking permission. It has nothing to do with the fact that honesty requires any taker, no matter how inconsequential his taking, to give credit to his sources.

Section 107 says that one author can quote another "for purposes such as criticism, comment, news reporting, teaching..., scholarship, or research" without infringing copyright. Teachers are permitted to reproduce copyrighted materials for classroom use if it is done spontaneously. This means that a teacher who finds an article in a magazine pertinent to the coursework can copy it without permission and distribute it to the students. However, if the article is of such value that

---

11. "Copyright Law Doesn't Protect Analysis of Historical Events, Court Rules," *Wall Street Journal*, 4 May 1990.

the teacher plans to make it part of the course, the law requires that permission be obtained from the copyright owner.

In determining whether a use is fair or not, section 107 requires courts to consider the following factors:

> (1) the purpose and character of the use, including whether such use is of a commercial nature or is for nonprofit educational purposes
> (2) the nature of the copyrighted work
> (3) the amount and substantiality of the portion used in relation to the copyrighted work as a whole
> (4) the effect of the use upon the potential market for or value of the copyrighted work.

Congress did not simply pick four principles out of the blue when it wrote Section 107 into the Copyright Act. Its definition of "fair use" was distilled from a number of court cases which, over the years, had recognized that the statute then in effect could not be enforced as it was written. Under its terms, any copying without permission, no matter how minor, was an infringement. Strict interpretation of the law would have stifled both scholarship and the market for popular literature, film, video and radio programming, and music. More than a century ago, courts began stretching the law to accommodate scholarly research and criticism of the arts. Thus, in 1841, in resolving a dispute between two biographers of George Washington, Justice Joseph Story wrote, "No one can doubt that a reviewer may fairly cite largely from the original work, if his design be really and truly to use the passages for fair and reasonable comment."[12]

Rosemont Enterprises v. *Random House,* 366 F.2d 203 (2d Cir. 1966); cert. denied, 385 U.S. 1009, 87 S.Ct. 714, 17 L.Ed.2d 546 (1967).

However, it was not until the middle of this century that courts became willing to extend the doctrine of fair use to protect works aimed at the popular market. The first case that did so is *Rosemont Enterprises* v. *Random House.* In it, the U.S. Court of Appeals for the Second Circuit established precedents on which Congress relied in drafting section 107. The book involved in this landmark case was a biography of Howard Hughes.

At one time, Hughes was a highly visible public figure. Born to wealth, he enlarged his inherited fortune by providing services to the oil industry, by producing movies, and by building aircraft during World War II. Physically attractive, he was the companion of the most beautiful movie stars of the era. But in his later years, he retreated from public view, living in elaborately guarded hideouts, seeing no one except a few trusted associates. He protected his privacy with unmatched zeal and discouraged all attempts to pry into his life. This made him even more a subject of public curiosity.

In 1954, *Look* magazine capitalized on that curiosity by publishing a series of three articles recounting some of the more interesting episodes in Hughes's life.

---

12. Folsom v. Marsh, 9 F.Cas. 342 (C.C.D.Mass. 1841) (No. 4,901).

Nearly a decade later, Random House commissioned a writer to prepare a hard-cover biography of Hughes aimed at the mass market. By that time, Hughes had become a recluse and refused all attempts to interview him. He tried to prevent publication of the Random House biography by buying the copyright to the *Look* articles and by filing a lawsuit for copyright infringement against the publisher. Pointing to the fact that the book, then in galley proofs, included accounts of incidents described in the magazine articles, he asked the court to issue an order forbidding the book from being published. Such prior restraint is one of the remedies provided by law against infringement.

A federal district judge in New York City ordered Random House not to release the book. He concluded that because it was aimed at a mass audience it was not scholarly and therefore was not entitled to protection under the fair use doctrine. The book contained only two direct quotations and one 8-line paraphrase that could be traced to language in the magazine articles. But the judge ruled that, given the popular nature of the book, even minimal copying was an infringement.

The court of appeals reversed, holding that the duplication of incidents did not prove infringement. Hughes was what he was and he did what he did. Biographers who portrayed him accurately obviously would describe many of the same incidents. As for the direct copying, the court held it was minimal and in any event justified because the book dealt with a matter of public interest. Breaking new legal ground, the court said that when a book serves the public interest it is protected by fair use, even though it is aimed at a mass audience. Hughes's life, the court said, reminds us that "initiative, ingenuity, determination and tireless work" are the keys to achievement "even in an affluent society."

During the decade between the second circuit's decision in *Rosemont* and the revision of the Copyright Act in 1976, courts expanded the idea that the public interest protects some copying of another's work. One of the more notable cases involved admitted direct copying, albeit in another medium, of frames taken from a movie film of the assassination of President John F. Kennedy.

Time Inc. v. *Bernard Geis Associates,* **293 F.Supp. 130 (S.D.N.Y. 1968).** When Kennedy was shot to death on the streets of Dallas in 1963, Abraham Zapruder, a dress manufacturer, just happened to record the event with his 8-millimeter movie camera. His film, in color, showed the president as the bullets struck him. *Life* magazine paid Zapruder $150,000 for exclusive rights to the film. Blown-up excerpts from it were used extensively by the magazine. Because there were no other photographs of the shooting itself, *Life* made copies of the Zapruder film for the commission named by President Lyndon B. Johnson to investigate the assassination. A number of still frames appeared in the final report with the notation that *Life* held exclusive rights to their use.

While the commission held that the evidence pointed conclusively to Lee Harvey Oswald as the lone assassin, others adopted the theory that the two bullets that struck the president had been fired from different locations. Among these theorists was Josiah Thompson, a professor of philosophy, who developed his belief into a book, *Six Seconds in Dallas,* published by Bernard Geis Associates, and distributed by Random House. Thompson tried and failed to get permission from *Life* to copy frames from the Zapruder film. However, his finished book was illustrated with charcoal drawings that were identified as "exact copies" of frames from the film.

When Time Inc., owner of *Life,* sued for copyright infringement, a U.S. District Court in New York City made two important findings:

1. The film, even though it recorded a news event, could be copyrighted because Zapruder had taken enough care in selecting his vantage point that he had created an original composition.

2. The assassination, and Thompson's two-gunmen theory, were of great enough public interest to justify such copying as Thompson had done.

In any event, the court reasoned, his book was not likely to diminish the value of the film. If anything, the book might stir up enough interest to lead some people to seek a copy of the film itself.

In 1986, the Second Circuit Court of Appeals further expanded the doctrine of fair use to condone extensive copying of interviews with women who had undergone abortions. It did so over the protests of the interviewer who had refused to give the author of the second work permission to copy from her book that reported the women's experiences. In its decision, the court held that interviews, like ideas, historical events, biographical data, and facts, are subject to less protection from copyright law than are other kinds of original compositions.

Maxtone-Graham v. *Burtchaell,* **803 F.2d 1253 (2d Cir. 1986)** — In 1973, right after the Supreme Court had made abortions legal,[13] Katrina Maxtone-Graham interviewed seventeen women who had abortions, or who had considered having one, and published her findings under the title, *Pregnant by Mistake.* The book sold about 2200 copies before it went out of print. When it did so, Maxtone-Graham acquired the copyright from the original publisher.

In 1976, James Tunstead Burtchaell, a Catholic priest and professor of theology at the University of Notre Dame, wrote an essay, *Rachel Weeping,* in which he quoted extensively from Maxtone-Graham's interviews and commented on them. The purposes of the books were diametrically opposed. Maxtone-Graham supported the right to obtain an abortion. Burtchaell's purpose was to show that women who choose abortion suffer long-term psychological effects. When Burtchaell decided to include the essay in a book by the same name, he sought permission from Maxtone-Graham to quote from the interviews. When she refused, the priest decided on advice of counsel to publish anyway. Maxtone-Graham filed a copyright infringement action in a U.S. District Court in New York City. That court granted summary judgment in favor of Burtchaell. On appeal, Judge Irving R. Kaufman, writing for a unanimous panel, conceded that

---

13. The Supreme Court held in Roe v. Wade, 410 U.S. 113, 93 S.Ct. 705, 35 L.Ed.2d 147 (1973), that laws forbidding abortions violate a woman's constitutional right of privacy.

"summary judgment on the question of fair use has been the exception rather than the rule" but held that it was justified in this instance. The decision is of interest not only because it expanded the scope of fair use but because it illustrates how courts apply the four principles in section 107 of the Copyright Act.

The court looked first at the nature of Burtchaell's book. It was commercial in the sense that it was written for a general audience. The book was published in a hardcover edition in 1982 by Andrews & McNeel and in a softcover edition in 1984 by Harper & Row. By the time the case reached the court of appeals, about 6000 copies had been sold. However, the court found that the educational elements of *Rachel Weeping* far outweighed the commercial aspects of the book. Burtchaell's purpose in writing was criticism and comment. Maxtone-Graham had reported the interviews almost verbatim. Burtchaell had analyzed the women's accounts of their experiences with pregnancy and abortion and had organized the material "into a topical framework to make the case against abortion." In doing so, he "applied substantial intellectual labor to the verbatim quotations, continually offering his own insights and opinions." The court concluded that Burtchaell's scholarship, even though it was flawed by taking some of the quotations out of context, outweighed the commercial purpose of his work. Thus, the first factor used in determining whether a use is fair was decided in his favor.

The court then turned its attention to the nature of Maxtone-Graham's work, *Pregnant by Mistake,* finding it essentially reportorial. This did not mean, the court said, that it did not contain "elements of creative journalistic effort." It did, but as a whole, "the book was essentially factual in nature." Referring to *Rosemont,* the court said, "Like the biography, the interview is an invaluable source of material for social scientists, and later use of verbatim quotations within reason is both foreseeable and desirable." This meant that the second factor, too, favored Burtchaell.

The third factor, the amount and substantiality of the copying, presented a more difficult problem for the court. Burtchaell had copied, and copied extensively, from Maxtone-Graham's book. He had directly quoted 7000 words, or 4.3 percent of *Pregnant by Mistake.* There were only 37,000 words in the title essay of *Rachel Weeping.* Thus nearly a fifth of the essay was made up of material taken from Maxtone-Graham's interviews. As copyright infringement cases go, this amounted to a substantial taking.

But, as the court noted, in weighing the third factor, there are no absolute rules. In some instances, courts have condoned wholesale copying. In others, they have found infringement in the taking of only "a tiny portion" of the original work. The inquiry must focus on the nature of what was taken. In this instance, Burtchaell took factual quotations. He said he had considered conducting his own interviews but had concluded he could not because women who seek abortions probably would not speak freely to a priest. Thus, the credibility of such interviews as he might be able to conduct would be open to question. Therefore, he had decided to rely on verbatim quotations from Maxtone-Graham's book to make his discussion of the problems arising from abortions more credible. In light of those facts, the court concluded that the priest's taking was reasonable.

The fourth factor, the effect of the alleged infringement on the market for the original work, is "the single most important element of fair use."[14] In this instance, *Pregnant by Mistake* was out of print. Maxtone-Graham said she intended to publish some copies on her own, but she had not done so. In any event, the two books served such different purposes that the market for one was unlikely to have an adverse effect on the market for the other. The court concluded it possible that readers of Burtchaell's book might even be led to try to buy *Pregnant by Mistake*.

With its conclusion that all four factors involved in fair-use analysis condoned Burtchaell's copying, the court ruled that the district court acted properly in summarily dismissing Maxtone-Graham's infringement lawsuit.

The cases in this section make abundantly clear that copyright law, as written by Congress and interpreted by the courts, condones some copying. Every writer about George Washington is not required to research government archives and major libraries for original documents bearing on his life. If the taking from secondary sources is not substantial, if it does not make up a substantial amount of the new work, and, above all, if it does not harm the commercial value of the copied work, it is a fair use.

Copyright Infringement

The Question of Access

Courts considering copyright cases have recognized that it is possible for composers, authors, and artists working independently to come up with works presenting the same themes in roughly the same way. Thus, the threshold showing in an infringement action is *access*. The copyright owner who alleges harmful copying must show by the preponderance of the evidence that the alleged infringer saw his or her work. If that can't be done, the copyright owner must show that there is such an overwhelming similarity between the two works as to rise above the level of coincidence. Sonya Jason was not able to prove either point and therefore lost an infringement action against Jane Fonda and others in 1981.

Jason v. Fonda, 526 F.Supp. 774 (C.D.Calif. 1981); aff., 698 F.2d 966 (9th Cir. 1982). In 1972, Jason had written and published at her own expense the book *Concomitant Soldier—Woman and War*. About half the press run of 1,100 copies was sold in New Jersey, where Jason lived. In 1977, some of the remainder were sold in Southern California. The general theme of the book dealt with the return of an injured soldier from war and the effect of his injury on the women in his life.

Jane Fonda toured military bases and hospitals during the Vietnam War and became active in the movement against the war. Those experiences gave her and

---

14.   Quoting from Harper & Row, 105 S.Ct. 2234.

Bruce Gilbert an idea for a movie, which they outlined to a writer, Nancy Dowd, in 1972. Dowd submitted a script to Fonda and Gilbert the next year. They submitted it to other writers for revision. The result was a movie, *Coming Home,* which was produced in 1977. Its theme, too, dealt with the return of an injured soldier and his effect on the women in his life. United Artists released the film in 1978, and it was used on the NBC television network the next year. Jason sued in the U.S. District Court in Los Angeles, alleging copyright infringement.

That court dismissed the action, holding that Jason could not prove that anyone connected with the film had seen her book. Further, the time sequence made it clear that most of the photography had been completed before Jason's book went on sale on the West Coast. Nor was there any substantial similarity between the book and the movie. While it was true that both dealt with the "effects of war on women, injured veterans and soldiers," these topics have been "the subject of countless works dating back for centuries." The book and the movie shared only themes, unprotectable ideas, and "commonly cited historical facts," none of which are subject to copyright. Aside from this, the movie was "substantially dissimilar to plaintiff's book," the court held.

Thus, if the author suing for infringement cannot prove that the other had access to her work, she must show that there is a substantial similarity between the two works. Such similarity must go beyond general themes or ideas into detailed plot development, situations, language, and characterization.

Fair Use or Infringement?

If the plaintiff in a copyright action can offer reasonable proof that the alleged infringer had access to the plaintiff's work, the court proceeds to an analysis of the competing works in light of the four factors found in Section 107. If the defendant's taking does not qualify as a fair use, the taking is an infringement, and the court can either prevent further sales of the infringing work or order its producer to pay damages to the plaintiff. Each case is considered in light of its own facts.

Because copyright law is defined by statute, courts usually decide infringement cases by strict application of the terms of the law. This is in accord with the principles of jurisprudence which hold that statutes are to be interpreted narrowly.

However, in the 1970s, some legal scholars and a few judges looked at the *Rosemont* and *Geis* decisions and found in them an intriguing element. In both instances, the courts had held that the public interest justified a fair use under circumstances that might otherwise have been considered an infringement. In *Rosemont,* the public interest was found in the lessons people might learn by reading the biography of an unusual person who had built a fortune through hard work and enterprise. In *Geis,* the public had an interest in the theory that President Kennedy had been shot by two assassins rather than the lone gunman identified by authorities. In the minds of some, these decisions raised a question: Weren't the courts saying that First Amendment values protect more copying than the bare words of the law seem to justify? In one instance, a federal district court judge in Miami held that the First Amendment justified the *Miami Herald*'s copying in an advertisement of the cover of *TV Guide*.[15] Other alleged infringers also invoked the First Amendment as a defense for their copying.

Harper & Row, Publishers, Inc. v. *Nation Enterprises,* **471 U.S. 539, 105 S.Ct. 2218, 85 L.Ed.2d 588 (1985)**

One of them was *The Nation* magazine, which scored a journalistic coup in April 1979 by publishing excerpts from former President Gerald Ford's not-yet-released memoirs, *A Time to Heal*. The excerpts, including 300 to 400 words of direct quotation from Ford's book, gave new insights into former President Nixon's involvement in the Watergate burglary and into Ford's subsequent pardon of Nixon. The article also contained Ford's candid appraisal of some of the leading political figures of the day. Victor Navasky, the editor of *The Nation* and author of the article, was correct in his belief that he had a newsworthy scoop. The article became the subject of widespread news stories and commentary.

The publication also had other effects. Harper & Row and the Reader's Digest association, coowners of the copyright on the book, had obtained Ford's permission to sell excerpts from the book to magazines and newspapers in advance of its publication. One of the purchasers was *Time* magazine, which agreed to pay $25,000 for the right to publish a 7500-word excerpt dealing with the Nixon pardon. It had paid $12,500 in advance and had scheduled its article to appear in mid-April 1979. When *The Nation* article appeared, *Time* canceled the deal. Harper & Row reacted by suing *The Nation* for copyright infringement. After a six-day trial, the U.S. District Court for the Southern District of New York found that there was indeed an infringement and awarded Harper & Row $12,500 in actual damages.

The Nation appealed, arguing that the district court had not paid enough attention to the First Amendment value of its newsworthy scoop. The U.S. Court of Appeals for the Second Circuit, the same court that had decided *Rosemont,* agreed that the disclosures were "politically significant." It held that it is not "the purpose of the Copyright Act to impede the harvest of knowledge so necessary to a democratic state" or "chill the activities of the press by forbidding a circumscribed use of copyrighted words."[16] The court reversed the district court's decision, holding that when First Amendment interests were considered, *The Nation*'s article was a fair use, not an infringement.

The Supreme Court agreed to take the case and reversed the court of appeals, six to three. In doing so, it placed heavy emphasis on the fact that no part of Ford's book had been released officially for publication at the time the article appeared. The Court said the right to control release of one's work, and to prevent others from using it prior to release, is a key factor in fair-use analysis. The Court noted that the timing of release not only is important to the value of a work, it also assures authors of the time "to develop their ideas free from fear of expropriation." The latter consideration alone, the Court said, "outweighs any short

---

15. Triangle Publications, Inc. v. Knight-Ridder Newspapers, 445 F. Supp. 875 (S.D.Fla. 1978); aff'd on other grounds, 626 F.2d 1171 (5th Cir. 1980).

16. 723 F.2d 195, at 197, 209 (2d Cir. 1982).

term 'news value' to be gained from premature publication of the author's expression.''

However, the Court also dealt with the First Amendment question raised in the lower courts. The Court noted that *The Nation* had sought to justify its copying of Ford's language "as essential to reporting the news story" embodied in his book. The magazine's lawyers argued in their brief that "the precise manner in which [Ford] expressed himself was as newsworthy as what he had to say." They argued further that the public's interest in getting that news as quickly as possible overrode the author's right to control the first publication of his autobiography.

Justice Sandra Day O'Connor, writing for a majority of the Court, rejected that argument. Adoption of *The Nation*'s theory of the law, she wrote, "would expand fair use to effectively destroy any expectation of copyright protection in the work of a public figure." Copyright would mean little, especially to public figures, if its protections "could be avoided merely by dubbing the infringement a fair use 'news report' of the book." The infraction is particularly grave, Justice O'Connor added, when, as in this instance, it preempts the author's right of first publication.

Turning directly to the First Amendment question, the justice noted that "the Framers intended copyright itself to be the engine of free expression." By protecting authors' right to profit from their work, "copyright supplies the economic incentive to create and disseminate ideas." At the same time, the law recognizes that First Amendment interests also are served by permitting some copying under limited circumstances. Justice O'Connor summed up the Court's position:

> In view of the First Amendment protections already embodied in the Copyright Act's distinction between copyrightable expression and uncopyrightable facts and ideas, and the latitude for scholarship and comment traditionally afforded by fair use, we see no warrant for expanding the doctrine of fair use to create what amounts to a public figure exception to copyright. Whether verbatim copying from a public figure's manuscript in a given case is or is not fair use must be judged according to the traditional equities of fair use.

With that said, the majority proceeded to apply the four-step analysis used to discriminate between a fair use and an infringement. It found that there was news in *The Nation*'s scoop, but that the magazine had exploited "the headline value of its infringement." Thus, the magazine's use of material from Ford's book was commercial. This weighed against its claim for fair use.

The Court viewed Ford's book as "unpublished historical narrative or autobiography." Copyright law recognizes a greater need to disseminate such works than works of fiction or fantasy. But the Court also found that the fact that the book was unpublished was "a critical element of its 'nature.'" The scope of fair use is narrower with respect to such works. Justice O'Connor clearly saw this as the crucial question. She wrote:

> In the case of Mr. Ford's manuscript, the copyrightholders' interest in confidentiality is irrefutable; the copyrightholders had entered into a contractual undertaking to "keep the manuscript confidential" and required that all those to whom the

manuscript was shown also "sign an agreement to keep the manuscript confidential."...A use that so clearly infringes the copyrightholders' interests in confidentiality and creative control is difficult to characterize as "fair."

The Court went on to find that while only 13 percent of Navasky's article quoted directly from Ford's manuscript, he had extracted precisely those portions for which readers were most likely to buy the book. Further, his taking had led to direct economic loss through *Time's* cancellation of its contract to publish an article based on the book. Therefore, *The Nation's* use was an infringement for which it could be required to pay damages.

Justice William J. Brennan, Jr., writing for the Court's minority, protested that the decision resulted in "an exceedingly narrow definition of the scope of fair use." He predicted that it would "stifle the broad dissemination of ideas and information" and limit "the robust public debate essential to an enlightened citizenry." In the minority's view, Ford's book contained important historical information that neither he nor his publisher should be permitted to monopolize.

However, the decision stands as the Court's major pronouncement on the First Amendment aspects of the doctrine of fair use. In the majority's view, the Copyright Act furthers First Amendment interests by protecting the right of creators to profit from their work, and thus it encourages free expression. The law also recognizes, through the doctrine of fair use, that there are times when the public interest in ideas requires that creators share their work with others. In writing the doctrine, Congress and the courts have taken First Amendment interests into account. In *Harper & Row,* the court said that those who would copy from the newsworthy works of important public figures have no First Amendment right to do so beyond that already included in the definition of fair use. This is particularly true if the work has not yet been released to the public by the author or the owner of the copyright.

The Market Value Test

The role of the market value test in copyright infringement cases is illustrated by two instances. In one, the taking was minimal, but the court nevertheless found an infringement. In the other, the copying was from letters found in university libraries. The author of the letters said he had no intention of publishing them, but the court concluded that if he should change his mind, his work might be worth thousands of dollars.

Iowa State University Research Foundation v. American Broadcasting Companies, Inc., 621 F.2d 57 (2d Cir. 1980).

The crucial factor in the first case, *Iowa State University Research Foundation* v. *American Broadcasting Companies, Inc.,* was the potential market value of a student-made film. Two students at Iowa State University made the film under supervision of a member of the faculty. Their subject was a fellow student, Dan Gable, an outstanding wrestler, who was destined to win a gold medal at the 1972 Olympics in Munich. The film was financed by the university's Research Foundation and Gable's parents. The foundation obtained a copyright on the film, reserving to one of the student producers the right to license its first television showing, but only with the knowledge and consent of the foundation.

The summer after the film was made, the student was employed by ABC Sports as a temporary videotape operator during the Olympic Games. When he heard producers Don Ohlmeyer and Doug Wilson talking about doing a biographical tape on Gable, he offered to show them the Iowa State film. They copied part of it. Three brief excerpts were used in the network's version of the Dan Gable story, which was aired three times.

When the Research Foundation asked the network to pay for its use of the excerpts, ABC denied taking any part of the film. But when a copyright infringement suit was filed, it admitted some copying, falling back on the defense of fair use. A federal district court held that there had been an infringement. When ABC appealed, the U.S. Court of Appeals for the Second Circuit affirmed. It focused on two elements in the four-part test: the commercial nature of ABC's taking—the network sold advertising spots at a premium during its coverage of the Olympics—and the potential harm to the market value of the student-made film. The court used strong language in condemning ABC's taking:

> The fair use doctrine is not a license for corporate theft, empowering a court to ignore a copyright whenever it determines the underlying work contains material of possible public importance. Indeed, we do not suppose that appellants would embrace their own defense theory if another litigant sought to apply it to the ABC evening news.
>
> Moreover, we must recognize that ABC's use of *Champion* was not motivated solely by its beneficence. While the fact that ABC sought to profit financially from the telecasts of the Olympics "does not, standing alone, deprive... [ABC] of the fair use defense,... it is relevant" that the film was used, at least in part, for "commercial exploitation." Thus, on balance, we cannot conclude that the purpose of ABC's use indicates the propriety of a finding of fair use.

ABC argued that the student film was designed for educational use and therefore had no significant television market. That was disproved, the court said, by the fact that Ohlmeyer and Wilson had found some of it good enough to use in their own filmed portrait of Gable. Furthermore, that and other filmed portraits ABC had used throughout its Olympic coverage were much like *Champion* in form and purpose. The court concluded that ABC had made its film on Gable to serve the same purpose as the Iowa State film. The taking of even a small portion of a copyrighted work under such circumstances was not a fair use.

Nor was it true that the Iowa State film was without value. Even before Gable had won his gold medal, the film had been widely circulated for a fee to civic groups and to schools. The court considered it quite possible that ABC's use of excerpts from it might have foreclosed wider use of it, perhaps even on television.

The court's award of damages was an arbitrary amount based solely on the trial judge's assessment of the case. He assessed ABC $250 for copying the film, a sum that had been mentioned by Ohlmeyer at the time as a possible fee. Additional assessments of $5000 were made for each of the three showings of the film. The judge held that Iowa State's attorneys were reasonably entitled to $17,500, which ABC was required to pay. Thus ABC was required to pay $32,750 to the foundation.

Salinger v. *Random House, Inc.,* **811 F.2d 90 (2d Cir. 1987); reh. denied, 818 F.2d 252 (2d Cir. 1987); cert. denied, 108 S.Ct. 213 (1987).**

A more recent case, involving a biography of J. D. Salinger, author of *Catcher in the Rye,* sheds light on several aspects of fair-use analysis. The biography, like the one at issue in *Rosemont,* was of a public figure who had chosen, for more than twenty years, to reject public attention. Salinger continued that rejection by refusing to cooperate in any way with the biographer.

However, over the years Salinger had written many letters to various private individuals who had given them to research libraries for safekeeping. The biographer used material from these letters, most of it in paraphrase. Salinger, who by law had the sole right to copyright those letters, said he had no intention of publishing them. Nevertheless, a federal appellate court held that if he should change his mind, the letters might have considerable value. Thus, the case is of interest because it illustrates that *Harper & Row* seems to have imposed limits on how far a biographer can go in copying the writings of a public figure.

In 1983, Ian Hamilton, literary critic of *The London Sunday Times,* began work on a biography of Salinger to be published by Random House. Hamilton informed Salinger of the project and asked for his cooperation. When that was refused, the biographer discovered that between 1939 and 1961, Salinger had written letters to several persons, including a famous U.S. circuit court judge, Learned Hand, and a noted fellow author, Ernest Hemingway. Some of the recipients, recognizing the probable historical value of the letters, had given them to libraries at Harvard, Princeton, and the University of Texas. Hamilton was able to read the letters at the libraries, but he also had to sign agreements that he would not publish the letters without permission from the library or "the owner of the literary property rights." Under the 1978 version of the Copyright Act, that owner is Salinger. Section 106(3) brought unpublished works under the Act's protection and gives their producers the right to publish them first.

Nevertheless, Hamilton drew extensively in direct quotation and paraphrase from the letters in preparation of a version of the biography that reached the galley proof stage in May 1986. One set of the proofs was sent to Salinger for his comment. He reacted by registering seventy-nine of his unpublished letters for copyright protection and by telling his lawyer to object to publication of the book until all the material taken from the letters had been removed.

Hamilton and Random House responded by revising the manuscript to remove all but about 200 words of direct quotation. Passages that had been taken directly from the letters, using Salinger's words, were changed to close paraphrases. Proofs of the new version were sent to Salinger in October 1986. He identified fifty-nine instances of what he believed to be direct takings from his letters. He filed suit to prevent publication of the book. Judge Pierre Leval of a U.S. District

Court in New York City granted a temporary restraining order, then ruled after trial that because the copying was minimal, Hamilton's biography made a fair use of Salinger's letters. On appeal, the circuit court reversed.

Judge Jon O. Newman quoted extensively from *Harper & Row* in holding that because the letters were unpublished the presumptions must run against the claim that Hamilton's taking was a fair use. Applying the fair-use factors found in section 107, he concluded that only one of the four factors—the nature of the biography—ran in Hamilton's favor. It was, the judge said, a scholarly work, a product of research. The material taken from the letters discovered by that research would add materially to the public's insights into Salinger's literary career. Further, the judge said Hamilton had every right to take facts and ideas from the author's letters because such content could not be copyrighted. But Hamilton had no right to take Salinger's method of expression, his "vividness of description." And, judging from excerpts in the footnotes to this case, some of Salinger's description—of Charlie Chaplin and Wendell Willkie, for instance— was quite vivid indeed.

Newman said the second factor in fair-use analysis—the nature of the copyrighted work—weighed heavily in Salinger's favor. The letters were unpublished. Even though they had been placed in libraries, Salinger had not lost control over them. Their content remained his. Only the physical form of the letters belonged to the recipients. Referring to *Harper & Row,* the court said that until Salinger chose to publish the letters, he retained absolute control over their content.

On the third factor—the amount and substantiality of the taking—the circuit court disagreed with Judge Leval's conclusion that the taking was minimal. Although relatively few of Salinger's words had been used in precisely the order in which he had written them, the paraphrases so closely followed the original passages as to constitute "a very substantial appropriation." If they did not take "the heart of the book," as in *Harper & Row,* "they are at least an important ingredient of the book as it now stands. To a large extent, they make the book worth reading. The letters are quoted or paraphrased on approximately forty percent of the book's 192 pages." Thus, this factor, too, weighed heavily in Salinger's favor.

In *Harper & Row,* the Supreme Court called the fourth factor—the effect on the market—"the single most important element of fair use." Salinger said he had no intention of publishing the letters. But the circuit court said that was not decisive: "Salinger has the right to change his mind. He is entitled to protect his *opportunity* to sell his letters, an opportunity estimated by his literary agent to have a current value in excess of $500,000." Thus, this factor, too, weighed in Salinger's favor.

The court said its ruling that the book infringed Salinger's copyright in his letters ought not prevent publication of a biography of the author. Judge Newman noted that the letters contain "a number of facts that students of his life and writings will no doubt find of interest, and Hamilton is entirely free to fashion a biography that reports those facts." That is what he did. Hamilton's book, *J.D. Salinger: A Writing Life,* was published by Random House in the summer of 1988.

The decision was widely criticized by authors who saw it as an undue restriction on biographers. In 1989, a federal district court judge in New York City said the *Salinger* precedent required him to rule that a biography of L. Ron Hubbard, founder of the Church of Scientology, violated copyrights on his published writings. The Supreme Court refused to review the decision.[17] Historian Arthur Schlesinger, Jr., said the decision "cast judges in the odd role of telling authors how they should write history and biography."[18] However, the U.S. Court of Appeals for the Second Circuit held in 1990 that Hubbard's biographer could quote from his published works without violating copyright. The court distinguished the case from *Salinger* by noting that Hubbard's writings, unlike Salinger's letters, were published.[19]

The Penalties for Infringement

The victim of a copyright infringement is entitled to an award of damages. Section 504 of the Copyright Act also authorizes the use of an injunction to prevent further distribution of the infringing work. Thus, copyright is another area in which prior restraints are permitted, notwithstanding the language of the First Amendment and the Supreme Court's reluctance to approve them generally. Restraint is justified in copyright cases on the theory that infringers ought not be permitted to prosper by passing off another's creative work as their own. Nor should piracy be permitted to rob the creator of the profit from the work. The law permits courts to use two methods to calculate the damages an infringer must pay to the copyright owner:

1. An award making good the copyright owner's losses from the infringement and taking the infringer's profits from it. The copyright owner has the burden of proof in calculating the infringer's gross revenue. The burden is then on the infringer to prove deductible expenses and other factors that might reduce the profit attributable to the infringement. Courts have held in cases involving movies that some part of the profit can be attributed to the box office appeal of the actors and actresses. A magazine publisher could show that a major part of its profits came from subscriptions and advertising contracts that were affected little, if any, by an infringing article. Calculations of profit and loss involve many such intangibles. Thus, it is seldom that a loss can be calculated with the precision of the *Harper & Row* case where the publisher could point to the $12,500 *Time* refused to pay for the canceled article after *The Nation* scored its scoop.

2. A statutory award fixed by the court. The copyright owner may elect this option at any time up to the point of final judgment. Such an award cannot

---

17. Stephen Wermiel, "High Court Declines to Hear Challenge on Line Between Banks, Securities Firms," *Wall Street Journal*, 21 February 1990.
18. Arthur Schlesinger, Jr., "The Judges of History Rule," *Wall Street Journal*, 26 October 1989.
19. "Copyrighted Writings Can Be Used in Critical Biography," *Wall Street Journal*, 25 May 1990.

be less than $250, unless the infringer was unaware of the taking, nor more than $10,000, unless the infringement is deemed willful, when the award can be raised to $50,000. If there are multiple infringements, the court may assess an award for each. This was illustrated in the *Iowa State* case where the court awarded the foundation $250 for ABC's copying of excerpts from the Gable film and $5,000 for each of the three subsequent uses.

Whatever method is used to calculate the damages, the victim of the infringement also is permitted to collect legal fees as part of the award.

Copying Machines, Computers, Jukeboxes, and Cable Television

Committees of Congress spent more than ten years in intermittent hearings before members could reach agreement on the version of the copyright law now in effect. Four areas generated considerable controversy, not all of which has been resolved. They are:

1. Codification of the definition of fair use

2. The widespread use of photocopying machines, especially in schools and libraries

3. Jukeboxes

4. Cable television

Fair use has been dealt with in the preceding sections. This section deals with the other three areas.

Educators and librarians went into the hearings essentially asking for a free hand to use photocopying machines as needed for classroom and research purposes. Publishers, particularly of specialized scholarly journals, saw this as the road to their ruin.[20] Negotiations were shadowed by a decision of the U.S. Court of Claims that seemed to give public research libraries the right to copy journals on a wholesale basis. The four-to-three decision in *Williams & Wilkins Co.* v. *United States* in 1973[21] reversed a district court's finding that the National Institutes of Health and the National Library of Medicine had infringed the copyrights on four medical journals by making thousands of copies of articles from them. The claims court held that the interest in furthering medical research was important enough to override copyright law. How close the question was is indicated

---

20. *Library Journal* followed the hearings on this point closely. See the issues of April through June 1976.
21. 487 F.2d 1345 (Ct.Cl. 1973); let stand by an equally divided Supreme Court, 420 U.S. 376 (1975).

by the fact that the Supreme Court took the case and split four to four, thus upholding the lower court's decision.

Publishers asked for a provision that would require makers of photocopying machines to pay an annual license fee on each machine in use, with proceeds to be split among copyright holders. This proposal foundered on its own complexities. Had it been adopted, someone would have had to keep records showing whose copyrighted material had been copied by each machine. However, Congress did try to impose limits on copying by libraries and educators. These are found in sections 107 and 108 of the Act and are explained in the House Judiciary Committee's *Notes* on the bill.[22] A teacher or student is permitted to make one copy of an article, a chapter from a book, or a sound recording for study purposes or for use in a classroom presentation. A teacher also can make multiple copies on a "spontaneous" basis for distribution to a class. But if such a copy is made a part of the syllabus and distribution becomes a planned part of the course, the use becomes an infringement. Libraries are not supposed to engage in copying that would substitute for buying the publication involved. Nebulous as these rules are, major publishers appear intent on trying to enforce them. In 1982, a group of publishers filed suit to restrain professors at New York University who allegedly were using a copying service to prepare collections of copyrighted works for student use.[23] The case resulted in an agreement by the professors to discontinue copying except on a limited basis without permission from the copyright owners.[24]

However, the U.S. Court of Appeals for the Ninth Circuit ruled that state governments, including universities, can reproduce copyrighted works without permission and without incurring liability for money damages.[25] The case involved unauthorized copying of computer software by members of the faculty at the University of California at Los Angeles. The court held that the suit was barred by the Eleventh Amendment, which prohibits suits against states in federal court. Such suits are permitted where Congress explicitly authorizes them or where states have waived their immunities. The Ninth Circuit held that neither exception applies to actions brought under copyright law. Because copyrights are protected only by federal statute, infringement actions cannot be filed in state courts. Conceding that its decision leaves copyright owners virtually helpless to prevent copying by state institutions, the court said the remedy lies with Congress.

Jukeboxes did not come into existence until after the Copyright Act of 1909 became law. Therefore, there was nothing in the Act which pertained to their repeated use of recordings bearing copyrighted songs. When the law was revised in 1976, Congress sought to resolve the problem by imposing an annual license fee on each jukebox in operation. These fees are paid to a Copyright Royalty Tribu-

22. House Report No. 94-1476.
23. "News Notes," *Media Law Reporter*, 4 January 1983.
24. David Margolick, "Publishers and N.Y.U. Settle Suit on College's Photocopying Rights," *New York Times*, 15 April 1983.
25. BV Engineering v. University of California at Los Angeles, 858 F.2d 1394 (9th Cir. 1988).

nal to be divided among the copyright owners of the recorded music on an equitable basis.

Because cable television also had not been foreseen in 1909, it, too, presented unusual copyright problems when it came into existence in the 1950s. The first cable systems were called "community antenna television systems" because that is precisely what they were. People in towns at a distance from a television station, or in localities shielded by mountains, would erect a common antenna on some high point so that they might bring in programs more clearly. The Supreme Court recognized the nature of such systems in 1968 in its ruling in *Fortnightly Corp.* v. *United Artists Television, Inc.*[26] In its decision, the Court held that cable distribution of signals picked up from distant television stations was not a "performance" as defined by the Copyright Act. Therefore, cable operators could not be required to pay royalties to the owners of the copyrights on the programs they distributed. In 1974, in *Teleprompter Corp.* v. *Columbia Broadcasting System, Inc.*[27] the Court reiterated that reasoning, even though cable systems had become considerably more sophisticated and could offer their users various kinds of programming. When the present law was enacted in 1976, cable systems were using thousands of copyrighted programs and sharing them with millions of users. If the new law had required cable systems to obtain the right to use and pay royalties on each copyrighted program, it would have involved cable operators and their suppliers in endless negotiation.

Therefore, Congress authorized the Copyright Royalty Tribunal to establish a system for distributing licensing fees imposed on cable operators. The initial formula, adopted in 1980, gave the lion's share to movie producers and syndicators of television programs shown previously on the major networks. Major league baseball was among the winners of a minor share of the pool. The three major television networks, whose offerings made up most of the programming available on cable systems, were given nothing.[28] They challenged the decision in court but lost.[29]

In 1984 the Copyright Royalty Tribunal was able to raise the fee cable operators must pay to retransmit movie, sports, and entertainment programs brought in from distant "super stations."[30] The principal targets of the increase were those cable systems using programs from WTBS-TV in Atlanta and WGN-TV in Chicago, which blanket the nation via satellite. The former carries most of the Atlanta Braves baseball games and the Atlanta Hawks professional basketball games. The latter carries the Chicago Cubs and White Sox baseball games, and the Chicago Bulls professional basketball games. When the increase was proposed, owners of other major league baseball teams were asking for the right to black out cable offerings of competing games in each team's home territory.

---

26. 392 U.S. 390, 88 S.Ct. 2084, 20 L.Ed.2d 190 (1968).
27. 415 U.S. 394, 94 S.Ct. 1129, 39 L.Ed.2d 415 (1974).
28. "Non-Network Firms Win Royalty Ruling on Cable-TV Shows," *Wall Street Journal,* 30 July 1980.
29. National Association of Broadcasters v. Copyright Royalty Tribunal, 675 F.2d 367 (D.C.Cir. 1982).
30. 49 F.R. No. 127, p. 26722, 29 June 1984.

That did not end the dispute, however. Cable system operators and the association that represents them challenged the system devised by the Copyright Royalty Tribunal to calculate how much each cable operator should pay. Under a district court decision the system was revised to reduce the cable industry's royalty payments from $100 million in 1985 to $60 million in 1986. On appeal, the U.S. Court of Appeals for the District of Columbia Circuit reversed.[31] It ruled that the law gives the tribunal authority to calculate the fee and that the district court erred in failing to defer to its judgment.

The Video Recorder and Copyright Law

When Congress revised the Copyright Act, its members could not foresee an advance in technology that extended copying into a new dimension. This was Sony Corporation's development of Betamax, a video copying machine that sold for less than a thousand dollars and could be operated by almost anyone. Betamax took the copying of television programs out of the studio and brought it into the home. This raised the fear among producers of movies and television programs that

Universal City Studios, Inc. v. *Sony Corporation of America,* **465** U.S. **1112, 104 S.Ct. 1619, 80 L.Ed.2d 1480 (1984).**

their works would be copied and sold in violation of copyright law. Their fears were heightened by Sony advertisements inviting television viewers to "record favorite shows" and "build a library" of "classic movies," sports events, and other entertainment. Fearing loss of revenue, Universal City Studios and Walt Disney Productions went to court, seeking an order that would bar further sales of Betamax. They argued that every buyer of a video recording device was a potential copyright infringer. Conceding the difficulty of going into the purchasers' homes to find out what was being done with copied programs, the plaintiffs asked the court to find that Sony was contributing to copyright infringement.

The district court rejected their plea, but in 1982, the U.S. Court of Appeals for the Ninth Circuit set Sony and other makers of home video recorders on their ears by holding that the devices did indeed contribute to copyright infringement. It passed the buck back to the district court to devise a suitable remedy. Sony reacted by asking the Supreme Court of the United States to intervene, which it did. In 1984, after hearing two rounds of oral argument in separate terms, the Court decided, five to four, that the copying of programs for one's personal use is a fair use, not an infringement. The majority decision, in *Universal City Studios, Inc.* v. *Sony Corporation of America,* was written by Justice John Paul Stevens. It concluded that most home copying is for convenience. Persons who cannot see a program when it is aired copy it so that they can see it at another time. This is called "time shifting." As long as the copies are not sold or used for other commercial purposes, there is no infringement of copyright law.

---

31. Cablevision Systems Development Co. v. Motion Picture Association of America, 641 F. Supp. 1154; 808 F.2d 133, 836 F.2d 599 (D.C.Cir. 1988); cert. denied, 108 S.Ct. 2901 (1988).

In reaching its decision, the Court rejected outright the argument that Sony was contributing to copyright infringement by selling its video recorders. Justice Stevens called this argument "an unprecedented attempt to impose copyright liability upon the distributors of copying equipment." He added:

> One may search the Copyright Act in vain for any sign that the elected representatives of the millions of people who watch television every day have made it unlawful to copy a program for later viewing at home, or have enacted a flat prohibition against the sale of machines that make such copying possible.

The dissenters, led by Justice Harry A. Blackmun, saw the decision as an erosion of the control that the Copyright Act gives to authors over the use of their works. They were not satisfied that most copying is authorized by implication because it does no more than change the time at which the program is viewed. They would have remanded for another trial at which the economic aspects of video recording could be explored more fully.

The precedent established by the Supreme Court in *Universal City* has had ramifications in other areas where technology has made copying easy. Copying of such things as computer programs, movies, and audio recordings has become so widespread that some authorities are wondering whether copyright law can continue to be enforced with respect to some media.[32] When compact audio disks, using beams of laser light rather than the conventional stylus to transmit sound, burst onto the market in the late 1980s, they seemed to be immune to copying. But in 1987, a Japanese firm announced that it was going to produce a digital recorder that was capable of copying compact disks. The record industry responded by asking Congress to enact legislation prohibiting the importing of such recorders unless they were altered to make it impossible for them to copy compact disks. That attempt failed when a Chicago firm announced that it was going to market its own version of a digital recorder.[33]

Movies Made Prior to 1978

A Supreme Court case growing out of the rerelease of Alfred Hitchcock's *Rear Window* and its transfer to videocassettes raised questions about the future of a thousand or more movies made before the present copyright law took effect in 1978.[34] Prior to 1978, copyrights were in effect for twenty-eight years and could be renewed for another twenty-eight years. Since then, they are in effect for the life of the author plus fifty years. An author's failure to renew his copyright on

---

32. James Lardner, "Annals of Law: The Betamax Case," *New Yorker*, 6 April 1987, p. 45 + ; 13 April 1987, p. 60 + . These articles not only give a detailed history of the Sony case but discuss its effect on copyright law.
33. Bob Davis, "House Panel Approves Measure to Block Sale of Digital Audio Tape Recorders," *Wall Street Journal*, 4 August 1987. The measure did not become law.
34. Linda Greenhouse, "Final Twist in 'Rear Window' Case," *Wall Street Journal*, 25 April 1990.

the short story that became *Rear Window,* and the subsequent sale of the renewed movie rights by his executor, laid the ground for the decision.

Cornell Woolrich wrote a short story, "It Had to Be Murder," which was published in *Dime Detective* magazine in 1942. Three years later, he sold the movie
rights to it and five other stories for $9250. The next year, a production company
formed by James Stewart, the actor, and Hitchcock bought the movie rights to
"It Had to Be Murder" from the original purchaser for $10,000. In 1954,
Hitchcock made the story into a movie which quickly became a classic and continues in such demand that it grossed $12 million in the 1980s. Woolrich promised
the moviemakers he would renew the copyright on his story but failed to do so
before he died. He left his estate, including his copyrights, to Columbia University. The bank that administered his estate renewed the copyrights in 1968 but
sold the renewed movie rights to "It Had to Be Murder" to Sheldon Abend, a
New York literary agent, for $650, plus 10 percent of all proceeds from exploita-
tion of the story. Abend also bought rights to about 100 other movies.

In 1971, when *Rear Window* was released for use on television, Abend notified
Stewart, Hitchcock's estate, and MCA Inc. that he owned renewal rights to the
copyright and warned them that any further distribution of the movie without his
permission would be an infringement. Nonetheless, MCA granted ABC television
a second license to show the film. Abend filed suit but agreed to dismiss it in
return for $25,000. Three years later, in a similar case, the U.S. Court of Appeals
for the Second Circuit held that the owner of a copyright in a derivative work,
which *Rear Window* is, could continue to use that right even if the grant of rights
in the original work had lapsed.[35] Relying on that holding, MCA proceeded to
release *Rear Window* through a variety of media, including videocassettes, vid-
eodisks, and cable television. Abend sued again. A federal district court dismissed his lawsuit, but the U.S. Court of Appeals for the Ninth Circuit reversed.
The Supreme Court agreed to review the case and, in *Stewart* v. *Abend,*[36] affirmed, six to three.

Justice Sandra Day O'Connor, writing for the Court, said that MCA's reliance
on the Second Circuit's decision was mistaken, because that decision was clearly
counter to the plain language of the copyright law in effect prior to 1978. Under
that language, the copyright of an original work, in this instance Woolrich's short
story, remains in full effect, even though it is incorporated into a derivative work.
Further, any rights granted for preparation of a derivative work, in this instance,
Rear Window, expire when the original copyright expires. If it is renewed, then
the owner of the derivative work must negotiate anew for the right to continue to
exploit that work. That's true, O'Connor said, even though the owner of the derivative right—Abend—makes demands "so exorbitant that a negotiated economic accommodation will be impossible." Abend was asking for half of MCA's
gross proceeds in excess of advertising expenses. In response to arguments from

35. Rohauer v. Killiam Shows, 551 F.2d 484, cert. denied, 431 U.S. 949, 97 S.Ct. 2666, 53
L.Ed.2d 266 (1977).
36. ___ U.S. ___, 110 S.Ct. 1750, 109 L.Ed.2d 184 (1990).

movie producers that the Court's reading of the law would lead them to withdraw many pre-1978 movies from the market, O'Connor said the remedy lies in getting Congress to change the law, not in the courts. The Court also rejected the movie maker's argument that *Rear Window* was a fair use of the short story, holding that it was an infringement.

As a result of the decision, Abend's $650 investment in the movie rights to a short story published in a dime novel fifty years ago entitles him to a share of the $12 million *Rear Window* earned in the 1980s.

TRADEMARKS

In its basic sense, the Copyright Act protects collections of words or an artistic composition such as a photograph, or a painting, or a piece of sculpture. Courts have held that no one can copyright individual words in common usage or even

James Stewart won critical acclaim as an actor in *Rear Window* more than thirty years ago, playing the role of a photographer confined to his apartment by a broken leg, whose pictures, idly taken through the windows, disclosed and helped solve a murder. Because Stewart also owned a piece of the highly successful movie, it helped make him a millionaire. Recently, the Supreme Court held that he and other surviving owners of *Rear Window* will have to pay part of their profits to the holder of the copyright on the short story which was the inspiration for the script. (The Museum of Modern Art/Film Stills Archive)

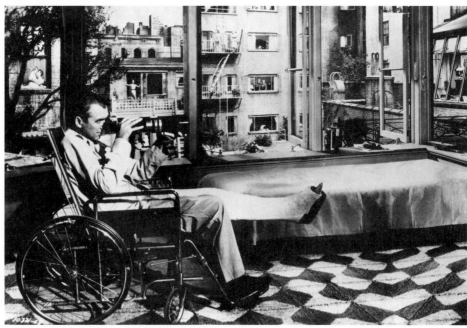

short collections of words of the kind likely to occur in common combinations. However, a federal law, the Lanham Trade-Mark Act,[37] can be used to protect words or symbols that clearly identify a business firm and its products. Such identifying words or symbols are called "trademarks." Normally such marks must be registered with the Patent and Trademark office if they are to be enforceable, and the owner must make an effort to prevent their unauthorized use. "Coke" and "Coca-Cola" are registered trademarks. A publication that uses either to refer to another kind of soft drink, or that fails to publish either word exactly as printed here, is likely to get a letter from a company lawyer reminding it that it has misused a trademark. Companies that do not protect their trademarks run the risk of having them become generic terms that anyone can use.

A case involving two clubs dedicated to serving young people illustrates both what a trademark is and how it can be protected. In 1987, officials of the Boys Clubs of America proposed changing the organization's name to the Boys and Girls Clubs of America. The purpose was to more accurately reflect the membership of the organization in an era when lines separating activities considered appropriate for boys and girls were being wiped out. The Girls Clubs of America began a trademark infringement action in a U.S. District Court in New York City. The Girls Clubs said that its name was a trademark clearly identifying it and its activities in the minds of the public. The club argued that the proposed name change of the Boys Clubs might lead potential contributors to believe the two organizations had merged. The court agreed that there was a likelihood of confusion and issued an order preventing the change until the trademark infringement action could be resolved.[38]

In this instance, the four words making up the name of the organization, "Girls Clubs of America," had become its trademark. If another's use of some part of that name could be shown to cause confusion in the public mind as to the identity of the two organizations, that use would be considered a trademark infringement. The National Geographic Society was able to win a partial victory in a trademark infringement action against a rival magazine publisher that took only one word, "traveler."[39] The publications involved in the dispute were the *National Geographic Traveler* and *Conde Nast's Traveler*. Both deal with travel, and both have circulations of about 800,000. National Geographic's magazine was on the market first. When it sued the newer magazine for trademark infringement, the court held that it was not entitled to an injunction preventing Conde Nast from using the word "traveler" in its title, but the court also held that Conde Nast should change its cover to give more prominence to the corporate name.

Congress amended the Lanham Act in 1988 to reduce the term of a trademark registration from twenty years to ten years.[40] Generally, a trademark must be

37. 15 U.S.C. §§1051-1127 (1982).
38. Girls Clubs of America v. Boys Clubs of America, 683 F.Supp. 50 (S.D.N.Y. 1988).
39. National Geographic Society v. Conde Nast Publications, 687 F.Supp. 106 (S.D.N.Y. 1988).
40. Julius R. Lunsford, Jr., "Trademark Owners' Relations with the Press," *Editor & Publisher*, 3 December 1988, p. 10T.

used to be kept in force. The Act says that any mark not used for two years is presumed to have been abandoned. However, another sentence in the same section says that a mark is abandoned "when its use has been discontinued with an intent not to resume."[41]

Allen v. *Men's World Outlet, Inc.,* **679 F.Supp. 360 (S.D.N.Y. 1988).**

In 1988, a U.S. District Court in New York City significantly extended the concept of trademark to cover an actor's physical appearance. The action was brought by Woody Allen, an actor, musician, and producer of movies, who became irked by advertisements using a model who looked like him to promote a video rental chain and stores selling men's clothing at a discount. He went to court to prevent what he considered to be an exploitation of his personality but was not altogether successful because the ads stated in fine print that the model was a "look-alike." When the clothing stores resumed their campaign by placing ads in *Newsday,* a Long Island newspaper, Allen's attorney sued to stop them, claiming trademark infringement. The court adopted his theory, holding that Allen was entitled to an injunction to prevent the clothing store and its advertising agency from using the "look-alike" in future advertising. The court held that the use of the look-alike created a likelihood of consumer confusion and therefore violated section 1125(a) of the Lanham Act.

The ad at issue showed Phil Boroff, who resembles Allen physically, holding a clarinet. Allen regularly played the clarinet with a jazz band at Michael's Pub in New York City. The court's decision said the ad copy "evoked the 'schlemiel' persona Allen cultivated up through his appearance in *Annie Hall.*" Below Boroff's picture, "in small lightface type," was a sentence, "This is a Ron Smith Celebrity Look-Alike." The court said that sentence kept Allen from having a case under laws preventing advertisers from using an entertainer's likeness to promote their products. It was reasonably clear that the man in the ad was not Allen. But with respect to the trademark infringement claim, the court concluded that Allen did have a case. Boroff's resemblance to Allen, heightened by the copy, was sufficient to create an impression that Men's World clothing was somehow associated with Allen. The court held, in effect, that Allen's likeness was a form of trademark and that Boroff "resembles him strongly." Further, it was logical to assume that there was some overlap between purchasers of discounted men's clothing and people who go to Allen's movies. Thus, there was a group of people who might be confused by the ad. Although there was no evidence that anyone had been confused by the look-alike, the Lanham Act requires only that there be the likelihood of confusion to support a finding of false representation. Given the diverse nature of *Newsday*'s audience, some part of it would not have the sophistication to conclude that Allen was not associated with the ad, the court held.

The court said Allen could not collect compensatory damages under the law because he would have to prove actual consumer confusion. Nor could he obtain

---

41. 15 U.S.C. §1127 (1982).

Which one is the real Woody Allen? He is at the left. On the right is Phil Boroff of Los Angeles, who was photographed, holding a clarinet, for newspaper ads promoting a video rental chain and men's discount clothing stores in New York City, where Allen lives. Allen was able to get a court order forbidding further use of the "look-alike" ads. (AP/Wide World Photos)

punitive damages because the Lanham Act makes no provision for them. The court did hold that he was entitled to a permanent injunction.

MISAPPROPRIATION ═══════════════════════════════

Every reporter borrows from the work of other reporters. Reporters working on newspapers in areas served by more than one paper are asked by their editors to follow up stories clipped from competing publications. Reporters from broadcasting stations find story ideas by reading the newspapers. A news feature may begin in one newspaper and then make its way, in altered form, through several others, and, perhaps, into the wire services, and end as a special on the evening television news. It's part of the game, and as long as a reporter doesn't take too much, too often, all is well. But starting as far back as 1918 in *International News Service* v. *Associated Press*,[42] courts have penalized the systematic taking of news, even when it is not covered by copyright.

---

42. 248 U.S. 215, 29 S.Ct. 68, 63 L.Ed.2d 528 (1918).

William Randolph Hearst established INS to offer his own newspapers and others an alternative to AP as a source of news. AP alleged that many of the stories distributed by INS were thinly disguised rewrites of stories gathered by its own reporters. Evidence supported the charge, and the courts condemned INS's piracy as a form of unfair competition. In a nice turn of speech, the Supreme Court said the Hearst service was reaping where it had not sown—it was using the fruits of another's labor, which gave it an unfair advantage. Even though the AP news service was not copyrighted and was widely used by its own members, the Court said INS could not take stories from that service and sell them as its own. Courts call such a systematic taking of another's work "misappropriation," a kind of distant cousin of copyright infringement. An important difference is that misappropriation is grounded in common law rather than in statute law.

In the middle part of this century, courts in several states used the concept to prevent radio stations from using in their newscasts descriptions of events taken from local newspapers[43] or to prevent one newspaper from copying advertisements from another. Implicit in all these decisions is the assumption that information is property. Thus the law of misappropriation is broader in scope than copyright law, which focuses on protection for the manner in which information is presented while offering little or no protection for the information itself.

Carpenter v. *United States,*
484 U.S. 19, 108 S.Ct.,
316, 98 L.Ed.2d 275 (1987).

In 1987, a majority of the Supreme Court decided an unusual misappropriation case and endorsed the concept that information is indeed property, which its owner can protect against misuse. The case was unusual in that it pitted a newspaper against two of its employees who were charged with using unpublished information gathered in the course of their employment to make a profit in the securities markets for themselves and others. The newspaper is *The Wall Street Journal,* a financial newspaper with a circulation of more than a million. One employee was a reporter who frequently wrote the newspaper's "Heard on the Street" column, which discusses factors that might affect the price of a company's stock. The reporter, R. Foster Winans, noticed on occasion that share prices rose or fell significantly after his column had appeared in the morning newspaper. Because he knew what was going to be in the column, he decided to take advantage of that fact by trading in the affected stock before the market closed on the day before the column appeared. He enlisted his roommate, David Carpenter, a copy clerk at the *Journal,* in the scheme. Their trading pattern soon was noticed by their stockbrokers who proposed that they, too, benefit from the inside information by trading on their own accounts and giving Winans and Carpenter a share of the profits. Over a four-month period, the brokers made a net profit of about $690,000 from information provided by Winans. The reporter's share was $31,000.

The trading pattern also was noticed by officials of the Securities and Exchange Commission, who began an investigation. As the net tightened, the participants in the scheme quarreled, and Winans and Carpenter told the SEC what

43. The most frequently quoted case is Pottstown Daily News v. Pottstown Broadcasting, 192 A.2d 657 (Pa. 1963).

had been happening. Winans, Carpenter, and the brokers were charged with conspiracy to commit securities fraud through insider trading. One of the brokers pleaded guilty. A federal district court jury found the others, including Winans and Carpenter, guilty. The verdict was affirmed on appeal. The U.S. Supreme Court agreed to review the decision and affirmed it unanimously.

The Court upheld the view that the trio's use of information taken from the *Journal* was a form of theft of property. It made no difference that Winans, acting as a reporter, had obtained much of that information from sources on his own initiative. As the Court saw it, that information belonged to the *Journal,* not Winans. Under *Journal* policy, the paper's employees are required to hold in confidence all information being prepared for publication. Justice Byron R. White, writing for the Court, said that the "'intangible nature' [of the information] does not make it any less 'property' protected by the mail and wire fraud statutes." The Court said there need not be any proof that the taking had cost the *Journal* any monetary loss. "It is sufficient that the *Journal* has been deprived of its right to exclusive use of the information, for exclusivity is an important aspect of confidential business information and most private property, for that matter." Winans was sentenced to prison.

Seen at one level, the decision gave the government a strong new weapon to use against persons accused of insider trading—of profiting from advance knowledge of information that will affect the market. Indeed the decision was hailed by the federal prosecutor in Manhattan who said: "It gives prosecutors a very clear road map on how to proceed."[44] Using that map, U.S. attorneys did indeed prosecute a number of insider trading cases, most of them against stockbrokers.

At another level, the case stands as a warning to anyone—including reporters, editors, advertising copy writers, corporate communicators, or public relations practitioners—who has knowledge of confidential information belonging to his or her employer. If that information could have an effect on securities markets, premature use of it can lead to prosecution. Indeed, a year after the Supreme Court's decision in *Carpenter,* S. G. "Rudy" Ruderman, a former *Business Week* news broadcaster, pleaded guilty to mail fraud for trading on information from the magazine's "Inside Wall Street" column. As a radio broadcaster employed by the magazine, Ruderman had access to articles before the magazine reached the public. In two and a half years, he used that access to earn about $15,000 by trading in securities that moved up or down after *Business Week* reached its subscribers.[45]

In the Professional World

Professional creators in any field are far more likely to benefit from the Copyright Act than they are to be restricted by it. Those who honestly attempt to do their own work, and they are in the majority, are highly unlikely

---

44. James B. Stewart and Stephen Wermiel, "High Court Upholds Conviction of Winans, Two Co-Conspirators," *The Wall Street Journal,* 17 November 1987.
45. Betty Wong, "Ruderman Pleads Guilty to Charges of Mail Fraud," *Wall Street Journal,* 9 December 1988.

to be infringers of copyright. Rarely does a court find that a reputable media organization has been guilty of copyright infringement. More common are cases exploring the outer limits of copyright law, as in the use of J. D. Salinger's readily available letters by his biographer, or *Nation* magazine's belief that a newsworthy "scoop" might justify copying from President Ford's memoirs.

Other recent cases have explored the limits of copying permitted by new forms of technology: computer software, data retrieval systems, and satellite dishes. A court has held that it is a violation of copyright to copy a computer program without authorization.[46] Apple Computer filed a copyright action to protect the way its programs display information on a video screen.[47] A legal publisher fought a three-year court battle to win a settlement recognizing that page numbers which are part of a highly refined system of case law analysis can be protected by copyright.[48] A court found a copyright infringement in the use of a satellite dish to bring professional football games to a bar's patrons.[49]

However, for most who work in the professional world, considerations of copyright law start with asking whether formalities of complying with the Act's registration terms should be observed. Since the law now assumes that works are copyrighted as soon as they take tangible form, why go to the bother and expense of registration with the Copyright Office? Registration not only involves payment of a $10 fee, it also requires filling out a form and mailing it, along with two copies of the work, to Washington, D.C. If a work has no market value, and the creator can be sure it is unlikely to have any, there isn't any point to registration. If a work does have value, however, and it is taken by someone else, the creator cannot pursue an infringement action unless the work is registered. Failure to place a copyright notice on the work may offer the infringer a defense, as an unknowing infringer is subject to minimum penalties.

The value of copyright protection for newspapers is debatable. Publishers vary in their use of the law. Some routinely copyright each edition. Others may copyright unusual stories, sometimes as a promotion device. Still others never copyright anything. Given the nature of most newspaper content—here today and forgotten tomorrow—newspaper articles are not likely to have much market value beyond the price paid by the subscriber. Publications of a more lasting nature, such as magazines or books, are almost always copyrighted. In the entertainment field, music, plays, television programs, videocassettes, moving pictures, and the like have such great potential value that they are always copyrighted. In the business world, such things as catalogues, instruction manuals, and specialized computer programs are given copyright protection.

---

46. E.F. Johnson Co. v. Uniden Corp. of America, 623 F.Supp. 1485 (D.Minn. 1985).
47. "Apple's Copyright Lawsuit Is Seen as Effort to Lock In Technical Lead," *The Wall Street Journal,* 21 March 1988.
48. Laurie P. Cohen, "Mead, West Publishing Are Expected to Settle 3 Suits over Legal Databases," *Wall Street Journal,* 26 July 1988.
49. National Football League v. McBee & Bruno's, 621 F.Supp. 880 (E.D.Mo. 1985).

In 1988, two firms, American Honda Motor Co. and Kawasaki Heavy Industries Ltd., carried copyright law a step further by using it to protect testing and safety documents related to products involved in lawsuits.[50] The firms' purpose was to prevent the plaintiffs' lawyers from copying the reports and giving or selling them to other lawyers who might be considering actions against the companies. Lawyers for Honda and Kawasaki argued that by copyrighting the documents they retained for the companies the sole right to decide how widely they might be distributed other than for their use as evidence in the lawsuits. Some commentators saw this as a misuse of copyright law, but in one of the cases a judge upheld Honda's right to restrict use of its reports.

The Woody Allen case is as noteworthy for the ethical questions it raises as for its value as a legal precedent. Should advertisers seek to capitalize on the value of popular entertainers or sports figures without paying them for their endorsement? Is it enough to explain in fine print that the reader is seeing only someone who resembles the entertainer? Might not some consumers conclude that a company willing to cheat in its advertising might also cheat in other ways?

The *Carpenter* case also raises prickly ethical questions. When the editors of *The Wall Street Journal* learned that a reporter had shared with others information that he had gathered, but the newspaper had not yet published, the editors treated the matter as a gross breach of the newspaper's code of ethics. The editors took the position that all members of the newspaper's staff were bound by that code neither to profit from information gathered for the newspaper nor to disclose it to others before it was published. Others argued that the rules were not all that clear. In any event, who owns the bits and pieces of information that ultimately take form as a story? What happens if the reporter, or an editor, concludes the bits and pieces do not add up to a story, but some of the bits point to what looks like a good investment? Should the reporter or editor have to forgo the investment? Or what happens if a reporter who is working on a long-range investigative project leaves one publication for another? Does the story, if it develops, go with the reporter? Or does it belong to the first employer? With the Supreme Court's holding that information gathered in the course of one's employment belongs to the employer, such questions are likely to spill out of the realm of ethics into the courts.

In less legalistic times, journalists who copied from others usually were dealt with informally but effectively. When this author became a Washington correspondent, he was welcomed by James Reston of the *New York Times,* who once had been employed by the author's publisher, James Cox. Reston offered advice on the rules of what was then a relatively small group of journalists. "You'll find you can't cover everything," Reston said. "None of us can. There'll be times when you may feel a need to copy a little from one of us. We all do it once in awhile. But if you copy too much, too

---

50. "Firms Use Copyright Law to Keep Documents Secret," *The Wall Street Journal,* 31 August 1988.

often, you'll soon be frozen out.'' It was sound advice then. It is sound advice yet.

FOR REVIEW

1. What is the purpose of copyright law? How is that purpose carried into effect? How does copyright law relate to the First Amendment?

2. What can be copyrighted? What cannot be? Illustrate with examples.

3. Explain the degree of protection provided by copyrighting a newspaper or a news story. What precautions should be taken by a reporter who is assigned to follow up another medium's copyrighted news story?

4. Define fair use. List and explain the elements that go into a determination of fair use. What is the significance of the *Rosemont Enterprises* decision with respect to the doctrine of fair use?

5. Compare and contrast the Supreme Court's decision in *Harper & Row* with the circuit court's decision in *Rosemont Enterprises* and the district court's decision in *Bernard Geis*. Collectively, what do they say about the First Amendment in copyright infringement cases?

6. On balance, does copyright law enhance or inhibit First Amendment interests? Justify your conclusions.

7. Define and illustrate with reference to cases an infringement of copyright. Which element of the test applied by the courts is most likely to prove decisive?

8. What rationale did the Supreme Court use in deciding the home video recorder case?

9. What is a trademark? In what ways is a trademark related to copyright law? What are the significant differences?

10. What must a trademark owner do to retain title to the mark?

11. Discuss the legal and ethical aspects of an advertiser's use in commercials of models who sound or look like popular entertainers.

12. Define misappropriation as the term applies to communicators. What is the probable significance of the Supreme Court's decision in *Carpenter* v. *United States* with respect to communicators and misappropriation?

CHAPTER 14

ANTITRUST LAW AND THE NEWS BUSINESS

Some Disapproved Business Practices
Antitrust Law and the Marketplace of Ideas

Tucson: Joint Operating Agreements / Los Angeles: One
Ownership in Adjacent Markets / Cincinnati: One Ownership in
the Same City

The Marketplace of Ideas Today
Joint Operating Agreements
Joint Ownership of Newspapers and Broadcasting Stations

THE DISTRIBUTION OF NEWS AND OPINION

TAXATION OF THE MEDIA

The First Amendment protects news, opinion, and advertising, as we have seen, but it does not grant the media immunity from laws regulating their business operations. At one time, some publishers attempted to argue that such things as minimum wage laws restricted freedom of the press, but the courts held otherwise. The general rule is that in their business operations, newspapers, magazines, book publishers, broadcasters, film makers, and cable operators must obey the same rules as nonmedia businesses. This means that they are subject to antitrust laws if they use predatory business practices to harm their competitors. They must comply with wages and hours laws, and they must pay normal taxes applying to other business entities. However, courts have held that the First Amendment protects the right to sell newspapers in public places and stands as a barrier against discriminatory taxation.

This chapter first examines antitrust law as it applies to the ownership of newspapers and broadcasting stations. In modern times, the law has been used primarily to challenge advertising rates and attempts by daily newspaper publishers to prevent the growth of free-circulation weeklies made up mostly of advertising. Despite an attempt by President John F. Kennedy and his brother Robert to use

THE NEWS MEDIA
AS BUSINESSES

antitrust law to encourage a competitive marketplace of ideas, the law has been ineffective in stemming the rapid growth of newspaper chains. However, regulations imposed by the Federal Communications Commission have limited newspaper ownership of broadcasting stations in the same city, and vice versa.

More than forty years ago, a persistent religious group, Jehovah's Witnesses, endured considerable persecution to establish that the First Amendment protects the right to disseminate ideas door to door or in public places. Today, the principles forged then protect the right of newspaper publishers to place coin-operated newspaper racks outside of supermarkets, or wherever else crowds are likely to pass by on foot in public places.

This book began with John Milton's argument against the licensing of printing in England. It will end by examining two decisions in which the Supreme Court held that discriminatory taxation aimed at newspapers, if unchecked, could do what the licensers of old sought to do—that is, suppress ideas considered harmful by government officials. The first of the two cases particularly serves as a reminder that the forces against which Milton argued so persuasively survive, even though, for the moment, they no longer prevail.

Major Cases

- *Associated Press* v. *United States,* 326 U.S. 1, 65 S.Ct. 1416, 89 L.Ed. 2013 (1945).

- *Citizen Publishing Co.* v. *United States,* 394 U.S. 131, 89 S.Ct. 927, 22 L.Ed.2d 148 (1969).

- *City of Lakewood* v. *Plain Dealer Publishing Co.,* 486 U.S. 750, 108 S.Ct. 2138, 100 L.Ed.2d 771 (1988).

- *Federal Communications Commission* v. *National Citizens Committee for Broadcasting,* 436 U.S. 775, 98 S.Ct. 2096, 56 L.Ed.2d 697 (1978).

- *Grosjean* v. *American Press Co.,* 297 U.S. 233, 56 S.Ct. 444, 80 L.Ed. 660 (1936).

- *Kansas City Star Co.* v. *United States*, 240 F.2d 643 (8th Cir. 1957).

- *Minneapolis Star and Tribune Co.* v. *Minnesota Commissioner of Revenue*, 460 U.S. 575, 103 S.Ct. 1365, 75 L.Ed.2d 295 (1983).

- *Syracuse Broadcasting Corp.* v. *Newhouse*, 319 F.2d 683 (2d Cir. 1963).

- *United States* v. *Times-Mirror Co.*, 274 F.Supp. 606 (C.D.Calif. 1967).

ANTITRUST LAW AND THE NEWS BUSINESS

When Congress adopted the Sherman Antitrust Act in 1890, its main targets were John D. Rockefeller's Standard Oil Company and Andrew Carnegie's United States Steel Company. These entrepreneurs had cut prices on a selective basis to freeze out competitors. They had made exclusive deals with favored customers. Their purpose was to establish monopolies that would let them charge what they pleased. Other targets of the Act were burgeoning monopolies in whiskey distilling, in the making of white lead for paints, and in sugar refining. Cartoons of the era picture such businesses as giant octopuses with tentacles reaching out across the nation. The original Act was strengthened by the Clayton Act of 1914, and the Robinson-Patman Act of 1936, which forbids discriminatory pricing.

It is doubtful, even when the Clayton Act was adopted, that anyone thought of antitrust law as applying to newspapers or magazines. First, there were no national newspapers in 1914, nor was there any dominant magazine. Second, publishing was a highly competitive business. As late as 1923, nearly half the cities with daily newspapers had two or more.[1] Finally, it was generally believed that newspapers, like other small businesses, were not engaged in interstate commerce. Therefore, they were presumed to be beyond the reach of federal law.

The Supreme Court demolished that assumption in 1934 with its decision in *Indiana Farmer's Guide Publishing Co.* v. *Prairie Farmer Publishing Co.*[2] It held that any publication that uses advertising or other content created in another state, or that sells copies by mail to residents of another state, is engaged in interstate commerce and therefore subject to federal laws. The Court also held that to become a monopoly, a business firm need not be a giant seeking to control a national market. A publisher is to be judged by the extent to which his or her magazine or newspaper dominates its market area. Because circulation of most newspapers is concentrated in what is called a retail trading zone defined by the shopping practices of their subscribers, the *Indiana Farmer's Guide* decision brought even the smallest newspapers within the reach of antitrust law.

---

1. Of the 1,297 cities with daily newspapers, there were competing ownerships in 502. In the Matter of the Cincinnati Joint Operating Agreement, Docket No. 44-03-24-4; Recommended Decision, 1 May 1979, p. 12.
2. 293 U.S. 268, 55 S.Ct. 182, 79 L.Ed.2d 356 (1934).

Associated Press v. *United States,* 326 U.S. 1, 65 S.Ct. 1416, 89 L.Ed. 2013 (1945).

The Court expanded the scope of its decision in 1945, when it rejected the argument that the First Amendment gives the news media immunity from antitrust laws. In this instance, the owner of the *Chicago Tribune,* the legendary Colonel Robert R. McCormick, had used his veto power as a director of the Associated Press to deny that agency's news service to Marshall Field's newly established morning *Sun.* The AP bylaws then in effect made it difficult and expensive for owners of a new newspaper to obtain the service if they were in direct competition with an existing member. This did not mean that they would be left without a wire service. At least two others, United Press and the International News Service, were then in competition with AP. However, Field took the position that AP was the best of the three, and that his newspaper would not be competitive without it.

The Department of Justice took up Field's cause and charged the Associated Press with violating antitrust laws. The government asked that AP's restrictive membership rules be declared illegal. The news agency offered two arguments in its defense, both grounded in the freedom of press clause of the First Amendment:

1. Because AP was engaged in the business of gathering and disseminating news, it should be granted immunity from antitrust law unless the government could show that its actions represented a clear and present danger to a vital government interest.

2. Because AP considered itself a cooperative news gathering agency, any government interference with its method of choosing members violated its First Amendment freedoms.

A United States district court in New York City rejected both arguments and ruled in the government's favor. AP took its case to the Supreme Court which, in *Associated Press* v. *United States,* upheld the district court's ruling five to three. Writing for the majority, Justice Hugo L. Black used reasoning that continues to be applied to the news media, not only in antitrust cases, but in other cases dealing with their business aspects. With respect to the first argument, he wrote:

> Member publishers of AP are engaged in business for profit exactly as are other businessmen who sell food, steel, aluminum, or anything else people need or want.... All are alike covered by the Sherman Act. The fact that the publisher handles news while others handle food does not, as we shall later point out, afford the publisher a peculiar constitutional sanctuary in which he can with impunity violate laws regulating his business practices.
>
> Nor is a publisher who engaged in business practices made unlawful by the Sherman Act entitled to a partial immunity by reason of the "clear and present danger" doctrine which courts have used to protect freedom to speak, to print, and to worship.... Formulated as it was to protect liberty of thought and of expression, it would degrade the clear and present danger doctrine to fashion from it a shield for publishers who engage in business practices condemned by the Sherman Act.

Justice Black was equally blunt in dismissing AP's second argument. He noted that the news agency was founded as a cooperative; that is, it was formed by newspapers who did no more than share local news of regional or national interest with one another. This sharing of news remained a principle of AP's operation in the 1940s and continues today. At the time of this case, AP's membership rules made it difficult and expensive for a direct competitor of an established member to enter the cooperative. The reasoning was simple: Why should an established newspaper be required to share its news with an upstart competing medium? In defending its rules, AP argued that if anyone who wanted the service had to be admitted to membership, the flow of news would be diminished. Where competition existed, no one would share news with the wire service until it no longer was news. Otherwise, the medium that got the news first would only be giving away its own scoop. Thus, as AP saw it, any change in the membership rules would restrict First Amendment freedoms. Justice Black disagreed:

> It would be strange indeed...if the grave concern for freedom of the press which prompted adoption of the First Amendment should be read as a command that government was without power to protect that freedom. The First Amendment, far from providing an argument against application of the Sherman Act, here provides powerful reasons to the contrary. That amendment rests on the assumption that the widest possible dissemination of information from diverse and antagonistic sources is essential to the welfare of the public, that a free press is a condition of a free society. Surely, a command that the government itself shall not impede the free flow of ideas does not afford non-governmental combinations a refuge if they impose restraints upon that constitutionally guaranteed freedom. Freedom to publish means freedom for all and not for some. Freedom to publish is guaranteed by the Constitution, but freedom to combine to keep others from publishing is not. Freedom of the press from governmental interference under the First Amendment does not sanction repression of that freedom by private interests. The First Amendment affords not the slightest support for the contention that a combination to restrain trade in news and views has any constitutional immunity.

This decision has helped make an important point: The main concern of the First Amendment is the protection of the dissemination of news and opinion. It cannot be stretched to give those in the business of disseminating news and opinion an exemption from laws generally regulating business activities.

Some Disapproved Business Practices

The Court's decisions in *Indiana Farmer's Guide* and *Associated Press* have opened the way for a variety of antitrust actions against the news media since World War II.

One of the few cases to reach the Supreme Court, *Lorain Journal Co.* v. *United States*,[3] was noted in Chapter 12. By systematically refusing to sell advertising to merchants and others who bought time on a competing radio station,

---

3.   342 U.S. 193, 72 S.Ct. 181, 96 L.Ed. 162 (1951).

the publisher of the *Journal* engaged in "bold, relentless, and predatory commercial behavior" clearly designed to harm the station. All of this took place in a limited marketing area served both by the newspaper and the broadcaster. There was little question that the publisher was engaged in a scheme tending to promote monopoly, thus violating the Sherman Act. Lower courts have cited the case as a precedent in condemning similar refusals to accept advertising in Las Vegas, Nevada,[4] where the target was a competing newspaper; in Haverhill, Massachusetts,[5] where a competing newspaper also was involved, and in Providence, Rhode Island,[6] where a rental information service was the victim.

Taken together, the cases suggest care in exercising the right to refuse advertising. If refusals are based on established standards of acceptance, and those standards are applied with an even hand, legal problems are unlikely. But if the pattern of refusals points to a conspiracy to harm a competing medium, or a firm in competition with a favored advertiser, it may be possible to prove a violation of antitrust law. The most recent of the three preceding cases, *Home Placement Service* v. *Providence Journal,* raises a special note of caution with respect to advertising offered by an arguably competing medium. Home Placement charged its customers a fee for providing them with a listing of available rental housing. This put it in competition with the *Providence Journal,* which sold classified advertising to owners of rental property seeking tenants. When Home Placement sought to advertise its service in the *Journal,* it was told it could not do so unless it agreed not to charge a fee for its service. Home Placement complied with the condition, but the U.S. Court of Appeals for the Second Circuit held that the newspaper's act violated antitrust law. This suggests that if a medium is offered an ad by a competing medium, it may neither refuse the ad nor insist that the ad be altered, unless it is demonstrably false or misleading.

Kansas City Star Co. v. United States, 240 F. 2d 643 (8th Cir. 1957). Media owners who have achieved dominant positions in their markets must take particular care in setting advertising and circulation rates and in other actions that may affect competing media. If that dominance results in abuse, it may result in an antitrust action. For instance, in 1957, the U.S. Court of Appeals for the Eighth Circuit held that the Kansas City Star Company's advertising and circulation policies tended to create a monopoly. In an action brought by the U.S. government, the court struck down a series of all-or-nothing package deals, coupled with a diligently enforced advertising policy that helped the Star Company dominate Kansas City's advertising market in the early 1950s. It published three newspapers, the morning *Times,* the afternoon *Star,* and the *Sunday Star,* and owned radio station WDAF and the city's first television station, WDAF-TV. People who wanted to subscribe to one of the newspapers were required to buy all three. Advertisers likewise had to buy space in all three papers in order to get space in one. Star executives rationalized the arrangement by contending that they published only one newspaper with thirteen issues a week. There also were

---

4. Greenspun v. McCarran, 105 F.Supp. 662 (D.Nev. 1952).
5. Union Leader Corp. v. Newspapers of New England, 284 F.2d 586 (1st Cir. 1960).
6. Home Placement Service, Inc., v. Providence Journal Co., 682 F.2d 274 (1st Cir. 1982).

advertising tying arrangements between the newspaper and the television station. In some instances, advertisers seeking to buy time on WDAF-TV were told they could do so only if they bought space in the newspapers.

It was a profitable arrangement. It also was alleged to have a devastating effect on competing media. A publisher of a competing newspaper in Kansas City, Missouri, had gone out of business during World War II, leaving the *Times* and *Star* alone. Seven other dailies continued to publish in the metropolitan area, but the largest of these, the *Kansas City Kansan,* had a circulation of only 27,873 in 1951. In contrast, circulation of the three Star Company newspapers exceeded 350,000 a day. In 1952, those newspapers received 94 percent of the money spent on newspaper advertising in the Kansas City area. With broadcasting revenues included, the company accounted for 85 percent of the total advertising revenue billed by all media.

In a criminal proceeding, the Department of Justice charged the Star Company with unfair competitive practices in violation of the Sherman Act. Witnesses told a district court jury that the newspaper's advertising executives had used threats and intimidation to discourage advertisers from using competing media, to the latter's harm. Star advertisers who ignored the warning found their ads placed in poor positions. A major league baseball player, who also owned a flower shop in Kansas City, was the target of another kind of threat. When he placed an ad in a competing newspaper, an advertising solicitor told him that even if he hit a hundred home runs a year, his name would never appear in the newspapers' sports pages except in the box scores.

A jury found in 1957 that the unit advertising system "was used...with the intent and effect of excluding competition." It also held that an effect of the unit circulation policy was to discourage subscribers from taking any other newspaper. Therefore, the Star Company was guilty of violating the Sherman Act. The court ordered the newspaper to pay a fine of $5,000 and the advertising director, $2,500. In addition, the company was ordered to stop its unit sales of advertising and subscriptions, to stop tie-in sales between the broadcasting stations and the newspaper, and to stop threatening advertisers who did business with competing media. The company appealed.

The newspapers had argued that the government's action was an attempt to intimidate a free press and therefore violated the First Amendment. The appeals court disposed of that argument as follows:

> Publishers of newspapers must answer for their actions in the same manner as anyone else. A monopolistic press could attain in tremendous measure the evils sought to be prevented by the Sherman Antitrust Act. Freedom to print does not mean freedom to destroy. To use the freedom of the press guaranteed by the First Amendment to destroy competition would defeat its own ends, for freedom to print news and express opinions as one chooses is not tantamount to having freedom to monopolize. To monopolize freedom destroys it.

The decision came at a time when many cities of a hundred thousand population and up had become one-owner towns, with formerly independent morning and evening newspapers coming under the same ownership. The decision sent them a message: They must not force advertisers or subscribers to take both or none. If they offered a unit advertising rate, they must leave the way open for an advertiser to choose one newspaper or the other. And they must not use their dominant position to try to squeeze out suburban newspapers, or other kinds of advertising media, which were beginning to emerge in response to changing patterns of urban living.

In the aftermath of the court action described above, the Star Company and the Justice Department entered into a consent agreement that is still looked to for guidance in setting advertising rates in cities where one owner owns two newspapers, two broadcasting stations, or any combination thereof. The agreement forbade compulsory combinations of the kind condemned by the court. But it permitted the publisher to offer substantial discounts to firms that were willing to place ads in more than one newspaper.[7] As long as such combination rates are not set unreasonably low, so as it make it impossible for other media to compete economically, and as long as they are not manipulated with intent to harm a media competitor, they do not violate antitrust law.

Syracuse Broadcasting Corp. v. *Newhouse,* **319 F. 2d 683 (2d Cir. 1963).** The principles established in the *Kansas City* case were reinforced in 1963 by the U.S. Court of Appeals for the Second Circuit. In its decision, in *Syracuse Broadcasting Corp.* v. *Newhouse,* the court said Newhouse was simply using good business practices to buttress its position as the dominant advertising medium in Syracuse, New York. The company owned both newspapers in the city along with WSYR-TV and its companion radio station, WSYR.

Syracuse Broadcasting Corporation, owner of WNDR radio, suffered financial problems in the early 1960s that it blamed on the Newhouse combination. It filed a civil antitrust suit alleging:

1. That WSYR stations got a better break in the newspapers, in both the news columns and in advertising, than it did. One of these breaks, it said, was free advertising space.

2. That the newspapers had established a joint advertising rate so low that it was particularly attractive to national advertisers who might otherwise buy radio time.

3. That the newspapers were picking on WNDR by publishing unfavorable news stories about its financial problems.

A federal district court held that Syracuse Broadcasting did not prove its case, and, on appeal, the circuit court agreed, holding that "inequality of treatment [in news and advertising] is not sufficient to prove a violation of antitrust laws." It was reasonable to believe that the newspaper's editors might pay more attention to their publisher's broadcasting stations than to others. Syracuse Broadcasting would have to show that it had been frozen out of the news columns altogether or

---

7. United States v. Kansas City Star Co., 1957 Trade Cas. (CCH) §68,857 (W.D.Mo. 1957).

that the publisher had told the editors to suppress news about its station. Nor could the plaintiff prove that WSYR stations were getting free advertising. More likely, the court concluded, there was a trade-off between the newspapers and the Newhouse stations that ended up as a bookkeeping transaction. Nor did the complainant prove there was anything unreasonable about the joint advertising rate. As for the news stories, they merely reflected a truth—WNDR was having newsworthy financial problems. Therefore, Newhouse was acting reasonably and was not in violation of antitrust law.

Obviously, what is reasonable is a matter of opinion. The advertising market in any community has become extremely complex and highly competitive. All but a few cities in the United States are served by only one daily newspaper owner, which leads to talk of a monopoly press. However, few publishers are without competition even from print media. The spread of population from core cities into the suburbs has led to a proliferation of weeklies and even dailies that cater to the news and advertising needs of specific neighborhoods. Some publishers have found it highly profitable to compile publications devoted almost completely to advertising that are distributed free of charge to every household in a specified area. Newspapers have also become distributors of glossy, full-color advertising supplements prepared by others. When they do so, they are, in effect, charging the advertiser to use their carrier distribution system. The purpose is to forestall the advertiser's resort to direct mail or some other methods of distribution that would shut out the newspaper altogether. Competition for the advertiser's dollar and for the consumer's attention also comes from billboards, the infinite variety of point-of-sale advertisements encountered in any retail store, locally published magazines, and zoned editions of national magazines, which carry advertising aimed at particular areas.

All of this says nothing of the electronic delivery of advertising. A city with one newspaper may have three or more television stations, several times that many AM and FM stations, and a cable system, all vigorously seeking to sell time to advertisers. Because television stations particularly can point to research findings that the average person spends more time watching or listening to electronic media than reading newspapers, competition from this quarter is formidable.

For any of these media, the setting of advertising rates is a delicate matter. The rates must be competitive, or the media will be bypassed by advertisers seeking maximum results for each dollar spent. But the rates must be high enough to cover expenses and return a profit, or the advertising medium eventually will fail. In addition, the owner of any medium that has achieved a substantial share of the market must be aware of possible antitrust action. A recent survey of antitrust actions involving the communications media showed that every aspect of advertising rate-setting, including the placing of newspaper ads in favored positions on the front or back of separate sections, is subject to challenge.[8] Most complaints founder on the rule of reason, but the possibility of antitrust action, civil, or criminal, is a factor to be considered in any rate decision.

---

8. Conrad M. Shumadine and Walter D. Kelley, Jr., "Antitrust and the Media," *Communications Law 1987*, vol. 1 (New York: Practising Law Institute, 1987), pp. 441–713.

Antitrust Law and the Marketplace of Ideas

"To monopolize freedom destroys it," wrote the U.S. court of appeals in the *Kansas City Star* case in 1957. Five years later President John F. Kennedy picked up on that idea and set in motion a series of actions that carried antitrust law onto new ground. His purpose was to preserve what he saw as a diminishing marketplace of ideas. He sought to promote competition for news, and a diversity of opinion, by attacking the economic forces and business practices that were creating one-newspaper towns.[9]

Kennedy's policy had its origins in several currents then running strongly through the media and society. Some were political, others economic. The principal motivating factors were:

1. Most newspapers that took positions during the Kennedy-Nixon campaign of 1960 backed the Republican candidate—as they had in every presidential campaign in the previous forty years. Adlai Stevenson, who had few newspaper backers in his two runs for the presidency, may have been the first to use the phrase "a one-party press," but he was not the only Democrat to complain about the phenomenon. When Franklin D. Roosevelt ran for a fourth term in the midst of World War II, he had the editorial backing of only 22 percent of the dailies with 17.7 percent of the national circulation. In no campaign from 1940 through 1956 did any Republican candidate for president have the support of less than 60 percent of the daily newspapers backing one candidate or the other. In 1960, Kennedy was supported by only 16.4 percent of the dailies, representing 15.8 percent of the circulation.[10]

2. At an accelerating rate, most cities in the United States were becoming one-newspaper, or one newspaper-owner towns. In 1923, 39 percent of the cities with daily newspapers had competing ownerships. By 1930, it was 20.6 percent. Thirty years later, when Kennedy was running for office, only 61 cities, or 4.2 percent of the 1,461 with daily newspapers, had competing ownerships.[11]

---

9. In this section, the author relies in part on conversations with attorneys who were with the Antitrust Division of the Department of Justice in that era, and on other sources in politics and in the newspaper business. The author was managing editor of the *Cincinnati Enquirer* and was to have been an expert witness in the divestment lawsuit directed at Scripps-Howard. The case was settled before it came to trial.

10. *Editor & Publisher* has surveyed daily newspaper endorsements of presidential candidates in every campaign, starting in 1932. Not until 1964, when President Lyndon B. Johnson ran against Barry Goldwater, did a majority of the editors making endorsements support a Democratic candidate. In each election since, a majority has endorsed the Republican candidate. In an editorial on 8 November 1980, the magazine noted, "The startling trend of these polls...has been the steady increase in the number of newspapers preferring not to take a stand with an editorial endorsement." In that year, nearly half the newspapers took no editorial position on the presidential election. That also was true in 1984 and 1988.

11. Raymond B. Nixon, "Half of Nation's Dailies Now in Group Ownerships," *Editor & Publisher,* 17 July 1971, p. 7.

3. Newspaper chains were growing at an accelerating rate. In 1960, more than half the nation's daily newspapers were independently owned. The long-established chains—Hearst, Scripps-Howard, Knight-Ridder, Newhouse, Cox—seemed to have stabilized. But a new phenomenon had begun to emerge: chain ownership of smaller newspapers in one-newspaper towns. The leaders in such acquisitions were Gannett, headquartered in Rochester, New York, and Thomson, owned by Lord Thomson of Fleet, a Canadian, with world headquarters in London. In part, the rapid growth of newspaper chains was a factor of heredity. The children and grandchildren of patriarchs who had founded newspapers early in the century lost interest in journalism. Another contributing factor in the trend toward chain ownership was the inheritance tax, which made it difficult to keep a small newspaper in the family. The estate had more to gain by selling the newspaper and using part of the proceeds to pay the taxes on the estate.

The trend toward chain ownership and one-newspaper towns was enough to convince the Kennedy administration that something needed to be done. As the president and his advisers saw it, people in too many cities were becoming a captive audience for one newspaper owner. Increasingly, that owner was not an individual who lived in the community, but a faceless corporation, with headquarters elsewhere, that was interested in only one thing: profit. Thus, the marketplace of ideas was becoming not a robust exchange for all kinds of political news and views, but a flabby monopoly offering one point of view, or, even worse, none at all. The president ordered the Antitrust Division of the Department of Justice to take action to preserve as much of the marketplace of ideas as still existed, and to try to restore what already had been lost.

Kennedy was assassinated before his order could be converted into action. However, his brother Robert carried on as attorney general under President Lyndon B. Johnson, who endorsed the program. Three antitrust suits filed in the mid-1960s against newspaper owners in as many cities were designed to send the news media a message. Each city was chosen to make a specific point. They were Tucson, Arizona, where two owners who long had shared common advertising, circulation, and printing operations, were about to become one; Los Angeles, where the Chandler family, owner of the *Times,* had bought the San Bernardino papers; and Cincinnati, where Scripps-Howard owned the *Post* and held 58 percent of the stock in the *Enquirer.*

Tucson: Joint Operating Agreements

The joint operating agreement in Tucson was one of the earliest, dating to 1940, and was typical of the way such arrangements operate. At the time it was

Citizen Publishing Co. v. United States, **394 U.S. 131, 89 S. Ct. 927, 22 L. Ed.2d 148 (1969).**

formed, two owners were in head-to-head competition. The *Star* was making a modest profit, but the *Citizen* had dropped into the red. The two owners reached an agreement and organized a third company, Tucson Newspapers, Inc., which, in effect, would become the city's only newspaper publisher. It sold advertising for, and distributed, both newspapers. It operated the printing plant. As publisher, it decided what to charge for advertising and set subscription rates. Profit was pooled and distributed to the two owners according to a formula on which they had agreed at the time the joint operation began. Executives of the two papers were bound by an agreement not to take part in a competing newspaper in the Tucson area, even if they lost their present jobs.

The arrangement worked well for more than twenty years. Then the family that owned the *Star* lost interest and the paper was offered for sale. The small Brush-Moore chain, centered in Canton, Ohio, offered to buy. William A. Small, Jr., owner of the *Citizen,* exercised his option to buy under the operating agreement. The Justice Department filed suit to prevent that sale and to require that the *Star* be sold to anyone but Small. The resulting legal battle went to the Supreme Court, which not only upheld the department, but held in *Citizen Publishing Co.* v. *United States* that the joint operating agreement violated antitrust law. The decision raised doubt about the legality of each of the twenty-two other agreements then in existence, and sent shock waves through the newspaper business.

Justice William O. Douglas, writing for the Court, found three fatal flaws in the Tucson agreement. Tucson Newspapers' control of advertising and circulation rates amounted to illegal price fixing. Profit pooling, with distribution by formula, also violated antitrust law. So did the restrictions on participation in competing newspapers. That was market control. The Citizen Publishing Co. could defend the arrangement only if it could prove that the *Citizen* not only had been failing at the time of the original agreement in 1940, but that there was no other buyer who might have saved it. Douglas held that the evidence did not support such a conclusion. If the *Citizen* was indeed failing in 1940, why would the publishers of the *Star* be willing to enter into an agreement giving it a fixed share of the profit?

The joint operating agreement could survive, the Court held, only if it was rewritten to permit each newspaper to set its own advertising and circulation rates, to distribute profit in a manner that reflected performance, and to eliminate the restrictions on future employment.

The message in this instance may have been stronger than the Department of Justice intended. The original purpose of the suit had been to make certain that competing editorial operations were preserved in joint ownership cities. The agreements were not to be used as easy vehicles to one ownership. But the effect of the Supreme Court's decision was to make each party to a joint agreement sink or swim on the basis of individual performance. Both could still operate out of the same printing plant, but if advertising and circulation rates were to be set independently, the owners almost certainly would have to separate those vital operations.

Congress, under prodding from some publishers, had anticipated the Supreme Court's decision, and sixteen months after the Tucson decision, President Richard M. Nixon signed the Newspaper Preservation Act into law.[12]

Briefly, that law wiped out the effect of the Supreme Court's decision. With it, Congress gave its approval to the agreements then in existence. It also restored

---

12. Joe Lewels, Jr., "The Newspaper Preservation Act," *Freedom of Information Center Report No. 254,* School of Journalism, University of Missouri at Columbia, January 1971.

the Tucson agreement, except for the section on market control. Future joint operating agreements elsewhere could be entered into only with the approval of the attorney general. In any such proposal, one of the newspapers clearly would have to be failing.

The Newspaper Preservation Act has withstood challenge in the courts.[13] The *Bay Guardian,* a monthly newspaper in San Francisco, attacked the constitutionality of the Act in a suit asking that the joint operating agreement between the *Chronicle* and the *Examiner* be dissolved. Judge Oliver J. Carter of the federal district court in San Francisco held that no constitutional issue was involved. The antitrust laws are an act of Congress, and what Congress does in one era it can modify in another to meet changing conditions. The Newspaper Preservation Act merely grants newspapers an exception from antitrust law under certain narrowly drawn conditions. The agreement in San Francisco met those conditions, Carter held.

However, that did not end the matter. Judge Carter held that the suit could continue on its merits to determine whether the newspapers' advertising and circulation practices violated the Sherman Act. The *Guardian* and its publisher, Bruce Brugmann, were joined by a department store that claimed that the papers' joint advertising rate was so high that it had been forced out of business because it couldn't afford to use the newspapers. The suit was settled out of court with the newspapers' agreement to pay the seventeen plaintiffs $1.35 million.[14]

Thus, while the court held that joint operating agreements do not in themselves violate the antitrust act, the case stands as a reminder that the Newspaper Preservation Act does not immunize the participating newspapers from the workings of antitrust law. If they take advantage of the Act to set rates that harm a competitor, or freeze out potential advertisers, they are vulnerable to an antitrust action.

Los Angeles: One Ownership in Adjacent Markets

Los Angeles has the distinction of pioneering three post-World War II phenomena: the freeway, urban sprawl, and smog. The three are interrelated products of America's love affair with the automobile. Not only has the automobile been an influence on urban patterns, it has had an effect on the daily newspaper.

As the 1960s began, editors and publishers in the nation's major metropolitan areas became aware of a trend with disturbing implications. The population of most central cities was declining, and changing in nature. The population of suburban communities was skyrocketing, sometimes by as much as 100 percent in a decade. Metropolitan areas became decaying cores populated by minorities and the poor, surrounded by affluent suburbs comprised of the mainly white middle and upper classes. Central cities became centers of commerce during the day, but were nearly deserted at night.

---

13. Bay Guardian Co. v. Chronicle Publishing Co., 344 F. Supp. 1155 (N.D.Calif. 1972).
14. Earl W. Wilken, "S.F. Printing Co. Settles Monopoly Suits Out-of-Court," *Editor & Publisher,* 31 May 1975, p. 7.

These changes proved to be especially troubling for afternoon newspapers published in the larger cities. Their old audience—working-class people who lived in neat rows of well-kept dwellings near the city's center—had been dispersed in the suburbs. Delivery trucks had to fight traffic to reach the new suburban communities, many of whose residents no longer had much interest in the news of the central city. They felt themselves part of new communities. Further, publishers of afternoon newspapers found themselves in competition both with fringe-area publications and with the evening news and entertainment on television.

Morning newspapers had fewer distribution problems. Their trucks could move over deserted streets in the early hours of the morning. But they, too, had problems finding the best mix of local, suburban, and regional news to meet the needs of their dispersed audience.

In the early 1960s, some publishers sought to solve their problems by buying newspapers, dailies or weeklies, on the fringes of their circulation areas. They reasoned that by doing so they could offer readers a package: the central-city paper for the big picture, including heavy doses of business and sports news, and the neighborhood daily or weekly for intense coverage of local news. One of the pioneers in this movement was the *Los Angeles Times*.

United States v. Times-Mirror Co., 274 F.Supp. 606 (C.D. Calif. 1967). By 1962, it had become the largest daily newspaper in Southern California, and one of the largest in the nation. It had competition from a Hearst-owned daily in Los Angeles, and from newspapers published in the rapidly growing suburbs, many of which had become cities in their own right. One of the latter in San Bernardino, a city of nearly a million population at the foot of the mountains sixty-five miles east of Los Angeles. For years prior to 1964, James Guthrie owned and published morning and afternoon papers there. In that year, he sold the papers to Norman Chandler, owner of the *Times,* to forestall sale to the Pulitzer family whose liberal political views were objectionable to Guthrie. To Chandler, the purchase made sense. He saw the *Times* as a metropolitan newspaper. It covered Los Angeles, to be sure, but its focus was on the larger picture, starting with California, and going on to include the West as a region, the nation, and the world. The *Times* had a large Washington bureau and, in cooperation with the *Washington Post,* was in the process of establishing more bureaus in foreign countries than any other paper except the *New York Times*. However, it could not begin to cover in detail the many communities in the Los Angeles basin. One of the functions of the San Bernardino papers would be to fill some of the gaps by covering that city and its neighbors. Thus, the three papers would serve complementary functions.

The Justice Department didn't see it that way. What it saw was a first step along the road that would take the *Los Angeles Times* to an even more dominant position than it already held. It filed suit in federal district court in Los Angeles asking that Chandler be ordered to sell the San Bernardino papers. Again, as in Tucson, the government was attacking a publisher's business practices under antitrust law in an effort to preserve competing editorial operations.

The *Times* brought in expert witnesses from universities who supported its view of the complementary nature of the publications. These witnesses argued that not only do newspapers function differently as to the extent of their news coverage, but that in doing so they serve different advertising markets as well. Thus, in the experts' view, the purchase would lead to no diminution in competition and therefore did not violate antitrust law.

The court did not accept that argument. In *United States* v. *Times-Mirror Co.,* Judge Warren J. Ferguson said the antitrust act "directed that the courts must look to the effect and impact of the merger. If its effect is anti-competitive, then there is a violation." The fact was that the merger wiped out a thriving small business and made it a part of the largest newspaper business in the area. As a result of that merger, the *Times*'s share of the weekday circulation in the relevant marketing area rose from 10.6 percent to 54.8. And on Sundays, the rise was from 20.3 percent to 64.3. This, he held, showed a prima facie violation of the Clayton Act.

Judge Ferguson also looked at daily newspaper publication in the entire Los Angeles metropolitan area. In a decade, the number of dailies had risen from fifty-two to sixty-four, but the number of independent ownerships had declined from thirty-three to fourteen. Additionally, one newspaper, the West Coast edition of the *New York Times,* had recently failed.

The divestiture order did not lead to an increase in the number of independent publishers. The San Bernardino papers were bought by the Gannett chain. However, the message was clear: The Justice Department would oppose an attempt by a major metropolitan newspaper to hedge its position by buying newspapers in its own circulation zone, or even on its far reaches. Each metro daily would have to make it on its own. Events were to prove that some, even in such cities as Washington, Philadelphia, Minneapolis, and Cleveland, could not.

Cincinnati: One Ownership in the Same City

Until the middle 1950s, Cincinnati was a three-newspaper city. Scripps-Howard owned the afternoon *Post.* Members of the Scripps family lived in the city. The Taft family, which had produced a president of the United States and a prominent U.S. Senator, owned the afternoon *Times-Star.* The morning and Sunday field was the sole province of the *Enquirer,* owned by the McLean estate and administered by a court in Washington, D.C. Because of that, it seemed ripe for buying by one of the two afternoon owners. To forestall that, employees of the *Enquirer* tried to buy it, but succeeded only in part. Scripps-Howard was able to buy 58 percent of the stock, but was content to operate the paper as a separate entity. When the Tafts lost the bidding battle, they sold the *Times-Star* to Scripps, which merged it with the *Post.* In 1960, when Kennedy was elected, Cincinnati was a one-owner city, although Scripps-Howard chose to exercise no direct control over the *Enquirer* management.

Both papers prospered under the arrangement. Looking to a time when both papers would need new presses, management began secret talks to explore the possibilities of a jointly owned printing plant. The Justice Department intervened in 1964 by filing an antitrust complaint. It asked a federal district court to order Scripps-Howard to sell one of the newspapers.

The government based its lawsuit on the premise that both newspapers were highly profitable, which was indeed true. Justice Department attorneys reasoned that there would be a more vigorous marketplace of ideas in Cincinnati if both newspapers were truly independent in all aspects of their operations. As evidence of the possibility of a monopoly in the field of news and opinion, as well as in the advertising market, the government pointed to the fact that Scripps also owned one of the three commercial television stations in Cincinnati and an associated radio station.

After several years of legal sparring, Scripps chose not to fight the suit. In 1968, it accepted a consent decree and put the *Enquirer* on the market. It was bought by American Financial Corporation, a locally owned holding company with interests in dairy stores, supermarkets, and banking, including ownership of one of the city's major banks. To comply with banking regulations, the new owner was also required to sell. The purchaser was Combined Communications, with headquarters in Phoenix. In 1979, Combined merged with Gannett.

The Marketplace of Ideas Today

With the benefit of nearly thirty years of hindsight, it is evident that the plan conceived by John F. Kennedy and carried forward after his death has failed. The trend toward one-ownership cities and newspaper chains, which he perceived and sought to forestall, has intensified. Whether the marketplace of ideas has been diminished by that trend is subject to debate. A great deal depends upon how one defines the market and identifies the sources of ideas competing for attention.

If one focuses only on daily newspapers, two facts emerge. The number of cities with truly competing daily newspapers is approaching the vanishing point. Further, newspaper groups own more than 70 percent of the nation's 1650 dailies, controlling more than 80 percent of the total daily newspaper circulation.[15]

A review of the present status of the newspapers involved in the antitrust actions examined in the preceding section is suggestive of the larger picture. Both newspapers in Tucson are owned by groups, the morning *Star* by the Pulitzer family, whose primary newspaper property is the *St. Louis Post-Dispatch*. The afternoon *Citizen* is one of Gannett's ninety dailies. The joint operating agreement condemned by the Supreme Court but largely restored by Congress through the Newspaper Preservation Act continues in effect. The *Los Angeles Times*, frustrated in its attempt to buy the San Bernardino papers, owns a substantial group, including the *Baltimore Sun*, the *Hartford Courant*, and *Newsday*, published in New York City's Long Island suburbs. Gannett owns the morning and Sunday *San Bernardino Sun*. Scripps-Howard continues to own the *Cincinnati*

---

15. John C. Busterna, "Trends in Daily Newspaper Ownership," *Journalism Quarterly*, Winter 1988, p. 831 + ; "Groups Still Own Most U.S. Dailies," *Editor & Publisher*, 28 April 1984, p. 76.

Post, but after suffering a decade of financial losses, the paper now is part of a joint operating agreement with the Gannett-owned *Enquirer.*[16]

During the 1980s, Gannett was the most noteworthy newspaper group. Under the leadership of Al Neuharth, it founded a national daily newspaper, *USA Today,* in 1982, which became marginally profitable at the end of the decade with a circulation of more than a million. In the middle years of the decade, the group shed its small-town focus by buying the *Detroit News,* the *Louisville Courier-Journal,* and the *Des Moines Register* to go along with the Cincinnati paper. These purchases helped it pass Knight-Ridder and Newhouse in the number of newspapers published each day, with more than 5 million.[17] For much of the 1980s, Gannett was also the largest group in terms of newspapers owned. But it yielded that position to Thomson Newspapers, a Canadian-British company, which owns about a hundred U.S. dailies. No other of the 132 groups listed by *Editor & Publisher* controls as many as fifty daily newspapers.

As group-owned newspapers have increased in number, cities with competing separate ownerships have decreased. The sixty-one such cities when Kennedy was elected president in 1960 had declined to twenty-eight in 1986, with a majority of them attributable to joint operating groups. The major cities served by only one daily newspaper owner, and in many instances by only one newspaper, include Philadelphia, Miami, Cleveland, Atlanta, St. Louis, Minneapolis, Baltimore, San Diego, Phoenix, and Kansas City. The trend reflects economic realities. Newsprint costs exceed $650 a ton. Reporters and editors are enjoying the highest salaries ever, which may still not be high enough, in light of newsroom turnover.[18] Competition for advertising has limited the extent to which newspapers can increase their rates and hence their revenue. Further, in cities with competing newspapers, advertisers tend to buy space in the paper that reaches the most potential customers. To be No. 2 can mean being left with too little advertising to support a newspaper.

The reality of today is clear. Most cities in the United States have only one daily newspaper. There is less than one chance in three that that newspaper will not be part of a chain.

Joint Operating Agreements Today

When the Newspaper Preservation Act became law in 1970, it gave government approval not only to the joint operating agreement in Tucson, but to others in effect in twenty-one cities. Competing newspapers in the same city would be permitted to enter into such agreements in the future only if one of them was failing, and then only with the approval of the attorney general. The Act's avowed purpose was to preserve competing news and editorial operations in cities then served by two newspaper owners. The Act has not been altogether successful in

---

16. *Editor & Publisher Yearbook 1990.* The yearbook annually publishes data on all U.S. daily newspapers and a listing of newspaper groups with their affiliated newspapers.
17. Busterna, "Trends in Daily Newspaper Circulation."
18. David H. Weaver and G. Cleveland Wilhoit, *The American Journalist* (Bloomington: Indiana University Press, 1986), pp. 99–100.

serving that purpose. Since 1974, when competing publishers in Anchorage, Alaska, became the first to take advantage of the Act, the number of new agreements has been offset by instances in which papers failed despite being parties to such agreements.

After nearly twenty years of experience with the Newspaper Preservation Act, the U.S. Supreme Court was offered its first occasion to rule on its propriety and, in effect, passed up the opportunity. It split, four to four, on an appeal from a U.S. circuit court decision upholding a joint operating agreement between Gannett and Knight-Ridder in Detroit. The Court did not issue an opinion, nor did it disclose how the justices voted, other than to note that Justice Byron R. White had abstained for "personal reasons."[20] The decision ended nearly four years of legal maneuvering and uncertainty starting when Gannett bought the *Detroit News* and entered head-to-head competition with Knight-Ridder's *Free Press*. Both owners held circulation and advertising rates down and promoted heavily, while seeking approval from the government of a joint operating agreement (JOA). The owners ran into strong opposition from Detroit merchants, labor unions, and the mayor of Detroit. During lengthy administrative hearings, followed by an appeal to the courts, Knight-Ridder's board of directors voted to close the *Free Press* if the JOA was not granted. The firm's losses were said to be $44,000 a day, despite circulation of 629,000.

Although both an administrative law judge and the Justice Department's antitrust department recommended disapproval of the JOA, former Attorney General Edwin Meese III overruled them on his last day in office. He said the *Free Press* was likely to close, even though it had not entered the "downward spiral" of circulation and advertising losses cited by the Newspaper Preservation Act as signs of a failing newspaper. Opponents of the JOA appealed to the courts, arguing that Meese exceeded his authority in overriding his own department and what they saw as the intent of Congress in drafting the law. The court of appeals for the District of Columbia Circuit ruled five to four that Meese acted properly. The Supreme Court's split vote let that decision stand.

The JOA went into effect early in 1990. The participants were expecting to effect production savings, coupled with increases in advertising and circulation rates, that would convert losses for both owners into the sharing of up to $100 million a year in profits.

The court's approval of the union in Detroit was followed by requests from publishers for approval of JOAs in York, Pennsylvania, and Las Vegas, Nevada.[21] A year later, E. W. Scripps Co. announced that it was paying Persis Corp. $40 million to end their JOA in Knoxville, Tennessee.

Of the several newspapers that have failed despite joint operating agreements, two of the most notable are the *St. Louis Globe-Democrat,* owned by the Newhouse group, and the *Miami News,* owned by Cox Enterprises. Newhouse announced in 1983 that continued heavy losses forced the closing of its St. Louis

---

20. George Garneau, "JOA OK'd," *Editor & Publisher,* 18 November 1989, p. 9 + .
21. George Garneau, "Why a JOA in York, Pa.?" *Editor & Publisher,* 15 July 1989; Jill Bettner, "Two Daily Papers in Las Vegas, Nev., Apply for Merger," *Wall Street Journal,* 9 August 1989.

The *Miami News* was one of several large-city afternoon daily newspapers that lost readers and advertising to a competing morning daily. In 1988, its owners, Cox Enterprises, announced it was for sale. When no buyer was found, the paper closed at the end of the year. (Maurice Cohn Band/The Miami Herald

paper. Another owner bought the paper but ceased publication in 1986, ending 133 years of *Globe-Democrat* publication. At the end of 1988, Cox Enterprises closed the *Miami News,* ending twenty-two years of publication under a joint operating agreement with Knight-Ridder, publisher of the *Miami Herald.*[22] Cox said the *News* would lose $9 million in 1988 despite the JOA. The newspaper's circulation was about 48,000.

As these episodes suggest, joint operating agreements are not a guarantee of profitable operation. At the best, they give two owners who are willing to work at it an opportunity to coexist as competing news operations and survive as business entities. Their continued existence in twenty or so cities serves as evidence that some publishers are willing to give it a try.

This chapter's focus on the problem areas of the business of journalism may contribute to an overly gloomy assessment of the future of newspapers. The problems are a product of changes in the nature of the newspaper business. Despite the notable failures of some once-powerful dailies in the nation's major cities, the number of daily newspapers remained constant over several decades at about 1750, before

22.   Martha Brannigan, "Cox to Close the *Miami News* at Year End," *Wall Street Journal,* 17 October 1988.

dropping to about 1650 in 1986.[23] Closings in the larger cities have been balanced by startups of suburban dailies and by an increase in Sunday newspapers. Suburban weeklies, many of them devoted almost exclusively to advertising, have proliferated.

One investment analyst looked back on the decade of the 1980s and called it "the best of times" for investors in publishing stocks.[24] An index measuring the performance of seventeen publicly traded newspaper companies advanced by 465 percent during that decade. In comparison, the Dow Jones Industrial Average, which measures the performance of thirty blue-chip stocks, advanced 241 percent. The top performer was the Washington Post Co. Its stock was ten times as valuable at the end of 1989 as it was in 1980, reflecting an increase in earnings from $2.44 a share to $14.31. In addition to its flagship newspaper, the Post owns a newspaper in Everett, Washington, and is part-owner of the *International Herald-Tribune,* published in Paris. The firm also owns *Newsweek,* four television stations, and more than fifty cable television systems serving 400,000 subscribers.

Several factors contributed to the profitability of newspapers in the 1980s. Advertising expenditures increased steadily, with newspapers holding their own in fierce competition with other media. Electronic composition and pagination greatly decreased composing room costs. New presses gave newspapers the ability to print high-quality color, rivaling that found in magazines. Computer-generated graphics gave editors a new dimension in which to present information. Condensation, sparked on one side by higher paper costs and on the other by marketing surveys, permits newspapers to offer readers more news and information in concise form than in earlier years.

However, as the decade of the 1990s began, profound changes in the nature of retailing, long the advertising mainstay of daily newspapers, led to a severe drop in revenue. In the first quarter of 1990, some publishers reported revenue declines of more than 10 percent.[25]

Joint Ownership of Newspaper and Broadcasting Stations

In the early days of broadcasting, many newspapers established radio stations and used them for promotion and as an additional outlet for news. In time, these stations became profitable in their own right, and many of the newspaper-owned broadcasters became pioneers in television. By the mid-1970s, there were 176 newspaper-radio combinations and eighty-three newspaper-television combinations.

In 1974, the Justice Department, again acting out of concern for the marketplace of ideas, asked the Federal Communications Commission to refuse to renew broadcasting licenses owned by newspapers in St. Louis and Des Moines.[26] Later, the request was expanded to include newspaper-broadcast combinations

---

23. Busterna, "Trends in Daily Newspaper Ownership."
24. Neil Nordby, president of Nordby International, "What a Decade!" *Editor & Publisher,* 10 March 1990, p. 7 + .
25. George Garneau, "Double-digit Declines," *Editor & Publisher,* 12 May 1990, p. 14 + .
26. "Justice Agency Urges FCC to Deny Licenses to 6 Stations It Says Are Newspaper Owned," *Wall Street Journal,* 4 January 1974.

Newspapers increasingly are using graphic devices both to present information in an easy-to-grasp form and to attract younger readers. This sampling, taken from *The New York Times, The Wall Street Journal,* and *USA Today,* ranges from graphs showing stock-price trends to a fanciful portrayal of forces affecting the nation's weather.

in Milwaukee and Salt Lake City. It chose to act through the FCC rather than go to court because Justice Department attorneys believed they would have an easier time proving that such combinations were not in the public interest than they would have proving violation of antitrust law. The FCC rejected Justice's request, but moved forward with its own study of the cross-ownership of newspapers and broadcasting stations in the same community.[27]

---

27. "Broadcast Licenses Renewed in Rebuff to Justice Agency," *Wall Street Journal,* 25 October 1976.

That study had begun in 1970,[28] and was to occupy the FCC and the courts for eight years, leading to a decision by the Supreme Court. By the mid-1970s, the FCC had agreed on the main thrust of a proposal: No newspaper would be permitted to start a new broadcasting station, or buy the license of an existing station, in its own community. All of the then existing cross-ownerships would have to be terminated within five years. This provoked a storm of protest that led to additional hearings. In the end, the FCC decided that diversity was not the only interest to be served. Some newspaper-broadcasting station combinations were doing a particularly good job of serving the public interest. In most instances the combinations had to meet vigorous competition from other broadcasting stations. When the proposal took final form in 1975, it still forbade future newspaper acquisitions in the same city. But the divestiture provision was limited to cities in which the only daily newspaper also owned the only broadcasting station delivering a clear signal to the community. The FCC identified only eighteen such communities, eight involving television stations. After further hearings, it ordered divestiture in sixteen.[29]

Federal Communications Commission v. National Citizens Committee for Broadcasting, 436 U.S. 775, 98 S.Ct. 2096, 56 L.Ed.2d 697 (1978).

That order came under fire from two directions. The stations involved, backed by organizations of broadcasters and publishers, thought it went too far. A consumer advocate group, the National Citizens Committee for Broadcasting, didn't think it went far enough. Neither did the Justice Department, which also intervened. If diversity of ownership was essential to a robust marketplace of ideas, as the FCC recognized in principle, then that principle ought to be carried as far as practicable. Both sides went to the Court of Appeals for the District of Columbia Circuit, which found for the Citizens Committee. Under its ruling, no newspaper-broadcasting combination could stand unless the owner could prove that it qualified for exemption under rules laid down by the FCC. The FCC joined the losing owners in going to the Supreme Court. Ruling in *FCC* v. *National Citizens Committee for Broadcasting,* the Court upheld the rule against future acquisitions, but reversed the appeals court on divestiture.

Justice Thurgood Marshall, writing for the unanimous Court, held that the FCC had acted reasonably and within its powers in concluding that forced divestiture carried too far might actually result in a weakening of the marketplace of ideas. Surviving newspapers, or surviving broadcasting stations, might in some instances be too weak economically to provide truly independent voices. One or both might no longer be able to afford a vigorous news and public affairs staff. Given the realities of broadcast and newspaper ownership patterns, a strong independent local owner might be replaced by an outside chain owner. The Court, then, concluded that the FCC had acted rationally in limiting its divestiture order to sixteen cities.

---

28. Further Notice of Proposed Rule Making (Docket No. 18110), 22 F.C.C.2d 339 (1970).
29. Second Report and Order, as amended upon reconsideration, 53 F.C.C.2d 589 (1975), 47 CFR, §§73.35, 73.240, 73.636 (1976).

The rules upheld by the Court authorized the FCC to grant waivers to permit joint ownership of broadcasting and newspaper properties in the same city to avoid the weakening of the marketplace cited in Marshall's opinion. The FCC granted such a waiver to permit Rupert Murdoch's News America Publishing company to buy the *New York Post* and to continue his ownership of the *Boston Herald*. He also owned television stations in both cities. In the closing hours of its 1987 session, Congress sought to write into law both a ban on joint ownership and repeal of the FCC's authority to grant waivers. Its effect would have been to force an immediate sale of one of Murdoch's media properties in each city.

Three months later, the U.S. Court of Appeals, District of Columbia Circuit, held that the provision violated both the freedom-of-the-press clause of the First Amendment and the due process clause of the Fifth Amendment.[30] Nevertheless, by midsummer, Murdoch had sold the money-losing *New York Post* to real estate developer Peter S. Kalikow for $37 million and had agreed to put up for sale Boston television station WFXT, valued at $35 million. Murdoch thus was able to retain television station WNYW-TV in New York and the *Boston Herald*.

THE DISTRIBUTION OF NEWS AND OPINION

The Supreme Court has drawn a fine line between the door-to-door sales of goods or services, including magazine subscriptions, and the door-to-door dissemination of ideas. Local governments may regulate and even prohibit the former. They cannot prevent the latter, even when some people find the ideas obnoxious or when the ideas are printed in pamphlet form and sold. As a result of the Supreme Court decisions, newspapers are one of the few products that have a constitutional right to be sold in public places.

Ironically, this right was not won through the efforts of newspaper publishers. Rather, it was defined in a series of cases carried to the Supreme Court in the 1930s and 1940s by a small religious group, the Jehovah's Witnesses. Because of their beliefs and their methods of spreading them, the Witnesses were the subject of persecution and legal discrimination prior to and during World War II.[31] Witnesses sought converts by distributing pamphlets and other church publications on city streets and door to door. Because the Witnesses' message angered some people, and others considered their methods of solicitation a nuisance, many communities adopted ordinances prohibiting distribution of handbills or licensing door-to-door solicitors. The Witnesses attacked these ordinances in the courts, eventually winning a remarkable series of Supreme Court decisions. Rights won by the Witnesses in those cases are enjoyed today by every person or group seeking support for a cause and by publishers seeking to distribute newspapers.

---

30. Bob Davis, "Murdoch Wins Ruling on Law Barring FCC Extensions on Ownership Rule," *Wall Street Journal,* 30 March 1988.
31. David R. Manwaring, *Render Unto Caesar* (Chicago: University of Chicago Press, 1962), pp. 163–86.

One of the more notable Jehovah's Witnesses cases, *Lovell* v. *City of Griffith, Georgia,*[32] is described in chapter 2, where it illustrates a form of prior restraint. In that decision, the Court also dealt with the right to disseminate ideas, holding: "Liberty of circulating is as essential to that freedom as liberty of publishing; indeed, without the circulation, the publication would have little value."

Later decisions involving Jehovah's Witnesses, labor unions, civil rights advocates, and political demonstrators have established a firm principle of First Amendment law: Government may impose reasonable restrictions of time, place, and manner on the dissemination of ideas on the streets and sidewalks, in public parks, and in other public places, but it cannot forbid such use. To do so is an unacceptable prior restraint.

In recent years that principle has been tested anew by attempts to regulate and license the placement of coin-operated newspaper vending machines. Such machines, commonly called newsracks, have been in use for many years, but they did not attract much attention until the advent of Gannett's *USA Today* in 1982. Planned from the start as a national newspaper designed for people on the go, it was distributed through vending machines placed in airports, commuter bus and train stops, and other public places. Publishers of other newspapers reacted by placing their own vending machines in the same places, if they were not there already. In some instances, local governments removed the machines or attempted to regulate or tax them. When Gannett and the *Miami Herald* challenged early attempts to both regulate and tax newsracks, U.S. courts of appeal in the Second and Eleventh Circuits agreed that the right to place the vending machines on public property is protected by the First Amendment. But they differed as to how far that protection goes.

The Second Circuit held that Gannett would have to pay a licensing fee to place its racks in the New York Metropolitan Transportation Authority's commuter railroad stations.[33] The court reasoned that the New York legislature had established MTA with the expectation that it would operate at a profit. Therefore, the authority could charge for the use of its property as any other property owner could. If Gannett objected, it could place its racks outside the stations. In pure *dicta,* the court noted that if the MTA was acting as an arm of government, it could not impose a license fee except to cover the expenses directly associated with its regulation of the racks.

The Eleventh Circuit's decision involved a licensing fee imposed by the city of Hallandale on newsracks placed on its sidewalks.[34] Under challenge by the *Miami Herald,* a federal district court held that the fee was an unconstitutional tax on the dissemination of ideas. The city appealed, leading to a ruling by the circuit court that the *Herald* had taken its case to the wrong forum. Because the city's fee had been imposed under authority granted by the state, the fee could be challenged only in state courts. However, the circuit court also held that because the law gave city officials arbitrary authority to remove the racks for reasons that

---

32. 305 U.S. 444, 58 S.Ct. 666, 82 L.Ed. 949 (1938).
33. Gannett Satellite Information Network v. Metropolitan Transportation Authority, 745 F.2d 767 (2d Cir. 1984).
34. Miami Herald Publishing Co. v. City of Hallandale, 734 F.2d 666 (11th Cir. 1984).

were not clearly defined by law, the law was void under the standards the Supreme Court established in *Lovell.*

Those decisions, with their "yes, but" approach to the First Amendment protection of newsracks, have proved to be representative of what has happened in the courts since 1984. Five years later, *Editor & Publisher,* the trade magazine of the newspaper business, commented, "Suits over the use of newspaper vending machines are proliferating and producing a mixed-up body of law."[35] The editorial traced the confusion to the Supreme Court's decision in *City of Lakewood* v. *Plain Dealer Publishing Co.,* which struck down an ordinance giving the city's mayor broad authority to forbid the placing of newsracks on public property. But the decision did not deal clearly with the question of how far local governments can go in regulating the placement of such racks. Ironically, when the Court agreed in March 1987 to hear the case, some publishers anticipated a holding that newsracks are protected by the First Amendment. What they got was an ambiguous and vague opinion that has left even the parties to the case wondering what the Court meant and who, if anyone, won.[36] Further, a minority of the Court stated flatly that the decision leaves cities free to ban newsracks from public property if they see fit. The four justices on the prevailing side called the reasoning supporting that conclusion "little more than legal sleight-of-hand" but did not say that the racks could not be banned. The decision is further clouded by the refusal of two justices to take part in it, which, with the resulting near-even split, resulted in an opinion that did not muster the five votes needed to establish a precedent.

***City of Lakewood* v. *Plain Dealer Publishing Co.,* 486 U.S. 750, 108 S.Ct. 2138, 100 L.Ed.2d 771 (1988).**

What the Court seemed to decide is reasonably clear. It affirmed a decision of the Sixth U.S. Circuit Court of Appeals holding that a statute giving the mayor of Lakewood unbridled discretion over whether to permit newsracks on city property was unconstitutional. The Court remanded the case to the circuit court for further proceedings to determine whether some parts of Lakewood's newsrack ordinance could be saved. Nothing more has happened. Lakewood adopted a revised newsrack ordinance before the Supreme Court heard the case, the city's law director said.

The reasoning supporting the decision deals more with procedures than with substance. In writing the Court's opinion, Justice William J. Brennan, Jr., skirted the question as to whether the First Amendment gives newspaper publishers a right to place newsracks on municipal property. Brennan did so by devoting most of his attention to the broader issue of the newspaper's right to challenge an ordinance with which it had made no attempt to comply. Beginning with the Jehovah's Witnesses cases in the 1930s, the Court has developed the doctrine that "when a licensing statute vests unbridled discretion in a government official over whether to permit or deny expressive activity, one who is subject to the law may challenge it facially without the necessity of first applying for, and being denied, a license." Brennan wrote that the "expressive activity" at peril in this

---

35. "Vending Machines," *Editor & Publisher,* 29 July 1989, p. 6.
36. Author's interviews with lawyers for both parties to the case.

case was "the circulation of newspapers, which is constitutionally protected." Working backward from that principle, Brennan held that an ordinance regulating the placement of newsracks has "a close enough nexus to expression, or to conduct commonly associated with expression, to pose a real and substantial threat" of censorship.

That threat, he said, came from language in the ordinance giving the mayor authority to grant or deny applications for annual newsrack permits. If the mayor were to deny a permit, he had to justify his decision in writing. His refusal could be appealed to the city council and from it to the courts. If a mayor were to grant a permit, the design of the newspaper rack would have to be approved by the Lakewood Architectural Board of Review before it could be installed. The rack's owner also would have to hold the city free from any liability resulting from its placement and would have to provide at least $100,000 in insurance. The ordinance also said the owner would have to comply with any "other terms and conditions deemed necessary and reasonable by the Mayor." It was those portions of the ordinance that the Sixth Circuit found objectionable on the grounds of vagueness. The Supreme Court plurality condemned those portions for the same reason, holding that nothing in the ordinance would require the mayor to do any more than hold that a request for a newsrack permit was not in the public interest. As Brennan saw it, this could be a mask hiding a mayor's decision to reject a permit because she or he didn't like the newspaper's policies. Because a permit would have to be renewed annually, a publisher might blunt coverage of the mayor rather than risk losing the right to place newsracks.

Justice Byron R. White wrote a sharply worded dissent. He saw the majority's position as "without precedent" and therefore as an "unwarranted expansion" of a doctrine "developed cautiously by this Court over the past fifty years."

White said Brennan's opinion was so written as to leave cities free, if they choose, to ban newsracks on public property, a position with which White agreed. He wrote:

> The Court quite properly does *not* establish any constitutional right of newspaper publishers to place newsracks on municipal property. The Court expressly declines to "pass" on the question of the constitutionality of an outright ban on newsracks....[O]ur precedents suggest that an outright ban on newsracks on city sidewalks would be constitutional, particularly where (as is true here) ample alternate means of 24-hour distribution of newspapers exist. In any event, the Court's ruling today cannot be read as any indication to the contrary: cities remain free after today's decision to enact such bans.
>
> Moreover, the Court expressly rejects the view, heretofore adopted by some lower courts, that any local scheme that seeks to license the placement of newsracks on public property is *per se* unconstitutional....It is only common sense that cities be allowed to exert some control over those who would permanently appropriate city property for the purpose of erecting a newspaper dispensing device.

Those two paragraphs set the tone for the 13 pages that followed. In the minority's view, newsracks are privately owned structures designed to sell a publisher's product. Cities may permit them to be placed on public property if they see fit but cannot be compelled to accept them. And although the First Amendment does protect the right to distribute newspapers, "the Plain Dealer's right to distribute its newspapers does not encompass the right to take city property—a part of the *public* forum—..., and appropriate it for its own exclusive use, on a semi-permanent basis, by means of the erection of a news box."

Lower courts seeking to apply whatever guidance they find in *Lakewood* are generally agreed that the right to distribute newspapers by whatever means is protected by the First Amendment. They also are holding that the right is subject to reasonable, content-neutral, time, place, and manner restrictions. What is reasonable seems to vary from court to court. A U.S. district court in New Jersey held that the Port Authority of New York and New Jersey could ban newspaper vending boxes from Newark International Airport.[37] The court upheld the authority's argument that the ban was necessary to ensure public safety, to permit the free flow of pedestrian traffic, and to protect the revenue of airport newsstands, which pay the authority a percentage of their sales. Gannett also lost a challenge to an ordinance regulating the placement of its vending machines on public sidewalks in Pennsauken, New Jersey.[38] However, the *Chicago Tribune* was able to prevent the city of Chicago and an airline from removing or relocating its vending boxes in an airport passenger concourse. The airline argued that the boxes would take revenue from its rent-paying concession stands and were a security threat.[39] And in Arizona, a federal district court judge awarded Phoenix Newspapers $66,000 in legal fees after it won the right to place its vending machines in the Tucson airport. The court said the airport authority's attempt to regulate and charge rent for placement of the machines violated the First Amendment.[40]

TAXATION OF THE MEDIA

As two of the cases above illustrate, one of the critical issues in newsrack regulation is the point at which a fee imposed to cover the cost of regulating a business becomes a tax on the distribution of ideas. The Supreme Court has held that the news media, as businesses, can be taxed as other businesses are taxed. But it also has held that any tax that singles out the media for special treatment, favorable or unfavorable, violates the First Amendment guarantee of freedom of the press.

Grosjean v. *American Press Co., 297 U.S. 233, 56 S.Ct. 444, 80 L.Ed. 660 (1936).*

In its earliest media tax case, *Grosjean* v. *American Press Co.,* the Supreme Court struck down a tax that was clearly designed to punish daily newspapers whose editorials opposed a state governor's rise to power. The governor,

---

37. Gannett Satellite Information Network v. Berger, 716 F.Supp. 140, (D.N.J. 1989).
38. Gannett Satellite Information Network v. Township of Pennsauken, 709 F.Supp. 530 (D.N.J. 1989).
39. Chicago Tribune Co. v. City of Chicago, 705 F. Supp. 1345 (N.D.Ill. 1989).
40. "Phoenix Dailies Win Legal Fees from Tucson Airport," *Editor & Publisher,* 17 June 1989, p. 4.

Huey P. Long, was one of the most flamboyant political figures of this century. In the 1920s, he established a political machine in Louisiana that permitted members of his family to rule that state for more than forty years. Long went on to become a U.S. senator and an aspirant for the presidency. His career was cut short by an assassin in 1935.

In 1934, at Long's request, the Louisiana legislature enacted what appeared to be a general tax law. It imposed a 2 percent levy on the gross receipts of newspapers, magazines, periodicals, or books having a circulation within the state of more than 20,000 copies a week. In actuality, the tax applied to only nine publishers of thirteen daily newspapers, all of whom had editorialized against Long's regime. The publishers promptly asked a federal district court to declare the tax void as a violation of the First Amendment. When it did so, the state appealed to the U.S. Supreme Court, which affirmed unanimously.

Justice George Sutherland, whose writing style usually could be described as dull, wrote an eloquent essay on the meaning of freedom of the press. He went back to Milton and examined the history of attempts to control the press. One such method was through taxation. In some instances, the British sovereign used the threat of taxation to bring publishers into line. If that failed, taxes could be imposed at such a level as to drive them out of business. The American Revolution, Sutherland recalled, was in part a protest against the Stamp Tax, which had newspapers and pamphlets among its targets. Such taxes, he wrote, properly were called "taxes on knowledge," explaining:

> That the taxes had, and were intended to have, the effect of curtailing the circulation of newspapers, and particularly the cheaper ones whose readers were generally found among the masses of the people, went almost without question, even on the part of those who defended the act.
> ...[T]he dominant and controlling aim was to prevent, or curtail the opportunity for, the acquisition of knowledge by the people in respect of their governmental affairs.

This tax was no different. Its purpose clearly was not to raise revenue as much as it was to punish Long's political opponents. It could be as vicious as direct censorship in diminishing the flow of vital information to the people. Therefore, the Court held, it was unconstitutional. But that did not end the matter:

> It is not intended by anything we have said to suggest that the owners of newspapers are immune from any of the ordinary forms of taxation for support of the government. But this is not an ordinary form of tax, but one single in kind, with a long history of hostile misuse against the freedom of the press.
> ...The newspapers, magazines, and other journals of the country, it is safe to say, have shed, and continue to shed, more light on the public and business affairs of the nation than any other instrumentality of publicity; and since informed public opinion is the most potent of all restraints upon misgovernment, the suppression or abridgment of the publicity afforded by a free press cannot be regarded otherwise than with grave concern. The tax here is bad not because it takes money from the pockets of appellees. If that were all, a wholly different question would be presented. It is bad because, in the light of its history and of its present setting, it is seen

as a deliberate and calculated device in the guise of a tax to limit the circulation of information to which the public is entitled.... A free press stands as one of the great interpreters between the government and the people. To allow it to be fettered is to fetter ourselves.

Those last two sentences should be engraved in the minds of every American. The First Amendment, Sutherland was saying, is not a special privilege for those whom fortune has placed in journalism. Journalists are protected because they are the only independent interpreters of what those in government do for us or to us.

Nearly fifty years after the *Grosjean* decision, the Supreme Court again rejected an attempt to impose a special tax on publications. This tax was not prompted by political vindictiveness, but by the state of Minnesota's need for revenue, tempered by special treatment for newspapers. In 1967, it adopted a retail sales tax on most items, but excluded newspapers. To protect the sales tax, it imposed a use tax on items bought outside the state but consumed in Minnesota. In 1971, the legislature amended the use tax to include the cost of paper and ink used in publication. No other items used in the manufacture of a retail product were subject to the tax. In 1974, the law was further amended to exclude the first $100,000 worth of paper and ink consumed by a publication in any calendar year. The effect was to exclude all but eleven publishers who produced 14 of the 388 paid-circulation newspapers in the state. Two-thirds of the revenue produced by the tax was paid by the Minneapolis Star and Tribune Co.

Minneapolis Star and Tribune Co. v. *Minnesota Commissioner of Revenue,* 460 U.S. 575, 103 S.Ct. 1365, 75 L.Ed.2d 295, (1983).

The newspaper company challenged the tax in the state courts and lost. Arguing that it was the victim of a special tax much like that in *Grosjean,* it carried an appeal to the Supreme Court. In *Minneapolis Star and Tribune Co.* v. *Minnesota Commissioner of Revenue,* the Court held in 1983 that although the comparison was not controlling, the use tax nevertheless violated the First Amendment. Justice Sandra Day O'Connor, writing for seven members of the Court, said the tax would have been proper had it been applied evenly to all kinds of business firms. But this one was not, failing the test of even-handedness in two important respects:

1. "It imposes a use tax that does not serve the function of protecting the sales tax."

2. "It taxes an intermediate transaction rather than the ultimate retail sale."

When the press is singled out for special taxation, Justice O'Connor continued, the state must prove that it has an overriding governmental interest for doing so. The power to tax is a "powerful weapon" that can weaken or cripple a target that stands by itself. But when all are treated equally, the realities of politics serve to restrain the hand of the tax collector.

Minnesota said it had imposed the tax not to harm the press but to raise needed revenue. But that reason, standing alone, was not enough, O'Connor said. The same amount of revenue could have been raised by a slight increase in a levy applying to all business firms. Or, she suggested, the revenue could have been raised by applying the sales tax to the price of newspapers. The state further argued that the use tax gave the press favored treatment, imposing levies on it at a lower rate than those paid by other businesses. That made no difference, the Court held. The point was that the press was given differential treatment. This point was highlighted by the fact that even within the press, most publishers paid no tax, while a few carried most of the burden. O'Connor concluded:

> Whatever the motive of the legislature in this case, we think that recognizing a power in the State not only to single out the press but also to tailor the tax so that it singles out a few members of the press presents such a potential for abuse that no interest suggested by Minnesota can justify the scheme.

In a later decision, the Supreme Court struck down the Arkansas sales tax as it applied to general interest monthly magazines.[41] Numerous items were exempt from the 4 percent levy, including newspapers, and religious, professional, trade, and sports journals, but not general interest magazines. One such magazine, *Arkansas Times,* asked to be exempted on the grounds that it published occasional articles on religion and sports. The Commissioner of Revenue refused the request and was upheld by state courts. The U.S. Supreme Court agreed to review the request and reversed the state courts. Relying heavily on the rationale of *Minneapolis Star & Tribune,* the Court said the tax was unconstitutional because it treated some magazines less favorably than others. The discrimination was "particularly repugnant to First Amendment principles," the Court said, because "a magazine's tax status depends entirely on its *content.*"

The following year, relying on the Establishment Clause of the First Amendment rather than on the Free Press Clause, the Supreme Court struck down a Texas law exempting religious periodicals from the state's sales tax.[42] The Court's majority held that the effect of the exemption was to subsidize certain publications solely because they served a religious purpose. The Court said that "there is no bar to Texas' imposing a general sales tax on religious publications." In effect, the decision gave the state the option of doing that or removing the sales tax from all other publications.

This chapter has reminded us that news and opinion media are like people with split personalities. In one part of their being, they are privileged vehicles for the dissemination of news and opinion, protected by the First Amendment. We have seen earlier that that protection is quite strong. The media are free to criticize government and government officials in the strongest terms, even to the point of calling for their overthrow. Nor is the First Amendment's protection limited to publications that are true, fair, or dedicated to a noble purpose. Freedom of the press protects some falsehoods lest strict insistence on truth dampen debate on public issues. The Supreme Court has said repeatedly that the First Amendment protects both fair and unfair opinion. The media are protected even though they

---

41. Arkansas Writers' Project v. Ragland, 481 U.S. 221, 107 S.Ct. 1722, 95 L.Ed.2d 209 (1987).
42. Texas Monthly v. Bullock, _ _ _ U.S. _ _ _, 109 S.Ct. 890, 103 L.Ed.2d 1 (1989).

choose to deal in what many members of society consider trash. This includes portrayals of sexual activity up to the point at which the portrayal is found obscence, of violence, and of ideas many members of society consider to be repugnant. Even advertising, long considered beyond the reach of the First Amendment, now is protected unless it is false or seeks buyers for an illegal product. In short, because of the First Amendment, the content of the media is almost beyond regulation except by the forces of the marketplace.

But in the other part of their being, media are subject to regulation, not only by the marketplace but by government. Whatever product they offer the public, the media are business organizations. They must take in enough money from customers and advertisers to cover their costs or go out of business. Obviously, many media organizations not only cover their costs but make a comfortable margin of profit. Some media organizations have become giant conglomerates with revenues from circulation, advertising, and the sale of products running into billions of dollars a year. Annual profits of 15 to 20 percent on investment are not uncommon.

Therefore it is not surprising that courts have held that in their business operations the media are to be treated like anyone else. More than forty years ago, in the *Associated Press* case, the Supreme Court held that the First Amendment does not protect the news media from laws regulating their business aspects. In that instance, the Court held that member publishers could not treat the Associated Press news service like a private club. Their attempt to deny the service's news report to publishers who were in competition with them violated antitrust law. In the *Lorain Journal* case, the Court expanded on that principle, holding that a newspaper violated the law when it used its power as a dominant medium to discourage advertisers from buying time on a competing radio station. More recently, the Supreme Court held in the *Tucson* case that it also violates antitrust law if one publisher buys a competing newspaper, unless one or the other is clearly failing. However, passage of the Newspaper Preservation Act now makes it possible for competing publishers to combine some of their operations if that is required to ensure continued publication of two newspapers. Such arrangements, called joint operating agreements, are in effect in about twenty cities.

However, even in their business aspects, the media are not without First Amendment protection. In two sensitive areas, circulation and taxation, the Supreme Court has limited the power of government. Through the efforts of a religious group, Jehovah's Witnesses, the Supreme Court has said that people have a right to disseminate ideas in public places. In modern times, this has led to decisions holding that the First Amendment protects the right to place newsracks in public places. These may be subjected to reasonable regulations designed to protect the rights of others to use the streets and sidewalks safely. The degree to which a fee may be imposed on newsracks is an open question, with most courts holding that it can be no higher than what is needed to cover the incidental costs ensuring that the regulations are complied with.

The Supreme Court has held that a discriminatory tax imposed on media of news and opinion violates the First Amendment. It makes no difference that the tax could be construed as treating newspapers more leniently than other kinds of business. The Court said that if it were to recognize a right to tax the media in ways not applied to other kinds of business, it would open the door for government to use the power to tax to influence or destroy its media critics. That, said Justice Sutherland in *Grosjean,* would restore the licensing power condemned by John Milton in *Areopagitica.*

In the Professional World

In the 1960s, President John F. Kennedy became concerned about what he saw as the disappearance of the marketplace of ideas. In part, his concern was political. Few newspapers had supported him editorially in his campaign for the presidency in 1960. He also knew that no Democratic presidential candidate, not even Franklin D. Roosevelt in the midst of World War II, had ever won much backing from newspaper publishers. But Kennedy also noted a steady decline in the number of cities with two truly competing daily newspapers and a growth in newspaper chains. And so he embarked on what has proved to be a losing battle to encourage competing, independent newspapers. Today, only a handful of cities support two newspapers, and more than two-thirds of all newspapers are part of a chain.

With the benefit of hindsight, it can be seen that President Kennedy's view of the marketplace of ideas was too narrow. The approximately 1650 daily newspapers are only a small part of the marketplace in which media, print and electronic, scramble for an audience and for advertising revenue. Daily newspapers are outnumbered by far by the 12,000 radio and television stations on the air. Further, studies consistently show that more people say they depend on television than on newspapers for news. Dailies also are outnumbered three-to-one by weekly newspapers, which have enjoyed their greatest growth in the suburbs around major cities. However, the belief on which Kennedy acted in planning a series of antitrust actions aimed at newspapers—that the publisher in a one-newspaper town is a monopolist—persists.

It is for that reason that publishers of daily newspapers, no matter what the size of their market, operate with constant awareness of antitrust implications flowing from their decisions. Failure to do so can lead to the expense of fighting an antitrust action. In recent years, publishers have come under attack because competitors concluded that their advertising rates were too low. Advertisers have attacked others for rates they believed to be too high. Publishers must take care if they decide to publish a weekly advertising supplement to be circulated free to some segment of their audience, or even if they establish zoned editions in which advertising is offered at a discount. Publishers also have encountered antitrust problems when they attempted to change from juvenile to adult carriers and vice versa, or to insist that carriers sell the paper for the price set by the publisher.

Nor is entanglement in the antitrust thicket confined to newspaper publishers. Cable television franchising arrangements and decisions by cable operators to carry some stations, but not others, have led to antitrust actions.

Thus, in the professional world there is a vigorous marketplace—for ideas and entertainment, to be sure, but especially for advertising. And, judging from a survey of the cases, that marketplace contains many operators who are on the alert for practices that seem to give others an unfair competitive advantage.

The competition for advertising is linked to equally intense competition for the audience. All media use market surveys to determine not only the nature of their particular audience, but to probe the likes and dislikes, the varied interests, and the spending habits of the audience as a whole. Television programs literally live or die by the Nielsen Ratings. Newspapers are moving toward shorter stories, and more of them, and to greater use of graphics and color in response to marketing surveys. Some have developed whole sections—on recreation, dining out, places to go, sports, and business—to meet the needs of particular segments of the audience. Some editors feel uncomfortable with the marketing approach to news content, arguing that it is a form of pandering. Most have accepted it, concluding that if some adjustments in content can ensure a financially secure newspaper they can afford to give the audience what they think it needs along with what the audience says it wants.

With newspapers, the competition for an audience has affected circulation methods, too. Traditionally, most dailies, particularly those outside the major metropolitan areas, have sold 95 percent of their copies by subscription. Newspaper readers were believed to be daily readers. However, the same marketing surveys that probed reader interest in content also led to the discovery that a considerable part of the potential audience neither reads nor wants to read a newspaper every day. Many people want to be able to buy a newspaper whenever they feel like it. That discovery, coupled with the rise of national and regional newspapers, has led to the proliferation of newsracks. In many cities with only one daily newspaper it is not unusual for shoppers to confront batteries of racks offering the local paper, *USA Today,* the national edition of the *New York Times,* the *Wall Street Journal,* and three or four regional newspapers. This is evidence that single-copy sales have become important to all publishers. It is for that reason that publishers challenge attempts to license racks or unduly restrict their placement. However, litigation usually is a last resort. Negotiation, coupled with a reminder that newspaper distribution is a protected First Amendment activity, is the preferred course. Lawyers advise publishers to cooperate with any reasonable regulations and to respond quickly and positively to complaints about service or potential hazards.

FOR REVIEW

1. Three principles applied by the Supreme Court in the *Indiana Farmer's Guide* and *Associated Press* cases have made virtually all media subject to antitrust law. What are those principles and what is their meaning?

2. Is it true to say that a commercial newspaper can refuse advertising in all circumstances? Why or why not?

3. What rule of law is applied by the courts to determine whether advertising rates or other business practices are in compliance with antitrust law?

4. What factors seem to have motivated President Kennedy's attempt to use antitrust law to preserve a marketplace of ideas? Was his view of that marketplace a valid one? What is the nature of the marketplace today?

5. Define a joint operating agreement. What is the purpose of such an agreement?

6. What did the Supreme Court say about such agreements in the *Citizen Publishing Co.* case? With the benefit of hindsight, what has been the long-range effect of that decision?

7. What message to publishers is implicit in the antitrust actions brought against the *Los Angeles Times* and Scripps-Howard in Cincinnati?

8. What is the law with respect to joint ownership of newspapers and broadcasting stations in the same city?

9. What is the connection between Jehovah's Witnesses and the newsracks that appear in many areas of heavy pedestrian traffic? What is the connection both have with Milton's *Areopagitica?*

10. What principles with respect to the taxation of the media were established by the Supreme Court in the *Grosjean* and *Minneapolis Star* cases?

APPENDIX

THE MEANING OF "LAW"

As used in this text, "law" has two general meanings, each quite different, but nevertheless closely interrelated. The primary meaning refers to law as the legal rules by which we live. These include statutes enacted by Congress and state legislatures, ordinances adopted by local governing bodies, the rules adopted by administrative bodies at all levels; they also include the decisions of courts interpreting all of the above or applying rules based on custom, which is known as the common law. In this sense, put in basic terms, laws are the words that define conduct required of us, or forbidden to us, for the common good.

In its secondary meaning, law is the system of courts, judicial processes, and legal officers through which the rules are applied. In this sense, it is a means of resolving disputes to reach an end loosely described as justice.

In the first meaning of the term, laws usually are classified as to their origin. The major sources of such law are described below.

Statute Law

Statute law is the great body of law that is a product of legislative action: by Congress at the national level, by legislatures at the state level, and by city and county councils at the local level. In theory, statute law is drafted to reflect the people's will, as perceived by their elected representatives acting in their behalf. Such law provides for punishment of wrongdoing, but it also defines and makes provisions for benefits. The Social Security system, for instance, is the product of a large body of statute law. Such law is said to be prospective in that we are supposed to know what it is and guide our conduct accordingly. In reality, none of us can know, except in general terms, what is in the thousands of statutes under which we live. Federal law alone fills twenty-four volumes of the United States Code, and every session of Congress adds more.

THE LEGAL SYSTEM

Common Law

Voluminous as the body of statute law is, it cannot anticipate, and thus forestall, every kind of dispute that is apt to arise between individuals. And yet there must be some orderly means of resolving disputes because the alternative may be a resort to violence. Indeed, at one time dueling was an accepted means of settling differences. Ten centuries ago, courts in Medieval England began to recognize that a duel did not determine who was right but only who was stronger. Thus courts began to apply common-sense principles to the resolution of disputes to which no statute applied. Some of these involved property rights. As early as the thirteenth century, courts began to deal with harm to reputation, which was seen as a form of property for which the victim of a damaging lie could be compensated. Over the centuries, a huge body of law, based on nothing more tangible than a court's sense of what justice required, has been established. This is known as common law. It is a product of cases, decided at a particular time on a specific set of facts. However, embedded in these cases are principles that editors of legal encyclopedias and digests have done their best to analyze and present in orderly form for the guidance of lawyers, judges, and students.

Because common law is a product of specific cases, it is more flexible than statute law. This is one of its strengths. It has survived and grown because it is adaptable to changing conditions. Some legal scholars hold that despite its flexibility it is, at bottom, based solidly on eternal principles, on verities, and on a sound sense of what the community will or will not stand for.

Administrative Law

In the last fifty years, Congress, to an increasing extent, has enacted laws stating broad objectives, leaving the details of reaching those objectives to administrative agencies. Under such laws, Congress sets goals and creates an agency charged with seeing that they are reached. The Environmental Protection Agency, for instance, was given the duty of holding air and water pollution to specified minimums. It is up to the agency to devise specific regulations and impose them on polluters so as to meet those minimums.

When regulations are drafted and adopted in accordance with procedures pre-scribed by Congress and the courts, they have the effect of law. They may be enforced through the agency's own hearing system, subject to an appeal to the courts. Because of the number of agencies empowered to regulate various as-pects of society, and the complexity of the problems with which they try to cope, the body of administrative law surpasses in volume the statutes enacted by Con-gress. Administrative law is of special concern to broadcasters and advertisers.

Constitutional Law

Constitutions, federal and state, are not dead collections of words. They have been kept alive by courts' interpretations of what the words mean when applied to a specific set of facts. The body of these interpretations is called constitutional law. Because the federal Constitution lies at the very base of the hierarchy of laws, constitutional questions permeate all other kinds of law. Much of this text deals with the large body of constitutional law generated by the courts' interpre-tation of the speech and press clauses of the First Amendment.

No one can say with certainty what any part of the Constitution means until the Supreme Court has decided what it means in a particular case. This does not mean that lower courts can't interpret the Constitution. The judge of even a lowest-level state court has the authority to do so. But such decisions are subject to appeal and review by courts at a higher level. The higher the court in the hi-erarchy, the greater is the weight carried by its decisions. But the Supreme Court of the United States is the final authority on all federal constitutional questions. Even its decisions are not carved in stone. On occasion, the Court has changed its mind.

This does not exhaust the kinds of law with which lawyers and courts deal. But it does attempt to define those kinds of law with which the journalist is apt to work.

With respect to the systems or processes applied to the law, three are of in-terest to communicators. These are described below.

Criminal Law

Society so abhors some conduct—such as murder, robbery, and drug abuse—that it provides for its punishment. The rules defining such infractions make up the body of criminal law. With rare exceptions, criminal law is statute law. The purpose of the legislature in defining a crime and its punishment is to deter law-breaking. All of us stand on notice that if we persist in writing checks when our bank account is empty, or take a bottle of expensive perfume without pausing to pay at the checkout counter, we run a risk of being arrested. If the victim persists in pressing charges and the prosecutor is agreeable, we may find ourselves in court, facing a judge.

If so, our fate will be determined by application of the processes of criminal law. Our offense no longer will be treated as a private matter but as an offense against society as a whole. Thus, in criminal cases, the state is the plaintiff and the prosecutor acts as its agent. However, the defendant is not helpless. The Constitution requires the court to assume that the accused is not guilty. The defendant may be tried by a jury if he or she so desires. In any event, the Constitution also requires the prosecutor to prove guilt beyond a reasonable doubt.

Criminal courts stand at the foundation of the legal system. In any jurisdiction, criminal cases, starting with traffic offenses and moving up the scale of the gravity of the infraction to murder, make up the bulk of the work of the courts. An earmark of criminal law is the nature of the penalty. Defendants can be deprived of property, by being required to pay a fine; of their liberty, by being sentenced to prison; or of their life, if the crime is serious enough.

Civil Law

When individuals disagree—over whether a physician's carelessness resulted in injury, whether a journalist's story defamed someone, or who was at fault in an automobile accident—they may ask a court to resolve their differences. Such disputes, and many others, become grist for the civil law system. While the state is not an essential party to a civil proceeding, it can be. If the state wants part of your land for a new highway, and you don't like what it offers to pay, the state may ask a court to decide on a fair price. The state also is involved in civil actions to the extent that it provides the forum—a court—and the rules for resolving the dispute.

The purpose of a civil action is to decide whether one party or the other has been wronged, and, if so, make good the victim's loss. If a precise dollar value can be placed on the loss, the award is for actual damages. If the claimed harm can't be measured precisely because it is attributed to such intangibles as mental anguish, humiliation, pain, and suffering, the award is for compensatory damages, sometimes called general damages. If the offending party's actions are considered particularly outrageous, the court may order an award of an additional sum designed to punish the offender and deter others. Such an award is for punitive damages. Some such awards can be quite large. They differ from the fines imposed in criminal cases in that fines are paid to the state. Awards of damages are paid to the victim.

Equity Law

One type of civil law, known as equity law, has assumed an identity of its own. It traces its origins to medieval England and to the belief that the king was the ultimate source of justice. When persons became embroiled in disputes that could not be resolved by reference to the common law, they looked to the king for relief. Originally, the monarch himself listened to the competing claims and made a decision based on the equities—that is, on a balancing of the rights of the one against those of the other in the search for a solution that would be fair to both.

In the United States, equity cases are heard by a judge. Usually, all that the disputing parties want is an order directing one or the other to perform a duty, or to refrain from performing an act considered harmful. If the duty is one required by law, the court may resolve the matter by issuing an order called a "writ of mandamus." The latter is a Latin word meaning "We command." Such a writ also can be issued to prevent one of the parties from committing an act forbidden by law.

If one party to the equity action is seeking a remedy not required by law, the court may resolve the dispute by issuing an injunction. A farmer who believes that a storm sewer designed to serve a proposed subdivision would pour water on his land could ask a court to halt work on the sewer. A judge would hear arguments from both sides and might even join in the discussion. The court's purpose would be to resolve the dispute with the least harm to both parties. This might be done by ordering the developers of the subdivision to revise their plan for the sewer. Or it could result in an injunction forbidding further work on it.

THE JUDICIAL SYSTEM

The courts, which make up the judicial system and bring law to life, are in all respects a separate and equal branch of government. They work with, but are independent of, the legislative branch, which writes statute law, and the executive branch, which sees that the statutes are carried into effect.

In a sense, however, the judicial system is superior to both, because it alone can decide what the state and federal constitutions mean. Thus, if a legislative body enacts a law in violation of some provision of the constitution, the courts have the authority, if asked, to nullify it. Likewise, if a president or governor acts in a manner not authorized by the constitution, the courts, if asked, can nullify the action. The proviso, "if asked," is important because courts cannot reach out and act on their own initiative. A case must be brought to them by someone who alleges harm. The courts, then, are the ultimate guardians of our constitutional rights. They stand as bulwarks against repressive acts of government, even those that may reflect the will of the people.

The United States has a dual system of courts, a fact that sometimes confuses the unknowing. Each state has its own courts, which deal with violations of that state's laws and constitution, and with civil actions involving its own residents. The federal government is served by a system of United States courts, which deal with violations of federal statutes, and with civil actions brought by residents of one state against residents of another. They also hear cases raising federal constitutional issues, although such cases may begin in state courts, too. The two systems are discussed separately below.

State Courts

At the lowest level, state courts dealing with minor offenses and small claims may be quite informal, not even taking a record of their proceedings. Names of such courts vary from state to state. Some may be called municipal courts; others, police courts, county courts, or small-claims courts.

The lowest-level trial courts of record also vary in what they are called. In most states, such courts operate at the country or parish level. (In Louisiana, a unit of government corresponding to the county is called a "parish." The name harks back to the time when Louisiana was owned by the French and governed with the help of the Roman Catholic Church. As another aspect of that heritage, Louisiana is the only state that has not adopted the English common law as the foundation for its legal system.) In some states, sparsely populated counties may be grouped together and served by one court called a district or circuit court. In a few states, lowest-level trial courts of record are called courts of common pleas. New York confuses the out-of-state beginning legal scholar by calling its basic trial courts "supreme" courts. Whatever the name, in these courts the great bulk of the legal work is done. Here individuals are tried on murder and other criminal charges, libel and other suits for damages are heard, and injunctions are sought.

Each state also has its system of appeals courts. In the more populous states, there are two layers of them, an intermediate appellate court, and a court of last resort. The intermediate courts in some states hear appeals from county courts in specified districts. In others, there may be two or more such courts, but they take appeals in rotation, no matter where they come from. Several states have specialized appeals courts, one branch hearing criminal appeals and another, civil.

However they are named or organized, appeals courts ordinarily don't conduct trials. Witnesses are heard and evidence is collected only in the lower trial courts. There a jury, or the judge, decides whose version of the facts to believe. Appeals courts are concerned with questions of law, which come to them through documents supported by legal citations called "briefs." Appeals courts permit lawyers representing the two sides to make limited oral arguments supporting their cases. Appeals are based on the contention that the trial judge erred in interpreting one or more points of law. Typical questions raised on appeal include: Did the judge improperly admit the defendant's confession as evidence? Were the instructions to the jury in accord with established principles of law?

Each state has a court of final appeal which usually also oversees the functioning of the entire judicial system. The name of this court also varies. Some are called "supreme courts"; others, the "court of appeals". Massachusetts calls its highest court the Supreme Judicial Court. Whatever its name, a state's highest court has the final word on any case that deals exclusively with interpretation of that state's constitution or statutes. If no federal question has been raised in the courts below, a litigant who is displeased with the verdict of a state's highest court has no further appeal. Thus it is in no sense correct to view state courts as somehow inferior to those in the federal system. They are coequal. It is a rule of judicial construction that in a case involving both state and federal questions, a federal court must honor a state supreme court's interpretation of the meaning of that state's constitution or statutes.

Federal Courts

Federal courts operate at three levels. At the trial level are the ninety-four U.S. district courts, which may be found in the major cities of every state. Some districts are divided into divisions, and a judge may hold court in two or more cities on a rotating basis to serve the convenience of the litigants. Districts are given straightforward geographical names. Thus, the cluster of federal trial courts in New York City is identified collectively as the U.S. District Court, Southern District, New York. The Northern District is headquartered in Albany; the Eastern, in Brooklyn; and the Western, in Buffalo.

The district courts in New York, Connecticut, and Vermont make up the Second Circuit for appeal purposes. Their decisions are subject to review by the U.S. Court of Appeals, Second Circuit, which has its headquarters in New York City. There are eleven such circuits made up of as few as three states and as many as nine. There is a separate U.S. Circuit Court for the District of Columbia, which hears many appeals from the decisions of federal administrative agencies as well as from the District Court for the District of Columbia. A thirteenth federal circuit court, simply called the "Federal Circuit," also sits in Washington, D.C. It hears appeals of cases involving government contracts and employees, patents, trademarks, and customs.

At the apex of the federal judicial pyramid is the Supreme Court of the United States, the only court established by the Constitution. Each of its nine justices supervises in a loose way one or more of the circuits. In practice, that means little more than that the justice has the power to hear and act on emergency appeals from his or her assigned circuit, while the Court is in recess.

Federal judges are appointed for life by the president, subject to approval by the Senate. Historically, federal judgeships have been used to reward faithful members of the president's political party. However, some recent presidents have made a show of consulting the bar association and others in seeking judges of merit. This is especially true at the Supreme Court level, although even there presidents have sought to influence history by choosing justices who are considered likely to interpret the Constitution to their liking. This has resulted in some surprises. Earl Warren, for instance, whom Dwight Eisenhower named chief justice in the belief that he was a conservative, led the Court through one of its most liberal eras in protecting the rights of individuals.

Federal district courts are trial courts. They hear cases involving violations of federal statutes. They are also the starting point for any civil suit to which the federal government is a party, or which involves residents of different states, provided the amount at issue is more than $10,000, or provided that a fundamental right is at stake.

A litigant who is dissatisfied with the verdict of a district court can appeal to the appropriate circuit court of appeals for a review of disputed points of law. A circuit court's decisions are binding as precedents only within its own circuit. Thus it sometimes happens that one circuit may rule one way on a disputed point of law, and another will rule just the opposite. If the subject matter is of any consequence, it is likely that the Supreme Court will take one or both cases in order to resolve the difference.

GETTING A CASE TO THE
SUPREME COURT

In our litigation-minded age, the Supreme Court of the United States is asked to resolve many kinds of questions. It is besieged with applications for review, which come to it in three ways:

1. By appeal

2. By application for a writ of certiorari

3. By certification

Most cases come to the Supreme Court through a petition for a writ of certiorari. The writ, if issued, is an order to the court below to deliver its file on the case to the Supreme Court for review. If petitioners are to have any chance of success, they must assert that the court below erred in applying a federal constitutional principle or a point of federal law to the decision of the case. Four of the nine justices must agree to take a case before a writ can be issued. In the overwhelming majority of cases, the Court refuses certiorari. Usually, no reason is given.

Until 1988, lower court decisions holding a state or federal law unconstitutional could be appealed directly to the Supreme Court. The Department of Justice also could appeal adverse decisions of U.S. district courts in criminal cases. This did not necessarily mean that the Court would hear the cases. In many instances, the Court would avoid a decision by blandly announcing that it found "no substantial federal question" at issue. Such direct appeals made up about a fifth of the 5000 cases reaching the Court each year. Public Law 100-352 (102 Stat. 662, 1988) eliminated the right of direct appeal to the Supreme Court in all but a few instances. Under the law's terms, a federal trial court decision declaring a law unconstitutional must be appealed to a U.S. court of appeals. If the appellate court affirms, the losing side can file for a writ of certiorari, which the Supreme Court can grant or deny as it does with other kinds of cases. Direct appeals still can be taken in certain civil injunctive actions, which, by law, must be decided in the first instance by a three-judge district court panel. This provision applies to congressional reapportionment cases and to certain cases arising out of the Civil Rights Act of 1964, the Voting Rights Act of 1965, and the Presidential Election Campaign Fund Act of 1971. Direct appeals also are permitted in a limited number of antitrust cases if the trial judge finds that immediate equitable relief is of "general public importance in the administration of justice."[1]

Certification seldom happens. The Court's procedures permit the circuit courts of appeal to ask it to clarify points of law essential to the decision of a pending case. The Supreme Court may choose to answer such questions, or it may ask that the case be sent up to it for decision.

---

1. For a history of the right of direct appeal and a discussion of Public Law 100-352 see Bennett Boskey and Eugene Gressman, "The Supreme Court Bids Farewell to Mandatory Appeals," *West's Supreme Court Reporter,* vol. 109, no. 1, pp. LXXXI–XCIX, 1 November 1988.

By these three methods, the Court is asked to review about 5000 cases each term, which runs from the first week of October until about the first week of July. Obviously such a tide of paper is enough to inundate the nine members of the Court who must, by necessity, assign most of the screening to their clerks. Because there is a limit to how much work the justices can do, they have become quite ruthless in rejecting cases. In recent years, their formal written decisions have been limited to about 140 cases a year.

HOW THE SUPREME COURT DECIDES A CASE

Cases submitted to the Supreme Court for review must be accompanied by briefs. Under the rules, these must state the issues presented by the case, and the questions of law it raises. The brief must contain a summary of the action taken in the lower courts, the arguments supporting the outcome sought by the litigant, and citations to cases, statutes or administrative rules believed to support the sought-after verdict. These briefs are of the utmost importance, for they frequently shape the Court's decision.

After the justices and their clerks have studied the briefs, a decision is reached on whether to schedule oral argument. If so, the maximum time permitted each side usually does not exceed an hour. Lawyers arguing their cases to the Court can never be sure that they will get to use all of their time as they had planned. One or more of the justices may choose to question a lawyer, or even to argue a point of law.

Each Friday morning, the justices meet in private to discuss cases awaiting decision. The chief justice presides. When a given case is under discussion, he asks each justice in turn, starting with the oldest in terms of years on the Court, to present his views. If the case is important, or deals with a topic on which the justices have strongly conflicting views, the discussion can get animated. When the time comes to vote, the oldest justice in terms of service votes first, and the balloting continues in order of seniority.

The next step, and it can be an important one, is the assignment of the justice who is to write the decision of the Court. If the chief justice is a part of the majority, he makes the assignment and can give the task to himself or another justice. If the chief justice is not a part of the majority, the assignment is made by the senior justice voting with the majority. The justice charged with the writing usually circulates preliminary drafts among his colleagues for their comments. Other justices may feel moved to write concurring or dissenting opinions. In a concurring opinion, the justice agrees with the Court's decision, but does not fully agree with the legal reasoning used by the writer of the leading opinion. When all of the opinions on a given case reach final form, the decision is announced in open court, usually on Monday of each week. Late in the term, decisions are announced more frequently.

The decisions and opinions of the Court take several forms. If the Court decides that a case does not raise new points of law but can be used as a vehicle for reiterating a point the justices thought they had decided previously, the decision may take the form of a *per curiam* opinion. The Latin words simply mean "for the court." Such opinions are never signed by an individual justice, although one or more may choose to write a supplementary opinion. *Per curiam* opinions are not looked to as strong precedents, although they can serve to clarify a confusing point of law.

If five or more justices agree with the legal reasoning used by one of their number in writing an opinion, that opinion becomes a majority decision of the Court. Such decisions express the opinion of the Court on legal questions raised by the case and thus establish precedents that all lower courts are supposed to follow in deciding similar cases. It makes no difference whether such decisions are joined by only five of the justices or all nine. A majority always speaks for the Court.

Some justices may agree with the outcome of the case, but disagree with the legal reasoning used by the author of the leading opinion. As a result, only four, or even fewer, justices may find themselves in agreement with any one version of the verdict. Such minority opinions are called "plurality judgments" of the Court. Lower courts may and do look to them for guidance in deciding similar cases, but they are not required to follow them. Obscenity law was thrown into confusion for more than a decade because no more than four members of the Court could agree on how far the First Amendment goes in protecting portrayals of sexual activity.

Decisions of the Court are not always models of precision. In theory, the Court deals in a decision only with specific points of law raised in the proceedings of lower courts. But, now and then, the justice writing for the Court will comment on points of law that are not at issue, and have no bearing on the decision. Such references are known as *dicta*. In theory, these do not carry the force of law, but lawyers and lower-court judges may nevertheless be guided by them.

CONSTITUTIONAL LAW

Courts are required by their nature to interpret or construe the meaning of the law, whatever its source, and of the constitutions, state and federal. In doing so, they are supposed to be bound by rules that are embedded deeply in custom and are designed to make the law reasonably predictable. Under these rules, courts are supposed to construe statutes strictly and literally. A law written by a legislative body represents the will of the people and means what the plain meaning of its wording says it means, no more and no less. If the words are not clear on their face, courts go to legislative committee reports and the record of the debate to discern the intent of the legislators, and are guided accordingly.

Constitutions are viewed more broadly as statements of principle. If the language is so clear as to admit no doubt as to its meaning, it is followed. But if there is room for a difference of opinion, courts look first to the decisions of other courts and then to the intent of the drafters, if that can be discerned. If all else fails, courts fall back on their understanding of the general purpose of the questioned passage and of the constitution as a whole.

In all such matters of construction, a court is supposed to be bound by the decisions of higher courts to which it is subject. Such decisions are looked to as precedents. As a general rule courts follow precedents rigidly. They act on the principle of *stare decisis*—that is, of taking at face value a decision on a specific point of law previously made by a higher court with jurisdiction over them. However, if the facts of a present case at issue are not exactly like those of the ruling case, or if the question of law involved can be stated in somewhat different terms, precedent can be ignored or modified. If a lower court's decision based on what it sees as a somewhat different case is upheld on appeal, then there is a new precedent. It is this process that keeps the law flexible—too flexible, its critics say. Thus, the meaning of the law can be stated with certainty only in terms of the latest appeals court cases.

However, at any given moment, a state's supreme court decisions offer the last word on the meaning of that state's statutes and constitution. The same is true of the Supreme Court of the United States with respect to the federal statutes and Constitution.

Very early in the nation's history, under the leadership of one of our most brilliant chief justices, John Marshall, the Supreme Court staked out ground it holds to this day:

1. When a federal question is raised during the trial of a state case in a state court, it creates a right to take the case to the Supreme Court of the United States. *Cohens* v. *Virginia,* 6 Wheat. 264, 5 L.Ed. 257 (1821)

2. When the Supreme Court concludes that an act of Congress, or an action of the executive, violates the Constitution, the Court can declare either null and void. *Marbury* v. *Madison,* 1 Cranch 137, 2 L.Ed. 60 (1803)

3. The Court also can declare null and void a state statute, or even a section of a state constitution, that violates the federal Constitution. *McCulloch* v. *Maryland,* 4 Wheat. 316, 4 L.Ed. 579 (1819)

4. While state courts are free to interpret and apply the federal Constitution, if the state court's decision is overruled by the Supreme Court of the United States, the latter decision prevails. *Martin* v. *Hunter's Lessee,* 1 Wheat. 304, 4 L.Ed. 97 (1816)

These remarkable decisions converted the government of the United States from what the founders intended—a divided depository of only such powers as the states had delegated to it—into a strong central government. Through those decisions the Supreme Court took unto itself the authority to determine how far the Constitution permits that government's power to reach. Marshall found his authority in Article VI of the Constitution:

This Constitution, and the laws of the United States which shall be made in pursuance thereof; and all treaties made, or which shall be made, under the authority of the United States, shall be the supreme law of the land; and the judges in every state shall be bound thereby, any thing in the Constitution or laws of any State to the contrary notwithstanding.

In that paragraph, the Marshall Court found the barrier against the tyranny of the majority that Locke and his disciples were seeking when they spoke of the "Law of Nature." That paragraph, buttressed by the Marshall decisions, gives the courts authority to protect our rights as citizens against oppressive acts of Congress. Because the Supreme Court's decisions on the meaning of the Constitution and of statute law become a part of the law, those decisions, too, are "the supreme law of the land."

Such power is not supposed to be used lightly. Courts are to assume that legislators do not willfully violate the Constitution. They, like judges, take an oath to uphold it. Therefore, if courts can avoid deciding a case on constitutional grounds, they usually will do so. If a law or executive order does not affect fundamental rights, courts assume it is constitutional until the weight of evidence proves otherwise. If fundamental rights are at stake, the burden of proof is turned around. The state must prove that its attempts to restrict them are constitutional. The power to declare a law unconstitutional has been used sparingly by the courts. The Supreme Court of the United States has found that only 121 acts of Congress violated the Constitution.

GLOSSARY

acquit   to release from guilt

actual damages; actual injury   see compensatory damages

actual malice   The publication of defamatory material with reckless disregard for the truth or knowledge of its falsity

adversary hearing   legal procedure in which evidence is heard from opposing parties

adversary proceeding   a legal action taken by opposing parties

affadavit   a written account of facts, sworn to as true

agency record   documents in physical possession of a federal agency and subject to the Freedom of Information Act

antitrust laws   laws designed to prevent businesses from forming monopolies and interfering with free trade among competitors

appellate court   see court of appeals

bail   money or a bond posted to release someone from legal custody

blasphemy   spoken or written words that insult a divine power

burden of proof   the duty to prove a claim in an adversary proceeding

censor   to forbid the public dissemination of written, printed, filmed, or other material considered offensive, immoral, or dangerous to the public welfare

censorship   the prohibition of public distribution of written, printed, filmed, spoken, or other material considered offensive, immoral, or dangerous to the public welfare

circuit court   a court with jurisdiction over several judicial districts

class action suit   a legal action brought by some injured parties on behalf of themselves and all others similarly injured

classified materials   information restricted in access to a particular group of people. Usually applied by government to documents considered vital to national security

commercial speech   advertisements that are entitled to limited protection under the First Amendment

common law   law that develops not from written statutes but from custom and usage

common pleas court   a trial court with jurisdiction over civil and criminal cases

commute   to change; to reduce a prison sentence

compensatory (actual) damages   the actual loss suffered by a complainant

common carrier   a bus line, telephone company, ferry, or other organization without competition in a particular region that must do business with all would-be customers

constitutional law   the area of law focused on the interpretation, violation, and enforcement of the U.S. Constitution

constitutional right   a provision guaranteed by the U.S. Constitution, such as the right to freedom of speech or assembly

constitutional privilege   see constitutional right

contempt   behavior that interferes with court proceedings, impugns a court's dignity, or violates an order of a court

contract   agreement in which one party assumes the obligation to perform certain acts, and the other party agrees to give consideration for that performance

copyright   the legal protection of original work that can be fixed in some tangible medium of expression

court of appeals   a court that reviews lower courts' decisions

Criminal Syndicalism Act   a law forbidding individuals to associate for the purpose of advocating violent changes in the form of government

cross-examination   the questioning of a witness by the opposing party

declassification   the process by which previously restricted information is made more widely available

defendants   parties against whom lawsuits are brought by plaintiffs or who are accused of crime

dicta   written opinions from judges that are not about issues essential to a case; dicta are not necessarily considered precedents for later court actions

discovery   the pretrial process in an adversary proceeding by which participants must answer all questions and produce all documents concerning the facts of the case

due process   the ordinary sequence of events in the provision of justice, to which everyone is entitled

entrapment   acts by police, government agents, or other public officials to induce suspects into committing crimes

equal opportunity   the legal requirement that everyone has the same rights to benefits such as jobs and, in the case of political candidates, to reach the public by radio or television

espionage   spying

fair use   the doctrine in copyright law holding that minimal copying of another's original material is permissible if it does not detract unduly from the commercial value of the original

felony   a serious crime

grand jury   a body of citizens who evaluates information about a crime with the aim of determining whether a suspect may be charged with having committed it

hearing   a legal proceeding during which evidence is heard so that the facts of a case may be established

hearsay   information not personally seen or heard but based on something heard or seen by someone else

impeach   to accuse or charge a public official with wrongdoing or to raise questions about the truth of a witness's testimony

indict   to charge a suspect with a crime

infringement   in copyright law, the substantial copying of another's original work or copying that detracts unduly from the original's commercial value

injunction   a court order that requires a party to stop committing some act

intrusion behavior that violates a person's right to privacy, for which a plaintiff may win damages

invasion of privacy the violation of a person's right to be free from outside interference or publicity

joint operating agreement in antitrust law, an agreement between newspaper owners to conduct the business of two newspapers in concert; considered legal unless the agreement harms a competitor or freezes out potential advertisers

landmark case a case often quoted by lower courts; a court case that acts as a turning point in the law

law of contracts and commercial transactions laws governing agreements in which one party assumes the obligation to perform certain acts, and the other party agrees to give consideration for that performance

libel the unjustified exposure of someone to public ridicule or hatred

matter of law a case that raises a question that can be resolved if the law is applied to the facts

misappropriation in copyright law, the systematic taking of another's original work

misdemeanor a crime considered less serious than a felony and punishable by prison, fine, or both

mistrial a trial canceled by a judge while it is going on because of prejudicial error by one of the parties or because the jury is unable to agree on a verdict.

motion to quash to request a court to make void a subpoena, indictment, or other order

natural rights according to Locke, the personal rights that were people's in the free state of nature

negligence failure to exercise the care justly expected of a reasonable and cautious person

neutral reportage the privilege of news media to report evenhandedly the claims and counterclaims in highly charged controversies without the need to investigate each accusation; the privilege exists even when an organization doubts the truth of the claims it reports

obscenity material that appeals to a prurient interest in sex or material that a jury finds arouses an obsessive or morbid interest in sex

ordinances city or municipal laws

pardon an order by the president or a governor releasing a party who has been found guilty of a crime

per curiam **decision** a decision from a court composed of more than one judge

permanent injunction a court order that permanently restrains a party from committing some act

plaintiffs parties who bring lawsuits against defendants

pleadings defendants' answers to questions

plurality opinion a judicial opinion offered by the greatest number of judges, but by less than a majority of the panel

police power the inherent authority of the state to protect the health, safety, morals, and general welfare of its residents

precedent a judicial decision that is later referred to as authority on a similar point of law

preferred position the status imputed by court decisions to First Amendment rights and certain others guaranteed by the Bill of Rights to protect against government attempts to prevent "harmful" speech; a doctrine used as a weapon against censorship

preliminary hearings   legal proceedings preliminary to a trial during which evidence is heard so that the facts of a case may be established; see pretrial proceedings

preponderance of the evidence   the weight or credibility of evidence; a test required in some civil actions that the weight of evidence clearly support a claim

pretrial proceedings   hearings held before the beginning of a trial, during which evidence that might not be admissible at a formal trial may be offered; see preliminary hearings

previous restraint   see prior restraint

prior restraint   any attempt by government or courts to mandate the content of printed matter; a form of censorship that violates the First Amendment guarantee of freedom of speech and press

privilege   a right, benefit, or immunity

probation   the court-ordered requirements of behavior and period of time for which a party convicted of a crime may stay out of jail

public domain   in copyright law, material that cannot be copyrighted and that can be used by anyone

public file   information about their operations that broadcasters must keep for public access, required by the Federal Communications Commission

punitive damages   an award made by a court to a complainant that exceeds his or her actual loss; the purpose is to punish the offender

restraining order   a court order that temporarily forbids a party from committing some act; a form of injunction (see injunction)

retraction   a statement confessing to a mistake in an earlier statement

right of publicity   the right of people, particularly celebrities, to control how others use their names

right to know   the right, imputed to the public, of access to all information about what their various governments are doing

search warrant   a court order authorized for good cause by a magistrate, allowing a search of private property

sedition   the crime of acting to overthrow a government

seditious libel   the crime of questioning the wisdom of a ruler's policies

separation of powers   the doctrine under which Congress makes the law, the executive branch puts it into effect, and the judiciary settles disputes that arise from this process

sequester   to isolate (a jury)

shield law   statute under which journalists are entitled to protect the confidentiality of their sources

slander   spoken words that falsely defame a person so that his or her reputation is harmed or others are deterred from dealing with him or her

statute   a law passed by a legislature

subpoena   a court order requiring someone to appear in court to testify

summary judgment   a court decision by a judge, which circumvents a full jury trial, usually sought when the adversary parties agree on the facts of a case

superior court   a court midway in authority between a lower, or inferior court, and a higher, or court of appeals; a trial court

temporary restraining order   see restraining order

tort   a private or civil wrong or injury, other than a breach of contract, for which one may recover damages

trade rules   regulations governing certain industries that are proposed and published by the Federal Trade Commission after administrative hearings

trier of fact   the person or people, usually a jury but sometimes judges, appointed to hear evidence and determine the truth from it

unconstitutional   forbidden by the Constitution of the United States

U.S. district court   a federal or state court with jurisdiction over a certain region

warrant   a court order empowering a police officer, sheriff, or someone else to arrest someone, search a house, or the like

CASE INDEX

Note: Entries in boldface type indicate major cases.

NAME AND ORGANIZATION INDEX

SUBJECT INDEX